Critical acclaim for *Naming Names*:

"Victor Navasky has written an important book about the McCarthy era. . . . What makes Mr. Navasky's book so striking is its fairness."   —*The New York Times Book Review*

"One of the indispensable books not only for understanding a critical era in Hollywood and in American political life, but for coming to grips with the whole subject of American films and the role they have played in twentieth-century American culture"   —*American Film*

"The most intense moral argument that I, at least, have seen brought to bear in a very long time. . . . Despite being addressed to the issues of the 1950s, it is current today. . . . Victor Navasky has given us a portrait of human beings under pressure which, in its fullness, is as lifelike as any Hollywood has ever given us. Anyone who thinks political choices are necessarily simple should read *Naming Names*."   —*Mother Jones*

"His achievement is unarguable. With *Naming Names* [Victor S. Navasky] establishes himself as that rare historian who can, like a novelist, illuminate the boundaries where power and conscience meet."   —*Time*

"*Naming Names* is the sort of book that ought to be required reading in the journalism classrooms of the nation as an example of how a writer can simultaneously convey a tough-minded point of view *and* be scrupulously fair."   —*New York Daily News*

PENGUIN BOOKS

NAMING NAMES

Victor S. Navasky, a graduate of the Yale Law School, is a journalist whose work has appeared in many forums, from the celebrated *Monocle*, which he helped to found, to *The New York Times*, where he worked as an editor. His previous book, *Kennedy Justice* (1971), was nominated for the National Book Award. Since 1978 he has been the editor of *The Nation*. He lives in New York City with his wife and three children.

Naming Names

Victor S. Navasky

PENGUIN BOOKS

PENGUIN BOOKS
Published by the Penguin Group
Penguin Books USA Inc.,
375 Hudson Street, New York, New York 10014, U.S.A.
Penguin Books Ltd, 27 Wrights Lane, London W8 5TZ, England
Penguin Books Australia Ltd, Ringwood, Victoria, Australia
Penguin Books Canada Ltd, 10 Alcorn Avenue,
Toronto, Ontario, Canada M4V 3B2
Penguin Books (N.Z.) Ltd, 182–190 Wairau Road,
Auckland 10, New Zealand

Penguin Books Ltd, Registered Offices:
Harmondsworth, Middlesex, England
First published in the United States of America
by The Viking Press 1980
This edition with a new afterword
published in Penguin Books 1991

3   5   7   9   10   8   6   4   2

LIBRARY OF CONGRESS CATALOGING IN PUBLICATION DATA
Navasky, Victor S.
Naming names.
Includes bibliographical references and index.
1. Moving-picture industry—United States.
2. Blacklisting of entertainers—United States.
3. Communism—United States—1917–
I. Title.
[PN1993.U6N4   1981]   791.43′09794′94   81-10519
ISBN 0 14 01.5235 0   AACR2

Printed in the United States of America

For Annie, Bruno, Miri,
and Jenny

Foreword

AT 10:35 A.M. ON MARCH 21, 1951, in room 226 of the Old House Office Building on Capitol Hill, Chairman John S. Wood of Georgia called to order the House Committee on Un-American Activities (HUAC). The subject: subversive activities in the entertainment industry. Congressman Wood's first witness was the actor Larry Parks, whose portrayal of the title role in *The Jolson Story* in 1946 had earned him overnight fame and, perhaps, the HUAC subpoena that accounted for his presence.*

That same morning, at the U.S. Federal Court in Foley Square in Manhattan, the government concluded its case against Julius and Ethel Rosenberg and Morton Sobell, charged with conspiring to commit wartime espionage for America's former ally, the Soviet Union. The most damaging witness against them had been Ethel's brother, David Greenglass. The other major espionage case of the late 1940s also reached its denouement as Alger Hiss, the forty-six-year-old former State Department official who had been convicted of perjury for denying that he had passed official papers to the Russians, prepared to enter prison for five years.[1]† His accuser, though not a family member, was nevertheless a man who had claimed to be his friend. Indeed, Whittaker Chambers was to go on to write *Witness,* one of the truly influential books of that era, in which he attempted to vindicate the informer as patriot, prophet, and moral hero.

---

* There is an argument over whether "HUAC" is a pejorative acronym for the House Committee on Un-American Activities used only by critics of the committee when "HCUA" is correct sequentially. Since HUAC has fallen into the popular language, I use it, with no invidious intent.

† The superscript numbers refer to the Notes on Sources, which begin on p. 428.

The congressional hearings into Hollywood had begun in 1947, when ten objecting witnesses (who came to be called the Unfriendly Ten or the Hollywood Ten) had been cited for contempt of Congress when they refused to give a yes or no answer to the question that marked that era: Are you now or have you ever been a member of the Communist Party? The hearings, suspended until the convicted Ten had exhausted their appeals and were imprisoned for terms of up to a year, were resuming with Parks as the lead-off witness.

By the spring of 1951, all parts of the federal government may have been united in a single battle against suspected subversives, but of course there are vital differences among the three branches. Whatever one thinks of the Hiss and Rosenberg trials, they followed formal indictments and took place in courts that provided at least some procedural protections. Government witnesses, including Greenglass and Chambers, were subject to cross-examination; moreover, if they were telling the truth, they were providing essential evidence unavailable elsewhere. Congress, however, cannot charge people with crimes; the Constitution in the Bill of Attainder clause specifically prohibits legislative incursion into this area. Yet witnesses before congressional committees have far fewer rights than defendants in criminal trials. And, as HUAC itself eventually revealed, congressional committees may already know the answers to the questions they are asking. Larry Parks was being called upon not to provide information that would lead to an acquittal or conviction, but rather to play a symbolic role in a surrealistic morality play.

Parks freely admitted to HUAC that he had joined the Communist Party in 1941 when he was twenty-five years old because it was the "most liberal" of the political parties and had left it in 1945 because of "lack of interest." Unlike the Hollywood Ten, he was willing to detail his own political autobiography, but he had compunctions about naming those who had served with him. "I would prefer, if you would allow me, not to mention other people's names. . . . This is not the American way," added Parks. "To force a man to do this is not American justice."

Chairman Wood said he was "not going to press the point, unless other members of the Committee wish to." And Congressman Francis E. Walter of Pennsylvania (who in 1954 assumed the chair himself) seemed to agree. "How can it be material to the purpose of this inquiry to have the names of people when we already know them?" he asked. "Why is it so essential that we know the names of all the people when we have a witness who may make a contribution to what we're trying to learn? . . . Isn't it far more important to learn the extent of the activity, and what the purpose of the organization actually was, than to get a long list of names of bleeding hearts and fools, suckers, hard-boiled Communist politicians? . . . As long as we have a witness willing and anxious to cooperate in carrying out what I conceive to be our purpose, I think the rest is all immaterial."

In the afternoon session Parks pleaded with the Committee: "Don't present me with the choice of either being in contempt of this Committee and going to jail or forcing me to really crawl through the mud to be an informer. For what purpose?"[2] But Parks's plea was rejected. The Committee went into executive session, and two days later it was leaked to the press that Parks had succumbed and named the names.* By talking about himself, he had waived the right to refuse to talk about others, the Committee insisted. Of course, the Committee could have granted Parks's request as a matter of decency, even if not of legal right, but it refused to do so. "The ultimate test of the credibility of a witness," Congressman Donald L. Jackson of California later explained, "is the extent to which he is willing to cooperate with the Committee in giving full details as to not only the place of activities, but also the names of those who participated with him in the Communist Party."[3]

It should be noted, however, that the issue of "credibility" did not go to the evidence being presented, for neither Jackson nor anyone else seriously disputed Walter's concession that HUAC already had the evidence it was allegedly seeking. Rather, the Committee was in essence serving as a kind of national parole board, whose job was to determine whether the "criminals" had truly repented of their evil ways. Only by a witness's naming names and giving details, it was said, could the Committee be certain that his break with the past was genuine. The demand for names was not a quest for evidence; it was a test of character. The naming of names had shifted from a means to an end.

From that day forward those called to testify were advised by their at-

---

* Parks's executive-session testimony was not released until 1953, when he wrote Chairman Harold H. Velde of Illinois his "clarifying" letter (see pp. 372–73). The rules governing the taking and the release of secret testimony are at best murky. According to HUAC's research director, executive sessions are held "(1) when the evidence or testimony at an investigative hearing may tend to defame, degrade, or incriminate any person; (2) when the interrogation of a witness in a public hearing might compromise classified information or might endanger the national security; or (3) when it is determined that the interrogation of a witness in a public hearing might tend adversely to affect the national interest" (letter from William G. Shaw to Arnold Green, 13 October 1972). In fact, HUAC sometimes held secret sessions as "rehearsals" before public sessions and, where there were not public sessions, often leaked secret testimony to the press for reasons of politics, publicity, or policy.

torneys that they had three choices: to invoke the First Amendment, with its guarantee of free speech and association, and risk going to prison for contempt of Congress like the Hollywood Ten; to invoke the Fifth Amendment, with its privilege against self-incrimination, and lose their jobs (Howard Da Silva and Gale Sondergaard, who followed Parks onto the stand that day, refused to answer the Committee, citing the Fifth Amendment, and were quickly excused and quickly blacklisted); or to co-operate with the Committee and name names and hope to continue working (as Sterling Hayden did, the first witness after Larry Parks to name names). The ground rules for the decade were set.

Playing the informer runs against the American grain, as Parks rightly indicated. As a people we start out with presumptions against certain ac-tivities, and among these proscribed undertakings are lying, theft, mur-der, incest, treason, and informing. And informing ranks high on this dark list. In the abstract, many Americans would probably subscribe to E. M. Forster's famous sentiment: "If I had to choose between betraying my country and betraying my friend, I hope I should have the guts to be-tray my country."[4]

Going into the 1950s, the image of the informer most Americans car-ried had been set, in no small part, by Hollywood. Thus in prison pic-tures, the only character more predictable than the sadistic guard or "Doc," the alcoholic medic, was the stoolie who gets his come-uppance. In *Brute Force* (1947), directed by Jules Dassin, who was later blacklist-ed, an inmate sums up the prevailing perspective when he says to Hume Cronyn, the sadistic prison guard who wants him to stool, "Captain, I'm a cheap thief. But I'm not an informer."

The informer was the wretched, hulking Gypo Nolan as portrayed by Victor McLaglen in John Ford's 1935 adaptation of Liam O'Flaherty's novel *The Informer*, the story of how Gypo, for thirty pieces of silver, be-trays his best friend, a revolutionary leader who comes out of hiding to see his mother before he dies of consumption. Who could forget the Brit-ish officer's look of contempt as he pushes Gypo's ill-gotten gains across the table with his swagger stick? To protect himself, Gypo accuses an-other man, the tailor Rat Mulligan, then tries to forget his sin in a night of revelry, but ultimately breaks down before the rebel forces' court of in-quiry. "One traitor can destroy an army," we are told, and Gypo has en-dangered "the lives of hundreds of other men who are fighting for what they believe in. . . . An informer is an informer. He's got to be wiped out like the first sign of a plague as soon as he's spotted. He's a common enemy. He's got to be got, Gypo." The generation of moviegoers and moviemakers who came of age in the late 1940s still carry with them the memory of the brilliant scene where, having collected his money, Gypo goes to visit the randy Katie (the dialogue is lifted directly from the novel):

"Ya," she said, "I knew ye were yellow. Have ye robbed a church or what? . . ."

"Shut up," he hissed suddenly, gripping at the word "robbery" and hooking a plan on it. . . . "It wasn't a church. It was a sailor off an American ship. . . . But if ye say a word ye know what yer goin' to get."

"Who? Me?" Katie laughed out loud and looked at him with emphatic scorn over her shoulder. "What d'ye take me for? An informer or what?"

"Who's an informer," cried Gypo, gripping her right knee with his left hand. . . . There was silence for a second. Gypo stared at Katie with a look of ignorant fear on his face. The word had terrified and infuriated him. It was the first time he had heard it uttered in the new sense it now held for him.

"What are ye talkin' about informin' for?" panted Gypo again, tightening his grip on her knee.

Part of our image is conditioned by the narrator's attitude: "Informer! A horror to be understood fully only by an Irish mind. For an awful moment each one present suspected himself or herself. Then each looked at his or her neighbor. Gradually rage took the place of fear. But it had no direction."[5]

For Christians, of course, mention of the informer invokes thoughts of Judas. Biblical scholars still debate whether Judas betrayed Jesus for thirty pieces of silver or because he was possessed by an agent of the devil. But aside from the third-century Gnostics, who briefly proclaimed the mystique of betrayal and celebrated the Gospel of Judas, most people—including those who regard his act as the fulfillment of scriptural prophecy—would agree that he came to symbolize the most repellent of traitors. Commentators have imputed to him every moral crime known to man. One tale casts him in the role of a criminal Oedipus, whose long life of crime culminates in the murder of his father and an incestuous marriage with his mother. Judas is unclean. As the second-century commentator Papias wrote: "His private part appeared more huge and loathsome than any man's 'shame.' Through it he passed pus and worms flowing together from every part of his body to his shame when he revealed himself. . . . "[6]

The informer fares worse, if anything, in the Jewish tradition. The Aramaic word for informer as found in the Book of Daniel is *Akhal Kurtza,* whose literal translation is "to eat the flesh of someone else." The so-called Minean curse, which was introduced as the twelfth benediction to the daily Amidah prayer, says, "And for the informer may there be no hope." Jewish law as found in the Halakah, the Talmud, and the responsa of various rabbis sees the informer as a threat to the entire community, the potential destroyer of a people. Thus Rabbi Abraham Rapaport defines the informer as "a person who informs against the life or property of another Jew to non-Jews." Jewish law requires reporting the informer to the Jewish legal authorities (the Beth Din) and forbids telling the non-Jewish authorities. Penalties for the informer range from flogging and imprisonment to branding the forehead, cutting out the tongue, cutting off the hand, banishment, and, most frequently, death.[7]

When the comic actor Zero Mostel was called in by the producer of a play in which he was appearing and told he had to clear his name, Mostel, the son of a rabbi, explained that he couldn't inform, because "as a Jew, if I inform, I can't be buried on sacred ground."[8]

Despite our culture's profound presumption against playing the informer's role, in the government investigations that followed upon Larry Parks's appearance before HUAC approximately one-third* of the witnesses who actually testified about subversion in the entertainment com-

---

* Professor Howard Suber of UCLA has reported in his unpublished Ph.D. thesis, "The Anti-Communist Blacklist in the Motion Picture Industry" (UCLA, 1968) that of the 90 witnesses from Hollywood who appeared before HUAC between 1951 and 1953, 30 named names. Other scholars have different counts. Larry Ceplair and Steven Englund report in *The Inquisition in Hollywood* (New York, 1980) that 58 of the 110 who were subpoenaed in the second set of hearings named names. In fact, some of those who were named avoided subpoenas by leaving the country, such as John Bright, Ben Barzman, Joseph Losey, Donald Ogden Stewart, and others. Prominent radicals, such as Ian Hunter, Arnaud d'Usseau, John Wexley, and others, were never subpoenaed. Since the various congressional investigating committees never released all of the testimony taken in executive session, and not all those who were subpoenaed actually appeared before HUAC, the precise figures cannot be known. But the estimate that one-third of those faced with the choice named names seems closest to the mark.

munity chose to name names, to "crawl through the mud," to collaborate with the Committee and, at least as it looked from the outside, to betray their friends.

It is my premise that most of the name-namers believed on some level that what they were doing was wrong; that these men and women would have preferred, had they been truly free (most of them waited until they were subpoenaed before they agreed to testify), not to collaborate with the likes of the House Committee on Un-American Activities, Senator Joseph McCarthy's Senate Permanent Subcommittee on Investigations, the Senate Internal Security Committee—all of which had been careless with individual rights and reputations and none of which had demonstrated a seriousness of public purpose; that they shared the revulsion with which our country, our culture, and the entire Judeo-Christian tradition view the informer and the presumption against playing the "squealer," the "fink," the "stoolie."

These were not people who believed, with James Burnham, William F. Buckley, Jr., and some other conservative thinkers of the 1950s, that on balance the investigative committees were engaged in an honest and honorable enterprise. Instead, these people believed (rightly or wrongly) that those they were asked to name had, like themselves and Parks, originally joined the Communist Party out of motives of social conscience at a time when it was in the business of fighting racism and depression at home and fascism abroad, and if there were Soviet espionage agents, which these people doubted, they operated outside the Party apparatus; that although they had supported the Soviet experiment and believed with Lincoln Steffens that it represented the future "and it works," they were patriotic Americans; that they had not engaged in any criminal or truly conspiratorial political activities; and most of all that HUAC was in the business of ruining lives without profiting the nation.

Having said that, I do not mean to preclude the possibility that some, or perhaps even most, of them believed—given the context of the times and the facts of their particular situations—that they were doing their best under all of the circumstances. The presumption against informing is, after all, only a presumption, and presumptions may be rebutted. Our society assumes the citizen's social obligation to report the hit-and-run driver and the legal obligation to testify against him in court. Even at the playground level the same children who are admonished not to be tattletales are also told to report any bullying activities to the nearest grownup. Although during the Watergate years many citizens suspected White House counsel John Dean's motives to be self-serving, most believed that he and the other Watergate felons did the right thing when they informed against Richard Nixon and his cohorts. And the consumer advocate Ralph Nader has called upon our most conscientious civil servants to "blow the whistle" on their superiors when they see them violate the public interest. The castration with a blowtorch of James Ragen, a Chicago racketeer and suspected government informer, by three syndicate executioners in 1947 is testimony both to the violence that the informer provokes and to the power his information has over the corrupt.[9] In other words, the informer's role is more complicated than the examples of E. M. Forster, Gypo Nolan, or Judas might lead us to believe.

There were, of course, witnesses before the congressional investigating committees who did not wait to be called, who were not reluctant, including those who were paid for their information. Some of these informers believed the subversion they were exposing overrode the presumption against informing. None of these quite substantial considerations, however, would seem to apply in the case of a Larry Parks or those who followed him. Congress has two recognized reasons for subpoenaing witnesses: to inform itself as to the need for legislation and to engage in its watch-dog function over activities of the executive branch. Even if the subversive-hunting committees had been interested in collecting information for legislative purposes (and the evidence is that they weren't), the request that each witness name names as a test was not in pursuit of such legitimate ends. Nor were Parks et al. government-connected, so HUAC was performing no real "overseer" role. The purpose of the hearings, although they were not trials, was clearly punitive, yet the procedural safeguards appropriate to tribunals in the business of meting out punishment were absent: there was no cross-examination, no impartial judge and jury, none of the exclusionary rules about hearsay or other evidence. And, of course, the targets from the entertainment business had committed no crime: "whistle-blowing" in this context injured only the innocent.

Yet HUAC couldn't seem to stay away from the motion-picture industry. For every witness from the worlds of labor, science, the armed forces, or education, there were a dozen from the wonderful world of show biz. The Committee undoubtedly enjoyed basking in the publicity glow generated by those it was interrogating. Also, the Communist Party had zeroed in on and attracted more than its share of showfolk, so Hollywood was a logical HUAC hunting ground. These were our pop heroes, the people who created America's stories.

The reason for my focus on the Hollywood informers, then, is not merely that congressional investigators singled them out but more importantly because I want to ask: How was it that so many went along, and with what consequences? What on the surface appears to be the most trivial case turns out to be the most interesting one because it promises to teach us most about the conditions under which good men do things they know or suspect to be wrong, about a political system that puts people in a position where they are encouraged to violate their values, about a republic that asks its citizens to betray their fellows.

If Whittaker Chambers told the truth at the Alger Hiss trial, he helped to uncover a plot to steal state secrets. If David Greenglass told the truth at the Rosenberg trial, he helped bring espionage agents to justice. And although the cold war atmosphere of the late 1940s and 1950s may have made the fairness of these trials problematic, the forum for their testimony, the courts, was the proper one for bringing people to justice. But if Larry Parks told the truth, he simply brought blacklisting upon himself and others like him, people who had joined the Communist Party because it looked like the most liberal party around. The actors, directors, writers, and publicity people called as witnesses before HUAC had no atomic secrets to steal, no vital war materials to leave unloaded on the docks, no opportunities to "poison" young minds in the classroom. It might be argued that the Hollywood people were in the ideal spot to create and distribute Communist propaganda to the American people. But, as the congressional hearings soon made clear (though I would dispute the propriety of conceding to them the right to conduct a propaganda search), the collective nature of work in the Hollywood studio system and on the broadcast networks precluded individual attempts at agitprop, and in any event the final products were available for inspection and criticism in motion-picture theaters and on television sets and radios across the country.

What follows is less a history than a moral detective story. After an introduction to the way in which the informer and what I call the Informer Principle—the naming of names as a test of virtue—determined and defined the cold war environment, I focus on the role of the informer in Hollywood and ask: How did it come to pass that scores of otherwise decent individuals were compelled to betray a moral presumption? What *are* the conditions under which good men do things they know to be wrong? *Are* there justifications for the informers' actions that reasonable men would regard as extenuating, or are there perhaps even mandating circumstances? Can it be that to live lives of moral equilibrium our values must never be tested, for when we adhere to them we destroy what we cherish (as happened to some of the uncooperative witnesses who were blacklisted), yet when we abandon them we destroy our sense of self (as happened to some of the informers)? What happens when a state puts pressure on its citizens to betray their fellows? What did the trade, professional, and voluntary associations, organizations, and institutions do, and by what mechanisms did so many of them undermine the values they were organized and constituted to uphold? How do the informers today feel about what they did yesterday? What are the consequences of betrayal and collaboration? What is the effect of the informer on those he named, on the community, and on himself? What good does thirty-year-old moral outrage and indignation do, and why does it survive in surrogates who will outlive the original participants? Is there—should there be—a statute of limitations on moral crimes? What, in other words, is to be learned from this episode in collaboration and betrayal American-style? These are the questions whose answers I pursue and occasionally suggest in the pages ahead.

V.S.N.

New York, 1980

A Note on Vocabulary

THE COMMUNISTS AND SOME LEFT LIBERALS called them "informers" and "stoolies" and "belly-crawlers." The investigating committees and American Legionnaires called them "patriots" and "courageous." Sometimes they called themselves "friendly" or simply "cooperative" witnesses.

Certainly many of those who named names resisted the informer label. Consider the exchange between the Committee and the writer-director Robert Rossen (*Body and Soul* [1947], *All the King's Men* [1949], etc.), who in 1951 refused to name names but appeared again in 1953 ready to go through the name-naming ritual. "I don't think," he told the congressmen, "after two years of thinking, that any one individual can ever indulge himself in the luxury of individual morality or pit it against what I feel today very strongly is the security and safety of this nation." Congressman Clyde Doyle of California tried to paraphrase Rossen's position: "In other words, you put yourself, then, in a position as a result of your patriotism or patriotic attitude toward your nation, which you came to subsequent to January 25, 1951, where you were willing to be labeled a stool pigeon and an informer, but you felt that was perhaps the privilege rather than a disgrace?"

MR. ROSSEN: I don't feel that I'm being a stool pigeon or an informer. I refuse—I just won't accept that characterization.

CONGRESSMAN KIT CLARDY: Well, Mr. Doyle means—

MR. ROSSEN: No; no. I am not . . . disagreeing with Mr. Doyle, but I think that is a rather romantic—that is like children playing at cops and robbers. They are just kidding themselves, and I don't care what the characterizations in terms of—people can take whatever positions they want. I know what I feel like within myself. Characterization or no characterization, I don't feel that way.[1]

Thus did the terminological terrain constitute a real, if obscure, battlefield of the cold war. Typically, J. Edgar Hoover, then director of the Federal Bureau of Investigation, ever-vigilant against enemy inroads on the semantic front, leaped into the fray. Writing in *Elks Magazine* in 1956, he denounced those who "indulge in sabotage by semantics":

> They stigmatize patriotic Americans with the obnoxious term "informer," when such citizens fulfill their obligations of citizenship by reporting known facts of the evil conspiracy to properly constituted authorities. It would require very little time for these critics to pick up a dictionary. Webster's unabridged volume specifically states that an "informant" is one who gives information of whatever sort; an "informer" is one who informs against another by way of accusation or complaint. Informer is often, informant never, a term of opprobrium.[2]

Although it may not do as a technical definition, for present purposes—and in accordance with what I understand to be popular usage—I define an informer as someone who betrays a comrade, i.e., a fellow member of a movement, a colleague, or a friend, to the authorities. Given this definition, and taking the objections of guilt-by-connotation into account, I think it is useful, when context permits, to call those who named names by their rightful name—informer. For the idea of "playing the informer" was part of what made the decision whether to name or not to name names so painful. The agony of a Larry Parks or even the delayed decision of a Robert Rossen was an acknowledgment that, however they behaved, in their hearts and minds they preferred *not to play the role of the informer.* Even the director Elia Kazan, who took out an ad in 1952 urging others called before HUAC to name names, conceded the presumption against playing the informer when he told a television interviewer in 1972 that although he doesn't feel called upon to apologize for what he did, his decision was not without ambivalence, since "there is something disgusting about naming things, naming names."[3]

By calling people informers, I do not mean to convert the presumption against naming names into an absolute prohibition. In principle, there may be circumstances where informing is the right thing to do, even as there may be circumstances where lying or murder (in self-defense, for instance, or in fighting a just war) is the right thing to do. If there is any literary strategy intended in my choice of vocabulary it is not to denounce by negative labeling but to reflect as accurately as possible the way the act was perceived at the time by "namers," "namees," and interested onlookers.

The writer-director Abraham Polonsky, a former Communist who was an unapologetic Fifth Amendment–invoking witness, explains the actor John Garfield's refusal to name names in terms that make clear the importance of the informer or stool-pigeon label. "He said he hated Communists, he hated Communism, he was an American. He told the Committee what it wanted to hear. But he wouldn't say the one thing that would keep him from walking down his old neighborhood block. Nobody could say, 'Hey, there's the fucking stool pigeon.' You see, that's what he was fighting against: He should be a stool pigeon because he can only gain from it, yet he can't do it because in his mind he lives in the street where he comes from and in the street he comes from you're not a stool pigeon. That's the ultimate horror."

Interestingly enough, Whittaker Chambers adopted the term "informer" when referring to himself in *Witness*. This was not because of any misapprehension about the word's dark connotations. Rather, Chambers, like HUAC, seemed to argue that informing was the inevitable hell through which the ex-Communist must pass on his road back to self-respect and redemption, and names were the bullets with which ex-Communists might slay the red dragon. According to Chambers, when he was still in the Communist Party in the 1930s and a friend urged him to break with it, he said: "You know that the day I walk out of the Communist Party, I walk into the police station." He meant, he later wrote, that the question which first faces every man and woman who breaks with the Communist Party is: Shall I become an informer against it? "My answer stopped the conversation, for to my friend as to me, 'informer' is a word so hateful that when, years later, in testifying before a grand jury I came to that word and my decision to become an informer, I could not at once go on."

In fact, says Chambers, his distaste for the idea of informing was so great that even after he broke with the Party, determined "to immobilize it, and if possible to smash it," he was not ready to become an informer. "Informing involves individual human beings, and neither then nor at any subsequent time were my actions directed against individual Communists, even when, perforce, I had to strike at the Communist Party as a political organization. I therefore decided to try first of all to smash the secret apparatus by myself."

It took him seven years, Chambers wrote, to realize he had no choice. Finally, he says, fearing that the Communists in government would give subversive policy advice, he flew to Washington, D.C., to tell all to A. A. Berle in the State Department. He recorded his thoughts, he tells us, at the time:

To be an informer . . .

Men shrink from that word and what it stands for as from something lurking and poisonous. Spy is a different breed of word. Espionage is a function of war whether it be waged between nations, classes, or parties. Like the soldier, the spy stakes his freedom or his life on the chances of action. Like the soldier, his acts are largely impersonal. He seldom knows whom he cripples or kills. Spy as an epithet is a convention of morale; the enemy's spy is always monstrous; our spy is daring and brave. It must be so since all camps use spies and must while war lasts.

The informer is different, particularly the ex-Communist informer. He risks little. He sits in security and uses his special knowledge to destroy others. He has that special information to give because he knows those others' faces, voices, and lives, because he once lived within their confidence, in a shared faith, trusted by them as one of themselves, accepting their friendship, feeling their pleasures and griefs, sitting in their houses, eating at their tables, accepting their kindness, knowing their wives and children. If he had not done these things, he would have no use as an informer.

Because he has that use the police must protect him. He is their creature. When they whistle he fetches a soiled bone of information. . . . He has surrendered his choice. To that extent, though he be free in every other way, the informer is a slave. He is no longer a man. . . . He is free only to the degree in which he understands what he is doing and why he must do it.

Let every ex-Communist look unblinkingly at that image. It is himself. By the logic of his position in the struggles of this age, every ex-Communist is an informer from the moment he breaks with Communism, regardless of how long it takes him to reach the police station. . . .

I hold that it is better, because in general clarity is more maturing than illusion, for the ex-Communist to make the offering in the full knowledge of what he is doing, the knowledge that henceforth he is no longer a free man but an informer. . . . Those who do not inform are still conniving at that evil. That is the crux of the moral choice which the ex-Communist must make in recognizing that the logic of his position makes him an informer.

For Chambers, one was an informer not out of choice but "out of necessity." The question for the ex-Communist was not whether to inform but when and how. "On the road of the informer it is always night," he wrote in his inimitable, melodramatic way. "I who have traveled it from end to end, and know its windings, switchbacks and sheer drops—I cannot say at what point the ex-Communist must make his decision to take it. . . . If he means to be effective, if he does not wish the act merely to be wasted suffering for others and himself, how, when and where the ex-Communist informs are matters calling for the shrewdest judgment."[4]

One doesn't have to accept Chambers' apocalyptic perspective or his ideological baggage to understand why he used the word informer the way he did—not to condemn, but rather to signify a process of personal betrayal said to be necessary for the greater good of mankind and the redemption of his soul.* He incarnated the Informer Principle—an unwritten law that came to underlie and govern so many cold war situations that by the time HUAC announced its second round of entertainment investigations in 1951, naming names seemed less a taboo-ridden activity than a 1950s folkway.

Chambers, it should be noted, represents only one type of informer that emerged during the cold war years—we may call them, as they called themselves, the espionage-exposers. If people like Chambers and Elizabeth Bentley (who purported to identify a number of Washington spy rings) were telling the truth, it would be dubious indeed to attack them as betrayers without honoring them as espionage-exposers. As it

---

* Having said that, it is important to note that the occasion for Chambers' ruminations may not have involved informing at all. For his message to Berle fell far short of his subsequent message to the world. He named for Berle the members of what he alleged to be a Communist cell operating out of Washington, but, according to some scholars who have examined Berle's notes of the meeting, he made a point of denying what he later was to charge—that Alger Hiss was involved in espionage. If Chambers later told the truth when he laid the theft of the so-called Pumpkin Papers to Hiss, then on the day in question, with Berle, he was less an informer than a liar, for it would have been lying-by-omission to fail to report the Pumpkin Papers espionage. (And if he *later* lied, then he was never an informer vis-à-vis Hiss, merely a lying accuser.) Thus Chambers' willingness to be called an informer may be an act of penance or a grand strategy of obfuscation; to denounce himself as an informer lends credibility to his credentials as an accuser.

happens, there are so many unanswered questions of fact surrounding their charges that it is impossible to say with certainty who belongs to this class of informer-as-spy-catcher. But whether history reveals Chambers to have been liar or truth-teller—the debate still rages—it seems indisputable that he helped to bring about the metamorphosis of the informer's image from rat to lion, from stoolie to patriot. Chambers himself was originally an object of obloquy, and when he first appeared before the Committee he appeared disheveled, disturbed, mercurial. After his HUAC testimony in 1948, his espionage charges later in the same year, the conviction of Hiss in 1950 for perjury, and the publication of *Witness* in 1952, which was featured for eight weeks in the *Saturday Evening Post* and selected as a Book-of-the-Month, Chambers began to seem respectable, and so, by that time, did the informer as a social type. By their example, the espionage-exposers gave informing a good name, and undoubtedly the prestige that was conferred on them by the culture was not lost on those ex-Communists with no espionage to expose but nevertheless a subpoena to contend with. In addition, their revelations lent a tone of urgency to the political situation, which was invoked by others to justify the suspension of traditional personal and political loyalties.

A second type of informer was the so-called professional witness—a person who would move from tribunal to tribunal "exposing" Communists and Communism, often for a fee—men such as Louis Budenz, former editor of the *Daily Worker;* John Lautner, who was expelled in 1950 from the Party under suspicion of being an FBI informer (he wasn't at the time but became one later, out of bitter disillusionment at the Party's failure to heed his protestations of innocence); or Harvey Matusow, the former Young Communist Leaguer, who eventually informed on the informers. The testimony of these people resulted in the conviction of scores of Party leaders under the Smith Act, for "conspiring to advocate the overthrow of the government by force and violence." These men and women elaborated their stories before federal, state, and local legislatures as well as in private forums, and their accusations cost hundreds of citizens their jobs.

As a class these professional or "kept" witnesses, as the journalist Richard Rovere called them,[5] played fast and loose with the facts and in time returned to the informer his bad name. But the immediate effect of their scary reports on the anatomy of the red dragon was to confirm a secondary message—that the informer was a Saint George who could slay the dragon, and the culture would reward him for such work.

Third, there were those whom Mr. Hoover called "confidential informants"—anonymous folk planted in or recruited from the Communist Party (or other allegedly subversive organizations) by the FBI, who reported regularly to the bureau. These people were, for the most part, police spies and/or agents provocateurs, and when they filed their reports, it was less a matter of betraying a friend than of simply doing a job, dirty work though it may have been. Some of them, like Angela Calomiris and Herbert Philbrick, first surfaced to testify in the key 1949 Smith Act trial in Foley Square and then moved on to become professional witnesses. There is no reason not to call such operatives "confidential informants"—although some of them plunged so exuberantly into their double and triple lives that they made (and ended up having to betray) intimate friendships and consequently faced much the same dilemma as the non-professional informer—for they supplied much of the material used to build dossiers on their unwitting comrades. These people also, like the espionage-exposers, contributed to the growing myth of the informer as folk hero—through the publication in newspapers and books, serialization on radio, on television, and in movies, of their tales.*

Finally, there were the private citizens like Parks and Rossen, many of whom had left the Communist Party more than a decade before, who appeared as one-time-only informers before a congressional committee and, under (but not always because of) the threat of being blacklisted, named names. This book is focused on this last group of informers—many of them reluctant, in the sense that had it not been for a subpoena and/or the pressure, they wouldn't have done it.

The espionage exposers, the kept witnesses, and the confidential informants had in common that they were ultimately volunteers, enthusiasts of betrayal; nevertheless, to the extent that their betrayal was shown as the price of patriotism, they served as role models for reluctant informers in academe, the sciences, government, and, most visibly and volubly, the entertainment community. They were fixtures on the landscape, against which the citizens hauled before congressional committees and asked to name names measured themselves when deciding what to do. Most of these citizens thought of themselves as informers, and that is what I call them.

---

* Occasionally the categories overlapped. Thus Elizabeth Bentley was both a self-styled espionage-exposer and a professional witness. Leo Townsend named names before a congressional committee but also testified at a deportation proceeding. Philbrick was a confidential informant who graduated to professional witness. And so on.

Contents

INTRODUCTION
THE INFORMER
AS PATRIOT

WE CALL IT THE COLD WAR but it was really three simultaneous conflicts: a global confrontation between rival imperialisms and ideologies, between capitalism and Communism, between the United States of America and the Union of Soviet Socialist Republics; a domestic clash in the United States between hunters and hunted, investigators and investigated, guardians of internal security and protectors of individual liberty, a war between "red-baiters" and "reds"; and, finally, a civil war amongst the hunted, a fight within the liberal community itself, a running battle between the anti-Communist liberals and those who called themselves progressives, the so-called anti-anti-Communists.

The dilemma confronting reluctant informers such as Larry Parks can't be fully understood outside the context of the cold war, but a true understanding of the cold war itself, including how it was experienced at the time, requires also an appreciation of the role of the *un*reluctant informer in each of these three wars. In fact he emerged as our authorized biographer of Communism—shaping and confirming its image as a worldwide, ideologically driven conspiratorial monolith. His first-person accounts in books, in articles, and in volumes of testimony before courts, committees, and secret tribunals conveniently supplied the evidence for prosecutors, arguments for legislators, illustrations for historians, premises for philosophers, anecdotes for journalists.

Mixing memory and fantasy, insight and paranoia, fact and fiction in a brew of bitterness, informers linked the Comintern to the Communist Party USA to Communist fronts to the Progressive Party to New Dealers to liberals—providing ideological ammunition to cold warriors on all three fronts.

The espionage-exposer served the state and justified the expansion of state power in the name of national security because in reporting on the activities of spies he confirmed the notion that many Americans had of all Communists as "agents of a foreign power." The professional witness served the state's internal-security bureaucracy by dipping into an apparently bottomless well of memories of subversion and producing endless lists of names to check, trace, process, subpoena, and harass. The citizen-informer served the liberals by providing them with seemingly plausible grounds for simultaneously denouncing the hunters and dissociating themselves from the hunted.

In all these capacities, many of those who played the informer stretched, distorted, inflated, and otherwise decomplicated the truth. They contributed to the cartoon history of the cold war as a struggle between the good guys (us) and the bad guys (you know who).

Perhaps sensing the informer's singular contribution to the cold war zeitgeist, the American state and American culture gave him employment, conferred prestige upon him, and conspired and collaborated to improve his image. Our courts protected him, our Congress praised him, our mayors honored him, our entrepreneurs employed him, our media romanticized him, our intellectuals legitimized him. He was simultaneously the repression's radar and its role model.

Each of the three great conflicts had emblematic informers, cold war correspondents who sent America its images of the enemy and, simultaneously, heated up the conflict. If any single individual can claim credit for establishing the link between the international cold war and the domestic one, between Soviet aggression abroad and the red menace at home, it is Whittaker Chambers. The conviction of Alger Hiss following Chambers' charges that he had been a Russian spy established the fundamental cold war assumption that to be a Communist was to be an agent of a foreign power.

A second great political case, the 1949 Smith Act trial of eleven leaders of the Communist Party in New York, wrote the script for a series of similar trials across the country, which in addition to smashing the Communist Party helped to set the tone for the domestic cold war and provided the legal framework for a decade of political harassment that, at best, operated at the margins of the law. The only "evidence" at these trials in addition to quotations from Marxist-Leninist classics was provided by a parade of FBI informants and ex-Communists, many of them professional informers. The conviction of the Party leadership in the Dennis case, as it was called (after one of the defendants), came to stand for the proposition that to be a Communist was to be a revolutionary conspirator, dedicated to the overthrow of the government by force and violence.

If the informers in these two instances functioned as agents of the right, smearing the New Deal, liberals, and fellow travelers, the informers in the civil war among the liberals played a quite different role. The liberal informer functioned as a litmus test for the left, whose ostensible purpose was to exonerate rather than expose by proving liberalism was free of any Communist taint. An emblematic example is James Wechsler, editor of the fiercely anti-McCarthy tabloid *New York Post*. By handing Senator McCarthy a list of names of former Communists even while denouncing him, Wechsler (and other reluctant informers, including many of those I shall consider later) hoped to establish the proposition that it was possible to be anti-Communist and anti-McCarthy at the same time. But in the contemporary context, the liberal informer was important less for what he had to reveal about those he named than what he revealed about himself. If the effect of the informers in the larger conflicts at home and abroad was to damage the left, those in the liberal community who named names or lent support to that action had as their goal to preserve and fortify their "liberal" outpost by means of this ultimate anti-Communist gesture.

HUAC's assault on Hollywood was at once a response to international tensions, a battlefield in the war between the hunters and the hunted, and an intervention in the war between the liberals. But its attempt to cleanse the cultural apparatus can be understood only within the larger framework of the efforts to cleanse the political apparatus. In both of these dubious enterprises the informer was the nonsecret agent, the instrument of the purge.

1.

The Espionage Informer

BY MARCH 1946, when Winston Churchill made his famous speech in Fulton, Missouri, the cold war was already under way. "From Stettin in the Baltic to Trieste in the Adriatic, an iron curtain has descended across the Continent allowing 'police governments' to rule Eastern Europe," he said. Although his analysis was defensible, his speech had about it the air of a self-fulfilling prophecy.

The years which followed saw the dialectic of escalating suspicions, mistrust, and armaments speeding up. The Russians rejected U.S. aid. The United States announced the Truman Doctrine and the Marshall Plan of economic and military aid to stop Communism. The Russians rejected the American offer to neutralize the "secret" of the atomic bomb through international controls and instead exploded one of their own. The diplomat-scholar George Kennan, writing as Mr. X, elaborated a doctrine of containment of Soviet Communism, a notion that guided American foreign policy for the next decade. The Russians blocked traffic to and from Berlin and appeared to be suppressing one East European government after another. The United States joined what was euphemistically called a "police action" against North Korea after its army had crossed the 38th parallel into South Korea.

Revisionist historians argue that the roots of Soviet actions lie more in national fears going back to Peter the Great than in the ideological imperatives of Marx and Engels, that its moves in Eastern Europe might be more usefully understood in terms of Russia's postwar needs for markets and raw materials than any demon drive for world conquest, that Truman rather than Stalin was the true father of the cold war. But whether or not this is the case, the fact is that in the 1950s the domestic American consensus was that the United States was defender rather than aggressor in the cold war. A major contributor to this "wisdom" was the ex-Communist whose testimony helped to create, confirm, and fix the image of the Soviet Union as subverter of American capitalism, to link Soviet imperialism abroad to the "red menace" at home, to persuade Americans that "the Russian fifth column in the United States is greater than Hitler's ever was."[1]

Of all of the ex-Communists, Whittaker Chambers left the most indelible imprint. After Alger Hiss sued Chambers for libel, Chambers, who on sixteen previous occasions had denied that any espionage was involved in his past Communist activities, reached into his pumpkin, pulled out five rolls of microfilm, and changed his accusation against Hiss from mere Party membership to one of espionage. The next day Congressman Richard Nixon was on the front page, waving the microfilm rolls and calling them "secret government documents" that provided proof, "conclusively established," of the existence of a vast Soviet spy network operated by members of the Communist Party in America. Looking at the microfilms for the press with a magnifying glass, Nixon was quoted under banner headlines saying, "This conspiracy comprises one of the most serious series of treasonable activities which has been launched against the government in the history of America."[2]* In *Witness,* Chambers wrote, "Alger Hiss is only one name that stands for the whole Communist penetration of government."[3] Whether or not Hiss was guilty, Chambers was certainly correct about what he symbolized.

Nonetheless Chambers, despite the increasingly accusatory nature of his tale, the inconsistencies in his story, and his chronic inability to distinguish fact from fantasy, was transformed in the public eye from nut to prophet. A gifted short-story writer and translator (*Bambi* was his), he quickly put his story into powerful best-seller form and critics hailed his autobiography as a literary and political masterpiece. Arthur M. Schlesinger, Jr., compared it favorably to the *Autobiography of Lincoln Steffens,*[4] and John Dos Passos put it "somewhere between Dostoievsky's *The Possessed* and the narratives of the adventures of the light within like *Pilgrim's Progress.*"[5]

The real messages in Chambers' pumpkin had nothing to do with

---

* Only two strips of microfilm were introduced at Hiss's trial. The others, it was said, were held back for security reasons. Twenty-five years later, a Freedom of Information Act suit brought by Hiss and William Reuben, a Hiss-Chambers biographer, sprung the three unintroduced rolls from the U.S. attorney's office in the Southern District of New York; one of them turned out to be blank, while the two others were faintly legible copies of Department of the Navy documents relating to life rafts and fire extinguishers. (National Emergency Civil Liberties Foundation, press release, 31 July 1975.) Whatever the truth about the Hiss case, the microfilms seem far less menacing than Nixon had suggested.

Hiss's guilt or innocence. They were: that to be a Communist Party member was to be a spy; that to be a Russian was to foment worldwide revolution; that to be an informer was to be a patriot; that to be a New Dealer was to be a dupe; and that other ex-Coms should be heeded, no matter how improbable their tales. Along with Chambers came Elizabeth Bentley, whose story of life in the red underground had been discounted when she first approached the FBI in 1945. As with Chambers, it is impossible to know where Miss Bentley's truths stopped and her fantasies began, but that is part of the point—the press, for the most part, didn't bother to try to make the distinction. There is no reason to doubt that the "blonde spy queen," as others called her, or the "red spy queen," as she called herself,[6] had been the lover of one Jacob Golos, an admitted Soviet agent, as she claimed; and there is every reason to believe that he tried to use her to obtain information for his government. (The pattern of Soviet male diplomat-agents using women for espionage purposes is well-known in other countries and contexts.) What can be said with certainty is that her gift for the telling example gave resonance to her stories of the Soviet menace.

One example is Bentley's claim that she brought her Soviet lover the exact timing of the D day invasion of Europe. Her ability to summon up such detail lent her stories an air of verisimilitude and made good copy, since it gave the American reader concrete images of the long reach of the Soviet conspiracy. (As it happens, this particular "recollection" may have been flawed. Because of weather and logistics, the Allies had set a time bracket rather than a specific date for the invasion; the decision to proceed on June 6 was not taken until June 5; according to Winston Churchill and the head of our own military mission to Moscow at the time, the Allies kept the Soviets posted on invasion planning all along, including the approximate date. Despite this, Bentley was unflappable in carrying out her professional activities as anti-Communist witness. Time and again she repeated her D day story and others no less shaky.)

Bentley's symbolic importance to the state was less than Chambers', since no great spy case hinged on her testimony. Yet, since her map to the espionage underground had received wide dissemination and acceptance in official circles, the government had a stake in preserving her fragile reputation: Miss Bentley had charged in more than a score of witnessings before various juries, committees, and other tribunals and in her memoir, *Out of Bondage,* that she was in touch with forty spies and two spy rings—one headed by Nathan Gregory Silvermaster, an economist with the Farm Security Administration, and the other by Victor Perlo, an economist with the War Production Board. The depth of the state's commitment to the good reputation of her testimony is well seen in the unhappy case of William Remington, a Commerce Department employee who attacked her veracity: he denied her allegations that he had passed secret government documents to her, documents she claimed she then gave to Golos, her NKVD lover.

There were a number of obvious and real parallels between the Remington and the Hiss cases (two bright Ivy Leaguers accused in congressional hearings by ex-Communists of having transmitted classified information to the enemy and subsequently convicted of perjury); there were also differences that needn't concern us here, but one of them was that in February 1950 Remington won a $9000 settlement in a libel suit against his accuser. By the spring of 1950, Miss Bentley was in trouble. Her usefulness to the government as a witness was declining, and she supported herself by lecturing and writing about her career as a spy. But none of the other persons she had publicly named as spies was prosecuted, and Remington had been cleared by the government's loyalty review board fifteen months earlier. If his version of events were now permitted to stand, Miss Bentley's already sagging reputation might be fatally undermined. A new grand jury was convened in May 1950, and in addition to Remington, his former wife, Ann Moos Remington, was called as a witness.

The extraordinary pressure put on Ann Moos Remington to discredit her ex-husband's testimony becomes comprehensible only in the context of the government's interest in protecting the reputation of one of its more visible informers. Remington was indicted and tried twice.* (The guilty verdict at the first trial was reversed on appeal but the indictment stood.) At the second trial, which began in January 1953, he was convicted on two counts of perjury. On appeal the grand jury minutes of the original indictment surfaced—in the course of a dissenting opinion by Judge Learned Hand that resists paraphrase:

> For myself, the [original grand jury] examination [of Mrs. Remington] went beyond what I deem permissible. Pages on pages of lecturing

* A complicating factor: the foreman of the grand jury in the first trial in 1950, one John Brunini, turned out to be providing editorial assistance to Miss Bentley for the book she was planning to publish with the Devin-Adair Company. Although counsel for the government knew the facts of the Bentley-Brunini relationship at the time the first indictment against Remington was returned, he did not notify the defense. (Brief for Appellant, *United States* v. *William Walter Remington*, U.S. Court of Appeals for the Second Circuit, 81–85.)

repeatedly preceded a question; statements of what the prosecution already knew, and of how idle it was for the witness to hold back what she could contribute; occasional reminders that she could be punished for perjury; all were scattered throughout. Still she withstood the examiners, until, being much tried and worn, she said: "I am getting fuzzy. I haven't eaten since a long time ago and I don't think I am going to be very coherent from now on. I would like to postpone the hearings. . . . I want to consult my lawyers and see how deep I am getting in." This was denied, and the questioning kept on until she finally refused to answer, excusing herself because she was "tired" and "would like to get something to eat. . . . Is this the third degree, waiting until I get hungry now?" Still the examiners persisted, disregarding this further protest: "I would like to get something to eat. But couldn't we continue another day? Or do I have to come back?" Thereupon there took place . . . what proved to be the *coup de grace,* after which she made a full disclosure of what she knew: a very large part of it what Remington had told her during their marriage and before they separated in January 1947.

. . . I shall assume for argument that, had there been nothing more than I have mentioned, the indictment might have stood up. It is the added circumstance that, as I have already said, a very large part of Ann Remington's testimony consisted of confidential communications from her husband to her, that satisfies any doubts I might otherwise have had. That was testimony as much privileged in a federal court as in a state court; moreover, the privilege extends to a proceeding before a grand jury. Although I have found no federal decisions, I accept it also as the law that her later separation and divorce from Remington did not open the witness's mouth; indeed, any other view would be completely inconsistent with the theory of the privilege. It will have been observed how important a part this played in the result, for in his final admonition that effected her breakdown, Brunini [foreman of the grand jury] not only threatened her with contempt proceedings, but expressly told her that she had no privilege. His language is worth repeating: "Now, I have already pointed out to you that you have a question from the Special Assistant to the Attorney General: Did your husband or did he not give this money to the Communist Party? *You have no privilege to refuse to answer the question.*" Read literally, that was true; but, read as the witness must have understood it—that is, whether her husband had not told her so—it was altogether false.[7]

Thus William Remington, a minor figure in Elizabeth Bentley's tales of Washington spy rings (she had said she dropped him because he never had any useful information), suddenly became extraordinarily important—for the reason that he had chosen to fight back at her. As his counsel, Joseph L. Rauh, Jr., argued in his 1953 appeal brief:

> In their five-day examination of Remington, both Brunini [the foreman] and Donegan [the prosecutor] likewise demonstrated their preoccupation with the rehabilitation of Bentley. Again and again they came back to the question of Remington's libel suit against Bentley and demanded to know why he thought the $9000 settlement was a "vindication" in his struggle against Bentley. They asked him about his relations with Daniel Lang and Alan Barth who had written pieces in *The New Yorker* and *The Washington Post* siding with Remington in his battle against Bentley. They asked who was financing his fight against Bentley, who was paying his investigator, Mr. Bielaski, whether the American Civil Liberties Union was paying anything, and what Bielaski had found out about Bentley. They asked what Remington's own lawyers had told him about Bentley and denied the relevance of the attorney-client privilege before the grand jury. . . . On an even lower level, [Remington] was asked irrelevant questions concerning his divorce, whether he had ever struck his wife, whether he had ever committed adultery, whether he had ever had psychiatric treatment, whether he had sought to avoid combat service during the war, and whether he had ever shared the same bed with a male roommate.[8]

Since Remington had appeared before a federal grand jury in New York City in April 1947 and had not been indicted, and before another grand jury in the District of Columbia in May 1950 and had not been indicted, Rauh's conclusion was that the main reason Remington was summoned yet again later that month was to rehabilitate Bentley. Rauh's analysis of the motives for the prosecution seems persuasive, and remains so even if Remington was guilty of perjury. The state had rehabilitated one informer by creating another, albeit a reluctant one. (Ann Remington frankly told the prosecutor that she preferred not to testify against her former husband, because if he were convicted that might imperil the support payments he gave for the children.)

———

If the state legitimized and then protected the informer by assaulting his detractors, the media romanticized him. As Whittaker Chambers moved from the congressional committee room to the top of the best-seller list, other espionage exposers were celebrated on stage, screen, and radio, in print, and even in the streets. There were ceremonies, awards, and banquets in their honor. Boston declared a Philbrick Day to honor the man who led three lives (as Communist, as FBI informant, and as private citizen). It was even suggested that informers be given medals for gallantry like those awarded to soldiers who had distinguished themselves on the field of battle. After Morris Appleman told HUAC he became a Communist because his father was an atheist, he returned to Denver, where he was asked to appear before the board of the Denver Hospital, where he worked as executive secretary, to hear his fate. On Sunday morning, January 13, 1952, *The Rocky Mountain News* editorialized that unless Denver rewarded his honesty after thirteen years as an agent of a foreign power, there would never again be a chance for "honest fugitives from the tyranny of the Communist Party to expect sanctuary or understanding, to encourage them in ever breaking with the Party." That Sunday afternoon the hospital board gave Appleman a unanimous vote of confidence and, as NBC reported it, "All Denver commended him and stood by him."[9] Pittsburgh declared Matt Cvetic Day in 1951 on the occasion of the film premiere of *I Was a Communist for the FBI,* ostensibly based on his real-life exploits. After a luncheon in his honor, Cvetic marched through downtown Pittsburgh in a parade which passed in front of the courthouse where a Smith Act trial just happened to be in progress. Angela Calomiris, a witness in the Dennis case, won a citation for patriotic assistance to the FBI, and this was announced in a press release during the course of the trial.

Although television was just coming into its own, its view of politics-as-entertainment infected all major media and seemed especially suited to the task of dramatizing the ways in which informer Davids fought the Communist Goliath. As the sociologist Edward Shils has written, "The new technique of reporting, the tone of the news in the popular press which was interested in sensation, in the dramatic and the scandalous . . . influenced the tone of political discourse. The journalist . . . brought into political reporting an imagery and a conception of the world which pushed politics into the direction of melodrama and crisis." Shils found that the popular journalist's interest in an event only if it is at its most intense level of melodrama matched "the journalist's own professional view that the world is a melodrama and that practically all that falls outside the extremes is dead, stale stuff which can interest no one and which is of no significance."[10] The red menace of the early 1950s was ready-made for such reportage. Religious and moral considerations aside, what made the media's presentation of the informer-as-intrepid-hero an undertaking at once Herculean and delicate were the incessant distortions, fabrications, inaccuracies, and outright lies attributable to those who specialized in exposing the red blueprint for world domination, the red fifth column.

Thus Joseph Alsop pointed out in 1950 in his syndicated newspaper column that Louis Budenz, after giving the FBI three thousand hours of his most cooperative time over a four-year period and telling it all he knew based on his experience in the Party, had *not once* mentioned the name of Owen Lattimore, of the Institute of Pacific Relations, as a Communist. In 1947, when a State Department investigator asked Budenz, he had said he "did not recall any instances" that suggested Lattimore was a Communist. In 1949 he had told his editor at *Collier's* magazine that Lattimore, "though misguided," had never "acted as a Communist in any way."

Then in March 1950 Senator McCarthy followed up his charge that there were however many "card-carrying Communists" and "Comsymps" in the State Department with a promise to name "the top Russian espionage agent in the United States." The Tydings Committee, a subcommittee of the Senate Foreign Relations Committee chaired by Senator Millard Tydings of Maryland, which was directed to investigate the loyalty of State Department employees, assembled in emergency session to hear the news. McCarthy said Lattimore was Alger Hiss's boss in the espionage ring in State, and if anything went wrong on this one the subcommittee shouldn't listen to him on anything else. By the time Lattimore was summoned back from Afghanistan to deny all and produce vast documentation including letters from Chiang Kai-shek and others to prove his loyalty, McCarthy had amended his claim: what he had really meant to say was that Lattimore was "the chief architect of our Far Eastern policy" and as such was "a policy risk."

But when the Tydings Committee found no evidence of subversive activities in Lattimore's file, McCarthy took action. He produced Budenz, who swore that in 1944 his superiors in the Party had told him "to consider Owen Lattimore as a Communist." Asked to explain why Lattimore's name had not come up in his earlier testimony or in either of the two name-crammed books he had written about life in the Party, Budenz said, "In another book which I am writing, Mr. Lattimore is very prominent." He had lied about Lattimore to his *Collier's* editor and the State Department investigator, he said, because he followed the rule of making disclosure to the FBI alone, and the FBI hadn't asked him about Lattimore until a few days earlier.

Lattimore was indicted for and finally in 1955 cleared of perjury, but the image of Lattimore-the-red and, more importantly, the image of a Soviet Union with tentacles extending to the inner reaches of our policy-making apparatus lingered on. Once again, an ex-Com had done his work.

Informers received both psychological and material gratification from exaggerating the truth, as the writer-lawyer Frank Donner suggested in an article in the spring of 1954 for *The Nation,* in which he reported any number of informer-lies. Consider the informer Paul Crouch, about whom Richard Rovere reported in a 1955 article on "The Kept Witnesses" in *Harper's* magazine, a man who had been court-martialed in 1925 for revolutionary activities in the Hawaii Communist League ("fomenting revolution, in both the garrison and the civilian population of Hawaii," said the press) and sentenced to forty years in jail. (The sentence had been commuted to three and he was released from Alcatraz in 1927.) In 1925 he had told the court-martial, "I am in the habit of writing letters to my friends and imaginary persons, sometimes to kings and other foreign persons, in which I place myself in an imaginary position." Later he went to Moscow where, he said, Marshal Tukhachevsky gave him plans "they had formulated for the penetration of the American armed forces."

A jury awarded Armand Scala of the Transport Workers Union $5000 in a libel suit against the Hearst publications because of what Crouch had written: having told HUAC in May 1949 that he didn't know if Scala was a member of the CP, twelve days later Crouch wrote that Scala "has been the chief Communist courier to Latin America, making trips without charge on Pan Am as far as Rio de Janeiro, Brazil, and Buenos Aires, Argentina." Crouch also named former FCC commissioner-attorney Clifford Durr and his wife, Virginia, and the newspaperman Joseph Lash, as Communists. Virginia Durr—Justice Hugo Black's sister-in-law—called him a "grinning, lying dog,"[11] Clifford Durr tried to punch Crouch in the nose, and Lash wrote, "Paul Crouch lied in his statement about me."

The informer Manning Johnson placed the West Coast labor leader Harry Bridges (at his second trial in 1949) at a Communist convention in New York City on June 17 or 28, 1936, but Bridges produced a half-dozen witnesses and documentary evidence that proved he couldn't have been there. In 1951 Johnson admitted to patriotic lying.

Q. In other words, you will tell a lie under oath in a court of law rather than run counter to your instructions from the FBI. Is that right?

JOHNSON: If the interests of my government are at stake. In the face of enemies at home and abroad, if maintaining secrecy of the techniques and methods of operation of the FBI, who have responsibility of the protection of our people, I say I will do it a thousand times.

When it was pointed out during cross-examination in a Pennsylvania sedition case (a so-called little Smith Act case) that his testimony in a deportation proceeding in 1948 "was not correct," Johnson answered: "No, it wasn't precisely, because I could not at that time reveal the fact that I had supplied information to the FBI. . . . I think the security of the government of the United States has priority over . . . any other consideration."[12]

Given this record, one might conclude that the political informers' public image was beyond repair. Yet, as Richard Donnelly wrote then in the *Yale Law Journal,* "Curiously enough, the political informer, spy, or agent provocateur is not now regarded with the same opprobrium as his brother who participates in other types of crime. Public opinion being what it is, his credibility is at a premium. His veracity exceeds that of his more orthodox and less eccentric fellows. He may admit to all kinds of past knavery and mendacity but the greater his self-abasement the greater his claim to belief. That he now acts from patriotic motives is conclusively presumed."[13]

The popular culture also got into the act. Hollywood made more than thirty-five anti-Communist movies, starting in the late 1940s and running through the mid-1950s, although, as Dorothy Jones noted, they all lost money;[14] and films such as *The Red Menace* (1949), *Walk East on Beacon Street* (1952), *I Was a Communist for the FBI* (1951), and *Iron Curtain* (1948) were so stereotyped that their message was scarcely believable. Nora Sayre has hilariously pointed out:

These movies instruct us especially on how American Communists look: most are apt to be exceptionally haggard or disgracefully pudgy. Occasionally they're effeminate; a man who wears gloves shouldn't be trusted. However, in films that feature dauntless FBI agents, it's very difficult to tell them apart from the enemy, since both often lurk on street corners in raincoats and identical snap brims while pretending to read newspapers, and also because many B-actors lack distinguishing features: they simply look alike. Just when you assume that the miscreants are massing to plot, they turn out to be the heroes. But you can sometimes spot a Communist because his shadow looms larger and blacker than his adversary's. Also, movie-Communists walk on a forward slant, revealing their dedication to their cause. Now and then, they're elegantly dressed, equipped with canes and stick-pins—which prove them hypocrites. But most are scruffy.

In many of these movies, there's a figure whom my notes identify as the Bad Blonde: in the 1950s, you knew that there was something wrong with a woman if her slip straps showed through her blouse; in this context, it meant treason. Communists also defile chaste American institutions—by meeting in the Boston Public Gardens amid the swanboats, or by carrying a copy of the *Reader's Digest* or a TWA flight bag in order to recognize one another—and they do frightful things to flags. Bereft of any humor, they grimly demand explanations of "jokes," and are incapable of asking civil questions, except when they're offering "More scotch?" to a possible recruit. . . . Moreover, Communists are cruel to animals. . . . Often, they can be detected by their style of inhaling: they expel smoke very slowly from their nostrils before threatening someone's life, or suggesting that "harm" will come to his family.

Communists "never keep their promises," and they tend to go berserk when they're arrested. But they devote so much time to spying on one another that it's hard to see how they could have any free time for serious espionage. While almost all are raving villains, a few are permitted "reasons" for joining the party, such as the Depression or fighting fascism abroad, and a couple were snared by their own "idealism." These movies dispense the fantasy that when such souls repent and try to resign, their comrades either expose their membership to the FBI—so that they'll be jailed or deported—or kill them. Above all, these fictional Communists are murderers, especially of their own kind: they don't hesitate to hurl their associates in front of trains or out of windows, or to "hound" them to suicide. All in all, the movies suggest that Communists were so adept at eliminating one another that there was little work or glory left for the FBI.[15]

My real point here is that in all these anti-Communist movies there was no such thing as a Communist who wasn't also somehow involved with espionage or plotting the overthrow of the government. (It was fitting that the film that offered the most sophisticated example of the informer, *On the Waterfront* [1954], on the surface had nothing to do with Communism.) The core of the Hollywood effort to present the anti-Communist informer as culture hero may be found not on celluloid but in the books that came out after *Witness*, a number of which were later converted to radio, television, and movie properties—*I Was a Commu-*

nist for the FBI (Matthew Cvetic), *I Led Three Lives* (Herbert Philbrick), *This Deception* (Hede Massing), *Out of Bondage* (Elizabeth Bentley), *This Is My Story* (Louis Budenz), *Red Masquerade* (Angela Calomiris), *My Ten Years as a Counterspy* (Boris Morros). Here is not the place to consider either the theoretical attacks on Communism by American social democrats or the real literature of anti-Communism—the work of writers such as George Orwell, Arthur Koestler, or Boris Pasternak who, as John Strachey pointed out in a brilliant essay called *The Strangled Cry,* had in common with Whittaker Chambers the rejection not merely of dialectical materialism but ultimately of eighteenth-century rationalism and the Enlightenment itself. (The only hope, Strachey concluded, lay in the rediscovery of spiritual values, the power of redemptive love, the reaffirmation of personal connections and loyalties.[16]) No such lofty themes found their way into the vulgar popular culture of the day—in print and on the air—which was openly dedicated to refurbishing the image of the anti-Communist informer.

For the most part the anti-Communist morality plays, in the guise of autobiographical revelations, exude two dominant and simple themes. First, there is the presentation of Stalin's plan for world domination. On behalf of this plan secrets are stolen, defense plants and unions infiltrated, liberals duped, and reds restricted to a shadowy world involving the black arts. "After all," Budenz tells us, "the planned use of the 'proletarian' groups as fifth column throughout the world under Stalin's leadership could not be more clearly stated." As the ex-Communist James Burnham reminded us in *The Web of Subversion* (1954), Lenin wrote that "Legal work must be combined with illegal work. . . . The party that . . . does not carry out systematically all-sided illegal work in spite of the laws of the bourgeoisie and of the bourgeois parliaments is a party of traitors and scoundrels."

Second, but not less important, is the theme of what might be called the challenge of informing. Here the reader is asked to sympathize with the author, who makes it clear that like the rest of us the last thing he ever wanted to do was spy on his fellow citizens. Asked to report on the Communists, Philbrick tells the inquiring agents, "It's just that I don't like the idea of being a spy even for the FBI. I'm not the type."

Who, then, is the type? Spying, after all, involves self-sacrifice and risk. "If you are exposed publicly as a Communist Party member you may lose your job, and you cannot claim the FBI to justify your position," Philbrick tells us he was told (although why once exposed he couldn't do what in fact he did, i.e., surface as a public witness, is never explained).[17]

In *Red Masquerade,* duty, not dough, is clearly Angela Calomiris's primary motive:

> "I want to do it," I said. But Ken wanted to point out all the risks and dangers.
>
> "There's no glory and no dough," he said flatly.
>
> "And you're completely on your own," Bill put in. "If you get into trouble, the FBI doesn't know you."

What sort of trouble? Danger. Miss Calomiris, a photographer who ended up as a membership secretary in her local Communist group before she testified as a Smith Act witness, reports that her agent told her:

> "We don't want to scare you, but we want you to know that people have disappeared. At the very least, the comrades might break your windows or annoy you in the street. They might find ways of making life unpleasant for you—they might try to scare you with threatening letters for instance, or tell lies about you. Lies that would hurt. If you had a good job, they'd try to get you fired. They could always prove that you were a card-carrying member of the Communist Party, and in most business organizations, open Communists don't get very far."
>
> "Yes, but in that case I could prove that I wasn't really a Communist," I pointed out.
>
> Ken smiled gently. "You could try, but we couldn't publicly recognize you."

No mention is made in these accounts, of course, of how the FBI, through its "Cominfil" program, routinely caused Communist Party members grief, harassing them with anonymous letters to employers, spouses, and comrades, a systematic unpleasantness that often resulted in loss of job, marital stress, political suspicion.

There is always a patronizing comment for those who resist the idea that one has a duty to betray. Miss Calomiris tells of friends who questioned what she did and then would admit "grudgingly" that

> "It may have been necessary but I don't like the idea of spying just the same. I'd hate to have the government pry into my life."
>
> At this point, I was often tempted to ask why they would mind being observed if they had nothing to hide. But I found that the most effective reply was a direct question: "What would you have done if the FBI had gone to you instead of to me?"

Most Americans don't like to admit it, but all established governments have always had to use spies. The blunt facts are that there will be undercover agents as long as there are conspirators who can be detected in no other way.[18]

═══

Whether the espionage informers told most of the truth most of the time is a historically interesting question, but even if one knew the answer, it would not begin to resolve the deeper questions of the ultimate causes of the international cold war, the real nature of Soviet intentions. Yet somehow the collective witness of the self-styled espionage exposers contributed mightily to Americans' belief that here was an international red menace and that these particular ex-Communists deserved our thanks and respect for blowing the whistle on Stalin and his blueprint for world domination.

George Kennan has written of the image of totalitarianism in these years that "it is both a reality and a bad dream, but its deepest reality lies strangely enough in its manifestation as a dream."[19] The espionage exposers specialized in selling the red nightmare.

2.
The Conspiracy Informer

THE DOMESTIC CIVIL WAR IN THE 1950s between the hunters and the hunted was fought at the national, state, and local levels, in the media, in private enterprise, in educational and nonprofit institutions, and even in the home. It polarized American society, pitting "patriots" (the hunters) against "subversives" (the hunted), right against left, the ins against the outs—even as the international cold war seemed to split the planet between those who sided with "the free world" and those who identified with "atheistic Communism." "There is no room in America today for the neutral patriot!" said Earle Cocke, Jr., national commander of the American Legion in 1951. "You cannot be indifferent toward Communism any more than you can be indifferent toward cancer."[1]

Ostensibly the internal-security bureaucracy was hunting subversives, but in fact it bagged not only Communists but ex-Communists who wouldn't recant, "fellow travelers," "pinkos," and liberals—especially those who had signed petitions, given money, or otherwise supported resisters to what they saw as repression. The Communists indeed set up some organizations and dominated others, but informers' tales of Communist "fronts" and Communist "infiltration" into schools and trade unions often were exploited to alarm the population, to fan the hysteria. No one would be safe from the red menace.

The success of the hunters depended on their ability to link the menace without to the menace within. Thus Chambers' allegations against Hiss were seized on not merely by the government to prove espionage but by the right to discredit the entire New Deal. Perhaps because of Hiss's Harvard Law School background, the fact that he had been recommended for his clerkship with Justice Oliver Wendell Holmes by Felix Frankfurter, the well-known New Deal impresario, his experience with the Agricultural Adjustment Agency, a New Deal creation, his presence at the

Yalta Conference and at the founding conference of the United Nations in San Francisco—all institutions and events closely associated with the Roosevelt presidency—many observers on both sides of the issue came to see his case as one where the New Deal was on trial. When his first trial ended with a hung jury, Congressman Richard Nixon, who had not attended a single session of it, denounced it as "stacked." And when Dean Acheson, with whom Hiss had worked at the State Department, came to his support, resentment against New Deal intellectuals came to the surface with a vengeance. "I look at that fellow," Senator Hugh Butler of Nebraska exploded, "I watch his smart-aleck manner and his British clothes and that New Dealism, everlasting New Dealism in everything he says and does, and I want to shout, Get out, Get out. You stand for everything that has been wrong with the United States."[2]

The most visible and noisiest hunters were on the political right— HUAC with its heritage of Dies and Rankin* backed up by Catholic and veteran organizations. But the hunters soon co-opted many of their natural enemies. Although President Harry Truman's initial reaction was to dismiss the red hunt as a "red herring," a combination of a flood tide of daily memoranda from J. Edgar Hoover on different aspects of the red menace and policies at home and abroad that anticipated domestic political pressures eventually set in motion forces that the president did not control. To underwrite the costs of containment abroad, Truman oversold the Communist menace at home. Ten days after promulgating the Truman Doctrine for Greece and Turkey, in March 1947, he signed Executive Order 9835, which established a loyalty and security program for all federal employees and revived the attorney general's old list of subversive organizations.

Many former isolationists quickly adapted Truman's anti-Communist foreign policy to their own "politics of revenge" against the New Deal. And of course the conditions for the hunt were improved in the years 1948 and 1949 by events abroad—the Communist coup in Czechoslova-

---

* Congressman Martin Dies of Texas was chairman of a temporary Special Committee on Un-American Activities, a forerunner to HUAC, from 1938 until 1944. In 1945 Congressman John Rankin of Mississippi moved to make it a permanent standing committee and served as an influential member on it from 1945 to 1948. Together they yielded the Committee a heritage of vicious and demagogic anti-Communism. As Professor Robert Carr wrote of Rankin in *The House Committee on Un-American Activities* (Ithaca, 1952): "It is his basic notion of what constitutes un-American activity that has dominated the work of the Committee even in its most calm and fair-minded moments."

kia, the Russian blockade of Berlin, the expulsion of Yugoslavia from the Soviet bloc, the frame-up trials of national Communists in Eastern Europe, and the persecution of the Jews in Russia itself.

Disloyalty, under Truman's order, was defined not merely as sabotage or treason but as advocacy of forcible overthrow of the government, or unauthorized disclosure of documents or information of a nonpublic character obtained through government employment "acting so as to serve the interests of another government in preference to the interest of the United States," which was where the attorney general's list came in. Under the infamous attorney general A. Mitchell Palmer, the list—which was discontinued with his departure in 1921—contained only twelve organizations. When during World War II the liberal attorney general Francis Biddle revived it, the number of organizations proscribed (with no hearing, but after an FBI investigation) went up to forty-seven. In theory the list was private, but in March 1948, when it contained six categories and seventy-eight organizations, it was published in *The Congressional Record.*

Since it was the FBI's job to conduct the loyalty checks and to investigate for the attorney general's list as well as to develop candidates for its own Security Index (a list of persons to be rounded up in the event of a national emergency), the bureau took on the character of an ideological police force, and until Hoover's death in May 1972, it was in the vanguard of an extraordinary internal-security bureaucracy.

By the end of Truman's presidency in 1952, this bureaucracy included a Subversive Activities Control Board (SACB), which was established under the Internal Security Act of 1950, a law passed over Truman's veto and based on legislation originally drafted by Representatives Karl Mundt of South Dakota and Richard Nixon of California. The Internal Security Act declared that participants in the Communist movement in effect repudiated their allegiance to the United States and transferred it to a foreign country. The movement's purpose, said the act, was to establish a "Communist totalitarian dictatorship throughout the world" by "treachery, deceit, infiltration . . . espionage, sabotage, terrorism and any other means deemed necessary." The SACB was the tribunal with which "Communist action" and "Communist front" organizations were supposed to register. Since registration required that the name and address of every member of a "Communist action" organization and every officer of a "Communist front" be provided, along with an accounting of all monies received and spent, to register was to accuse one's members of collective traitorship.

Registered Communist Party members were not permitted to apply for passports or to hold government jobs or defense jobs. No organization that registered with the SACB could send communications through the mails or broadcast over radio or television to more than two persons, unless the material were labeled Communist propaganda. The law also included a criminal sedition clause and an Emergency Detention Act, intended for use in time of national emergencies.*

Under the Immigration and Nationality Act of 1952, the 2.5 million aliens who resided in the United States could be arrested without warrant, held without bail, and deported for an action that was legal when committed. Among the grounds for deportation was membership in any subversive organization as defined by the Internal Security Act. Information from anonymous informers could be invoked at the deportation hearings, and no hearing needed be granted to deportees if the disclosure of evidence was found "incompatible with national security."

Thus the international cold war fed the internal red hunt and vice versa. It was only a matter of time until a master demagogue with the instinct, skill, and recklessness to exploit what the English writer David Caute has called the "great fear" came along, and he, of course, was the junior senator from Wisconsin, Joseph ("Tailgunner") McCarthy, who first came to national attention when he was reported in the Wheeling, West Virginia, *Intelligencer* as telling a Republican women's club, on February 9, 1950, "I have here in my hand a list of 205 that were known to the secretary of state as being members of the Communist Party and are still making and shaping the policy of the State Department."

The technique of reckless charge, paper-waving, shifting numbers soon took on the name of its most prominent practitioner. McCarthy repeated the same tactics in different forums throughout his reign, which lasted from 1951 to 1954 (when he was censured by his fellow senators on two

---

* The Emergency Detention Act had originally been offered by liberal legislators as a substitute for the Internal Security Act. Sponsored by Harley Kilgore of West Virginia, Paul Douglas of Illinois, Frank Graham of North Carolina, Herbert Lehman of New York, and Estes Kefauver of Tennessee, it authorized the attorney general during presidentially declared internal-security emergencies to detain persons who he had "reason to believe" might act subversively. One member of Truman's staff called it a "concentration-camp bill." As often happens with arcane legislative strategies, the senators outfoxed themselves, and Scott Lucas of Illinois, the Senate's Democratic majority leader, added the detention bill to the omnibus Internal Security Act, and the country got the worst of both worlds.

Although no one was ever successfully registered under the Emergency Detention Act, as late as 1961 the courts were still upholding its basic provisions. Eventually, in 1965, the Supreme Court held that registration amounted to self-incrimination.

counts that interestingly had only a tangential relation to "McCarthy-ism": for his refusal to explain a financial transaction and for his abuse of other senators). Like all great pitchmen the senator kept his audiences mesmerized with patter and chatter, as he recycled names and allegations and innuendoes served up by informers who had frequently popped up in other contexts earlier, only to be rediscovered by him as he talked of "a conspiracy on a scale so immense as to dwarf any previous such venture in the history of man. What is the objective ... of this conspiracy?" he would ask. "To diminish the United States in world affairs, to weaken us militarily, to confuse our spirit with talk of surrender." To what end? "To the end that we shall be contained and frustrated and finally fall vic-tim to Soviet intrigue from within and Russian military might from with-out." The senator's message was very much in the public domain. The evangelist Billy Graham's opening prayer for the Senate in 1952 referred to "barbarians beating at our gates from without and moral termites from within."[3]

At the time the strength of these moral termites seemed limitless. As early as September 1946 the Chamber of Commerce published a thirty-eight–page booklet entitled *Communist Infiltration in the United States: Its Nature and How to Combat It,* 683,000 copies of which were distribut-ed by Republican Party officials prior to the 1946 elections. The pam-phlet, which identified the New Deal as preparing the way for Communist ideology, was followed in January 1947 by a fifty-seven–page booklet called *Communist Ideas, Loyalty and Espionage.* As the chamber put it, "Americans do not normally think in terms of espionage and sedi-tion. We reserve such 'cloak and dagger' material for war time, or for mystery stories centering on the turbulent Balkan region. We would con-sider even peaceful espionage as fantastic. Certainly we are not prepared for mass espionage, motivated ... merely by fanatical devotion to the So-viet Union. Yet the June 1946 *Report* of the Canadian Royal Commission describes a pattern which is not confined to Canada...." It called for the dismissal of all Communists from government.

FBI Director Hoover in May 1947 called the 74,000 members of the Communist Party USA "masters of deceit" and pointed out that they represented a larger percentage of the population than Lenin's Bolsheviks did in Russia in 1917. And when Party membership fell to 54,000 in Feb-ruary 1950, Hoover helpfully observed that there were 486,000 fellow travelers* in the background and "each is regarded as a potential spy."[4]

---

* David Caute wrote, "So indiscriminately and aggressively was the term [fellow traveler] bandied about during the post-war American witch-hunts that it came

In truth, however, by the early 1950s the Communist Party USA was in pitiful shape. Not a red dragon waiting to uncoil, not even a paper tiger, but rather, as David Caute has put it, "a flea on the dog's back." Indeed at its peak it had never been very much, and the notion of the CP as subversive, conspiratorial, and revolutionary was profoundly misleading. Founded in 1919, the Party had quickly fragmented amid sectarian disputes; various factions went underground in the early 1920s, mainly to avoid government persecution; and it emerged only in 1929 as CPUSA, a full-fledged above-ground member of the Communist International. Historians tell us that the Party didn't really go underground again and make formal contact with Russian agents until January 1949—and again in response to U.S. governmental persecution—when its national committee set up a small undercover operation based in Mexico, whose purpose was to maintain a sort of leadership in exile and to secure the leadership against both physical and prosecutorial attack.[5]

Occasionally (as in their dedicated effort to free the Scottsboro Boys, nine poor blacks accused in 1931 of raping two Southern white women), and despite their overblown and predictable rhetoric, the Communists demonstrated a reasonable ability to use the media on behalf of worthwhile causes. Yet even Communist successes, for instance their influence in the CIO, were overstated. To say, for example, that they had "infiltrated" the CIO is to lean toward melodrama: when the CIO was being formed they were warmly and openly welcomed. Where Communists won power it was because they stayed late when liberals left early. For the most part, however, CPUSA was a relatively ineffectual organization—officially fighting against racism, fascism, and the Depression and unofficially following the Party line.

Why, the joke went, is the Communist Party like the Brooklyn Bridge? Answer: Because they are both suspended by cables. It is true that the CPUSA followed the twists and turns of the Soviet Party line: it stopped "fighting fascism" for the duration of the Stalin-Hitler Pact; adopted the slogan "Communism is Twentieth Century Americanism" for the duration of the wartime Soviet-American alliance; and took an abrupt turn to the left after Jacques Duclos, the second-ranking French Communist, published a famous letter at the end of World War II in which he con-

---

to signify anyone who received *Pravda* through the post, anyone who took the First or Fifth amendments, anyone who defended the constitutional rights of those who did, anyone who had doubts about the guilt of Alger Hiss, or anyone who dared to contend that Russia had made a major contribution to winning the war." (*The Fellow-Travellers* [New York, 1973], pp. 2–3.)

demned as soft Earl Browder's policy of working with rather than against democratic capitalism. But such reflexive ideology was more transparent than effective. Also, as we learn from Alexander Bittleman, the Party's major theoretical and economic adviser during the cold war years, the leadership got its so-called "orders from abroad" by his clipping American and foreign press articles containing the speeches of influential Communists—he would underline passages that struck him as important and pass them on to the leadership. As Peter Steinberg has concluded, "If this was a conspiracy it was the most inefficient the world has ever seen."[6]

The Party never achieved a membership approaching one percent of the American population. Its high—when we were wartime allies with the Soviet Union—was put at around 75,000. By 1950 it was down to 31,608 and by 1957 it had sunk to 10,000, including a healthy contingent of FBI undercovermen. The Communists ran William Z. Foster for president in 1932, and he got only 102,791 votes (compared, for instance, with 915,490 votes for Eugene V. Debs on the Socialist ticket in 1920); they ran Browder in 1936 and he got only 80,195, which fell to 46,251 next time out. After that they supported FDR in 1944, Henry Wallace in 1948 on the Progressive Party ticket, and Vincent Hallinan, Progressive, in 1952. The Party never elected a single congressman on its own ticket, although the New York congressman Vito Marcantonio, elected as a candidate of the American Labor Party, seemed faithful to Party policies.

Moreover, as the writer and editor Carey McWilliams pointed out at the time in the small-circulation *Chicago Jewish Forum,* precisely those aspects of Communism most commonly regarded as threatening doomed Russian-style Communism to lasting failure in the United States. Even the image of the CP as "the agent of a foreign power" isolated it from the American masses, who resist orthodox Russian propaganda; the CP was said to have had successes running front organizations—but the "broader" the front, the less control they had, and the narrower, the fewer members. The CP was said to be "menacing" because of the iron discipline it exercised over its members, but the system of "democratic centralism" made for maximum individual irresponsibility because it worked to inhibit real self-criticism. Also the attempt of the Party to dominate too large a sphere in the lives of its members resulted in ex-members outnumbering members by a ratio of ten to one.

Hoover called his book about Communists *Masters of Deceit* (1958), but when CP-ers succeeded in getting a front group to adopt their "line," they advertised the fact for all to see. "Secret" organizations don't work in America. The Communists were supposed to be for "force and violence," but the history of the labor movement shows how such tactics alienated potential public support. As McWilliams noted, a sound policy might have been to protect the Communists' right to advocate force and violence from every soapbox; nothing would better insure their failure to capture American opinion. Their Manichaean view of the universe precluded compromise. Their zeal was remarkable but chiefly in contrast to liberal, middle-class indifference.[7]

That Party members, acting on behalf of Soviet definitions of the American interest, often distorted the goals of the non-Party organizations they joined may or may not be true. But they were never the "internal menace" portrayed by the myth. J. Edgar Hoover and the Justice Department put out copious memoranda and public statements referring to "15,000 potential Smith Act defendants," in reality the number of names that had serendipitously found their way onto the FBI's Security Index. President Truman himself contributed to the misunderstanding when he confused the Smith Act indictments for *conspiracy* with the prior grand jury investigation for *treason*.[8] Not even the cumulative misinformation, however, can account for the durability of a myth which has lasted for decades. Historians have advanced a variety of theories to explain this delusion. Some attribute McCarthyism to the Republicans' twenty-year absence from power, which led them to fantasize that a conspiracy was keeping them out—the revenge, as Peter Viereck put it, of twenty years' worth of noses pressed against the windowpane.[9] Others see it as an expression of status anxiety—a form of nativism that has always identified those who threaten the status quo as "foreign," "radical," "unclean," merely the latest and most shameful in a series of American episodes that include the Haymarket Riot, the trial of Sacco and Vanzetti, the persecution of the Wobblies, the Palmer Raids after World War I, the "criminal syndicalism" statutes, the Lusk Committee hearings, and the various precursors to HUAC. Richard Rovere would give McCarthy himself his share of the credit. Some blame the atomic bomb. Yet others see it as part of a worldwide counterrevolution, the petite bourgeoisie joining forces with finance capital to maintain the status quo. And some would say Stalin and CPUSA brought it on themselves.

Without presuming to identify the critical causes of the war between the hunters and the hunted, it is evident that professional informers and FBI informants were undispensable to the former. They provided info and ammo in the form of names to be subpoenaed, suspended, harassed. And even as the Hiss affair helped to establish the image of the American Communist as agent of a foreign power, so the Dennis case did much to confirm the image of the American Communist Party as a revolutionary, subversive internal conspiracy, committed to the overthrow of the government by force and violence. And the Dennis case was the model for further Smith Act trials; the prosecution would put FBI informants and former members of the Communist Party on the stand to identify the defendants as Party officers and testify that they saw the works of Marx, Engels, Lenin, Stalin, et al. being sold, distributed or discussed at Party functions. These writings were then introduced as evidence to establish "the nature and character and aims and objectives of the Communist Party." The witnesses would then testify about what they heard some Communist teacher or Party member say in a class or meeting about the "principles of Marxism or Leninism" or the policies of the Communist Party. As the attorneys A. L. Wirin and Sam Rosenwein pointed out in *The Nation* in December 1953, "The FBI informant relates what some third party—not subject to confrontation or cross-examination—said . . . in a classroom or meeting usually in some city or state far distant from the one where the case is being tried, or where any of the defendants were present."

Defense lawyers regularly objected to this kind of testimony as hearsay, to no avail. The objections were generally overruled on the grounds that in a conspiracy the acts of co-conspirators are binding on all members of the conspiracy, whether or not present. There was a certain poetic justice in this harsh rule. Since the real defendant was the Communist Party, it did not matter that much of the evidence introduced and admitted had little or nothing to do with the particular men and women on trial.

As Richard Rovere has truly written, our entire system of criminal justice would collapse if we were not free to compel testimony from third parties in criminal proceedings.[10] But the joker in the Dennis and other Smith Act cases is that in reality they were *political* as much as *criminal* trials. The Dennis case deserves close attention because in it the political informer was presented in the guise of criminal witness—thus confusing the issue, enhancing the informer's persona, and launching a number of informers on careers. At the same time it embodied and helped reveal the Informer Principle.

The Informer Principle held not merely that there was nothing wrong with naming names, but that it was the litmus test, the ultimate evidence, the guarantor of patriotism. If the witness was "cooperative" in the legislative hearings, he was generally (though not always) permitted to return to society. If not, he remained on the political index, which at a minimum meant career purgatory. It was a corollary of the Informer Principle that the act of informing was more important than the information imparted.

As for the executive branch, President Truman's loyalty order required that hundreds of thousands of federal employees be investigated, the principal evidence against them (and this was also the case in thousands of deportation proceedings) being provided by anonymous informants. As the persecution of Remington suggests, this informer information was treated as fact until rebutted, reversing the constitutional presumption that a person is innocent until proved guilty. It was another corollary of the Informer Principle that protection of the informer's reputation (and in some cases his identity) was more important than the accuracy of the information. Hence in many administrative proceedings, as well as in most legislative investigations, the requirements of internal security were thought to negate the need for such traditional truth-gathering guarantees as the right to cross-examination. Thus the anonymous informant (whose information was untested) wrote the dossier on the reluctant informer (whose information was unneeded). "The accuser speaks; the next morning's headlines announce the accusation; and the accused is marked thereafter as a traitor to his country," Joseph Alsop wrote at the time.[11] It was yet another corollary to the Informer Principle that to attack an informer's credibility was to attack the informer system. To attack the system was to attack its sponsor, the state. Ergo, to question informer information was a subversive activity.

It was in the judicial arena that the Informer Principle was officially codified and its implications spelled out.

The Smith Act had been passed as a little-noted rider to the Alien Registration Act of 1940—so little noted, in fact, that Zechariah Chafee, Jr., perhaps the leading civil-liberties lawyer of his day, later confessed that he hadn't known about it at the time. The act made it a crime for anyone "to knowingly or willfully advocate, abet, advise or teach the duty, necessity, desirability or propriety of overthrowing or destroying any government in the United States by force or violence." Attorney General Francis Biddle, who said he opposed seditious conspiracy prosecutions on principle, nevertheless in 1941 authorized the first prosecution under the Smith Act.[12]

The defendants were members of the Socialist Workers Party, a Trotskyist group that had adopted a Declaration of Principles explicitly advocating the overthrow of capitalism by force and violence "if necessary." (After passage of the Smith Act, the declaration was suspended, but the government argued that this was cosmetic.) The real reason for the prosecution, the historian Michal Belknap has shown, a prosecution that by the way was enthusiastically supported by the Communist Party (which regarded Stalin's exiled rival, Leon Trotsky, as the enemy), was White House pressure. FDR couldn't have cared less about the Trotskyists, but he did care about the Teamsters' president, Dan Tobin, who had supported him during the 1940 campaign and was having trouble in his union with a dissident affiliate, controlled by the Socialist Workers Party, which voted in early June 1941 to join the CIO. Tobin wired FDR, and two weeks later federal marshals raided Party headquarters in Minneapolis. Eighteen men were convicted and went to jail under sentences of a year to sixteen months. On appeal the constitutionality of the Smith Act was upheld by the federal circuit court, and the Supreme Court declined to hear the case.

The other major Smith Act indictment before the Dennis case came in July 1942, again under pressure from FDR, when a District of Columbia federal grand jury indicted thirty-three Nazi sympathizers who had been publishing hate literature against minority groups and, incidentally, attacking FDR's handling of the war. Again, the Communists were enthusiastic supporters of the government's effort to jail the right-wing propagandists. They saw the courtroom as a combat zone in the propaganda fight against the Nazis. The trial, which was chaotic, ended in a mistrial after eight months (the record runs eighteen thousand pages) when the harassed and exhausted Edward Eicher, chief judge of the federal court for the District of Columbia, died. Eventually the charges against the Nazis were dropped, over the objections of the Communist Party, whose press as late as July 1947—with Hitler dead and World War II over— still pressed for legal action against the fascists.

A year later the Party had reason to regret its Smith Act stance. For since mid-1947, a New York grand jury had been hearing testimony from Elizabeth Bentley and other ex-Communists who purported to describe a vast underground Soviet spy network in this country. But when indictments were finally handed down on July 20, 1948 (in between the conventions of the Democratic Party, which nominated Harry S Truman, and the Progressive Party, which nominated Henry A. Wallace to run against him), the defendants—Eugene Dennis, the CP's national secretary, and the rest of the Party's national board—were charged not with spying or espionage but, rather, with violating the Smith Act. The indictment said that starting on or about April 1, 1945 (the date when Browder's old Communist Political Association had been reconstituted as the Communist Party), the twelve members of CPUSA's national board had *conspired* with each other to "organize as the Communist Party of the United States, a society, group and assembly of persons who teach and advocate the overthrow and destruction of the Government of the United States by force and violence, and knowingly and willfully to advocate and teach the duty and necessity of overthrowing and destroying the Government of the United States by force which said acts are prohibited by the Smith Act."

One hundred percent of the government's "evidence" at the Foley Square trial of Dennis and his co-defendants was provided by thirteen ex-Communist informers and FBI informants, most notably Budenz, Philbrick, and Calomiris. And 90 percent of the evidence had nothing to do with Dennis or his co-defendants but, rather, related to the meaning of Marxist-Leninist classics. The government's theory was that the postwar transformation of Earl Browder's ecumenical Communist Political Association signaled the end of the united front, which had emphasized the peaceful pursuit of common objectives by both Communists and non-Communists, and the beginning (or recommencement) of the Party as a militant, tightly disciplined conspiratorial organization, whose ideology dictated violent measures to achieve the proletarian revolution. The ex-Communists offered "expert" testimony on the meaning of the classics, and to a lesser extent they recounted specific incidents involving the defendants' role in the conspiracy. As Professor Herbert Packer described the proceedings, "The 'classics' occupy the center of the stage and the ex-Communists appear in the Talmudic role of glossers on the text."[13] In the Dennis case this task was discharged mainly by Budenz, an assistant professor of economics at Fordham University, former editor of the *Daily Worker,* and recent reconvert to Catholicism. Budenz made two contributions to the prosecution that effectively settled the central issue of the case; the first, the defendants argued, was improperly admitted into evidence, and the second was absurd on its face. First was his interpretation of the lead sentence in the CPUSA constitution: "The Communist Party of the United States is the political party of the American working class, basing itself upon the principles of scientific socialism, Marxism-Leninism." Budenz's gloss:

Lenin and Stalin . . . have specifically interpreted scientific socialism to mean that socialism can only be attained by the violent shattering of the capitalist state, and the setting up of a dictatorship of the proletariat by force and violence in the place of that state. In the United States this would mean that the Communist Party of the United States is basically committed to the overthrow of the Government of the United States as set up by the Constitution of the United States.[14]

Budenz's second and more famous contribution—that Communists often spoke in "Aesopean language"—was designed to take care of the loophole created by the first, namely the many passages in Communist texts that disavow the need for violence. Budenz testified that these were, like Aesop's fables, in effect written in code and that no matter how innocent the language might seem on its face, the initiate always understood the sinister underlying message: violent overthrow is necessary.

After Budenz came the Party's former literature director for the New England region ("District One"), Herbert Philbrick, in red, white, and blue bow tie. He read a passage from Lenin's *State and Revolution* which, he said, had been used in a class he attended: "The replacement of the bourgeois by the proletariat state is impossible without violent revolution."[15] Philbrick's appearance for the prosecution, plus the revelation that he had been in contact with the FBI since 1940, shocked the defense camp. The defendant Gil Green recalls, "We called Boston to ask if they knew Philbrick, and they said sure, he was a nice guy. He was always inviting us to use his office mimeograph machine." The Party's Boston leadership was soon on the streets with leaflets and fliers branding him "a Judas, a cheap informer, a stool pigeon, a labor spy, and a spinner of fantastic tales."[16]

From the Communist viewpoint, Central Casting could not have improved upon some of the government's key witnesses. These included, in addition to those already mentioned:

William Odell Nowell, who had worked as a "labor spy" for the Ford Motor Company and was presently engaged in undercover work for the Immigration and Naturalization Service.

Charles Nicodemus, who had a history of nonpolitical trouble with the law after he quit the Party in 1946 (among other problems, he had been arrested in 1948 in a Pittsburgh motel room for carrying a gun without a license); he reported on a Party meeting where someone said that in order for the revolution to succeed in the United States the Red Army might have to march from Siberia through Alaska and Canada to Detroit.

William Cummings, a black who had established his dedication to the Stalinist cause by his energetic recruitment of new Party members, including three close relatives, to whom he neglected to mention that he was reporting to the FBI throughout his six years in the Party.

The Party's response to this parade of informers, after its initial shock at the quantity of betrayal from within its ranks, revealed another corollary of the Informer Principle—that the informer's by-product is more important than his product. The Party tightened security, regarded all newcomers and many senior members with suspicion, and commenced a violent anti-informer campaign. In court the Party's lawyers argued that the evidence gathered by the FBI informants was inadmissible because the presence of such persons at private meetings violated the defendants' First Amendment rights and that this method of collecting information violated their Fourth Amendment right to privacy and Fifth Amendment protection against self-incrimination. Out of court they carried on an agitprop campaign to alert CP-ers and non–CP-ers alike to the menace. Gil Green wrote in *Political Affairs,* a party journal, in May 1950 about the "scummy stool pigeons" and "Gestapo agents" of the FBI at Foley Square.

But the Party critique lacked force on a number of counts. First, its support of the earlier Smith Act prosecution of non-Communists undermined the credibility of its newly claimed commitment to civil liberties. Second, its lawyers' obstreperous tactics at the Dennis trial, while undoubtedly triggered by Judge Harold Medina's arbitrary rulings, nevertheless obfuscated serious consideration—in or out of court—of the merits of their argument. Third, the Marxist idea that law is the instrument by which the ruling classes oppress the proletariat confirmed the Party in its misconceived strategy of attempting to achieve in the streets what they assumed they could never achieve in court. The Communists were never able to make an adequate political issue of their oppression partly because in refuting the information used against them they felt obliged to insist that they weren't even theoretical revolutionaries, a problematic position at best.

If the government had stopped with Dennis, the case's chief importance would be that the Supreme Court used the occasion of reviewing it to replace the old standard of a "clear and present danger" with Judge Learned Hand's less stringent formulation of the basis on which the government is permitted to curtail free speech ("the gravity of the evil discounted by its improbability"[17]). But after the Dennis case, the government indicted and tried fifteen defendants in Los Angeles, twenty-one so-called "second string" Communists in New York (in fact, they included people like Elizabeth Gurley Flynn, who wasn't second-string at all), two in Honolulu, five in Pittsburgh; subsequent cases were brought in Seattle, Detroit, St. Louis, Philadelphia, Cleveland, and elsewhere. Before it was finished the government had indicted 141 alleged conspirators, and the scheduling gave rise to a booking system that encouraged professional witnesses to move from trial to trial. The government prosecutors found it advantageous to have some of the same witnesses at each trial, since with practice they were able to perfect their stories, anticipate defense objections, and generally present a more credible front.

———

The Dennis case also revealed that perhaps the most insidious corollary of the Informer Principle was its obverse: refusal to inform was interpreted as the ultimate evidence of conspiracy.

A legal formula—the waiver doctrine—was invoked to give this interpretation currency. When asked by a 1948 grand jury to identify her successor in the Party, to whom she had turned over her records, one Jane Rogers, former treasurer of the Party's Denver section, anticipated the later position of people like Lillian Hellman, Pete Seeger, and Arthur Miller and said she was willing to talk about herself and even admitted to having held office, but she wouldn't name her successor's name. The Supreme Court confirmed her jail sentence for contempt of court on the ground that she had "waived the privilege" provided by the Fifth Amendment by making the admission about herself and that she could not then refuse to identify her associates.[18]

Once the waiver doctrine was on the books, the state discovered it was able to use a defendant's reluctance to inform as a way of stigmatizing him, holding him in contempt, or preventing him from testifying in his own behalf. This process, which recurred throughout the Smith Act cases, began when the U.S. attorney in New York questioned John Gates, one of the Dennis defendants, on what Party position Dennis had held. Gates said he was willing to testify about himself, but not others. Even though Eugene Dennis's job as general secretary of the Communist Party was a matter of public record, Gates was "reluctant to play the stool pigeon." Judge Medina ordered Gates to answer, he refused, Medina dismissed the jury to hear legal arguments on the matter, and Dennis (who was serving as his own lawyer) immediately agreed to stipulate to all Party offices he had held at the time in question. Medina refused, saying that if he accepted the logic of the defendants' position, they would be free to testify or not testify at will and he couldn't allow that.

Defense lawyers then offered the court a memorandum that set forth all of the defendants' Party jobs, and although Judge Medina agreed to accept it, he still insisted that Gates answer the question. Gates finally did so, but then the prosecutor pressed for more names. He asked Gates to identify those who had served with him on the Party's national veterans committee. After a brief recess, Gates named two men who were co-defendants with him (Thompson and Winston), but he refused to give other names and claimed his right not to do so under the Fifth and First amendments. The prosecutor also asked him to name the persons who had helped prepare a pamphlet called *Who Ruptured Our Duck* and he refused. Judge Medina again excused the jury, advised Gates that under the Supreme Court's *Rogers* decision he did not have the right he was claiming, pronounced him in contempt of court, and remanded him to jail until he should either purge himself by answering the question or serve thirty days.

To refute the testimony of Herbert Philbrick the defense called three Communist Party officials from the Boston area. The prosecutor, unable to discredit their testimony, solved the problem of how to embarrass these defense witnesses by asking them questions whose answers would require them to name names, which he knew they would not do.

Over and over, Judge Medina, extremely agitated over what he regarded as improper defense tactics (and extremely sensitive to the fate of the late Judge Eicher, who had expired during the explosive Smith Act trial of the alleged Nazis), pointed out that "this so-called stool-pigeon rule does not exist."

Since it was Budenz's testimony that had done most damage to the defendants, the appearance as a defense witness of his former assistant at the *Daily Worker,* Alan Max, was the one chance the defense had to seriously damage the prosecution case. When defense counsel asked Max about a meeting originally mentioned by Budenz, Judge Medina intervened to ask who was present at the meeting. Max repeated the names Budenz had given, but refused to mention anyone else. The prosecutor insisted that the government needed the additional names for rebuttal. Judge Medina said he would order Max to answer and jail him if he refused. As a result, defense counsel withdrew the original question, leaving Budenz's credibility unimpeached.

In trial after trial defendants (and sometimes their witnesses) would be asked to identify persons as Communists. Reluctant to subject others to possible prosecution and certain loss of jobs, they would generally refuse. One result was that many defendants ended up declining to testify in their own behalf. Others were charged with criminal and civil contempt of court and usually imprisoned for the duration of their trials. In the Los Angeles Smith Act case, Oleta O'Connor Yates, one of the defendants, declined on cross-examination to name some names and was jailed. When the trial was over, she was given sentences of one and three years' imprisonment for alleged criminal contempt, in addition to a five-year sentence on conviction on the Smith Act charge. These sentences for criminal contempt (eventually set aside on appeal) were also in addition to an order that Mrs. Yates continue to be jailed, pending her appeal from the Smith Act conviction!

Elizabeth Gurley Flynn served double thirty-day contempt sentences in 1952 for not answering questions she was asked about two people named by the prosecutor. "I'm very sorry," she said, "but I can't identify people as Communists." She based her refusal to answer on her desire "not to degrade or debase myself by becoming an informer."[19]

Probably the most cynical manipulation of the refusal to inform, however, came when the government used that refusal as grounds to deny defendants bail. When the government followed the Dennis case conviction by arresting seventeen more Communist leaders on June 20, 1951, four of the convicted Dennis defendants jumped bail and went "underground." (This strategy was adopted, after bitter internal Party debate, on the theory that the United States was headed for fascism, that there would be mass roundups of Party members, and that these fugitives would provide leadership for the duration of the repression. Indeed, when their co-defendants were released from prison five years later, the remaining two fugitives—the others had been caught—turned themselves in.) As a result, the Civil Rights Congress (CRC), a nonprofit trust fund that had put up bail totaling $500,000 for various Communists, forfeited $80,000—and the CP's reputation as a revolutionary conspiracy was confirmed.

The CRC itself was on the attorney general's list of subversive organizations and was generally recognized as a Communist front. It was born of two earlier organizations which had mobilized the campaign to save the Scottsboro Boys. It had also put up the bail for Gerhardt Eisler, the man accused, probably wrongly, of being the top Communist in the country, who had fled the United States in 1949 while awaiting deportation proceedings. Since it is part of the duty of a surety to secure the appearance of the bailee, the court was within its rights in ordering an investigation of the CRC. In fact, however, nobody in those fearful days *but* CRC was available to put up money for Communist defendants. The government moved to revoke the bail posted by the CRC for the "second string" Smith Act defendants and to prevent it from ever again underwriting bail in a New York federal court. As part of the process, it called the trustees of the bail fund to ask them, Who put up the money? The trustees, including the writer Dashiell Hammett, declined to inform and were sentenced to prison, and the fund was barred from putting up any more bail.

So the Communist defendants' refusal to inform deprived them of witnesses, their own testimony, counsel, and bail, and landed some relatively innocent bystanders in prison for contempt of court. Hammett, for instance, was really an honorary trustee of the fund, with no interest in or knowledge of the membership list that he refused, on principle, to turn over to the state.

The Dennis case lawyers were cited for and convicted of contempt of court, too. Because half the lawyers were sent to prison (in handcuffs) immediately following the trial, their clients were deprived of their most knowledgeable counsel on appeal, and other attorneys got the message of what happened to lawyers who vigorously argued against the forced naming of names in Smith Act cases. Defendants in the second Smith Act case, which began in August 1951, had such difficulty obtaining counsel that Judge Sylvester J. Ryan had to assign eight attorneys to take the case. All of them asked to be relieved of the court assignment, including one who commented, "I don't propose to shorten my life to defend these people." Steve Nelson, a Party leader indicted for sedition in Pennsylvania, sounded out 162 lawyers before he found one willing to take his case.[20]

If the Party was a conspiracy, then it made sense—at least in the popular imagery of the day—that Party lawyers were part of the conspiracy, and so, in the future, only a handful of courageous non-Party lawyers, most of them affiliated with the National Lawyers Guild, which had been founded in 1937 to counter the American Bar Association's exclusionist tendencies, would even consider taking on Smith Act defendants.

On August 28, 1953, Attorney General Herbert Brownell moved to list the National Lawyers Guild as a subversive organization on the ground that it "had become the 'legal mouthpiece' of the Communist Party."[21] In an address to the delegates' assembly of the American Bar Association, he made the disclosure that he had served notice on the organization to show cause why it should not be designated on his subversive list.

It was particularly pernicious that critics of the informer system were attacked not merely as Communist-inspired but as "Communist-lawyer"-inspired. J. Edgar Hoover and other spokesmen for the internal-security bureaucracy took every opportunity to link lawyers who questioned the informer system with those who questioned the American system. As late as October 3, 1955, Hoover told the International Association of Chiefs of Police that informers are "used as a means of establishing truth"; they are "as old as man." But they are victims of a "determined . . . campaign of vituperation" that is part and parcel of a Communist strategy, devised "for the most part" by Communist lawyers, "skilled in concealing foul and despicable acts behind the Fifth Amendment." These lawyers employ "unscrupulous tactics shunned even by the underworld mouthpiece. It is the technique of the smear."

Intentionally identifying the political with the criminal worlds, Hoover said, "We cannot minimize the hate of the underworld whether it be the underworld of hoodlums or the underworld of subversive traitors and its urgent desire also to identify and discredit the confidential informant. There needs to be a greater effort to protect those who risk their lives for the protection of society."[22]

When Richard Rovere of *The New Yorker* wrote to the Justice Department on December 20, 1954, to inquire about the government's use of professional witnesses, he was sent a couple of speeches that cited court cases showing the practice to be legal. A Mr. Tompkins of the Internal Security section wrote: "It has become increasingly clear that the current attack against governmental witnesses . . . has its roots in a Communist effort."[23] Such comments could be explained partly as the expression of the internal-security establishment's ideology and partly as simple smear technique, but they were also the result of the state's increasing stake in the good reputation of its informers. For it was another corollary of the Informer Principle that the reputations of the government and of informers were commingled. They served as each other's fact guarantors, confirmed each other's charges, tainted each other's accusers. In the eyes of the state, to question the accuracy of one was to jeopardize the credibility of both, and to taint one informer was to libel the informer system.

We have already seen the lengths to which the state went to protect the reputation of an "espionage-exposer" like Elizabeth Bentley in the Remington case. Now, as Smith Act cases followed on each other and state, local, and federal agencies held more and more investigations, when a professional witness was shown to have perjured himself (and perjury seemed an occupational hazard; since the informer is paid for information, when the accusations stop, so do the checks), the state through its various agents chose less to suffer the consequences of having used liars than either to ignore the lies or to go after those who uncovered them.

An indication of the state's attitudes on these matters may be found in the pressures brought to bear on one Charles Carroll, a local district attorney in the state of Washington who naïvely sought to prosecute a professional witness for perjured testimony.

The case arose out of the testimony of one George Hewitt (and other professional witnesses) given in 1949 before the Canwell Committee of the Washington state legislature, a committee which used such devices in investigating higher education as showing a faculty-member witness a list of "suspects" and asking him to identify anyone on it who was "red by reputation."[24] The Canwell Committee had undertaken to investigate subversion at the University of Washington, and to its happy surprise found that it had the full cooperation of the Board of Regents, who "welcomed" the investigation, and the president of the university, who saw "no abridgment of academic freedom."

Hewitt charged that a philosophy professor named Melvin Rader was a Communist, and he gave as his evidence his recollection of a Communist Party meeting in Kingston, New York, at which he claimed to have seen Rader. Rader unequivocally denied the charge and produced documentary proof that he couldn't have been at the meeting. When the district attorney, Carroll, issued a warrant for Hewitt's arrest on a charge of perjury, he found that the warrant could not be served, for the Canwell Committee had flown Hewitt to New York on the day following his appearance as a witness.

Soon the district attorney's phone started ringing. Two inspectors from the U.S. Immigration Service called to insist that the charges against Hewitt be dismissed since they might jeopardize the testimony he was to give in upcoming immigration proceedings. Then Carroll received a visit from a political reporter on the powerful Seattle *Post-Intelligencer,* who demanded that the complaint against Hewitt be dismissed because the Canwell Committee would have trouble getting more funds if its key witness were indicted for perjury. As an added fillip, the paper's managing editor told Carroll they would "blast him out of office" if he didn't dismiss the prosecution against Hewitt.

Nevertheless the intrepid district attorney persisted and moved to have Hewitt extradited from New York. Argument on his request for extradition was heard in New York, where the government produced another professional witness, Manning Johnson, who supported Hewitt's testimony and complained that Carroll was out to get him. The New York judge then declined to have Hewitt returned to Washington on the grounds that to do so "would be to send him to eventual slaughter." Later that year Hewitt collapsed while testifying in a New York deportation proceeding and was rushed to Bellevue Hospital, where he was confined to the neurological ward for a condition diagnosed as aphasia, a disease of speech and memory impairment caused by either a brain lesion or a functional disorder. When he was released a month later his wife told an Associated Press reporter, "Sometimes he can't remember things."

Or consider the case of Harvey Matusow, who after seven years in the Party and four years as an informer (against various Communist Youth organizations, folk singers, and the Boy Scouts) repudiated his career as a professional witness in a book, *False Witness* (1955), in press conferences, and before a grand jury. Between 1951 and 1954, he consulted with and testified for the Justice Department (in the second New York Smith Act trial), the Subversive Activities Control Board, the Permanent Investigations Subcommittee of the Senate Committee on Government Operations, the Internal Security Subcommittee of the Senate Judiciary Committee, the House Committee on Un-American Activities, the Ohio Committee on Un-American Activities, and the New York City Board of Education. By his own count he had testified in 25 trials and deportation proceedings and identified 180 persons as Communists as he worked his way up from the sticks to the informers' Palace—the McCarthy Committee. He also lectured for the American Legion, campaigned for candidates who could meet his fee (he once campaigned for McCarthy himself), wrote for the Hearst papers, and at one point had a radio program with fellow informer Howard Rushmore called *Out of the Red.* "Pretty good for a mama's boy from the Bronx, wouldn't you say?" he says.

It was his account of his dealings with Senator McCarthy's counsel, Roy Cohn, that got Matusow into trouble. When in 1951 Cohn, then an assistant U.S. attorney in New York, let him know that the prosecution wished to get into evidence at the second Smith Act trial a particularly incendiary passage from Andrei Vyshinsky's *Law of the Soviet State,* Matusow conveniently allowed as how he not only had read the book but had discussed passages from it with defendant Alexander Trachtenberg—the very one Cohn was after. In his book, Matusow claimed that this was perjury and that Cohn had suborned it.

Instead of prosecuting Cohn the government prosecuted Matusow. And instead of prosecuting him for perjuring himself during his years as a government witness (which would have meant reopening countless cases) they prosecuted him for perjury in his story about Cohn. As Richard Rovere observed at the time, "Neither the Department of Justice nor any other agency of government . . . has given any indication that the Matusow incident has led it to reconsider the moral, juridical and political effects of the whole practice of retaining professional witnesses. On the contrary, it would appear that the government's principal concern at this stage is to prevent Matusow's latest set of confessions from discrediting the testimony of its other professionals." (Once the case against Matusow was won, Thomas Bolan, the successful prosecuting attorney, left government and went into private practice . . . with Roy Cohn.)*

Matusow was not the only recanter to receive such treatment. When Marie Natvig recanted the testimony she had given before the FCC that she had known as a Communist one Edward Lamb, whose television license was in question, the Department of Justice indicted her, too, not for the perjury she claimed, but for lying in claiming it.[25]

Beyond the courts, as ex-Communist informers became more familiar figures on the cold war political-cultural landscape, there were systematic attempts to assist them as a class. Morris Ernst spoke for many when he wrote in an introduction to *This Deception* (1951), the memoir of Hede Massing, who had volunteered to testify against Alger Hiss at his second trial (about a single disputed meeting fourteen years earlier), "We cannot get people out of this movement and ask them to aid us in getting all of the facts, and then at the same time ostracize them socially and economically for being of aid to us. Do we believe in possible repentance and salvation for murderers and not for Communists?" There even came to be a radio series devoted entirely to encouraging disillusioned Communists to come out of the closet and turn themselves and their comrades in.[26] Called *Last Man Out,* it won awards for "Programs that Combat Communism and Educate Americans" and *TV-Radio Life*'s award as "the outstanding documentary series giving special service in telling the true story of Communism and exposing the various ways Communism has of tearing down the American way of life."

The main message of each weekly episode was ostensibly directed at active Party types, urging them to go to the FBI, but since by the early 1950s only a few thousand members were left, the program was really agitprop

---

* Matusow is a special case, of course. One can't really blame the government for not knowing what to believe. When I last talked with him in 1979 he was threatening to come out with a new book called "The Matusow Case," in which he would maintain that he never was a fink for the FBI or the Committee at all but, rather, inspired by a book entitled *Undercover* by Roy Carlson, about a man who joined the Ku Klux Klan to expose it, that he joined the Communist Party intending from the outset to go to work for Communist hunters in order to expose *them*. And if that sounds far-fetched, says Matusow, in January 1950, before he ever volunteered his services to the FBI, he made out an affidavit to this effect, had it notarized by his father, and put it in a safe-deposit box.

for the hunters, aimed at influencing the larger listening audience's view of ex-Communists and informers. To that extent the real message of the program was always the same—honor the informer, it takes guts to be one. Richard English, *Last Man*'s producer,* was ingenious in stimulating sympathy for and empathy with some rather dubious characters.

Thus during the premiere episode based on the life of Paul Crouch, listeners heard nothing about his court-martial in Hawaii or his fantasy letters. They did hear about how his little boy, a victim of hemophilia, received blood transfusions from " 'regular' Americans, and not from Party-member Americans." And they heard about how after Crouch and his wife had left the Party their little girl was pointed out by other children as "daughter of a stool pigeon," "daughter of a traitor."†

At the close of a two-parter on Harold Sunoo, a Korean teacher who seemed to confuse religion with Communism but ultimately redeemed himself by testifying in the Smith Act trial of six Communist Party leaders in Seattle in 1952, it was revealed that although he was again active in church work he had been unsuccessful in getting a full-time teaching job. The plea is made to the listening audience: get ex-Communists of Sunoo's "caliber" back into their profession; "refrain from condemning a man who has made a mistake."

The final program of the series introduced John Butler, who had joined the Communist Party in 1944 and was a member of the Mine, Mill and Smelter Workers Union, which, on February 15, 1950, was expelled from the CIO as Communist-controlled. His first real contact with a Party

---

* Mr. English specialized in writing anti-Communist movies (he collaborated with HUAC investigator William Wheeler on *Big Jim McLain* [1952], starring John Wayne, which was based on Wheeler's HUAC experiences in Hawaii) and anti-Communist articles (he collaborated with Edward Dmytryk, one of the Hollywood Ten, on a *Saturday Evening Post* [19 May 1951] article explaining why he decided to return to HUAC and name names after his release from prison).

† The fact that pandering producers used these devices in a primitive radio show does not of course mean that the CP didn't occasionally stoop that low. For instance, J. Peters, a CP functionary, did give advice—in a pamphlet called *The Communist Party: A Manual on Organization*—on how to treat Party enemies: You "mobilize the children and women on the block ... to make his life miserable; let them picket the store where his wife purchases groceries and other necessities; let the children in the street shout after him or after any member of his family that they are spies, rats, stool pigeons. . . . Chalk his home with the slogan 'So-and-so who lives here is a spy.' Let the children boycott his children or child; organize the children not to talk to his children," etc. (Quoted by Howard Suber in his unpublished Ph.D. thesis.)

member was with Henry Collins, a veteran of the Abraham Lincoln Brigade that fought in the Spanish civil war. After Butler broke with the Party he went to live with his daughter on her farm and was approached there by the FBI, who called to ask him to testify against Collins. "Although he knew his daughter might die of cancer while he was away, John Butler made the decision and went to Pittsburgh, Pennsylvania, to give the testimony his Government needed to deport Collins as a Communist. The U.S. Immigration and Naturalization Service flew Butler back in time to spend the last hours at the bedside of his daughter." (Why the deportation couldn't have waited on the cancer we aren't told.)

———

Underlying all was the doctrine of conspiracy, whose most articulate proponent was the ex-Marxist philosopher Sidney Hook. His 1950 essay "Heresy, Yes—But Conspiracy, No" was expanded into a book that became the bible for liberals unwilling to fight for the rights of Communists. Hook's argument: Communists were not heretics whose unpopular ideas deserved First Amendment protection, but conspirators who were out to subvert not merely the government but also the very exchange of ideas the First Amendment was designed to protect. Our moral obligation "is to the toleration of dissent, no matter how heretical, not the toleration of conspiracy, no matter what its disguise."[27] Given the conspiratorial definition of *all* Stalinist activity (and often enough, by inference, all radical activity), Hook carved out an area of exception to the Bill of Rights, and the distinction between the Stalinist espionage apparatus and the legal activities of the Party was eliminated.

It was only a matter of minutes before this conspiracy theory entered the domain of private employment, most notably in the academic community. Perhaps the most effective response to it came from Michael Harrington, one of a small band of socialist intellectuals writing in such small-circulation journals as *Anvil, Commonweal,* and *Dissent,* who indeed did attack both Stalinism and McCarthyism—as did many liberals—but also defended the rights of Communists as part of the American premise. "If a Communist or a liberal, or a conservative, or a fascist, turned the classroom into a soapbox for political agitation, or if he discriminated against students who disagreed with his views, or engaged in any other form of incompetent academic conduct, he should be sacked for cause after a due process determination of his peers. But if his politics were vile, including advocacy of detestable and even treasonable ideas, but his teaching met rational standards, then he must not be fired."[28] As Harrington noted, "Sidney Hook took a legal doctrine which had begun at three removes from a vaguely defined criminal activity ['conspiracy' (1) 'to teach' (2) 'the advocacy of' (3) . . .], turned it into a metaphor, and discovered an educated conspiracy. The conclusion was, of course, that Communists should not be allowed to teach."[29] And thus the attorney general's list found its way not only into schools but personnel offices of every irrelevant variety throughout the country, and the informer became a critical supplier of data, the professional serving as model for the amateurs.

The Informer Principle took on a bureaucratic momentum of its own, and eventually the hunters were as happy to have a former Communist go through the motions of naming names—even in the privacy of an executive session—as to use him to expose the revolutionary nature of the Communist conspiracy. The government's use of "spies," as in the Smith Act cases, resulted in the breakdown of confidence in social and family life, Zechariah Chafee, Jr., observed: "Intercourse is poisoned if one never knows whether his fellow guest at dinner is going to report his casual statements to the secret police."[30] Yet throughout the period it was the special job of the professional informer (who was, after all, paid witness fees which averaged $35 per diem plus expenses) to instruct the rest of us on the *evils* not only of the Communist Party but of Communists themselves. The hunters never had any public doubts that if their means were shabby their ends were noble—to deliver us from the evils of the internal conspiracy.

The function of the investigating committees was to discharge aggressions that already existed in society. "America: Love it or leave it"; "Go back where you come from"; "If you don't like it here why don't you go to Russia?" were slogan-themes of the 1950s. What the hunters were doing was pronouncing a tribal judgment—you're not our kind; get out of town. The classic way to make such judgments stick is to label the hunted person as "foreign" and then to identify him as conspiratorial, unclean, and immoral. Charlie Chaplin was driven out of Hollywood partly because he had radical (foreign) ideas, and also because he was unclean; he had fathered a child out of wedlock. It was a function of the professional witnesses to distort a political environment by defining the Communist conspiracy as not merely alien but also immoral.

3.

The Liberal Informer

IN 1976 LILLIAN HELLMAN published a brief memoir of her experiences during the blacklisting years which she called *Scoundrel Time*. In the course of her essay she told about how in 1952 the House Committee on Un-American Activities turned down her offer to answer questions about herself provided she not be required "to bring bad trouble to people who, in my past association with them, were completely innocent of any talk or any action that was disloyal or subversive." She described how her attorney, Joseph Rauh, helped her win a brief public-relations victory by passing out mimeographed copies of her letter to HUAC which contains her justly famous sentiment: "But to hurt innocent people whom I knew many years ago in order to save myself is, to me, inhuman and indecent and dishonorable. I cannot and will not cut my conscience to fit this year's fashions, even though I long ago came to the conclusion that I was not a political person and could have no comfortable place in any political group." And she explained why she rejected Rauh's advice that she cite the *Daily Worker*'s negative review of her play *Watch on the Rhine** to prove to the Committee that she was not a Party-liner. She felt that using the *Worker*'s attacks on her would amount to attacking them at a time when they were being persecuted and she would, therefore, "be playing the enemy's game." But Rauh kept coming back to his suggestion and, as Hellman remembers it:

> We were, on this issue, to have our first and last sharp words: I said we were wasting time, I was not going to change my mind, and what was the matter with him? He said that James Wechsler of the *New York*

* The anti-fascist play was produced during the period of the Stalin-Hitler Pact; later, the *Worker* praised the movie (1943), which opened after the Soviet Union was invaded by Germany.

Post was an old and close friend and he had talked over my case with Wechsler. I interrupted him much too sharply by saying that I had never met Wechsler, didn't like what he wrote, and wanted no advice from him. We batted all that around for so long that I said I would like Joe to stop analyzing me, it had already happened, and I didn't need another analyst, I needed a lawyer. (It has been my experience that most lawyers now consider themselves psychiatrists and should quit it.) Rauh didn't like my attack on his friend Wechsler, but when Wechsler was later called before the Committee, I know Joe could not have liked the fact that his friend not only was a *friendly witness* but had high-class pious reasons for what he did [my italics].[1]

On April 22, 1976, James Wechsler sent a letter to Little, Brown, the publisher of Miss Hellman's book, objecting to her reference to him as a "friendly witness," which he considered a "defamatory" portrayal. Since he had clearly been an "adversary witness," the objectionable phrase should be removed from all future editions of the book. When George Hall, senior vice-president of Little, Brown, acknowledged Wechsler's letter and promised to review the "concerns" he raised and to be in touch with him again, Wechsler replied that his letter was not merely an expression of "concerns," but a demand that a "libel" be deleted.

Miss Hellman's response, after due deliberation with her attorney, the noted civil-liberties lawyer Ephraim London, was to notify Wechsler that in future editions of *Scoundrel Time* she would drop the "friendly" and instead refer to Mr. Wechsler as a "cooperative" witness. Mr. Wechsler didn't like this any better but when last heard from nobody had gone to court.[2]

The law of libel (which has to do with harm to one's reputation in the community) aside, was Wechsler a "friendly" witness or wasn't he? In fact, he was what one might call an unfriendly informer. Before the McCarthy Committee he accurately and angrily accused Senator McCarthy of trying to intimidate him and the *New York Post* as punishment for the *Post*'s anti-McCarthy editorials and articles, but in his first appearance Wechsler also answered questions about members of the Young Communist League he had known (the *Post* writer Murray Kempton among them), and when asked by the chairman to prepare a list to be submitted to the Committee at a later date, Wechsler said:

> I would just like to say, on that point, Senator, that I am here as a responsive but not a friendly witness.
>
> I would like to add the obvious point at this moment that I have severed my connections with the Communists as of nearly sixteen years ago.

I trust you will recognize that the list I give you would be as complete as a man's memory might be. I don't know that you would be able to do very well with a similar list of any organization you were connected with sixteen years ago.[3]

On the surface the dispute between Mr. Wechsler and Miss Hellman is one of semantics. At the time there were so few witnesses who denounced the Committee and nevertheless named names, that there was no word to describe the breed. Terms like "friendly" or "cooperative" were euphemisms for naming names, and terms like "uncooperative" or "unfriendly" meant what they said. Obviously it is the connotation rather than the denotation which is at issue. From Hellman's vantage point the fact that Wechsler gave names makes him an informer. From Wechsler's view the spirit in which he gave them made him a more effective opponent of McCarthyism, for it deprived the senator of the chance to denigrate him for "hiding behind the Fifth."

That Hellman and Wechsler are still at it twenty-eight years later is merely another piece of evidence of how deep were the divisions that beset the liberal community in the third great cold war conflict—the war between those who thought of themselves as progressives and those who inhabited what they liked to call the Vital Center.

If the function of espionage exposers such as Chambers and Bentley was to confirm that to be a member of the Communist Party was to be an agent of a foreign power, and the function of professional witnesses such as Budenz and Philbrick was to confirm that to be a member of the Communist Party was to be a member of a revolutionary conspiracy, the function of a reluctant informer like Wechsler had less to do with the image of the Communist Party than with the reputation of the liberals and their organizations. Their goal was to demonstrate to the state and the culture at large that, contrary to what right-wing ideologues said when they lumped liberals with Socialists with Trotskyists with Communists, it was possible, indeed desirable, in fact inevitable, to be liberal and anti-Communist at the same time. Their means of achieving this goal was to dissociate themselves from those involved with the CP. From their perspective the internal-security bureaucracy drew the dividing line at precisely the right place—between those like themselves, whose politics were simply the appropriate exercise of the privileges and immunities of citizenship; and those like the Smith Act defendants, who had forfeited such rights by virtue of their membership in a subversive conspiracy. The decision to name names was often taken reluctantly but was nevertheless taken, time and again, by liberal informers.

Three organizations provided the battleground on which the war within the liberal community took place, and constituted the context within which it was decided by so many to name names: the American Civil Liberties Union (ACLU), the Americans for Democratic Action (ADA), and the American Committee for Cultural Freedom (ACCF).[4]

If the weapons in the international cold war were blockades and pacts and military- and economic-aid programs, and the weapons in the cold war between hunters and hunted were subpoenas and executive orders and jury verdicts and judicial opinions, the weapons in this third cold war were more subtle—primarily articles in small-circulation magazines, newspaper columns, letters to the editor, interpretations of actions as much as the actions themselves. But the stakes were no less significant, the emotions no less bitter. As one admirer of ADA described what happened in 1947 and 1948 when the war among the hunted really got under way: "In the course of this battle liberals attacked liberals with more venom than they had ever directed at any economic royalist, the labor movement was to divide and choose sides between the two protagonists, and a political party was to arise and die in a matter of months."[5]

Charles Morgan, who headed the ACLU's Washington office during the days when it led the fight for impeachment of Richard Nixon, dates the start of the cold war within the liberal community as far back as May 7, 1940, when Elizabeth Gurley Flynn was kicked off the board of the ACLU because she was a member of the Communist Party. This was a startling turn of events since the Union's *raison d'être* is supposed to be the defense of civil liberties, and here it seemed to be imposing the sort of political test it had long opposed as "guilt by association" and a violation of the spirit of the First Amendment; Flynn had been reelected to the ACLU's board in 1939, two years after she had openly stated at an ACLU board meeting that she had joined the CP; and only a year earlier the same board had authorized publication of a leaflet entitled *Why We Defend Free Speech for Nazis, Fascists and Communists.*

The fight to knock Flynn off the board was a bitter one, coming as it did right after the Nazi-Soviet Nonaggression Pact of August 1939, the outbreak of World War II in September, and the Soviet invasion of Finland in November. The chairman, Reverend John Haynes Holmes, broke a 9–9 tie, voting against Miss Flynn and for a purge resolution that had been rejected earlier in the year. It read:

> The Board of Directors and the National Committee of the American Civil Liberties Union . . . hold it inappropriate for any person to serve on the governing committees of the Union or on its staff, who is a

member of any political organization which supports totalitarian dictatorship in any country, or who by his public declarations indicates the
support of such a principle.

Within this category we include organizations in the United States
supporting the totalitarian governments of the Soviet Union and of the
Fascist and Nazi countries (such as the Communist Party, the
German-American Bund and others); as well as native organizations
with obviously anti-democratic objectives or practices.[6]

This "slick maneuver," as Flynn called it, plagued the organization for
many years. In 1975, when Jerold Auerbach, a historian from Wellesley
College commissioned to write up this epoch in an authorized history of
the ACLU, concluded that in practice the desire to limit association to
those who believed in liberty "yielded to a policy that limited association
to those who disbelieved in Communism,"[7] Roger Baldwin, founding father and first executive director of the ACLU, demurred. In an extraordinary footnote—which again shows the present-day resonance of these old
sectarian battles—he wrote: "The author's account is incorrect, biased
and misleading. The sufficient answer to its assumption that the resolution was a departure from principle is that it has remained in substance
Union policy ever since."[8]*

Actually, another event that preceded the expulsion of Flynn also signaled trouble ahead. In 1939, shortly after Martin Dies, chairman of the
newly established House Special Committee on Un-American Activities,
had attacked the ACLU as Communist, he was visited for off-the-record
cocktails by co-counsels Morris Ernst and Arthur Garfield Hays on behalf of the ACLU, after which he announced, "There is not any evidence
that the ACLU was a Communist organization."[9] Was this a deal (the
ACLU would purge itself of Communists like Flynn if Dies would lay
off), or a simple change of mind? Either way, the 1940 resolution anticipated what was ahead. In 1951 the ACLU wrote the 1940 resolution into
its constitution and began to include a statement affirming its opposition
to Communism in all its relevant legal briefs.

The ACLU's new cautiousness where the Communist issue was concerned revealed itself in a number of ways:

• The ACLU changed its position on the right of unions to disqualify
Communists from running for office; it failed to protest the refusal of

* But in 1976 the ACLU reinstated Flynn (who had died in 1964), stating that the
1940 expulsion "was not consonant with the basic principles on which the ACLU was
founded." *The New York Times,* 27 June 1976.

government to give permanent employment status to Communists; and, with the advent of the "police action" in Korea, it dropped its opposition to military conscription.

• Where it could not avoid participation in law cases concerning Communists, as in the Smith Act cases, the ACLU deferred involvement until the appeals stage, where it could come in as *amicus curiae*, or friend of the court, and thereby, it hoped, insure that the public didn't "confuse" the ACLU position with the (Communist) views of those it was defending.

• When the philosopher-philanthropist Corliss Lamont was subpoenaed by McCarthy in the fall of 1953, and after denying past or present Party membership nevertheless refused to answer any further questions because he claimed the Committee had no jurisdiction to ask them of private citizens, the ACLU delayed coming to the defense of one of its own board members. Lamont became the center of a policy dispute and, after a lot of bureaucratic infighting which Osmond Fraenkel properly called "a shabby business," Lamont resigned from the ACLU (as did some of those who opposed him) and put his ample resources behind a new civil-liberties organization, also non-Communist, but ready, eager, willing, and able to defend the rights of Communists—the Emergency Civil Liberties Committee. The ECLC was composed of libertarian stalwarts such as Thomas Emerson of Yale, H. H. Wilson of Princeton, Carey McWilliams of *The Nation,* the journalist I. F. Stone, and a few others who had in common that they were non-Communist libertarians who vigorously fought domestic repression but refused to advertise their reservations about Communism, believing that such rhetoric at the time would be self-serving and at the expense of the civil liberties of those under attack in this country.*

Whatever the shortcomings of the ACLU's public positions, at least they were public and publicly arrived at. Morris Ernst's meeting with

---

* Thomas Emerson, for example, ran for governor of Connecticut on the Progressive Party ticket in 1948, but when the liberal Chester Bowles, with whom he had worked at the wartime Office of Price Administration, won the Democratic nomination, he withdrew. He spoke for the rights of Trotskyists at the same Bill of Rights rally in 1949 where Paul Robeson and others called for their conviction under the Smith Act. All the while he was turning out students at Yale with a deep commitment to and understanding of the Bill of Rights, which orthodox Marxists of the day considered bourgeois nonsense. By the mid-1970s his critique of the intelligence community came to be widely accepted and Emerson himself won a nationwide reputation as a civil-liberties scholar.

Dies, however, in addition to inspiring recurring rumors over the years, turns out to have constituted a precedent of sorts for a form of behind-the-scenes collaboration that occurred throughout the 1950s and continued to haunt the ACLU through the 1970s. Some of the details came to light in 1977 as a result of the ACLU's own Freedom of Information Act suit, which revealed that various members of its staff had been regularly exchanging confidences and information with the FBI.

Irving Ferman, for instance, director of the ACLU's Washington office from 1952 to 1959, sent a note to FBI assistant director Louis Nichols about two people who urged the ACLU to join the campaign against HUAC. Asked about this in 1977, Ferman explained that Nichols had been of great help to the ACLU in killing a potentially damaging HUAC report that was "exceedingly irresponsible" and by keeping "such anti-ACLU groups" as the American Legion "at bay." Ferman thought behind-the-scenes collaboration with the FBI was a good investment, since it liberated the ACLU to spend its time and energy "protecting civil liberties rather than being absorbed in defending itself."

If FBI internal memos are to be believed (and that is always a fair question), Patrick Murphy Malin, the ACLU's executive director from 1950 to 1962, asked Nichols in 1956 to be "tipped off" to CP-ers on ACLU's local-affiliate boards. And we learn that Morris Ernst, who called himself "Hoover's lawyer," alerted the FBI to anti-FBI sentiment among ACLU members and to the plans of some of them to attack the bureau. Ferman gave the bureau minutes of ACLU affiliate meetings in Colorado, Oregon, Pennsylvania, Michigan, and Illinois.[10]

Thus our premier defender of civil liberty had publicly purged members from its ranks because they failed precisely the sort of political-association test it opposed when applied to others; privately and behind the scenes it had collaborated with various wings of the same internal-security establishment it was supposedly keeping honest; instead of questioning the utility and wisdom of the bureau's informer system, it had joined it.

━━━━━

If the ACLU's attitude toward the constitutional rights of Communists was ambivalent, the Americans for Democratic Action had no such uncertainty. The ADA was born in January 1947 when more than four hundred New Dealers, trade unionists, and others met in Washington, D.C., in response to a "call for action" from the Union for Democratic Action (UDA), which had been founded as a non-Communist liberal organization in 1941. Arthur Schlesinger, Jr., a founding member, had it right in 1954 when he upbraided Richard Nixon for harping on the sinister nature of ADA and suggesting that it was in any way a rationalizer or dupe of Communism. As he wrote in a *New York Post* column (October 3): "I cannot believe that Nixon does not know that ADA was founded to combat the Communist influence within the American liberal community, that it spearheaded the fight against the Communist-operated third party in 1948 and that it has consistently called for firm policies of resistance to Soviet aggression—far more so than Nixon's right-wing Republican colleagues who have voted consistently for slashing the defense and foreign aid budget."

The ADA—organized by such as Schlesinger, Wechsler, Rauh, Reinhold Niebuhr (the theologian whom Schlesinger called "the architect of the ADA foreign policy"[11]), Hubert Humphrey (then mayor of Minneapolis; he stormed the Democratic Party's platform at the 1948 convention on behalf of a liberal civil-rights plank), and others—identified its political position with the New Deal, FDR, the triumph over the Axis, Eleanor Roosevelt's do-goodism, and most of Truman's foreign policy, and it was a noisy critic of McCarthy—the man and the method. It was founded within a week of the founding of the Progressive Party, and in February 1948 it condemned the Progressives' presidential candidate, Henry Wallace, and stressed that the Progressive Party was Communist dominated, that it opposed the Marshall Plan, and that third-party candidates would only help to elect an isolationist and reactionary president. In literature and on the stump, the ADA suggested that Wallace was a puppet of the Communist Party.

Many of these anti-Communist liberals identified with not the left but the center, with not the masses but the intellectual elite. They celebrated rather than criticized the social order and had given up the old ideal of the perfectibility of man in favor of a new "realism" about his inherent corruptibility (and the need for institutions beyond those prescribed by the founding fathers to keep these tendencies in check).

Progressives and revisionist historians have charged that these liberals were in the red-baiting business. But a close reading of the articles, journals, and speeches of the epoch suggests that what many of them were in was the dissociating business. The historian Mary McAuliffe was right when she wrote, "As conservatives sought to brand Democratic liberals with pro-Communist sympathies, liberals responded by trying to dissociate themselves . . . from the old popular-front left and by stressing their own anti-Communism."[12]

On the one hand, the liberals wanted their confreres to know that they were anti–witch-hunt; and on the other, they wanted to let the hunters know that they were anti-Communist. A. A. Berle, Jr., a founder of New York's anti-Communist Liberal Party, in his collection of papers *Navigating the Rapids: 1918–1971* (1973), makes clear the theory of liberalism as a two-front struggle: primarily against the left and secondarily against the right. It is their desire to advertise their anti-Communism that helps to account for the liberals' otherwise surprising support of positions that even President Truman couldn't stomach.

Thus in 1950 they opposed the internal-security bill of 1950 which proposed to register all "Communist action" groups and "Communist fronts," on the grounds that such registration violated due process; but in its place they supported the draconian emergency-detention bill. President Truman vetoed the measure, but to no avail.

Arthur Schlesinger, Jr., in his book *The Vital Center* (1949) defined the liberal as standing midway between the totalitarians of left and right. The very phrase Vital Center may be seen as a kiss good-bye to the left, an attempt at trouble-avoidance through strategic labeling. It is appropriate that its coiner should have been its most insistent proselytizer not only in his book but also in letters to the editor, speeches (given by himself or written for political candidates he favored), articles, and a weekly column he wrote for his friend and colleague, James Wechsler of the *New York Post*. The column was called "History of the Week" but was really the View from the Vital Center.

A typical example of Schlesinger in top 1951 form was his July 7 column on the Smith Act, which he opposed. He opposed it not because as applied it was used to harass, intimidate, and suppress a bona fide political party, however distasteful that party might be, but rather because it was not the best way to get at "the real threat" posed by the Communists. "For the last five years the American Communist Party has been bending its energies toward a single end—that is, the laying of foundations for espionage, sabotage and subversion in case war should come between the Soviet Union and the United States." His own proposal: pick up the idea mentioned by Mr. Justice Jackson in his concurring opinion in the Dennis case, where he argued that "the Communist Party is, above all, a criminal conspiracy, employing espionage and perjury as official and approved tactics. . . . The government . . . should name the Communist Party as a criminal conspiracy, serving notice that all who remain associated with it would be subject to prosecution as co-conspirators."

Advocating the outlawing of hard-core Communists was a simple way of advertising to the hunters that the ADA-ers were not to be confused with them. More complicated problems, however, arose in the case of those whom Schlesinger regarded as fellow travelers, but he did not shrink from the task. Thus he devoted his September 2, 1951, column to mocking a letter that proposed a civil-liberties conference because it was signed by "Thomas Emerson of the Progressive Party, Carey McWilliams of *The Nation*, and Stringfellow Barr of the solve-the-Russian-problem-by-giving-them-money school." Wrote Schlesinger:

> None of these gentlemen is a Communist, but none objects very much to Communism. They are the typhoid Marys of the left, bearing the germs of infection even if not suffering obviously from the disease.
>
> A civil liberties conference is vitally needed, but it should be called by men who deeply believe in civil freedom. Those whose belief in the importance of civil freedom is so feeble that they could collaborate with Communists in the 1948 election at home and extenuate Soviet expansion abroad are clearly less interested in civil liberties than they are in something else. I doubt whether many liberals will fall for the Emerson bait. There can be no compromise between liberals and doughfaces.

Consider Schlesinger on the attorney general's list: "The Attorney General's list of subversive groups (whatever the merits of this type of list as a form of procedure) provides a convenient way of checking the more obvious Communist-controlled groups. . . . The Attorney General's list, however, leaves out organizations like PCA [Progressive Citizens of America], which have a large proportion of non-Communist members, but rarely, if ever, oppose Communist objectives."[13] Instead of questioning the propriety of keeping such a list, the concern seems to have been with its accuracy as an instrument of detecting pros and antis. To Schlesinger the categories "pro-Communist" and "anti-Communist" were "clearly fundamental," and he quickly warmed to the phrase "anti-anti-Communist." As he explained it, "This label applies to those who think it is fine to be anti-fascist, anti-Republican, or anti-Democratic but who squirm and wince when someone in exactly the same sense is anti-Communist. All forms of baiting are okay for the 'anti-anti-Communist' except red-baiting. Some of the 'anti-anti-Communists' are not substantively pro-Stalinist. They just have a feeling that a Communist is a rather noble, dedicated fellow who deserves special consideration in a harsh and reactionary world."[14]

As it turned out, there was only a short distance between denouncing anti-anti-Communists and endorsing the act of informing. For many of those ridiculed by Schlesinger were people who risked career and financial penalties rather than abandon their beliefs, one of which was that naming names must be rejected as a test of loyalty. From the perspective of the Vital Center liberal, however, how better to prove that one was not a "Comsymp" than to name those one was falsely accused of aiding? Or, if one had no names to name, one could at least identify the "typhoid Marys." Or, if one preferred to stay out of the name business altogether, one could endorse the names test as being a legitimate political credit standard. Thus Schlesinger did not forbear praising some of those who named names, and denounced those who objected.

And he endorsed Wechsler's testimony (without mentioning the name-naming), saying simply (May 24, 1953), "the response to James Wechsler's courageous defiance of Senator McCarthy shows that a good many Americans are tired of taking the Wisconsin Senator lying down. The outburst of editorials across the country . . . was a heartfelt tribute to Jimmy Wechsler's display of personal wit and courage in face of the great national bully. The Walter Mittys of the American press found in Wechsler's performance a happy moment of identification and fulfillment."

———

While the ACLU was doing backstairs business with the FBI, the Congress for Cultural Freedom (CCF) and its American affiliate, the American Committee for Cultural Freedom (ACCF), both widely advertised for their commitment to human rights, turn out to have been taking money from the CIA.[15] Exactly how much in the way of CIA funding was used to support the activities of either organization is still unknown. Originally organized in the late 1930s under the auspices of a group that included the philosophers Sidney Hook and John Dewey, the ACCF was revived after the Waldorf Peace Conference in 1949, which was denounced by many intellectuals as dominated by Communists and fellow travelers. Sidney Hook, who was the first chairman of the American affiliate, and Irving Kristol, who was its first executive director, played major parts in the congress. Other members included Schlesinger, Elliott Cohen of *Commentary*, Elia Kazan, the critic Diana Trilling, and Wechsler. Hook frankly said that among the congress's goals was the aim "to expose Stalinism and Stalinist liberals wherever you find them."

During the ACCF's most active phase, Sol Stein, formerly a political analyst on Voice of America's ideological advisory staff, served as executive director. The combative Stein saw his job as that of attacking "the residues of Communist influence frontally."

A favorite tactic of the American Committee for Cultural Freedom was to confuse support of a man's right to hold unpopular views with endorsement of the view. Fowler Harper of the Yale Law School (and associated with the Lawyers Guild and ECLC) charged with some truth that ACCF's position was, "whatever the Communist Party is for, they are against; whatever the Communist Party is against, they are for. . . . They are not free men because they fear that some position they may take will 'associate' them with the Communist Party." A favorite target was the already-mentioned Emergency Civil Liberties Committee. Despite the fact that not even the attorney general considered this organization subversive, the ACCF insisted that it was "Communist-dominated and dangerous." In anticipation of a 1953 ECLC conference, Irving Kristol wired conferees such as Reinhold Niebuhr (who was also a board member of the congress): "Are you aware that this organization is a Communist front with no sincere interest in liberty in the United States or elsewhere?" He asked Niebuhr to persuade the chairman of the conference, Paul Lehmann, to resign, and singled out McWilliams, Emerson, and I. F. Stone as suspect. He added, "There are, of course, non-Communists who are also taking part, but no one who can be legitimately described as an anti-Communist."

When Roger Baldwin, also an ACCF member, wrote Kristol that he thought the telegrams "most unfortunate" since there was no proof that the ECLC was a Communist front, Kristol complained that ECLC "has no intention whatsoever of protesting the destruction of civil liberties in Communist-dominated countries, or indicating its detestation of the Communist movement even while defending its rights."[16] (In fact, the ECLC had announced at the outset that its concern was domestic, not foreign, affairs, although it did put out a statement condemning double standards of political conduct and condemning anti-Semitism in the USSR.)

But eventually the American Committee for Cultural Freedom fell apart with defections left and right. Whittaker Chambers joined it in 1954, although he was at first reluctant to belong to any organization that included J. Robert Oppenheimer. By 1955 even Arthur Schlesinger felt that the committee's anti-Communism was becoming "obsessive." Wechsler resigned in January 1956. And James Burnham, the once radical political scientist who had veered to the far right, resigned in 1954 when the congress subsidized a book critical of McCarthy. *McCarthy and the Communists,* by James Rorty and Moshe Decter, argued that the trouble with McCarthy was he was messing up the fight against Communism. "Should a witness," Rorty and Decter ask, "testify frankly not only about his own past as a Communist or fellow traveler but about that of his friends and associates as well?" Dissociation from Communists is one thing; turning over a comrade to the authorities is something else again, especially when the authorities have demonstrated how careless they are with other people's lives and careers. Here is their own answer:

> The question poses delicate considerations of personal honor and responsibility. But it would seem to be the part of the wisdom as well as of courage to answer it affirmatively. Speaking out fully and frankly serves to establish the credibility of the witness. It is probably also the best method of vindicating one's own values.
>
> The Communist Party has profited greatly by the reluctance of liberals to be considered "red-baiters." Conversely, a former Communist who testifies frankly about his past associations often thereby helps to expose dangerous current activities of the Party.
>
> Frank testimony of this sort does not make one an "informer," with all the distasteful connotations of that word. On the contrary, if a silent witness must be protected in his right to invoke the Fifth Amendment, a forthright witness must be equally protected from slanderous insinuations against his reputation and idealism. The man who testifies frankly about the past Communist record of former friends and associates performs the same public service as the witness who testifies to his personal knowledge of the past Nazi or Fascist record of former friends and associates.
>
> Both may be patriots who place the highest value on safety of their countrymen. They may be persons who believe so deeply in the value of freedom and democracy that they will sacrifice the comfort of their own silence and the emotional ties of personal attachment to the ideals they honor.[17]

In the context of the anti-Communist crusade of the 1950s, in other words, citizenship required the betrayal of friendship. If such a skewed conception had been limited to right-wing congressional demagogues or an embittered handful of social democrats, traumatized by the American Communists' unwillingness or inability to face the reality and implications of Stalin's purges and what followed, that would be of historical curiosity. If those called upon to name the names had regarded the request as justified—turning in a bona fide spy who happened to be a friend or relative—that could have posed a profound Forsterian dilemma. In fact, however, the assumption that even those guilty of nothing more than past membership in an organization later labeled subversive ought to betray past friends as the price of present employment had quietly entered the liberal mainstream. Harvard University, for instance, discreetly made the willingness to name names the test for employment in the cases of Sigmund Diamond, a young historian, and Robert Bellah, then a graduate student in sociology, whose past records of Communist affiliation had been brought to the university's attention by the FBI.[18] M. I. Finley, the eminent classical scholar now at Cambridge University, was forced to leave Rutgers University in 1952 after invoking the Fifth Amendment before the McCarthy Committee. He recalls the dean saying to him, "Look, we don't give a damn what you tell the Committee. Tell them anything. Just clean your skirts. Say you were a spy—we don't care what you say as long as you're not accused of not having cooperated." *The New York Times* penalized employees who were noncooperative at congressional hearings and invoked the First Amendment by reducing their editorial responsibilities and prospects for advancement; they fired those who took the Fifth Amendment. Less lofty institutions took less lofty and noisier action.

———

It was against this background that a man like James Wechsler, who had voted against the expulsion of Elizabeth Gurley Flynn from the ACLU board in 1940, had to decide what to do when called.

Wechsler had never made any secret of his life in the Young Communist League, which he left when he was twenty-two, in 1937. He resigned from the newspaper *PM* in 1946, charging that he felt compelled to leave because it was Communist-dominated. He had fought to eliminate Communist influence in the American Newspaper Guild, and his case is worth looking at in some detail since in addition to his ACLU affiliation he was a founder of the ADA and, along with his friend Schlesinger, a member of the ACCF. He was a prototypical liberal.

Wechsler was summoned before the McCarthy Committee on April 24, 1953, shortly after the *Post* had run some sensationally negative series on Senator McCarthy himself and also on such McCarthy enthusiasts as the columnists Jack Lait and Lee Mortimer and the political hit man

Walter Winchell. McCarthy's aides Roy Cohn and G. David Schine had recently returned from their famous tour of USIA libraries abroad, and the ostensible purpose of Wechsler's hearing was to ask him about his books in USIA libraries. (There were four, and two of them, *Revolt on Campus* and *War Our Heritage,* were written when he was still a Young Communist.) The hearing was barely under way when McCarthy leaped in to ask him to name any YCL-ers or former YCL-ers at the *New York Post;* Wechsler replied, "I will say that I am going to answer that question because I believe it is a citizen's responsibility to testify before a Senate Committee whether he likes the Committee or not."[19] He named the writers Murray Kempton and Robert Bendiner, and a man named Jack Casey as former Communists, and the writer Joseph Lash as someone who had followed the Party line—all of them, he said, would be happy to tell the Committee why they left the Party.*

That same year, in his book *The Age of Suspicion,* Wechsler explained why he answered the Committee's questions "despite my belief that they were far beyond the scope of the Committee's authorized inquiry":

> I had resolved much earlier that silence was suicidal in dealing with McCarthy. I know some thoughtful people differ with me, and that there are some who believe I should have refused to answer any questions dealing with the policies and personnel of the newspaper I edit. But I was persuaded then, and I have not changed my opinion, that McCarthy was hoping I would refuse to testify so that he could use my silence to charge that I had something to hide. . . . To put it simply, I did not believe that my answers would tend to incriminate or degrade me but I was quite certain that silence would.

To prove his anti-Communist bona fides to the Committee, Wechsler cited a statement issued by the National Committee of the Communist Party blaming the poor electoral showing of the Progressive Party on "the policies of the Reuthers, Dubinskys, Wechslers, et al. . . . " He said he had long believed "that the most effective opponents of Communism in America have been the liberals and labor leaders associated with the non-Communist left." He mentioned an article he had written for

---

* In 1977 Kempton told me he told Roy Cohn in the 1950s that while he would be happy to testify about himself he would decline to name others because he couldn't afford the commercial consequences in years to come—it would hurt his marketability among the liberals, his natural allies.

Harper's magazine on "How to Rid the Government of Communists" and a letter he had received from Richard Nixon praising his *New York Post* editorial endorsing the finding of guilt against Alger Hiss.

Wechsler had indeed played a major role fighting Communists at the newspaper *PM,* in the American Veterans Committee, and, more recently, on any occasion where he had the opportunity. Back in 1947 in an article in the *Guild Reporter* he had written:

> It would be nice if the world were prettier, but it isn't; espionage and sabotage are facts of modern life. I have no brief for anybody who refuses to testify before a congressional committee; no matter how foolish or fierce the committee, an American ought to be prepared to state his case in any public place at any time.

When Wechsler asked for the release of his testimony, Senator McCarthy said that would happen as soon as he furnished a complete list of those he had known as Young Communists. Before the hearing was over McCarthy asked him if he felt intimidated and Wechsler countered: "Why of course I have been abused. The suggestion that my break with Communism was not authentic is the greatest affront you could recite anywhere. I have fought this battle a long time, longer than you have, Senator, and I have taken plenty of beatings from the Communists in the course of this fight. So I feel very strongly about this." Outside the hearing room he told the assembled reporters that he was going to bring the session to the attention of the American Society of Newspaper Editors (ASNE).

There followed an exchange of telegrams, with Wechsler asking for a transcript of his testimony so that he could turn it over to the ASNE, McCarthy replying that the Committee's practice was not to release a transcript until the testimony was complete, including the requested list of names. As Wechsler reconstructed it in his book:

> The notion of placing any names in his hands was repugnant to me, yet to refuse to do so meant to abandon the argument or let him shift it to ground most favorable to him.
>
> I am an active anti-Communist; McCarthy wanted to prove that I must be pro-Communist because I am opposed to McCarthy. I did not see how I could persuade my perplexed countrymen that unwillingness to entrust such a list to McCarthy was different from the now stereotyped refusal of Communists to answer questions before congressional committees. It seemed to me that any function I might serve was to es-

tablish beyond dispute that an American might be as resolutely anti-Communist as anti-McCarthy, and that being anti-McCarthy did not involve any sentimentality about Communists or Communism. I had contended that the true issue in McCarthy's attack was freedom of the press; I believed that on the ground he might finally be challenged by editors and publishers who had been nervously pampering him, and I knew that McCarthy was hoping to obscure that issue by picturing me as just another reluctant witness in a procession of evasive Communists. Having decided that silence was exactly what he was inviting, I had chosen to talk; I could not balk now.

So Wechsler telegraphed McCarthy that he would submit his list "because I do not propose to let you distort or obscure the clear-cut issue of freedom of the press involved in this proceeding," but he would "ask your committee at that time to decide whether the inclusion of such a list in the record is proper or desirable."*

Wechsler arrived at his second hearing on May 5 with a press release announcing that he was turning over his list of names only because McCarthy had insisted he do so before a transcript would be released. McCarthy outmaneuvered him in his opening remarks by stating that he would make the record public regardless of whether Wechsler turned over the names or not. But, as Wechsler put it, "He was still seeking the opportunity to tell the world that I had refused to talk, and thus to consign me to the netherworld of silent witnesses. . . . Strong impulses counseled me to leap at the chance to withhold the list from McCarthy and tell him that I would instead give it to the FBI, although the bureau had not requested it. But equally strong instinct cautioned me to fight for time to think." So Wechsler took the occasion to read his press statement into the record. He then said: "The mediations and struggles of con-

---

* Wechsler had arrived at his strategy after hurried consultation with his friend and fellow ADA founder, the lawyer Joseph Rauh, who was en route to Mexico at the time. Today Rauh says, "We had a failure of communications. I said, 'There is no *legal* way to refuse to name names and not take the Fifth Amendment under the present law.' He thought I was telling him to name names. In fact I wasn't at all. I thought it was a good risk [neither to name names nor to take the Fifth]." Throughout this period, Rauh was looking for ways to beat the Committee at its own game. He had represented Lillian Hellman in 1952, who combined "taking the Fifth" with her statement that "I will not cut my conscience to fit this year's fashions," which captured the headlines and used the Committee's publicity against itself. Later, in 1956, Rauh represented Arthur Miller, who risked a contempt citation by speaking about himself but not others, and claimed the constitutional protection of only the First Amendment.

science I have had do not involve people whom I have reason to believe—
by their present affiliations with the *Daily Worker* or other obvious Communist associations—are still Communists. I am deeply concerned about
the fact that half of this list includes names of people about whose political whereabouts I have no idea." He asked Senator Stuart Symington
whether it was safe to turn over the list to the Committee, and Symington
said, "Well, the Chairman has said he would not release the list without
discussing it in executive session with the rest of the Committee. On that
basis, based on your telegram to him, I would submit the list at this
time."* Wechsler then asked for a recess in which he consulted with his
publisher, Dorothy Schiff. Mrs. Schiff had earlier stunned Wechsler by
telling him in the midst of his deliberations that she had not known of his
Communist past when she hired him; now she told him that she believed
it important to cooperate with duly authorized committees of the Congress, but what he did was up to him. According to Mrs. Schiff, he also
consulted with Senator Symington's fellow Missourian the influential
lawyer Clark Clifford.

After the recess Wechsler handed over his list. McCarthy looked at it
with Cohn and Committee consultant Howard Rushmore (whom
Wechsler had known as an anti-Communist journalist), and said: "I have
a list from Mr. Wechsler and I have had Mr. Rushmore and Mr. Cohn
check it. They tell me at this point that apparently there are no names on
here except names of those who have been publicly known as Communists or Young Communist Leaguers."

"Sir," Wechsler responded, "that is not a true statement, and I do not
believe Mr. Rushmore could make it under oath." He didn't.

Subsequent to the hearings Wechsler turned the transcript over to the
ASNE. A committee of eleven was appointed to study it; only four of
them saw the session as raising the sort of threat to freedom of the press
which required them to speak out, so although a minority report was
available to be read, the ASNE took no position on the matter. Wechsler
did not achieve his goal of getting the ASNE on record against the senator and his tactics. He did, however, win a warm endorsement from *The
New York Times,* whose editorial approving his conduct reflected the pa-

* At his publisher's instigation, Wechsler had earlier met privately with Senator Symington to discuss what he would and would not say before the Committee. Wechsler
says that at this meeting Symington assured him the list would not be put in the public
record. Senator Symington says that at this late date he cannot recall what assurances
he gave.

per's own policy toward its in-house ex-Communists—that the better
course of action was to cooperate, to name names:[20]

FREEDOM AND FEAR

... We have repeatedly said that the investigative function of congressional committees is an important and a desirable one. We believe
it is the citizen's duty to respond fully and frankly to congressional investigators (as Mr. Wechsler did), just as it is the duty of the investigators scrupulously to observe the citizen's constitutional rights. We
think that newspapermen are no more immune from investigation in
respect to allegedly subversive or seditious activity than anyone else.
The mere fact that a man works on or writes for a publication does not
give any special privilege if, as and when his loyalty comes under scrutiny.

But there is another basic American principle involved here, too,
and that is the principle of freedom of the press. The real question is
whether or not Mr. McCarthy was using his undoubted right of investigation as a cover for an attempt to harass and intimidate Mr.
Wechsler as an editor who has bitterly and uncompromisingly opposed
Mr. McCarthy. It is our opinion after reading the transcript that this is
just exactly what Mr. McCarthy was doing.

Wechsler now says, "The whole issue hinged on my relations with the
American Society of Newspaper Editors, where I was fighting very hard
to get them to move in. They had made it perfectly clear that if the issue
bogged down on my not giving the 'list' I was going to get nowhere. I
have to add ... that I have grave doubt that I'd do that today. Certainly
it was not something that I thought was simple or easy.

"I will say with respect to the list, I know only one person who ever
suggested that he had been hurt by my putting his name on it. He was a
businessman who said that something happened to him about a visa. Roy
Cohn was probably quite accurate when he exploded after I gave him the
list and said, 'You're not telling us anything we didn't know.' There were
no secret names on this list. There were people who, in one way or another, had all been identified. But that doesn't totally satisfy me—I
would certainly feel better if I could look back on that period and say
that I testified freely about myself ... and I would still hold on the position that if I had known anyone working in a secret atomic laboratory
whom I knew was still a Communist, that I did have an obligation to
name that person.

"As far as the Hellman thing is concerned, I am outraged by the notion that it was wrong to go before a committee and say that it was perfectly clear that I had fought the Communists in the Newspaper Guild and so on. Well, I never believed that it was red-baiting to say that somebody was a Communist in the guild. I felt very strongly about that.

"I suppose I also felt, in terms of dealing with McCarthy, that I really had him—that was my mistake in the beginning, because I didn't anticipate the list issue arising, as I should have. I rather welcomed the invitation to go before the Committee.

"And then there was that fateful moment—not fateful, but absurd moment—after I'd introduced all the editorials of the *Daily Worker* denouncing me, and he asked me, with that bland face, 'Did you write them?' I don't think I ever printed this, but there was one point in the hearings when Leonard Lyons told me that Joe McCarthy was in New York and that he'd be happy to meet with me in his hotel and Leonard felt that he could work this whole thing out. I could have made a deal with the Committee. Leonard was a very close friend of Roy Cohn's, and it was very painful to him. His feeling was that I was his friend and Roy Cohn was his friend and therefore how could we possibly be arguing? Leonard's view of life was that his role was to bring such people together. But nobody has ever brought me together with Roy Cohn and will not in the time that remains. But this was a sort of side comedy.

"The interesting thing, in the context of that period as distinct from now [1976], is that if I had challenged the Committee on that issue [the list] and McCarthy had said, 'The hearing is over, we're going to cite you for contempt,' the ASNE would not have gone with me. In the end, as you know, they split anyway. The appalling thing is the sense we all had then that it was almost impossible to make this case without yielding on the list issue.

"This was a time when there was a sense that advertisers would punish the paper, that there was real danger. I never felt any sense of great personal hazard in this. I had a kind of instinct for combat, and I really looked forward to it. The thing that really shadowed the whole business was Cohn's cleverness in forcing me into a corner on the list issue. If it hadn't been for that I would have been proud of myself."

Wechsler's experience with the Committee suggests a number of lessons for anyone who would understand the circumstances under which decent men decided it was their duty to play the informer.

First, his threatened lawsuit against Lillian Hellman reveals how deeply ingrained are the attitudes, values, assumptions, and perspectives which people had in those cold war days. The policy-reason behind the threat, he says, is to prevent Miss Hellman from misleading a new generation as to what happened. But Wechsler's own memoir, *The Age of Suspicion,* is itself misleading or at least self-serving, since it does not sufficiently emphasize that all of his agonizing over whether to turn over a sealed list of names came *after* he had already openly mentioned a shorter list of names. When asked if he knew the names of his fellow Young Communist Leaguers he had responded:

"Do you want a long list? A short list? How do you want this?" And when the chairman said, "I think all of those that you can think of," Wechsler had said, "Joe Cadden was a Communist at that time. Bill Hinckley was, to the best of my knowledge, a Communist. And here I would draw only what to me is a legal distinction as to whether he held a card. Celeste Strack was, of course, an active Communist in that period. Bert Witt, who subsequently became an active Wallace Leaguer on the West Coast. . . . Kenneth Born, who was another with Wallace in 1948."

Moreover, as Wechsler conceded, in 1948 he had given Louis Nichols, of the FBI, YCL names on the occasion of "straightening out Nancy's dossier [his wife had also been in the YCL]."[21] It is certainly a distinction to say, I will give names to the FBI and not to Senator McCarthy, or, I will give publicly only a short list of those names already known, or, I will give names in secret but not to be read aloud; but all three positions assume the right of the state to ask for the names, which is the position Miss Hellman attacked then and attacks now.*

Second, the press response to Wechsler's testimony reveals something of the media environment surrounding the cold war congressional investigations. Few newspapers were willing to challenge McCarthy, but even those that were, as Richard Rovere has pointed out, were not up to running a "McCarthy lies" feature next to a "McCarthy says" feature, and since no other senator took the trouble to answer his charges, McCarthy benefited from the myth of "objective" reporting.[22] As it happens Wechsler told the truth, but the press, which acted as press agents for unreliable professional informers, rarely attempted to check out such allegations on its own. Nor did it generally bother to report on the gap between the Committee's legitimate functions as an agent of Congress and its dubious ones as a punisher-through-publicity.

* It should be pointed out, however, that in *Scoundrel Time* Hellman, in elaborating on her refusal to bring trouble to others, added, "I do not like subversion or disloyalty in any form, and if I had ever seen any, I would have considered it my duty to have reported it to the proper authorities." It may have been a sign of the terror, or simply loose terminology, that led even Miss Hellman to refer to "subversion" when she might have said "espionage."

That even *The New York Times,* which editorially fought many lonely battles against McCarthyism, chose to endorse Wechsler's stand of denouncing McCarthy publicly and naming names semiprivately is, however, a more intimate index of prevailing media assumptions. As Alden Whitman, who worked on the *Times* and was called before the Senate Internal Security Committee as a former Communist, recalls: "It's one of the country's greatest disgraces. Moral issues were involved, but they weren't seen that way at the time. Even a liberal like Judge Thurman Arnold [then Whitman's lawyer] never thought of it in moral terms. He offered to get me out of the situation. He said, 'I know Jim Eastland and I'm sure I can arrange for you to go up in executive session, tell them what you know, and you'll never be identified publicly.' That's a lawyer trying to help his client. I couldn't make him see that there was anything more involved than litigating a case. This was the framework in which he'd become accustomed to live.*

"Politically I felt that under the Constitution anybody should be able to advocate anything he wanted to and the penalty shouldn't be retroactive. On moral grounds, I felt that when you implicate somebody where he'll be held up to public obloquy, lose his job, be called before a [congressional] committee, you're taking onto yourself far more than any one individual should be called to take on with respect to another. I didn't know about any conspiracies and I didn't know anyone who did. What the Committee wanted were names. You're not telling the Committee anything they don't know."

Whitman was assistant copy editor at the time, next in line to replace the head of the city desk, who was due to retire. "I was bumped all the way back to the rim," he says.

Contrast the *Times*'s eloquent endorsement of Wechsler's noisy but *de facto* collaboration with its silence on the plight of the co-founders and editors of the more radical *National Guardian.* Cedric Belfrage had

---

* The *Times,* according to Whitman, had a triple policy: "First there was this letter from the lawyer Louis Loeb and Punch's father [Arthur O. Sulzberger, then the publisher] which said they expected all to cooperate, but if one didn't judgment would be suspended until all legal proceedings were exhausted. Loeb interpreted this as follows: If you took the Fifth Amendment and were in the news operation you got fired. If you were not in the news operation, you didn't get fired, but you could work on the index, printing, etc. Second, you had to confess internally, whatever you did. Third, if you took the First Amendment, you weren't fired. The Fifth had a bad reputation. For some reason you could be a First Amendment former Communist and not a Fifth Amendment former Communist."

been named by Elizabeth Bentley, and he and James Aronson were summoned before McCarthy in May 1953 after they had been publicized by Walter Winchell, who described the *Guardian* as "a pro-Commie rag" because of its defense of Alger Hiss and the Rosenbergs and its opposition to the Korean War. They invoked the Fifth Amendment rather than the First, as Aronson explained it in his book *The Press and the Cold War* (1953), because:

> Our lawyer had reasoned in a four-hour argument that if we invoked the First we would almost surely be cited for contempt, be convicted, and, in the existing climate, go to prison. He said the *National Guardian* would suffer and perhaps even be forced to suspend publication if its two chief editors were jailed. In effect he put the issue as one of survival of the paper as against the issue of personal principle, however valid that principle might be.
>
> We also explained to the reporters why we had refused to answer questions about the *National Guardian* and our association with it. If we had conceded association with our newspaper, the next questions probably would have been . . . Who are the other staff members? Who contributes financially to the paper? Will you produce your subscription files? We felt that such questions went beyond the jurisdiction of the inquiry; that they would seek to intimidate us and through us, our readers; that we had a moral obligation—as did any newspaper editor—to keep the trust of privacy with our readers, among whom were Communists, Republicans, vegetarians, agnostics, Jehovah's Witnesses, and agrarian socialists.

The day after the hearings Belfrage, a resident alien from England, was arrested and taken to Ellis Island as a "dangerous alien." After an unsuccessful two-year deportation fight and months in jail, he left the United States as his only alternative to imprisonment.

I. F. Stone wrote at the time, "*The New York Times* spoke up for Wechsler of the *Post,* but the *Post* did not speak up for the *National Guardian.* True, Belfrage's case is more difficult: He neither confessed, recanted nor informed. But the difference clarifies the real issue which must be faced if freedom of the press is to be preserved."[23] Aronson argues that the real issue and fact was that those who fought "not only against McCarthy's methods but against his basic premise that there was an international Communist conspiracy (with an American branch) which endangered the American way of life" were, apparently, indefensible.

Today Wechsler says he didn't comment on the *Guardian* because he believed that Belfrage was a Communist and he believes people should be open about their affiliations. I pointed out to him that Belfrage denies he was a Communist, and Wechsler said, "Perhaps I was misinformed."

A leading (or certainly vocal) liberal critic of the internal-security establishment became an informer in carrying out a plan to involve his peers (the ASNE) in the fight against McCarthyism, and then they didn't get involved. He prevented Senator McCarthy from winning a political public-relations victory by permitting him to win a substantive one. He granted the senator his most damaging premise—the right to demand names—and thereby reinforced the very system his editorials had opposed. Along with *The New York Times,* he attacked McCarthy for attempting to intimidate the liberal press, but when the *National Guardian* came under attack both the *Times* and the *Post* kept their silence.

The espionage exposers, it could be argued, were patriots engaged in counterespionage; the Smith Act witnesses were conspiracy-revealers— radar against the revolutionaries; the confidential informants were information-providers engaged in police work; the professional witnesses were—at their best—making their living by doing their duty. The anti-McCarthy, ex-Communist liberal informers like Wechsler were veteran political infighters trying to beat the Stalinists at their own game. Betrayal may have been a part of, but it was not central to, their respective enterprises. And yet, speaking the language of conspiracy, these last were major contributors to the cultural context and the moral environment that routinized betrayal. Endorsed by the state and promoted by the media, they were an essential part of the machinery for the mass production of the citizen-informer.

Let us assume that Chambers told the truth about Hiss, that the Rosenbergs were indeed spies who, as Judge Irving Kaufman suggested in sentencing them to death, were responsible for the death of fifty thousand American boys in Korea. Let us assume that Elizabeth Bentley was reporting fact rather than fantasy when she called herself a Soviet spy courier, and that her "spy rings" were the real thing and not merely Marxist study groups. Let us assume that Crouch and Johnson and Hewitt and Cvetic and witnesses like them told the truth much of the time. Let us stipulate that Stalinism meant purges and death camps and a mockery of the socialist vision and that the American Communist Party took its orders—via the Comintern—from the Kremlin. Let us assume that the witnesses in the Smith Act cases told the truth and were correct and that classic Communist doctrine called for the overthrow of the government by force and violence. Let us grant that James Wechsler and many other ex-Communist veterans of the political wars of the sectarian left were persuaded that Stalinist takeovers of the trade-union movement, the American Veterans Committee, and various key political organizations constituted a clear and present danger. Let us assume that the internal-security establishment was acting in good faith and that HUAC believed that the Committee had an honest and valid mandate to investigate Communist infiltration into the entertainment community for the purpose of proposing legislation that would do something about it. And let us stipulate that many of those summoned to appear before the Committee who ultimately named names had become genuinely disenchanted with the CPUSA years before, preferring capitalism to Communism, democracy to dictatorship, America to Russia.

Even assuming all this, it remains true that the Communists in Hollywood (actually most of them were ex-Communists by the time of the mass naming of names in 1951) and the entertainment industry in general posed the smallest threat to the security of the Republic—either in theory or in fact—yet yielded the greatest per-capita number of citizen-informers. How did it happen?

PART I
NAMING NAMES

THERE WERE RELUCTANT INFORMERS, like Larry Parks and the writer George Beck, who preceded his name-naming by telling HUAC that he would rather not, because, "It is just that the majority of these people are very close and good friends of mine and I like them and I know very well; that is, in my own mind, these are not people who could by the furthest stretch of the imagination be considered bomb throwers."[1]

And there were enthusiastic informers like the screenwriter Bart Lytton, who closed his office and invited his staff to see the show. He told the Committee that he would be "very pleased" to testify. "If a traffic police officer gives me a ticket," Lytton said, "I don't tear it up, so let's put it that way."[2]

There were informed and philosophical informers, like Robert Rossen, who returned in 1953 to give the Committee a detailed rundown of Communist Party practices including its system of tithing the salary of members. He said he had changed his mind about naming names because, given the changed political circumstances, he could no longer "indulge himself in the luxury of individual morality."[3]

And there were uninformed informers, like the bandleader Artie Shaw, who wasn't sure whether he had been a Party member—"I was certainly a bad Communist. It was never my intention to be one, and to the best of my knowledge I have never been one, although these people may have assumed I was, as I could probably assume some of those people were." He admitted, "I was a dupe," and said that in the future he would not sign anything "unless I had the advice of seven lawyers and the granting of permission or clearance by this Committee."[4]

There were truth-telling informers, like the novelist Budd Schulberg, among whose grievances was the Party's attempt to interfere with his literary output, especially his Hollywood novel, *What Makes Sammy Run?*

There were informers like the writer Danny Dare, who initially lied to the Committee in executive session and denied his Party membership, and only later confessed to Party membership and named names in public.[5]

There were combative informers, like the playwright Clifford Odets, who lectured the Committee on the meaning of poverty. When asked, "Didn't you write later on Communist themes?" he answered, ". . . When I wrote, sir, it was out of central, personal things. I did not learn my hatred of poverty, sir, out of Communism." And there were groveling informers, like Nicholas Bela, the Hungarian-born writer who made a point of standing up out of respect for the Committee. "I would like to stand . . . I want to humbly apologize for the grave error which I have committed and beg of you to forgive me."[6]

There were denigrating informers, like Harold Hecht, who told the Committee that George Willner, an agent for many blacklisted people, had threatened him that morning at the luncheon recess saying, "I understand you are going to be a stool pigeon." Or Leopold Atlas, the screenwriter who described a Party meeting where Alvah Bessie, one of the original Hollywood Ten, was "dripping venom" in his denunciation of a fellow comrade. There were exculpatory and laudatory informers, like Rossen, who made it a point to mention that as far as he knew the writer John Bright was no longer a Communist. The playwright John Wexley recalls that "Leo Townsend, who named me, named me in the guise of a eulogy. He doubled the salary I was getting and praised my writing. He was like a PR man. He liked me and my wife very much."[7]

There were noisy informers, like the director Elia Kazan, who took an ad in *The New York Times* urging others to do as he had done. There were quiet informers, like the director Michael Gordon, who appeared in secret session in a hotel room long after the furor had died down and went through the name-naming ritual on condition that there would be no publicity.[8]

There were comic informers, like Abe Burrows, who had no trouble identifying those he saw at CP meetings but, when it came to himself, made clear that while he may have looked like a Communist and talked like a Communist and hung around with Communists, and others were justified in thinking him a Communist, "In my own heart, I didn't believe it."[9] This from the songwriter who gave us "You Put a Piece of Carbon Paper Under Your Heart and Gave Me a Copy of Your Love."

There were husband-and-wife informers, like the writer Max and his wife Mildred Benoff, each of whom named names but in separate testimony denied knowledge that the other was in the Party.[10]

There were informers-by-dispensation, like the writer Ben Maddow, who first invoked the Fifth Amendment but years later decided to cooperate[11] after, he told a friend, he had run into the left-wing union leader Harry Bridges at a party, and Bridges had said, "Forget it, you've been on strike long enough. Go back to work."

There were informers who volunteered to testify, like Schulberg, and there were informers under duress, like the writer Virginia Viertel, Schulberg's first wife, who told a friend that when she was subpoenaed her husband Peter was in the Reserves and the Committee was alleging that she had served as a Communist courier, so she testified fully and named names to protect him.[12] The choreographer Jerome Robbins was rumored to have turned informer to keep the Committee's investigators from publicizing evidence that he was a homosexual, at a time when our society attached a cruel stigma to such sexual preferences. Robbins denies that this was his motive, although his demeanor before HUAC was so compliant that his appearance had about it the aura of social blackmail.[13]

There were informers who had never joined the Party, like the agent Paul Radin, who nevertheless said that the director Joseph Losey and his wife Louise had brought him to a Party meeting.[14]

There were resister-informers, like the director Edward Dmytryk, who went to prison as one of the Hollywood Ten rather than desert his comrades and cooperate with HUAC, but who, after the Korean War broke out, decided to name names; before the Committee and in a long article in the *Saturday Evening Post* he denounced those who questioned his right to do so.[15]

Sterling Hayden, star of *The Asphalt Jungle* (1950), named his former mistress. The screenwriter Melvin Levy (*The Bandit of Sherwood Forest* [1946]) named his collaborator. Richard Collins (who wrote *Song of Russia* [1944]) named a creditor. Clifford Odets, the Group Theatre playwright who had given the eulogy at the actor J. Edward Bromberg's memorial service (where he blamed HUAC for Bromberg's death), named J. Edward Bromberg. And Martin Berkeley, a screenwriter specializing in such animal pictures as *My Friend Flicka* ("I always maintained that was because he couldn't write human dialogue," explains Ring Lardner, Jr.), named 161 names.[16]

Although this orgy of informing was a response (albeit a Cecil B. De Mille–sized one) to the national red hunt, it would be simplistic to regard it as an inevitable result of the national repression. Certainly Joe McCarthy, Roy Cohn, J. Edgar Hoover, and the rest contributed to the atmosphere of urgency. None contributed more than the agent of repression in Hollywood, the House Un-American Activities Committee, which violated so many of our values and used unethical and possibly unconstitutional means to achieve dubious ends and in the process recklessly mangled lives and careers.

Nevertheless, to pronounce the Hollywood community a victim of HUAC, a casualty of the war between the hunter and the hunted, is too easy. For Hollywood, with all its contradictions, was not merely the compliant company town, willing to endure a little repression in exchange for the cash and profit to which its inhabitants had grown accustomed. Hollywood *was* a company town, but a fragile one, which had earned its coherence by holding violently contradictory tendencies in balance: culture vs. commerce, message vs. entertainment, formula vs. originality. HUAC helped to shatter this fragile network of delicate balances, but Hollywood was an active contributor to its own predicament. The architects of repression created the conditions under which good people and organizations betrayed their friends, but that is really all they created. They opened the door to the informer, but they did not determine who would hold the door open, who would walk through it, and who would stand idly by watching the traffic.

To understand why so many in Hollywood came to accept rather than contest HUAC's assumptions and permit them to dominate the motion-picture industry for a decade, would require hundreds of individual case studies. I have not the expertise, data, or inclination to attempt such an excavation into the deep psychological and personal histories that undoubtedly contributed to individual decisions to inform, to collaborate, to tolerate. It is possible, however, to describe the conditions under which so many people failed to follow their better instincts. I should quickly add that putting the Hollywood informers in context is intended not to relieve them of responsibility for the consequences of their actions but, rather, to locate that responsibility more precisely.

The making of an informer involved more than the receipt of the infamous pink slip from a HUAC process server. As the writer Sylvia Richards recalled, her lawyer urged her to "cooperate"; her therapist made clear that since she had quit the Party, taking the Fifth Amendment would be a self-destructive if not suicidal act; and her boss, a former Communist for whom she felt respect and loyalty, had himself become an informer. And all of these people saw themselves as liberals. Add to such confidants talent agents who saw the failure to name names strictly as a career impediment; religious, political, and trade-union organizations

that endorsed the naming of names as a way of distancing their membership from charges of Communism; and those majorities and minorities
who simply found it easier to avoid the fray than to risk personal or organizational injury. One then gets a sense of an informer subculture that
was as real a presence in the community as the HUAC hearings that oc-
casioned it. The informers, in other words, had an active support system
within the liberal community. In addition to friends and advisers, there
were those we may call collaborators, who worked with HUAC and the
blacklisters but whose motive (or rationalization) was to benefit the "innocent" (i.e., non- or repentant Communists); and those we may call the
guilty bystanders—individuals or groups who knew better and in some
cases even set out to fight the informer system and the blacklist but somehow ended up perpetuating it. It is possible that without these two
groups, there would have been no informers; it is probable that without
the informers, HUAC would not have kept coming back for more. A retrospective look at what happened when HUAC came to Hollywood
makes it clear that the Hollywood community cannot avoid its share of
responsibility for what happened.

4.

HUAC in Hollywood

HUAC APPEARS TO HAVE CHOSEN the entertainment industry as its special target for three reasons. First, the Committee was the tail on the Communist Party's kite, following wherever it flew. The Party itself had focused on Hollywood starting in 1936, when V. J. Jerome, a cultural commissar, and Stanley Lawrence, a CP organizer,* journeyed out to the West Coast to set up a movie-industry branch of the Party. Hollywood represented the prestige of its stars, a source of financial support, and a chance to influence or control "the weapon of mass culture," although John Howard Lawson, who ran the Hollywood branch, quickly understood that the collective process of moviemaking precluded the screenwriter, low man on the creative totem pole, from influencing the content of movies. As the Party's national chairman, William Z. Foster, told the faithful in a secret meeting at Dalton Trumbo's house in 1946, "We can't expect to put any propaganda in the films, but we can try to keep anti-Soviet agitprop out."[1] Lawson and Ring Lardner did run a writer's clinic that tried to analyze scripts from the viewpoint of a Marxist aesthetic, but submission and compliance were mostly voluntary, and the project never got very far.

Second, HUAC chose Hollywood for its glamour. The anthropologist Hortense Powdermaker called Hollywood "the dream factory." But if its inhabitants were in the business of manufacturing our dreams, they were also in the habit of living them. Not only their salaries but also their cars, pools, breasts, alimony payments, mansions, muscles, psychiatrists' bills, talents, and images were, like the images on the silver screen, larger than life. HUAC saw a chance to bask in the publicity glow of Hollywood's

---

* Lawrence was killed in Spain during the Spanish civil war under ambiguous circumstances. See p. 244.

stars. And as Edith Tiger, current director of the Emergency Civil Liberties Committee observes, "They were our royalty and if you want to scare a country you attack its royalty."

The Party at the time, and independent commentators subsequently, have maintained with some credible evidence that HUAC was in the thought-control business and out to break the left. Whatever its collective motive, HUAC stayed with Hollywood because it succeeded where such earlier red hunters as Congressman Martin Dies, who first went after Hollywood in 1940, and State Senator Jack Tenney of California's Joint Fact Finding Committee on Un-American Activities, had failed. HUAC put its nickel in the slot machine in 1947 when J. Parnell Thomas held the hearings that resulted in the incarceration of the Hollywood Ten, but it was not until four years later that it hit the political jackpot.

The industry's initial reaction to HUAC in the spring of 1947 was negative. "Hollywood is weary of being the national whipping boy for congressional committees," complained the Association of Motion Picture Producers (AMPP). "We are tired of having irresponsible charges made again and again and again and not sustained. If we have committed a crime we want to know it. If not, we should not be badgered by congressional committees."[2]

When Chairman Thomas announced open hearings in Washington in the fall of 1947, he miscalculated: the subpoenaed witnesses were either "friendly" ones who didn't really know any names (like the movie mogul Jack Warner, Ginger Rogers' mother, and the actor Robert Taylor) or "unfriendly" ones who wouldn't give them. From the friendlies who led off the testimony, such as Warner, HUAC got lists of so-called Communists; these turned out in fact to include names of non-Communists (like Howard Koch) whom Warner resented for participating in the famous 1945 strike against his studio. (Later Warner admitted to having been "carried away. I was rather emotional," he said.) Robert Taylor, only slightly more circumspect, allowed as how "... I can name a few who seem to sort of disrupt things once in a while. Whether or not they are Communists I don't know. ... One chap we have currently, I think, is Mr. Howard Da Silva. He always seems to have something to say at the wrong time." Taylor said if he had his way the Party would be outlawed and "they would all be sent back to Russia or some other unpleasant place." Lela Rogers repeated her testimony of the previous spring, this time omitting the story of how her daughter Ginger had been required to speak agitprop in a 1943 Dalton Trumbo picture called *Tender Comrade* (the offending line—"Share and share alike, that's democracy").

The proceedings had comic overtones. Walt Disney described attempts to subvert Mickey Mouse by taking over the Cartoonists Guild. The novelist and objectivist Ayn Rand found Communist propaganda (which she described as "anything which gives a good impression of Communism as a way of life") in the smiling faces of Russian children in *Song of Russia*.[3] And Lester Cole was fingered as the subversive screenwriter who had a rabbi address a group of death-camp-bound Jews, after the fashion of the Spanish Communist La Pasionaria, that "It is better to die on your feet than live on your knees."[4]

The following week came the unfriendlies. Only eleven of the nineteen who had been subpoenaed and announced that they would not cooperate were called; the eleventh, the playwright Bertolt Brecht, when asked if he had ever made application to join the CP, answered "No, no, no, no, no, never,"[5] and within hours fled the country. The other ten were backed by a planeload of stars organized under the banner of the Committee for the First Amendment; Humphrey Bogart and Lauren Bacall, Groucho Marx, Frank Sinatra, and others flew to Washington to provide visible and vocal support. The film community seemed united.

Notwithstanding Billy Wilder's quip that "of the Unfriendly Ten, only two had any talent, the other eight were just unfriendly," the Ten included some of the most talented writers in Hollywood, and politically the most active. Most of them either had been or were still members of the Communist Party. To take them alphabetically:

• Alvah Bessie, who worked on screenplays such as *The Very Thought of You* (1944), *Hotel Berlin* (1945), and *Objective Burma* (1945), had fought in Spain and written a good book about it called *Men in Battle*, served as drama critic for *New Masses,* and received a Guggenheim fellowship for creative writing. He was an active and somewhat dogmatic member of the Communist Party.

• Herbert Biberman, married to Gale Sondergaard ("The Spider Woman"), who was herself called as a witness in the early 1950s and took the Fifth Amendment, had directed such movies as *Meet Nero Wolfe* (1936) and *The Master Race* (1941). The Bibermans, too, were in the Party.

• Lester Cole had written thirty-six films (*Objective Burma, High Wall* [1948]) and was running for reelection of the Screen Writers Guild executive board when he was subpoenaed. Cole was a vocal and hard-line Communist from a working-class background; he had not gone to college.

• Edward Dmytryk had directed twenty-four films between 1929 and

1949 (*Till the End of Time* [1946], the anti-anti-Semitic *Crossfire* [1947], *Hitler's Children* [1943]). He had left the Party in 1945.

• Ring Lardner, Jr., the son of the great American humorist, was co-author of the Academy Award–winning screenplay *Woman of the Year* (1942). One of the youngest members of the Ten, he also was something of a Marxist theorist, but was moving away from the Party at the time of the hearings.

• John Howard Lawson, founder and first president of the Screen Writers Guild when it was organized in 1933, was head of the Hollywood branch of the Communist Party. His expressionist play *Processional* had won good reviews; he wrote authoritative texts on the theater and film and two of the more celebrated movies coming out of World War II, *Action in the North Atlantic* (1943) and *Sahara* (1943).

• Albert Maltz, O'Henry Award winner whose short stories were widely anthologized, had probably the best literary credentials of any member of the Ten and was a frequent contributor to controversy in the world of Marxist periodicals. The previous year his writings on socialist realism had triggered a major Party controversy. His movies included *This Gun for Hire* (1942), *Pride of the Marines* (1945), and *Destination Tokyo* (1944).

• Sam Ornitz had written twenty-five films between 1929 and 1949, none particularly notable. He was best known for his novel, *Haunch, Paunch and Jowl*. In deliberations as to what posture they should take before the Committee, it was Ornitz who advised, "Let us at least be as brave as the people we write about."

• Robert Adrian Scott was a writer-producer whose career was just taking off when the blacklist descended. He had produced such films as *Crossfire* (1947) and *Cornered* (1946), both with Dmytryk, and the very successful *Murder My Sweet* (1944). His starlet wife wanted him to cooperate with the Committee and left him when he didn't.

• Dalton Trumbo, in addition to being one of the highest-paid writers in Hollywood, had written a prizewinning novel, *Johnny Got His Gun*. Trumbo, whose films included *Kitty Foyle* (1940), an Academy Award nominee, *Thirty Seconds Over Tokyo* (1944), and *Our Vines Have Tender Grapes* (1945), was in such demand that his contract omitted the standard "morals" clause (whereby a studio could cancel an employee's contract if it had come into public disrepute because of his actions) but included a stipulation that story conferences would be held in his house, where he preferred to sleep days and work nights in a bathtub with a special cross-board to hold his typewriter. Trumbo had worked as a baker for eight years before coming to Hollywood, where his first job was editing the *Screen Writers Guild* magazine. Although close to the Party for many years he didn't actually join until 1943.

Each of the Ten arrived at the HUAC session in Washington with a prepared statement denouncing the Committee, which none but Maltz was permitted to read, and each challenged the Committee's right to ask questions relating to political affiliations. Although to avoid conspiracy charges they maintained the fiction that each had arrived at his stand in consultation only with his own attorney, in fact there had been a series of strategy meetings to arrive at a collective stand: they would refuse to answer questions about Party membership and base their stand on the First Amendment's guarantee against incursions on free speech rather than the Fifth Amendment's protection against self-incrimination. A public-relations defect of their collective legal strategy had to do with their decision not merely to tell the Committee that they refused to answer because it had no right to ask, but, rather, for each to add, "I am answering your question, but in my own way."* In the event, this tactic turned out to be unwise, since it murked the First Amendment issue. And John Howard

---

* The full charge against the Ten has been that the CP lawyers who were part of the original Nineteen's defense team were secretly caucusing and setting Party strategy, which was then visited on unsuspecting others. Susan Rossen, widow of Robert Rossen, believes, "The reason these guys [the Ten] were handled so poorly is that when the Dies Committee called certain people and asked if they were CP members, on advice of attorney at that time under oath they said no. It's my opinion that it was to protect these one or two people that they wouldn't tell the truth under penalty of perjury. So the CP lawyers gave bad advice to everybody, and that's how you got the cover-up. From that point on it went down the drain."

If indeed she is right, or even if for whatever reasons the Party manipulated the other lawyers and defendants, there is no warrant for such deception.

The evidence, however, suggests otherwise. Lardner recalls that over drinks he and Trumbo invented the strategy that ultimately prevailed. Koch has told of how he refused to go along with the majority and even took ads in the trades outlining his position. And two of the lawyers, the Republican Bartley Crum, who had been hired by Dmytryk and Scott, and Robert Kenny, former attorney general of California, were not merely non-Communist, but were men of sufficient experience, legal learning, sophistication, and honor; it is not credible without hard evidence to assume that they were manipulated by the Communist lawyers. As the attorney Martin Popper says, they arrived at the First Amendment defense openly and knowingly, and he still believes that if subsequent witnesses had adopted it they might have served themselves and the country better. ("To Whom It May Concern," in Howard Koch Collection, Wisconsin Center for Theatre Research.)

Lawson's aggressive ripostes to the chairman's hostile and bullying directives upset many of those in the audience who thought they had come to cheer on a group of civil libertarians and instead found themselves listening to what sounded suspiciously like Party rhetoric.

On November 24, 1947, Congress voted to cite the Ten for contempt, and fifty top Hollywood executives met for two days at the Waldorf-Astoria Hotel in New York to consider what their position toward the Ten should be. Eric Johnston, president of the Motion Picture Association of America, who had earlier promised, "As long as I live I will never be party to anything as un-American as a blacklist," announced after the meeting that the Ten would be suspended without pay, and that thereafter no Communists or other subversives would "knowingly" be employed in Hollywood. Liberal Hollywood, which had been with the Ten on arrival in the East, abandoned them as they left—partly out of shock at the confrontation with the Committee, partly in reaction to the indictment for contempt of Congress, and partly out of fear, after the Waldorf meeting, that they themselves would be tainted. The Committee for the First Amendment, which had announced a major propaganda campaign on behalf of the Ten, folded almost as fast as it had formed.

Dore Schary, the liberal writer-turned-producer who was assigned the unpleasant task of informing the Screen Writers Guild (SWG) of the Waldorf decision, which he had opposed, to this day tries to give it a happy gloss. Schary's personal position (and he so testified before HUAC at the time) was that since a California law explicitly prevented the denial of employment based on political affiliation and since no law prevented anyone from being a Communist, blacklisting was illegal. As an executive at RKO he opposed the firing of Dmytryk and Scott, "despite the fact that they had lied to me about their having been members of the Communist Party." And since the executives' decision at the Waldorf-Astoria was not to employ Communists "knowingly" and since "the only *known* Communists, as far as I knew, were the guys whose cards were called," Schary claimed a narrow victory. He voted against and declined to fire Dmytryk and Scott, so somebody else fired them, and along with other liberals, he supported the establishment of a Motion Picture Industry Council (MPIC)—a council of management *and* the talent guilds— whose purpose would be to fight the blacklist, to let the public know that Hollywood was innocent of the charges of subversion. Schary speaks for many liberals when he says, "I felt the Committee acted with absolute banality, the producers acted cowardly, but the Ten acted stupidly—they were trying by their hysterical acting to get the Committee to admit error. They should have quietly but firmly refused to cooperate with the Committee and then held a dignified press conference where they said eight of us are Communists, but all of us are Americans and patriots, and the public and the press would have backed them one hundred percent."

In the summer of 1949 the liberal Supreme Court justices Frank Murphy and Wiley Rutledge died, and the following spring their conservative successors, Tom Clark and Sherman Minton, helped to constitute the Supreme Court majority that refused to review the Ten's convictions. The Ten went to prison for sentences of up to a year. (So did the chairman of the Committee, J. Parnell Thomas, who in 1948 was convicted of taking kickbacks from his staff and locked up at the federal correctional institution in Danbury, Connecticut, where his fellow inmates included Ring Lardner, Jr., and Lester Cole.) Not long after, the Supreme Court decided *Rogers* v. *U.S.,* the case that established the waiver doctrine (i.e., if a witness talked about himself he couldn't refuse to talk about others).*

The Hollywood investigation, suspended while the Ten's case worked its way through the courts, was reopened in 1951 with John Wood at the helm and Larry Parks as the first witness. Thereafter the informer came into his own, and the blacklist became institutionalized. No Hollywood Communist or ex- who had ever been accused, or called to testify, or refused to sign a studio statement would get work in the business—at least under his own name—unless he went through the ritual of naming names.

For every Hollywood informer there are two who refused to go along—and many of these seemed to revel in their resistance. The gravel-voiced Lionel Stander volunteered to identify "a group of fanatics who are desperately trying to undermine the Constitution." He was, of course, referring to the Committee itself, and he offered "to name names."[6] The folksinger Pete Seeger wouldn't name names, but he offered to sing songs and when Chairman Francis Walter demurred, Seeger noted, "I know many beautiful songs from your home county, Carbon and Monroe, and I hitchhiked through there and stayed in the homes of miners."[7]

Or, to cite a positively existential moment, consider Congressman Donald Jackson's attempt to explain to Zero ("After my financial standing in the community, sir") Mostel that he had aided the Communist cause by appearing at a benefit for *Mainstream* magazine. All I did, Mos-

---

* Also in 1950, in *Blau* v. *U.S.,* the Supreme Court decided for the first time that unwillingness to admit Communist Party membership was adequate grounds for invoking the Fifth Amendment.

tel argued, was "an imitation of a butterfly at rest. There is no crime in making anybody laugh. I don't care if you laugh at me."

Mr. Jackson: "If your interpretation of a butterfly at rest brought any money into the coffers of the Communist Party, you contributed directly to the propaganda effort of the Communist Party."

But, argued Mostel, suppose I had the urge to imitate a butterfly somewhere?

Mr. Doyle: "Yes, but please, when you have the urge, don't have such an urge to put the butterfly at rest by putting some money in the Communist Party coffers as a result of that urge to put a butterfly at rest. . . ."[8]

═══

The hearings quickly gave rise to free-lance blacklisters—some of them nonprofit, like the American Legion, the Catholic War Veterans, or Hollywood's Motion Picture Alliance for the Preservation of American Ideals (MPAPAI); others free enterprisers of the blacklist, like the American Business Consultants and Aware, Inc., which published, listed, and cleared names for pay. The Committee itself got into the act with annual reports that conveniently listed names and namers in the appendix, which could be clipped and pasted by the free lancers. Not only in scandal sheets such as *Confidential* but in national magazines and newspapers, political and gossip columnists supplemented and subtracted from the "official" lists by giving two-line case studies in repentance and/or subversion.

At least the Committee—contrary to what propaganda from the left alleged—was an "honest" red hunter. By the 1950s it went after Party members and former Party members exclusively, and subpoenaed nobody who had not already been identified as a Communist by at least two sources. As the staff investigator William Wheeler understood, "They would kill you if you made one mistake." (Among the relatively few mistakes the Committee made was with Martin Berkeley, whose eight-score names included as many as a dozen misidentifications. "I told him not to do it," says Wheeler, "but his ass-hole lawyer, Edward Bennett Williams, insisted." Williams, incidentally, represented a number of informers, including Robert Rossen.) Because the Committee was fastidious in its targets and relatively rigorous in its ritual (nobody got the redeeming "thank you" from the chairman unless he had named the names), its procedures had the virtue of their predictability.

But the free-lance vigilantes made no such distinctions. Between HUAC's errors and this network's wider definition of the red menace, the blacklist extended well beyond those with direct links—past or present—to the Communist Party.

Of all the extra-governmental agencies in the listing business, by far the most powerful, feared, and effective was the American Legion.[9] After all, the Legion had 17,000 posts, 2,800,000 members and another 1,000,000 associates in its auxiliaries and was in a position to do damage. From the earliest Hollywood hearings until as late as 1960, the Legion monitored the entertainment business. And coming after the war it had credibility.

The sequence of the Legion's involvement is classic: first, at its 1951 National Convention in October, the Legion directed its officers to undertake a "public information program" that would disseminate data on "Communist associations" of people in the entertainment industry. In November its Hollywood post called for the picketing of theaters showing pictures that had been worked on by people who hadn't cooperated with HUAC. The Legion advised its members to organize groups to write, telephone, and telegraph television programs, networks, and sponsors employing entertainers with a record of belonging to Communist fronts.

The next month, the *American Legion Magazine* published an article, presumably as part of this "public information program" (though actually it had been in the works for some time), that caused tremors throughout the entertainment industry. Its author was J. B. Matthews, who had been one of the first informers to testify, along with ex-Communist Rena Vale, before the Dies Committee in 1938. He had gone on to become HUAC's research director, and eventually he went back to work for Joe McCarthy on the Senate Committee. His article, whose title asked "Did the Movies Really Clean House?" answered no. Matthews listed sixty-six examples of what he was talking about, including with each name the appropriate motion picture and the political credits. To be listed in the *American Legion Magazine* was to be graylisted in the industry.

I shall examine the vicious consequences of such lists (see below, Part IV); here, let it merely be said that although the blacklist system dominated the movie business throughout the decade, after that conference at the Waldorf-Astoria in 1947 nobody wanted to talk out loud about it. Its force came from the mystique that surrounded it. Now you see it, now you don't. The Motion Picture Association of America denied that the industry kept a blacklist, but it said that no Fifth Amendment takers (or

First Amendment takers either, for that matter) who hadn't purged themselves before an appropriate congressional committee could work in Hollywood. The Screen Actors Guild (Ronald Reagan speaking) said, "We will not be a party to a blacklist," but it banned Communists and noncooperative witnesses from membership. One would have thought that the publisher of the so-called bible of blacklisting, *Red Channels,* or one of the other publications that purported to list Communist and Communist-front activities with which individuals had been publicly identified, might have conceded the existence of the blacklist, but no, they were a sort of political credit-rating service, like Dun & Bradstreet, and as an attorney for Aware, Inc., observed, "nobody ever accused Dun & Bradstreet of running a blacklist."[10] In other words, there was no such thing as a blacklist; it was just an ugly rumor started by movie, radio, and television people who couldn't get work because of their political associations. As recently as 1979, George Murphy, who was a Hollywood song-and-dance man before he became a U.S. senator, deplored the "myths" of McCarthyism. "The blacklisting that everyone talks about," he remarked, "only happened in New York, it didn't happen in Hollywood."[11]

Perhaps inevitably, the blacklist was barely in business when it spun off an ancillary enterprise with yet more complicated rituals of its own, called "clearance." Getting off the blacklist soon became as ritualized as getting on: the principal distinction between the two enterprises was that one got on the list against one's will as punishment for adhering to one's values, whereas one got off as a reward for violating them. And of course everyone denied that there was a clearance process. Logically, they had a point. How could one be cleared to get off a list that did not exist?

A prototype of how the clearance process worked is available in John Cogley's *Report on Blacklisting:* "When a former member of the Party came to Brewer* for help ... the first thing [Brewer] insisted on was that the ex-Communist go to the FBI with all the information he had. Then the ex-Communist was put in touch with the House Committee and some kind of public repentance was worked out. The ex-Communist was

---

* Roy M. Brewer was a pudgy Nebraskan who was brought in to help clean up the racket-ridden International Alliance of Theatrical Stage Employees (IATSE) in the mid-1940s. When he found himself in the midst of a bitter jurisdictional dispute in 1945–46 with a rival organization called the Conference of Studio Unions, his solution was to call its progressive leader, Herbert K. Sorrell, a red. He quickly became one of Hollywood's most visible anti-Communists.

expected to testify (which meant naming names in public session), denounce the Party at union meetings, and, if he was prominent enough, make some kind of statement for the press . . . or in some other way publicly express his new feelings."[12]

Brewer sat on the MPIC board that Dore Schary had helped set up "to fight blacklisting," and before anyone could go back to work, his okay—among others—was required. Because he was such a visible and powerful anti-Communist willing to help a "repentant" ex, his influence was unique. He could call up studio executives and say, "Listen, so-and-so used to be in the Party, but he's not now and he's trying to make a new life for himself. Why don't you give him a break?"[13] And they would.

It was appropriate that the clearance presidium be inhabited by the same folk who instituted the blacklist in the first place. For if the blacklist made a clearance procedure inevitable, the clearance process helped the blacklist to continue. For one thing, by weeding out cases of mistaken identity it helped the blacklist avoid a black eye. Sometimes people were confused with someone else. Sheridan Gibney, whom Jack Warner had incorrectly listed as a Communist (undoubtedly because he was president of the Screen Writers Guild in 1948 when it decided to sue the industry and try to break the blacklist), continued to be graylisted even after Warner retracted. The actress Martha Scott suffered from her confusion with the singer Hazel Scott, who in addition to being married to the controversial congressman Adam Clayton Powell, performed for many left-wing–cause organizations. José Ferrer, John Garfield, and Edward G. Robinson had all taken up HUAC on its open invitation to persons falsely accused to clear their names, but since as non-Communists they had no definite CP names to name, the process was tricky. Garfield and Robinson both appeared before the Committee twice and in Garfield's case, he died before he straightened out his political problems. Ferrer and Robinson, after much negotiating and self-abnegation, went back to work. Moreover, the lines of those who were ready to go before HUAC to get a clean bill of health became longer than had been anticipated, and HUAC quietly canceled the service.

It took until March 1952 before the movie industry and its adjuncts had organized procedures by which one could get off the graylist as predictably as one got off the blacklist. Any number of organizations, individuals, publications, and journalists were ready to step in as guardian at the gate of rehabilitation. The American Business Consultants, publishers of *Red Channels,* and Aware, Inc., which published *Counterattack,* were ready to use the same data bank that put people on the blacklist to take them off. The American Legion, with two publications of its own, the *American Legion Magazine* and *Firing Line,* was also in the clearance game. The Motion Picture Alliance for the Preservation of American Ideals, Hollywood's collection of reactionary right-wingers including Adolphe Menjou, John Wayne, and Ward Bond—some of whom had already testified before HUAC, others of whom had helped to run the short-lived anti-Communist union of screen playwrights—was in on the act. Newspaper columnists such as George Sokolsky, Victor Riesel, Walter Winchell, Jack O'Brian, and Hedda Hopper were as happy to fill their spaces by getting the deserved off the list as by putting the blameworthy on.

As the clearance process became defined, it involved liberal lawyers, humanitarian social organizations, and even a psychotherapist or two. Why not, after all, help "innocent" people to go back to work?

The way in which the entertainment industry decided to work with rather than against the American Legion is in some respects a metaphor for the ways in which individuals persuaded themselves to name names or otherwise go along with corrupt practices. Their motives were "honorable," in the sense that they were trying to protect the innocent. The atmosphere was fear; the strategy was the politics of the possible.

After Matthews' article appeared in the *American Legion Magazine,* the leading executives of the major motion-picture companies first panicked and second called for a conference with the Legion, which was held on March 31, 1952, in Washington, D.C. Representatives of the major Hollywood trade associations came along with the moguls to meet with Donald Wilson, national commander of the Legion, and James F. O'Neil, director of Legion publications. The industry asked the Legion to give it "all the information it had—large or small—that tended to connect any of their employees with Communism," and the Legion agreed. The producers, for their part, agreed to cure a "defect" in the agreement made at the Waldorf-Astoria in 1947 to not "knowingly employ a Communist." What liberals like Schary had thought of as a stratagem was now seen as a loophole. How could Hollywood know whether witnesses who refused to answer HUAC's questions were now or had ever been Communists? The producers added "those who had taken refuge in the Fifth Amendment" to their ban.

Spyros Skouras, president of Twentieth Century-Fox, had another good idea. Prior to filming *Viva Zapata* in 1951 he had taken out some political insurance. He had asked all suspect members of the company to send him letters explaining why their politics presented no problem, so that if questions were raised he had evidence of having taken advance precautions. He had tested the notion on the columnist George Sokolsky, who thought it a splendid idea and even offered to print portions of such a letter in his column. Would the American Legion, Skouras asked in 1952, accept such letters as a form of clearance for those on the graylist?

The Legion, it turned out, would do more than that. It offered to distribute the confessional letters to posts throughout the country—just in case they were thinking of picketing a film featuring a purified suspect. And to make sure that the studios didn't omit any names, one month later, on April 3, 1952, James O'Neil circulated to the studios a twenty-page list of three hundred names with the request that they check it for factual errors. After each name were the person's alleged transgressions—some as modest as "close associate of Dalton Trumbo," or "lecturer, Actor's Lab brochure."[14] (As Czeslaw Milosz noted in *The Captive Mind* [1953], attacking interrogators makes one the enemy.) Pens scratched all over town, and all but thirty of the three hundred were ready, willing, and apparently able to explain away their pasts.

The Motion Picture Industry Council now had a decision to make. It had been organized in the wake of the conviction of the Hollywood Ten with the objective of "the combatting and containment of vigilante actions against the industry such as boycotting and picketing and similar attacks." Now it had reached a new consensus: "(1) That we should seek to work in a 'friendly way' with the American Legion. (2) That we should seek to afford those who are being unfairly accused an opportunity to affirm their one hundred-percent Americanism and their hatred of Communism." Ronald Reagan even suggested that MPIC might send everyone in Hollywood his record, so that each could decide whether a reply was warranted. MPIC didn't go that far, but it did ask that those subpoenaed "tell the truth, the whole truth and nothing but the truth," and it deplored those who stood on constitutional privilege. It started a file called Hollywood Against Communism.[15]

To avoid charges of conspiracy, neither MPIC nor the Legion functioned as an official clearinghouse, although each of them, along with MPAPAI, Brewer himself, Sokolsky, and a few other people and institutions did favors, and people in trouble might go to them to get out of it. Basically, however, each studio undertook to screen its own employees' letters before passing them on to anyone else, and each studio had its own clearance officer, whose title varied from place to place.[16]

As Hollywood developed this internal-security bureaucracy, a variety of epistolary strategies and negotiations were devised by lawyers, studios, the accused, and other intermeddlers such as Brewer. Paramount, for instance, balked at an insufficiently detailed letter from the actress Paulette Goddard because "this does not give us the kind of declaration that we would want from her, namely, that she is not and has never been a Communist and that her allegiance is to the USA." But eventually they went along because Goddard was a big box-office draw and because her attorney, Martin Gang, came armed with a good argument: he told Paramount's Sam Katzman that "to ask her for any more than what is written here would only open a can of peas and she might get up on her high heels and kick."[17] This referred to the fact that Goddard had been married to Charlie Chaplin, then in exile; the thought of resurrecting the controversial Chaplin saga was too much for the studio that had invested so much in her, so they relented.

There were abject letters, ambiguous letters, quasi-defiant letters, and what was known simply as the "Voltaire Letter." What you said, explains the screenwriter Henry Ephron, who sent a Voltaire Letter, "was that the reason you signed that petition for the Ten was not because you agreed with what they had to say, but because you believed they had the right to say it." There were also honestly troubled letters, like the one which the writer-director Don Hartman sent to the vice-president of Paramount (Y. Frank Freeman) on the occasion of an offer to become production supervisor of Paramount provided he file a letter. His five-and-a-half-page single-spaced letter, dated May 20, 1952, begins as follows:

Dear Frank:
    The idea of a man explaining his present or past behavior to any but legally constituted authorities who request an explanation is not something that I believe in or am anxious to be a party to, but because of my position in the industry and of your faith in me and because of the tenor of the times, I believe there are extenuating circumstances. I should therefore like to "bend with the wind" and have decided to tell you voluntarily something of my association with liberal organizations that have since been named subversive. I want to do this to stop once and for all, all the rumors and/or accusations or insinuations of every kind and description against my good name and reputation. I have worked too long and too hard all these years to allow anything or anyone to do harm, however slight, to me or to an industry that I love or to a company that has been, through the years, extremely kind to me.
    I should also like to make clear at the outset, that I believe a man may be completely innocent of any wrongdoing and still *not* write a letter to anyone explaining his behavior for reasons or convictions of his

own. I sincerely hope, therefore, that any letter will in no way be a reflection on others who decide not to write letters explaining themselves. . . .[18]

As letters were accepted or returned, rejected and revised, the standards were refined, until by the end of 1952, Donald Wilson, the national commander of the American Legion, after apologizing for the premature banning of José Ferrer's film *Moulin Rouge* (1952) (Ferrer had appeared as an obsequious witness before HUAC but had named no Communists because he himself had not been in the Party), listed five tests, passage of which would qualify any letter writer for clearance:* The "suspect" must denounce and repudiate all past Communist Party or "front" associations; appear before HUAC and make "full public disclosure of past Communist-front activities" by "identifying all those responsible . . ."; join organizations that are "actively and intelligently combatting Communism"; publicly condemn Soviet imperialism; and promise not to do it again.[19] Depending on circumstances, some got by with less.

Even with such subtle standards, individuals such as Judy Holliday, who made a friendly appearance before the Senate Internal Security Committee, wrote and rewrote letters, and found she had to hire her own researcher to clear her by checking out her past and finding nothing damaging.[20]

Each studio was also supposed to do its own checking. Nate Spingold of Columbia, for instance, maintained extensive files in his East Coast office and eventually employed the services of one Ken Bierly, a former FBI agent who had a company called the Research and Security Corporation. For a fee he would check out a person's record and rate him as "See" (could find nothing), "Bee" (questionable background), or "Very Que" (Very Questionable). If *X,* for instance, had been a Communist and not

---

* The list of questions the American Legion gave its letter writers was: Is this charge accurate? Why did you join the listed organization? Who invited you to join? Whom did you invite to join? Did you resign? When? (From *X* [a group of Hollywood writers], "Hollywood meets Frankenstein," *The Nation,* 28 June 1951, quoted in Ceplair and Englund, *The Inquisition in Hollywood,* 393.)

Questions three and four, it should be noted, are identical to the two questions (reported by Robert Tucker and Stephen Cohen in their introduction to *The Great Purge Trial*) asked by the NKVD during the great purge. Who recruited you? Whom did you recruit? The difference between answering the Legion's questions and those of the NKVD are too obvious to elaborate. The issue in the United States was not, Do I answer or go into a slave labor camp? It was, Do I answer and get to go back to work?

clarified his position before HUAC he would be rated "Very Que." Here is a typical Bierly report, this one for Raymond Bell of Columbia Pictures, dated July 21, 1953, on Peter Viertel:

Dear Ray:

For identification purposes, Peter Viertel is reported to have been born in Dresden, Germany, Nov. 15, 1920. His name appeared on the Amicus Curiae brief in support of the Hollywood Ten in September 1949. The coast reports he was a friend of Hanns Eisler and it appears he joined with Eisler in issuing an invitation to a social function at Malibu, Calif., in Feb., 1948. The return address appearing on the invitation at that time was Box 10, Route 1, Bonsall Drive, Calif.

Viertel's wife, Virginia, was formerly married to Budd Schulberg. She was identified as a Communist Party member by Martin Berkeley and Elizabeth Wilson, who testified in Sept. of 1951. From their testimony it appears Virginia Schulberg was a Communist in 1937 and later, and there is nothing in the record which would indicate she subsequently disaffiliated from the Communist Party.

There is some confusion about Peter Viertel's mother.* The records indicate his mother's name is Salomea, and that his father's name is Berthold. A Salka Viertel has been active in several Communist enterprises on the coast. It is possible that Salka is a contraction of Salomea, that Salka is Peter's sister and not his mother, or, that Salka is no relation to him. In any event, Peter Viertel's *mother* is reported to have been friendly with Hanns Eisler and to have served on a Committee in his support in Dec. of 1947. *Salka* Viertel's name appeared on the Amicus Curiae brief for Lawson and Trumbo, in support of the Hollywood Ten, and she has also been listed as a member of the Progressive Caucus (Communist) within the Screen Writers Guild, who supported Lester Cole and Ring Lardner Jr. for office in Nov. of 1948.

In view of the foregoing, I would suggest Peter Viertel be listed as *very que.* It is true that information linking him to the Communist apparatus is scant. Nevertheless, the fact that there is a record of a slight degree of affiliation, plus the fact that his wife has been identified as a Party member, plus the fact that his mother has been identified with Communist organizations and causes, makes Viertel's present status

---

* Salka Viertel ran a well-known salon in Hollywood at the time, attended by such German intellectuals and members of the left as Thomas Mann, Bertolt Brecht, Kurt Weill and Hanns Eisler. See her memoir *The Kindness of Strangers* (New York, 1969).

highly questionable and suspect. Unless he is able to clear up these
points in a statement, I feel his employment might be highly embarrassing to the Studio.

With best regards,[21]

Not all letter writers believed they were playing the internal-security
establishment's game, even though once one had written such a letter, the
principle of having nothing to do with the clearance apparatus was
breached. A vivid example of one who worked to get off the list without
breaching his own sense of propriety may be found in the case of the
songwriter E. Y. ("Yip") Harburg. His series of letters and lunches as
much as any show the thin line one had to walk to be true to oneself and
still get by.

Harburg, whose credits include lyrics for *The Wizard of Oz* (1939) and
A Day at the Races (1937), had never belonged to the Communist Party
but had belonged to and worked with a number of left-liberal organizations, including some that had found their way onto the attorney general's list.

When he was asked by an executive of Metro-Goldwyn-Mayer to write
a clearance letter in 1950 to neutralize his listing in *Red Channels,* he ex-
coriated the blacklisters even as he tried to exonerate, without compro-
mising, himself. "As a firm, almost fanatical believer in democracy, as a
proud American, and as the writer of the lyric of the song 'God's Country,' I am outraged by the suggestion that somehow I am connected with,
believe in, or am sympathetic with Communist or totalitarian philosophy."

He argued that the theory of guilt by association "is an old European
doctrine which has always been repudiated in this country, and it is
about time that decent liberals and good Americans fought back against
this European theory." He explained his joining such organizations as
the National Council of Soviet-American Friendship, the Hollywood
Writers Mobilization, and the League of American Writers by saying
that he had hoped the poets might succeed in their attempts at peace
where the politicians had failed. He annexed copies of his songs "God's
Country" and "Brother, Can You Spare a Dime?" because "they speak
for themselves as well as for me."

Two years later, still unemployable, he wrote to another M-G-M executive arguing that whatever he had joined, he had joined as an independent thinker. "I feel that I have a contribution to make which can bolster
the American spirit in these troubled times. Words and music play a vital
role. Laughter and entertainment are crucial to our national defense."

He met with Brewer, he lunched with the American Legion's O'Neil ("It was a warming experience to meet with you and have you devote your time on my behalf," he wrote O'Neil), he answered the "charges" against him one by one, and sent along two other songs—"Chin Up! Cheerio! Carry On!" and "The Son of a Gun Who Picks on Uncle Sam."[22]

The letter project, the Bierly clearance, the Brewer lunch, the Sokolsky mention, the anti-Communist article, were all ways in which the graylisted, the "innocent" or the "duped" could go back to work. The "guilty," i.e., the Communist Party member, had to name names.

———

It is important to emphasize that the most vicious vigilantes were also in the forefront among those who favored the "rehabilitation" of sinners willing to bare their souls and name the names. Aware, Inc., even went so far as to publish a twelve-step how-to-do-it pamphlet called *The Road Back (Self-Clearance): A Provisional Statement of View on the Problem of the Communist and Communist-Helper in Entertainment Communications Who Seeks to Clear Himself.* This little pamphlet begins with a biblical quotation—"That they should have a change of heart and mind, performing deeds fitting this change" (Acts 26:20)—and goes on to describe the required intellectual and moral transition and "voluntary surrender to the exigencies of reality, of truth, of love." Hatred of Communism "is like hatred of sin and error: a moral obligation. This does not mean hatred of individual Communists. It means 'informing' in the noble sense of warning, educating, counselling. The sinful informer sells, for money or selfish advantage, that which he knows to be right."

Step one on the road back was to question oneself, step twelve was a return to religion, and in the middle, of course, was the "voluntary and cooperative" interview with the Federal Bureau of Investigation and "a written offer to cooperate, as a witness or source of information" with the Committee on Un-American Activities, House of Representatives, room 225A, Old House Office Building.[23]

The clearance apparatus, whose ostensible purpose was to help people get off the blacklist, actually strengthened the blacklist system it was designed to circumvent. For to agree to the ritual of rehabilitation was in the first place to acknowledge the legitimacy of the blacklisters, to affirm publicly their values, to dignify and strengthen their moral position; in the second place it frequently meant implicating others—which was the heart of the process. It was not long before the same people and processes at work in Hollywood invaded the entertainment industry on the East Coast. Again, in the guise of rehabilitating the penitent, the blacklisters worked to get the industry to hire the name-namers, which by implication further validated their right to blacklist the unrepentant. "In radio and television," wrote Martin Berkeley in *The American Mercury* magazine in August 1953, quoting "my good friend" George Sokolsky, "some of those who have worked hardest for the success of this [anti-Communist exposure] program are still controversial persons because some lazy bureaucrat in the advertising firms along Madison Avenue ... finds it easier to kill a man's career than to [hire a cooperative witness]."

One of the worst aspects of the insistence that one inform before one was restored to civilized society is that anything short of naming names became, for those who wouldn't do it, an ethically defensible position. Denouncing one's past, for example, which in other circumstances would be thought degrading, became acceptable. The clearance system, presented as an escape from the blacklist system, was in fact an adjunct to it; together they comprised the social structure underlying the mass informing.

It is understandable how the American Legion and Aware, Inc., and Brewer and MPAPAI and Berkeley and the other rabid anti-Communists—those who believed that Communists should *not* have the right to work in the industry—got mixed up in this clearance enterprise. But to appreciate how the blacklist system flourished for so long, why the Informer Principle was permitted to govern, how it was tolerated in a community that only a few years earlier had been making movie after movie condemning the Nazi practice of having children turn in their parents, one must look at some individuals and institutions who opposed the repression and who had worked closely with the Communists in organizations such as the Hollywood Anti-Nazi League and in popular front groups during the war, even on behalf of the Hollywood Ten—people and institutions whose later claim was that they worked with HUAC and the Legion and the Sokolskys not because they agreed with them but because they believed it was the humanitarian thing to do.

5.
The Collaborators

WHEN ASKED TODAY why they decided to cooperate in their appearances as witnesses before HUAC, many people have cited grandiose historical and political reasons, ranging from wanting to do their bit to expose totalitarian thought-controllers to disillusion over the Nazi-Soviet Pact and Soviet anti-Semitism. But these historical factors by themselves don't automatically determine the way individuals confronted with present and urgent moral dilemmas will react. At least as influential in shaping their immediate moral perspective may be those people one tends to take for granted, those to whom one turns in time of trouble—the sympathetic lawyer, the family doctor, the religious confidant, the professionals and institutions whose social function is to perpetuate a community's values, to serve their members as cushions for pain and sources of comfort in time of trouble, and to provide the energy and animate the resilience required to overcome temporary misfortune.

As it happens, one lawyer in Hollywood was extremely influential in representing the informers, and apparently he did so in a way that gave many of them a sense that they were preserving a vestige of dignity. One "doctor" (he turns out on closer examination to have been a lay therapist), who was in and out of the Party, had enough informer-patients to justify an inquiry as to whether he was indeed converting his patients into informers, as alleged, whether under his care they persuaded themselves that informing was a sign of emotional maturity. And one community-based organization actively tried to mediate between the accusers and the accused and, indeed, helped many "innocent" victims get back to work. A brief examination of the role played by each of these three gets us closer to the values at the core of the informer subculture, and it also helps us to understand the moral environment within which so many succumbed to the temptations of betrayal.

In the early 1970s the California ACLU planned a major fund-raising dinner to obtain money for the defense of Daniel Ellsberg in connection with the Pentagon Papers case. The chapter chairman, who had not been on the scene in the 1950s, asked Charles Katz, a member of the legal team that had represented the Hollywood Ten, to appear on the dais along with another Hollywood attorney, Martin Gang, whose clients now included stars of the magnitude of comedian Bob Hope. "Appear with Gang?" asked Katz incredulously when he heard the lineup. "That's like asking me to appear with Torquemada's adjutant."

Martin Gang, a typical liberal Hollywood lawyer, was a Democrat and a member of the antiestablishment National Lawyers Guild. In the 1940s his clients included such progressive types as Parks, Trumbo, and the director Lewis Milestone—all members of the original Hollywood Nineteen. In 1947 he had signed an *amicus curiae* brief on behalf of the Ten. But by the middle of 1951 he had become the symbol of collaboration: in fact, he represented more informers than any other single attorney in Los Angeles, among them Lee J. Cobb, Sterling Hayden, Abe Burrows, Mrs. Burrows, Lloyd Bridges, Richard Collins, Sylvia Richards, Roland Kibbee, and Meta Rosenberg. He also helped Norman Corwin, Paulette Goddard, Burt Lancaster, and John Houseman with their political problems. Allen Rivkin, a former writer who served on the executive board of the Screen Writers Guild, describes coming to New York with Gang in the early 1970s for a meeting of the American Bar Association: "Some dear friends of ours threw a party for us, and I asked if I could bring Martin Gang. They said of course. We got there and the party got started. . . . Martin looked around the room and I saw him smiling, so I said, 'What's the matter?' He said, 'You know, I was looking around. I got every son of a bitch here off the hook.' "

How did Martin Gang, an entertainment lawyer who had been active in a variety of Jewish fraternal organizations and who numbered among his clients many Communists and former Communists, end up as "Torquemada's adjutant"?

His critics say he did it for the money, and rumors of his fee varied. The blacklisted actor Phil Brown says, "I was told to put myself in Martin Gang's hands and for five hundred bucks he'd get me off." Millard Lampell writes of a clearance lawyer in Hollywood whose "established fee was $5000." But others report that Gang worked for court costs when the client couldn't afford more, and Gang himself claims that his partners once compiled the time he put in representing one year's worth of informers and concluded that he cost his firm $50,000 in free (or under-compensated) time. "I am convinced," he says, "that the function of a lawyer is to help people who need help. I would have felt terrible if I was too cowardly or too stupid to do what I did knowing that I couldn't please everybody. No, I'm not unhappy that I did it now, though, as my partner kept pointing out, it cost a lot of money. But we don't live by bread alone. (Is that a Communist statement?)"

Early on, Gang seemed to see the issues in terms of tactics rather than ethics, of style rather than substance, of immediate benefit or loss rather than long-range principle. He felt it was better to work with rather than against the House Un-American Activities Committee. Thus, although he was a member of the Committee for the First Amendment, in November 1947 he wrote to Robert Kenny and Bartley Crum, two of the non-Communist lawyers on the team representing the Hollywood Ten who had just been cited for contempt of Congress.* His argument: unless some real service could be performed by the eight remaining members of the Nineteen following the procedure the Ten followed, "they should not sacrifice themselves to no useful end." His proposal: a public-relations campaign when the hearings resumed; each individual would answer the questions put to him subject to his statement that he was doing so voluntarily without conceding the right of the Committee to ask, but since the issue had been raised and would be decided by the courts he was answering the questions under protest. "This will prevent such persons from being discharged or blacklisted."[1]

Almost before the battle started, Gang had implicitly conceded what may have been a critical point—that non-Communists had no constitutional stake in standing up for the rights of Communists.† Even in advance of the Ten's appearance, Gang counseled caution. He met with Kenny and some of the Nineteen and a Party lawyer and advised that they get as counsel, rather than a liberal or radical, the prestigious and sympathetic former deputy secretary of war, Robert Patterson, "to make a dignified constitutional case." Instead, as he saw it, "the tactics were strictly dictated by those lawyers who were members of the Communist Party. And the tactics were to have a confrontation, which they did. . . .

---

* Gang made it clear that although he represented some of the original Nineteen on other matters, they did not know about the letter that he was writing "entirely on my own responsibility."

†An ironic concession in view of the fact that, unbeknownst to Gang, his client Larry Parks had indeed belonged to the Party.

As a result they got a lousy piece of law, because [given] that conduct the courts were bound to come down with a lousy decision—which they did."

According to Gang, a lawyer's obligation is simple—to serve his client's best interests. And in the case of his Hollywood clients, their best interests were served by not being blacklisted. So Gang devoted himself to working out a variety of formats to clear them. "I didn't tell them what to do; I only told them what the choices were."

His first attempt to clear a client—before the HUAC hearings began in earnest but after the Hollywood Ten had been cited for contempt of Congress—was aimed not at the Committee but at the FBI. The actor Sterling Hayden, who had joined the CP after his work in World War II with Tito's Partisans, came to Gang in 1950 fearful that his past might cost him his future. Gang went right to the top: he wrote to J. Edgar Hoover about an unnamed client who had joined the Party as a youthful indiscretion, now regretted it, and wanted to clear his name. "Hoover said, 'We don't have anything to do with it,' " Gang recalls, " 'but if your client feels that way about it, talk to the local FBI people, so that if anybody subsequently makes a complaint we'll know he's all right as far as we're concerned.' "

A year later Hayden was subpoenaed to appear before HUAC. Gang recalls that he and Frank Tavenner, HUAC's general counsel, worked out a format for pretested testimony that was to serve as a model for virtually all the cooperative testimony in the hearings that followed.

"I'll never forget how mad the general counsel got at me. I said, 'Look, I'm not going to let you crucify my client by asking "Are you now or have you ever been ... " without first laying a foundation: why he became a Communist, what he did.' Tavenner was mad. He said, 'You're not going to tell me how to examine.' I said, 'If you want the witness to help you, if you want him to testify, you're going to do it my way or he's not going to testify.' Hayden came out a hero (which he was, by the way). He testified why he became a Communist, what he did to help Tito—sailing ships into Yugoslavia and all that—and the papers made a hero out of him. Sterling wasn't hurt one goddamned bit by telling the truth—he also didn't have any names because he didn't know any names, so he didn't hurt anybody. As I said, he ended up a hero and rightly so.*

"And that's when I first met the Committee and Tavenner and Wheel-

---

* Gang's memory is only half-right. Hayden ended up a hero in the press but he named his former mistress, Bea Winters (his agent's secretary), who had recruited him into the Party. He also named, among others, Robert Lees, Karen Morley, Maurice

er, and I established a relationship with them which at least permitted us to talk. Even after we laid a foundation I wouldn't let them ask the question, 'Are you now or have you ever been . . . ?' I said, 'That's a compound question and it can't be answered right.' "

Why was Parks blacklisted and Hayden hired? Parks was the first of the name-namers and openly reluctant, whereas Hayden was apparently enthusiastic, but also Parks had a New York lawyer who, though he apparently shared the values of the Committee, operated outside its rituals. "It just didn't have to happen that way," says Gang. "It didn't happen with any of my people."

Gang also insists that none of his clients named new names, but the record does not bear this out. What is true, however, is that he told his clients, "Don't guess: unless you saw a card or it was a closed meeting, you can't be sure someone was a member of the Party, so you shouldn't name him." The Committee's investigator, William Wheeler, went along, wishing neither to be embarrassed by a case of mistaken identity nor to push a cooperative witness to the point of noncooperation.

Gang shortly became the informers' preeminent defense attorney. As more and more witnesses appeared before HUAC the ritual was refined. How to tell, then, when a so-called cooperative witness was *really* cooperative? How to avoid Parks's situation, where one named names, yet also offended the internal-security auditors? Gang worked out a routine with the chairman, who would excoriate the resisters but always closed by thanking the adequately penitent. The closing "thank you" quickly took on operational significance when there might otherwise have been a question as to the adequacy of a witness's contrition. The writer Michael Blankfort, for example, who had written reviews for the *Daily Worker,* the Communist newspaper, and had been named as a Communist by Louis Budenz, insisted he was never a Party member and therefore had no names to name. He recalls that at the end of his otherwise cooperative and friendly testimony, "The chairman, Walter, forgot to thank me for appearing. So Martin Gang got hold of him after the session and said, 'You forgot to thank Blankfort.' Walter called the court reporter of the Committee over and told him to put in a thank you so that I could be clear of the blacklist, and that's what he put down." Thus readers of the Committee's record see the closing statement of Blankfort's testimony as a comment from Congressman Walter: "We appreciate your cooperation,

---

Murphy, and Abraham Lincoln Polonsky. The result was that he ended up as a hero to the public but a coward to himself, as he makes clear in his 1964 memoir, *Wanderer.*

and it is only because of the willingness of people like you to come here and give us a full statement of the facts as you know them that we are able to point up to the American people the danger of this conspiracy. We are deeply appreciative of your efforts to assist us."[2]

Gang mixed the social and the political, the public and the private. "Working with the Committee" did not mean merely in the Committee room. It meant strategic socializing. Says Gang: "I got to be very fond of Bill Wheeler. I think I kind of educated him, because I used to take him to dinner with people who were on his list. . . . A lot of people who he was personally convinced were okay, he never pursued them. He met them and talked to them and made up his own mind. . . . There used to be a Japanese place—I remember taking him to dinner with two clients of mine whom he wanted to talk to. And he became convinced they were in the clear, and he never bothered to subpoena them. So there again I think I did my clients a favor and I also did Wheeler a favor. I don't know what it proved about me, but Wheeler was doing a job, and what I tried to do was to present the facts to him in such a way that my clients would not be unnecessarily hurt. And if that's a crime you can convict me.

"During the time of the Spanish Inquisition," Gang says today, as he peers out the window of his splashy California-style rock-and-glass Sunset Boulevard law office, "I suppose if a poor son of a bitch was supposed to be a Jew but wasn't, he had to go to a lawyer and try to convince the Inquisition he ain't a Jew. . . . What are you going to do? What would a lawyer do in a case like that? What would you do if you were in my position? You would try to help them, wouldn't you?" Thus he represented Danny Dare, who had first denied past CP membership, "and then the poor son of a bitch came to me. I straightened that out with Wheeler. I had to. I said, 'The guy made a mistake,' and we cleaned it up. He was never prosecuted. There again, what else could you do? The man would go to jail for that. . . . I had to."

Another Gang technique was a HUAC executive session in the privacy of his office. Wheeler recalled, "We interviewed witnesses in his offices—like Mrs. Burrows. Gang was always present during my sessions until I got to know the people well. Then later on, probably with either his permission or the permission of the witnesses, I talked to them independently. It's a sensitive subject, but [there were times when] a congressman would fly out here and be appointed by the chairman and swear the witness in and leave, and I'd take the testimony. But this was never released.

"That's what happened with Lloyd Bridges. He was a member of the CP, and he came up to Gang's office, and my wife was waiting for me when he walked in. Well, she recognized him from high school. They used to go out together. Lloyd didn't know too much [about the Party]—he was sucked in. So I just took the statement in Gang's office. Now how many congressmen were there? I don't know that there were any."

Gang did not merely prep witnesses. He followed up, like a good employment agency. On July 8, 1952, he wrote Max Arnow of Columbia Pictures and told him that Sylvia Richards had appeared before Congressman Jackson voluntarily at the Hotel Roosevelt in New York (Wheeler took the testimony) and testified "fully, completely and cooperatively."[3] (So hire the woman.)

On Lloyd Bridges' behalf on April 14, 1953, he wrote to IATSE head Roy Brewer in his role as clearance maven:

> Ron Lubin [of the Jaffee Agency] got the impression it was you who said Bridges was unacceptable. I told Ron this must be a mistake since Lloyd Bridges was one of the people who had come forward voluntarily to testify about his short contact with the Communist Party in 1944; that he had testified to the best of his ability cooperatively; and that in the 1952 Annual Report . . . he is listed on page 40 as one of the witnesses who had helped the Committee and was thanked and commended for it.
>
> After talking to [Brewer's assistant] and giving him what information I had yesterday, I called [the producer]. . . . He told me he did not wish to get in the middle, but that he had been given a list in New York, he did not remember who gave it to him . . . and on the list was the name of Lloyd Bridges listed as politically unacceptable.
>
> When I told him that Lloyd Bridges had been a cooperative witness, had been commended by the Committee and so listed officially in the 1952 Report, he was amazed since he had no idea of what had been going on in this field.
>
> He did tell me if you said that Lloyd Bridges was politically okay that would be good enough for him.

Gang closed by emphasizing the importance of cleaning and organizing "the lists." In other words, it is too bad they are using lists, but if we are going to have them let's make them accurate, alphabetical, up-to-date, and so on. Let's make them *usable.*[4]

Undoubtedly Gang's ex-Communist clients took solace from his novel legal theory, adhered to by no other attorney at the time, that they were precluded from pleading the Fifth Amendment. As he explains it, "The Fifth Amendment couldn't honestly be taken if a man was no longer a member of the Communist Party . . . because if that person had been a member of the Communist Party and had gotten out, he had no right to plead the Fifth Amendment because he was not guilty of any crime unless he had lied about not having gotten out."

Other attorneys took the position that because of the possibility that conspiracy charges might be leveled at witnesses, former Communists could plead the Fifth Amendment with impunity. Not Gang. He claimed that since their motivation was to avoid informing, admittedly an insufficient legal reason to invoke the Fifth, they had no valid recourse to the privilege against self-incrimination. "When I told people that was my legal position, that I could not represent a client who to my knowledge was going to plead the Fifth Amendment when I did not think it applied— they left me and went to another lawyer."

Perspective on Gang's *modus operandi* may be gained by listening to one who chose not to avail himself of Gang's services—Howard Koch, a writer whose screenplays included *Sergeant York* (1941), *Casablanca* (1942), and *Mission to Moscow* (1943). (Written at FDR's request, this film, based on Ambassador Joseph Davies' book about his experiences in Russia, got him into trouble as a Stalinist apologist.) Koch wrote to a friend, the expatriate actor Philip Brown, then living on a houseboat in England, to explain why he did not want to "walk the Gang plank," even though he considered himself graylisted. Koch had gone to Gang after three bad experiences: Joseph L. Mankiewicz had wanted to buy a script of his called "The Island," but the project was "sabotaged" by United Artists because of his name; Monica McCall, his agent, had received an acceptance for his play about Woodrow Wilson from the Theatre Guild for its U.S. Steel television show, but the advertising agency vetoed it because of his name; and finally, John Houseman had requested CBS to let Koch assist him with the writing of his new *Seven Lively Arts* television program and CBS said no. Koch wrote:

> Three strikes were out, and I asked Monica not to submit my stuff— except to Broadway—until this thing was cleared up.
> By this time the Kohner office was working on the problem in Hollywood. They went to the [Screen] Writers Guild and were advised to approach Martin Gang. This was done without my knowledge and I was not very happy about it but anyway I sent him a statement of my political history which [was] asked for. It was a description of the aims and methods of the organizations I'd been connected with and, since it was factual, it was in essence a defense of those things I worked for and

the people I worked with. On the Communist question I merely repeated what I've always maintained—that I wouldn't know one from an Eskimo, and cared less—and that in all my activities I had never seen or heard anything that could remotely be called subversive.

Mr. Gang replied that he had given my statement to Mr. Wheeler . . . who said that . . . in appearing before the Committee (this was the first mention of it to me) I should be prepared with certain more "specific" answers and that Mr. Wheeler was interested enough in getting me reinstated, that he would help "jog my memory" in a preliminary conference. . . .

We had this talk in New York last week. Mr. Gang appeared to me a very troubled man, who was more anxious to impress me with his political wisdom and virtue than in solving my problem. However, he assumed that I was going to follow his suggested procedure and he gave his instructions while I listened. He advised that I should not appear before the Committee members in New York because their attorney here was "not to be trusted." In Hollywood he and Mr. Wheeler would arrange an appearance before a relatively sympathetic member but first I would have to "bone up" on the testimony of others like Bob Rossen since it seemed from my statement that some of the "ulterior designs" of some of my co-workers had evidently eluded me. . . .

Koch told his friend Phil Brown that he hadn't wanted to do it on the basis of anybody else's hindsight. Why couldn't he do it like "Yip" Harburg, "a simple and dignified procedure"? "At this point Mr. Gang reversed himself completely, agreeing that this approach was more suitable in my case and 'less work for both of us.' " Koch wrote his agent Paul Kohner asking him to find a studio executive who would take the chance, "assured there would be no opposition from the Committee," although there might be squawks from the lunatic fringe and columnists.

I should point out, Phil, that as a last resort appearing before a member of the Committee is no longer an impossible procedure to contemplate. It depends, I should say, on how skillfully one is able to walk the tight-rope, balancing between what they want and what you're willing to say. It's not a question of being asked to name names—that's out with us. . . . However, for a long time I've looked on this as somewhat of a token distinction without much practical value inasmuch as the Committee has all the names. I happen to feel there are other ways of disavowing ideas and friends besides calling them Communists. I realize there can be honest differences of opinion on this question but I can't but feel that in renouncing past beliefs there is a danger of finding oneself with a whole new set of premises that require more of a psychological adjustment than one is aware of in the beginning. Mr. Gang himself is a good example of this schizoid process. I felt as if I were talking to two people, one identifiable with a progressive past, the other committed to an unprogressive present and future. For those of us who feel this way, the business of "clearance" is perhaps more complicated than if we were Communists—or at least repentant Communists.[5]*

As Gang developed relationships with blacklisters and expertise at the craft of meeting their objections, it was only natural that he should be able to service his clients with ever finer stratagems and distinctions. The matter of clearance letters raised points jesuitical and talmudical. Where exposure would be harmful, he would arrange for only limited circulation of the letter. Where favorable publicity was needed to get the word out, he would mimeograph copies of letters of testimony and send them off himself to prospective employers.[6]

Consider, for example, Gang's handling of the request made in 1952 by Columbia's B. B. Kahane, vice-president in charge of security, for a statement "under oath" from Rita Hayworth explaining the circumstances under which she had lent her name to such alleged Communist fronts as the Hollywood Democratic Committee, the Hollywood Independent Citizens Committee for the Arts, Sciences and Professions, the Sleepy Lagoon Defense Committee, and so on. "The statement," Kahane wrote, "should set forth the fact (if, as I assume, it is a fact) that she is not now and never has been a member of the Communist Party. It should also contain a positive, forthright affirmation of her loyalty to the United States and I hope, a strong condemnation of Communistic subversive groups and ideologies."[7] Gang's partner Robert Kopp wrote back on May 27 that Kahane should be satisfied with "a statement" rather than "a private loyalty oath. . . . If Nicholas Schenck has enough confidence in the employees of Loew's Inc., many of whom he does not personally know, so that he merely requests explanatory letters and not loyalty

---

* Koch's ability to work in Hollywood eventually was reestablished—after seven years—by Edward Bennett Williams. "It is my understanding," Koch wrote to the Wisconsin Center for Theatre Research, "that he accomplished this by his personal endorsement of my political and personal loyalty after looking up the records of my activities during the period in question and by making it clear to the Legion and the Motion Picture Alliance that he considered any further efforts on their part to prevent my employment as actionable at law."

oaths, it would seem to me that you . . . should exhibit an equal degree of trust when you are asking for an explanation for Miss Hayworth with whom you have a personal acquaintanceship."[8]

When the American Legion sent around its "for instance" list of people with dubious records who were still on the Hollywood employment roles, Gang got agitated because "innocent people who didn't even know they were on the list might be hurt."[9] He went to the Legion's James O'Neil on behalf of one client, and to the columnist George Sokolsky on behalf of another. It did not apparently occur to him to ask (as Dalton Trumbo once did), "How can there be innocence where there is no guilt?"

A further refinement in Gang's clearance methodology had to do with knowing over what sorts of issue it was permitted to display indignation. After he filed with M-G-M a seventeen-page document to refute false charges against the radio writer Norman Corwin and the studio hired him, Gang was able to display splendid indignation when another studio made Corwin a job offer but then wanted a whole new document. In a rational world, getting off one list should mean getting off all lists. "I was exasperated enough . . . to call Mr. Brewer and get him involved. . . . Most of the trouble came from the Motion Picture Alliance. . . . Somebody [there] like Ward Bond would pick up the phone and complain to the executives, and we would have trouble all over again. Roy Brewer, I thought, was the one voice of sanity in that group, and he was also, personally . . . a decent and honest man. . . . I used to take him to lunch at the Brown Derby with the client." Since in this case the client was an uncompromising intellectual, "it took quite a bit of time before Mr. Brewer was honestly convinced that my client was not a Communist." But even after that, "Brewer said to me he [was having] trouble convincing Ward Bond and that Bond could always pick up the phone and make trouble."

Gang introduced Corwin to James O'Neil so that O'Neil "could get to know him and talk to him and realize, as I did, what a fine human being he was and how unjust this whole atmosphere was, and I use [the word] 'atmosphere' advisedly." Corwin, whose whole thrust was to oppose the blacklist, ended up urging with O'Neil that he, as an old newspaperman, ought to know better than to participate in such a tragi-farce.

One might argue that the employers set the rules and Gang merely made sure that his clients qualified under them. But the employers' public posture was that there was no blacklist, so how could there be ways of circumventing something which didn't exist? Gang understood that. As he saw it, his job was to convince the employer that my client was "a person for whom the employer would have an answer if the pressure group picketed or attacked or wrote letters or picked up the phone and said, 'Why are you hiring a Commie or a member of a Communist front or a fellow traveler?' It was my job to convince the employer that it was a wrong accusation and see to it that he had a proper answer for it so he in his own good business judgment could hire such a person without subjecting his stockholders to a possible loss. That was a difficult job to do in many cases." Gang saw himself as "a frustrated crusader. I was trying every which way to remedy the situation, and ran into nothing but roadblocks."[11]

But if Gang, who considers that the blacklist was reprehensible, doesn't consider himself reprehensible, who *was* responsible? "The people who were responsible were the people who ran the studios. They should have taken the position that Eddie Mannix—alav hasholom—took: We're responsible for what goes on the screen, so we hire whom we please. That's the position they were going to take until they hired Jimmy Byrnes as counsel* and he told them to back away.

"All of these decent people—yet nobody but Mannix, an uneducated man who came up the hard way (he had been a bouncer at Palisades Park), had the guts. He took the decent position, the logical position, the defensible position.

"To me the big failure of the time—I blame most of it on CP tactics— was that decent people like Lillian Hellman didn't attack it on principle.[†] They could have won, because in my opinion the [government] would never prosecute anybody who on moral principle refuses to name names. No jury would ever convict."

Why didn't he test that in court?

"Because I don't go looking for business. If people come to me I help them the way I can. A crusader I'm not."

———

The hidden premise or, rather, the not-so-hidden premise underlying Martin Gang's labors to get his clients back to work in Hollywood was

---

* James F. Byrnes had been a secretary of state in the Truman administration, and was an important leader of the conservative wing of the Democratic Party.

† Hellman actually did precisely what Gang says she should have done. The difference is that she relied on the Fifth Amendment, whereas Gang maintains that the "moral" position would require the First Amendment.

that only non-Communists or publicly repentant ex-Communists were entitled to job security. This premise informed the decision to work with rather than against the internal-security establishment in achieving the goal of full employment for non-, anti-, and repentant ex-Communists—a policy that had unforeseen and tragicomic consequences, especially within California's Jewish community.

In addition to being a leading member of the Hollywood bar, Martin Gang was also a leader in another California establishment—that of organized Jewry. Indeed, he had originally joined the National Lawyers Guild "because Jews didn't get very far in the ABA." And since the movie business was and is very much a Jewish business, it is not surprising that the interests of the Jews as a group and of the motion-picture industry were thought to intersect. Indeed, many Jews, especially in the days when the anti-Semitic John Rankin was serving on the Committee, believed that HUAC went after Hollywood precisely because it was something of a Jewish preserve, a dozen Yiddish-speaking moguls—Sam Goldwyn, Louis B. Mayer, William Fox, the Warner brothers, the Schencks, the Selznicks, Harry Cohn, Jesse Lasky, and Adolph Zukor—who more or less created the studio system. Walter Goodman gives a fair summary of the Rankin-HUAC heritage:

> The source of Rankin's animus against Hollywood—and he made no particular effort to conceal it—was the large number of Jews eminent in the film industry. "I have no quarrel with any man about his religion," he explained after a Committee investigator was reported to have warned some liberal Jews [in 1945] to "watch their steps" lest the fate of Germany's Jews overtake them. "Any man who believes in the fundamental principles of Christianity and lives up to them, whether he is Catholic or Protestant, certainly deserves the respect and confidence of mankind." In Rankin's mind, to call a Jew a Communist was a tautology. His convictions led him to attribute all the horrors of the Russian revolution to Trotsky and to see Stalin as a kind of reformer, a seminary student who opened the churches, got rid of the commissars, and drove the local Reds to America. "Communism is older than Christianity," he would explain from time to time. "It hounded and persecuted the Savior during his earthly ministry, inspired his crucifixion, derided him in his dying agony, and then gambled for his garments at the foot of the cross." In the halls of Congress he called Walter Winchell "a little slime-mongering kike" and he took glee in baiting his Jewish colleagues, particularly [Adolph] Sabath and [Emanuel] Celler. One day he referred to the latter as "the Jewish gentleman from New

York." When Celler protested, Rankin asked, "Does the member from New York object to being called a Jew or does he object to being called a gentleman? What is he kicking about?"[12]

The question of naming names was at some level a struggle between the right and the left within the Jewish community. Jews on both sides were for the most part secular, second- and third-generation people who had migrated west in search of the American dream and, in large part, thought they had found it. Here was an affluent community that could afford ideological dispute and dialectics. It was also a community that had less a religious or theological sense of Judaism than a cultural one.

The specter of anti-Semitism persisting after the Holocaust and the war undoubtedly helps to explain the proliferation of Jewish fraternal, social, and protective organizations in the late 1940s. Not the least of them was Hollywood's Community Relations Committee of the Jewish Federation Council. The CRC, as it was known, was a sort of United Nations of all the local and national organizations concerned with anti-Semitism—the Anti-Defamation League, the American Jewish Congress, the Jewish Labor Committee, the Jewish War Veterans, the Council of Jewish Women, and thirty-two others. Its chairman, appropriately enough, was a prime Hollywood establishment figure, one Mendel Silberberg, an eminent Republican who served also as vice-president and general counsel of Columbia Pictures; he had also represented other studios and he had taken part in the 1947 deliberations at the Waldorf-Astoria. He was close to Governor Earl Warren on the state level, President Dwight D. Eisenhower on the national level, and perhaps most important, was the contact man with the corrupt labor leader Willie Bioff on the local level. As Paul Jacobs, who belonged to the CRC first as a member of the American Jewish Committee and later as a CIO representative, told me, "Silberberg controlled the slush fund which the producers kept available for bribing purposes—to pay for sweetheart contracts to keep embarrassments quiet, to buy people off." When in 1945 George E. Browne, president of IATSE, and Bioff, its Hollywood representative, were convicted for extortion and conspiracy, Bioff was replaced by Roy Brewer, who became one of the central figures in both the blacklisting and clearance businesses. Silberberg was close to him too.[13]

The CRC, called by Joseph Roos, its executive director, "the public face of the Jewish community in Los Angeles and California," like the Anti-Defamation League on the East Coast concerned itself primarily with quietly representing Jewish positions to the Gentile community, and with the prevention and cure of anti-Semitism. Its director, like the Anti-Defamation League's general counsel, Arnold Forster, soon found himself in the rehabilitation business, helping "innocent" victims of McCarthyism go back to work. "I was an investigative reporter for movie stars," is how Roos defines his job. "I spent time with those stars and drew them out in order to develop a good dossier that Martin Gang could use." Thus when Mendell Silberberg asked him to help the graylisted Jewish actor Edward G. Robinson, Roos says, "I did this by going through check stubs and showing how giving to this or that organization declared subversive after the fact didn't prove anything about him, since I could show who else gave."

Roos takes credit for introducing Martin Gang to HUAC investigator William Wheeler. "The CRC was a natural place for the process to take place," Paul Jacobs told me, "because you had the studios represented through Silberberg; you had the Jewish war veterans there, who were able to go to the Legionnaire types, and you had other people who were close to union people who could go to Brewer; and you had in the case of Roos himself a very knowledgeable, sophisticated political guy. Roos came out of the German Social Democratic movement, he was a refugee, he knew a hell of a lot about the CP and all about CP activities."

As the cold war heated up, so did the Jewish community's fear of McCarthyite anti-Semitism. First, it was a fact that many Jews were or had been in the socialist movement, and the professional patrioteers were unable or unwilling to distinguish between socialist and Communist. Also, as Irving Howe points out in *World of Our Fathers,* the Communist Party had helped to acculturate Jewish immigrants, beginning in the early 1920s, when it built up a network of Yiddish-speaking social and cultural institutions based in New York City:

First came the *Freiheit,* the Yiddish Communist daily started in 1922 [which delighted in polemicizing against the Social Democratic *Daily Forward,* an intramural distinction lost on the nativists and investigators of the 1950s]. . . . All through the twenties the Communists had built up dissident fractions within the Workmen's Circle, tearing away from it both a number of children's schools and the New York summer camp, Kinderland. In 1930 they started their own fraternal society, the International Workers Order, which would prove to be a rich source of recruitment and finances. Meanwhile, they were building a maze of local groups devoted to Yiddish folk singing, cooperative housing projects (in the northeast Bronx), mandolin ensembles, sum-

mer camps (Nitgedaiget—"No Worries"—in Beacon, New York),
amateur theatre, sickness and death benefits, radical Jewish schooling,
not-quite-modern dance, and literary discussion.[14]

But second, and more important, since there was a general national
failure to distinguish between the Communist as theoretical Marxist and
the Communist as espionage agent, with the arrest of Julius and Ethel
Rosenberg in July 1950 as "atom spies" (and the arrests of other Jews
such as Judith Coplon, Robert Soblen, Jack Soble, Morton Sobell, et
al.), many leaders in the American Jewish community came to fear "the
establishment of a link between being a Jew and being a 'Communist traitor' in the popular mind," as Arnold Forster, general counsel of ADL,
recalls. "There was an evident quotient of anti-Semitism in the McCarthy
wave of hysteria. Jews in that period were automatically suspect. Our
evaluation of the general mood was that the people felt if you scratch a
Jew, you can find a Communist."

On both coasts establishment Jewish organizations responded to the
cold war with a double reflex.[15] There was the traditional civil-libertarian
response—a resistance to and attack on McCarthyism as the denial of liberty and due process. Thus the executive board of the American Jewish
Committee annually promulgated statements on civil liberties that deplored actions that endangered "the dignity of the individual," "essential
freedoms," "unjustified interrogation and attack," and "intolerance of
dissenting opinions and unsubstantiated attacks on loyal individuals."
Yet at the same time, the board carefully refrained from denouncing
HUAC or McCarthy by name.

The mood of the Jewish left at about the time HUAC heard the Hollywood Ten had not yet jelled. In November 1947 the American Jewish
Committee board member Sidney Harmon of Studio City, California,
wrote to John B. Slawson, the AJC's executive director, proposing that
the AJC take up the fight against HUAC by documenting the charge that
"one of the prime purposes of the Un-American Activities Committee is
to spread anti-Semitism." He quoted the film director Billy Wilder on
how Hitler had charged the Jews who owned Germany's motion-picture
business with being Communists, wiped them out and scared them out,
and then dedicated the industry to propaganda. He added, "the salient
fact is that motion-picture policy is, for the most part, conceived and carried out by Jews." Harmon argued that a recent *Fortune* magazine survey
"finding the far west the center of the greatest percentage of anti-Semitism implies that the reason for this is that California is the home of the

movie industry . . . and everyone knows the Jews make the movies." He then noted "the insistent declaration on the part of the Thomas Committee and the Hearst press that Hollywood is Communist dominated"; since Hearst's theme, that "the movies are dominated by the Communists," assumed that everyone knew they were made by Jews, what Hearst was really saying was that Jews were Communists.

It's more than coincidence, wrote Harmon, that ten of the nineteen Hollywood people subpoenaed by HUAC were Jews (Milestone, Collins, Kahn, Maltz, Rossen, Ornitz, Lawson, Bessie, Biberman, Cole) and six of the Ten indicted were Jews. "What position is the American Jewish Committee to take in relation to the ten Jewish unfriendly witnesses? Doesn't the constitution of the American Jewish Committee say something to the effect that the American Jewish Committee is organized to come to the defense of those Jews whose civil rights are being threatened?"

It took Slawson six weeks to answer but on January 20, 1948, he responded that the AJC could not act on the case of the Hollywood Ten, because it was not one that had an impact "directly on members of minority groups" but rather "a most important legal problem affecting the rights of all citizens, be they Jews, or Methodists or freethinkers. It is, in short, a matter in which an organization like the American Civil Liberties Union, but hardly one like the American Jewish Committee, should be concerned. The fact that a majority of the defendants in this particular case are Jewish does not alter the fact that the issue involved goes beyond our proper area of functioning."

The AJC's real response to HUAC was to decide that a little protective housecleaning of their own might be in order, so they retained a full-time staff member to conduct exhaustive research into the degree and identity of Communist infiltration into Jewish communal life. One result of this investigation was the expulsion from the AJC of the Jewish People's Fraternal Order.*

The JPFO had indeed been created by the Communist Party, but it was in all other respects a harmless fraternal organization where left-wing Yiddish-speaking Jews came together for mutual economic and cultural benefit. But because it found its way onto the attorney general's list, the Community Relations Committee also moved quickly to expel it. As Roos recalls, "The CRC created a committee, and it assembled informa-

---

* An AJC memorandum on the JPFO was used to expel the latter from local centers in ten communities "where it had gained a foothold in Jewish life."

tion about the Jewish People's Fraternal Order which proved that its first objective was not a Jewish objective. The argument was that if there would be a Jewish Republican club it could not become a member because its objective is really to help the Republican Party; the same thing with a Jewish Democratic club. And on that basis they were thrown out—we said their first objective wasn't Jewish. I think this is the only time when Jews really went the wrong way during the red-baiting period. Let us assume that red-baiting can be justified. The Jewish People's Fraternal Order could not have made the entire Jewish community non-kosher. They were a bunch of *alte cockers*. The only paper they would read was a Yiddish paper. This was a sad experience."

The event that gave rise to the AJC's most active behind-the-scenes role was, not surprisingly, the Rosenberg case. The Communist Party had initially been silent on the Rosenbergs, but after their trial, when the Party joined, if not inspired, a campaign to attribute their conviction and death sentence to anti-Semitism in the American government, the AJC joined "with other Jewish community-relations agencies" to make clear that there was no evidence of anti-Semitism in bringing the Rosenbergs to justice.

The Rosenberg case split the Jewish community and raised many troubling questions. "It is conceivable," Paul Jacobs wrote in 1965, "that had they not been Jewish, they might not have received the death penalty from the Jewish judge who presided at their trial. Perhaps he invoked the death penalty from an unconscious feeling of a need to demonstrate that a Jewish judge could be as harsh on Jewish traitors as any other judge."[16]

Questions which were not asked out loud at the time: Was it because the Rosenbergs were Jewish that they were tried before a Jewish judge and prosecuted by a Jew? Was it a coincidence that both the Rosenberg lawyer and the prosecutor used their jury challenges to prevent any Jews from sitting on the jury? Were the Jewish organizations that so vocally supported the death penalty motivated, at least in part, by the fear that the conviction of the Rosenbergs might spur anti-Semitism?

Given all of the murkiness surrounding the conviction of the Rosenbergs on charges of conspiracy to commit espionage, one would have thought that organizations like the AJC might consider at least two strategic possibilities: (1) dissociate Jews in general from alleged spies and subversives like the Rosenbergs; (2) question the fairness and accuracy of the Rosenberg verdict—and thereby disqualify the symbolic connection between the Jew and the subversive at its source. The AJC chose the first course. Thus it subsidized publication of a book reaffirming the Rosenbergs' guilt, *The Rosenberg Case: Fact and Fiction* (1953), written by S. Andhil Fineberg, of the AJC staff. It seems not to have occurred to the AJC that the Rosenbergs might have been innocent, as it did not to most of America at that time.

The AJC's contemporary preoccupations are revealed in a six-page interoffice memorandum sent by a staff person to Executive Director Slawson on July 31, 1950. It was aptly titled "Public Relations Effects of Activities of Jewish Atom Spies."*

Considerable concern has been expressed over public disclosures of spy activities by Jews and people with Jewish-sounding names. The present situation is regarded as being potentially more dangerous than the situation which obtained during World War II; for now the enemy is seen as Communist Russia rather than as Nazi Germany.

The main reason for concern is the belief that the non-Jewish public may generalize from these activities and impute to the Jews as a group treasonable motives and activities. . . .

We miss yet another bet in the use of our investigative staff. During recent years we infiltrated into rightist organizations to explore them, etc. Why can't we do this with Communist organizations, also using our knowledge to scare off Jews?

Because it seems likely that the AJC will undertake some kind of propaganda campaign in connection with these problems, I should like to make some constructive suggestions along propaganda lines. The principle underlying these suggestions is that the propaganda of the deed or propaganda of facts may have greater positive value than propaganda of exhortation. . . .

Instead of arguing exhortatively that Jews are not Communists, that they hate Communists, that they hate Russia, that Russia hates Jews, more positive approaches based on propaganda of fact can be used. One of the difficulties of propaganda of exhortation is not only that links may be established where none now exist, but also that there will always be instances to prove the exception of the propaganda claim; that is, there may be more Jewish atomic spies or more Jewish Communist leaders who will be arrested and tried and found guilty.

The following propaganda of fact ideas may be tried out:

1. Stories about how Russia stifles and oppresses its various minorities, including Jews, despite its claims to the contrary.

* Note the pop term "atom spies."

2. Stories about how Russia recruits spies and controls Communist Party members in this country. (Such an exposé would be most useful in Yiddish and Anglo-Jewish newspapers.)

3. Stories of American party systems and voting, showing how parties cut across all religious and ethnic lines. Possibly attention could be paid even to third-party groups and parties left of center.

4. Exposés on how Communists work in this country, infiltrating into various institutions such as labor unions, etc., and

5. Stories of how Communists are fought in this country through institutional means such as labor unions (Dubinsky kicks them out) and through government, featuring the work of such U.S. attorneys as Irving Saypol. (In this connection it should be pointed out that Saypol and other Jews on the "right side" may have as much or as little chance of recognition as do Jews on the "wrong side.")

6. Stories and reprints of stories on Russian attacks against Israel, against Zionists, against use of the Hebrew language.

7. Reprints and stories of Israel siding with the United Nations against Korean aggression.

8. Stories of how the present government in Israel keeps down Communists. . . .

The issue, never satisfactorily resolved, kept reasserting itself every time a Jewish Communist surfaced. Nine months later Fineberg sent out a "For Private Circulation / Not for Publication" memo on "Public Comment on the Atomic Spies" in which he argued that it was better not to try to anticipate anti-Semites who say Sobell, the Rosenbergs, and Greenglass are Jews (and *think* Fuchs is a Jew) and conclude all Jews are spies, because such anticipatory comment might just stir up trouble. He also noted that when the *Daily Mirror* cited Bernard Baruch, Lewis Strauss, and Adam Gimbel as "good Jews," this wasn't so good for the Jews either, because such an editorial "reinforces the concept of group responsibility" and "the *residue* in the mind of the average person for whom the editorial is intended to influence, is likely to be, 'But why is it all those atomic spies are all Jews?'" Fineberg said that the CP-ers are trying to tie the Jews' conscience in with the spies and argue that a Jewish judge can't be trusted to handle such cases because he may lean over backward. "The implications of the idea are devastating." Fineberg's recommendation was for Jews to reply to such charges that "Criminals operate as individuals, not as members of religious or racial groups."

The obsession with the Rosenberg case continued well into the 1950s, so that in August 1955, when HUAC held special hearings on The National Committee to Secure Justice in the Rosenberg Case, Fineberg sent AJC Executive Director Slawson a memorandum bringing him up-to-date. First, a reminder:

> The activities of the Rosenberg Committee were such that it was necessary for the American Jewish Committee and other Jewish community-relations agencies to issue a statement in May 1951 warning that " . . . Attempts are being made by a Communist-inspired group called The National Committee to Secure Justice in the Rosenberg Case, to inject the false issue of anti-Semitism into the Rosenberg case. . . ."

Second, a self-congratulatory observation: "Chairman Walter of his own volition also put into the record my memorandum of June 2, 1951, 'The Communists Find a New Opening,' which fully exposed the Rosenberg Committee and was widely distributed as a mimeographed item." In summary the HUAC hearings established that the Rosenberg Committee and the Sobell Committee were Communist-dominated and were therefore about to be put on the attorney general's list. "William A. Reuben, the instigator and one of the principal writers and speakers of the Rosenberg Committee," he added, "went into hiding and could not be subpoenaed." (It is a mark of the mystification that surrounded the Rosenberg case that the inability of HUAC's subpoena-server to find the vacationing Reuben is rendered as his having gone "into hiding." Reuben, as it happened, was miffed that he didn't get a chance to tell his story to HUAC and says, "I would have given anything to be there—I could have sold copies of my book, *The Atom Spy Hoax*, and told people my point of view.")

A third way of tackling the association of spy and Jew would have been to distinguish Communist espionage from Communist ideology and indeed from the CPUSA itself, which was—Sidney Hook and the Smith Act prosecutions to the contrary notwithstanding—a battered and tainted but nevertheless still legal entity. There was little sentiment within the organized Jewish community for such an undertaking—on either Marxist or Jeffersonian grounds.

Nevertheless, there continued to be internal tensions, as illustrated by the argument in 1952 between AJC staffers Edwin Lukas and Morris Fine over whether to distribute a pamphlet called *Loyalty and Democracy*, written by Maxwell Stewart, a former editor of *The Nation*. Fine, who said he believed the testimony of Budenz, Bentley, et al., objected to the pamphlet because it did not emphasize Soviet imperialism, the existence of a worldwide Communist conspiracy, and the revelations about Communist fronts, infiltration, and espionage within the United States. In addition, he questioned "the propriety of the AJC's associating with the Public Affairs Committee, in view of the accusations leveled against its director, Maxwell Stewart, as a Soviet symphathizer"; the reprinting of a panel discussion which included "such fellow travelers as Carey McWilliams and Thomas Emerson"; and "the listing in the bibliography of a book by James Davis." On the other side of the battle was Ed Lukas, who felt that Fine was exaggerating the threat of Communism, underestimating that of McCarthyism, and ignorantly impugning the integrity of libertarians such as McWilliams and Emerson.

It was not merely that the Jewish community, like the community at large, was agitated by the Communist issue and that its agitation was increased by the interaction of anti-Communism with anti-Semitism. Another factor helps to explain what happened next. In the days leading up to and during World War II, when the Federal Bureau of Investigation was hunting Nazis, Jewish organizations had gone out of their way to assist it.* These contacts with the FBI persisted into the McCarthy years and extended beyond the bureau to other elements in the government's internal-security bureaucracy.

It was the heritage and the style of the Jewish establishment to work with the internal-security establishment even while opposing its values. When McCarthy's hearings about the Voice of America and the USIA program were telecast on March 24, 1953, featuring a hostile witness named William Mandell, the response of the AJC was not to attack the investigation as misplaced, nor to question what valid purpose was served by asking Fifth Amendment witnesses a string of questions that the Committee knew, given the waiver doctrine, would not be answered. Rather, the AJC's reflex was to ask whether something couldn't be done to prevent giving witnesses such as Mandell, whom they regarded as an embarrassment to the Jewish community, a forum. Mandell, pointed out the staffer Morton Clurman in an internal memo, was "an extremely unpleasant, evasive, unctuous character who reinforces every stereotype of the Communist Jewish intellectual. Repeatedly he refused to say whether he had engaged in espionage for Russia, whether he would bear arms for the United States in a war with Russia, or whether he was, in fact, a

---

* HUAC itself, with various Jewish groups cheering it on, had conducted some half-hearted hearings into native fascist movements in the late 1930s.

member of the CP. . . ." Mandell raised the Jewish issue, which gave Mc-Carthy a chance to say nice things about the Jews, and as a result:

> McCarthy and Dirksen came out looking like Abraham Lincoln and Thomas Jefferson compared with the witness. . . . We should try to find out through careful approaches to Roy Cohn or anyone else on the Committee accessible to us how much of this testimony was anticipated or, in fact, rehearsed in executive session. . . . With a view to preventing future incidents of this type, it would be advisable to screen witnesses and testimony in executive session so that future Mandells would not get a chance to spew their poison at public expense.

When Louis Harap, the editor of a small journal named *Jewish Life,* generally believed to reflect the CP line, testified before the House Un-American Activities Committee three months later and charged that HUAC was creating conditions "under which six million Jews were murdered" and that the Jews in the Soviet Union were better off than the Jews in the United States, a private conference was arranged between Marcus Cohn of the American Jewish Committee, Herman Edelsberg of the Anti-Defamation League, and Bernard Weitzer of the Jewish War Veterans with Robert Kunzig, chief counsel of HUAC; Frank Tavenner, then its chief investigator (he had been chief counsel under the Democrats); and the Committee chairman, Harold Velde of Illinois. The purpose of the meeting, Cohn explained in a memorandum to his boss, John Slawson, was to "avert a repetition of the unfortunate publicity which had been given to the testimony of Dr. Louis Harap." Taking advantage of having HUAC's ear, they took the occasion to bring up a number of collateral incidents "to help the Committee in its own public-relations problems. It was evident that our advice and suggestions were appreciated."

When Kunzig noted that it was impossible to predict what witnesses, even witnesses who had been through an executive session, might say,

> I [Cohn] replied that in the case of a professional Communist such as Harap, it should have been obvious that he was waiting for an opportunity to spread the Communist line as consistently purveyed in *Jewish Life. It was also pointed out that if the Committee had consulted the files of the AJC and the ADL, it would have been prepared to deflate and deflect Harap's testimony.* We also pointed out that there is a large amount of literature demonstrating the incompatibility of Communism with Judaism as well as with democracy [my italics].

Herman Edelsberg, in a report to Arnold Forster, his superior at ADL, stated that "Velde and counsel agreed then and there that in the future, Committee investigators would be sent to ADL and AJC for material on prospective witnesses."

My point is not that meetings with the Committee were per se either evil or counterproductive. One can cite countless examples where public-interest groups and others engaged and still engage in creative behind-the-scenes lobbying; such informal meetings were a feature of the civil-rights pressures of the 1950s and 1960s, for example. (In fact, the AJC joined other interested groups in attempting to reform HUAC: in January 1954 a three-and-a-half-hour dinner which included representatives from the National Catholic Welfare Conference, the National Council of Churches of Christ, and Ed Lukas of the American Jewish Committee, was held with the Committee, where various proposals were made to improve HUAC's procedures for protecting witnesses' rights—all of which were "taken under consideration.")

The significant fact, though, was that in their attempt to protect the reputation of the organized Jewish community, these Jewish organizations with the best of motives accepted the premises of the internal-security establishment with whom they were collaborating behind the scenes. The perhaps unintended result was to strengthen its premises, legitimize its assumptions, enhance its ability to operate, and generally to expand its capacity to "define the situation." In other words, such contacts gave HUAC a more respectable frame of reference, thus dignifying a committee whose conduct deserved to be denounced, and making it acceptable to ordinary people.

In this general context it was only natural that the Community Relations Committee, the umbrella group of thirty-seven Jewish groups whose ostensible purpose was to fight anti-Semitism in California, set up its own Committee on Communism in the Jewish Community. The specific circumstances that brought this into being are illuminating. When I asked Martin Gang in 1976 why such a committee was needed he gave this reply: "Because the FBI had passed around a list of institutions that wouldn't get the preparedness plans if there were an atom bomb attack. The Mount Sinai Hospital was Jewish-sponsored, and we were tipped off by the FBI that they couldn't give the Mount Sinai Hospital the defense plans because there was a Communist on the staff. So we had to get a Committee on Communism. Paul Jacobs was my expert, and I was the chairman. That's where I met Paul. And we found out that a lady who was very prominent in the Party was a mistress of one of the Mount Sinai directors, so the FBI wouldn't give them the goddamn defense plans in case somebody dropped a nuclear bomb on L.A. Our job was to try to find out what the facts were, so that the hospitals and other such institutions wouldn't get into trouble by running into problems like that. It was self-defense in that lousy atmosphere."

Instead of challenging, exposing, or merely questioning the FBI's curious criteria, Gang's impulse was "self-defense." So organized Jewry in California made private peace with the internal-security establishment while publicly proclaiming its concern with the threat of McCarthyism.

Only in this "lousy atmosphere" is it possible to comprehend how the best and the brightest, the most liberal and activist members of the Jewish community almost ended up with a HUAC of their own making.

It started as an effort to combat a vigilante organization with heavy Jewish representation called the Joint Committee Against Communism in New York, whose three promoters were Rabbi Benjamin Schultz, executive director of the American Jewish League Against Communism; Alfred Kohlberg, chairman and chief backer of that organization (not to mention of the China Lobby); and Theodore Kirkpatrick, of *Red Channels*. The Joint Committee's charges were responsible for keeping Jean Muir (hired to play Henry Aldrich's mother) off the air and banning from the radio "Old Man Atom," a Columbia Records release (whose message was, "Listen folks, here's my thesis/Peace in the world, or the world in pieces").[17] This inspired the AJC's Ed Lukas with an idea for a counter-committee. The idea was simple: an ad hoc group "to neutralize the witch-hunt." On September 7, 1950, Lukas prepared a letter to Fred Lazarus, chairman of the Committee for Economic Development's Subcommittee on National Security and Individual Freedom, to ask whether Lazarus's group would be the agency to set up such an outfit. When they refused, he asked Gang. On March 10, 1952, Gang exposed his plan for what he called the Citizens Committee for Cooperation with Congress, and he wrote to key Hollywood and East Coast entertainment executives. "We would like to get moving on this fast because the Committee [HUAC] has set further Hollywood hearings for April 21, 1952."[17] His plan was for a committee of private citizens representing all branches of the entertainment world, whose function would be to "provide for the first time effective liaison between the entertainment industry and the House Committee on Un-American Activities." It was needed, he said, because Hollywood was vulnerable to attack from headline-hunting crackpots, and " . . . the work of the House Committee itself is beginning to suffer damage. Its motives are being misunderstood, its work beclouded by those who usurp its functions."[18]

The argument was that irresponsibles were mucking up the fight against Communism. HUAC should be the central repository, should insist that cooperative witnesses be hired, and an entertainment-industry committee should share information with it. The trouble, said Gang, is that "fanatics are given the same space as sincere patriots. We have to stop that. Effective exchange of information together with machinery for mutual assistance between show business and the House Committee will do away with the damage caused by ex officio superpatriots who misguidedly or deliberately fire irresponsible accusations."

The functions of Gang's proposed committee were as follows:
1) to serve as clearinghouse between HUAC and entertainment world;
2) to request that HUAC insist that it be the agency to handle all charges;
3) to reiterate HUAC's stand that "cooperative witnesses should be given employment . . . ";
4) to aid in publicizing the good work of HUAC and the fairness of its procedures;
5) to exchange information with HUAC;
6) to make HUAC more effective by exposing fanatics.

At first Gang attempted to enlist Hollywood's unions and guilds, the American Legion, and various executives from the networks (he succeeded in gaining the support of the executive vice-president of CBS, the general counsel of NBC, and the president of ABC), and to have HUAC issue a statement. On May 27 Gang sent a draft statement to James O'Neil in order to get Legion support (telling him that HUAC's counsel said they were "interested"). Again, the impulse was ostensibly humanitarian—to let "innocent" victims get their careers back. The draft said, among other things:

The Committee has been informed of instances in which persons who have been named as members of the Communist Party under oath before the Committee on Un-American Activities and who have cooperated with that Committee in its investigation and have been commended by the Committee, subsequently have been refused employment in the entertainment field. Such ill-considered actions not only are unfair and un-American but are detrimental to the work of this Committee in that employment is denied to cooperative witnesses just as it is denied to persons who have pleaded the Fifth Amendment or who have failed to deny present membership in the Communist Party. The failure to distinguish between cooperative witnesses who have been commended by the Committee for their assistance and the unfriendly and uncooperative witnesses impedes the work of this Committee and should be ended.

Gang then proposed that his group publish a list of all witnesses with indications as to what they did to clear themselves:

> This list, it seems to us, affords the employers a sound basis for exercising a reasonable judgment as to the employability of prospective employees. Those witnesses who have cooperated with the Committee should without question be employable and no discrimination should be exercised against them.
>
> It has been pointed out that complaints have been and may in the future be made with reference to the employment of persons not so named as Communists. It is the position of this Committee that if any person believes that others are or have been connected with subversive activities within the purview of this Committee, such information should be brought to the attention of the Committee and if the evidence warrants it the accused person may be subpoenaed and required to testify under oath before the Committee. If such person cooperates before the Committee, there should be no question with reference to the employability of that person.

While Gang was pushing his West Coast plan, on the East Coast the AJC had commissioned the respected constitutional scholar Professor Robert Cushman of Cornell to come up with recommendations on what to do about the entertainment industry's predicament. Cushman advanced a plan (on June 12, 1952), and it too involved setting up an independent tribunal. Cushman began with a strong libertarian premise:

> The entertainment industry is uniquely dependent upon public opinion. As a result there has come about an unexpected and wholly intolerable state of affairs in the entertainment field. Self-appointed censors of other people's loyalty, capitalizing on this disturbed state of the public mind and operating commercially, have wholly discarded the time-honored American doctrine that a man is innocent until he is proven guilty, and are using threats of economic boycotts and virtual intimidation to induce advertisers and sponsors to drop, or not to employ, entertainers on the basis of charges of disloyalty or Communist affiliation, which are frequently unsupported by facts or evidence, or which are subtly implied by circulating lists of entertainers "duped" into joining questionable organizations.

But he quickly added:

> It is clear that American entertainers, advertisers, and broadcasting
> companies are determined not to sponsor, nor be associated with,
> Communists or those known to be disloyal or subversive. It is impor-
> tant that the entertainment industry should protect itself against Com-
> munist infiltration in any of its forms.

The rest of the memo spelled out how this protection might be provided.

Five days later Lukas of AJC, East Coast division, wrote Gang of
AJC, West Coast division, and pointed out the proposed committee
would provide a means by which victims, now frustrated by the lack of
an adequate procedure, could "clear" themselves. "The people we had in
mind for such a tribunal would be of the caliber of Judge Learned Hand,
Herbert Bayard Swope, Judge Harold Medina, Elmer Davis, Paul Hoffman, Herbert Hoover, and maybe even Harry Truman after November,"
Lukas added, and then, after asking Gang's views on its potential, he provided the ubiquitous disclaimer: "I think you ought to know that, personally, I regret it as an unfortunate expedience; it should be unnecessary for
people living in a democracy to have to resort to plans of this nature in
order to secure those rights which, under normal conditions, are deemed
vouchsafed."

In a follow-up letter, Lukas elaborated and explained:

> I am now trying to be a pragmatic libertarian . . . serving the cause I
> cherish with you: the cause of pure principles. I have a conviction that
> if we were to resort to this procedure, and a fairly representative group
> of victims of lists in the entertainment industry were to appear before a
> distinguished screening panel during the first, say, six months of its ex-
> istence, such a large proportion of them would be "cleared" that the
> creators of these lists would be discredited from pursuing their tactics,
> and the public would have been taught, in a dramatic fashion, how un-
> reliable the lists and the listers are.

Gang, still pushing his own idea, went after officers of the Screen Actors Guild (SAG), the Screen Writers Guild (SWG), and the American
Federation of Television and Radio Artists (AFTRA). They were reluctant to take any action until HUAC appeared to sanction the idea, lest
they be accused publicly of trying to do what they claimed privately they
were trying to do, i.e., undermine the blacklisters. On January 13, 1953,
Gang wrote to representatives of SAG, SWG, and AFTRA, pointing out

that although "for various and sundry reasons" HUAC never issued such sanction, its "report for 1952 does contain the gist of what was sought":

> The report in its foreword refers to instances in which persons who have been members of the Communist Party but who have testified under oath before the Committee, are commended. The employers of such persons are likewise given praise . . . and those employers who refuse to employ such witnesses are criticized.
>
> The report contains an alphabetical list of all persons who have been named as present or former members of the Communist Party in hearings affecting the entertainment industry. . . .
>
> . . . This report . . . seems to me to afford the entertainment industry, including employers, employees, unions, advertising agencies and advertisers, a sound basis for exercising a reasonable judgment as to the employability of prospective employees.

He suggested that a committee consisting of representatives of the major broadcasting networks and movie-industry organizations be set up, and said he hoped that this would be a permanent solution to the problem.

Not hearing sufficient enthusiasm for the plan from the guilds, Gang reevaluated his view of Professor Cushman's proposal and a month later sent Lukas a letter reiterating that the HUAC Report of 1952 laid a "great foundation" for the operation of the sort of committee that Cushman had proposed. He also mentioned a Walter Lippmann column that had praised President Eisenhower for "improving" government screening procedures by making "security" rather than "loyalty" the test. The entertainment community should do the same thing, he thought. And then he got to the meat of the matter:

> The Committee could also consider whether or not it might state that employers in show business may take it as principle that they need not employ people who have been called Communists under oath and who have not denied it; people who have been called Communists and who have pleaded the Fifth Amendment. Starting from this base, you would eliminate 99% of the problems if not more.

Gang, now enthusiastic about the Cushman plan, made a number of other points:

> Learned Hand will be a good chairman and might be available. . . .
>
> The lay committee, in addition to acting as a buffer between pressure groups and the entertainment industry, should actually have a staff

which will operate somewhat as Dun & Bradstreet does for the business world and as the Thoroughbred Racing Service does in protecting racetracks against bad horses, jockeys, crooks, and gamblers. I have investigated the law of California and I am convinced that such a committee could operate within the protection of the law rendering confidential reports to subscribers. . . .

I think the function should be first to examine all screening procedures and to issue a general report on how they have operated, how unfair they are, what harm they do and make general recommendations for the protection of the industry and the elimination of all screening procedures except the ones this committee institutes. That of course would not be a screening procedure but would be an investigation and a report which would be made available to any person who is a subscriber to the service of the committee and who helps finance it. This would come within the nature of the confidential reports mentioned above. . . . If a person in the industry thought he wasn't being hired because of an adverse report, that person could then come to the committee and ask the committee to look at his special case and advise him of what the facts were so that if the report was adverse he would have an opportunity to get the help of the committee in correcting it if the committee believed it should help.

On March 18, 1953, Lukas wrote to Gang that they were making "slow but real progress." He had talked to George Heller and they still needed a formula to make everybody happy. Hand was not available.

We are thinking of persuading an outstanding citizen, like Paul Hoffman or Gerard Swope, to issue an invitation to all of the principals. It is hoped that Eric Johnston would accept such an invitation to discuss, along with the networks, advertising agencies, sponsors and artists guilds, as well as the American Legion, Catholic War Veterans, etc., some device along the lines of the Cushman proposal to sift the responsible and irresponsible charges. . . .

As it happened, what might be called the kosher HUAC never came to pass. But what killed this oxymoronic conception were not protests from the liberal left—who, for the most part, never heard about it.

It was more because of the prospective problems. Gang et al. had difficulty coming up with the right chairman, perhaps because all the names that were floated (from Hand to Truman) had only one thing in common—not one of them was Jewish. They had difficulty coming up with an acceptable sponsor, perhaps because their criteria of selection—an establishment organization with impeccable credentials—precluded their finding any acceptable takers. They lacked the cooperation of free-lance blacklisters, who may have regarded the scheme as potential competition that could put them out of business.

So this particular affirmative-action program for informers was aborted. It is revealing, however, that its chief proponents should have come from the one community that one would have thought was sensitized to the dangers of dealing with the enemy. The psychoanalyst Ernest Jones wrote, apropos the phenomenon of collaboration, "The key to understanding Quislingism and the other phenomena connected with it, is that they are all based on a peculiar inability to face or even to recognize the enemy. By an enemy I mean someone whose interests and endeavors run diametrically counter to one's own, so that one has no other emotional relationship to him than the attitude of sheer opposition."[19] Yet the premise of Martin Gang seems to have been that the problem with the real HUAC, and even more so with *Red Channels* and *Counterattack* and Aware, Inc., and the Legion, was that they went after the wrong guys, that they weren't *careful* Communist hunters, that their procedures were inadequate to the task of separating apparent Communists from real Communists.

Nothing is intrinsically wrong with a division of labor among pressure groups, and theoretically it would have been fitting and proper had the ACLU concentrated on protecting free speech and the CRC and AJC concentrated on protecting the reputation of the Jews. But in this case one suspects that a benign intention may have contributed to the maintenance of a less than benign system, one which was bad not only for the Jews but for everyone else as well. By working with rather than against HUAC both groups routinized betrayal, denied the reality of the enemy, and contributed to a moral numbing that long outlasted the blacklist which helped give rise to it.

When I asked Martin Gang in 1976 whether he was sorry his plan had never gone through, he told me, "I'm glad it never came to anything because on second thought, who needs some more private courts? It would have been terrible, to have a private court. That's what it would have amounted to, you know. Even if you had a fellow like Learned Hand sitting there, to me it would have been disgraceful. When I look back at it, it was a lousy idea. Looking back, between you and me I think it was better to have us individuals trying to straighten it out. At least you didn't give it the dignity of making it official or semiofficial."

When I first heard stories about a shrink who converted his patients into informers, I didn't believe them. I assumed it was all part of the paranoid folklore of the old left. After all, one rumor said he was an FBI man in disguise. Another said he was an FBI informant who turned over tapes of his private sessions to the House Un-American Activities Committee. A third rumor even had him flying tapes of his patients' free associations to Washington on his own private plane, a Taylor Bird. And yet from 1951 on, the rumors of a therapist who was taking people out of the Party persisted. As early as April 14, 1943, Victor Lasky had written of "a Hollywood psychiatrist" who "did a very good business with people who wanted to leave the Communist Party." He said, "Not every psychiatrist is equipped politically to do this job."[20] Novels about the period, like Arthur Laurents's *The Way We Were,* refer to "a rumor of a popular psychoanalyst who is employed by the FBI part time."[21] And memoirs gave fuller accounts—although, since no names are mentioned, it is difficult to tell whether they all are referring to the same person. Thus Alvah Bessie wrote in *Inquisition in Eden* of the time in 1949 he went for help (after dreaming that an FBI man was sleeping with his mother):

> [The] time came when I could not seem to cope with the enormity of our problems, and I finally did make an appointment with a highly recommended man (who was also guaranteed to be a Marxist with no Freudian nonsense about him) and spent fifty minutes spilling my guts, to all of which he made no reply except, "Um."
>
> Then he informed me that he would like me to start writing my autobiography: "Writers work better that way," he said, and he said he would refer me to another man as he was too busy to take me on.
>
> "Obviously," he said solemnly, "you need deep analysis, and it may take several years."

About two years later, Bessie wrote, he found out that the fellow

> had worked with a great many Hollywood writers and actors, and it was a matter of some astonishment to discover that at least six of his patients turned up at subsequent investigations of The Industry (in 1950 and 1951)—and every one of them was a stool pigeon. It also appeared that the man was not a psychiatrist at all; he was not even a

psychologist—but apparently he *was* an FBI man (if not the one who had slept with my mother).

In all justice, however, it must be said that the task that the so-called Marxist psychiatrist set me to must have acted as a form of self-therapy that lasted several years, for the depression disappeared and my ability to work returned. . . .[22]

Sterling Hayden sounded in his memoir *Wanderer* (1964) as if he might have been seeing the same man. He paid $500 a month, $25 an hour, and, he complained, "I did all the talking." Hayden reproduces the dialogue verbatim:

> "All right now, Doc, let's come to grips with something. I've got the toughest decision to make that has ever hung over my head. I'm in the Marine Corps Reserves. Since the war in Korea started, I've felt this thing closing down around me. Suppose they call me up and we come to the loyalty part: 'Are you now or have you ever been a member of the Communist Party?' What do I do then? If I say no, I perjure myself. If I say yes, and the word gets around, then I'm dead.
>
> "Every studio in town has blacklists. Some of them have a half-dozen lists. . . . I had a talk yesterday afternoon with my lawyer about how to protect myself. He thinks we should write a letter to J. Edgar Hoover asking if there isn't some way I can admit having been in the Party without screwing my whole life up."
>
> "That seems reasonable."
>
> "I'm not so sure. The FBI isn't going to let me off the hook without my implicating people who never did anything wrong—except belong to the Party."
>
> "Didn't your attorney suggest the FBI would probably treat this information confidentially?"

Hayden tells his "doc" that if he had his druthers he'd take a two-page ad in the trade papers and say yeah, he was a Communist and so were a lot of others but so what—it's HUAC and the self-proclaimed patriots who are the danger, not the innocents who happened to believe in a planned social order.

> "Why not do it then?"
>
> "Because I haven't got the guts, that's why. Maybe because I'm a parlor pink. Because I want to remain employable in this town long enough to finish this fucking analysis. Because when it comes time for

the divorce I'd like to be able to see my children, and the courts downtown are full of judges who would look askance at a divorced man who
was an ex-Communist to boot. That's why. How many reasons do you
want, sitting there on your throne?"

What's left of the hour is passed in total silence.

Hayden sees the FBI with his lawyer, one Martin Gang, and tells them
he'd prefer not to name others. They tell him it's up to him what he says,
but if he really wants to cooperate it's best to tell all and that's what he
does. Later, on the couch, Hayden says:

"Son of a bitch, Doc, I'm not sure I can take much more of this. . . .
I'll make no bones about it, I'm thinking of quitting analysis. . . . I'll
say this, too, that if it hadn't been for you I wouldn't have turned into a
stoolie for J. Edgar Hoover. I don't think you have the foggiest notion
of the contempt I have had for myself since the day I did that
thing. . . . Fuck it! And fuck you, too."

By analytic hour number 300 Hayden has received his subpoena to appear before HUAC, has met informally with William Wheeler, the Committee's chief investigator, and is scheduled to appear. Our patient is as
conflicted as ever:

"Doc, I can't go through with it. Since the subpoena two weeks back
I've tried and tried to convince myself. They know I was a Party member—they don't want information, they want to put on a show, and I'm
the star. They've already agreed to go over the questions with me in advance. It's a rigged show: radio and TV and the papers. I'm damned no
matter what I do. Cooperate and I'm a stool pigeon. Shut my mouth
and I'm a pariah."

"I suggest, Mr. Hayden"—the analyst's sober voice—"that you try
and relax—just lie down. . . . Now then, may I remind you there's
really not much difference, so far as you yourself are concerned, between talking to the FBI in private and taking the stand in Washington. You have already informed, after all. You have excellent counsel,
you know, and the chances are that the public will—in time, perhaps—
regard you as an exemplary man, who once made a mistake."[23]

There was, as it turned out, one man at the center of the rumors, the
memoirs, the myths, and the folk legends, and his name is Ernest Philip
Cohen. He was not a psychoanalyst and he never even got his degree as a

psychologist, although he had done three years of graduate work in psychology at the University of Chicago. He came briefly to Hollywood in 1937 to begin practicing as a therapist. In 1939 he went up to Seattle for more graduate work at the University of Washington. There he met his wife, Liz, and joined the Communist Party.

He returned to Hollywood as a lay analyst in 1942 and like the Unidentified Guest in T. S. Eliot's *The Cocktail Party,* he seemed to take over the lives of everybody in the room. Only in Cohen's case the room was the weird Hollywood red subculture of the 1930s and 1940s, where the line between artist and hack, capitalist and Communist, Marxist and Freudian was always thin, frequently invisible, sometimes nonexistent. And whatever charisma this ordinary-looking man might have possessed on his own, it was augmented by the policy conflicts his peculiar role inevitably generated.

Underlying his influence was the fact of the Communist Party's then-current rule against its members going into psychoanalysis. Freud and Marx were regarded as antithetical. On the most elementary level, as Dr. Isidore Zifferstein, a politically liberal Beverly Hills analyst observes, "There were ideological reasons for feeling that being psychoanalyzed was not the Marxist thing to do: you were subjecting yourself to the propaganda of the enemy. Psychoanalysis is basically the tool of the class enemy to justify the inequities of society by attributing them to flaws in personality rather than the system."

So the Party had a double fear: that the analysand would be ideologically poisoned; and since it is a rule of psychoanalysis that the patient reveals everything, that the Party's security as a secret organization would be compromised.

There was never unanimity on these matters, however, and the ideological battle was fought out in the journals of the left. Thus Joseph Wortis had written in the *New Masses* in 1945 that although psychoanalysis made a lot of important advances and contributions to our understanding of personality ("it strengthened scientific materialism at a time when religious idealism was influencing certain schools of psychiatry, it helped shatter taboos against an examination of sexuality and the family," etc.), it nevertheless had four basic defects that it would never overcome: first, the Freudians' belief in the preponderant influence of the unconscious "stood everything on its head by regarding social situations as the expression of people's ideas or unconscious strivings"; Freud had lost interest in the internal physiological basis of mental function, whereas the Party believed Pavlov had demonstrated its centrality; Freud's scientific method was "antiquarian" rather than sociological; and Freud's social framework was too narrow—an implicit acceptance of middle-class standards. (This last Wortis found revealed in Freudianism's attitude toward women, in its notion of what is normal, in its standards of success and failure, in its attitude toward social progress, and in its fundamental pessimism. "It is fascinated by the past at the expense of the present.")[24]

Five years later a critique in the Party journal *Political Affairs* by Henry Winston was essentially the same:

> There follows from Freudian psychoanalysis a Freudian sociology which sees the driving force of the history of class societies, not in class antagonisms and class struggle, but in the instinctual drives and conflicts of the individual. . . . Who owns what means of production, the class struggle and the role of class ideologies in the formation of consciousness are all ignored. The result is that analysis ends up as a tool and rationalizer of imperialism since one can make no concessions to Freudianism . . . without serving reaction.[25]

Although many did their best to reconcile Freud and Marx (including whole schools of therapies built around such figures as Erich Fromm and others) the dominant Party view as late as 1954 was expressed by Joseph Clayton in *Political Affairs*. It was natural, he thought, in a period of what he viewed as decay, frustration, confusion, and (thus) mental illness that the people should be told that:

> their mental disturbances bear no relationship to the sick, corrupt society in which they live, but rather are caused by certain inborn, unchanging, biologically determined, bestial "instincts" repressed in their "unconscious" minds.
> [It is] a major ideological weapon to use against the Marxist interpretation of history, against the working-class method of class struggle, and against the scientifically based perspective of growing sections of humanity that the path to the solution of all major problems lies through the reorganization of society in Socialism and Communism.[26]

Despite the ideological resistance to and the bureaucratic edicts against psychoanalysis, Phil Cohen was an example of the Party's concession to the American—or at least the Hollywood—reality. Hollywood had the prestigious personalities, the generous donors, and the potential for influencing mass culture that the Party wanted, but only the Freudians had access to the psychic relief the talent needed. The deceptively simple solution: send the patient to a Party therapist. For although the Party had no faith in the bourgeois principle of doctor-patient confidentiality, it did have confidence in Party discipline. This had an ideological advantage as well, since Communist Party therapists were expected to temper Freud with Marx. The "referral mechanism" was often the doctors' unit, a local subsection of the CP, whose members-in-good-standing took on Party patients.

Enter Phil Cohen. He established Party contacts in Los Angeles in the 1940s and soon had a thriving practice, as first members of the Party's doctors' unit and then friends recommending friends sent patients his way. He was, despite his lack of formal training (not unusual in those days), effective in his work and his reputation quickly spread in Party circles. Before he left Seattle Cohen had become disillusioned with and disappeared from the Communist Party—although he never really let the Party know the extent of his disaffection and he kept most of his patients. There were only a handful of acceptable therapists for Party people and, given the pressures of left-wing Hollywood life of the day, more than enough patients to go around. So Cohen got more than his share. These included, in addition to Hayden, the actors Lloyd Bridges and John Garfield; the actress Dorothy Comingore; a script girl, Judy Raymond; Joan LaCour, a writer and activist in many progressive organizations; writers—Leo and Pauline Townsend, Richard Collins, Isobel Lennart, Elizabeth Wilson, Ann Roth Richards and Robert Richards, David Hertz, and Sylvia Richards; and the agent Meta Rosenberg.

Today Cohen is in his early sixties and looks like a mild-mannered dentist—baldish, slightly portly, glasses. I interviewed him in Los Angeles in the spring of 1974 at the Château Marmont Hotel. He had come down from Santa Barbara, where he teaches photography at an arts institute.

He told me that as an undergraduate at the University of Washington he had majored in premed and psychology. Then from 1936 through 1938 he did graduate work at the University of Chicago toward a Ph.D. in psychology, earning his way as a photographer until "the dollars ran out." He "went into practice in Hollywood for a year or two," then "up to Seattle," where he did another "two or three years" of graduate work in sociology and was a teaching assistant in social work. He also practiced there as a part-time therapist. In 1939 he joined what he now says was an open section of the Communist Party in Seattle and worked as a section organizer in the Negro community. "I joined the Party as an anti-fascist," he says. "That was during the Popular Front or United Front period, whatever it was called." The Party meetings were open to the public; most of the members registered to vote Communist. "There was no attempt to conceal it."

Asked how he felt about the Nazi-Soviet Pact, he says, "I saw it as a tactical move and never felt there was any entente between them, and I don't see how anyone could have."

At the outset of the war, a medical examiner pronounced him unfit for military duty. In the early 1940s he returned to Hollywood, where he was to practice therapy for the next decade.

Cohen says, "I dropped out of the Party officially some time around 1941 or 1942, when I first came down here. I never appeared at any Party meetings." Asked why, he says, "I began to feel that the Party was not an adequate instrument." In Seattle he had discussions with Party officials on such matters as, "What happened to the democratic front?" "What is the true role of the Soviet Union?" "Why are you deceiving the American Party members and saying it is not really an extension of the Soviet Communist Party?" He was called to account for teaching Marxism in a non-Marxist way. But whatever his formal relations with the Communist Party, informally he was in good enough graces to be on the list of approved therapists. So when the Party ordered its members to drop out of analysis with non-Party therapists, "The CP became reconciled to me as one of two or three doctors they didn't insist on their people leaving."

During the 1940s, for better or worse, Cohen was a fixture in the Hollywood left. Other therapists cite at least three reasons for Cohen's success: that psychologists and social workers charge lower fees than psychiatrists; that radicals distrusted M.D.'s, which by definition psychiatrists are; and that there weren't enough therapists who were Party members to go around. Whatever the reasons, his practice thrived.

Sterling Hayden is not the only one of his former patients who has attributed his decision to cooperate with the authorities in part to Cohen. The screenwriter Sylvia Richards recalls that everywhere she turned—her boss, her therapist, her lawyer—she got the same message: cooperation with the House Un-American Activities Committee seemed the courageous and the correct thing to do. "I was the [sort of] person who wanted to please my friends, please my analyst, take care of my kids, and not be associated with the Communist Party. I thought of that line from E. M. Forster—but loyalty to my friends meant loyalty to people like Dick Collins, who was a cooperative witness, versus loyalty to the 'state,' which meant loyalty to the USSR and the Party. I thought I was choosing my friends."

Cohen gained his influence in part as one of a triumvirate of opinion trustees—the others were Gang and William Wheeler, the Democratic "good guy" investigator for HUAC who was willing to make it as painless as possible for those who were willing to play the game. The three of them, who saw themselves as basically humanistic liberals, functioned collectively as a support system for those ripe for cooperating with the investigators.

Progressive Hollywood was a small town, and as in any small town, the views of "doc" carried no little weight. And this particular doc's style was to socialize with his patients. It should be said that with fewer than three hundred card-carrying Communists in the Hollywood contingent, and the leftist habit of socializing among the faithful, even if Cohen had scruples against patient-association it might have been difficult to obey them. Also, he seems to have been drawn to celebrities. Sterling Hayden first got in touch with Cohen on behalf of his mother, who had problems of her own, but after one session Cohen told him, "Mr. Hayden, I have talked with your mother. . . . But I'm just wondering, Mr. Hayden, about you. . . . "[27] He was also attracted to the ladies.

"It was weird," recalled Pauline Lauber Finn, who was active in any number of left-wing causes of the day and whose husband was a leading attorney for many of those who had run afoul of HUAC. "Right off, he asked a physician I knew to bring me to dinner. His wife had a backache and rarely appeared socially."

Although the Party didn't like analysis, it accommodated itself to a certain amount of idiosyncrasies and attitudes when the Party member/patient was important enough. But when the member was of no particular consequence the Party could be quite adamant. The screenwriter Joan LaCour, who was blacklisted and wrote under a pseudonym, recalls becoming a patient of Phil Cohen's. "My sister knew about him and I had a breakdown. He was weird. He would get me slightly swacked on brandy to get me opened up. But he did help me personally at the time with my problems. He helped me buck up.

"He caused a tremendous commotion in the political arena because analysis was grounds for dismissal from the CP. This position was rigid in 1948. I know because I volunteered that I was in analysis and objected to the concept that it was incompatible with being a good Party member. I said they'd have to kick me out. I was subsequently visited by a Party functionary, who met me at my house and gave me my walking papers."

Whatever the Party's views on Freud, Cohen was something more (or less) than an orthodox Freudian. I asked him whether he felt socializing with his patients was appropriate. "It is not the function of the therapist to direct people's behavior," Cohen told me, but, he added, people would ask his political advice on social occasions—patients and ex-patients and spouses of patients among them—and occasionally he would give it. He made a distinction between "supportive" therapy ("there isn't any problem there about seeing and advising people socially") and "analytic depth" therapy ("there, there can be a very big problem").

Whether or not Phil Cohen violated Freud's classic canons on the doctor-patient relationship is less important than the larger issue of what the appropriate role is for the therapist who believes his patient is about to commit career suicide as the result of irrational, conflicting inner drives. For that was the way he regarded Elizabeth Wilson, the actress-writer—according to her friend Helen Levitt, who was married to a blacklisted writer, and a person very much on the scene as John Garfield's secretary. All Mrs. Wilson remembers about those sessions is her therapist's "deafening silence," but at the time, says her friend, "Betty would come and tell me what Phil was telling her. 'The blacklisted people are not facing the reality of concentration camps,' is what he was telling her." One assumes Elizabeth Wilson's personal circumstances and background as well as her therapist led to her decision to name names. Another close friend of hers speculates, "Betty was afraid of going to jail because she would be leaving a two-year-old. It had to do with her own experience as a child. Her mother had left her father, and Betty had had to help take care of her younger brother."* Without presuming to know why she did what she did, or what Phil Cohen did or did not say to Elizabeth Wilson, who prefers not to talk about it, one notes that in September 1951 she appeared as a cooperative witness before the House Un-American Activities Committee.[28]

The mix of CP secrecy, the mystique of secrecy, and Cohen's peculiar style undoubtedly contributed to the feeling on the left—especially after a number of his patients turned informer—that he was at best not to be trusted, at worst working with (or for) the FBI. As one of his peers put it, "I've always thought of him as a psychopath—not a guy motivated by a

---

* When I asked Mrs. Wilson for her comment, she wrote, "As for my being afraid of going to jail, that is such an over-simplification of my dilemma (though a kindly one, well meant, I suspect by whomever) that anyone who knows me would reject it as just that."

serious commitment to a social philosophy, but one who did whatever his conflicting drives motivated him to do and then rationalized it."

Had the screenwriter David Hertz been anyone else's patient, his strange disappearance and death would probably have been attributed to his tragic emotional problems, and he might have been mourned and eventually forgotten by all but a few close friends. But Hertz was a patient of Phil Cohen's, and so his death became part of the Cohen legend. As Pauline Finn recalled it: "David Hertz returned from the war with problems, including a separation from his wife. He went to Phil Cohen and was so enthralled with this father figure that he felt he needed to fly an airplane like Phil. Phil felt that would be good therapy. David had told me he got nauseated whenever he went up; he almost died when he went up solo. Soon after that, he took the plane one night over the ocean, and he never returned. Some said it was suicide, others that it was incompetence at the wheel. There was an all-night vigil at the writer Paul Jarrico's house and all anyone could talk about was Phil Cohen. He had so many patients."

As might be expected, there were other sides to the story. Phil Cohen, who told me, "I don't discuss my patients with anybody," offered a different version: "Hertz came back from the army and found his wife living with a man in their home, and she wouldn't leave him or kick the man out, and she wouldn't divorce Hertz or give him the time of day. Then, when he was lost, all of a sudden she became the tearful, loving wife and played it for all it was worth and she was very hostile to me. I think . . . her hostility was because I knew about her true role."

The significance of such specific case histories has less to do with the disputed facts—which will never be known to outsiders—than with the mythic quality of the Rashomon-rumors about Cohen's practice. Even Pauline Finn, however, who regarded him as "a most unattractive man to socialize with," conceded that as an ex-Communist with the blessing of the left wing he seemed to be helpful in "making one a more useful member of the left. One patient said she'd never been able to get up [in political meetings] and make a speech, but with Phil Cohen's help she was able to get up and second a motion. He helped women writers get over their blocks. I remember he had Judy Raymond [who also became an informer] write out her life on sheafs of paper."

A number of his patients who informed before the Un-American Activities Committee deny that he had much, if anything, to do with it—at least insofar as they could tell at the time or figure out twenty-five years later. Richard Collins, who is quite explicit about the circumstances and people who contributed to his decision to cooperate with the Committee, says, "Phil Cohen may have said something but I don't remember if I was still going to him or not, but he may have. . . .

"I think if you had gone in and said to Phil Cohen, 'I'll take the Fifth,' he would have gone along with that. I don't think it was his role to convert. But the fact is that some people who went to him did take the Fifth; my ex-wife was one of them—Dorothy Comingore."

The screenwriter Leo Townsend has an equally benign recollection. "Well, he knew a lot of people in the Party. Whether he was in the Party or not, I wasn't sure. I knew he had been, I thought he had been. But when I went to him, I had already left the Party. I went for other reasons. Not to get out of the Party. I was already out of it. And I told him.

"I testified after I had had sessions with him but not through him. I went to him for personal reasons, not political. And I didn't tell him I was going to testify. I wasn't his patient at that time. This was completely on my own. . . ."

Townsend recalls Cohen as "a charming man. Yes, very much so. Shy, but a nice man. And his wife, Liz—she's Irish and Phil's Jewish. They had a good marriage. I think they still have it. Pauline and I saw them quite a bit; she had been in the Party, too, up in Washington state. So naturally we talked a lot about the Party and it would be in that area that he might have subliminally suggested leaving. . . . During the professional hour he never did. I think he never said a goddamn thing to me. He'd say, 'What do *you* think?'"

Townsend says: "I left the Party because I wasn't a person. I just did what I was told. I went to Phil Cohen because I had an ego problem. It wasn't there."

Sylvia Richards' former husband Bob and his new wife, Ann, both took the Fifth before the Committee but told her that Phil Cohen attempted to influence them. "I don't think that Phil actively set out to make me take any positions about HUAC," she says. "I look back and see he assumed I had free will. But the slightest remark from him, I'd follow. I agreed with him on the Party." Once she had decided to inform, "Phil set up a meeting with an FBI guy named [Mark] Bright. And Dick [Collins] and Phil and I met at Phil's house with Wheeler."

The truth, in a way, is less important than the mystery. Abe Polonsky, the writer-director who when his turn came before the Committee invoked his constitutional privilege not to talk, says, "We're still trying to find out if Cohen worked for the FBI. I know he was reporting confidences to the FBI. There's no question about that. And he was turning patients into stool pigeons. He didn't reveal his politics until the last minute. The dates are very important. We know Phil Cohen was pretending not to be that, up to the minute when he became that other kind of character. So he carried on his fantasies over at the FBI. But not out in reality where other people can notice and see that they are going to be involved in this great favor he is doing them."

Amidst the welter of rumors, charges, memories, and speculations, these things can be said for certain: first, at least a dozen of Cohen's patients cooperated with the Committee, but some of his patients did not; second, he did fly a private plane, but, as Leo Townsend told me, "I knew damn well his little Taylor craft couldn't get to Washington, D.C., because one weekend we flew up to see some mutual friends and we damn near didn't get to Grass Valley"; third, Cohen used to attend football games with Bill Wheeler, the HUAC investigator. As Wheeler recalls, "The agent George Rosenberg had season tickets to the Rams games, and we all used to go. (George and his brother were brought up by the Hearsts. Incidentally, Richard Collins used to go to the games, too, and his ex-wife, Dorothy Comingore, is the one who played Charles Foster Kane's girlfriend in *Citizen Kane*.) George's wife, Meta Rosenberg, came before the Committee and she was a cooperative witness."

In talking with me Cohen explained his role without apology.* He denied that he tried to convert anybody into anything, insisting that as a therapist he merely attempted to assist his patients to gain insights into

---

* After our interview was under way (but not as a ground rule for it), Cohen expressed the preference that I omit his name from my book on the grounds that his current employer, a "superpatriot," would fire him for having once been a Communist. I told Cohen that while I was not out to embarrass him, I could not make such a promise since his name and role were a part of the history and record of the epoch, but that after I completed the book I would decide what to do, taking into account not only what he had said but also my other obligations.

There is always a tension between the claims of history and the claims of privacy, but in this case the former seemed to me to have an edge for a number of reasons. First, Cohen's request for anonymity posits the possibility of a specific injury that on its face is improbable. (Given his own role as a supporter of HUAC in the 1950s, it seemed to me that even a "superpatriot" boss could forgive him his forty-year-old indiscretions.) But more important, anonymity precludes historical cross-examination, after-the-fact checking and cross-checking, the testing of specific memory, the pyramiding of scholarship. Those people who worked with congressional investigators behind the scenes made their secrecy bargains with the Committee, but such understandings are precisely the sorts of contracts whose hidden clauses journalists and scholars ought to scrutinize, if only in the interest of preventing their recurrence. It is because the facts were hidden then, that it seems useful to open them for inspection now, while enough survivors remain to improve and refine the record.

their problems and the strength to deal with them. And he denied ever violating the therapist-patient rule of confidentiality and said he never turned over the "life stories" of his patients (not all of whom were asked to write them) to the FBI. In fact, he told me it was the Party and not the bureau or HUAC that tried to get him to break his professional code. "It actually was raised with me one time by the Party: they felt I ought to inform them of any anti-Party things that came up in the course of therapy. I wouldn't do it. They would ask me, 'What about so-and-so?' I'd say, 'I'm sorry, I can't discuss so-and-so with you in any way. He has become a patient and I don't discuss my patients with anybody; I don't discuss them with my wife and I don't discuss them with the Party.' . . . The implication was that the therapist for the Party should try to influence people toward the Party positions, that you should think of the Party before you think of the welfare of the person."

He confirmed, however, that he did have independent ties to the law-enforcement community in California while he was a therapist, although he insists that these had nothing to do with politics. Cohen is vague about exactly when he got into law enforcement, estimating that it was "in 1948, 1950—long after. But the law-enforcement work that I was involved in at that time still wouldn't have anything to do with that. I was involved in criminal activity, not political." He worked as a captain in the sheriff's office in Inyo County, ranking third under the sheriff and deputy sheriff. There he wore a uniform and served as chief of detectives in a small department "involved in street-level enforcement" and "investigations." He also worked as a training officer, organized an air squadron, and was in charge of search-and-rescue operations.

"Later, when Pat Brown was the attorney general of California [1951–58], I became a special agent in the state Department of Justice. But my assignment was organized crime. Syndicate operations. As far as I knew, they didn't even have a political unit." When Brown became governor in 1959, Cohen returned to the sheriff's office as a consultant and in the early 1960s "drifted back accidentally into photography."

He recalls that "some time after I had left the Party, [Special Agent] Bright came to see me. He phoned and made an appointment. He talked to me about myself and my own participation in the Party. . . . He and I developed a personal relationship of sorts. As I got involved in law enforcement—these two events are not connected, the law enforcement and the political thing—then, obviously, he was one of my contacts at the bureau."

Cohen first met Wheeler "at a football game. And then I got involved in law enforcement and we had mutual friends in the law-enforcement community. So if he subpoenaed somebody, then there was no secret that he knew, and then I would talk to the person, and I would say, I want your permission to talk to Bill Wheeler." And when he got that green light Cohen would say to Wheeler, " 'When so-and-so left [the Party] he really left.' That kind of thing. And I would often, when talking to so-and-so, persuade him he was better off talking to Bill rather than holding back and trying to be a hero against his own conviction."

Cohen's personal attitude on the informing issue may be indicated by his observation twenty-five years later, "I think most of them could turn around with justice and say, 'I was the one who was betrayed originally. I was lied to and used by these people.' It's a matter of who's the betrayed person: the person in the Party who lied to you about the objectives of the Party and whom you later turned in, or you?"

Even as Cohen's practice thrived because of Party referrals, whether from the doctors' unit or through informal contacts—tales of writers' blocks broken, speeches made, or what have you—once his patients started to be known as cooperative witnesses before HUAC, his role as red therapist was quickly over: "There was a very very strong campaign on to break me, to try to persuade people not to refer to me. The breaking point was in 1951—after the group of cooperative witnesses testified.* At that point my income suddenly went down seventy-five percent. And that's when some of the people who were still in the Party and were still coming to see me were given absolute orders that they couldn't come back, which was very distressing for them. I had a hard time referring them to somebody else for therapy." At that point Cohen says he got more heavily involved in law enforcement. "For a long time I was doing both and maintained my practice as well, but of course by then I couldn't make a living from my practice, though I maintained it for ten years more."

Townsend agrees that "the Communists did Phil Cohen in. He lost patients—so much so that he could not afford office rent, and that's when he went back into photography."

* The first three cooperative witnesses after Parks—Sterling Hayden, Meta Rosenberg, and Richard Collins—were all Cohen patients (and, inter alia, Gang clients). In an affecting, albeit politically charged, memoir published in the mid-80s in Hilton Kramer's new *Criterion*, a neoconservative journal, Sterling Hayden's stepson asserts that the anonymous therapist in Hayden's memoir was not Phil Cohen. He provides no evidence for this claim, but if he is right, it does not change the fact that the therapist, whoever he was, played the same role as Cohen in facilitating Hayden's journey on the informer's path.

William Wheeler is quite definite about what Cohen did and didn't do. "Because he had been in the CP, he got all the referrals from the doctors' unit. And then Phil started taking [his patients] out of the Party. He didn't help me, in the sense that he didn't tell me who his patients were. I never questioned him on who his patients were. He was giving me too much help. And then, when this stuff broke wide open, well, then, these Communist doctors said, 'He's unreliable,' and they broke his business. He had a booming practice—John Garfield and a lot of top-flight movie stars—and they destroyed him."

How did Cohen help Wheeler?

"He said, 'If you subpoena one of my patients, I'll try to condition him to testify.' "

Condition or convince?

"What's the difference? It was part of the therapy. The whole thing."

The point is not whether the left is right or wrong in believing Cohen leaked confidential data to the FBI and in other ways knowingly violated his professional ethics. And certainly the point is not how the Party broke his practice when they had reason to believe he was "unreliable," especially since the Party was responsible for building up his practice in the first place. It is interesting that Cohen himself talks of a double life as hip therapist and Dick Tracy cop and at least in his own mind is able to keep these existences separate, even though he evidently mingled them at football games and at the FBI, but this schizo quality (whether real or fantasized) is less significant for its singularity than its typicality. He was not alone in muddying the boundaries between the public and the private, the political and the social, the patriotic and the subversive. He was a master of manipulation operating at the murky crossroads where the mystique of Freud met the mystique of Marx.

Cohen got into memoirs and novels and once received an anonymous reference in an exposé in *Frontier* magazine,[29] but he never really made the papers at the time. He never was named as a former Communist by any of his informing friends or patients. It did not seem unusual that he defined the requirements of his profession in terms of the requirements of the state. He was part of the Hollywood system, the informer system, and the Communist Party system. What makes this fantastic character interesting and significant is that he was regarded as part of the landscape.

———

Martin Gang, acting under what he discerned to be the lawyer's ethic, put the interests of his clients first, and the result was to get *them* back to work but simultaneously to validate the blacklist system that kept others out in the cold. His style of translating moral problems into tactical ones undoubtedly facilitated the transformation of many of his clients from accused radical to informer. Whether their long-run interests were served by this transition is a question I shall explore (see below, Part V).

The Jewish organizations also lived up to what they saw as their professional ethic—to protect the reputation of the Jewish community (and thereby curtail the rise of anti-Semitism) and to assist Jewish victims. But they, too, through their back-room dealings, not only ended up strengthening the chief agents of the repression but did so at the expense of other Jewish constituents and non-Jewish citizens in the community at large, and at the expense of the broader principles of political and civil rights they were organized to uphold.

Phil Cohen is perhaps too fantastic a character to be emblematic. And yet his links left and right, his role as double agent (of his patients and of the repression), was no less real than that of Gang or other blacklist intermediaries. His viewpoint—that to throw away one's career and risk prison to protect principles one has long ago discarded is a disguised death wish—was held by many in and out of his profession.

It was perhaps poetic justice that the Party's covert nature made the FBI's job easier since it had only to cultivate links with a handful of "approved" professionals—doctors, lawyers, and therapists—to tap into the whole red subculture.

Collectively these case studies are most significant in their suggestion that none of these collaborators felt he had violated professional obligations. Each firmly believed that serving the immediate needs of the client, the constituency, the patient, would contribute to the common good.

6.

Guilty Bystanders

IF THE INTERNAL-SECURITY BUREAUCRACY and its anti-Communist crusade defined Hollywood's political environment, and the collaborators both shaped and reflected the community's moral environment, it was the motion-picture industry itself that dominated, and indeed constituted, the economic environment.

Many analysts blame worries over the industry's economic condition for the studios' overnight accommodation to HUAC. Hollywood had reached a prosperity peak in 1946. "Every night," said *Variety*, "was Saturday night." Eighty to ninety million moviegoers paid over half a billion dollars for the weekly habit. But with the war's end began a decline, and by 1957 weekly attendance had fallen by half and profits by more than 70 percent. Changing consumption patterns (related to the so-called postwar baby boom), the advent of television (the number of television sets sold annually went from fourteen thousand in 1947 to 32 million in 1954), the currency freeze abroad (studios could build up currency credits in foreign countries but not take the money out), and the 1948 Supreme Court decision in the Paramount case (putting an end to a variety of industry practices leading to forced disvesture, so that the corporations that produced and distributed films could no longer also own the chains of theaters in which they were exhibited)—combined to scare the old moguls. They were not in a mood to risk further box-office decline due to political controversy. Concern verged on panic.

At the end of the war, the motion-picture industry had been dominated by five major companies—Warner Brothers, Loew's (which owned M-G-M), Paramount, RKO, and Twentieth Century-Fox—which collectively accounted for nearly 70 percent of the box-office receipts in three thousand theaters, mostly in metropolitan areas, across the nation. These major companies were responsible for 75 percent of the top-billed features each year, half the total output of the industry. Each had a stable of contracted writers, directors, producers, cameramen, and other artists and technicians.[1]

"I think if at the very beginning the heads of the studios had stood up to the Committee, none of this would have happened, or it would have happened on a very reduced scale," speculates Leon Kaplan, who worked as general counsel for M-G-M during the blacklist years and now is a senior partner in one of Hollywood's largest law firms. "If they had said, 'Look, we have zealously watched the content of our motion pictures, and you can't point to one sequence or one picture that is of the Communist line or destructive to the American ideals, and we're going to continue to do that, and beyond that—what a man does politically—it's not our business, and if you want to take us on you're going to have the whole weight of the industry fighting you,' I think this posture would have ended it."

Whether or not Kaplan is right, the fact is that not merely the majors went along. In addition to the big five there were the little three—Universal, Columbia, and United Artists—who had all-important, though limited, exhibition access to the screens of the big five's theaters. After the Paramount decision they were able to distribute even more of their pictures, particularly those by independents, in the best first-run houses. United Artists, the leading distributor for independent producers, experimented on the margins of the blacklist—that is, distributing a number of movies written by blacklisted writers under pseudonyms—but they never challenged it openly.

There were two major talent agencies (William Morris and Music Corporation of America); three powerful talent guilds—the Screen Writers Guild, with over one thousand members, the slightly smaller Screen Actors Guild, and the Screen Directors Guild, with just over eight hundred members;[2] a vast array of trade and craft unions, organized (after a vicious jurisdictional dispute culminating in the violent Hollywood strikes of 1945 and 1946) by the International Alliance of Theatrical Stage Employees (IATSE), affiliated with the American Federation of Labor; an Association of Motion Picture Producers (AMPP) made up of the majors and a few independents, which served to negotiate on behalf of the studios with the guilds and unions; and two daily trade papers, *Daily Variety* and *Hollywood Reporter,* the "bibles" of the industry. As the Hollywood columnist and critic Ezra Goodman observed, "The Hollywood press does not merely chronicle the show. It is part of the show itself."[3] And then there were the gossip columnists, who did the political addition and subtraction that enabled people to keep track of who was supposed to be in and out of trouble (marital, political, you name it).

Under the reigning political philosophy—what fashionable academics liked to call "pluralism"—the political economy of Hollywood could not have been in better shape, despite the troubling economic trends. According to the prevailing political folklore, our lives, our liberty, our pursuit of happiness are creatures of our diversity. This was a political elaboration on Adam Smith's economic proposition that the pursuit of individual self-interest results in the public good. Or, as James Madison wrote in *Federalist 51,* a society "broken into so many parts, interests and classes of citizens" was the best guarantee of civil and political rights.

This theory of countervailing powers had a pleasant symmetry. And yet, after HUAC arrived in Hollywood, it didn't seem to work. Each element of the community indeed sought its own goals, worked for its own ends, fought for its own interests, yet the result was not a series of benign cancellations of evil. Fifth Amendment–invokers and name-namers did not offset each other. The Motion Picture Alliance for the Preservation of American Ideals (whose Statement of Principles said, "It knows that co-existence is a myth and neutrality is impossible: that anyone who is not FIGHTING Communism is HELPING Communism") was not offset by the Committee for the First Amendment. The talent guilds seemed to play more of a self-preserving than a countervailing role. The informer system was not challenged by the many who believed that naming names violated elementary canons of personal loyalty and decency. Rather, it permitted those whose actions reinforced it to harbor the illusion that they were opposing it. The clash of private interests resulted not in the public interest's being served but in the blacklist and, with it, the triumph of corruption, the institutionalization of betrayal, collaboration, and defection from responsibility. Pluralism, at least in the land of the happy ending, didn't work. The informer was both a casualty and a causer of this process.

Each player in the game discovered the best of reasons not to protest its unjust rules. Before he died in 1972, the writer Robert Aurthur recalled complaining about the blacklisting of an actor to producer Fred Coe, and asking him to do something about it. And Coe told him what they could do:

> "Right on this phone we will call the newspapers and summon a press conference for tomorrow. I will let you use this office, and you can tell the reporters exactly what's going on. At the end of the confer-

ence I will roll a carpet from here to the elevator and I will have photographers lining both sides taking your picture as you leave." Coe looked me right in the eye. "You will then get into the elevator," he said. "The doors will close and you'll never come back." A pause, and then he said, "But you'll be a big hero."[4]

William Wheeler sits on the patio of his home in the redwood forests of northern California and looks back: "The idea was to prove that these people were Communists. It didn't make a hell of a lot of difference who they were, in a sense. In retrospect, I just wonder if I did what was right. I often wonder. I've thought a lot about this. But you see, I was a cop. I'd been trained as a cop. And when you work for Congress you say to yourself, 'If this is what I'm assigned to do, I'm going to do it and I'm going to do a good job.' But if I had known as I know now, I don't know. I destroyed a lot of people and I think they destroyed themselves."

At the outset, it appeared as if the profit ethic might subordinate itself to the anti-Communist ethic. How else explain what happened to Howard Da Silva, the actor who appeared as a belligerently uncooperative witness before HUAC immediately after Larry Parks's tearful *mea culpa*? "He cried, so I shrieked. What else do you do?" asks Da Silva. Whatever his motives, his well-publicized appearance caused a problem for Irving Allen, the producer of an upcoming RKO film called *Slaughter Trail* (1951), which included footage of Da Silva as a captain of the U.S. cavalry. Because he was the first uncooperative witness after the Ten, it was important that a symbolic example be set. The solution: Allen announced that Da Silva's role would be spliced out and reenacted by Brian Donlevy at a cost of $100,000. In fact, what appeared to be a patriotic act was probably a financial calculation. The producer would invest $100,000 in splicing and reshooting as a form of insurance to avoid the possible millions in revenue losses not only from possible picketing of *Slaughter Trail* but from potential trouble on future projects.[5] After this episode Da Silva embarked on a personal crusade against the blacklist. A friend remarked, "Even when he was talking to a group of Hadassah ladies he would work in a pitch against the blacklist."

It would have been ironic indeed if the free enterprisers of the American Legion had been unwilling to accommodate themselves to the capitalist ethic. But their interest was in consolidating political influence, and they were only too happy to bend the blacklist system to the requirements of the studio system. In this respect the blacklist proceedings slowly took on the aspect of a gigantic charade, with all players going through the motions but none under any real illusion that they were serving any higher god than the Mammon of self-interest.

Even such compromises, however, were transacted in the language of capitalism footnoted by the language of anti-Communism. Two letters written in 1952 from Paramount's Frank Freeman to the Legion's O'Neil tell it like it was. The first letter (June 9) explains why Paramount had not fired an assistant to the director of the movie *Roman Holiday,* even though he had invoked the Fifth Amendment before HUAC after the voluble screenwriter Martin Berkeley named him as a Communist:

> Several years ago, Paramount Corp. acquired the stock of Liberty Pictures, Inc., a company which had contracts with the director William Wyler. One of the conditions of employment of Mr. Wyler by Liberty, and a condition Paramount accepted when they acquired the stock, was he would have a right to select his assistants and also any writer he desired to work for him so long as the obligation created for the writer's services did not exceed $50,000, without the approval of Liberty and later of Paramount.
>
> At the time Paramount acquired the stock of Liberty, William Wyler had as one of his assistants a young man by the name of Lester Koenig. Mr. Koenig was under contract to Liberty on an annual basis. . . . When [this] renewal took place, none of us here at Paramount had any knowledge or idea that Lester Koenig had ever been a member of the CP, for had we such knowledge we would not have permitted the renewal of the contract regardless of Mr. Wyler's right to select his own assistant. . . .
>
> I have had several conversations with Lester Koenig in connection with his actions before HUAC. I have strongly urged him to again appear before the Committee and answer all questions and to give them any facts, if he has any, that might be helpful to them. I have been told by Mr. Koenig that William Wyler has also requested him to do this.
>
> When in New York I explained to you the problem that confronted Paramount in connection with Lester Koenig and the urgency of getting the picture *Roman Holiday* started and completed. To accomplish this, the services of Lester Koenig in helping William Wyler to coordinate and to bring together the elements necessary to complete the work were essential. The failure to have him do this could have seriously jeopardized the whole venture. Mr. Koenig's name will in no way appear in connection with the production of this picture. . . . When his contract expires in August it will not be renewed. It may be a few weeks beyond the expiration date of his contract will be necessary for the completion of the picture.

It is my belief, although I can give no assurance of this, that upon Mr. Koenig's return to America after completion of the picture, he will appear before the House Un-American Activities Committee of his own accord and will then and there answer the questions which he refused to answer at the hearing in Los Angeles in 1951.*

The second letter (July 30), concerning a writer named by Berkeley, is self-explanatory:

Last week Ward Bond called my attention to the fact that Richard Weil had received screen credit along with Fred Rinaldo and Robert Lees on a picture named *Jumping Jacks*, produced by Hal Wallis and released by Paramount. The picture features Dean Martin and Jerry Lewis.

First let me say that Paramount has no control over writers employed by Hal Wallis. His contract with Paramount is an autonomous contract in which he has complete authority in the employment of actors and writers and I did not know at any time, until Ward Bond called it to my attention, that Richard Weil had anything to do with *Jumping Jacks.* . . .

When Ward Bond called my attention to the fact that Richard Weil had been given credit as a writer on *Jumping Jacks* I called Hal Wallis and asked him if he had any knowledge of the fact that while Weil was employed by him he had been named by Berkeley as a Communist. Hal Wallis stated to me that Weil had called this matter to his attention and volunteered to give him a complete statement for his record. Weil did give him a statement under date of September 26, 1951, and I am enclosing twenty photostatic copies of this original letter. This letter stands as a complete denial and since there is a conflict here and Weil has been named by Berkeley in his testimony before the House Un-American Activities Committee I am sure they will subpoena Weil when they have their hearings here in Los Angeles in September and the matter can be clarified for the record one way or another.

Had I known about the employment of Weil at the time, I would have done everything in my power to persuade Hal Wallis to then insist that Weil appear before the Committee, or terminate his employment. Unfortunately, I did not know of this.

Whether Weil is guilty or innocent I do not know. He makes a definite statement that he is not and never has been a member of the Communist Party. Martin Berkeley said that he was.

* Koenig did no such thing.

The statement Weil had given to Wallis denied that he was or had ever been a Communist and began by saying, "Martin Berkeley lied in his teeth." More interesting, however, was Weil's version of how "one of the smartest attorneys I know" persuaded him to resist the impulse to sue. "As of right now," he said his attorney had told him, "you're just *one* name—and a pretty small one at that—in a list of a hundred and fifty. The whole stinking mess will be yesterday's news in a couple of minutes—but if you take *any* action, you'll spotlight *your* name, and then it *won't* be forgotten. The people who know you know it isn't true—and the others don't matter."[6]

Taken together, these two letters suggest how the combination of big money already on the line and intercorporate contractual commitment carried the day. Henry Maine has written that the history of civilization is the movement of society from status to contract, and what higher compliment could a mature blacklist system pay capitalism than to recognize the priority of its contracts over the First Amendment to the Constitution?

After the November 1947 Waldorf-Astoria meeting nobody expected the major studios to risk financial capital for political principle. Even the most iconoclastic of the moguls, Sam Goldwyn, who had spoken against the blacklist at the Waldorf, was unavailable for battle. When the director William Wyler suggested that he employ one of the Hollywood Ten, Goldwyn declined. "I'm sorry. It would be a dishonorable thing to do," he explained. Once he had agreed to sign the Waldorf statement, "I couldn't go back on it."[7]

Resistance in Hollywood to HUAC, to the blacklist it spawned, and to the informer system it assumed, would have to come from elsewhere, from groups or professionals or classes of people free from financial entanglement and primary identification with the fortunes of the major studios, yet with sufficient incentive to challenge them. Aside from heroic individuals and those simply adhering to Party discipline (cooperation was verboten), there were a number of groups whose avowed purpose, whose natural function, whose job definition or sense-of-self recommended them as potential candidates for exposing and/or resisting the corruption and collusion endemic in the situation. Among these were the press, which had only to report the facts to injure the system; the talent representatives, whose principle of compensation gave them a percentage stake in the fortune of their clients; the talent guilds, organized to protect the political and economic rights of the membership; the independent producers, an unconventional crew, a number of whom chose to operate outside the structure of the studio system precisely so that they would be free of bureaucratic constraint or political and aesthetic interference from above; and, finally, the racial and other lonely minorities who were so far out of the system, such victims of injustice, that they had nothing to lose by opposing it. On paper, each of these groups had the potential capacity, motive, maneuverability, and—with the exception of the outcasts—arguably the duty to sound the alarm. Although outside of the formal studio system each of these groups were participants rather than spectators in the life of this unique company town. Yet in the event, despite a number of well-meant challenges to the system, each ultimately chose to play the role of moral bystander.

Publicity is the natural enemy of secrecy. Since secrecy was intrinsic to the maintenance of the blacklist mystique, one suspects that an aggressive press might have exposed and by exposing ended much of the corruption, injustice, and absurdity of Hollywood's surrealistic anti-Communist crusade. But, if anything, the media camouflaged rather than covered (not to mention uncovered) the problem. William Wheeler remembers how "journalists like Howard Rushmore and Ed Nellor and Willard Edwards would write an article and then give it to their pigeon—like [J. Parnell] Thomas or [Joseph] McCarthy—who would put it in *The Congressional Record,* and therefore you couldn't sue!"

After he named names before HUAC, Sterling Hayden subscribed to a press-clipping service. "They sent me two thousand clips from papers east and west, large and small, and from dozens of magazines. Most had nothing but praise for my one-shot stoolie show."[8] The national press wasn't really interested in muckraking the situation. Elizabeth Poe Kerby recalls that when she came out to California in March 1953 for the press section of *Time* and *Life* and told Thomas Pryor of *The New York Times* that she wanted to do an exposé of the blacklist for *Frontier,* a small-circulation liberal magazine, "He took two steps backward, and he wouldn't even talk about it. . . . The general press just didn't want to admit what was happening. My husband and I," says Kerby, "were the only non-Communist journalists in the western United States willing to write about it. It was shocking that Pryor didn't 'know' about it. When I finally published my article in May 1954, he wrote two paragraphs as part of his weekly column."

Kerby (who later became a consultant to John Cogley's study) next went to see the editor of *Daily Variety,* Joe Schoenfeld. "He sat down and talked to me for one and a half hours, and he said he knew but couldn't prove that people in Hollywood were naming others so they could keep their jobs." The trade press in fact covered what it sometimes called "the nonexistent list," and even reported details on how to write an effective clearance letter; but when it came to prevailing political assumptions, it functioned as little more than a house organ for the industry, reflecting rather than challenging it.

The real war correspondents were the gossip columnists, but for scribes such as Walter Winchell and Hedda Hopper, the line between name-dropping and name-naming was so thin that they ended up as adjuncts of the blacklist process, doing the sorting out that made the job of the monthly and annual blacklist compilers so much easier. The political pundits—Victor Riesel, Westbrook Pegler, and the relentless George Sokolsky—also used their newspaper columns as vehicles for tainting, painting, and turpentining alleged reds. For blacklisters in doubt on how to regard the politically active Paul Draper, for example, who had tap-danced to Handel, Bach, Beethoven, and Brahms, Pegler referred to him as a "mincing twirp" with "twittering toes."[9] Sokolsky came to rival Roy Brewer as a doctor who could cure people with political malaise: columns on such matters were less journalism than criminology, as he indicted, convicted, pardoned, paroled, and granted clemency according to his own rules of evidence. Thus on October 6, 1947, his column explained why it was important to reward ex-Communists:

> I have among my friends and acquaintances literally dozens of men and women who during the Hitler-Stalin Alliance were so ashamed of Soviet cynicism that from ardent Communists they became ardent anti-Communists. Such a man was Dr. J. B. Matthews, while never a Communist, was associated with that party as a fellow traveller.
>
> In fighting Communists, our Government is absolutely dependent upon the ex-Communists; yet it does nothing to protect them from the brutality of Communist lawyers. . . .
>
> If the government is seriously trying to tackle the Communist menace, then the first step is to employ qualified experts. . . . Amateurs can bring only discredit upon the government. Every effort should be made to ensure the cooperation and protection of friendly witnesses. . . . The cooperation of witnesses should receive the highest public commendation from the presiding officer of such proceedings.[10]

And of course the columnists did double duty as advice to the politically lovelorn. A classic example of this is seen in Sokolsky's "correspondence" with Humphrey Bogart concerning Bogey's trip to Washington at the time of the Hollywood Ten's appearance before HUAC:

Dear Humphrey Bogart:

I received your mimeographed letter in which you say:

> "My recent trip to Washington, where I appeared with a group of motion-picture people, has become the subject of such confused and erroneous interpretations that I feel the situation should be clarified.
> "I am not a Communist.
> "I am not a Communist sympathizer.
> "I detest Communism just as any other decent American does.
> "My name will not be found on any Communist front organization as a sponsor for anything Communistic.
> "I went to Washington because I thought fellow Americans were being deprived of their constitutional rights, and for that reason alone.
> "That trip was ill-advised, even foolish, I am very ready to admit. At the time it seemed like the thing to do.
> "I have absolutely no use for Communism nor for any one who serves that philosophy.
> "I am an American.
> "And very likely, like a good many of the rest of you, sometimes a foolish and impetuous American."
>
> *(signed) Humphrey Bogart*

Confession is good for any man's soul. And you display great courage and manhood to confess error. Yes, that trip was foolish. . . .

Next time, however, I hope you will look before you leap. Things are not always what they seem. . . . For instance, you people out in Hollywood had an idea . . . that this country had an ally during the war. You were asked to portray Soviet Russia as a glorious, free, democratic country that was allied to us. You may recall that Hollywood produced some pictures along that line.

Of course that was never true. Soviet Russia was never an ally. Germany's war on Russia coincided, more or less, with our war on Germany and the Russians were ready and willing to take advantage of that situation. We gave them $11,000,000,000 of lend-lease and we shipped them airplanes and tanks and machinery. But they never coordinated. . . . They blackmailed us at Teheran and Yalta. . . . Only enemies . . . act that way.

If you are genuinely contrite for a very foolish bit of exhibitionism, you ought to go further. You might tell us who suggested that trip to Washington. Whose brainchild was it? Who projected you and your wife to take the lead?

Your wife, Lauren Bacall, is a beautiful young lady and you are a popular actor. . . . They stuck you out front because you did not belong to them. That is an old trick. . . . But somebody was using both of you. Who is that somebody? . . . It would be a great service if you told all—and gave him a sock.

Anyhow, I am glad to see you among the Americans. . . . You show first-rate manhood in taking the people who admire you into your confidence. Now do something for your country that is really constructive. Tell us who suggested and organized that trip. If you have no better way, use this column for that purpose. It gets around.

Best regards to the lady,

George E. Sokolsky[11]

When in 1947 Robert Kenny announced in California that Henry Wallace would probably run for president, Sokolsky provided helpful information (July 28): "It is interesting to note that Robert W. Kenny is a vice chairman of the PCA [Progressive Citizens of America]. He has been affiliated with the following organizations, some of which have been designated as Communist fronts by the Dies Committee and the Attorney General of the United States . . . "[12]

The columnists also performed a literary function by explicating symbolic victories. It took Ed Sullivan, for instance, to salute Elia Kazan's symbolic victory, his success an invitation to others. Thus in 1955 Sullivan wrote:

Elia Kazan's spectacular series of successes this season—*On the Waterfront, East of Eden, Tea and Sympathy, Cat on a Hot Tin Roof*—have been four giant blows in freeing the movies and the Broadway Theatre of Communist influence. Kazan loosened the Commie grip on entertainment by demonstrating that denunciation of the party didn't lead to personal disaster in the movies or in the theatre. He punctured the legend. . . . In [his] fierce denunciation of the Commies, Kazan invited their hatred and his own disaster. . . .

Far from being destroyed, Kazan went on to his greatest triumphs. In another field, that of ballet, Jerome Robbins denounced the Commies. Recently his production of *Peter Pan* on TV played to the greatest single audience in history. . . .

So this season should be forever remembered as a blue-ribbon event
in the movies and in the legitimate theatre, a shining experience for
those of us who in earlier years fought the Commie invasion of theatre
to the best of our ability.[13]

The attitude of the writer Edward Eliscu, who had left Hollywood for
the East Coast to work in television in 1950, provides a fair reading of the
extent to which the media environment adapted itself to the blacklisting
system. "One day the boom fell," recalls Eliscu. "My agent said, 'If you'd
like, I can have you meet George Sokolsky. You're in trouble.' I said I'd
walk on two feet, not on four, and I gave up that agent.

"Then a story editor took me for a cup of coffee and said my producer
subscribed to a checking service and they checked me out and got back
two pages of entries." Was Eliscu bitter? Not at all. "I had been friendly
with Dan O'Shea, the chief clearer of CBS—I had known him from my
days at RKO. O'Shea was *really* friendly and sympathetic and he
thought it was an unjust situation because I could have done the job well.
I knew it was nothing personal."

———

That reporters had internalized the assumptions of the industry they
were assigned to audit should not astonish students of media habit; especially since in this case the industry in question was itself a mass medium.
Independent filmmakers, however, were by definition antagonistic to studio values. Some were independents because they were incapable of functioning other than on the margin (and on the cheap). And it seems fitting
that one of these, the King brothers, should have made it a regular practice to employ blacklisted personnel under pseudonyms—not as a protest
against repression but as a calculated risk, a shrewd economy, getting top
talent for minimal money. It was the King brothers who hired Dalton
Trumbo to write *The Brave One* (1956), the movie that helped break the
blacklist by embarrassing the academy when its writer-of-record, one
"Robert Rich" (named after a King Brothers nephew who served as messenger boy) failed to show up to accept the Academy Award. Trumbo
finally admitted authorship about two years later. "The King brothers
had a hell of a lot of plagiarism suits," Trumbo explained to me, "and
they needed a body to defend themselves. The story is about as original as
Androcles and the Lion or *Beautiful Joe* or *Black Beauty* or *The Yearling*
or *State Fair*. *State Fair* is a girl and a sheep; *The Yearling* is a boy and

deer; *The Brave One* is a boy and bull. What the hell—it was wide open for plagiarism—and they were all there."

Among the independents-by-choice—those who were successful and socially committed enough to negotiate their freedom from the formulas which life within the studio system implied—opposition to, indeed contempt for, the moguls, their values and *modus operandi*, festered. None among their number seemed more vocal, more liberal, more pugnacious than young Stanley Kramer. On any list of independents expected to challenge the powers-that-be, the producer Stanley Kramer would have been at the top.

Kramer and the writer-director Carl Foreman were two of the more autonomous spirits in Hollywood. In 1946 they went into business together with the idea of making A movies on a B budget. George Glass, the publicist, would get the word out, and Sam Katz, the former M-G-M executive who had founded the Balaban and Katz chain of movie theaters, would run the business. Among their pictures were *Champion* (1949), starring Kirk Douglas as Ring Lardner's cynical prizefighter; *Home of the Brave* (1949), one of Hollywood's first attempts to deal with anti-Negro racism (based on Arthur Laurents's play about anti-Semitism); *The Men* (1950), a film about paraplegics starring Marlon Brando; *Cyrano de Bergerac* (1950), with José Ferrer; and *High Noon* (1952), starring Gary Cooper as the cowboy who refused to go along, who stood alone against the forces of evil.

Kramer made much, in private conversation and public press conferences, of his status as an independent, and on March 18, 1951, when he and movie mogul Harry ("King") Cohn of Columbia Pictures announced what Cohn called "the most important deal we have ever made," he became the biggest independent. Said Cohn, "Never before has an arrangement of this kind been concluded between a major corporation and a completely self-operating independent organization."[14] Columbia would put up $25 million and Kramer's group would make thirty pictures. Kramer claims to have approved the deal "only after assurances of complete autonomy." His average budget as an independent had been under $500,000, and now he was free to spend up to $980,000 per picture before he had to ask anybody's (i.e., Cohn's) approval.

Independence was important to Kramer and Foreman because they wanted to be free of the studio system—the politics, bureaucracy, aesthetics, and economics it entailed. According to Kramer, they didn't want "some illiterate telling us what to do." Thus when Carl Foreman was subpoenaed in September 1951 by the House Committee on Un-

American Activities he assumed that with Kramer's support he might be able to survive the political trouble—especially since his *High Noon* had been such a success and Gary Cooper, no radical, had told Foreman he wanted to buy into the business, HUAC or no HUAC.

Foreman, who had joined the Party with his wife in Hollywood a few years after they were married but dropped out in disillusionment in 1942, had a more complicated idea. Although he was unwilling to be an informer, he was also reluctant simply to invoke the Fifth Amendment and tell the Committee nothing. He had heard that a New York lawyer, Sidney Cohn, had worked out a format that had enabled the writer-director Robert Rossen and the writer Leonardo Bercovici to tell the Committee what was on their minds without naming names, and he was interested in something like that for himself.

"I knew I could not live with myself as an informer," he told me in London some twenty-five years later, "but I was also not a member of the Party, and the Party members were taking the straight Fifth. I arranged to meet Sidney and went up to see him in his hotel room, and said, 'Why don't I take the straight First? The worst that can happen is a fine and six to nine months in jail.' And I did feel that my partners would have enough loyalty to take care of my family. Common criminals do that. I had been to two well-known lawyers on the Coast and told them what was on my mind, and they called back and wouldn't represent me. I needed someone who would represent me with the Committee but also with my partners. So I went to see Sidney Cohn but I told nobody. Hollywood was full of gossip at the time and I wasn't interested in feeding it. I told Sidney about myself and what I wanted to do. He said, 'I see no reason for you to go to jail. You're a husband and a father and not a union leader. My job is to keep you out of jail. I've got an idea I would like to try.' "

Cohn's idea was that Foreman could deny present membership in the Party, as Rossen and Bercovici had done, and refuse to name names from the past, as they had done, but he would also deny past membership year by year backward until they got to 1942, the year he quit the Party. That would make clear to the Committee the duration of his break without, in Cohn's judgment, waiving his right to plead the Fifth Amendment on the issue of past membership or the corollary issue of naming names.

Foreman's hope was that by establishing his clean break with the Party some years earlier, he and the Kramer company could "ride out the storm." But the hoped-for didn't happen. Four months after Foreman testified,[15] his partner George Glass chose to appear before HUAC as a cooperative witness. Although Glass denied CP membership, he told the Committee in January 1952 he had attended a half-dozen Party meetings and at the Committee's request named his fellow attenders.[16]

"I got kicked out of my own company by Kramer," says Foreman. "We had a contract with Columbia. As a group there was no way our films could have been attacked for being subversive. Instead, [Columbia] said the pressures were too great. I'm not talking only about the right-wingers, who told Kramer and Katz to get me to cooperate [with HUAC]. If Stanley had had the guts to ride it out we might have won— Gary Cooper wanted to invest. But Stanley was scared. In the crunch he said he was not prepared to have his career destroyed by my misguided liberalism.

"And then when it became known that George Glass was becoming an informer—I never even knew he was involved with the Party!—my position was seen as untenable. I tried to explain, but Stanley wouldn't listen. He said to me, 'What are you going to do when you go before HUAC? Are you going to take the Fifth?' I said, 'Yes, Stanley, but I am going to take the qualified Fifth.' He said, 'Don't tell me about the qualified Fifth. They'll say, "Do you know Stanley Kramer?" and you'll take the Fifth and then *I'll* be in trouble.' Stanley wouldn't listen. He was scared."

(Another party interested in Foreman's testimony was the CP itself. They sent the screenwriter Eddie Huebsch to interview Foreman: "I was assigned by the Party to find out what Foreman's testimony was going to be. I had lunch with him—he was doing *High Noon* at the time. I sat for eleven hours with him. We went to Lucy's, the fanciest restaurant in Hollywood—across from Paramount. I could not get him to assert that he would take an anti-Committee position. So I reported that he was an informer. Nothing he has said then or since has convinced me I was wrong. I asked him to state it for me. I think he got it from Sidney Cohn: 'Did you know these men in the CP?' 'No, I didn't know *those* men.' You'd say who wasn't, not who was. That was sufficient for him to be an informer. The main point is, Carl wouldn't tell the Committee to go fuck themselves. Had anyone asked me [and had Foreman still been a member of the Party] I would have recommended expulsion.")

Estelle Foreman, Carl's then-wife, thinks to this day that "Stanley behaved very badly. I always call him a fair-weather liberal." What she remembers is that "when Carl was subpoenaed, Stanley was out of town. Carl called him to explain what had happened, and Stanley said, 'Not to worry, we'll stick together.' But when it came down to it, Stanley wouldn't stick his neck out. He forced Carl out of the company ... barred him from the studio, you know, nasty things like that. ... And at

Stanley's instigation this other partner, Sam Katz, tried very hard to persuade Carl to inform [before HUAC], because George Glass, who was subpoenaed at the same time, did inform. He remained with the company but Carl was forced out."

As might be anticipated, Stanley Kramer puts a different cast on the events that led to Foreman's departure from the studio, from Hollywood, and eventually to his expatriate life in England:

"We supposedly were a closely knit group, he and George Glass and the rest of us. But I didn't know anything about their politics, and I protected Foreman to an extent. He had an attorney, and I told him and Katz that whatever the norm figure was for a company that hadn't yet made a picture, he would be bought out for it. And I think he got two hundred eighty thousand dollars or something like it.

"Columbia capitalized on the disagreement between us in a press release, but what I really told them was that I had nothing to say about Foreman, any more than I had anything to say about [Joseph] Losey or [Ben] Maddow, who were good friends of mine but chose on their own to leave [my employ] when they thought they would be subpoenaed. Foreman was in a different position because he had stock. Whether or not these fellows wanted to be cooperative witnesses or not as far as I was concerned was between them and their conscience.

"What I did tell Columbia was that I was in total disagreement on a personal basis with the way Foreman was acting and what he was doing. But that wasn't because of the way he was going to behave before the Committee. That was because he hadn't confided in me at all. In fact he sounded like he was making threats. Later I went out on a limb for something much more dangerous when I made *The Defiant Ones* [1958] with the blacklisted Ned Young; because the guy was warm and truthful I was willing to take a stand with him. In the case of Foreman it would have pleased my sense of rebellion to have said 'Screw you, Harry Cohn' at that time and 'Screw you, Sam Katz,' because this is what I believe. Katz wanted Foreman out of there, and I didn't like Katz. I didn't even want to be at Columbia—the other guys wanted to be there for the money. But it would have pleased my ego very much, because I was young and I was very aggressive about what I believed, and I really didn't care about the financial aspects of all these things.

"But in my negotiations with Foreman there was this veil of unspoken ideas about how my past connections could militate against me depending on how the negotiations turned out. I had what was called at that time a 'liberal' background. I had been at the People's Educational Center, which was on some list. Now Carl was not somebody who could be discharged, period. He owned stock in the company and therefore he was bought out from that stock and left with a packet of money. What is the morality of that? There are two sides to it. He took a stand, he went before the Committee, and he didn't name any names. If he had leveled with me, if I had known all the facts, that would have been one thing. But he really didn't, and that's why it got to the point where Columbia finally released a story which said I was in disagreement with Foreman. Well, I was in disagreement with the way he proceeded with regard to me, not the Committee. We had a couple of meetings in which I locked the door and looked him right in the eye, and I just felt he didn't look me back in the right way, and we parted. That's it.

"You sit with a man in a room and he says, 'How do you think we ought to handle this? What should we do?' A man should say, 'Here's what the problem is, here's the danger, here's what can happen to the company.' It was never explained to me. I never heard the phrase 'qualified Fifth.' All I got from Foreman was the threat, 'I could name other names besides these.' I don't want to get into that business because it's all shit—and not only that, it's not true, because I never was a part of it [the Communist Party]."

In other words, Kramer feels Foreman wasn't acting in a principled way, and as a result he himself can't be blamed for acting to preserve the corporation rather than to preserve Foreman. Whether the threats were real or in Kramer's imagination or attributable to the paranoia endemic in those enmeshed in blacklist, Kramer thought he heard them. In fact, his relationship with Harry Cohn—already strained because his movies were losing money (only the last, *The Caine Mutiny* [1954], was financially successful) and because his independent style upset the "King"— ended not long thereafter.

It is true that when he was back on his own in 1958 he made a picture with the blacklisted Ned Young, although he didn't know Young's status when he hired him. (Young was still writing under the pseudonym of Nathan E. Douglas.) After he found out, Kramer says, he told Young, " 'I'm going to make this picture, but you've got to stop saying fuck 'em to the press and everyone. I don't want you to change your position. I just want you to stop saying fuck you.' That's the only agreement we had.

"In the meantime I went on nationwide television and had a debate with the head of the American Legion. The issue was, Was *The Defiant Ones* a red-inspired property? I really let them have it. I said I was an independent entrepreneur, that I had a perfect goddamn right to buy any property I wanted to buy. I didn't know who wrote it, and I couldn't care less. I bought the property, period, and what appeared on the screen was going to be what I thought it should be, and go drop dead."

In 1952 Foreman went to England, where he lost his American passport and his wife, and gained a new career on the "black market." Among other projects, he wrote the screenplay that became (with the help of a rewrite by Michael Wilson) *The Bridge on the River Kwai* (1957). It was released in the United States as written by Pierre Boulle, the author of the novel on which the film is based but who could not, as it happened, write in English. Says Foreman of Boulle, "He had the good taste not to return in person to accept the Academy Award."[17]

One of the reasons Foreman chose to return to America was that in the midst of *Kwai* his lawyer, Sidney Cohn, telephoned him in England with the news that "if I hurried to the States there was a great chance that Columbia and I could make an end run around HUAC and I could come out from under the table."

Cohn was an unusual attorney in the sense that he differed from most attorneys who represented political witnesses before HUAC, who were either, like Ben Margolis, Charles Katz, or Robert Kenny, at arm's length from the Committee and represented only uncooperative witnesses or, like Martin Gang, "fixers" who worked with the Committee and specialized in clients who named names. Most left lawyers felt that to work "with" the Committee behind the scenes was a cop-out. But Cohn's theory was, "You play the game. Go in quietly, work with the Committee, but challenge it in a legal fashion." He succeeded in 1956 in getting Foreman (and Bercovici and Rossen) their passports back (Foreman's had been confiscated on July 4, 1953) by persuading the judge that Secretary of State John Foster Dulles's brief in opposition to Foreman's request for it was so inadequate it could only be an embarrassment to the government to have it on the record.

"We have achieved the impossible, thanks to you," Foreman told Cohn. "They said it couldn't happen and it did. Why don't you try to get some sort of an amnesty declared in the U.S. so that I and others like me can come back to work?" Cohn took up the suggestion and in short order had cooked up a deal with Congressman Francis Walter.

Cohn had his own idea of how witnesses before HUAC ought to behave. "I felt no man should be made to be an informer to prove his patriotism, but also if a man left the CP for his own reasons, there was no need to take the Fifth Amendment, period." Which is how he came up with the idea of the diminished Fifth, which permitted witnesses to say no to present membership. But through it all he never represented any cooperative witness. "I must tell you, he said in 1973, "I'd be uncomfortable representing anyone who would buy his own freedom by exposing others."

Cohn was constantly experimenting with new ways to circumvent the blacklist system. He was able through affidavits to convince CBS of the absurdity of Martin Berkeley's charges: "I got [the actor] Jack Gilford cleared with an affidavit—a disclaimer of advocacy of overthrowing the government through force and violence."

Cohn had first tried to arrange for Foreman to come back through Edward Bennett Williams, who had had some success working with the Committee. "Williams came in to see me. He was a good friend of Scott McCleod at State* and had the reputation of being a violent anti-Communist. I gave him Carl's affidavit before State *re* the passport, with a full statement of Carl's position, and he read it over and said, 'I want a fifty-thousand-dollar fee and ten percent of his earnings.' That didn't faze me because I had an offer from Spyros Skouras and Buddy Adler to give Carl a bonus of a million dollars if he would be a good boy, clear himself with the Committee, and come back to work for Fox. Williams came back and said he'd read the affidavit; he could arrange for a private hearing [before HUAC]; Carl would not have to get into anything deeply, but he'd have to supplement the affidavit with some names. For a private hearing to confess you're a sinner and name names, you didn't need Edward Bennett Williams at fifty thousand dollars and so I said thanks but no thanks."

Next, Cohn went directly to Congressman Walter with the argument that since the Committee now had all the names it needed, it could get nice publicity for itself and perform a service for the country by hearing repentant ex-Communists denounce the Party *without requiring them to become informers.* As Cohn outlined it, this would bring a new wave of witnesses, glory for the Committee, and public education on the Communist menace. They had several meetings, and finally Congressman Walter said, "By God, that's not a bad idea. If your friend Foreman ever comes back and you find him receptive to it, I'd like to talk to him." As Cohn recalls it, Walter would "listen to what I had to say, and then as a subcommittee of one he'd vote for it. And that would open the gates."†

---

* R. W. Scott McCleod was the director of security at the State Department, and a very powerful figure throughout the early 1950s.

† The probability is that Representative Walter agreed to try the Foreman tactic primarily to placate his daughter, who was getting flack from her classmates at Sarah

And that, according to legend, is what happened: Cohn negotiated a contract between Columbia Pictures and Foreman—conditioned on Foreman's making an appearance before HUAC and not utilizing the Fifth Amendment; on August 8, 1956, Foreman and Cohn met in Washington, D.C., in executive session with Congressman Walter, and Foreman testified as planned. He denounced himself but no one else, Walter thanked him, and declared the session closed. But when word leaked out that Foreman was back at work without naming names, instead of opening the gates to others, Walter himself came in for such criticism from his allies on the right that he decided to stop the procedure.

Foreman, however, was cleared and back at work. The uniqueness of his experience and the mystification that surrounded the whole blacklist *apparat* naturally gave rise to a number of rumors. Mike Connelly, a columnist for the *Hollywood Reporter*, wrote at the time (March 14, 1957) that HUAC "plans holding executive sessions to probe a report that one of its members received money to clear a show-business personality suspected of being a Red." Paul Jacobs in *The Reporter* magazine on May 15, 1958, wrote that the "suspect" was Foreman, and he told me in the early 1970s that he believed Columbia Pictures had paid Congressman Walter $25,000 "under the table." When I asked Foreman about this in London in 1973, he said it was the first he had heard of it, "But don't get me wrong—I would have been happy to pay twenty-five thousand dollars to go back to work. I would have paid fifty thousand without batting an eye." And the late writer Michael Wilson told me the rumor that the way Foreman got around the naming-of-names requirement was that a HUAC person showed him a list of names, held it up, and asked, "Do you have any names to add to that?" and he said, "No, I don't." To this day Stanley Kramer and others find it difficult to believe that Foreman did not name names to Walter.

Foreman observed to me that it was "unfortunate" his hearing had taken place in executive session, since that had caused all these rumors. When I asked to see a copy of the transcript, he demurred, on the grounds that he was saving his story for his own memoirs and that he should talk to his lawyer first. (His lawyer demurred on the grounds that he should talk to his client.)

But a number of people who *have* read the testimony confirm that Foreman named no names. The blacklisted director and expatriate Joseph Losey says, "I saw his testimony. It was terribly well-maneuvered.

Lawrence, some of them children of blacklist victims, over the activities of the Committee.

He saw a subcommittee of one, which was a maneuver that was brilliant and cost a lot of money. He did not name any names—that was perfectly true. But he made statements that would have stuck in my throat. I never understood how he could do that. I'm reasonably sure he didn't believe what he said, and I charged him with this privately. But he said, 'Well, you don't appear before people like that if you aren't prepared to give them something. What did you want me to do?' "

Foreman's former wife also saw the testimony. "Yes," says Estelle Foreman, "I read it and it's as Carl reported it to me. I was opposed to the whole thing. I said, 'Fuck them all. Who needs them? You're earning a living and why reappear before the Committee?' But Carl and Sidney convinced me that if Carl could get by with it perhaps others could too, and it might be a break in the blacklist. So on that basis I agreed to it. But no one else was able to do that—at least not that I know of."

Indeed, Foreman's appearance failed to set a precedent; it also incurred him some enmity. His former friend, the screenwriter Hy Kraft, also a blacklist victim and sometime expatriate, wrote, apropos Congressman Walter's invitation to return to the United States if he ever wanted to cooperate: "What an irretrievable opportunity! Others such as Elia Kazan, Carl Foreman, and Abe Burrows had accepted the offers, embracing them as if they were pacemakers. . . ." Kraft said, "No sale." To him, Sidney Cohn's tactics were unacceptable: to sell HUAC on the proposition that writers were naïve types—moved to radicalism by the plight of Negroes and Jews—who didn't understand the realities of politics.

A fellow writer told me that Cohn thought of presenting the idea to Lillian Hellman. I knew Miss Hellman well enough to predict her vigorous and violent rejection of any proposal that would lend even a microscopic shred of dignity or standing to the Committee. It was convenient for people to lose sight of this basic principle. You don't give up smoking by cutting down to two or three cigarettes daily. You say, "Cigarettes don't exist for me." That's how those of us who have declined to accept the waiver of immunity feel about the Committee: It doesn't exist. It's to be avoided at all costs.[18]

Thus Stanley Kramer drew the line at bringing down his company, and for all intents and purposes his company was brought down. Carl Foreman denounced himself to open the gates for others, and the gates remained shut. Sidney Cohn refused to represent informers but got cozy with and perhaps thereby strengthened those who insisted on the informer litmus test. In this way did the entertainment industry's foremost independents challenge the system of blacklist-by-informer.

———

Milton Gelman, a screenwriter and former agent who now teaches in the Department of Communications Arts at Loyola Marymount University in Los Angeles, says of the McCarthy period, "If MCA [Music Corporation of America] had gotten together with William Morris and said, 'We're going to pull all our shows off the air,' they could have broken the whole goddamn operation to begin with. The sponsors would have had nothing to show. But everyone ran scared."*

Indeed, since an agent's income and performance are both measured by the success of the client, in theory the Hollywood agents should have been on the barricades suing, threatening, and negotiating the blacklist into oblivion. In fact, the idea that the Hollywood agent of the 1940s and 1950s would represent any interest other than his own (though where possible and convenient, his clients' too) struck the hundreds of Hollywood people I talked with, including a number of agents, as hilarious.

Inquisition in Eden (1965), Alvah Bessie's biting memoir on life before, during, and after prison as a member of the Hollywood Ten, paints an unforgettable picture of the prototypical agent. The time, the early 1940s. Bessie had been living on a farm in Vermont because he couldn't afford to live in New York. He was the underpaid drama critic for the *New Masses* and broadcast for fifteen minutes every Sunday morning on station WQXR for free. He had published an unsuccessful novel and had received an offer of $50 a week plus expenses from the International Workers Order, a mutual-benefit insurance society, to go on tour and speak about the war. When Warner Brothers offered him $150 a week to go to Hollywood, his agent went to the Stork Club in New York to celebrate.

---

* By the late 1940s the networks had surrendered control of programming to the advertising agencies and big-business sponsors. The rise of television as the most effective advertising medium for national advertisers raised the cost of a one-hour show to hundreds of thousands of dollars. With giant corporations dealing through a handful of agencies, Gilbert Seldes pointed out, "The calamitous effects of a change of agency by any one of the ten leading advertisers haunts the hucksters' dreams. In these conditions, everyone concerned looks for insurance against failure." (Quoted in Bert Cochran, *Business in American Life* [New York, 1975], 293.)

There he ran into Jack Warner, and the following conversation took place:

> AGENT (*to Warner*): What kind of a shit you got working for you in your New York office, anyhow?
>
> WARNER: Why, what's wrong with him?
>
> AGENT: He offered my writer, Bessie, a lousy one hundred and fifty dollars a week.
>
> WARNER: That's what I told him to offer.
>
> AGENT: Bessie don't have to work for you for a lousy one hundred and fifty. He's a drama critic for a national magazine. He's got a house in the country. He's got his own radio program. He's got a best-selling novel on the stands that would make a great picture. He's going on a nationwide speaking tour.
>
> WARNER: Well, I don't know that I want him, anyhow. I hear he's a red.
>
> AGENT: Warner, you guys make me sick. The reds are saving your goddamn moving-picture business on the Stalingrad front tonight!
>
> WARNER (*enthusiastically*): You're *right*! I'll give him three hundred dollars.

At the time the two major agencies—William Morris and Music Corporation of America—represented most of the talent. It is probably true, as Gelman suggests, that if either of them had refused to go along, if they had told the studios, "Blacklist one of our clients and you get none of our clients," the blacklist might have been broken. But at the contemporary level of commerce and consciousness, such a gesture was inconceivable.

Besides, the old Fred Allen quip about how an agent's heart would fit in a flea's navel and there would still be room left over for two aspirin and an acorn, was apt. The agent was seen as a sleazy wheeler-dealer. The blacklisted agent George Willner, who specialized in progressive clients, recalls a fellow agent at the Goldstone Agency: "He'd advance a writer five hundred dollars [on the eventual sale of a property] and say, 'We'll own one-third if we sell it, nothing if we don't sell it.' He'd neglect to mention that it had already been sold. And then he'd take the five hundred dollars back *and* the third off. Another agent would say of a script he had already sold, 'We can't possibly sell it but I'll do you a favor and buy it outright'—for a pittance. And that's what he'd do."

By definition an agent is supposed to serve or represent his client. But

with only a handful of exceptions, such as Willner himself and Ingo Preminger, the Hollywood agents served not their clients but the studio system.
Thus they routinely urged their clients to cooperate with HUAC. Partly
that was because the agents' own survival depended on their ability to function within the prevailing system, but partly it was simply because they
made more money with working writers than with blacklisted ones.

Abe Polonsky's agent tried to convince him not to plead the Fifth
Amendment before HUAC in April 1951. Twentieth Century-Fox didn't
want to fire him, but he had publicly made the startling declaration that
he saw nothing wrong, for example, with Communist firemen. He was
given notice, fired, and appeared before the Committee a few days later
(where he invoked the Fifth Amendment).[19]

The writer George Sklar recalls that Mary Baker, head of the literary
department of the Jaffe Agency, tried to persuade him to go and have a
talk with Martin Gang. " 'What have you got to lose?' she asked. She
called the day after Berkeley named me."

Ned Young testified in 1960 in a blacklist suit against the Motion Picture Association: "Within two days of my appearance and testimony before the House Committee [in 1953] I called my agent, Gene Corman of
MCA, who asked to be released from his contract as my agent. Corman
pointed out that I had been a valuable property . . . but I was no longer
employable in the industry. I agreed."[20]

Howard Koch, one of the original Hollywood Nineteen, also felt agent
pressure. He had never been a member of the Communist Party and
therefore seemed a good prospect for "rehabilitation." He had been
"named" by Warner because he was so visible in progressive politics and
was of interest to HUAC because his movie, *Mission to Moscow,* although
made at FDR's request, nevertheless seemed the one concrete example of
pro-Soviet propaganda that the Committee could point to. Koch fought
for a decade to get off the blacklist without naming names. The message
was always the same. Consider this wire which he received from his agent
Paul Kohner:

> DISCUSSION WITH ROY BREWER INDICATES YOU DEEPLY IN-
> VOLVED AND IDENTIFIED WITH IMPORTANT ACTIVITIES EVEN
> AFTER SO-CALLED DUPES HAD LEFT. SINCE YOUR RECORD SUB-
> STANTIAL PERSONALLY APPEARING HERE AND UNEQUIVOCALLY
> ANSWERING ALL QUESTIONS ONLY WAY REHABILITATING YOUR-
> SELF WHICH BREWER INDICATED COULD BE ACCOMPLISHED. RE-
> GARDS, PAUL.[21]

As late as October 31, 1958, Koch received a letter from the Alvin G. Manuel Agency which went:

> I just had a talk with Martin Gang and he was very nice, but he says there are only two ways of clearing up the matter. Either appear before the Committee and let them publicize the appearance, or get some employer who is willing to take an affidavit and use you on an assignment. I don't know how rugged the Committee meetings could get, but from your background I'd think they would be glad to get you out of there as soon as possible.
>
> I wish you would reconsider appearing before them. I know Martin Gang recommends it, although he deplores the necessity.[22]

Generally, of course, the agent was merely one more voice in the chorus of those who urged cooperation. The experience of the screenwriter Robert Richards was typical. As he recalled it in 1960: "Borden Chase, a screenwriter with whom I had worked at Universal, called me to suggest that I contact William Wheeler, a House Committee investigator. I told Chase that Wheeler and I had nothing to discuss. Subsequently I repeated [this] conversation to my attorney. He advised me to contact Wheeler, and I did so. Wheeler and I met for lunch at the Tail of the Cock restaurant on Ventura Boulevard, North Hollywood, California. I opened this conversation by telling Mr. Wheeler that I assumed he knew all about me and therefore there was very little to be gained by my appearance before the Committee. Wheeler tried to appear sympathetic, but despite his efforts, he finally came out and said that my appearance and testimony before the Committee were essential. According to Wheeler, this was my time of crisis. I asked him whether it would be possible to discuss my own political affiliations and associations without identifying others. Wheeler said, 'No.' He told me what my attorneys had already told me, i.e., that by answering one question about my political associations, I would waive my right to refuse to answer others. I then said I would not become an informer. Wheeler told me that this was a very foolish decision on my part inasmuch as it would destroy my career in the industry and would stigmatize my children for life. I asked him whether he thought it fair to stigmatize little children for something they knew nothing about. He replied that it was unfortunate, but, in a time of national crisis, 'That's the way it is.' We finished our lunch and went our separate ways.

"That day, or a few days thereafter, I saw my agent George Rosenberg and told him what had happened. He urged me to 'cooperate' with the Committee, and asked if it were possible [for me] to name just 'a few little people.' While he agreed that there was no moral or logical distinction between naming some people [and] not [naming] others, he continued to urge me to 'cooperate' because otherwise I would be permanently 'dead in the industry.' "

On September 20, 1951, Richards appeared before the Committee, but he did not cooperate because "the very core of the Committee's methods of interrogation, the single and sole criterion of 'cooperation,' was the identification of other people. This, in all conscience, I could not bring myself to do, knowing them to be as innocent of any wrongdoing as I was myself, and knowing the economic and social consequences which would inevitably follow for many who in turn would be hailed before the Committee."[23]

It was not always possible to know an agent's motive. Paul Kohner telephoned Michael Wilson before his HUAC appearance "and begged me not to ruin my career," Wilson recalled before he died. "When I decided not to heed his advice, he sent his deputy agent, Ilse Lahn, to attend my hearing, and she remained a devoted friend and in fact later got me a couple of black-market jobs."

Shortly after Wilson's appearance before HUAC, Kohner was at a bullfight in Tijuana, where he saw John Wayne. Kohner walked up to him and said, "Hello, how are you?" Wayne stared at him and said, "I don't shake hands with people who represent Commies," and turned on his heel and walked away. "This did it for Kohner," as Wilson told the story. "He knew from that time forward he was not going to represent me. He would let his assistant Ilse Lahn do it, but not he himself. He never took a militantly hostile position toward any of the blacklisted people, but he didn't go out of his way to try to get them work with the independents—and he did have such contacts."

The natural state of the Hollywood writer's relationship with the agent is one of love-hate, since talent may be forgiven for assuming—often incorrectly—that unemployment is the agent's fault. Conversely, during the blacklist years, which were also tight money years for the studios, agents often found it simpler to hint to their less talented clients that their difficulties were political rather than intrinsic. Since agents as a class follow the money, it is perhaps a clue to the environment of fear within which they operated that, for example, the Berg-Allenberg Agency was, even in late 1948, ready, eager, willing, and able to lose its most profitable client, Dalton Trumbo (at $3000 per week he was one of the highest paid writers in Hollywood)—and this even before the more general system of blacklisting had gone into effect.

Trumbo's talent as a screenwriter being second only to his virtuosity as a letter writer, it is appropriate that the last word on the matter of the behavior of agents during the blacklist years should have been written by him in a letter to Meta Reis Rosenberg, then of the Berg-Allenberg Agency, in response to the agency's request for 10 percent of monies Trumbo had collected. Here are some excerpts:

Dear Meta: December 17, 1948

... I have certain doubts about the firm of Berg-Allenberg which I feel you should know. As a matter of fact I have five specific doubts, and for the sake of clarity I shall enumerate them below.

(1) The last time Mr. Berg granted me a private audience—I believe it was during the first week of April in 1948—he spoke fully and frankly to me, and I have remembered what he said, as I always remember the words of people who have got on in the world. He spent considerable time criticizing me for "making long speeches" when I was on the congressional carpet before that rascal—now happily indicted for defrauding his government—the Hon. J. Parnell Thomas. ...

This statement, coming from an employee of mine, from an employee whose job it was to keep my best interests constantly in mind, gave me considerable pause. For according to the record he said he had read, my testimony before the Committee on Un-American Affairs comprised only four and a half pages, and my longest "speech"—as Mr. Berg and later the prosecuting attorney at my trial insisted on calling those brief statements I was able to get into the record—my longest "speech" counted exactly 75 words.

What caused me especially to think upon the matter was the fact that Mr. Samuel Grosvenor Wood, at the time of the hearings a client of Berg-Allenberg, testified for 14 pages, and his longest speech counted 148 words; that Mr. James Kevin McGuinness, at the time of the hearings a client of Berg-Allenberg, testified for 18 pages, and his longest speech counted 400 words; that Mr. Adolphe Menjou, at the time of the hearings a client of Berg-Allenberg, testified for 17 pages, and his longest speech counted 671 words; that Miss Ayn Rand, at the time of the hearings a client of Berg-Allenberg, testified for 9 pages, and her longest speech counted 1,636 words. ...

(2) During this same conversation Mr. Berg suggested to me a scheme whereby I and my nine colleagues, if they agreed to it, might be received back into the motion-picture industry. He stated to me that

Mr. Westbrook Pegler, a journalist of the fascist lunatic fringe, was a good friend of his; and that he would pay Mr. Pegler's expenses to the Coast and arrange a meeting between him and the ten, or him and me alone; and that by talking freely to Mr. Pegler and revealing to him the motives which prompted us to behave as we did before the indictee Thomas, we would deliver ourselves from the onus allegedly attached to our names and make possible our return to our jobs.

I held my silence while this went on, for I was so nauseated that to speak would have been to lose my temper, and to lose my temper is to become completely incoherent. I never again took the matter up with Mr. Berg for a reason which he should understand as well as I—namely, that Westbrook Pegler is one of the most dangerous, malicious, and outspoken anti-Semites in the country. . . .

(3) In the course of this same conversation I brought my financial condition to Mr. Berg's attention. Three times during the previous six months Mr. Berg had assured me that if I needed money I had only to ask for it. Moreover, part of the fee I had been paying Mr. Berg over the years was in consideration of business management—a fact which both Mr. Berg and Mr. Allenberg had called to my attention at various intervals. They had even gone so far as to urge me to discharge my business manager and avail myself of the business service for which I was paying them. So it was also in his capacity as my business manager that I approached Mr. Berg about money.

I had previously sent him a statement of the $80,000 investment in my ranch, together with an inventory of chattels prepared for insurance purposes by the United Appraisal Company, listing them at $40,000 current value. I asked Mr. Berg either to lend me $10,000 outright; or to take a $10,000 trust deed on the ranch; or, if he found himself unable to do either, to guarantee a first mortgage at the bank against both ranch and chattels in the sum of $15,000.

Mr. Berg replied that for business reasons and for reasons of his reputation he could not possibly afford to appear to be sponsoring me or backing me or guaranteeing me in any way, no matter how large the security nor how safe the investment. He did, however, authorize his associate, Mr. Jack Nerdrum, to look around for private money against ranch and chattels, with the clear understanding that in so doing Mr. Nerdrum did not represent Berg-Allenberg, and that the firm had no interest or connection with the transaction. . . .

Now the point of this grimy little narrative is this: that for reasons of business Mr. Berg could not afford to be the medium by which money flowed into my pocket, no matter how firm the security or how legitimate the transaction. Such a connection with me would somehow be harmful to him in the conduct of his affairs. But this brings us even a larger question, and one which greatly perplexes me and has caused me sleepless nights. If money flowing through Mr. Berg to me would injure him, is it not true that money flowing through me to Mr. Berg would be equally injurious to him? The stain would be on it, and no amount of rationalization can wash it off. You can understand then, why I shrink from the responsibility of placing him and his firm in such jeopardy. . . .

Now in view of the fact that association with me or advocacy of my cause or involvement in a mortgage or business deal with me would be harmful to Mr. Berg's reputation, I am moved to ask what kind of people are not harmful to his reputation? Would he, for example, hesitate to enter into a legitimate deal with . . . any of the dozens of perverts, homosexuals, and lesbians who work prominently in motion pictures, or any of that legion of men—some of them even Mr. Berg's associates for all I know—who perjure themselves in their marriage vows by later acquisition of concubines? I doubt that Mr. Berg would hesitate to deal with any of these people. I am quite sure that he has, at one time or another, dealt with practically all of them. . . . But I am dangerous to his reputation, perhaps because I do not sin in a way that Mr. Berg understands.

In view of all this, and understanding the delicacy of Mr. Berg's feelings and the quality of his reputation, I fail to see how it is possible for him to sponsor me, to back me, to accept the incriminating dollar from me, unless he publicly admits a close economic association with me and begins to fight vigorously for my right to work. I don't see how this is possible for him unless he is willing, at this late date, to make a moral compromise; and I should hate to think him the sort of man to whom moral compromise comes easily; and regardless of how difficult the struggle, if it came at all, then he would not be the kind of person I should wish to employ as my representative. . . .

(4) There is still another matter which puzzles me, and concerning which I suspect that Mr. Berg cherishes naïve illusions. I employ him for two purposes: (1) to find employment for me—which he has not been able to do for over a year; and (2) to collect payment for my work—which he has been conspicuously unable to do in, for example, the case of *Angel's Flight*. I have therefore been compelled to employ my attorney, Mr. Martin Gang, to enforce my contract and to collect the funds which Berg-Allenberg were unable to collect.

The expense of filing the various suits, of court fees and what not, have run into a considerable cash sum, all of which I myself have paid out of pocket. At the outset I suggested to the firm of Berg-Allenberg that they participate in this expense, since their normal ten percent commission was involved. But they thriftily refrained from sharing any of the costs—not even ten percent to protect their own interest in the suit. Apparently they believed that some deeply charitable impulse on my part would cause me to advance cash for the legal costs of their percentage as well as my own. Unfortunately, they overestimated my benevolence. . . .

(5) There is only one more major point, and then this letter shall come to an end. It's been *so* long since I've heard either from Mr. Berg or Mr. Allenberg. In the old days when they were the two most highly paid men in my employ, I heard from them very often. From every spa between Miami and Rio de Janeiro came their cheerful little wonderful-vacation-wish-you-were-here postal cards. One such even came from Mr. Berg amidst the storm and stress of seagoing life aboard his yacht as it plowed its way through the Caribbean waves. But I have not heard from them lately. I have not heard from them at all. My last letter from Mr. Berg was mailed March 3rd, 1948, and the most recent from Mr. Allenberg was dated June 1, and even then was in answer to a letter of my own. During all these intervening months—nothing. No more vacation notes. No more photographs of tropic splendors.

I worry about this, Meta. I worry, and then I wonder: aren't they taking vacations any more? What can be wrong? And then a hopeful thought comes to me: why obviously if they're not flying down to Rio or challenging the peril of the tropic seas, then it must mean that they are too busy for relaxation, that they are working. And then the gnawing thought: busy with what? working for whom? For you see, Meta, I receive no word from them about the state of employment in the motion-picture industry. They have made no suggestions about how I might proceed to get work. They have given me no hint of the story market, of what stories are needed by what stars, of the general trends of the market. I have received no advice from them whatever, business or otherwise. They tell me nothing of their ceaseless efforts to get me a job. They render me no account of the rebuffs, the heartbreaks and the high resolution which attends their efforts in my behalf. In fact they do not write me at all. Just . . . silence. Six long months of silence. I thought I had been forgotten, I assumed that our relationship was over, that I was on my own, that this sensitive pair were addressing themselves to other and higher matters. And then your wire—! . . .

Cordially,
Dalton Trumbo[24]

Three years later Meta Rosenberg, the talented and buxom recipient of the letter, appeared before HUAC as a cooperative witness and named names. She received a telegram from the playwright Nunnally Johnson in London, who wired, "I always said politics was for flat-chested girls." Twenty years later, in 1971, she saw Trumbo again for the first time. George Willner, who had been knocked out of Hollywood and forced to sell his $750,000 interest in the Goldstone Agency for $25,000, had climbed back to the top and was working with the International Famous Artists Agency. "Trumbo had done a screenplay of *The Fixer* (1968), and the producer and the director on the film wanted Alan Arkin to play the lead," recalls Willner. "Meta represented Arkin [on the West Coast]. Arkin wanted a conference, and Meta said she ought to be there; but then she found out Trumbo was coming, and she was scared to death she would lose Arkin as a client. She asked me as a favor to call Trumbo and make sure he wouldn't cost her my client. I called Dalton and after cursing her out he said, 'You tell Meta if I see her at a business meeting I'll say hello but if I see her socially I'll kick her ass.' Usually Meta talked her head off but that day she didn't say a word."

———

It is often forgotten that "Are you now or have you ever been a member of the Communist Party?" was the second question asked the Hollywood Ten. The first was, "Are you now or have you ever been a member of the guild?"—the Screen Writers Guild for eight of them, the Screen Directors Guild for the other two. Although all three major guilds—writers, directors, actors—were resented by the moguls, and their potential power was such that bitter political contests were fought for internal control of them, these organizations were indeed *guilds* more than unions. Despite the high hopes and ideals of their founders, they were composed of people uncomfortable with the kinds of strike mechanisms or mass appeals common to other forms of trade unionism. By virtue of their stake not only in the Hollywood system but in a social structure in which hundreds of millions of dollars were spent on maintaining their new life-styles, they were particularly vulnerable to the sort of pressures in which HUAC and its allies specialized. The guilds did not distinguish themselves in representing the interests of those members who were under attack; arguably, however, their performance was consistent with the values of the culture which gave birth to them.

Ever since 1933 when John Howard Lawson, Lester Cole, John Bright, and seven other writers founded the Screen Writers Guild, the producers saw SWG as the enemy, and vice versa. Lawson, its first president, whose vision of the guild was formed by his experience in the workers- and experimental-theater movements in the East, saw its avowed aim as nothing less than winning for the writer "creative control" over his materials—not to mention a minimum-standard contract, a system of arbitrating credits, a means of enforcing collective bargaining, and a guild shop.

Leonard Spigelgass, past vice-president of the guild, recalls that its beginning coincided with the terrifying earthquake of March 10, 1933. "And first, like all the terrible movies we'd ever written, the schools fell apart and the bridges fell down because the people who had built them had cheated. It was like a bad B picture. And secondly, I was at Fox and my salary check bounced—it came back marked 'insufficient funds.' And thirdly, Roosevelt closed the banks. And fourthly, we were asked by the studios to take a fifty percent salary cut, which we all agreed to do on the assumption that everybody was taking it. Well, the only people who took it were the actors, writers, directors and, I suppose, the technical people. We discovered to our absolute horror that the producers didn't take it, the exhibitors didn't take it, and nobody else took it. And that was the agony that turned the old Writers' Club into the Screen Writers Guild. From thirty-three to thirty-six we were kind of an underground movement."

The guild survived the producers' attempt in 1936 to break it with a company union, the so-called Screen Playwrights. Writers were summoned into Irving Thalberg's projection room and given an ultimatum by the M-G-M producer and boss: resign from the guild and join Screen Playwrights, or be fired. "Six months after I joined the guild," Trumbo told me, "I was approached by the same man who had recruited me, and he told me I should resign and join the Screen Playwrights." Thalberg had formed an alliance with a small group of affluent, older right-wing writers, and the guild membership, then approaching a thousand, plummeted to fifty. Ultimately, the company union failed. This was partly because some of the top talent refused to go along, and according to Spigelgass, "Nobody else could put it on paper. There was a literacy shortage." But the guild was really saved when its officers and organizers—some of whom went "underground," keeping their union activities secret—successfully established that screenwriters were "labor" and had a right to unionize; in 1938 they petitioned the National Labor Relations Board for a binding election in which the writers would cast secret ballots to choose their union and the Screen Writers Guild won, 267 to 57.[25] From that time forward, despite informal blacklisting of guild activists, red-baiting, the dangling of long-term contracts to potential guild members, and the reorganization of the studios into "unit" production—which meant fewer on the studio payroll and a vastly increased pool of unemployed—the guild became the writers' sole bargaining agent in Hollywood.

The Screen Writers Guild sided with the labor leader Herbert Sorrell's progressive Conference of Studio Unions in its 1945–46 jurisdictional dispute against the racket-ridden International Alliance of Theatrical Stage Employees. (In the late 1930s, the golden years of IATSE, its president, George E. Browne, and his Hollywood representative, Willie Bioff, as in "buy off," would shake down the studio executives on a regular schedule in return for limiting the union's demands. Louis B. Mayer, the Schenck brothers, and other studio executives later conceded that they had probably saved $15 million by buying off Bioff and Browne.[26])

The result of this battle was that the defeated Screen Playwrights converted themselves into the militantly right-wing pressure group the Motion Picture Alliance for the Preservation of American Ideals); IATSE got a new leader, the fiercely anti-Communist Roy Brewer; and the members of the Screen Writers Guild had their political consciousness, not to mention their parliamentary skills, raised as they attempted to navigate the guild through the turbulent political waters of the period, when organizations like the Communist Party, the League of American Writers, and the Hollywood Writers Mobilization were all vying for influence.

When HUAC invaded the entertainment community, one would have expected the Screen Writers Guild to constitute a bulwark of resistance. Instead, the guild fought its own version of the war between the liberals, who had been fragmented in Hollywood ever since the Nazi-Soviet Pact. The most serious rift concerned the executive board elections of November 1947. On one side was the "Progressive slate," which had carried the 1946 elections, including Communist writers such as Lardner and Cole but also non-Communists such as Frances Goodrich and Albert Hackett, whose dominant idea was to involve the guild in the political struggles of the day. And on the other side was the "All-Guild slate," led by the screenwriter Allen Rivkin (who in 1950 became president of the Motion Picture Industry Council) and including liberals like Spigelgass, who describes it as "a merger of innocent liberals like myself and some very right-wing people, but more non- than anti-Communist." These folk shared the view of screenwriter Art Arthur, who felt the guild had been "infiltrated" by Communists and that "we had to restore control to the people who would use it for the purposes for which it was intended, the protection of writers' economic interests."[27] The All-Guild slate secretly rounded up hundreds of proxies and sprung them in a surprise maneuver the night of the vote, which they won by an overwhelming majority.

The guild made it a priority from that time forward to protect its reputation from charges of Communism, and by the end of 1947, although it was a vocal critic of HUAC's practices, it had accepted Section 9H of the new Taft-Hartley labor law, which required officers of all trade unions to sign a non-Communist oath, purged its committees of Communists, and abandoned the Hollywood Ten. When Emmett Lavery, outgoing guild president, testified before HUAC in 1947, he spent much time establishing his own non-Communist bona fides and dissociating the Writers Guild from its Communist members, but he also strongly condemned HUAC's tactics.[28] This pattern—of condemning the Committee's tactics but conceding its premises—was endemic to all the talent guilds.

The Screen Actors Guild (SAG) was in any event more talk than action. It was not that the actors were less brave than their writer or director counterparts. Countless acts of individual defiance are part of the honor role of the period. Thus the actor John Randolph, who denounced the blacklist whenever he was in telephoning distance of the press, recalls arriving in Chicago, where he was booked for a summer-theater performance, only to be told by the manager that a letter from the head of the local American Legion post included (a) a dossier on Randolph and (b) a threat—fire Randolph or we'll picket and shut down the show. Randolph, who had been hit before, assumed the manager might want to call in an understudy, but the show went on as scheduled. After it was over, Randolph said with relief, "Well, I guess it was a bluff." The theater manager set him straight: "Now I can tell you what happened. The head of our Legion post is a florist. I called a Teamster friend and told him about the threat. He called the florist and said, 'Don't give me any of that shit. You picket that show and your trucks don't roll.' So they didn't picket."

Frank Wilkinson, executive director of the National Committee Against Repressive Legislation (who himself went to prison for contempt of Congress when in 1956 he invoked the First Amendment before the Committee), describes Randolph on a stage tour in 1955–56. "Every time he came to a city—L.A., San Francisco, Seattle, Chicago—he called in advance and said to get all the people from radio and television who have been hurt and I'll tell them what's going on. You'd look at the faces of these people, they were just so discouraged. He would tell them how things were improving here and there, how the tide had changed. It was like a religious revival. By the time he left everybody was picked up. . . . And this was a real risk in the mid-fifties."

But where isolated individuals rushed in, organizations—even those representing these same individuals—feared to tread, a particular inconvenience for performers. Writers could always hide behind pseudonyms, but as the actor Lee J. Cobb said, "It's the only face I have." Zero Mostel used to say, "I am a man of a thousand faces, all of them blacklisted."[29] Even where SAG passed an anti-blacklist resolution, its subsequent lack of action spoke louder than its occasionally brave words. In March 1951, Gale Sondergaard, famous up to that point as the Spider Woman and wife of Herbert Biberman of the Hollywood Ten, wrote SAG on the eve of her first appearance before the Un-American Activities Committee and asked it to denounce the Committee's attempt to intimidate witnesses and to say "that it will not tolerate any industry blacklist against any of its members who see fit to act upon a unanimous decision of the Supreme Court and avail themselves of the privilege against self-incrimination which is once more available for the purpose for which it was originally established—as a barrier to political and religious persecution. . . ." SAG's board of directors replied that it "totally rejects" the Communist Party line that HUAC was in the "witch-hunting" business:

> The deadly seriousness of the international situation dictates the tone of our reply. This is not the time for dialectic fencing. Like the overwhelming majority of the American people, we believe that a "clear and present danger" to our nation exists. The Guild Board believes that all participants in the international Communist Party conspiracy against our nation should be exposed for what they are— enemies of our country and of our own form of government.
>
> It is not the province of the Guild Board to decide what is the best method of carrying out this aim. . . . We will watch with extreme interest the way in which the hearings are conducted. . . .
>
> The Guild as a labor union will fight any secret blacklist created by any group of employers. On the other hand, if any actor by his own actions outside of union activities has so offended American public opinion that he has made himself unsalable at the box office, the Guild cannot and would not want to force any employer to hire him. That is the individual actor's personal responsibility and it cannot be shifted to his union.[30]

Other actors' organizations showed not much more bravery. Actors' Equity condemned the blacklist as "iniquitous" when General Foods fired the actress Jean Muir from *The Aldrich Family,* but nine months later, in June 1951, when asked whether Equity would protect those called before the House Un-American Activities Committee, the Equity council issued "a general statement of principle" using language identical to SAG's.

By June 1953, Equity's council still condemned blacklisting, and the "regular" slate beat the "conservative" slate 16 to 2, but even the so-called regulars had pledged to sign the non-Communist (and nonfascist) oath. In September of that year the organization voted to expel any member proven "by due process of law" to belong to the Communist Party or to be guilty of any subversive act; and it pledged to use its influence and prestige to support the government against the "legally proven plan of the Communist Party to overthrow the government."[31]

On August 10, 1955, the American Federation of Television and Radio Artists (AFTRA) passed a national referendum (3967 to 914) that if a member refused to answer the question whether or not he was or ever had been a Communist he "shall be subject to the charge that he is guilty of conduct prejudicial to the welfare of AFTRA" and the local board could at its discretion "fire, censure, suspend or expel the accused from membership in accordance with the constitution and by-laws of the local, subject to such appeals as are provided."[32]

And the directors were no more immune to the prevailing cultural climate than their officers were to the loyalty-oath provisions of Taft-Hartley.[33] When Joseph L. Mankiewicz, who had written and directed such films as *A Letter to Three Wives* (1949) and *All About Eve* (1950), was elected president of the Screen Directors Guild (SDG) in 1950, he signed the officers' oath. That the oath was mandatory for officers, however, did not mean that it was mandatory for members, and Mankiewicz was elected at least partly because he was against a mandatory membership oath. Cecil B. De Mille, a founding member of SDG and perhaps the most successful money-director in Hollywood, had a different idea. He was a right-wing activist whose Cecil B. De Mille Foundation regularly provided "information" to California's little HUAC, the Tenney Committee, and to the real HUAC in Washington, and he had proposed that SDG members be required to file reports, which would be available to prospective employers, on the politics of those they had worked with after the completion of every film.

In July 1950 De Mille took advantage of Mankiewicz's absence on a two-month trip to Europe to mobilize the SDG's board of directors and pass a "mandatory loyalty oath" bylaw. Under the guild's constitution, once the board took such action, all that was required from the members was a courtesy ballot checked "yes" or "no." Since the ballots were open and signed, and the political climate was oppressive, such ballots were generally considered *pro forma,* and the measure had been adopted by a large majority by the time Mankiewicz returned to Los Angeles in September.

In addition, De Mille instituted a campaign to discredit Mankiewicz. He leaked items to the trade papers hinting that Mankiewicz was a "pinko," a "fellow traveler," an unreliable intellectual. And he went so far as to show what the director Robert Parrish has called "a secret Joseph Mankiewicz film festival," whose purpose was to identify the subversion and agitprop in such films as *The Philadelphia Story* (1940), *If I Had a Million* (1932), and *Million Dollar Legs* (1932).

In October De Mille followed his move to impose a loyalty oath on the SDG membership with an effort to kick Mankiewicz out of office via the circulation of a ballot to "recall" the recently elected president. He sent out a 650-word telegram to the SDG senior members asking for Mankiewicz's ouster and accusing him of being "dictatorial" to the extent of rendering impossible "the democratic procedure of the board." Joseph Losey recalls De Mille sending around a corps of motorcycle cops (his private force) collecting proxy signatures for the recall. When a pro-Mankiewicz caucus heard of De Mille's effort, it mobilized to intervene. Under the bylaws, the only way to do that was to petition for a special separate meeting of the full membership to consider the proposed recall. The signatures of twenty-five members in good standing were needed to call such a meeting, and they had to be collected, signed, notarized, and turned in to the executive secretary (who happened to be a De Mille man and was making himself scarce) before the recall votes were collected and counted. If not, according to Parrish, who was part of the pro-Mankiewicz faction, "all was lost."

"It was a Friday," says Losey, "and we had to get the signatures by midnight to head him off. I remember it was a warm day, and Fred Zinnemann, John Huston, and I and various people decided to get together a group of directors at Chasen's at seven that night and we spent the afternoon rounding up others. The meeting occurred and Mankiewicz insisted on bringing Martin Gang. When we gathered we found we had twenty-three or twenty-one, not twenty-five. We went out into the restaurant and collected directors as they came in for dinner until we got at least twenty-five. Then Joe Mankiewicz said, 'Look, if we're going to fight this vicious thing we've got to be clean ourselves, and I suggest that we jointly declare that we are not members of the Communist Party.' In other words he was proposing that this group do exactly more or less the same thing which had been proposed by De Mille."

Parrish remembers that Gang, who didn't take a fee, pointed out that according to the new bylaw, "a member was not in good standing unless he had signed a loyalty oath and that any signatures on petitions would be invalid unless each signing member also swore that he was not a member of the Communist Party and did not support any organization that believes in or teaches the overthrow of the U.S. government by force or by any illegal or unconstitutional methods."

A lot of people around the table opposed the idea, including Losey. There was a noisy debate at which one heard "the usual arguments" about the need to "fight fire with fire" versus the need to adhere to the principles Mankiewicz had campaigned on—the secret ballot, an end to blacklisting, no loyalty oath. Losey remembers that "Martin Gang, as it happens, was sitting next to me and at one point he leaned over to me and said, 'I don't know whether you're in the CP or not but you're not under oath so it won't be perjury—sign it!' And I did. We all signed it. Every fucking one of us." Huston was number one, Losey was number seventeen, Billy Wilder was number twenty-one, and Walter Reisch, sitting in a booth, was cornered as the last signer, number twenty-five.

The full membership meeting, which was held at the Beverly Hills Hotel on October 22, lasted six and a half hours. De Mille made a speech attacking Mankiewicz's supporters as unserious, subversive, and "foreign born" (boos and hisses), and a De Mille man charged that Mankiewicz leaked to *Variety* (laughter). Mankiewicz made a speech on why he opposed the blacklist and the mandatory oath, and why he favored the secret ballot. George Stevens, the director of *Giant*, asked De Mille to recall the recall. John Ford asked De Mille to apologize or resign. Finally, the assembled gave Mankiewicz a unanimous vote of confidence, with four abstentions, and De Mille and the entire board were forced to resign.

Four days later Mankiewicz sent a letter to all SDG members asking them "as a voluntary act in affirmation of confidence in your guild" to sign the loyalty oath since it had been made mandatory by the August membership vote. Members were told to "set aside whatever reservations you may have concerning any aspect of our oath or its method of adoption, and sign it now!" So the loyalty oath went through as the first act of Mankiewicz, who had been elected to stop it—the first mandatory loyalty oath in a Hollywood talent guild. At Christmas that year, Mankiewicz sent the twenty-five directors photostatic framed copies of the document they had all signed. "I'm not pleased to be on that list," says Losey. "If the loyalty oath hadn't gone through the guild, history might have been slightly different, because it started the ball rolling."

It was the Screen Writers Guild suit, however, that seemed to hold the most promise. Initiated in 1948 in response to the Waldorf statement, *Screen Writers Guild, Inc.* v. *Motion Picture Association of America et al.* charged the producers with collusion and its specific purpose was to squelch the blacklist. Since Thurman Arnold, the New Dealer who founded the prestigious Washington firm of Arnold, Fortas and Porter, had been retained to handle the case, everyone was optimistic. But in January 1953 Arnold went to dinner with the SWG's executive committee, and after much wine they agreed that although SWG would probably lose at the district court level, it might prevail in the higher courts. They also agreed that as a result of that assessment they had best reassess their own position.

"What I am afraid of," Arnold said, "and you must face, is an attack on the guild itself being subversive for bringing this suit. Senator McCarthy will be in greater power than he ever was before. It has worried me considerably—the guild's being called before the Committee to explain why this suit is being pursued. It can be explained, but it is a problem in [view] of the press. I know that many of you as individuals are committed to this suit, but whether the guild itself can face the initial adverse decision, even though I anticipate a favorable decision a year later, I don't know. If it were an individual, I would say go ahead and sue. But can the guild maintain its organization and morale under that kind of possible attack? . . .

"If you can do it, I think it would redound tremendously to the credit of the guild, because no other organization in the United States has taken such a public-spirited action on behalf of civil liberties, but how much strain can you stand?"

The decision taken was akin to Senator George Aiken's proposal, made in the waning days of the Vietnam war, that the United States proclaim "victory" in Southeast Asia and then retreat. According to the minutes of the guild meeting at which it was discussed, the guild decided that since Eric Johnston, president of the Producers Association, had denied any industry-wide collusion in the deposition he filed in connection with the case, if his position—that there was no blacklist—were interpreted as a promise for the future, this in effect was a victory. And so they voted to recommend to the guild's board that, "If Mr. Johnston's statement under oath that the producers do not act in concert nor do they intend to is reaffirmed, the guild will withdraw from the case."[34]

The SWG was more adamant, however, when it came to protecting its right to arbitrate credits. This, after all, represented one of its most important and critical early victories, and when the blacklist, at the insistence of the late Howard Hughes, threatened to take it away, SWG fought back. It all happened over a picture called *The Las Vegas Story* (1952).

It is fitting that according to the so-called *auteur* theory, the real "author" of a film is not its writer but its director. Historically the writer has always been relatively low on Hollywood's totem pole. The first movies, the one- or two-reel "flickers," didn't even use writers. And when writers were eventually signed on, it was simply to write titles to accompany the action. With the advent of talkies, writers became more or less indispensable, but their status didn't improve all that much. Maybe it's because moviemaking is a collective enterprise and writing is a solitary occupation—whatever the reason, the screenwriter has always been seen more as a worker on the assembly line than inventor of the product.

It is not merely that the writer is only one among a score of creative contributors to a picture, but also that a script usually goes through more than one rewrite by more than one writer, and frequently it builds on, is added to and/or subtracted from, an amalgam of preexisting scripts by a variety of other writers. It is not unusual to see a list of credits that might include "Screenplay by . . . " "Adaptation by . . . " "Additional scenes by . . . " "Additional dialogue by . . . " "Original story by . . . " "Suggested by a story/novel/play by . . ." "Based on a character from a play by . . ." et cetera. Since a writer can't take credit for the film itself, he takes credit for his credit. Like the scholar who must publish or perish, the screenwriter's job, prestige, and salary are functions of his list of credits, especially his last one. It was the spectacle of producers passing out unearned screenwriter credits to friends and relatives that was a main motivation for John Howard Lawson, the SWG's first president, in his fight for the establishment of an effective guild in the 1930s. "A writer's name," he said, "is his most cherished possession. It is the basis of his economic life, and the 'trademark' which establishes his competence and craftsmanship. It is more than the means by which he earns his bread. It is his creative personality, the symbol of the whole body of his ideas and experience."[35]

And indeed, one of the guild's enduring achievements was to secure for its members so-called Minimum Basic Agreement with the producer, which specifies precisely how credits are to be allotted. Under the agreement, first secured in 1941 and renewed just before the Hollywood hearings of 1951, the Screen Writers Guild won the final right to say to whom screen-writing credits could go. Any writer who had worked on a picture had the right to object to the award of credit and appeal to a committee of three SWG members chosen from a rotating panel. These panels acted as arbitrators, and their decisions were considered final.

Barely a month after SWG won a renewal of its right to arbitrate credits, the screenwriter Paul Jarrico, who had worked on the screenplay for the upcoming RKO movie *The Las Vegas Story*, starring Jane Russell and Victor Mature, took the Fifth Amendment before HUAC, and Howard Hughes, then owner of RKO, moved to take away his credit. Jarrico appealed to the guild, and its arbitration committee awarded him the credit. Hughes still refused to yield and went to court asking for a declaratory judgment asserting that Jarrico had violated the "morals" clause in his contract by taking the Fifth Amendment before the House Committee on Un-American Activities. Jarrico filed his own cross-claim asking for damages; and SWG sued Hughes for breaching the bargaining agreement it had with the producers. At first RKO offered to pay Jarrico a bonus if he would let them drop his name from the credits, but in the midst of the negotiations the volatile Hughes called them off and joined the MPAPAI. Thereafter, his high-powered lawyers prevailed, as the California Supreme Court ruled that SWG lacked power to enforce the arbitration provisions of its contract with the producers, since the dispute was between a writer and his studio. This finding appeared to place in jeopardy the entire Minimum Basic Agreement. If SWG couldn't enforce its credit arbitrations, what good was it?

The guild met with RKO and the Association of Motion Picture Producers and by 1952 they worked out a "compromise," which was approved by the guild membership on April 23, 1953, by a 241–61 vote.[36] Under the new understanding, the language of the Minimum Basic Agreement would be amended so that in the future SWG would again legally arbitrate credit awards, but in exchange for that SWG officially ceded to the producers the right to deny credit to a writer who admitted membership in the Communist Party or falsely claimed he was not a member, who appeared before a committee of Congress and refused to answer questions, or who refused to answer a producer's questions about membership in the Communist Party. (The amendment was kept in the contract when it was renewed in 1955, and remained until 1977 when it was finally removed.)

In short, to preserve the right to arbitrate credits in general, SWG ceded the producers the right to take away credits for political "crimes."

An unintended byproduct of this concession was that it made life easier for the producer who was inclined to use black-market writers "under the table." No longer need the producers fear that a black-market writer would blow his cover and insist on his credit, to the embarrassment—and possible financial detriment—of the studio. Activity on the black market picked up, and dormant projects were revived. For example, for some years Allied Artists had been sitting on Michael Wilson's script for *Friendly Persuasion*, afraid to make the movie for fear Wilson would demand credit. In 1956 they shot the film and on March 26, 1957, sent SWG a letter informing it that they were exercising their option to deny Wilson screen credit, even though the guild's arbitration committee had awarded it to him. As Wilson recounted the situation nineteen years later: "William Wyler, the producer-director, chose to list as co-authors of the screenplay his brother Robert and Jessamyn West, the author of the short stories on which my screenplay had been based. I appealed to the guild for an arbitration and was later informed that a panel of my peers had ruled unanimously that I was the sole author of the shooting script. When Allied Artists was also so informed, a company spokesman reminded the guild that I did not have to be given credit because I had been a naughty boy. Very well, said the guild spokesman, but you can't give credit to another writer. And so for the first and perhaps the only time a Hollywood picture was released that wasn't written by anyone."

Later *Friendly Persuasion* (1956) won a Writers Guild Award and the Palme d'Or at Cannes, "so my noncredit on the film gained me more recognition than I would have received had my name been on it."[37]

Despite the boom on the black market it would be a mistake to say that the agreement improved the lot of the writers it most affected. Albert Maltz, for instance, wrote some black-market scripts for vastly reduced fees, but in a land where credit is all, Paramount exercised its option to omit his name from the remake of *This Gun for Hire* (which the guild arbitrators had ruled should read "Based on a Screenplay by Albert Maltz and W. R. Burnett"). Others fared no better.

"Which side are you on?" asked the chorus of a militant folk song popular with the progressives of the 1940s. Had a poll been taken, the membership of the Hollywood culture guilds might have been hard put to answer. The Screen Actors Guild was against the blacklist but refused to defend blacklistees. The directors' caucus signed a loyalty oath to defeat a loyalty oath. The liberals in the Screen Writers Guild objected to the Communists because they employed underhanded parliamentary maneuvers to work their will, and defeated them by employing underhanded parliamentary maneuvers. And to protect its right to arbitrate credits, SWG gave up its right to arbitrate credits. In each case these organizations or their officers and councils set out to protect the rights of their members; in each case they ended up on the sidelines. In each case they began by supporting a principle; in each case they ended by claiming victory for an interest.

As they saw it, their membership—the majority of whom were not directly affected—had much to lose by pursuing lost causes. But what about those who had nothing to lose? What about those whose treatment by the industry had been so shabby that their only real choice for advancement as a class was by opposing and helping to transform it? What about the sense of solidarity and comradeship that is presumed to bind the underclass, the underdog, the victim?

On July 18, 1949, Jack ("Jackie") Roosevelt Robinson, the first black to break the color line in major-league baseball, was called as a witness before the House Un-American Activities Committee.

When Branch Rickey hired Robinson to join the Brooklyn Dodgers organization in 1947 he had extracted a number of promises from him, one of them that he would stay out of politics. But as Robinson himself mentioned to the Committee in 1949 in explaining why he was happy to accept its invitation, "the question of Communist activity in the United States isn't partisan politics." First Robinson acknowledged his discomfort in appearing before such a controversial forum:

> I have had a great many messages come to me, by wire, phone and letter, urging me not to show up at this hearing. And I ought to make it plain that not all of this urging came from Communist sympathizers. Of course, most of it did. But some came from people for whom I have a lot of respect and who are just as opposed to Communist methods as I am.
>
> And so it isn't pleasant for me to find myself in the middle of a public argument that has nothing to do with the standing of the Brooklyn Dodgers in the pennant race—or even the pay raise I am going to ask Mr. Branch Rickey for next year!
>
> So you'll naturally ask, why did I stick my neck out by agreeing to be present and why did I stand by my agreement in spite of the advice to the contrary.[38]

Robinson attributed his appearance to his "sense of responsibility." And he made it clear that he had few illusions about the lot of blacks in America, and that he intended to fight Jim Crow *despite* rather than because the Communists "kick up a big fuss over racial discrimination when it suits their purposes."

Whether he knew it or not, he then got to the reason he had been invited to testify: "I've been asked to express my views on Paul Robeson's statement in Paris to the effect that American Negroes would refuse to fight in any war against Russia because we love Russia so much. I haven't any comment to make on that statement except that if Mr. Robeson actually made it, it sounds very silly to me. . . ." After Robinson finished his statement, various Committee members complimented him. Congressman Morgan Moulder of Missouri observed that "it is not the purpose of this Committee in conducting these hearings to question the loyalty of the Negro race. There is no question about that. It is to give an opportunity to you and others to combat the idea Paul Robeson had given by his statements." Congressman Francis Case of South Dakota asked Robinson a few questions about whether he found any support for Robeson's attitude in the army or school among Negroes and Robinson said that he had not.

There was, although it was not remarked on publicly at the time, a *de facto* double standard when it came to blacks. Unlike whites, blacks interested in getting back to work were not automatically required or expected to name names. Instead, they had a number of options, among which the most effective was to denounce Paul Robeson.

Robeson had been larger than life. An All-American football player at Rutgers University—where he won prizes in oratory, a Phi Beta Kappa key in his junior year, and letters in baseball, basketball, and track—he had gotten a law degree from Columbia University while supporting himself by playing professional football on weekends, before he turned to the theater.

Eugene O'Neill put him in *All God's Chillun Got Wings,* and in 1924 he played his most famous role, O'Neill's Emperor Jones, after which he appeared in *Showboat* on Broadway singing "Ole Man River" and in *Othello* in London in 1930. It wasn't until 1943, in the middle of the war, that a black man could kiss a white woman on an American stage; Robeson did it as Othello and the play ran for 295 performances, a Shakespearean record on Broadway. He cut short his own movie career after making eleven films, leaving Hollywood in 1942 because the movie industry stereotyped blacks as "plantation Hallelujah shouters."

He ran into virulent race prejudice in Nazi Germany in 1934, but he was celebrated in the Soviet Union, and later spoke of "the principles of scientific socialism," and he had gone to Spain to sing for the antifascist troops. His testimony before HUAC in 1956 anticipated a number of the themes and some of the rhetoric of the black-power, black-nationalist, and other militant and not-so-militant black groups of the 1960s, but at that time, it was too much. He lost his passport in 1950 and his income dropped from $104,000 in 1947 to $2000 in 1950. His name was removed from the list of All-Americans and in 1952 he accepted a Stalin Peace prize.

Robeson invoked the Fifth Amendment when he appeared before HUAC although he apparently never joined the Communist Party; but he had taken Party-line positions on a number of issues, such as the resolution calling for restored civil liberties for members of the Socialist Workers Party. At a Bill of Rights Conference sponsored by the Civil Rights Congress at New York's Henry Hudson Hotel on July 17, 1949, Robeson opposed a motion on behalf of the Trotskyist Smith Act victims by asking, "Would you give civil rights to the Ku Klux Klan?"

"No," chorused the delegates.

"These men are the allies of fascism who want to destroy the new democracies of the world," the singer shouted (according to *The New York Times*). "Let's not get confused. They are the enemies of the working class."

Robeson also used the occasion to reaffirm his earlier statement that the Negro people would not take part in "an imperialist war."

Following his address, a resolution affirming that "Paul Robeson does indeed speak for us in his fight for Negro rights and in his fight for peace" was adopted unanimously by the 346 Negro delegates.[39]

It was not until he died in 1976 that Paul Robeson was once again celebrated in the white media. Television shows honored his memory[40] and editorialists the country over lamented his fate. Many quoted his famous 1956 retort when asked by Congressman Gordon Scherer of Ohio if he felt so free in Russia why he had not stayed there. "Because my father was a slave, and my people died to build this country, and I am going to stay here, and have a part just like you. . . ."[41]

Canada Lee and Harlem's fabled congressman, Adam Clayton Powell, had been boys in Harlem together. Violinist, boxer, actor, Lee had played Othello, Bigger Thomas in *Native Son* on Broadway and Kid Chocolate in *Body and Soul*. Then, as Stefan Kanfer has reported: "In 1949, reduced to penury, he called a press conference to protest his anti-Communism. 'I refer to the drivel that has come from the so-called secret files of the FBI about one Canada Lee,' he said. 'I am not a Communist. This is a simple fact.' " By the summer of 1952 he had been banned from forty television shows after the American Tobacco Company dumped him from those it sponsored. "How long can a man take this kind of unfair treatment?" he had asked in a letter to the editor of *Variety*.

Not too long, as it turned out. That same summer, Lee delivered himself of an attack on Paul Robeson, and Hollywood rewarded him with the role of Reverend Stephen Kumalo in Alan Paton's *Cry, the Beloved Country* (1952), filmed near Johannesburg, South Africa. (Unbeknownst to the general public, the author of the screenplay of *Cry* was John Howard Lawson, in his last serious effort for Hollywood.) Lee returned to the United States, his blood pressure high, and his mood depressed by the apartheid scenes he had witnessed on location. He was offered television roles, but the offers were withdrawn as sponsors waited for someone else to use him first. He went to his friend Walter White, executive secretary of the NAACP. "I can't take it anymore," he said. "I'm going to get a shoeshine box and sit outside the Astor Theatre. My picture is playing to capacity audiences and, my God, I can't get one day's work." Walter White told him not to make waves and predicted the trouble would disappear. A few weeks later, penniless and alone, Lee died, and the *Daily Worker* commented:

> ... those who joined with the torturers three and a half years ago now vulture-like seek to embrace their victim. Like one, the red-baiting obituary writers of the commercial press seize upon two sentences from the Negro actor while he was on the economic rack: "I am not a Communist or a joiner of any kind. ..."
>
> They could not make Canada Lee into a cold war stool pigeon. He fought for his dignity, even when he did not understand the nature of that fight. ...[42]

Kanfer has written that Leonard Lyons disagreed: "The *Worker* is trying to claim Canada Lee," he wrote. "The fact is that Lee worked with anti-Communist groups for the past three years. After he made *Cry the Beloved Country* he told me: 'I'd rather be the lowest sharecropper in Mississippi or Georgia, than live in South Africa. America is the best place for the Negro, for no place else is there any real hope for decent living.'"[43]

Joshua Daniel White, the black folksinger who made his "St. James Infirmary Blues" the anthem of a college generation, had a more successful rehabilitation. He appeared before HUAC on September 1, 1950, at his own request, as he explained, "for my own sake, and for the sake of many other entertainers who, like myself, have been used and exploited by people who give allegiance to a foreign power."

White portrayed himself as a dupe, an artist who knew "mighty little about the ins and outs of 'movements' and parties" despite his many Communist-front appearances. He told of his childhood years: "I was seven years old when I left my home in Greenville, South Carolina . . . to lead a blind man while playing the tambourine. Before I was eight years old I knew what it meant to be kicked and abused. Before I was nine years old I had seen two lynchings. I got to hate Jim Crow for what it did to me personally and because Jim Crow is an insult to God's creatures and a violation of the Christian beliefs taught by my father."

White then explained how he became a folksinger, recording first at the age of sixteen under the name "Joshua White, the Singing Christian." Then, said White, he had some bad luck. He hurt his hand and for five years it remained paralyzed, until his prayers were answered, the paralysis ended and he got a role in a play, *John Henry,* in which Paul Robeson had the lead.

> I have a great admiration for Mr. Robeson as an actor and great singer, and if what I read in the papers is true, I feel sad over the help he's been giving to people who despise America. He has a right to his own opinions, but when he, or anybody, pretends to talk for the whole race, he's kidding himself. His statement that the Negroes would not fight for their country, against Soviet Russia or any other enemy, is both wrong and an insult; because I stand ready to fight Russia or any enemy of America.

White went on to explain how, although not officially a member of the Party, he had been duped by it. He didn't know that any of the Communist fronts for which he performed were fronts until he learned "the hard way," when in 1947 he read about the attorney general's list and saw all of their names on it. "It was an awful blow. I realized that I had been played for a sucker." He discussed the matter with his manager, who put him in touch with Howard Rushmore, the newspaperman "who knows a lot about the Communist rackets and could give us some guidance."

White explained that whenever he sang the powerful antilynching song "Strange Fruit," he coupled it with "The House I Live In or What Is America to Me."[44] The Committee had no questions, White was dismissed, and shortly thereafter he went back to work.

Not all blacks were required to denounce Paul Robeson. One important exception was the poet Langston Hughes, who had included a chapter on the Un-American Activities Committee in his book *Simple Speaks His Mind* (1950), and had been named as a Communist by two professional witnesses, Louis Budenz and Manning Johnson, in 1953. Hughes, who was represented by the black attorney Frank Reeves when he was called before the McCarthy Committee in 1953 in connection with its investigation into the United States Information Agency (two hundred copies of his sixteen books were to be found in fifty-one USIA libraries abroad), was required to denounce only his previous naïveté and his work. He told the Committee he thought some of his early books "definitely" did not belong on USIA shelves. In addition, he came forward with what he called "affirmations"—examples of his work that "affirmed" the American way of life. He asserted unequivocally that he was not then and had never been a member of the Communist Party. He told the McCarthy Committee he thought his story "When a Man Sees Red" was an example of the free speech allowed in America and on those grounds conceivably could have some useful life in USIA libraries. He also noted that since large portions of the books were written in Harlem slang and Negro idiom, foreigners might find it difficult to understand or translate and on those grounds it might be inappropriate to include them. His poem "Goodbye, Christ" was, he said, his most misunderstood poem: intended ironically, it was misinterpreted as antireligious. He proceeded to quote from another poem, "Ma Lord" to prove his religiosity. Throughout the next years he was constantly compiling dossiers, answering misinformed mail, correcting magazine and newspaper comments that suggested that his politics were other than he had represented them to be before the Committee.

After he appeared he spoke with the liberal lawyer Lloyd Garrison and wrote to his own attorney, Frank Reeves, on a number of points, among them:

> ... if you think wise (and I do) you might send the FBI a copy of the transcript of my testimony for their files with a brief covering note, since Cohn told us Hoover once used "Goodbye, Christ" in a speech, and perhaps should therefore be advised that this no longer represents my views in any way. Please let me know your opinion on this, and I'll be guided thereby.
>
> Lloyd Garrison feels that we might also draw up a brief statement using portions of the transcript of the open hearing to send the American Legion ... who might pass the word down to the red-baiters in

their Indianapolis office who've been sending out mimeographed material à la *Red Channels* on a number of writers and artists, to correct
their material on me, at least to the extent that it conform with my
sworn testimony.... All of my publishers are pleased with the out-
come of the hearings, have backed me up beautifully, and are going
ahead with their publishing plans in relation to my work. But it would
do no harm to have a brief résumé and interpretation of my testimony
on tap, if needed, and I'll draw one up (getting your and Garrison's
OK before giving anyone copies) as soon as I get the transcript.[45]

The fact was, Hughes was untypical. For the most part, those blacks
who did not denounce Robeson settled their problems quietly. The singer
Lena Horne, for instance, was permitted to work out her difficulties behind the scenes. After the New York paper the *Journal American* tried to
have her barred from a scheduled appearance on Ed Sullivan's television
variety show, *Toast of the Town*, her manager, Robert Harris, announced
that Miss Horne had "made her peace" with *Counterattack* by conferring
with ex-FBI agent Theodore Kirkpatrick, its publisher. The substance of
what she told him was not revealed, only the purpose of the conversation:
"to clear up once and for all the propaganda emanating from *Counterattack* charging her with having been associated with 'subversive' causes
and implying that she was therefore unfit to entertain Americans....
Most of these things have now been straightened out," Harris said.
"She's been given a clean bill of health. But she'll try to avoid groups
which are *called* subversive."[46]

Not that it did that much good. As the black actor William Marshall
told me, "Lena Horne never had much of a film career to speak of. She
would always be set off in white and make a guest appearance but she
never had any career. If you are black it's very difficult to know if you're
being whitelisted—which is what I call it. Because you don't know.
Horne had little before and little after."

Another politically controversial black who had won favor with a
white audience was Harry Belafonte. Dubbed by the disk jockey Sym-
phony Sid as "the Cinderella gentleman" (because, in January 1949,
when he was twenty-one, he had walked into New York's Royal Roost
one night, done a number, and was signed up on the spot for twenty
weeks), Belafonte, singing songs of social significance like his own "Recognition," had quickly become a cult figure and then later a national pop
star with his "Banana Boat Song." His introduction to Hollywood came
in 1952 when he starred in *The Bright Road*, and then in 1954 he was

offered the lead in the film *Carmen Jones* (1955), playing opposite Dorothy Dandridge. It was to be the first Hollywood production in which a black man played a leading role. But his contract was conditioned on his clearing himself. For advice, and his blessing, Belafonte went to the man he most respected in the black community, Paul Robeson, and said, "I'd like to write a statement saying, 'I did "Caravans for Wallace" because I was paid for it.' Is that bad?" Robeson said, "No, there are few enough jobs for blacks as it is and I wouldn't tell a black what to do."

Belafonte was visited by a representative of the Un-American Activities Committee and "she said she knew about the time I put my hand through a car window in February 1953, the night the Supreme Court turned down the Rosenberg appeal. I said to myself, It could only be one man who told them that—the motherfucker who was driving the car. And I told that to Paul Robeson, but Paul said, 'Wait a minute. Look at what this is doing to us, the insidious suspicion it is creating. Maybe that poor fella went to a poker game the next night and said do you know what that crazy Harry Belafonte did? He broke my car window because of what the Supreme Court didn't do. So it wasn't only one person who could have finked. Maybe it was seventeen!' "

Belafonte never had to name names either, but that did not stop people from thinking he had. He remembers that "Sidney Poitier saved me one night at a bar in Harlem from a man with a knife who came at me—he was part of the left—because he thought, how could I have possibly gotten on the Ed Sullivan show unless I finked?"

Why the double standard for blacks? William Marshall, who played "de Lawd" in the Broadway revival of *Green Pastures* and has made something of a career playing nonstereotypes, says: "It seems to me the oligarchy wanted to avoid the mistake of letting other black men become martyrs to the black people, as happened with Paul Robeson. That's why they caused white men like Parks and Kazan to lay themselves bare in public, but not blacks. They wanted to use blacks, not humiliate them." At later points in American history, Marshall points out, Martin Luther King, Jr., Malcolm X, and Medgar Evers were each assassinated at the point at which the white oligarchy could no longer use him, and he believes that in a metaphorical sense, this is what happened to Robeson. Robeson lost his international forum when he was deprived of his passport, his domestic forum when blacklisting and intimidation cost him his concert bookings. By having blacks denounce him, suggests Marshall, the idea was to isolate Robeson from his own people.

Whites, then, either dismissed him as a Communist dupe or regarded him with regret as a tragic figure whose astonishing promise remained unfulfilled. For many blacks, he was the sun around which all else revolved. Because blacks already lacked stature in the Hollywood scheme of things, nothing was to be gained by subjecting them to the humiliation routinely visited on whites. They were called upon to degrade not themselves, but their star. And he, in turn, granted indulgences to those blacks who chose collaboration over unemployment on the theory that they had enough problems without shouldering the additional burden of opposing the white man's list. It wasn't their fight.

———

The talent blamed their agents, and the agents blamed the studios, and the studios blamed HUAC, and HUAC blamed the pressure groups. The pressure groups blamed their members, said their hands were tied. (However, when the national commander of the American Legion told Martin Gang that the Legion helped to circulate the names of subversives only because their members insisted on it, his fellow attorney Milton Rudin made a tour of Legion posts across the country, only to find that few of the members really cared.[47]) Lawyers blamed their clients, and clients blamed their lawyers. Blacks blamed The Man.

Thirty years after the documented fact, George Murphy asserts that there never was a blacklist. Denial of fact can always be disproved by evidence; not so denial of responsibility.

Yet Dore Schary wasn't responsible for the producers' Waldorf-Astoria decision—after all, he voted against it—he was merely the messenger who brought the bad news. William Wheeler wasn't responsible for his work on HUAC—he was just a cop doing his job. The gossip columnists weren't responsible for tarnishing names—they were just reporting facts. The producers weren't responsible for making decisions to keep from being picketed—they were simply trying to protect declining profits. Martin Gang wasn't responsible for his clients' pleas before the congressional committees—he told them their options and they made their choices. Phil Cohen wasn't responsible for his patients' decisions—he simply tried to strengthen their ability to cope with their problems. The Jewish agencies weren't responsible for hounding the guilty—their job was to help the innocent. The director Lewis Allen wasn't responsible for the blacklisting of the writer Lewis Allen—he wrote a letter only to clarify the confusion and clear his own name. Agents weren't responsible for clients who refused to listen to common sense, who refused to tell the studio or the state what it wanted to hear so they could go back to work. Stanley Kramer wasn't responsible for Carl Foreman's failure to be "totally forthright"—his first obligation was to the independence of his enterprise. The Mankiewicz faction in the Screen Directors Guild weren't responsible for the loyalty oath they signed to protest a loyalty oath—they were simply following the advice of counsel. The letter writers weren't responsible for the maintenance of the principle of self-abnegation as a condition of employment—they were simply trying to go back to work without hurting their friends. The guilds weren't responsible for the well-being of members whose politics interfered with profits—their primary obligation was to protect the interest of the membership at large and that required strategic restraint. The blacks weren't responsible for what William Marshall calls the whitelist. . . .

The buck, in other words, stopped nowhere, and the informers were afloat in a sea of nonresponsibility.

But being a spectator, going along, even pitching in at one remove is one thing; betrayal is another. And on the evidence of their testimony few of the informers were ready to admit—at least to HUAC—that they were afloat in a sea of nonresponsibility. The ritual required that they, of all the players in the big charade, take responsibility upon themselves. At the time, they did so, loudly if not gladly. Why were they required to do it? Why did they say they did it, and what do they have to say about it now?

PART II
STARS, STRIPES, AND STIGMAS

7.
Elia Kazan
And The Case
for Silence

A STORY IS TOLD that in 1955, after Arthur Miller had finished *A View from the Bridge,* his one-act play about a Sicilian waterfront worker who in a jealous rage informs on his illegal immigrant nephew, Miller sent a copy to Elia Kazan, who had directed his prize-winning smash Broadway hits *All My Sons* (1947) and *Death of a Salesman* (1949), but had broken with him over the issue of naming names before HUAC. "I have read your play and would be honored to direct it," Kazan is supposed to have wired back. "You don't understand," Miller replied, "I didn't send it to you because I wanted you to direct it. I sent it to you because I wanted you to know what I think of stool pigeons."

Apocryphal? Perhaps. But the story had credibility and currency because after Kazan's April 1952 testimony before HUAC, Miller and Kazan, once the closest of collaborators and the best of friends, no longer spoke. Kazan was not asked to direct Miller's next play, *The Crucible* (1953), and as Sam Zolotow delicately reported, "It is known that a disagreement—nothing to do with the play, though—exists between them that would make their further association incompatible."[1] They had planned to collaborate on a movie about the waterfront to be called "The Hook," but now Kazan went on to do his own waterfront picture, *On the Waterfront,* in which Terry Malloy comes to maturity when he realizes his obligation to fink on his fellow hoods. And Miller wrote *View,* which tried simultaneously to understand and condemn the informer. Kazan emerged in the folklore of the left as the quintessential informer, and Miller was hailed as the risk-taking conscience of the times. "One could almost say," said Richard Rovere, "that Miller's sense of himself is the principle that holds informing to be the ultimate in human wickedness."[2]

If we are to understand why so many otherwise high-minded people agreed to lend themselves to HUAC's degradation ceremonies, Kazan is a good place to begin. Not because he is typical—he was too successful, articulate, self-aware, and visible to be that—but because in his life, his politics, and his art he has done as much to defend the naming of names as his old colleague Miller has done to challenge it.

"If Kazan had refused to cooperate [with HUAC]," speculates one director-victim of the day, "he couldn't have derailed the Committee, but he might well have broken the blacklist. He was too important to be ignored." Probably no single individual could have broken the blacklist in April 1952, and yet no person was in a better strategic position to try than Kazan, by virtue of his prestige and economic invulnerability, to mount a symbolic campaign against it, and by this example inspire hundreds of fence sitters to come over to the opposition.

Even Kazan's harshest critics conceded he had earned his success and power through talent and effort. Born in 1909 in Istanbul, Turkey, to the Kazanjoglouses, a family of Anatolian Greeks who emigrated to the United States when he was four years old, Kazan worked his way through Williams College and Yale Drama School as a waiter. "I think the reason why I later joined the Communist Party and turned against everybody was born at Williams. I had this antagonism to privilege, to good looks, to Americans, to Wasps."[3]

An alumnus of the already legendary Group Theatre of the 1930s, in the late 1940s Kazan along with Lee Strasberg had helped to found the Actors Studio, which gave America the Stanislavski-based "method" and such outsize talents as Marlon Brando, Julie Harris, Lee J. Cobb, Montgomery Clift, Shelley Winters, and James Dean. Besides Miller's plays, Kazan directed such classics as Thornton Wilder's *The Skin of Our Teeth* and Tennessee Williams' *A Streetcar Named Desire*. His burgeoning career as a screen director was marked by the successes of *A Tree Grows in Brooklyn* (1945), the controversial *Gentleman's Agreement* (1948), the documentary-style *Boomerang* (1947), and the poetically powerful screen version of *Streetcar* (1951). From 1946 on he had *de facto* first-refusal rights on any Broadway-bound play. And since the blacklist never dominated the New York theater as it did Hollywood, the conventional wisdom was that he wouldn't have, in the vernacular of the day, to sing for his supper.

Kazan had a hard-won reputation for caring about the social content of his work. As an actor in the Group Theatre he was the taxi driver in Clifford Odets's *Waiting for Lefty* who held up his fist at the end and yelled "Strike!" as the audience yelled "Strike!" right back, in unison. As a member of the proletarian theater movement, he had co-authored a play with Art Smith (on whom he was later to inform) called *Dimitroff,* subtitled *A Play of Mass Pressure.* It told how the pressure of the world proletariat forced the release of the Bulgarian Communist Dimitroff after he gave a stirring courtroom speech and refused to confess falsely to the setting of the Reichstag fire. The villain of the play was the informer Vander Lubbe, who had been persuaded by Hitler and Göring to put the finger on Dimitroff. The hero of the play, the authors explained in an introductory note, is "mass pressure."[4]

On Broadway, the plays Kazan directed dealt with problems of conscience, responsibility, and personal honor in a materialistic society, and even in Hollywood he traded in such socially significant themes as anti-Semitism (*Gentleman's Agreement*), racial discrimination (*Pinky* [1949]), and revolution (*Viva Zapata* [1952]).

It was because Kazan seemed to take the social content of his art so seriously that his appearance before HUAC caused such astonished dismay among many of his friends and colleagues. He was in rehearsal in Boston on *Flight into Egypt,* George Tabori's play about a group of refugees from Austria awaiting passage to America, when he was first subpoenaed by HUAC and the rumors started to fly. He went to Washington for a hearing in executive session on a day when he and Tabori had been scheduled to observe the waiting room of a local hospital (on the theory that since much of the action of the play took place in a waiting room, maybe they would pick up some usable business). On his return, Kazan asked Tabori what he had seen, and the playwright, who felt that Kazan's own confusion about his HUAC appearance was distorting his perspective on the play and its theme of betrayal, was said to have replied, "They cut a man's tongue out."

The late Kermit Bloomgarden, who had produced *Death of a Salesman,* told me, "I do remember that any number of times in the course of the investigations Kazan would say he had been [in the Communist Party], he was not now, he wanted no part of the Communists, but if they wanted him to give names, he'd tell them where to get off. He told me that as late as six weeks before he testified.

"I had an office at 1545 Broadway on the first floor. Kazan had one on the fourth floor. My office had a window then. He waved to me through the window to come down and have a drink with him at Dinty Moore's. He told me he'd been to Washington and met with J. Edgar Hoover and Spyros Skouras and they wanted him to give names and he was going to call the people whom he had to name. Gadg [Kazan's nickname] wanted to know what I thought, and I said, 'Everyone must do what his conscience tells him to do.' He said, 'I've got to think of my kids.' And I said, 'This too shall pass, and then you'll be an informer in the eyes of your kids, think of that.' Finally we left Dinty Moore's and we walked down the block and he went his way and I went mine and we didn't see or speak to each other for fifteen years.* I immediately called Miller and I said to Arthur that it was ninety-nine percent sure that Gadg was giving names. Miller went over to see Gadg and Molly [Kazan's wife], and then he and Gadg walked for hours through the woods in Roxbury, Connecticut, where Miller told him he would regret it for the rest of his life and tried to talk him out of what he was going to do. When he couldn't, Gadg went to Washington and Miller went right up to Salem and wrote *The Crucible.*"

Kazan appeared before the House Un-American Activities Committee twice, the first time in January 1952, when he answered all questions except the one about what people he knew to be members of the Communist Party between the summer of 1934, when he joined it, and the spring of 1936, when he left. In April he told the Committee he had come to the conclusion "that I did wrong to withhold these names before, because secrecy serves the Communists, and is exactly what they want." Now his testimony, written in advance, was articulate, tough, and detailed as he named eight members of his Group Theatre unit and some Party functionaries. He split with the Party, he said, over its attempt to use him to take over the group:

> . . . I was instructed by the Communist unit to demand that the group be run "democratically." This was a characteristic Communist tactic; they were not interested in democracy; they wanted control. They had no chance of controlling the directors, but they thought that if authority went to the actors, they would have a chance to dominate through the usual tricks of behind-the-scenes caucuses, block voting, and confusion of issues.
>
> This was the specific issue on which I quit the Party. I had enough regimentation, enough of being told what to think and say and do, enough of their habitual violation of the daily practices of democracy to which I was accustomed. The last straw came when I was invited to go through a typical Communist scene of crawling and apologizing and admitting the error of my ways. . . .
>
> I had had a taste of police-state living and I did not like it.

---

* They met again when Bloomgarden was in the hospital after a heart attack and Kazan brought him some books.

Had he simply told his story and named his names along with the scores of other witnesses, he might have been denounced on the left, celebrated on the right, and his testimony forgotten. But Kazan was not content to let his affidavit speak for itself. First, he appended to his testimony an annotated bibliography *cum apologia* which listed and "explained" the entire history of his twenty-five professional forays as a director. This seemed to his critics unnecessary bending. Most of the items on his list were comparatively harmless, and Kazan said so, but whenever there was the possibility of an interpretation at odds with prevailing dogma, he anticipated the objection. Thus:

Boomerang (picture), 1946: Based on an incident in the life of Homer Cummings, later Attorney General of the United States. It tells how an initial miscarriage of justice was righted by the persistence and integrity of a young district attorney, who risked his career to save an innocent man. This shows the exact opposite of the Communist libels on America.

All My Sons, by Arthur Miller, 1947: The story of a war veteran who came home to discover that his father, a small manufacturer, had shipped defective plane parts to the Armed Forces during the war. Some people have searched for hidden propaganda in this one, but I believe it to be a deeply moral investigation of problems of conscience and responsibility.

Gentleman's Agreement (picture): Picture version of the best-selling novel about anti-Semitism. It won an Academy Award and I think it is in a healthy American tradition, for it shows Americans exploring a problem and tackling a solution. Again it is opposite to the picture which Communists present of Americans. . . .

Pinky (picture), 1949: The story of a Negro girl who passed for white in the North and returns to the South to encounter freshly the impact of prejudice. Almost everyone liked this except the Communists, who attracked it virulently. It was extremely successful throughout the country, as much so in the South as elsewhere. . . .

Viva Zapata (picture, my most recent one), 1951: This is an anti-Communist picture. Please see my article on political aspects of this picture in the *Saturday Review* of April 5, which I forwarded to your investigator, Mr. Nixon.[5]

The day after his testimony was given (in executive session), it was released, and the day after that (April 12, 1952) Kazan took an ad in *The New York Times* explaining his position and exhorting others to do likewise. Its logic—that the way to fight totalitarian secrecy was with free-world openness—seemed impeccable, if one accepted its premise (that all Communists were totalitarian conspirators), its asides (that the employment of liberals was threatened "because they had allowed themselves to be associated with Communists," rather than because some free-lance vigilantes had joined with HUAC to create and enforce a blacklist), and its rhetoric (Communist censorship is "thought control" but HUAC intimidation is unmentioned). It will be recalled—although Kazan didn't mention it in the ad—that part of the reason he left the Party was because they wanted him to confess error and humiliate himself.

Here is the ad:

A STATEMENT
by Elia Kazan

In the past weeks intolerable rumors about my political position have been circulating in New York and Hollywood. I want to make my stand clear:

I believe that Communist activities confront the people of this country with an unprecedented and exceptionally tough problem. That is, how to protect ourselves from a dangerous and alien conspiracy and still keep the free, open, healthy way of life that gives us self-respect.

I believe that the American people can solve this problem wisely only if they have the facts about Communism. All the facts.

Now, I believe that any American who is in possession of such facts has the obligation to make them known, either to the public or to the appropriate Government agency.

Whatever hysteria exists—and there is some, particularly in Hollywood—is inflamed by mystery, suspicion and secrecy. Hard and exact facts will cool it.

The facts I have are sixteen years out of date, but they supply a small piece of background to the graver picture of Communism today.

I have placed these facts before the House Committee on Un-American Activities without reserve and I now place them before the public and before my co-workers in motion pictures and in the theatre.

Seventeen and a half years ago I was a twenty-four-year-old stage manager and bit actor, making $40 a week, when I worked.

At that time nearly all of us felt menaced by two things: the depression and the ever growing power of Hitler. The streets were full of unemployed and shaken men. I was taken in by the Hard Times version of what might be called the Communists' advertising or recruiting technique. They claimed to have a cure for depressions and a cure for Naziism and Fascism.

I joined the Communist Party late in the summer of 1934. I got out a year and a half later.

I have no spy stories to tell, because I saw no spies. Nor did I understand, at that time, any opposition between American and Russian national interest. It was not even clear to me in 1936 that the American Communist Party was abjectly taking its orders from the Kremlin.

What I learned was the minimum that anyone must learn who puts his head into the noose of party "discipline." The Communists automatically violated the daily practices of democracy to which I was accustomed. They attempted to control thought and to suppress personal opinion. They tried to dictate personal conduct. They habitually distorted and disregarded and violated the truth. All this was crudely opposite to their claims of "democracy" and "the scientific approach."

To be a member of the Communist Party is to have a taste of the police state. It is a diluted taste but it is bitter and unforgettable. It is diluted because you can walk out.

I got out in the spring of 1936.

The question will be asked why I did not tell this story sooner. I was held back, primarily, by concern for the reputations and employment of people who may, like myself, have left the Party many years ago.

I was also held back by a piece of specious reasoning which has silenced many liberals. It goes like this: "You may hate the Communists, but you must not attack them or expose them, because if you do you are attacking the right to hold unpopular opinions and you are joining the people who attack civil liberties."

I have thought soberly about this. It is, simply, a lie.

Secrecy serves the Communists. At the other pole, it serves those who are interested in silencing liberal voices. The employment of a lot of good liberals is threatened because they have allowed themselves to become associated with or silenced by the Communists.

Liberals must speak out.

I think it is useful that certain of us had this kind of experience with the Communists, for if we had not we should not know them so well. Today, when all the world fears war and they scream peace, we know how much their professions are worth. We know tomorrow they will have a new slogan.

Firsthand experience of dictatorship and thought control left me with an abiding hatred of these. It left me with an abiding hatred of Communist philosophy and methods and the conviction that these must be resisted always.

It also left me with the passionate conviction that we must never let the Communists get away with the pretense that they stand for the very things which they kill in their own countries.

I am talking about free speech, a free press, the rights of property, the rights of labor, racial equality and, above all, individual rights. I value these things. I take them seriously. I value peace, too, when it is not bought at the price of fundamental decencies.

I believe these things must be fought for wherever they are not fully honored and protected whenever they are threatened.

The motion pictures I have made and the plays I have chosen to direct represent my convictions.

I expect to continue to make the same kinds of pictures and to direct the same kinds of plays.

Kazan's status, testimony, apologetic curriculum vitae, and advertisement, and rumors that he could make a big-money deal with Spyros Skouras contingent on his naming names—these collectively established him on the left as the ultimate betrayer, even as he was hailed on the right as patriot and applauded by centrist liberals for doing the difficult but right thing. He went on the letterhead of the American Committee for Cultural Freedom (which condemned Miller for being insufficiently vocal in his condemnations of Soviet totalitarianism), and his first post-HUAC film, *Man on a Tightrope* (1953), had an overtly anti-Communist theme. The *Daily Worker,* picking up on Kazan's having named his old *Dimitroff* co-author, Art Smith, asked with characteristic rhetorical overkill: "Isn't it clear that Kazan, like Vander Lubbe, is repeating the same old vicious lies the Nazis invented to cover up their murderous aggression! And for a similar purpose—to aid Wall Street's drive to world power?"

The *Worker* went on to observe that in Scene One of *Dimitroff*, Hitler puts his arms around Vander Lubbe and says, "This is the greatest moment of my life." Said the *Worker:* "Kazan's belly-crawling statement calling upon U.S. intellectuals to prostrate themselves before the Big Money sounds as if he too really believes (one can visualize the chairman of the Un-American Activities Committee putting his arm around him), 'This is the greatest moment of my life.'

"It is the lowest moment of Kazan's life, one which will haunt him forever."[6]

It soon became clear that whatever Kazan's motives, his reputation as the epitome of a betrayer would outlast the Party's ritualistic indignation.

When HUAC asked the folksinger Tony Kraber, another Group Theatre alumnus who had been named by Kazan, whether they had known each other in the Party, Kraber responded, "Is this the Kazan that signed the contract for five hundred thousand dollars the day after he gave names to this Committee?"[7] To the day he died in 1977, Zero Mostel, who made it back to a stardom he had never known before he was blacklisted, referred to Kazan as "Looselips." Sidney Zion, the editor of *Scanlan's Monthly,* a brash magazine that flourished briefly in the 1970s, once ran an article called "Hello, Informer," and to accompany it, he republished Kazan's 1952 ad and sent him a check for $150. No matter how unrelated the occasion, few serious interviewers fail to ask Kazan about his informing.

Today, Kazan declines to discuss his twenty-odd-year-old decision to name names. He has, he tells me—in person and by mail—received dozens of requests for interviews on this subject, but with one partial exception he has turned them all down. He gives a number of reasons, some personal, some general, depending on who is doing the asking. It is, he says, not all that important. If he had the same decision to make again, he might decide the same way. In any event, he is now busy with other things—writing novels and traveling—and that's what he would prefer to talk about. He will "do that scene" in his own way in his own good time, and he doesn't intend to undercut his future effort to write about the 1950s. Another thing: the decision to name names was a difficult decision, and a difficult decision brings pain no matter which way one goes. "The liberals who think I did it for the money are simplistic. I've turned down million-dollar deals." Besides, he would prefer to describe his position outside the "envelope" of someone else's words. After all, he was there, and he is a novelist, and to capture the complexities requires a novelist's ability to re-create context. He has been reading over his voluminous papers (which he donated to Wesleyan University, under terms that render them unavailable to the public until he has finished using them for his own purposes), and he finds them unique and personal and full of unexpected turns. The trick is not to attack others, but to try to understand some of the painful events in a context where personalities and past experiences and pressures interlock, and who is better qualified than he? The materials, after all, include intimate diaries, including his own notes following sessions with his therapist, letters from and to such varied personalities as Miller, Marilyn Monroe, Tennessee Williams, et al. It is all so intimate that he "wouldn't show it to my own brother."

The partial exception is Michel Ciment, the French critic who regards Kazan as one of the great film directors of all time and who was granted permission to ask Kazan whatever he wanted, provided Kazan had final editing privileges on the taped interview. Although they discussed the subject only briefly, what he told Ciment in 1971 was not inconsistent with his more generalized comments when ostensibly refusing to discuss the matter with others, a cross between ambivalence and justification:

> I don't think there's anything in my life toward which I have more ambivalence, because, obviously, there's something disgusting about giving other people's names. On the other hand . . . at that time I was convinced that the Soviet empire was monolithic. . . . I also felt that their behavior over Korea was aggressive and essentially imperialistic. . . . Since then, I've had two feelings. One feeling is that what I did was repulsive, and the opposite feeling, when I see what the Soviet Union has done to its writers, and their death camps, and the Nazi pact and the Polish and Czech repression. . . . It revived in me the feeling I had at that time, that it was essentially a symbolic act, not a personal act. I also have to admit and I've never denied, that there was a personal element in it, which is that I was angry, humiliated, and disturbed—furious, I guess—at the way they booted me out of the Party. . . . There was no doubt that there was a vast organization which was making fools of the liberals in Hollywood. . . . It was disgusting to me what many of them did, crawling in front of the Party. Albert Maltz published something in *New Masses*, I think, that revolted me: he was made to get on his hands and knees and beg forgiveness for things he'd written and things he'd felt. I felt that essentially I had a choice between two evils, but one thing I could not see was (by not saying anything) to continue to be a part of the secret maneuvering and behind-the-scenes planning that was the Communist Party as I knew it. I've often, since then, felt on a personal level that it's a shame that I named people, although they were all known, it's not as if I were turning them over to the police; everybody knew who they were, it was obvious and clear. It was a token act to me, and expressed what I thought at the time. . . .

> I don't say that what I did was entirely a good thing. What's called "a difficult decision" is a difficult decision because either way you go there are penalties, right? What makes some things difficult in life is if you're marrying one woman you're not marrying another woman. If you go one course you're not going another course. But I would rather do what I did than crawl in front of a ritualistic Left and lie the way those other comrades did, and betray my own soul. I didn't betray it.[8]

If Kazan had fully refrained from discussing the issue of informing, that would indeed be unfortunate, since he has so much to tell us. Happily for students of the phenomenon, however, Kazan has been talking about informing for twenty-five years, although he has frequently put out his message in disguised form. Indeed, it can be argued that his film *On the Waterfront,* with its screenplay by Budd Schulberg (who also named names*), makes the definitive case for the HUAC informer or at least is—among its considerable other achievements—a valiant attempt to complicate the public perception of the issue. The image of the informer is transformed from thirties-McLaglen to fifties-Brando.

After he unwittingly sets up young Joey Doyle to be pushed off the roof, the hero, Terry Malloy (Marlon Brando) reflects, "He wasn't a bad kid, that Joey," but he is quickly reminded, "He was a canary," which by the waterfront ethic is supposed to justify the brutal murder.

The movie is rife with talk of "rats," "stoolies," "cheesies," "canaries." Terry Malloy has to choose between the waterfront ethic, which holds ratting to be the greatest evil, and the Christian ethic, which suggests that one ought to speak truth to power. The former is represented by the vulgar, vicious, cigar-chomping corrupt labor boss, Johnny Friendly (Lee J. Cobb, also a real-life informer†), and the latter by the clean-cut, gutsy, straight-talking priest, Father Barry (Karl Malden). Terry comes to maturity and wins the girl (Eva Marie Saint) when he gains the courage to inform. In addition he achieves heroic stature as he single-handedly takes on the mob at the risk of his life and in the process comes to true self-knowledge. "I been ratting on myself all these years," he tells Johnny Friendly, "and I didn't know it. I'm glad what I done."

A particularly poignant moment occurs when Terry's protégé, Tommy, who has helped him tend Joey Doyle's pigeons on the roof, confronts him after he has turned informer and throws a dead bird at his feet. "What's that for?" asks Terry. "A pigeon for a pigeon," says Tommy. Even here, however, the message is clear: The injunction against informing is all right as a guideline for an adolescent street gang like Tommy's Golden Warriors, but it won't do for adults who are obliged to look at each situation in its own moral context. (What's ratting for them is telling the truth for you.) Squealing is relative.

Whatever else it may be, *Waterfront* seems an allegory for 1950s anti-

---

* See below, p. 239.

† See below, p. 268.

Communism, with the Waterfront Crime Commission an analog for HUAC. The critic Peter Biskind has gone further, ingeniously elaborating a religious metaphor. According to Biskind, when Terry decides to become a stool pigeon he fuses the spiritual and secular realms:

> In Christian terms, Terry voluntarily assumes the role of the meek (the dove); in secular terms he assumes the role of the stool pigeon (the informer); and the one transfigures the other. The political informer as Christian saint.
>
> Terry is well on his way to crucifixion before he testifies. He puts his hand through a plate-glass window (stigmata) and later when his friends avoid him after his testimony he experiences the abandonment of Christ on the Cross.[9]

But one needn't accept either the cold war or religious analogies to recognize the fact of Kazan-Schulberg's achievement: the creation of a context in which the naming of names is the only honorable thing to do—the maximum case for informing.

Kazan says life is ambiguous and his movies are meant to avoid black-and-white portrayals. "The liberals' answer to HUAC is simplistic. That's what I think is wrong with Arthur's plays," he says, "and you know how I like him. But he's always striving for an absolute, a single answer. That's what I object to about Lillian [Hellman]. I respect her work but she's an either-or person." Yet Kazan-Schulberg leave no room for ambiguity in *Waterfront.* The most memorable moment in the picture is the taxicab scene where Terry tells his brother Charlie (Rod Steiger) that Johnny should have taken better care of him ("I couldda been a contender"). If his informing had meant that the loyal and loving Terry would be sending his brother to prison or perhaps the electric chair, then the dilemma posed by the act of informing would have been real. But Kazan-Schulberg have the mob rub Charlie out, thereby giving Terry a socially sanctified personal motive (revenge) for testifying against the mob, as well as the political one (anti-corruption): This denies the audience any opportunity for genuine consideration of the ambivalent and dangerous complexities of the informer issue. "Squealing" may be relative, but in *Waterfront* it is mandatory.

Waterfront is not Kazan's only indirect reference to his HUAC experiences. In novels, films, and interviews he frequently includes material that justifies informing. After writing his number-one best-seller, *The Arrangement,* which was published in 1967 by Stein & Day (whose co-founder is the same Sol Stein who was formerly executive director of the American Committee for Cultural Freedom), and making it into a movie, Kazan let it be known that he was forsaking moviemaking, which had lost its magic for him, for full-time novel-writing. But two best-sellers later, he returned to the screen with a quite powerful low-budget movie he filmed at his country home in Connecticut, and which he directed at the request of his son Christopher, who had written it. *The Visitors* (1972) is the story of a gentle Vietnam vet who informed on two Calley-type buddies whom he had witnessed raping a Vietnamese girl in a My Lai situation. The film tells what happens when the brutal men he testified against are released from the stockade and journey up to Connecticut to terrorize him and his girlfriend.

In a number of conversations with me, the ostensible purpose of which were to (1) get to know each other but (2) explain why he wouldn't talk about his naming of names, the subject of informing kept coming up spontaneously. John Dean was appearing before the Senate Watergate Committee, in its televised hearings, as we talked one time, and Kazan observed that Dean's mouth seemed to move apart from the rest of his face; neither of us was unaware that Dean was an informer who might be said to be engaged in socially constructive betrayal. As if to demonstrate that informing can be essential to justice, Kazan told me about a jury on which he served (with the critic Alfred Kazin) which was forced to rely on the evidence of a wired police informant to convict a guilty man. He lent me the transcript of a trial involving a Jewish Defense League police informer who was being persecuted by the police. And when we ran into each other on a Broadway bus a few days after Solzhenitsyn's *Gulag Archipelago* was published, Kazan observed, "Isn't it interesting that all of that was going on while all of what you're looking at was going on?" The implication: If he was right about Stalinist brutality, perhaps he was not altogether wrong to name the names of those who denied Stalinist brutality.

Even if Kazan had really found it possible to resist the temptation to revisit the scene of his alleged crime, his historical connection with Arthur Miller probably of itself guarantees that for him there is no escaping the issue. For Miller, preoccupied as he is with the relationships between public and private morality, between the claims of the state and the claims of conscience, has returned again and again to the theme of betrayal, and each journey serves to remind those who care of Kazan's counterpoint role.

Miller's *The Crucible,* set in Salem during the witchcraft trials of the

1600s, tells the story of a community in the grip of terror.* Its central character is John Proctor, who prefers to die rather than to give false testimony. When the prosecutor Danforth asks John Proctor to name names, he says:

> I speak my own sins; I cannot judge another. I have no tongue for it. . . . I have three children—how may I teach them to walk like men in the world, and I sold my friends?
> DANFORTH: You have not sold your friends—
> PROCTOR: Beguile me not! I blacken all of them when this [a false confession he has prepared] is nailed to the church the very day they hang for silence![10]

Miller had written the play from documents he uncovered in research, and it was his conviction that "the fact that Proctor and others refused to give false evidence probably helped to bring the witch trials to an end. Their character was such that it penetrated the mob. When it came time for Rebecca Church to be hanged, the mob surged in and had to be stopped by cavalry."[11]

The critic Eric Bentley and others attacked the implicit analogy in the play between Massachusetts and Washington on the grounds that there hadn't actually been any witches in Salem, whereas there *were* Communists in Washington. As Miller recalls it, "*The Crucible* appeared to some as a misreading of the problem at best—a 'naïveté,' or at worst a specious and even sinister attempt to whitewash the guilt of the Communists with the noble heroism of those in 1692 who had rather be hung than confess to nonexistent crimes. . . . The truth is," Miller argues, "the playwriting part of me was drawn to what I felt was a tragic process underlying the political manifestation. . . . When irrational terror takes to itself the fiat of moral goodness somebody has to die. I thought that in terms of this process the witch-hunts had something to say to the anti-Communist hysteria. No man lives who has not got a panic button and when it is pressed by the clean white hand of moral duty, a certain murderous train is set in motion."[12]

---

* An index to the terror of the times in which Miller wrote this play is that when *The Crucible* was produced in Belgium in 1954, the U.S. government denied Miller a passport to travel to see it, and the American ambassador in Brussels had to take Miller's bows for him, which led the playwright to observe, "It didn't harm me, it harmed the country; I didn't need any foreign relations." (*Newsweek,* 3 February 1964, 52.)

Miller might have added that there was another sense in which his allegory was appropriate. The word "Communist" had come, as we have seen, to signify an amalgam of traitorous espionage-agent and conspiratorial, violent revolutionary, yet Kazan and the other entertainment-community witnesses called before HUAC were not, and never had been, either of these. In that sense HUAC was hunting in Hollywood for something that wasn't there.

To the charge that his play was agitprop against the McCarthy witch-hunt, Miller, like Kazan, had a complicated answer:

> It is not any more an attempt to cure witch hunts than *Salesman* is a plea for the improvement of conditions for traveling men, *All My Sons* a plea for better inspection of airplane parts. . . . *The Crucible* is, internally, *Salesman*'s blood brother. It is examining . . . the conflict between a man's raw deeds and his conception of himself; the question of whether conscience is in fact an organic part of the human being, and what happens when it is handed over not merely to the state or the mores of the time but to one's friend or wife.[13]

Even as Miller argues that critics have misread the symbolic meaning of *The Crucible*, Kazan has suggested that it is wrong to read *On the Waterfront* primarily as an allegory in defense of his behavior before HUAC. "It was aimed at something more universal," he told two interviewers in 1971. He cited the Mafia trials and the My Lai investigations as examples of situations where good people are conflicted between the social duty to expose and the ethic of silence. "That's a very characteristic and very genuine inner conflict of man."

"As a matter of fact," says Kazan, "*On the Waterfront* did not start with Budd Schulberg, it started with Arthur Miller." And he tells the story of how, long before he knew Schulberg, long before his HUAC testimony, he went to Arthur Miller and said, "Let's do a story about the waterfront!" They actually got as far as Miller's drafting the screenplay of "The Hook," which was scheduled to be made by Columbia Pictures. "Then I got a phone call from Art," says Kazan, "saying that he had decided he didn't want to do it. I still don't know why he did that."[14] (The reason, according to Miller, is that Harry Cohn, Roy Brewer, and the FBI all suggested that Miller should substitute reds for racketeers as the force terrorizing the waterfront workers. When Miller said no, Cohn fired off a telegram to him which said, "Strange how the minute we want to make a script pro-American, Miller pulls out."[15])

Miller did not get around to his own waterfront drama until 1955; *A View from the Bridge* is the story of Eddie Carbone, an Italian immigrant who lives on the waterfront with his wife Beatrice and his niece Catherine, for whom he has an irresistible attraction. When a Sicilian cousin, Rodolpho, who has entered the country illegally, wins Catherine's love, Eddie, consumed with incestuous jealousy, informs on Rodolpho to the immigration authorities, and soon thereafter suffers the fatal consequences of his betrayal.

Whatever Miller's intention (he later told me, "We don't want to forget the enemy—it wasn't the informer. It was the state which forced people to inform"), the anti-informer theme is inescapable. The injunction against informing is underlined at the outset as Eddie explains to his family why it is best that they tell nobody about the illegals:

EDDIE: I don't care what the question is. You—don't—know—nothin'. They got stool pigeons all over this neighborhood they're payin' them every week for information, and you don't know who they are. It could be your best friend. You hear? *To Beatrice:* Like Vinny Bolzano, remember Vinny?

BEATRICE: Oh yeah. God forbid.

EDDIE: Tell her about Vinny. *To Catherine:* You think I'm blowin' steam here? *To Beatrice:* Go ahead, tell her. *To Catherine:* You was a baby then. There was a family lived next door to her mother, he was about sixteen—

BEATRICE: No, he was not more than fourteen, cause I was to his confirmation in Saint Agnes. But the family had an uncle that they were hidin' in the house, and he snitched to the Immigration.

CATHERINE: The kid snitched?

EDDIE: On his own uncle!

CATHERINE: What, was he crazy?

EDDIE: He was crazy after, I tell you that, boy.

BEATRICE: Oh, it was terrible. He had five brothers and the old father. And they grabbed him in the kitchen and pulled him down the stairs—three flights his head was bouncin' like a coconut. And they spit on him in the street, his own father and his brothers. The whole neighborhood was cryin'.

CATHERINE: Ts! So what happened to him?

BEATRICE: I think he went away. *To Eddie:* I never seen him again, did you?

EDDIE: . . . Him? You'll never see him no more, a guy do a thing like that. How's he gonna show his face? *To Catherine:* Just remember kid, you can quicker get back a million dollars that was stole than a word that you gave away.

In an effort to reconcile an impulse he doesn't understand, Eddie forgets what happened to Vinny and why. He consults the lawyer-narrator Alfieri, a sort of Greek-chorus character. And when Alfieri understands what is on Eddie's mind he says:

I'm not only telling you now, I'm warning you. . . .
You won't have a friend in the world, Eddie! Even those who under-
    stand will turn against you, even the ones who feel the same will de-
    spise you. Put it out of your mind! Eddie![16]

Eddie is powerless to resist. And by his act of informing he betrays not only Rodolpho but the people he loves most. He has no place to go, as the people who knew him and accepted him—the neighborhood—reject him. And so he dies.

By the time Miller was called to appear before HUAC on June 21, 1956, he had already found his way onto a number of blacklists, including that of the New York Board of Education, which canceled a contract with him to write a film on street gangs. His performance before the Committee almost lived up to his art.

Like Proctor,* Miller was willing to talk about himself—and he did, at considerable length—but not to name others. Thus, asked why the Communist Party produced his play *You're Next,* he remarked, "I take no more responsibility for who plays my plays than General Motors can take for who rides in their Chevrolets." He also told the Committee, apropos his brief flirtation with organized Communism, that "I have had to go to hell to meet the devil" (which led Lillian Hellman to quip that he must have gone as a tourist). But when asked whether he had attended a Communist Party meeting at the home of one Sue Warren, which was chaired by Arnaud d'Usseau, author of the play *Deep Are the Roots* (di-

---

* Actually John Proctor's crucial confession is the admission that he had an illicit relationship with his chief accuser. And one of the turning points in *The Crucible* concerns Mary Warren's unwillingness to testify accurately as to what she was doing in the forest with the other girls. We are heartened as an audience when we think she is going to testify against her friends, and we feel dismay, consequently, when she recants under pressure from her erstwhile colleagues. Thus did Miller the artist recognize a more complex position than Miller the citizen articulated.

rected, as it happens, by Kazan), he declined to answer. Unlike most resisting witnesses, however, he did not invoke the Fifth Amendment's protection against self-incrimination. Instead, he invoked the First Amendment's guarantee of free speech and, by implication, the right to silence.[17]

Whereas the straight Fifth would, under prevailing doctrine, have definitely kept Miller out of jail, "taking the First" risked incurring the fate of the Hollywood Ten. Under these circumstances, many people on the liberal left perceived him as something of a heroic countersymbol to the prevailing informer-as-hero type. But the reality was somewhat more ambiguous than that, since Miller conceded the Committee's right to inquire into his own political opinions, which is more than many resisters wanted to grant; also, by 1956 the worst ravages of the anti-Communist terror seemed to have passed, and Miller after all had at his side his fiancée, the nation's reigning sex queen, Marilyn Monroe: The reason he wanted a passport in the first place (the ostensible subject of the hearings) was to take her to London, where they planned to honeymoon and see one of his plays. Finally, although if convicted he was subject to a maximum sentence of $1000 and a year in prison, he was so polite that Chairman Walter thanked him for his testimony, leading some to believe he might never be cited for contempt; in the event, he was fined $500 and given a suspended thirty-day sentence.

In arguing on appeal from his contempt of Congress citation, Miller's attorney, Joseph Rauh, was able to ask a unique rhetorical question: "What could have a more restraining effect on a man's future writing than forcing him publicly to perform an act openly condemned by his current writing?"[18] At the very moment the Committee was interrogating Miller, *A View from the Bridge* was being performed in various parts of this country and was being readied for production in England.

It was not only those who agreed with him who saw Miller as the archetypal anti-informer. The liberal Richard Rovere found that what Miller did before the Committee involved "a certain amount of moral and political confusion." Even if Miller was morally justified in refusing to bow to the Committee's procedure of testing the good faith of witnesses by demanding that they name names, Rovere thought, he was wrong in trying to elevate the refusal to inform into a "universal principle." Otherwise, wrote Rovere, we should supplement the Fifth Amendment with another one saying, "No man could be required to incriminate another," and if we did that, the whole machinery of law enforcement would collapse because, "If any agency of the community is authorized to undertake a serious investigation of any of our common problems, then the identities of others—*names*—are of great importance."[19]

But Rovere attributed to Miller a position he never took. Miller the witness was articulating a point of conscience, not a legislative program.

Miller the playwright never pretended to take his characters beyond their context. Moreover, although Miller may have been the informer's most visible symbolic enemy, his own attitudes on the matter were in flux. Marilyn Monroe, who had worked with Kazan at the Actors Studio and had an affection for him, got the two ex-friends back on speaking terms. Miller revised *A View from the Bridge,* so that it was less a condemnation of Eddie Carbone-as-informer and more a legend of the human condition. In the final version the lawyer Alfieri makes a new speech that gives Eddie a dignity he originally lacked:

> Most of the time now we settle for half and I like it better. But the truth is holy, and even as I know how wrong he was, and his death useless, I tremble for I confess that something perversely pure calls to me from his memory—not purely good, but himself purely, for he allowed himself to be wholly known and for that I think I will love him more than all my sensible clients. And yet, it is better to settle for half, it must be! And so I mourn him—I admit it—with a certain ... alarm. . . .[20]

In 1963, when Miller and Kazan—who had separately dreamed of working with a national repertory theater—were invited to serve as resident playwright and director, respectively, of Lincoln Center for its first season (1963–64), the reconciliation between these two was hard for many to understand, much less accept. This was especially true since the play on which they were to renew their collaboration was Miller's autobiographical *After the Fall,* which had as its protagonist Quentin (Jason Robards), a one-time Communist who breaks with a friend about to turn informer before a congressional committee. At the time most of the gossip focused on blond, beautiful, vulnerable Maggie, modeled, it seemed, on the late Marilyn Monroe, but the insiders knew that Kazan was also directing an informer-character based on Kazan. The *New York Times* critic wrote at the time, the play recalls "those who would name names and those who wouldn't. . . . *After the Fall* seeks to understand, not to judge."[21]

One member of the company recalls: "I couldn't believe what was going on. Gadg in his own really paranoid way thought he was the hero of this play—not that he ever asked Arthur. He thought it was about him, not Marilyn. He and Jason had a big battle about that long naming-names speech. That's when Jason vanished—went off on a week's binge and they couldn't find him. It was a bitter, dark, and terrifying fight they had over that speech.

"At first Miller thought Kazan understood his play—then he thought Kazan used Barbara Loden (Maggie) to take it away from the central issue. I mean, he looked at things sexually instead of intellectually—he made her play it in a see-through dress—and that was a road to escape.

"The problem with Arthur is that he *was* an 'informer.' He was informing. Gadg kind of had one over him because he was really 'naming' Marilyn and the rest of them. The invasion of privacy is what made it so sick."

Miller never accepted the criticism that he had invaded Marilyn Monroe's privacy. The critic Tom Prideaux probably had it right when he wrote, "For many years, whoever sees *After the Fall* will be haunted by Marilyn's golden image. It comes with the territory. . . ."[22] Miller points out that those who were vicious to her alive were most quick to condemn the alleged portrayal of her dead. "The hypocrisy which bewildered and finally enraged her in life indeed seems to be following her in death."[23]

Many of Miller's friends never forgave him for reuniting with Kazan. "The irony of Kazan doing *After the Fall,*" notes Norman Rosten, a friend of Miller and Monroe, "was that Miller thought he was getting the same man who directed *Death of a Salesman,* and Kazan was not the same man. It was not the same setup. Miller was looking for a replay of his past triumphs and the plays were different, the times were different. Kazan—because of what he had gone through—was not the same man and the chemistry was different."

Kermit Bloomgarden, too, blamed Miller for the play and its director. "He gave the Kazan-character a flag of honesty and then he attacked the people who took the Fifth Amendment."

Even Miller's close friend and publicist on all his plays, James Proctor, stopped talking to him for two years. He remembers the day in 1958 he was to appear before the Un-American Activities Committee: "At seven-thirty in the morning my doorbell rang and it was Arthur. He was there to bolster my morale." Now Proctor was baffled as to why Miller, who had never wavered on what he himself would do, would allow Kazan to direct his play. (But then, Proctor had what some might characterize as a bias. He had been named by Kazan—specifically, Kazan had told HUAC that Proctor had signed Molly Kazan's name as a sponsor of the Waldorf

Peace Conference—the 1949 popular-front gathering attacked for its Communist participants—without her permission, and that he had later apologized for this.) Proctor is a moralist who says, "I've always believed that *why* a subject behaved as he did was a proper subject for medical study, but *how* he behaved was a proper basis for judging a person."

"It was a time when everybody became an expert on everybody else's life," says Conrad Bromberg, the son of the actor J. Edward Bromberg, who was named by Kazan and appeared before HUAC under compulsion and against doctor's orders. He declined to cooperate and died shortly after. Conrad (who has written and rewritten a dozen drafts of a play called "The Dream of a Blacklisted Actor," the titular character being based on a combination of his father, John Garfield, and Edward G. Robinson) observes, "There was a great Brownie point system set up, depending on which way you wanted to jump. Who was more cowardly? Who was more courageous? Lee Strasberg [director at the Group Theatre and Actors Studio] was a big adviser on what to do. His position was that artists have no place in politics, and if you get caught you get out. Everybody was meeting in living rooms and everywhere the same argument occurred. On the basis of what do you take that position? It was not so much a defense of the USSR as a question of how far do you bend in order to survive? If it doesn't bother you, you bend all the way, with the knowledge that it will affect others. For two years my father ducked subpoenas. But that didn't matter. Anything this side of giving names and addresses of your best friends was okay. Whether you talk to them or lie to them or evade them didn't matter.

"You were constantly in the position of asking, Who am I in relation to other people? Do I trust my impulses, my humanity, my own sense of living, or do I follow others? Is it a matter of power? Arthur Miller made a decision, in spite of an awful lot of advice the other way. People said, 'You are blowing your career.' Either he was braver or smarter than they were or he could not be in the company of corrupt men for too long and live well with himself. There's a kind of healthy arrogance that many creative people have. They don't want to be bothered with hustlers. And you certainly don't want your life controlled by them. Would *you* want to be a prisoner of Victor Riesel, who could tell you to appear at a certain meeting? That's what it came down to—that you belong to somebody else who was not even your peer."

Conrad thinks "Kazan made a very pragmatic decision. He takes the offensive whenever possible. Clifford [Odets] named names out of ego—he never liked to be made to look like a schmuck, and something like taking the Fifth Amendment smelled, and I don't think he liked that. But Gadg knew that nobody opposed the Committee and came out with a whole career. You knew that up front. And he wasn't about to be destroyed. Business was involved, too. Twentieth Century-Fox had pictures in the can directed by Kazan. In a sense he had leverage. He also had a contract for several hundreds of thousands of dollars. So if he did a number for them they had to do a number for him.

"I've seen Gadg since. . . . I ought to be angry at him but I'm not. The obligation fights the reality. When I see him, I keep thinking he's a figure out of my childhood."

Conrad Bromberg is a man who has come to terms with personal ambiguities. Others see his father, Joe Bromberg, as victim, perhaps martyr, and Kazan as victimizer. These nagging I.D.'s won't go away. When in 1972 Kazan appeared on WNBC-Television's hour-long interview show *Speaking Freely,* to discuss with Edwin Newman among other things his latest novel, *The Assassins* (which has an informer-character in it), two-thirds of the way through the following exchange took place:

> NEWMAN: Some of [the Group Theatre's actors] got into political difficulty in Hollywood which is a subject that I really cannot avoid. In 1952—and this is, I suppose one of the things for which you were most criticized—you appeared before the House Committee on Un-American Activities and confessed that you had been briefly for eighteen months a Communist when you were young. And you named I think it was seven other people who had been Communists. A good many people thought you shouldn't have named any other names whatever you said about yourself. You have never over the years said much about that. Is there anything you want to say about it?

> KAZAN: Well, not really, in the brief context of a program like this, Ed, because I'm going to write about it. I think when it is understood from the point of 1972 it is one thing and when it is understood in the context of what was going on in 1952 and how we felt in 1952 [it is another]. Also then I think there is something disgusting about naming things, naming names and all that, that I felt ambivalent about. But on the other hand, when we knew about what Khrushchev reported in his book, we had close contact with it. We knew about a society that the left was idealizing then, the Russian society. We knew that it was a slave society. We had a good idea how many people were being killed. I've often wondered how some of the people who criticized me went through those years and stayed behind

Russia, ... continued to idealize it when they knew what was happening. ... I've felt sad about it or bad about it, and I've sometimes felt—well, I would do the same thing over again. ... To talk about regrets, I do have some and I don't have some. I think I spoke up not for any reason of money or security or anything else, but because I actually felt it. If I made a mistake, then that was a mistake that was honestly made. ... It was a part of a thing that has to be understood in terms of that time. Now, when I look back on it, you know, humanly I feel some regrets, and as a symbolic gesture I don't. I feel that I didn't tell a lie, I didn't tell any falsehoods, I didn't speculate, I didn't do a lot of the things that I would feel dishonorable about. And as I say, to write about it, to speak about it, very briefly and simply, I think is not what I want to do. I'd rather in my own time, in my own way speak about it at length.[24]

One evening in 1978 I was driving home from the country and the radio talk-show host Barry Gray announced that his next guest would be Elia Kazan, who as it happened was plugging his latest novel, *An Act of Love*. Before the program was over Gray asked Kazan about his HUAC experience, and inevitably the listening audience was duly informed that that was in the past, that nobody, especially Kazan, was really interested in it anymore, that it wasn't worth talking about, that the subject was in any event too complicated to cover in two minutes on the air but that he was writing a book about it where he would tell his side, and so forth.

There is method to Kazan's reticence. It's a strategic silence, as much mystification as anything else. There is about it the strong hint that were he at liberty or inclined to tell all, had he but the time to say his say or get it on paper, the painful nobility of his action would at last be appreciated. But don't get him wrong, it was a tough decision either way and he is as ambivalent today as he was then.

At the time, Kazan urged all former comrades to follow his example and fight totalitarian secrecy with "the facts." Now he prefers to keep his counsel, to take, as it were, a retrospective Fifth.

It says something that those like Miller and the Hollywood Ten, who claimed their right to silence then, now miss no opportunity to tell their tale, whereas many, like Kazan, who talked at the time, citing the compulsion of history, today invoke their preference for silence.

Kazan has written, "My favorite quote is from Jean Renoir: 'Everyone has his reasons.' "[25] And yet for his own reasons he hasn't fully shared his reasons. His thesis—that in certain contexts to inform can be an act of honor, and that therefore it is simplistic to condemn all informers—sounds reasonable. But it begs the question of whether his own "token" betrayal occurred in such a context.

His silence, however, has resonance. Without giving a single American interview on the subject, he has sent the message that the decision he made was a painful but honest one, that given the same context he might do the same thing again, that the Communists rather than the informers were the betrayers, that he injured no one by his conduct, that perhaps Kazan really believed what he said, that he will tell his story in time, and that the whole thing is not really all that important, not worth talking about.

In fact, it is so "unimportant" that he refuses to talk about it. Yet each of Kazan's hints are themes that anticipate or echo more elaborate justifications advanced by other informers more willing or able to share their experience, to explain and try to understand out loud why they did what they did, to subject their "reasons why" to the tests of conversation, consideration, logic, analysis.

8.

The Reasons Why

AS A GROUP, the Hollywood informers of the 1950s exhibit even today many of the symptoms which the sociologist Erving Goffman once described as characteristic of the stigmatized: They adopt their own group postures, styles, standards, associations, and tests. In the early 1970s, for instance, Kazan was awarded the Handel Medallion, New York City's highest civilian medal, for his contribution to the arts, and his publisher, Sol Stein, arranged a reception at the New York Public Library. The crowd—Budd Schulberg, Jerome Robbins, Abe Burrows, et al.—lent the gathering the air of an informers' alumni association. "A characteristic task," wrote Goffman of representatives of the stigmatized, "is to convince the public to use a softer social label for the category in question."[1] "Cooperative witness"?

In lancing an especially obstinate boil, Studs Terkel observes, it is not the doctor who feels the pain.[2] Being asked in the 1970s why they informed in the 1950s, how they felt and feel about it, is for many of the subjects a painful experience. Informers have a sense of privacy, too, and a number of those I contacted perferred not to talk. Some, like David Lang (the cartoonist and writer who named Carl Foreman and years later tried without success to renew acquaintance with him), simply said, "I'd just as soon not talk about it—it happened a long time ago and there's nothing to be gained by going over it." Others, like the actor Marc Lawrence (who told HUAC that the actor Lionel Stander had recruited him into the Communist Party by telling him that in the Party you "get to know the dames more"), couldn't resist combining a refusal to talk with a denunciation of the interviewer. In 1972, shortly after Eric Bentley's play *Are You Now or Have You Ever Been?* opened in Los Angeles and *Only Victims,* a study of the blacklist by Robert Vaughn (best known as the star of the television series *The Man from U.N.C.L.E.*), was published, I telephoned Lawrence, who is mentioned briefly in both, in connection with an article on the blacklist I was writing for *The New York Times Magazine*. "It's a ghoulish exercise!" he shouted over the phone. "Some schmuck did a play on it. Another asshole did a book on it. It's like opening a grave. It's like opening a cancer and asking, 'How did you get it?'

"The Committee weren't heroes. Maltz is not a hero. Trumbo is not a hero. If he said he was a Communist then he'd be a hero. I had to do it because they caught me with my pants down. I lied to them. They gave me a list of people. It was sick. You want to kill somebody, why don't you shoot Nixon?

"*The Times* is going into this? That Robert Vaughn is a ghoul. Eric Bentley is a ghoul. You are a ghoul. The investigators came with a list of names. All I know is I came out of an asylum to testify. I was very sick. Do you think this helps me? I left the fucking country—got out of here for ten years, and now you're digging up the garbage. You're creating another blacklist.

"Anybody who had the guts to say, 'I'm a Commie and you want to cut my throat because that's what I believe?'—that's gutsy. But nobody said that. They were frightening everybody.

"I wasn't proud of anything I said. I went to Europe. I would appreciate it if you don't mention my name. Arthur Miller at least had the decency not to name names. You guys shouldn't name names."

Some less volatile than Lawrence also preferred to attack the interviewer rather than answer his questions. "You are doing it for the money." "Your mind is already made up." "You are engaged in a new form of blacklist." Here let it simply be noted that some of these assaults seemed "authentic" in the sense that I had pushed a button that elicited an immediate and powerful, if antagonistic, emotional response; others seemed more calculated, tactical maneuvers for dealing with (or avoiding) the press—akin to the mystifications engaged in so much more artfully by Kazan. Most, however, had simply never been asked about their experiences, and of these many had much they wanted to say. If there is pain and unpleasantness in much of the talk which follows, that is because lancing a boil means letting the pus out.

I came to these interviews armed with questions and a tape recorder. My questions, however, were designed for more than eliciting specific answers—the idea was to get people talking, to say their say, to free-associate, to open up. What follows are the informers speaking for, informing on, themselves. I have omitted my questions and other material where it

seems clearly beyond the borders of relevance. I have left in certain rep-
etitions from interview to interview ("I only named those who were
named before"; "I didn't hurt anybody") because they faithfully convey
commonly held preoccupations. It is difficult, at least it was for me, to
hear these men and women talk and not to feel compassion. Since that,
too, is part of the story, I refrain from interrupting these "reasons why"
with analysis of their adequacy, which can wait until after the informers
have had their say.

RICHARD COLLINS

The screenwriter Richard Collins was thirty-seven years old when he
named twenty-six names before the Un-American Activities Committee
on April 12, 1951. His attorney was Martin Gang, his therapist was Phil
Cohen, and he worked closely with the FBI and with HUAC investigator
William Wheeler in preparing his testimony.

One of the original Hollywood Nineteen, Collins was one of the few
Hollywood Communists thought to be a serious student of Marxism. His
testimony was of special interest because he had received joint credit
(with his friend Paul Jarrico) for the screenplay of *Song of Russia*, which
the actor Robert Taylor had said he filmed against his better judgment
and the writer Ayn Rand had told HUAC was pro-Soviet propaganda
because it showed so many smiling Russian children. Also, as a key Party
functionary Collins was in a position to know the inner workings of the
Hollywood faction and the names of virtually all of its members. (The
day he was to testify he called Cleo Trumbo to tell her that he was not
going to name her husband, Dalton, who was about to be released from
prison. "Why he did that, I'll never understand—the shit!" said Trumbo,
many years later.)

Collins had been earning up to $1500 a week at Warner's when his
work was cut off in 1947. From 1947 to 1951 he did some ad hoc "under
the table" writing and worked in New York for a couple of years in the
pattern business. "I didn't really do well during those years." In 1953 he
was hired by the independent producer Walter Wanger, wrote the successful *Riot in Cell Block 11,* and was back in business. When I saw him
in 1975 it was in a trailer on the back lot of M-G-M, where he was executive producer of the then successful television series *Firehouse.*

In the course of his HUAC testimony he told of the Party's interest in "cultural workers," and went into detail about a celebrated moment in the Party's cultural history—when in 1946 Albert Maltz, after severe Party criticism, recanted the views he expressed in an influential article on art, culture, and politics.* Collins described the Party's attempt to influence the Screen Writers Guild before the 1947 board elections, told of how Budd Schulberg left the Party after its harsh criticism of his Hollywood novel, *What Makes Sammy Run?*, and when asked if any effort had been made to influence his testimony, he told of a visit from his old collaborator, Paul Jarrico:

> ... He understood I was out of the Party, but he wanted my personal assurance that I would not give any names. I didn't give that assurance.
> We then had a long political discussion. Paul Jarrico feels the justice of his position, and he went over the situation that he believes the Soviet Union is devoted to the interests of all people and is peace-loving as well.... I looked at my watch and it was a quarter of twelve, after four hours of discussion.... I said "I will give you my personal assurance that I will not give any names if you will give me your personal assurance that in the event of a war between the United States and the Soviet Union you will do nothing to help the Soviet Union."
> Paul said, "You know my answer to that." He didn't explain the answer, but it was that if it was an aggressive war of the United States he would not support it.
> I said, "I am not interested in whether it is aggressive. I want your personal assurance...."
> Since he could not give me this assurance, I would not give him mine, and since we would not lie to each other, we had no further conversation.

Collins also told the Committee that had he been called before it with the Hollywood Ten in 1947, he would have done as they did, although he was then already disillusioned with the Party. "At that time it seemed to me that purely on American democratic constitutional grounds there was a question of the propriety of asking a man his political beliefs. Without going into the question of its propriety today, there has been a marked change in the world situation since 1947, and there had been as great a

* See below, p. 288.

change in me. It is hard to tell where one thing begins and the other ends."

Collins told me he was also reevaluating his aesthetic assumptions. "I remember the time [my co-worker] Sylvia Richards said, 'You've got to read Tennessee Williams' *The Glass Menagerie*—you'll love it.' And I had read nothing really but didactic material for years. So I read Tennessee Williams' play and I was enchanted with it. It was magic as far as I was concerned. And it occurred to me that there was a kind of writing that could be done that wasn't necessarily involved with pushing a particular position."

Even after he went back to work, in his own mind he did intermittent battle against the falsification of ideas. Thus when he was doing some television writing for Ronald Reagan's *General Electric Theater*, he was asked to work on an anti-Communist two-parter. "When we started to work on it Reagan had a scene he wanted to put in, some idiot thing where the Communist mother slaps her child because she finds him praying or something like that. I said, 'You can't do that. It's just absolutely out of the question.' So I left it half-done and it was completed, and then he got unhappy with me because I said, 'I didn't write it, so, obviously, I won't put my name on it.' So we had a go-around over that."

A year and a half after his testimony Collins got involved in a highly publicized, vicious custody battle for his children with his former wife, Dorothy Comingore. Miss Comingore (best known for her portrayal of Charles Foster Kane's mistress, Susan Alexander, in Orson Welles's *Citizen Kane*) had take the Fifth Amendment a few weeks earlier (October 6, 1952) and was accused of being an unfit mother because of alcoholism and Communist leanings.[3] (William Wheeler told me she actually was picked up on a prostitution charge while the HUAC hearings were going on, which led the right-wing writer Morrie Ryskind to comment, "That Wheeler plays rough"—on the assumption, which Wheeler denies, that the charge was a setup.) Collins was accused in the custody proceedings of welching on his child-support payments and his debts. According to Abe Polonsky, one of his creditors, "When the people from whom he had borrowed money tried to get it back, he claimed the statute of limitations had run. . . . *More* than the statute of limitations had run; the statute of all limitations had run.

"Collins is interesting because his role is more complex than the normal informer who went before the Committee and did his thing and [then] tried to forget this business. He was reporting to the FBI while he was still ostensibly a member of the Party.

"Dick Collins disagreed totally during these last years with the whole attitude of the Communist Party toward literature. . . . He was for freedom of aesthetic attitudes, and he was always disagreeing about this stuff. And he was attacked for that by people who were doctrinaire mechanical Communists, following out the policy as handed down in the [Party] newspapers. He defended left-wingers who violated the rule of keeping the truth that is handed down by the CP. No one knew that he was also turning in names. He was treated as a man who disagreed with the CP, and some people in the radical movement didn't like him for that. I liked him. It was a great shock for me to find out that he was an informer. I thought he was an honest intellectual who disagreed. He was also a dishonest man pretending to be a radical when he wasn't."

Why did Richard Collins do it?

"I had gone to Washington in 1947 with the so-called Hollywood Nineteen, and they called ten and didn't call nine, and the nine who were not called didn't work unless they sent a letter to the producers saying they had made a terrible mistake—or whatever was supposed to be said at the time. I didn't know about that, actually, but an agent whom I'd had for years, Allen Miller, said to me at lunch one day, 'Are you still in?' I said, 'No, I haven't been in for years.' He said, 'Then why don't you say so?' and I said, 'Well . . .' And he explained to me that there had been people who had written these letters. So I thought about it and decided I didn't like that.

"I think in my testimony I discussed the Korean War and the fact that I was upset about Americans who were being killed in Korea. And also I had been out [of the Party]. I was out in forty-seven, as a matter of fact, but in forty-seven it didn't seem reasonable to say so—in terms of the men whom I had been with for many years. I was fond of them and for some of them I had a great deal of respect and some affection. But four years later I didn't feel the same way. I don't think that my *view* of the world changed, rather than that the *world* changed so radically.

"I don't think that anyone on either side came off very well. But my feeling was that I had been out [of the Party] for a great many years and had a certain hostility toward the Soviet Union (but certainly not toward the men whom I had been in with, because I understood them and I knew that in the main they were very well motivated). I felt I was not a friend of the Soviet Union and in the event of a war, I would certainly not be—and in those days I thought a war was more likely than I think it is now [1975].

"When I first testified [in 1951]—and this was true of, say, Meta Rosenberg and the actor Sterling Hayden—there was no feeling that you [would get] work, because the experience was that you wouldn't. The only experience of a cooperative witness up to that time was Larry Parks. I can't speak for subsequent witnesses, but in our time we didn't take that position because we felt that we'd be working. . . .

"I hadn't actually worked except under the table since 1947. So it was not for me a matter of, 'Well, I'm going to bounce back and go to work.' It turned out that that's what happened finally, but that was not the primary consideration. The primary consideration was that I just thought it was ridiculous to go through life as a member of the Party—which taking the Fifth in effect said publicly you were doing—when I wasn't. You know really you get further away as you get further away.

"The decision to not take the Fifth came about in a very peculiar way. I was sitting with Meta Rosenberg and Martin Gang at the Brown Derby, and we were talking about taking the Fifth, which was considered at the time the only thing you could do. Meta had been subpoenaed, and I had a subpoena hanging over from 1947. Gang had a partner who died subsequently, Bob Kopp, a very nice man, and he came and sat down at the table and he listened to the discussion, and he said, 'You can't take the Fifth, it's ridiculous.' He went on to explain what he thought was reasonable. At that lunch it was decided that we would cooperate.

"And then Meta and I got together and we talked about how we were going to handle this. First we came up with a list of guys and ladies who were dead, and I said to Meta, 'I don't think that's going to work. That's a little soft; they're going to figure that one out.' So, between us, I suppose, or at least just to speak for myself, I must have known at least three hundred people from the Party. I had been in for ten years. I had been— what did they call it?—on the section committee, and in various branches, in fractions, and so forth, and so I really did know probably everybody. Maybe there were three or four people I didn't know. So we finally ended up with three categories. One was the ones who had died; the second was the ones who had been called [to testify], because we figured that they were stuck already; and the third—and this was my mistake—were the ones who had left [the Party] a long time before. I had no idea that they would be bounced as hard as they were. I figured that having been out for ten years or nine years, like Schulberg, for instance, that everybody would see that they *had* left. It was a tremendous mistake, because firstly *The New York Times* headlined Schulberg on the front page because he was a novelist of some importance, which is something that stupidly had never occurred to me. Then Martin Berkeley [whom I named], who had been out six or seven years, turned out to be the most voluble, I guess, of the witnesses. I never realized the panic which set in with Berkeley. I mean, I never recognized it as possible.

"Looking back on it, it was a mistake, a stupid thing. At any rate, that's how we came to give the people named.

"I know that in every case where someone cooperated, there was tremendous anguish because it wasn't considered a very pleasant or even, I would have to say, a decent thing. The alternatives were to get stuck with something. In many cases, the cooperative witnesses really weren't in the Party anymore; they were out. They didn't feel like standing up as the people who were still in felt they had to do. And rightfully. The Party is really a religious operation, and if you have religion it's fine to suffer for it, and if you don't, well maybe you don't want to. But I'm not taking any moral positions on that, because I never felt that it was a marvelous thing to do. I think it took a certain amount of guts. In a sense it was harder to be cooperative than not.

"And strange things happened. In many cases a man would be urged by his wife to take the Fifth and I don't think she recognized the consequences of it. A year later a lot of wives said, 'Well, how are we going to live?' It was uncharted territory for us—for everybody. I don't think anybody quite knew what was going to happen. (And you know the motion-picture producers met and really threw in the sponge. They wouldn't hire some of the people who had taken the Fifth and then some of the unions went along and I think the Screen Writers Guild itself, finally.)

"Another problem in my time was that even with Larry Parks we didn't know just what he had said; it was not revealed; we just knew he had named names but we didn't know whose—I didn't know whose names they had. I had no idea. So I just took the ones who had been called which were a matter of common knowledge, and I expanded that by the third category of people who had been out for a while. I think there were more than Budd [Schulberg] and Martin Berkeley, but I don't remember.

"I was ashamed, really, of my role when I thought back on it. Not the thought-control, but the little punk who had some power and who swung it. I knew people who were older, wiser—I'm not talking just about Schulberg, I'm talking about people who had been in the Party for years—and I was giving them the law. I was the priest. I have to say, I was a son of a bitch, a miserable little bastard. It was unfortunate but true. I was a good boy, doing what you're supposed to do.

"A friend of mine in military intelligence [during World War II] said to me when we were in the army together, 'Look, do me a favor. If they ever ask you whether you are in the Party, don't say no because they have everything. They have not only what meetings you went to, who was there, but what you discussed.' So I remembered that, because it was an extraordinary thing in a way—an act of friendship. I guess he knew through Army Intelligence. When he said, 'I'd like to hire Collins,' they probably said, 'Well, you got to know that he's in the Party.' He said, 'I don't care, I want him anyway'—or whatever. I remember him as a guy who was not in but knew I was, so I wasn't revealing anything and I went to him and told him. I asked him the question and he said, 'If you really want to get out, I think it's perfectly reasonable as long as you don't name anyone.' So that's what I did.

"[Edward] Dmytryk urged me to cooperate and said he was going to, and I said, 'I don't think I'm ready to do that.' When I was ready I called the FBI and I said, 'I'm Richard Collins and I'd like to come down and see you,' and there was about a nine-second pause while they must have looked up the file and they said, 'By all means, come down.' I called the guy in charge. I told him my little story and what I was going to do, and he said 'Fine,' and he called in another man, Mark Bright. Mark went with me into a little room and he said, 'You can certainly talk about John Howard Lawson because we all know about John Howard Lawson,' and I said, 'Well, I can't talk about anybody.' Except for a little urging they accepted what I had to say without pressing me. They seemed to know about inner Party attitudes. They knew I was a shining boy. How they found out I don't know.

"I used to go to lunch with a guy around the time of the Korean business, and he wanted me to contribute some money to something or other, and I did and I felt ridiculous about it. Here I was giving money to the Party in areas that I didn't agree with because I hadn't the guts to say, 'I'm out.' I hadn't gone to any meetings in a long time. My friend said, 'A lot of people look up to you. When are you going to come back?' This was six months or more before I was subpoenaed. I said, 'Well, I'm not.' But I didn't say, 'I'm out and I don't agree.' I was diddling.

"I didn't have any place to live, because the fact is, if you've been in the Party for ten years you don't have anything else. There are no other people you know. Fortunately my wife was around, so I had her and my children, but I didn't know anyone, except for a few people who were out of the Party. I finally came to a conclusion: I had to do something. And I got the word around that I was out, and so the Party made life a little harder for me. . . .

"When it comes to a decision like [whether to inform], you really can't talk anybody into it. If a person's not considering it seriously, nobody's going to push him into it. Nobody's going to push a man to take the Fifth or to cooperate, both of which positions have their own problems, unless he or she is really considering it. It's too big a decision. And they weren't children, any of these people. If you're very young and your father says, 'You shouldn't marry that girl,' maybe you'll listen. But by the time you're of age, you know, in your thirties or forties or whatever, you have got to account for the conclusion yourself. You couldn't take somebody who was firmly embedded in the Party and persuade them to cooperate. That is impossible."[4]

EDWARD DMYTRYK

Edward Dmytryk, born in Grand Forks, British Columbia, thirty-nine years before he appeared as one of the Hollywood Ten, was the only member of the Ten to recant. Perhaps that is why Helen Manfull, who edited Dalton Trumbo's letters, and others believe that the requisites for being cleared from the blacklist had been "largely established by Edward Dmytryk."[5]

Dmytryk had started in pictures at the age of fourteen, working after school at Hollywood High as a messenger for Paramount. In 1939 he was naturalized and began directing B pictures, and by 1943 he had moved to A pictures. The year of the HUAC hearings he was nominated for an Academy Award for Best Director for *Crossfire*, the anti-anti-Semitism picture he had made with Adrian Scott, another member of the Hollywood Ten.

Like many others in Hollywood, Dmytryk's domestic life was in little better shape than his political life during this particular time of trouble. After the Ten were cited for contempt of Congress but while their case was on appeal, Dmytryk went to England to direct some pictures. Two letters signify some of the pressures he was under. On November 23, 1948, Albert Maltz wrote to him in London:

> Here is a somewhat delicate note to write you. Believe me, I do so without any desire to interfere in your personal affairs, and I write at the request of our steering committee.
>
> On November 30th Lester Cole's civil suit vs. Metro goes to trial before Judge Yankwich, a jury trial. It is the pilot case for all the contract

men and very critical.* Our lawyers have prepared for it by literally months of research, study, etc. Our case is excellent and a victory might mean the breaking of the blacklist and a good financial settlement of all the cases. We have only one weakness: prejudice. The MPA lawyers will, of course, red-bait. If they prejudice only one juror the jury will be hung.

All of this to explain our request: We heard by grapevine that you have instructed your lawyer to institute an action to reduce your son's allowance. Couldn't you postpone this for a few weeks or a month? Lester's case will take two or three weeks of trial. Any action you wish to take after it is over is your own affair, of course. But we are afraid that the Hearst press may deliberately blow up your personal action in order to affect the jury in the Cole case.

We hope that you will appreciate the situation and see it as we do and instruct your attorney to postpone your action until the end of December or January. . . .

The second letter, written six months later, was from Dmytryk's new wife, Jean Porter Dmytryk, to one of his lawyers, Robert Kenny. The new Mrs. Dmytryk was concerned because Eddie's ex-wife, who already had the $60,000 house and a big car, was trying to get *her* ranch, which Eddie had given her as a $16,000 wedding present (half down); it might even mean Eddie would be forced to sell his plane. "*Do something!*" she pleaded. As he said in his own letter to Kenny of February 12, 1949, "How vicious can you get?"[6]

Dmytryk and Maltz (who had stood as best man at Dmytryk's 1948 wedding) had served three months of their prison terms at Mill Point Prison Camp in West Virginia when Jean paid the only visit their finances would allow. According to Dmytryk's 1979 memoir, *It's a Hell of a Life But Not a Bad Living,* among the things they talked about were his getting "not just out of jail, but out of my real imprisonment, my associations." Even before being sentenced, he had reached a tentative decision, he writes, to take some sort of action, but "I knew that if I broke

---

* After the secret meeting of the Motion Picture Association of America (MPA) was held at the Waldorf-Astoria Hotel on November 24, 1947, RKO fired Scott and Dmytryk, Twentieth Century-Fox fired Lardner, and M-G-M "suspended" Cole and Trumbo without pay. The other five members of the Hollywood Ten were not under contract at the time and so there was no need to fire them. Cole's suit, charging breach of contract and conspiracy to blacklist against Loew's, Inc. (M-G-M's parent company), won at the trial level in December 1948, was reversed on appeal, and dropped in January 1952.

with the Ten before going to jail, everyone would think I was doing so to avoid prison, so I decided to postpone any move until I had served my sentence."

But the waiting was too much. He told Jean to call his lawyer Bartley Crum, and she was "ecstatic." "Ever since I had refused to take part in the last of the fund-raising campaigns, the hard-core members of the group had been uncertain of my continuing cooperation. Jean, who aside from this sad business, had never had anything in common with the other wives, was also considered a weak link. From time to time, one of these dour-faced women would call on her to keep her firmed up. She was actually a little frightened of them and didn't want them working on her. So, until the announcement came out in the press, no one was to know. Naturally, I didn't confide in Maltz."

Dmytryk's statement, witnessed by the prison warden on September 9, 1950, said that although he still believed he was right in his refusal to cooperate with HUAC, "in view of the troubled state of current world affairs I find myself in the presence of an even greater duty and that is . . . to make it perfectly clear that I am not now nor was I at the time of the hearings . . . a member of the Communist Party . . . and that I recognize the United States of America as the only country to which I owe allegiance and loyalty."

Dmytryk's agents worked quietly to "ease" him back into the industry, and once he was out of prison they had Harry Cohn talking about a $60,000 deal. "Then Herbert Biberman knocked on my door."

Biberman and Dmytryk, with six-month sentences, had both been denied parole and were both now out of prison. The other eight men, with one-year sentences, were making parole applications, and Biberman wanted Dmytryk to write the parole board urging that they be granted. Dmytryk agreed, on condition that the eight not publicize his name, because of the delicate state of his contract negotiations with Columbia Pictures. "Two days later, it was plastered over the front pages of both trade papers, and Feldman [his agent] phoned to tell me that as a result Cohn had called off our deal.

"That was the last straw. I was boiling mad. I had been walking a tightrope between abandoning an extremely distasteful affiliation and protecting my few friends in the Party. And my 'friends' were giving me no help whatever. Of course, I had another choice; I had received offers of work from J. Arthur Rank and other European producers, but Jean and I had decided that the U.S. was our country and this is where we wanted to live, work, and raise our family. Now, thanks to Biberman's 'humanitarianism' all hope of work had disappeared. . . .

"Bart Crum and I had been looking into every possible means of breaking the blacklist. There was only one: I had to purge myself. Hollywood's right wing had to have its pound of flesh. They were rising high just now, and there was no way they were going to let anyone off the hook. It was an eye-for-an-eye attitude, but who could blame them?"

So Crum contacted the Motion Picture Industry Council, which gave Dmytryk several requirements, "some merely suggested as desirable, some absolute. The suggestions involved primarily public-relations activities which they felt important in paving the way for favorable acceptance by the public at large. The absolute was a second appearance before HUAC, with full and open answers to all questions asked."

Dmytryk met the voluntary requirements by writing, with the help of the free-lancer Richard English, who specialized in anti-Communist subjects, an article for the May 17, 1951, issue of the *Saturday Evening Post* entitled "What Makes a Hollywood Communist?" "We spent a couple of weeks together," Dmytryk has explained, "during which he questioned and cross-examined me like a prosecutor. He edited the material down into a lengthy and fairly comprehensive article explaining my involvement with the Communist Party."

In the article Dmytryk said, "While like any guy I hope to work one of these days, that isn't why I'm talking now. . . . It's fellows like myself that give the Party its strength and its camouflage. If they walk off, the rest won't be hard to handle."

In reaching the decision to reappear before the House Un-American Activities Committee, Dmytryk says he "weighed the facts. I had long been convinced that the fight of the Ten was political; that the battle for freedom of thought, in which I believed completely, had been twisted into a conspiracy of silence. I believed that I was being forced to sacrifice my family and my career in defense of the Communist Party, from which I had long been separated and which I had grown to dislike and distrust. I knew that if it ever got down to a choice between the Party and our traditional democratic structure I would fight the Party to the bitter end.

"On the other hand, I would have to name names, and I knew the problems this would cause. Though the principle remained the same, my decision was made easier by the fact that my experience as an actual Party member had been rather meager, and I couldn't name anybody who hadn't already been identified as a Party member. Weighing everything, pro and con, I knew I had to testify.

"I was put in touch with Committee investigators. Naturally, they were pleased that I was going to cooperate. They were tired of getting hit on the head with the bladder of 'freedom of thought' by people who would have abolished it overnight if their positions had been reversed. They (as did the FBI in future interviews) laid down one stricture: they did not want to hear a name mentioned unless his (or her) membership in the Party was certain and verifiable. None of the names I gave was a surprise to them, though they were interested in some of the Party procedures. I found out at this time that Larry Parks was also going to testify before the Committee, and we discussed the timing of our appearances. I suggested that I be called first, but for some reason which escapes me, Larry wanted that position. His tortured testimony was so copiously reported that it haunted him throughout the rest of his life."

On April 25, 1951, Dmytryk told the Committee he had changed his mind because of the changed world situation, that he believed the Communists to be behind North Korea's invasion of South Korea, and he wanted to make it clear he would fight for America in a war against the Soviet Union. He also mentioned the trials of Alger Hiss and Judith Coplon (a Justice Department employee accused of espionage in 1949) and said, "I don't say all members of the Communist Party are guilty of treason, but I think a party that encourages them to act in this capacity is treasonable." He talked of Communist attempts to infiltrate the various guilds in Hollywood and provided the Committee with his own definition of "informer": "An informer, roughly speaking, is a man who informs against colleagues or former colleagues who are engaged in criminal activity. I think the Communists, by using this word against people, are in effect admitting they are engaged in criminal activity. I have never heard of anybody informing on the Boy Scouts." In the course of his testimony Dmytryk named twenty-six people as Communists, including six directors, seventeen writers, and three others.

Finally, it should be noted, he told of one of the Party's cruder (but unsuccessful) attempts to impose its politico-aesthetic line, and cited the episode as "the thing that actually got me out of the Party." It had to do with *Cornered,* a picture he made with Adrian Scott in 1945, about a Canadian pilot who went to Argentina looking for the Nazi who had killed his wife, a member of the French underground. As Dmytryk recalled the incident:

> In that picture we had an opportunity to say many things about fascism, which we did. While the first script was being written by John Wexley I found the script had long speeches, propaganda— they were all anti-Nazi and anti-Fascist, but went to extremes in following the Party line. I objected—not because of this, but because

the picture was undramatic, too many speeches, and I suggested to Adrian that we get another writer, which we did.... After they were making prints to go out to the theaters, so that I knew no changes could be made in it, Adrian Scott received a note from Wexley saying he wanted to have a conference with us...

The meeting was at my house. I was surprised to see the meeting was of Communists, and the whole meeting was along Communist lines. Adrian Scott and I were attacked by Wexley and by two people he brought with him at the time, Richard Collins and Paul Trivers....

The whole attack on us was along this line: by removing Wexley's line, we were making a pro-Nazi picture instead of an anti-Nazi picture. To say the least we were startled.

... Of course, we refused to admit any of the charges made by Wexley and the other two. Nevertheless, they asked for a further meeting. At the further meeting they brought John Howard Lawson, who was the "high lama" of the Communist Party at that time.

MR. TAVENNER [HUAC's counsel]: Why do you say that?

MR. DMYTRYK: He settled all questions. If there was a switch in the Party line, he explained it. If there were any decisions to be made, they went to John Howard Lawson. If there was any conflict within the Communist Party, he was the one who settled it. We had a third meeting at which Adrian Scott brought Albert Maltz, who was a more liberal Communist, to defend us. These meetings ended in a stalemate. There were several by-products of these meetings. I think Albert Maltz had been concerned with the lack of freedom of thought in the Communist Party for some time, and this was the trigger for the article he wrote for the *New Masses* on freedom of thought which was so widely discussed.*

MR. TAVENNER: Is it your view that this incident you have described had a very strong effect upon Albert Maltz?

MR. DMYTRYYK: I know it did, because I talked to him about it, and he was very much concerned with this effort to control the thought of members. So he wrote the article which he later had to repudiate or get out of the Party, and he chose to repudiate it....

"There was no new or startling information in any of my testimony," Dmytryk writes. "Its chief value was that it was a confirmation of the committee's statements by an actual former member of the party. Every-

* See below, p. 288.

thing I said had been verified by the committee's investigators in advance. For the first time in three and a half years, I felt free of guilt."

After he testified, Dmytryk says, he still had trouble finding work, until the King brothers hired him to make a small-budget film called *Mutiny* (1951). Then he got an offer that put him back in business: "Stanley Kramer, a noted 'chance taker' and progressive filmmaker, approached me with a four-picture deal. Manna from heaven. Maybe after four years of famine, the harvest would be full again." He joined Kramer at about the time Carl Foreman left, and his career was back on its way.

Asked if he felt a revulsion against informing, Dmytryk told a television interviewer in 1973:

> Not necessarily. . . . It depends. For instance, if you belong to an organization you're proud of—are you ashamed to say that the president of the organization is so-and-so? You'll tell me who the head of the union is, won't you? Without any question. Now the Communist Party was a legal party and actually the officers of the Communist Party—except during a short time when the Smith Act was involved— . . . weren't being thrown in jail; nothing was being done to them.
>
> It isn't as though a man becomes a hero under certain conditions—it's like a spy. A spy is considered a horrible man by the enemy but a hero by his own country, isn't he? And it's the same thing here. . . . It's a little childish, this business of "tattletale" or "singing." If a man like Valachi, for instance, talks about the rest of the Mafia, now it's amazing . . . people in general consider him some sort of horrible person. And yet what is he doing? He's trying to help the public in general to overcome a very horrible conspiracy of gangsters. And there's really nothing wrong with it, except that he was involved in it himself for so long and sinned exactly himself. But what if an FBI man came out and delivered all that same information? He would be a hero. . . . We call it squealing in America, something bad, you know, connected with the idea of squealing or singing, but I don't think it's legitimate, no. . . .
>
> Not a single person I named hadn't already been named at least a half-dozen times and wasn't already on the blacklist. Because I didn't know that many. I only knew a few people, literally a handful of people, all of whom had been in the Party long before I was, all of whom were known by the FBI and were known by the Committee. There was no question about that. . . .
>
> With me it was [that] defending the Communist Party was something worse than naming the names. I did not want to remain a martyr to something that I absolutely believed was immoral and wrong. It's as simple as that.[7]

BUDD SCHULBERG

Two days after he was named by Richard Collins, Budd Schulberg sent the following telegram to HUAC:

> I HAVE NOTED THE PUBLIC STATEMENT OF YOUR COMMITTEE IN-
> VITING THOSE NAMED IN RECENT TESTIMONY TO APPEAR BEFORE
> YOUR COMMITTEE. MY RECOLLECTION OF MY COMMUNIST AFFILI-
> ATION IS THAT IT WAS APPROXIMATELY FROM 1937 TO 1940. MY
> OPPOSITION TO COMMUNISTS AND SOVIET DICTATORSHIP IS A
> MATTER OF RECORD. I WILL COOPERATE WITH YOU IN ANY WAY
> I CAN. BUDD SCHULBERG, NEW HOPE, PENNA.

Born March 27, 1914, the son of B. P. Schulberg, one of the original Hollywood moguls, Budd was known less for his screenplays than for his best-selling novels, *What Makes Sammy Run?* (1941) and *The Disenchanted* (1950), the latter a fictionalization of F. Scott Fitzgerald's last years. He appeared before the Committee on May 23, 1951, and told Frank Tavenner, HUAC's counsel, that he had "voluntarily made known" his status to "an investigative agency of the federal government" prior to his being named by Collins.

The Committee told Schulberg it had heard testimony of "efforts made by the Communist Party in Hollywood to influence the work of writers in Hollywood." Schulberg told the Committee how the Party tried to influence his own writings, how from 1937 to 1939 Party members had criticized his short stories. When he told them he was going to write a book, that was acceptable, because books could be "useful weapons," but when he told them his plan to convert his 1937 *Liberty* magazine short story "What Makes Sammy Run?" into a novel,

> The reaction . . . was not favorable. . . . The feeling was that this was a
> destructive idea; that . . . it was much too individualistic; that it didn't
> begin to show what were called the progressive forces in Hollywood;
> and that it was something they thought should be either abandoned or
> discussed with some higher authority . . . before I began to work on
> it. . . .
>   I believe the one who either felt most strongly or was most responsi-
> ble at that time was Richard Collins.

Collins suggested Schulberg consult with John Howard Lawson, and "Either in the group or through Lawson it was suggested that I submit an outline and discuss the whole matter further," to see if the novel would be useful, i.e., would be a "proletarian novel." They said he needed to submit himself to "self-discipline," which he regarded as discipline having nothing to do with the self.

> I decided I would have to get away from this if I was ever to be a writer. I decided to leave the group, cut myself off, pay no more dues, listen to no more advice, indulge in no more literary discussions, and to go away from the Party, from Hollywood, and try to write a book, which is what I did.

Schulberg went to Vermont in 1939, wrote *Sammy,* and returned to Hollywood in March 1940. This resulted in another visit from Richard Collins, who upbraided him for not giving proper notice, not getting a "transfer," turning in his book to his publisher without prior Party consultation. "Are you in or out of this thing?" Collins asked. "As far as I'm concerned, since I left in May I am out," Schulberg answered.

Schulberg nevertheless went to see John Howard Lawson, who gave him a severe critique, and finally he had a talk with the Party's cultural commissar, V. J. Jerome, or rather he listened.

> . . . I remember being told that my entire attitude was wrong; that I was wrong about writing; wrong about this book; wrong about the Party; wrong about the so-called peace movement at that particular time . . . a kind of harangue. When I came away, I felt maybe, almost for the first time, that this was to me the real face of the Party. . . . I felt I had talked to someone rigid and dictatorial who was trying to tell me how to live my life, and as far as I remember, I didn't want to have anything more to do with them.

Schulberg recalled that the *Daily Worker*'s book reviewer, Charles Glenn, called the book "*the* Hollywood novel," and Schulberg was then told there would be a public meeting at which the reviewer would be called to account and "the real Party line on the book would be laid down." Schulberg was asked if he wanted to attend, and "I said that I didn't believe any writer should defend his book in public." After the meeting Glenn wrote a second review recanting the first, and pointing out the defects in *Sammy,* for example that it had not sufficiently emphasized the Party's role in building up the Screen Writers Guild.

Schulberg, elaborating his theme, went on to say, among other things, that in the Party a writer was in a sense looked upon as a soldier who was given certain "social commands." If he didn't follow them, he was out.

After his testimony Schulberg, who named fifteen names, went back to work and wrote the screenplays for *On the Waterfront, A Face in the Crowd* (1957), and a number of other pictures. He has devoted his life to his novel-writing and a variety of other causes, such as the Watts Writers Workshop, which he founded following the riots in Los Angeles in 1964; he continues to work with black ghetto kids on their writing to this day. At cocktail parties, in bars, and whenever he is confronted by critics of his informing, he has engaged in verbal duels, arguing that while he might have preferred not to name names, he didn't hurt anybody and did the right thing, given the choice as he saw it: HUAC versus the USSR.

When Herbert Biberman, of the original Hollywood Ten, died on June 30, 1971, an obituary the next day mentioned that he had been identified as a member of the Communist Party by Budd Schulberg. Later that evening Schulberg walked into the Lion's Head Tavern in Greenwich Village, and Doug Ireland, a local wit, asked him, "What are you doing here? I thought you'd be sitting shiva for Biberman." Schulberg, Muhammad Ali's biographer and a fight fan, took a swing at him but Joe Flaherty, the boxing writer, moved in and broke them up.[8]

Jack Desmond, associate Sunday editor of *The New York Times* and Schulberg's neighbor in Quogue, Long Island, appeared the next day at the *Times* with a page fresh from the typewriter of the actress Geraldine Brooks, Budd's third wife. Geraldine Schulberg's memo said it was "to be appended to *The New York Times* obit of Biberman in order to represent true historical fact rather than lie through innuendo so that readers of *The New York Times* in the future shall not be misled as were readers of the original obit. . . .* This mythical version," she wrote, "must not be perpetrated." The memorandum said:

. . . The fact was that Biberman, as one of the most outspoken of the original Communist leaders, had been mentioned by many previous witnesses before the Committee. Schulberg simply corroborated a list of names that had already been corroborated many times over.

The gist of Budd Schulberg's testimony was that he became disenchanted with official Party pressure to censor and even to question his

---

* The writer of the original obit was Alden Whitman, the *Times* man who had invoked the First Amendment when asked about his own Communist past and that of others by the Senate Internal Security Subcommittee.

right to write his first novel, *What Makes Sammy Run?* Schulberg was subsequently expelled (at the same time resigning) from the Communist Party for his refusal to accept Party discipline of artistic work. He related this to the system of vilification, exile and death of leading Soviet writers. He explained to the Committee that the reason he became a co-founder with Arthur Koestler of Funds for Intellectual Freedom [FIF] was to convince all authors to support financially and politically those writers in totalitarian countries who were being sent to concentration camps, whether fascist or Communist, because their literary works did not follow the official line. To say that Schulberg's experience in the Party, '36–'39, had made him a left-liberal anti-Communist is one thing; to single him out as Biberman's only accuser seems neither in the interest of good journalism nor fair play.[9]

Today Schulberg says, "My guilt is what we did to the Czechs, not to Ring Lardner. I testified because I felt guilty for having contributed unwittingly to intellectual and artistic as well as racial oppression. In a small way I helped to bring down McCarthy and I can show it.

"These were not civil libertarians. Look at what they did to Charles Glenn, who was forced to retract and reverse his opinion of *Sammy* once Lawson and the rest went to work on him. Anyone who attended the meeting called to denounce the book—unless he was under Party influence—would know that these were thought controllers, as extreme in their way as Joe McCarthy was in his. Actually it was the first book to speak positively of the strike at the guild. It's probably the only time the same book has been reviewed on successive weeks for reasons of political pressure.

"The Communist Party is a totalitarian society. You're under strict discipline. You're in a cell. You have special assignments every evening to work in a group. You have to request time off to write a novel. Once they say you can't write the book or you have to discuss it with them in order to get their permission, they have a strong hold on you. When Lawson says there was no pressure put on me, he is lying in defense of the Communist Party. The discipline of the Communist Party is something not understood by the Communist Party.

"Get off the idea that these are civil libertarians. . . . And don't talk to me about socialist realism. Dalton [Trumbo] wrote one good novel and that's it. Most of these people never tried to write any social realism. I think maybe [they had some] guilt about making two thousand dollars a week and doing nothing. You could make it up by paying ten percent dues [to the Party], and maybe that made you feel better about being a hack. Most of them settled for being hacks.

"These people, if they had it in them, could have written books and plays. There was not a blacklist in publishing. There was not a blacklist in the theater. They could have written about the forces that drove them into the Communist Party. There was practically nothing written.

"Nor have I seen these people interested in social problems in the decades since. They're interested in their own problems and in the protection of the Party. You show me where these people have fought for the poor. What stopped these people for thirty years or more? I really think you'll find that they became a kind of new establishment. Not to belabor Watts—but where the fuck were they?

"It's Dostoevskian. There *were* people who weren't just interested in getting a job in Hollywood, who loathed the Committee, who didn't like the Communists, who were troubled, worried about coercion, fighting for the lives of people in Russia. By the time I went to testify I had signed with [Arthur] Koestler saying I'd give ten percent of my income to FIF, to help writers not only in Russia but everywhere.

"There's some justification for saying, 'I'll take the First.' I felt immediately I couldn't take the Fifth at a time when I was raising money against Soviet aggression, but taking the First passed my mind.

"They had all been named—there wasn't much new I could add. While I didn't like the nature of HUAC—I thought it was a sleazy Committee and I denounced it—I saw no way I could say [that its inquiry] was going to incriminate me. I also had doubts about the idea of a clandestine organization in our democracy, and Communist Party members were not telling the truth when they spoke out as 'liberals' on the Korean War.

"There were other people who had a need to belong to an in-group— Dalton, Lillian, Ring (though he's nice). All of these people helped by their silence to create not a blacklist but a deathlist.

"When I asked Lillian Hellman, 'What about [the Russian writer] Isaac Babel?' who was sent to a death camp and killed, she said, 'Prove it!' I told Lillian, 'Better writers than you or me have been killed.' She said, 'Prove it.' I said, 'They put out an annual book; instead of shouting at me at a cocktail party, read it.' But I have to 'prove' that Babel is dead, Olesha is dead, Pilniak is dead! They are nonpersons. Isaac Babel doesn't exist. When the Soviet world comes to Park Avenue, Babel becomes a nonperson.

"After the war Yuri Jelagin, who wrote *Death in the Arts,* escaped to this country. He came to see me and told me that he had gotten a postcard with nothing on it which told him where Babel was. When I went to the Writers Congress in the USSR in 1934 as an avowed Young Communist, Babel spoke, and I hadn't been aware it was the first time he'd [spoken publicly] since 1928. It was a fantastic congress. Bukharin was our leader. Everyone was there. Babel said he was clinging to the right to write badly, but I was still a partisan and didn't understand what he meant.

"Later on, it struck me that every single one of the speakers—every single one—went to their death or disappeared. And these people—Lillian, Dalton, and Ring—bullshit about freedom. These are Nazis posing as libertarians. If the Lawsons and Hellmans ever got into power I think no one would have any freedom. It's a real battle. Until people are able to hear the story, they'll never know the truth.

"I think it would be very hard to get Lillian to criticize the death of a Soviet writer. They could be stretched on the rack at Lubianka Prison and Lillian would go back on the ferry to Martha's Vineyard. I think they have been toads. They have been unwilling to attack [Russia].

"Stanley Lawrence [a CP organizer who, with Jerome, set up the Hollywood branch of the Party] was the first international Communist I ever met. This gets into life and death, and if you're going to listen to [the blacklisted writer] Ian Hunter and Ring Lardner and people who want to make it in Hollywood, hear this. He came to us—we were young people searching for a sense of socialism with a human face. He brought us into [the Party] and sent us into scary things, like organizing the farmers in Ventura Valley. Posses came after us—Steinbeck things. Then a whole new group came in—Lawson, Jerome, and the rest. They accused Lawrence of misunderstanding the situation. He was using these sons of rich producers as organizers in the valley when he should have been using us to take over the [entertainment] industry—he had missed the point. He was sent to Spain and then it was announced in the *Worker* that he had been shot as a traitor. I didn't understand it. Orwell did.

"All of this will simply amuse the Ian Hunters and Lawsons. They think I support the blacklist. I think they support the deathlist—by their silence. If you want to test it out ask them about Lawrence, and they will say, 'What about the Scottsboro Boys?'

"Ninety percent didn't give names [before HUAC] because they were under Communist Party discipline. I say most of these people are without any feeling about the death of their fellow artists because they are so driven by the spell of the Communist Party. It took me years to get over it. I'd ask questions about the purge trials, and they'd say, 'That will be explained when comrade so-and-so comes to town.' You hand over your conscience to the Party.

"It's easy to say that the Communist Party here was weak—but it was a splinter in the heart of the United States. What's overlooked is the mind control they were able to exert, and the organizational control through superior organization and concentrated energy. To see the Party as just another caucus is a seventies' point of view. It was the only game in town.

"You're called by HUAC, and you don't want to act to endorse its thought control, but you know the greatest thought control you've experienced was from the Party. I expressed doubts [about naming names]—it would be inhuman not to. But I truly felt the Communist Party was a menace. It was hard for me to see myself doing anything to help the Communist Party. It was especially a menace for the left and liberals. The CP uses them for protective coloration.

"I thought that what was happening in Russia was more repressive than anything we were doing in this country, and I didn't trust people who didn't want to fight it. All of that affected what I did before the Committee.

"The great majority of the unfriendly witnesses were under Party discipline; a small number were [simply] under Party influence; and a few were speaking their own conscience—there were a few police spies, too.

"Of the friendly witnesses there were people who were pressured through fear of losing their jobs, although that's somewhat exaggerated. Then there were some who spoke out of conscience. These people had experienced Communism and had a healthy distaste for it, and were against it for a different set of reasons than Senator McCarthy, who I think was trying to split and destroy the democratic movement. The irony was that both the Communist Party and McCarthy tried to throw a blanket over all the left. In that odd way they met on this matter.

"I spoke to Arthur Koestler about my doubts. I respected him as someone who had gone through that fire. You should look at his chapter in *The God That Failed*. What he describes there is what I went through. It's like a three-stage rocket. First, you argue inside yourself: I'd write notes to myself about the Moscow show trials, the Nazi-Soviet Pact. Second, you go out of the Party, but you feel that to make it public would play into the hands of reaction; you are still anti-fascist and you don't want to shore up the reactionaries if you can help it. Third, as Koestler said, you realize you have not been true to yourself. He realized he would not be true to himself if he did not speak out on something he thought was a scourge.

"Without being paranoid, once I realized that all the writers I'd met in the USSR were dead (or nonpersons) I felt that if the Jeromes were in power here, I'd be in the same kind of salt mine. So I didn't feel ashamed [in front of the Committee]. I felt sad. It's always sad to talk about something that disappoints.

"I said to Koestler, 'I hate the Communists but I don't like to attack the left.' He said, 'You've got to get over that. They're not left, they're East.' I don't think a lot of them knew that. They never got over it. They never faced the true impact.

"They question our talking. I question their silence. There were premature anti-fascists but there were also premature anti-Stalinists."[10]

LEO TOWNSEND

Leo Townsend, a lapsed Catholic, came to Hollywood in 1935 by way of a college humor column that he wrote when an undergraduate at the University of Minnesota and a job with Dell Publishing in New York. Townsend's therapist was Phil Cohen. His wife, Pauline, also an informer, was also in therapy with Cohen in the late 1940s.

Townsend's best-known screen credit is for *Night and Day* (1946), the Cole Porter story starring Cary Grant and Alexis Smith. After he testified, he wrote such movies as *Beach Blanket Bingo* (1965) and *Bikini Beach* (1964).

Townsend joined the Communist Party in 1943, left it in 1944 for a few months during the war when he worked for the Office of Strategic Services, and then rejoined in July 1944, "when the USSR was our ally." He joined "because I didn't want any friction in the family. Pauline—my wife—was a member of the Party. I really wasn't a dedicated Communist, ever."

John Wexley, a fellow Communist and friend until Townsend testified, believes that Townsend got a "bum rap" from the Party because of his intellectual curiosity. "He was reading *Monthly Review* and liking what he read and talking about it, and you weren't supposed to do that." In any case Townsend became disillusioned with the Party and in 1950, at the suggestion of the producer Floyd Odlum (whose wife, the former script girl Judy Raymond, became an informer), called the FBI, who sent out two agents to interview him at his home. In 1951 he contacted or was contacted by the Un-American Activities Committee and Wheeler. Townsend says his testimony was his own idea and voluntary, but nonetheless there was a subpoena. On September 18, 1951, his attorney Martin Gang drove him to the Federal Building in Los Angeles, where his testimony took all morning and afternoon.

In the course of his testimony he gave a lengthy speech on why he left the Party, and before he named his thirty-seven names he assured Chairman Wood: "I feel that the purpose of this Committee is an investigative one so that the Congress of the United States may intelligently legislate in the field of national security. As a loyal American interested in that security, I feel I must place in the hands of this Committee whatever information I have."

He went out of his way to commend Warner Brothers for promising to keep him employed. "When I received my subpoena last week," he said, "I went to the heads of the studio, told them I had a subpoena, told them what I had planned to do here, that I was going to testify before the Committee. They told me that my testimony would in no way affect my employment at their studio."

He said the problem he faced as a Communist was one of conflicting loyalties to the United States and the Soviet Union, a conflict sharpened by the Party's "conspiratorial" and "treasonable" nature. Several years ago, he said, "all of us fought with all our might against German and Italian fascism. Today there is a section of people who shut their eyes to Soviet fascism . . . and if what I say here and if what this Committee does here can help these people, I think this will show a large measure of success."

He then quoted "just a couple of sentences" from "an interesting article I read" in a recent issue of *The Saturday Review of Literature* by Peter Viereck, then an associate professor at Mount Holyoke College:

> This kind of liberal tends to avoid the real fact of Soviet Russia, such as the enormous aid given to Germany during the Hitler-Stalin Pact; the Stalinist purge of all Lenin-Marxist associates; the postwar anti-Semitic drive in the Soviet Union; the slave labor camps; increasing class lines and pay differentials between Soviet rich and poor, so much greater than the capitalist United States.

All members of the Committee effusively thanked and praised him for his testimony.

In 1953 he also appeared as a government witness at deportation hearings against Reuben Ship, the Canadian who made "The Investigator," a phonograph record satirizing Senator Joseph McCarthy.

Townsend left the Party in 1948. "In 1950 I became really worried about what the Party in the U.S. was—it was a conspiracy, I thought, a conspiracy against our country. And I called the FBI and I said, 'I am a former member of the Communist Party here in this area. . . .' So two men came out to my home, and I told them all I knew. I discovered they knew more about it than I did; they knew every meeting I went to, they knew who was there. The names I gave them were names they already knew—I wasn't revealing anything. . . . Then in 1951 I got a call from a man named Bill Wheeler who was an investigator for the Committee and he asked if he could come out to see me—he said he'd heard I'd been in the Party. . . . He asked would I testify and would I accept the subpoena—of course I would have to accept the subpoena and I said yes I would volunteer, I didn't need a subpoena.

"The Committee had all those names. When I testified, they knew all the names. Someone else had mentioned the names. . . . I didn't name anyone who hadn't been named. . . .

"I brought out this point about anti-Semitism [in the Soviet Union] before the Committee. I had researched this and I made sure I was right. . . . Many Jews were killed [in Russia] but secretly—at least Hitler did it publicly, if that's an advantage. Oh, and the Communists in this room just gasped—they didn't believe that, because a lot of them were Jewish, you know . . . they read only their own papers. And then I compared communism with Nazism and fascism. They didn't like that, either.

"I would like to impress you with the fact that from my standpoint I did it out of my conscience, as I'm sure Dalton and Ring did it out of theirs. I was not *pressed* to do it by anyone but myself. I was testifying for the government. If I had taken the Fifth Amendment I would have been lying, because I had left the Party, I had hated it. I had found out what evils were in it, especially that anti-Semitic thing. And I really spent a lot of time making sure I was right, because if I'd been wrong I'd have been killed.

"I wasn't subpoenaed. I volunteered, I wanted to get it off my mind. And I knew it was going to hurt me. . . . I said, 'I will not regret it because I've thought of it for almost three years now and I want to clear my conscience.' I knew they were in town, and I said, 'My name is Leo Townsend and I've been a member of the Party.' And they said, 'Yes, we know.' And I said, 'Well, I will testify for the government.' And they said, 'What?' So that was how it started.

"I never would have testified before the McCarthy Committee because I was opposed to everything he stood for. Testifying before McCarthy would have been like taking the Fifth Amendment—I didn't believe in that.

"Wheeler said, 'I've got to tell you that you have to name names. It's going to hurt you, and you won't want to do it, but it's the only way if you want to cooperate.' So I met with the Committee in private session a couple of times before I testified publicly."[11]

DAVID RAKSIN

David Raksin is one of the leading composers in Hollywood. His credits include the music for *Modern Times* (1936), *Laura* (1944), *The Secret Life of Walter Mitty* (1947), *Forever Amber* (1949), and many others. In the 1960s he served as president of the Composers and Lyricists Guild of America; today he lives in comfort in the Hollywood hills, works regularly for television and films, and is professor of music at USC and UCLA.

In the 1930s, Raksin had belonged to various organizations such as the pro-Loyalist Musicians' Committee to Aid Spanish Democracy; he joined the Communist Party in August 1938, and left it again not long after the Nazi-Soviet Pact of August 1939.

On September 20, 1951, the day Raksin officially became an informer, his marriage was coming apart, his character—as he saw it—was weak, and his lawyer was Martin Gang.

Reading his testimony before HUAC today, one is struck by how careful he was to make distinctions, not to be pushed into saying more than he wanted to. He named eleven names.

He told the Committee, "I didn't cease to be a liberal, sir, when I left [the Party]. In fact I left because I was a liberal." He said he opposed a law being passed making the Communist Party illegal, and he believed in the free expression of thought. Asked if he thought the Committee was doing a valuable job, he replied:

> I would say this, strange as it may sound coming from me, I think this Committee has done an extremely beneficial thing and that is that heretofore there has been a notion abroad in the United States that Hollywood is infested, it's overrun—you may choose the word—with Communists.
>
> I think this investigation has proved and will continue to prove that at most there were not more than a couple of hundred and that only a

small few were zealots who have remained and that the notion is once
and for all dispelled that subversive doctrines were insinuated into
films. I never heard of one being in a picture.

Raksin offered the Committee three examples of his own deviations
from the Party line. First, he told them he was incensed over the Soviet
government's disciplining of the composers Shostakovich and Prokofiev.
When Tavenner asked him whether it was the Party's view that these
men should "use art as a weapon," he said, "Oh, I wouldn't say as a
weapon, but that they felt they should submerge any desire to do anything special or extremely personal which might not be understood by everybody, and that my own feeling was that this is not possible to a
composer of any kind."

Asked how he was disciplined for his views, he said he wasn't really,
even though he had once said that if "the economic directors and commissars of the Soviet Union had as much ability at their jobs as Mr. Prokofiev had at his, there would be no economic problem in the Soviet
Union." And, without evident irony—though his own circumstance was
expressive of the very situation he described—he told the Committee that
the Party had accused him of subscribing to bourgeois thinking for expressing the view that, "whenever means arrive at a point where they
themselves are so terrible that they debase the man that does these deeds,
it is time to examine not only the substance of the means but the end itself."

Finally, he mentioned that he had been criticized for thinking that it
was a mistake to attempt to inject novels with socialist realism. "Those
men who did this deliberately at the expense of the work of art itself,
were making a great mistake and producing neither something which
would affect people nor something which would be a good work of art,
and I submitted as an example the *Comédie Humaine* of Balzac."

But when the Committee asked him whether these views had been considered dangerous by the Communists, he answered carefully, "It wasn't
considered dangerous, sir, if I may say so. It was just thought and expressed to me that other people, who were perhaps less capable of making such 'fine'—and I put that word in quotes—differentiations would
perhaps be thrown off the path of possible action in some cause or other."

A gentle man, David Raksin cried several times during our talk as he
recalled the pain he had brought to himself and others.

"I remember I got a call, and the man said, 'I've named you, so don't
try to lie.' Then Louis Russell, the FBI man who worked for HUAC,

came to see me and gave me a summons and asked me not to talk about it. I was coming to the end of my M-G-M contract, and they were about to give me another one, and I didn't know what to do about it because I didn't want to embarrass them. So I called my agent and told them to pull an artist thing—tell M-G-M I'm too busy on other things to sign. Later [the producer and M-G-M executive] Eddie Mannix called and said, 'I understand what you did and I must tell you that was a hell of a fine thing to do.'" In other words Raksin had saved M-G-M embarrassment at the cost of his own job security.

"The only thing a decent person could do was not talk—I still believe that. But my English wife helped pull the rug out from under me. She was no help at all. I was muddled and frightened and decided I needed some shoring up. So I picked out the two persons of integrity I most admired and told them about it. I said, 'This is what I wanted to do—not talk.' They said, 'You have to ask yourself, Why do you want to commit suicide?' One was a physician and the other a musician and an all-around marvelous person. I remember talking to these guys and I had this crazy vision of that story about the nightingale and the rose, where the nightingale has to press herself against the rose and then dies from the thorn. This thing sapped my resolve.

"The whole thing was some kind of insane ritual. None of this could have happened if society was not mad. I said to myself, 'This is like the Spanish Inquisition, so maybe the best I can do is to come out of it alive.'

"Martin Gang didn't understand that there are some things I was just not going to do. He wanted me to vomit all over the place. It was debasement disguised as patriotism. I knew that the chances of anybody understanding that [my testimony] was not capitulation were minor, but I said, 'If I can do this and not eat dirt, I can live with that.' Also, I didn't want people to think that this particular brand of progressive ideology was something I was ready to destroy myself over. (You know, at the end of Brecht's *Galileo* there's a monumental confusion. The student says, 'Now I understand—you capitulated to write your book.'*)

---

* In Brecht's play, Galileo, after being forced by the Church publicly to repudiate his belief in the Copernican theory that the earth moves around the sun, is visited by a disciple. He reveals to his student that he is secretly writing his *Dialogues*, summing up his life's work in astronomy. Part of the confusion Raksin refers to is that Brecht leaves open the question of whether Galileo has recanted in order to continue his studies or simply to save his life.

"It may have been that at that moment we were required to rise to a stature we just didn't have. . . .

"There were people I knew they knew I knew about—and I left them out and they didn't care! I still don't understand what pulled Tavenner away from my throat.

"I'm beginning to feel that I didn't deserve the punishment I have inflicted on myself all these years. I have condemned myself in a way I wouldn't condemn the Jews of the Spanish Inquisition. If I'd been willing to take the consequences, I'd be more justified in feeling sorry for myself. But it took guts to say, 'Yes, I was in [the Party], now I'm out, and you guys ought not to run around and embarrass us,' and that's what I said. At the end of the hearing, [Congressman Donald] Jackson started after me and made a speech about Hiss being a traitor and all. I realized he was just orating, and he didn't nail me. Then somebody paid me a gratuitous compliment, and that didn't sit well, but I wasn't about to say, 'Don't compliment me.'

"It's possibly a delusion that I was less of a fink than some other guys. I did what I thought I had to do. I'm tougher on myself than I ought to be. The honorable thing is to respond to your own code, not other people's. It's minor league to suffer from 'their' attitude of disapproval. But I had feelings. This is the kind of issue you die over."[12]

ISOBEL LENNART

Isobel Lennart, born in 1915, was fired from a job in the M-G-M mail room at the age of nineteen for organizing a union. She returned to M-G-M two years later as a script girl and stayed in what she called "the family" for the rest of her life.

In 1938 she joined a Communist "study group," in 1939 she joined the Party, and in 1944 she met the strongly anti-Communist John Harding, a *New Leader* columnist, actor, and writer, who became her husband. She left the Party soon after, primarily, she told the Un-American Activities Committee, because of the Party's new postwar militance. By the time she appeared as a cooperative witness on May 20, 1952, naming twenty-one persons as Communists, she was one of the top musical-comedy writers in the movie industry, and her screenplays included *East Side, West Side* (1949), *Anchors Aweigh* (1945), and *Meet Me in Las Vegas* (1956). She wrote the screenplays for twenty-six film musicals and won the 1966

Laurel Award (given by the Screen Writers Guild) before she died in 1971 in a car crash.

When first visited by Wheeler in 1951 Lennart told him she did not want to give names. Because she didn't testify but nevertheless continued to work, it was reported in the *Hollywood Reporter* that she was the beneficiary of a deal. But in fact, she was the beneficiary of a pregnancy—her obstetrician refused to give the Committee an opinion that she could appear as a witness without serious danger to her health. She explained her situation and change of mind on the matter in 1952 to HUAC:

> Well, that brings us up to Mr. Wheeler's visit in 1951, and I had said I would like to talk on why I told him a year ago that I did not think if I were subpoenaed, I would give names and why I obviously have changed my opinion on this today. I would like to say why I didn't want to give them a year ago. In the years since I have been married, my life has changed a great deal. I no longer saw the people I had once known. I have lost track of most of them. The whole subject of the Party was one I kept pretty closed. I knew that my convictions had changed. I felt that my conscience was clear, that I was doing nothing that could hurt this country in any way. I thought it was more than likely that many of the people I had known once had changed as much as I had, and I couldn't bring myself to damage anyone in a way that I felt I was going to be damaged because I thought that when I testified, that career I had worked hard at for a long time would be over. I was also in the third month of a pregnancy. I was emotionally not too stable and I just couldn't get myself to do it.

MR. WOOD: What made you believe that? Do you know of any person who had been called to testify before an authorized body of people or a committee of Congress with reference to Party affiliation in the Communist movement, who has done so, freely, honestly, who has been penalized on account of it, with reference to their position?

MISS LENNART: No, I do not, since that time. But, Congressman, may I say that this was before the hearings. There was an awful lot of talk in town. Nobody knew what was going to happen, you know, and I was in quite a turmoil about it. I must confess that after my meeting with Mr. Wheeler I relaxed a little about the whole matter. I live in comparative isolation from the political zone in Hollywood and from the social zone. We live quite a bit out of town, and between working and bringing up my children and running my house—I have another child besides the new one—I don't get around much. I have lost touch with what was going on. . . . I heard rumors for the first time that were very shocking and horrifying to me. This one I didn't hear directly—but I was told that it was commonly supposed that the reason I was still able to work even though I had been mentioned at the last hearing last year was that I had made a deal with someone, and this was pretty revolting for me and for this Committee, too, I felt. The other, opposing rumor was that I was the last active, powerful Communist in Hollywood, that for some reason I was such a powerful Communist I couldn't be touched. This rumor was appalling to me too.

MR. WOOD: I think it appropriate at this point to let the record be perfectly clear that there has never been any deal entered into by this Committee or any member of the Committee, so far as I know, or any member of its staff.

MISS LENNART: I don't consider the Committee's consideration for a woman who is busy having a child a deal. I call it something I am grateful for. . . .

MR. TAVENNER: . . . But actually, when you look back upon your experience don't you agree that a person cannot be a member of the Communist Party without doing harm, because by being a member you are lending your moral assistance and your aid to those of the Communist Party who are out, unquestionably, to do harm.

MISS LENNART: I most certainly believe that now. Most certainly. I believe with you. You can't be as irresponsible as to think that what you specifically are doing is all there is to it. You have to see how this ties in with what other people are doing, and you have to consider yourself a party to it, and that is why I did not want to be in it.

Before she died Isobel Lennart taped an interview with the actor and writer Robert Vaughn:

"When they came to me and they wanted names, I could have hurt—I felt—an enormous number of people, because I knew a great many people [who had been in the Party]. I told them that since I was out of the Party, I didn't know who else was out of the Party. . . .

"They said, 'What position would you take if you're subpoenaed?' And I said, 'I will answer all questions about my own activities.' And they said, 'We don't think your activities have made you an enemy of the state.' And I said, 'I don't either. I'll answer all questions about my activities and none about anyone else.' That was before that stand had ever been taken by anybody, and they said, 'Well, in that case you'll probably go to the clink.' And I said, 'Yes, I'll have to.' Jack and I discussed this. I was very brave at that point.

"They disappeared, and then suddenly they came back, and I really steeled myself. I was miserable, but I still was very close to having been in the Party. . . . I loved these people. They came back about a week later, and they had been told by somebody that I was pregnant. Which I was. Which I hadn't mentioned—I didn't think it was relevant. I was about three or four months pregnant, and they felt that for a pregnant woman to test them on this ground would be bad publicity. They buzzed around. Somehow through M-G-M, I think, they found out who my obstetrician was and went to him. They wanted an affidavit saying that I could testify without danger to my health. My obstetrician, who was a very wise man, said certainly not, he would sign an affidavit saying it would definitely endanger my health. I didn't know this was going on at all. This was all very subterranean. I was Rh negative, which was a big thing in those days—grounds for divorce in some states, I believe.

"They came back two weeks later and said, 'We withdraw the subpoena.' I said no. By this time I felt I was going to get away with it, too. But I said no because it had been hanging over my head for a year or so. I knew . . . that I might as well learn this way, and I would prefer to testify. They said that was it, and they wouldn't be back. . . .

"The FBI came back a day after I got out of the hospital and asked me a million questions. . . . They said they had information that I had been a member of the Young Communist League when I was sixteen in New York, and they asked me a great many questions about theater people. I had forgotten I had been in YCL. They wanted to know about John Garfield and Bromberg. They came back twice, and my husband said, 'Stop harassing my wife.' I had two sessions when they asked me about names . . . and I answered quite honestly that I had a different feeling about the FBI than I did about the Un-American Activities Committee. The FBI was not in the business of stopping people's employment and ruining their lives. They had tremendous information which they didn't use in any way unless you were insecure [sic].

"Then M-G-M called me in and said, 'We can't protect you any longer and this time you're going to have to testify. I had, I must say, a tremendous reversal of feelings about the Party at that time, but then I think it was [for] quite selfish [reasons]: my father had died, which made me know I would now be responsible for my stepmother and my brother. . . . On a personal level, I had come to feel that people don't sustain you, your work sustains you, and I knew how to do absolutely nothing else but screenwrite. I didn't know how to live if I couldn't work. Now I'm sure I'm rationalizing, but there was an enormous difference in the situation for me.

"Every name that I knew had been mentioned by this time. The first time I could have hurt other people; this time I felt I could only hurt my-self. I had weeks of debate about what effect it would have on me, be-cause I felt it was wrong to cooperate. To the extent that I did talk [to HUAC] it *was* a deal. It was very important for them for me to testify; they told me so. My studio felt that if I could testify and still continue be-ing employed, it would prove that HUAC did not necessarily ruin lives. They were having a lot of trouble with people who had cooperated who then could not find employment. Hollywood wouldn't employ reds, and it wouldn't employ people who had informed on reds either. It was clear to HUAC that I would not mention new names. I did not—if you read my testimony you will see—I told them honestly it was a setup. I went through the testimony, and my criterion was that I would mention no name that had not been mentioned ten times before—not eight, but ten. I mentioned about ten to twelve names; they had all been mentioned over ten times. You know, George Willner, names like that.

"The Committee said, 'There is one name we will ask you that has not been mentioned,' and they said the name, and I said that he had been my collaborator and closest friend. I said I knew he was in the army, and most people who were in the army were asked to leave the Party in this community. I said he had been thinking of joining the Party when he went into the army and that altered it; he did not; and by the time he came back I was out. Tavenner and Wheeler said, 'We don't believe that,' and I said, 'That's your problem.'

"They said they wanted me to testify at a closed hearing, they felt that uncertain of me, and I said oh, what the hell, if I'm going to do it, let's do it. I went to Washington.

"They came to my hotel room the night before I testified and said again that they had to have this name, and they would ask me on the stand and what would I do? I said, 'I will get up and say you are trying to corrupt my testimony, since I told you I don't know about this man.' Wheeler said, 'You're lying,' and I said, 'Prove it.' They did not ask me on the stand. He was mentioned three weeks later by somebody else. Nevertheless he never talked to me again. I don't think I hurt anybody else. I hurt myself enormously. . . .

"I didn't want to go to the attorney whom all of the people who were going to cooperate went to. For a long time a kind of vanity kept me from feeling I was the same as they, and for a year or two I was not. But then I was, and it was time to stop kidding myself. . . . We (Jack and I) agreed at that time that if I were asked to name any new names . . . I would not cooperate. Yes, we made a stopping place, and I felt I could live with this. I couldn't live beyond that. I don't think anything would have made me mention a group of new names. It's a small device, but at least there's nobody who was ruined and informed on because of me, and that made it at least tolerable for me.

"I believe with all my heart that it was wrong to cooperate with this terrible Committee in any way, and I believe that I was wrong. I believe I did a minimum of damage, but I still believe it was wrong. I had a much bigger reaction to it than I thought I would. . . . It was shame and guilt and nothing else. I've never gotten over it. I've always felt like an inferior citizen because of this. But it was a consensus decision. . . . I am able to comfort myself by saying I hurt nobody, but I'm aware that this is a comfort device. . . .

"Dick Collins didn't testify out of fear . . . and he was much hated in this town for a long time. . . . Three, four years before he testified, he turned violently against the Communist Party for the most honest reasons. He testified out of conviction (and it's hard for me to say that). Martin Berkeley I always thought was a pig when he was a Communist and a pig when he stopped being a Communist. This was not true of Dick, who was a very rigid man and a fanatic. . . . On leaving the Party, a big effort has to be made not to become a reactionary. You have to catch it in yourself. It's one thing to throw yourself off a cliff for what you believe in. It's another thing to throw yourself off a cliff for what you don't believe in anymore."

Lennart's husband, John Harding, who served as a buffer when the Committee tried to lean on her, told me when I saw him in 1974: "Her final decision was one she regretted all her life. Isobel's final decision was based on pressure from me and her lawyer. Our argument was that everybody she knew had been named so she would not be hurting anybody.

"At that rehearsal the night before, Tavenner said, 'We know you know one name not yet named.' She said, 'If you force me to do that'—he had been a close friend of hers—'I'll take the Fifth.' But they wanted her to cooperate, so they said, 'Okay.'

"The *Daily News* headline read, 'Red Writer Saved by Army Lieutenant.' I was supposed to have converted her. When we came back [from Washington] there were constant telephone calls asking her to identify people.

"It had been in our mind that if she cooperated with HUAC, she'd continue to work—and she did, on *Skirts Ahoy!* I was always trying to get her away from screenwriting to write a book or play. But she had a certain security at M-G-M. It was her place, like a school. It was murder even trying to get her to go on loan-out to other studios."[13]

ROY HUGGINS

Born in 1914, the son of a Portland, Oregon, lumberman, Roy Huggins attended the University of Oregon, Pasadena City College, and UCLA, where he was graduated Phi Beta Kappa, *summa cum laude* in political science. He missed out on a graduate fellowship at UCLA, where he studied public administration, because they mistakenly thought he was a Communist. This so enraged him, he says, that he then joined the Party as the sort of open Communist who would carry his card in his wallet. What drew him to Communism was his hatred of the Nazis and his belief that only the Communist Party was doing anything about Hitler. When the Nazi-Soviet Pact was signed, he withdrew.

Huggins says he was blacklisted before he was named by HUAC witnesses, although his credits indicate that he worked steadily as a writer and director on such pictures as *The Fuller Brush Man* (1947) and *The Good Humor Man* (1949). He says he "insisted" on director's credit for *Hangman's Knot* (1952) and got that, too, before he appeared before HUAC on September 29, 1952, and named nineteen names.

Huggins is at home in the world of television, where he functions as writer-director-producer and works in tandem with Meta Rosenberg, the former agent. Over the years he has been responsible for such successful series as *Cheyenne, Maverick* (for which he won an Emmy in 1958), *Run for Your Life, The Rockford Files,* and *The Captains and the Kings.* In 1977 he was given UCLA's annual Professional Achievement Award, and chose the occasion to warn against government control of television licenses.

Michael Wilson told me in 1975 that on the night of the execution of Julius and Ethel Rosenberg, some Hollywood protesters were keeping an all-night vigil. "At two a.m.," said Wilson, "Roy drove by in his Cadillac and shouted, 'Go back to Russia!'" Whether or not he did such things, in the years after he appeared before HUAC he went out of his way to hire blacklisted writers and actors whenever he could.

Looking back, Huggins says he welcomed the opportunity to appear before HUAC in 1952 because it gave him the opportunity to criticize it. His "criticism" of the Committee came in response to a question from Congressman Clyde Doyle:

> I think you are in a spot, because there isn't any question in my
> mind at all but there is a great need for democracy to do something
> about the subversive drives which intend to overthrow it. This is one
> of the things that disturbed me deeply about the Communist Party,
> is that they do not believe in individual freedom, and yet they shout
> to the housetops in defense of individual freedom in all of the demo-

cratic countries in which they exist. They become champions of complete political freedom. The moment they get power, they will destroy political freedom. It seems to be one more evidence of their complete lack of integrity or scrupulousness or anything else.

So I think that to the Communist, capitalism is going to be in a sense an easy thing to overthrow, eventually, I suppose, because we do have a tendency to fail to fight our enemies properly, but I suppose one of the reasons for that is that it would be a terrible thing if we were to fight tyranny by becoming a tyranny ourselves, isn't that so. This would be a terrible thing if we are anti-Communist because we feel that Communists destroy individual freedom and liberty, and in fighting Communism, we destroy individual freedom and liberty. This would be a fight in vain.

So I think that is why I say this Committee is in a terrible spot, because I think that subversive elements must be fought, and I think democracy has to fight for its life, and it can't just sit back and say, "Well, history will take care of us." It has got enemies and it has to fight those enemies but it has to fight them within the framework of the democratic system or it might as well not fight at all, because it loses the battle in the means it chooses to use to fight that battle. I don't know whether that answers your question or not. . . .

MR. JACKSON: To what do you attribute the violence of the Communist attack on this committee? . . . Is it that the Communists are seriously concerned, let us say, with constitutional government as we know it in this country, or is it possibly . . . that exposure is to be avoided? . . .

MR. HUGGINS: Well, I think . . . both questions can be answered "Yes." I don't recall the exact source, but I know that even Marx himself wrote that the Communist parties must be prepared to make use of democratic freedoms; that this is one of the greatest weapons they have. That is why you have a real problem.

MR. JACKSON: Well, is the utility of a Communist who is exposed publicly in any way affected so far as the Party is concerned?

MR. HUGGINS: Well, I would say it depends on what his role is in society. I am sure that if a man is highly placed in Government, it is in the interest of the Communist Party not to have him exposed, or if a man is placed in any position where as long as he is unexposed can do something that the Communist Party thinks is worthwhile.

MR. JACKSON: Then from the standpoint of America, exposure is an excellent idea?

MR. HUGGINS: Yes; I would say so.

MR. JACKSON: Do you make any distinction in your own mind, Mr. Huggins, as between a Communist in the city of Los Angeles, and a

Communist in the North Korean or Chinese Red armies, philosophically?

MR. HUGGINS: I have a suspicion that they are very much alike in that they are both the dupes of the Soviet Union, and they are both being used for the purposes of the Soviet Union, and in that respect they are very much alike.

Roy Huggins was and is an extremely articulate and careful man. He had his own tape recorder ready to capture his reflections when I visited him in his office on the Universal lot.

"It was a period of absolute terror on the part of the whole country. Terror and paranoia. We were convinced that war was just around the corner. . . . Title Two of the Internal Security Act gave the president the right to put into detention—in other words, into concentration camps— anyone suspected of being a subversive when the president decided that the emergency required that action. It was called the Concentration Camp Bill. It was the creation of liberal [senators] like [Paul] Douglas and [Hubert] Humphrey and [Harley] Kilgore; the ADA, which was considered to be an extreme political group, was behind it. Now that gives you an idea of the mood of the period.

"So there I was faced with the possibility of being hustled into a concentration camp while having several people completely dependent upon me. I considered the possibility of being a hero and I couldn't quite make it. I said to myself, You know, I'd love to be a hero, I'd love to go to jail, except for one thing: Who the hell is going to take care of two small children, a mother, and a wife, all of whom are totally dependent upon me? But I was still terribly tempted [not to cooperate], because although I honestly believed that war was imminent, I also knew our system was under a terrible strain from people who didn't believe in the libertarian principles I believed in; but I still felt our system was one hell of a lot more to be preferred than the Russian system. So it was difficult for me to take a position, a public position, that would make it look as if I would indeed be supporting what everyone there considered to be the enemies just around the corner. . . . We were indeed at war in Korea.

"And so I concluded that I would meet with the Committee. But since I had no names to give—there was literally no one in the Communist Party whom I had ever known who hadn't already been publicly listed many, many times—I had what I thought was an understanding with the general counsel [of HUAC] that the question of names wouldn't come up. . . .

"The conclusion I came to was that I would state my reasons for having become a Communist, which were very critical of this society, and I stated them very strongly and in great detail. I acknowledged that if you were a Communist at this moment, you were probably an untrustworthy citizen of the United States, which might be going to war any day, but I never once apologized for having become a Communist because I didn't feel apologetic. I wanted to outline my reasons for having joined the Communist Party because I thought they were very good reasons and under the same circumstances I probably would do it again. I also wanted to criticize the Committee. . . .

"So I decided that I would testify because I welcomed the opportunity to state the historical reasons for someone like me joining the Communist Party and also to state that the Committee was possibly defeating its own ends by its methods. I had no names to put into the record. By the time I got the subpoena, everyone had been mentioned many times. It didn't occur to me that I'd be double-crossed, because I wasn't aware of the ritualistic aspect of the whole HUAC procedure. I was trapped into partaking of the ritual. I could have said, 'Sorry, screw you, I will not partake of this ridiculous ritual.' But I was unprepared. I ended up agreeing that people who had already been mentioned many times were indeed known to me as Communists.

"I afterward regretted that decision, because the ritual was terribly important to them and I hadn't realized that, and the names went into the record; the transcript, as I recall it, makes it look as if I had volunteered all those names, which I did not do. As a matter of fact, I wouldn't even tell Tavenner that I knew how to spell the damned names. He would put the name in the record, and I'd say, 'Yes, that name has been mentioned in the public press,'' and he would say, 'How do you spell it?' and I would say, 'I don't know.' But I don't regard that as a brave position.

"In retrospect, it is appalling to me that I cooperated with them in any way. But that wasn't obvious twenty years ago, especially when I had at that time a strong emotional reaction to Soviet Communism. Today I don't have any such emotional reaction. I feel that the Russians have got their form of government, and God bless 'em. It's unfortunate for the Russians that they happen to have a totalitarian and terribly repressive regime, but it's none of our damned business. I regard anti-Communism as another refuge for scoundrels. I think it is our business that the Greeks have a terribly totalitarian regime;* that is our business because we cre-

---

* He was speaking of the "colonels' regime," which lasted in Greece from 1967 to 1974.

ated it, but we didn't create the Russian one, so I feel that it's not proper policy now.

"I got one letter asking if I wasn't ashamed of myself for having mentioned so-and-so, because so-and-so was ill in the hospital and had been named eighteen times. But the truth is, I *was* ashamed of myself. When it was over I was sorry I had not insisted that the name was irrelevant, and if I hadn't been caught so unprepared, I would have. I was caught unprepared and had a failure of nerve. I don't think there's any question about it. There I was, facing this Congress and terribly aware that we were at war in North Korea and that they had just passed a bill called the Internal Security Act, and asking myself, Do I really want to go to a concentration camp for who knows how many years? I don't know if you remember, but during World War II the Japanese in California were suddenly rounded up and put in concentration camps. I happened to see it happen. I happened to be appalled by it. I couldn't believe it when the Supreme Court refused to act on it. It was one of the first blows—not the first, but it was one of the early blows to my faith in our libertarian traditions in this country.

"It was a failure of nerve. I really decided that. There was a long pause which never showed up in the transcript. I think I must have waited four or five minutes before I finally replied, 'Yes, that name. . . .'

"You know, when you're thinking of becoming a hero you feel like a slob. You feel, Do you really have a right to do that? But after you have decided not to be a hero, then you feel like a slob for not having done it. It's a battle you can't win.

"I have a deep sympathy for everyone who got trapped in that unspeakable moment of our history. It's very difficult for a man to face the prospect of a concentration camp because he is believed to be something he is not. If I'm going to go to a concentration camp I want to go for something I'm actually guilty of.

"When the Hollywood Ten took the stand, I was appalled by their lack of candor because they all pretended to be Jeffersonian Democrats, and they weren't. It was all so terribly dishonest. It was simply not a reflection of their total political commitment. You don't believe in the Bill of Rights if you happen to believe in the Soviet Union and the Communist revolution. And I really objected, because they missed a great opportunity to state their case. When I got on the stand I said, 'I want to tell you why I joined the Communist Party before I go into anything else.' And then I told the Committee in exactly those terms.

"From the hindsight of twenty years, I would have refused to cooperate with the Committee in any way whatsoever on the grounds that *they* were the subversive ones; there was no internal Communist danger—there might have been a very real external Communist danger but not an internal one; and I was not going to answer their questions. That's what I would like to have done. Then I would have been able to support my children after I got out of jail. In the meantime they would have had to look to other means.

"I would never have taken the Fifth, never. When I got the subpoena I said no, that is an unprincipled position and I will not take it. I will not get up there and come on as if I were a member of the Communist Party in complete sympathy with its aims and not take advantage of this platform I'm being given. I absolutely refused to consider that possibility. I only had two possibilities: to get up and state what I wanted to state and assume that Tavenner would not double-cross me; or, if he double-crossed me, to say, 'Screw you, Mr. Tavenner, we have an agreement and I'm not going to answer your question'—and then that would have put me in jail since I had chosen to answer the previous questions already. In other words, the only choice I had was the choice that was facing me while I was on that stand. When I say now that I would have done it differently, I'm saying that I wish now that I had said, 'As an American citizen I feel obligated not to go through with this ridiculous ritual. I am here to tell you I was once a Communist and why, because there were damn good reasons. I'm perfectly willing to do that.' I would never have taken the Fifth. I considered that to be an unprincipled position.

"While I was a simple American citizen adhering to the Democratic Party and in no way connected with the Communist Party, I was under surveillance by either the Los Angeles Red Squad or the FBI (I never found out which), but in 1938–39 a car with two men in it watched my apartment for weeks at a time. Anyone who was antifascist, anyone who was an activist in the antifascist movement, was automatically considered to be a subversive, which tells a lot about the history of that time. . . . That's one of the reasons I chose to come before the Committee and take the opportunity to state that, and then to say that I thought it was using a self-defeating tactic, that it was pointless to claim it was fighting for democracy and to use undemocratic means. Last year when I read my testimony in Robert Vaughn's book, I thought, Oh shit, Christ Almighty, was I polite! I said it, and they didn't like it—Vaughn even lists me as an unfriendly witness, by mistake—but it didn't make me happy at all.

"The naming of names was probably the most unspeakable and heinous aspect of the Un-American Activities Committee. To cooperate with it in that aspect, even though the names had already been men-

tioned, was, I believe, the wrong thing to do. And that's the only part of
my part in this thing that I really regret. I got caught off guard and I had
a failure of nerve. I don't think there's any question about it. I recognized
it immediately. As soon as the damned hearing was over I said, 'Jesus
Christ, you had your moment of truth—it came, and you should have
said, Stick it up your ass, and you didn't.' I . . . became a part of something I knew was wrong, and that I have regretted for twenty years."[14]

SYLVIA RICHARDS

Sylvia Richards, a former radio writer and contract employee for Walter
Wanger, had just started writing screenplays of her own—*Rancho Notorious* (1952), *Ruby Gentry* (1952)—when she appeared before HUAC on
March 25, 1953. She was a patient of Phil Cohen's, she worked as an assistant to Richard Collins, her attorney was Martin Gang, she had separated from her husband nine years before, and she had two small children
to worry about.

Her father was a Fabian Socialist, her mother voted for Norman
Thomas for president, and "Communism was in the air" when Sylvia
Richards was growing up. She joined the Communist Party after witness-
ing the May Day Parade of 1937, which she found profoundly moving—
it was emotionally connected in her mind with the Spanish civil war. But,
as she told the Committee:

> I became a Communist because I was young and was irresponsible
> and because I didn't want to think for myself. It was extremely com-
> forting to have all the answers in a series of books and I would never
> have to think again. . . . That is why a lot of people will continue to
> cling to Communist thinking, even when the facts don't fit, because it
> is a little painful to take responsibility finally for your own thinking
> and for your own mistakes. . . . A large number of people are in the
> Party because they don't want to think for themselves. They like the
> security for only the right answer and the unquestioned right answer,
> and therefore they don't dare to question these directives, because they
> are flung out in the cold world, where they have to figure out the an-
> swers themselves.

In 1944 she separated from her husband, Robert L. Richards, also a
Communist (who later invoked the Fifth Amendment before HUAC),

and she cited the Jacques Duclos letter condemning the American Party for softness toward capitalism ("a signal for the concerted attack on Browder . . . a signal the honeymoon was over") as the turning point when she began to realize the Party was not for her. She also cited the Party's political use of art as a reason for her disenchantment. At her last Party meeting, she objected to a discussion of "Contributions of Writers to the War" because the only writers mentioned were Communist writers, with the exception of the Spanish poet Federico García Lorca, of whom they said that had he not been executed by Franco's fascists, he would have become a Communist within the year. Sylvia Richards thought this presumptuous and said so, and when she emerged, she

> started to read the forbidden books of Koestler, all these wicked things. I read with great interest the controversy of Lysenko in the Soviet Union,* and I began for the first time to think what I had been in. . . . Then I read in Arthur Koestler a very interesting thing. He said in *Darkness at Noon:* "In the life of every Communist there comes a moment when he hears the screams." The first screams I heard were outraged intellect. But since then [I] have been able to see the slave-labor camps, and the fourteen million killed in China—or eleven million; the figures vary. So as I say, it takes a while to get out, but when you finally are out it is a complete change.

The "one thing" Richards told the Committee she felt "good about" was that the motion-picture industry had "made it possible" for people to announce they had been but were no longer Communists "without stigma or without being penalized." She attributed this to a number of factors:

> That the Committee itself, the procedures of the Committee, in that it has heard evidence and not wild hearsay and gossip, has been very reassuring to the industry. . . .
> Some of the first cooperative witnesses had a very rough time. One is a close friend of mine, and I know he had a rough time. But because of certain individuals I don't know—I understand Mr. Roy Brewer has worked very hard to get the industry to recognize this policy toward

---

* In mid-1948 the Central Committee of the Communist Party in the Soviet Union gave official blessing to Trofim Lysenko's theory of acquired characteristics, a theory that was discredited among reputable geneticists. Those Soviet scientists who disagreed with Lysenko were compelled to recant or lose their professorships and laboratories.

people who come before the Committee, and as a result, generally speaking, insofar as my knowledge is concerned, the industry is extremely friendly to people who come here and cooperate with the Committee.

In fact, despite her cooperative testimony, Mrs. Richards never really worked in pictures again. When I saw her in 1974 she had remarried, was helping to run a nursery school, and seemed more in touch with the values of the counterculture of the 1960s than with either side in the cultural cold war 1950s style.

"To say a year of your life was painful is gutless. That was a difficult time, a time of transition. I know if I were faced with anything similar I would not make the same decision but I would not make the opposite decision. On the one hand there were those who said, 'Take the Fifth,' and on the other hand, there were those who said, 'Cooperate.' But I never heard there was a third way to go. After all, you're not a member of the Communist Party unless you have a built-in passivity.

"[When I was in the Party] my friends were questioning it more than I, although I was called to task for taking Koestler seriously. And I thought Albert Maltz's article in the *New Masses* in 1946 calling for freedom for creative writers was a breath of fresh air. But Albert crawled— two issues later he took it back.

"Up until the time of the hearings the Party did exercise a considerable amount of power in Hollywood. When I stopped going to meetings, an agent from William Morris called on me and said it would be helpful if I stayed in the Party when it came to getting jobs. There was an implied threat there. I know that Dick Collins' recommendation, in his Communist Party days, would carry great weight with a producer.

"I was in desperate trouble [in the early 1940s]. My marriage broke. I had two children and a mother, and I'd never worked for a living, and I was down to a hundred and ten pounds. So Dick Collins sent me to Phil, and in the first two months he saved my life. Seven years later I was still going to him, but most of that was wasted.

"My decisions about HUAC were passive—those of a woman. I was going to Phil Cohen, who had been a member of the Communist Party. One day Phil said to me—a writer—that my first priority as a woman was to get married. The same thing with my lawyer, Martin Gang. I don't think he told me what to do, but I would never have bucked him. I was working with Dick Collins, and when Dick got subpoenaed, he told me what he was going to do, and no question, I was going to back him.

"I was going with Hans Habe, a European, liberal anti-Communist at the time. He encouraged me to take the anti-Communist position, but he warned me—I remember, it was on the Fox lot—that some day I'd be known as a 'premature anti-Communist.'

"My ex-husband was not helping to support the kids. Gang said, 'If you answer one question you are obliged to answer all of them.' I was young and scared of going to jail and I knew Bob couldn't take care of the boys.

"Dick Collins and I were writing something on speculation which we sold to John Garfield, but it was never made because Garfield himself was in trouble with the Committee. Dick set up a meeting for me with Wheeler. Then Phil set up a meeting with an FBI guy named Bright. And Dick and Phil and I met at Phil's house with Wheeler, and by plain good luck I gave them nobody new. I didn't deliver anybody over. That's not the point, though.

"I went out with Hans Habe the night before. Hans felt it was absolutely wrong to take the Fifth Amendment. I know Bob Richards regrets taking the Fifth Amendment—he also regrets not taking the third way. I remember sitting outside the courthouse and trying to think of a way out. Bob and Ann [his second wife] tried to talk me out of it. He had a nerve to tell me what to do! So I wouldn't listen.

"It was a form of self-hypnosis. Before, I had feelings of enormous turmoil. Then I [testified] in executive session and then in public. I went to Mexico the next day and for four days I drank margaritas.

"Then this passive persona took over, and I resisted thinking for a long, long time. Instead I was totally involved with my personal life. There's a certain amount of self-anesthetizing that goes on. It was a long, long time later that I started thinking about it.

"The hardest part afterward is to avoid the embrace of people you don't agree with. Like Wheeler. He lived in Anaheim and wanted to socialize. To try to find your own position afterward is extremely hard to do. My position was, I do not want to end up with people still thinking I'm in this ridiculous organization, the Communist Party.

"I don't think those who took the Fifth could have persuaded me [to do so], because I had broken with them on other things. The Fifth stands for nothing. It's the last hiding place of the Mafia. That's the hiding place for scoundrels who will get more than they deserve. Nothing was gained from it. The very words 'self-incrimination,' no matter how much they say that doesn't suggest guilt, to everyone who learns those words, it does.

"I wish I'd met some of the people I later met in the Gandhi Society and CORE who knew how to take an independent position and stick with it. They know how to resist in their own way and not make an organizational thing out of it. The CORE way is to say, I will not cooperate with injustice and I will say what I want to say. That has no constitutional amendment. I learned it later, and I was not the same person.

"It wasn't till I got to the civil-rights movement that I knew what I should have done. In 1953 I considered the Party a villain and the Committee a villain. The left chose a position to keep themselves out of jail. The cooperators chose a position which would keep them from being branded publicly as still sympathetic to Communism. Years later my son became a Freedom Rider and I went into CORE, and I realized that you can resist and risk jail. I saw what I could have done. But at the time I thought both decisions were lousy and I took the one I thought I could live with. I had no illusions that it would improve my standard of living. I've never worked since. I told Fox what would happen. I took a leave, my boy had an eye accident, and they never asked me back. They assigned my picture to somebody else, and because of my passive nature I folded up.

"To be honest, I did not want to be associated with the Party. But in the long run you're always on a higher plane if you're in opposition to the power of your own government. I can take that position today. I've lost economic fears. I've learned to live at rock bottom and feel no pain. In those days I had the feeling I had to provide for my kids. But we've all been liberated to some extent by young people who turned their backs on the plastic society. I've gotten into that part of the subculture where schools and food are cooperative, you buy your own bread at Aardvark, and you wear secondhand jeans.

"I don't think anybody on either side made a completely free decision. They were so locked into the Party structure and what-will-my-friends-think. Even a guy like Lawson had this aura to maintain.

"What I learned from the civil-rights movement was, if you're not afraid of them they can't hurt you. But it's too late for that. The wounds have healed. I have friends on both sides. I've become a lot stronger and more alive than I was then. I can deal with things now."[15]

LEE J. COBB

The actor Lee J. Cobb was named as a Communist before HUAC by Larry Parks in 1951, but he resisted the Committee for two years. During that time he ran out of work and money and his wife was institutionalized as an alcoholic. On June 2, 1953, in room 1117 of the Hollywood Roosevelt Hotel, Lee Cobb, testifying in executive session, became an informer.

Cobb was born Lee Jacob in 1911 on the Lower East Side of New York City, the son of a compositor on the *Jewish Daily Forward.* As a child he studied to be a violinist and he was a virtuoso on the harmonica, winning contests until a broken wrist ended his career. He ran away to Hollywood at the age of seventeen and returned after two months to study accounting at New York University. Cobb went back to California to work briefly at the Pasadena Playhouse, and when he was twenty-three came East and joined the Group Theatre, where he met the Party people who later were the source of his trouble with the Un-American Activities Committee. As a member of the Group he appeared in such productions as Odets's *Waiting for Lefty* and *Golden Boy.* He married the former Helen Beverly and they had two children. In 1943 he joined the Air Corps, where he made the film *This Is the Army.*

From Elia Kazan, Cobb received the script of Arthur Miller's *Death of a Salesman,* and with his 1949 portrayal of the play's protagonist Willy Loman, he was acclaimed "the next Barrymore," one of the major talents of the American theater. Critics awaited his Lear with great anticipation. His talent seemed to know no limits.

One day, not long before *Salesman* opened, Cobb was visited by his old buddy Alvah Bessie, now on hard times as one of the Hollywood Ten.* Now under indictment, Bessie needed a quick $500, but Cobb, earning $1500 a week, said no, although he was willing to pay Bessie's grocery bill. Bessie cursed him out and, as he reports in his memoir, Cobb showed him the door, saying, "I forgive you. I can understand how a man like you, who's been through what you've been through and who's going to prison, can say a thing like that to an old friend. I hope you'll come see me again. You're a revolutionary, you know. Go *on* being a revolutionary. Go on being an example to me."[16]

After more than two years of refusing to talk, Cobb went first to the FBI and then to the Committee. Not long after he testified, he had a massive coronary. Frank Sinatra appeared to pay his hospital bills "and saved my life."

---

* Back in 1940, according to Cobb, they were such good friends that Cobb's review of *himself* appeared under Bessie's byline, where Cobb-Bessie called his performances "pure, stunning, dignified and heartbreaking." According to Bessie, *he* wrote the review, received a fan letter from Cobb, who said Bessie "was the only critic who had ever properly evaluated what he was trying to do," and their friendship began then.

In the following years, he had some nice roles; in addition to Johnny Friendly in *On the Waterfront*, he got to play the father in *The Brothers Karamazov,* and he even got to play Lear in Lincoln Center. He also revisited his Willy Loman role in *Salesman.* But at the end he was reduced to playing in high-paying but second-rate television series.

Conrad Bromberg, the son of the actor J. Edward Bromberg, who was named by Elia Kazan and Cobb, recalls going to visit Cobb after he had testified in executive session. Young Bromberg did not know that Cobb had named his father. "I went backstage, and he saw me and put his arm up as if to shield himself from me and he backed away and said, 'Oh my God, I can't talk to you.' I was confused. I thought he was still so moved by Dad's death that he couldn't say anything. I knew something was wrong but I didn't know what."

In addition to naming twenty people as Communists, Cobb said in his testimony that Phil Loeb and Sam Jaffe "controlled" a left-wing caucus within Actors Equity called the Forum, although, he added, "I never knew them to be Communists." In the course of his testimony he described how a project was undertaken by John Howard Lawson "to rewrite the precepts of Stanislavski's method on acting, to try as far as possible to color it by the prevailing Communist ideologies." Asked why, Cobb elaborated: "The excuse was that however good Stanislavski was, he would be so much better if he were a Communist, and so the purpose was to add the Communist portion to Stanislavski which he was not endowed with by God."

At the close of his testimony, Cobb endorsed not only HUAC's right but its "duty to investigate Communists within any environment in the United States." When asked if he had anything further to add for the record, he said:

I would like to thank you for the privilege of setting the record straight, not only for whatever subjective relief it affords me, but if belatedly this information can be of any value in the further strengthening of our Government and its efforts at home as well as abroad, it will serve in some small way to mitigate whatever feeling of guilt I might have for having waited this long. I did hope that, in my delay to speak earlier, others of the people I had mentioned might have availed themselves of this opportunity for themselves to do likewise. I think by this time I can reasonably assume that those who have desired to do so have taken the opportunity to make their position clear, and I can only say that I am sorry for those who haven't and that more haven't done so.

When I visited him in 1974, Cobb had a new life. He was married to Mary Hirsch, a former schoolteacher, and had two new sons, who were then seven and eight.

"When the facilities of the government of the U.S. are drawn on an individual it can be terrifying. The blacklist is just the opening gambit—being deprived of work. Your passport is confiscated. That's minor. But not being able to move without being tailed is something else. Phone taps are expected, but the interception of the grocery bill? After a certain point it grows to implied as well as articulated threats, and people succumb. My wife did, and she was institutionalized. I had two babies then.

"As it happened I was one of the most effective resisters to the terror for two and a half years. That isn't well known because the purpose of the game was to keep it from being known. The cat-and-mouse game was they wouldn't put me on the stand. We'd meet—two representatives of the Committee and me—but I was of no use to them unless I cooperated, so to speak. I thought I was stalwart, brave, in adamantly refusing cooperation. I had the dubious honor of being adamantly admired by them.

"[In 1953] it was they who made the deal with me. I was pretty much worn down. I had no money. I couldn't borrow. I had the expenses of taking care of the children. You are reduced to the position where you either steal or gamble, and since I'm inclined more to gamble than steal, I gambled. If you gamble for stakes where you must win, it's suicidal. You lose. And that's what happened.

"All of this time I was out of touch with my colleagues—the people with whom I had shared these ideological tenets. When the chips were down you were abandoned. They ran when I was named. The very people I was protecting were beneath contempt. I called my lawyer and told him, 'I'm in political trouble,' and he said, 'Don't come up here, I'll meet you in the car.' He wouldn't suffer to be seen with me coming into his office. You became a thinly disguised pariah. You were really bereft of those closest to you. They threw in the towel, gave up. They would sympathize with me as I died—*that* human they would allow themselves to be. There wasn't a single exception to that statement. I'm talking about breakfast, not moral support.

"I was never even in the Party—but what use would it be to them, the Committee, if I said that? Besides, if you lived through the 1930s you had to be a Communist; no one feels injustice as keenly as the young. I was never a revolutionary except in spirit. And the American Communist Party [members] were a laughingstock—they were idealists, children. None of the revolutionaries of the world had any respect for the American Communist Party. However, we had been friends, not strangers, drawn [together] by revolutionary principle, and because we were co-workers in the theater. But suddenly it was every man for himself!

"The Committee representatives said, 'Any names we already have and have been confirmed and reconfirmed—all you have to do at this point (after two and a half years of living hell)—is concur.' And that was the first time—if it wasn't the rationale of a sick man—the issue clarified itself to me in these terms: What is the principle I am upholding? Why am I subjecting my loved ones to this? If it's worth dying for, I'm just as idealistic as the next fellow. But I decided it wasn't worth dying for, and if this gesture was my way of getting out of the penitentiary I'd do it. I had to be employable again. There were no two ways about it.

"Writers could write under another name. Directors could leave the country and direct under another name. The human animal is not noble. That's why we celebrate those few who are. Why should we be? But some are pettier than others. There were people I worked with who were taken aback, but were understanding. The interesting thing is those who were least implicated were most offended.

"No one has held out, that's my profound discovery. I discovered that what I thought was thoroughly principled resistance [to cooperating] really wasn't that at all. I had had this image of getting tied to the stake and saying, 'Do your worst, I won't cooperate.' I was profoundly selfish. I didn't want to cut myself off from my friends and colleagues. To risk alienating them would mean I'd be lonely in the profoundest sense. You can't turn around and say, 'Now I'll start making new friends.'

"I still have contempt for my former cronies. It was a joke. I never gave any money to the Communist Party. Today I won't sign a thing. I'm out to pasture. I'm grazing. I take no part in politics. I'm restrained. I have whatever is given me left to enjoy. I don't want to fight anymore. Oh, I can be driven against the wall. But I won't seek the fights I sought when I was young. I never recovered my health, which was impaired. I'm bitter about the anonymous unscathed revolutionaries who are today enjoying prominence and who from their lofty ideological perches sit in judgment on us. A cause does not necessarily ennoble its follower.

"When Elia Kazan testified I was shocked. I was offended. I wasn't in as deep. I thought, If I were in his boots I'd die before they'd break me. But Kazan acted out of principle. If I didn't think so, I could ask him, 'How could you name Tony Kraber—a selfless man, a Band-Aid if you scratch yourself?' So that must have been principled, if he reached that far. It didn't sit well.

"I didn't act out of principle. I wallowed in unprincipledness. One of my closest friends pleaded with me not to do a thing like this, as he ran to catch the boat for England. He was fleeing the country, but I was the coward. We haven't spoken since—and he became a well-known director. These are profound bereavements to me. In the theater the odds are so remote, but then comes the miraculous coincidence of a Kazan, Miller, and Cobb being contemporaries! If you spit in the face of that kind of good fortune it is unforgivable. If for so-called political reasons the breach is widened, that is deserving of criminal prosecution.

"No whipped dog is more pathetic than a supine brilliant man. Part of the Mephistophelian mystery that the reds have bequeathed to the world is the ability to make one confess without any truncheon marks on one's head. You start out by wanting to keep your friends. In a totalitarian country they want you to betray your friends—and you persuade yourself finally that it is your duty. On the tortuous road to that conclusion lie many bleached bones of others.

"If I had not been in need, I'd have never cooperated. By implication I did dignify the Committee. I went through as little of the charade as I had to. My friends had the attitude, 'I would rather eulogize you dead than have you as an imperfect contemporary alive.' There's a need to see people that way: The little man grows in stature, ennobles himself, by saying he hasn't done what you did; the least in jeopardy are the most intransigent nonunderstanders—I was going to say, nonforgivers. Some people need me so that I can be anathema to them.

"I remember the television producer who read in the trades that I had signed on to do a television series and he said, 'Lee, how could you?' Well, I'd rather not, but the man doesn't hear himself. They'd rather say at your funeral, 'He didn't give in—he died pure.' Where are these friends now? They're in hiding. Lee Strasberg's wife, Paula, once called me up and said, 'What are you doing? I haven't heard from you.' She said, 'I never realized how bad it was, really bad.' That's the last time I ever heard from her."[17]

ROLAND KIBBEE

Roland Kibbee, born in Monongahela, Pennsylvania, in 1914 and a Los Angeles City College dropout in 1933, calls himself these days "a hyphenate," which means that he is a writer-producer. He used to be a radio writer, and his credits include such all-time favorites as *The Fred Allen Show*, *The Fanny Brice Show*, and *The Groucho Marx Show*. He drifted into the Communist Party in 1937 by way of the Hollywood Anti-Nazi League, and he drifted out three years later by way of the Nazi-Soviet Pact.

In September 1951 he was named as a Communist by Martin Berkeley (who got the time and place wrong) and responded with a telegram to the Committee:

> TO THE BEST OF MY RECOLLECTION JOINED 1937 LEFT 1939. NO AFFILIATION SINCE THEN. PROMISE TESTIFY IMMEDIATELY UPON SCHEDULED RETURN LATE NOVEMBER.

At the time, Kibbee was on location in Italy. On his return in December he met with Wheeler and persuaded him that since as a member of an intelligence unit in the Air Force reserve he was handling classified documents, if he were to testify in public it would needlessly embarrass the military. And so on June 2, 1953, he gave his testimony in executive session at the Hollywood Roosevelt Hotel.

As he remembers his feelings at the time, "I was sympathetic to the people who had been called and supported them with time and contributions. I was appalled by the business of the Party as tactical adviser to them, recommending that they take the Fifth Amendment. I approved of Sidney Buchman's position [who preferred to stand on the First Amendment and offered to talk about himself but not about others]. I don't like the word 'self-incriminating' in the Fifth Amendment; nothing we had done was incriminating.

"I was out of the country on location when I got the telegram. I think I replied if I were subpoenaed I'd testify to any questions I felt were appropriate. That took the heat off for a short time. But when I got back Bill Wheeler contacted me. I told him (a) I had no new names, (b) I couldn't say under oath who was or wasn't a member of the CP, (c) I knew nothing. Finally I testified in executive session, with only Wheeler present. I named those who named me. I walked a narrow line. There wasn't a human being in the world I could have exposed. . . .

"I was given a hard time on the left in the Hollywood community; they didn't know how I had testified, and I was not going to run around and say, 'I fooled those bastards.' A great many others wouldn't talk to me because I didn't join the parade of Fifth Amendment takers."

Here are some excerpts from his testimony:

MR. WHEELER: Are you presently under subpoena?
MR. KIBBEE: I am not.

MR. WHEELER: You are giving this statement of your own free will?

MR. KIBBEE: I am.

MR. WHEELER: ... have you previously discussed your Party membership with me?

MR. KIBBEE: Yes, sir; I have.

MR. WHEELER: I believe the records show that we had such a discussion on December 14, 1951.

MR. KIBBEE: ... the first [Party] meeting that I recall going to ... was in the home of Budd Schulberg.... It was the home of someone of wealth, which is something that I was not familiar with. As nearly as I could make out, the part of the Communist Party that I saw in Hollywood at that time was partly a social organization. It didn't seem to devote any great attention to security....

At the meeting at Waldo Salt's house the name stands out in my mind of Luke Hinman. He was not a Hollywoodite. He was a trade-union organizer. The best grip I can get on that is that he kind of briefed us about this situation in the San Joaquin Valley. I believe he was associated with the Cannery Workers Union.

MR. WHEELER: How do you spell his name?

MR. KIBBEE: I would spell it H-i-n-m-a-n, and the first name, Luke, L-u-k-e. I don't know that I have ever seen it in print....

MR. WHEELER: Martin Berkeley identified you on September 9, 1951, as a member of the Communist Party. Do you recall him as being a member?

MR. KIBBEE: I have seen Mr. Berkeley and spoken with him since he testified.... We both agreed that we had not been members of the same unit, that we had been exposed to each other within the framework of the Communist Party, and as I said earlier in the testimony I don't contradict Mr. Berkeley's word. I simply have not been able to put my finger on the exact specific situation in which we met.

Mr. Berkeley's recollection is, I know, he told me, that I had attended a writer's fraction meeting on race relations. This is possible. I was not a qualified writer. It is certainly possible, as a self-proclaimed writer, I would have been at something of this sort, but I don't know with what organization.

Kibbee signed a Screen Writers Guild petition to nominate Albert Maltz for office in 1949, but when Wheeler asked him about it, he said, "It might have been on the basis of ... some salary raise.... I might have done it while I was drunk at some party, I am sorry to say. I just don't know how I came to sign it." He also said he signed for the Hollywood Ten but it was motivated by some "gimmick," such as their right to have their say before HUAC, or it might have been out of fear of Communist slander of him as an ex-Communist. About HUAC he stated:

> Well I think in my own case the Committee on Un-American Activities has been a blessing, Mr. Wheeler. We have referred before to the element of fear that is in a man as an ex-Communist. He never really comes out as anti-Communist. He is afraid of how it may be interpreted. It is not very pleasant to be dragged out, but I am grateful to have had the opportunity to speak freely without coercion, without any pressure of any kind, and that I have had an opportunity to express an open feeling of anti-Communism and take the position as an anti-Communist without its being felt that I am trying to wriggle out of my own responsibility for ever having joined.
>
> I think the Committee does serve the ex-Communist very well in that regard, and I feel that very strongly indeed.

When I asked him in 1975, sitting in his office-trailer (which he shared with Burt Lancaster's production unit), whether he was a "cooperative" or an "uncooperative" witness, Kibbee said, "I don't know what you'd call me. I don't think of myself as either."[18]

MICHAEL GORDON

Michael Gordon, born September 6, 1909, had attended the Yale Drama School with Elia Kazan, and in the 1930s directed a play entitled *Black Pit,* by Albert Maltz, joined the Group Theatre, and worked on such productions as *Golden Boy, Casey Jones,* and *Thunder Rock.* After World War II he directed *Home of the Brave* on Broadway and *The Male Animal* at the New York City Center, and in Hollywood his films ranged from *Another Part of the Forest* (1948) and *Cyrano de Bergerac* (1950) to *Boston Blackie Goes to Hollywood* (1942).

Like Robert Rossen, Gordon appeared before the Committee twice—in 1951 as a resister and, after two coronaries and little work, in 1958 as an informer.

Why didn't he name the names the first time? "The Hitler era was not yet over and the whole concept of being an informer was repugnant, repellent, against the principles of what the democratic way of life meant." Gordon, whom I interviewed in his faculty office at the University of

California at Los Angeles, where he is a professor-in-residence, was quite eloquent on why it was important to resist HUAC in the context of 1951 cold war politics. It was particularly frustrating for him not to have been able to testify because "the person who introduced my name in public testimony perjured himself with respect to me. He placed me in the CP in Hollywood at a time when I didn't live here. I was in New York at the time." Under the waiver doctrine, however, Gordon couldn't deny the false allegation without restricting himself to the choice between being an informer or being in contempt of Congress, and so he had kept his silence.

When I asked him why he changed his mind and named names in 1958, he seemed somewhat taken aback. His 1958 testimony has never been made public, and he was surprised I knew about it and asked me how I did. I had been told by a number of Fifth Amendment–takers that they believed Gordon had become an informer in the end, and I told him so. He shared these thoughts:

"The situation changed in eight or nine years from several points of view. First, personal imperatives. Second, social considerations: certain things exist at a given point in time as a burning issue—you struggle even at the cost of personal sacrifices—and a decade later it's not the same kind of issue. The historical character changes.

"It was an extremely complex situation. I had been in contact with certain people at the studios. The climate had thawed. In 1958 Ben Kahane at Columbia was trying to effect a rehabilitation for me. At his suggestion or insistence I spoke with—I can't remember whom I spoke with. The thing was *pro forma*. There were certain rituals. There wasn't a committee. It was quite a *pro forma* thing.

"It should be made clear that the nature of that reappearance was not before the Committee. I spoke with Congressman Jackson and a court reporter. I can't remember anyone else's being there. I doubt that the whole thing took an hour. It was not a highly publicized event. I don't believe there was any press on it. It was a totally different kind of event than it would have been eight years earlier.

"Ben Kahane gave me to understand it was a token affirmation of these names who had been self-acknowledged; and in a few instances these so widely known it was not a question. In the actual procedure itself, the names were read to me—and in the vast majority of cases I didn't know them. From 1943 to 1946 I wasn't in Hollywood, so I had no first-hand information."

Why did the Committee do it?

It was an attempt to corrode the moral fiber. "For a police state you have to alter decent behavior—loyalty to friends. Particularly when you are not talking about criminal activities. An act of self-abasement is required to regain respectability. I felt disloyal to a principle when I co-operated—though it no longer was of such urgency that it called for the supreme sacrifice of one's profession. My first engagement [after the 1958 hearing] was at Universal—I did *Pillow Talk* [1959], which started a pernicious trend in male-chauvinist pictures.

"Regardless of what utterances may have been made, I seriously question that anybody wanted to [cooperate]. People preferred not to. I don't know of anyone in that situation who didn't have the deepest ambivalence. People preferred not to name names, but they responded to the political and social imperatives as they saw them. Whether you were combative or grudging didn't matter.

"Many people had forgotten what had happened nine years before. This was a contributing factor to my estimate of the altered moral landscape. People had forgotten or never knew why I wasn't working—a lot of people have these ups and downs in career terms in this business, so why not Mike Gordon?

"I've talked to you because of the Santayana notion—that if you don't learn from the mistakes of the past you are doomed to repeat them. I've tried to avoid talking about this, I debated whether to have this interview. In the interest of accuracy I did not want to take a self-serving position with respect to these matters. At the same time I didn't want to take a contrary position. I don't think there was any individual who was not racked by the most tortured intellectual conflicts. Often the after-the-fact statements don't reflect the processes by which they arrived at the decision.

"There's a point at which if one retreats from a line of battle the battle will be lost. That's the way I felt about 1951. At another point that is not so. This second appearance—whenever one is asked to make a personal sacrifice one has to ask what the sacrifice is for.

"We weren't playing for nickels and dimes. We were playing for our lives. Nobody took anything lightly."[19]

9.
The Reasons Considered

MOTIVES, C. WRIGHT MILLS ONCE SUGGESTED, should be analyzed as answers to questions.[1] Did those who defended their naming names really believe in what they did or is it all after-the-fact rationalization? Were they simply turning in others to save themselves?

Abe Polonsky, the blacklisted writer-director, makes the persuasive argument that since the informers didn't turn in names *before* the Committee put pressure on them, we (and in some cases they) can never know whether they acted from noble or ignoble motives. As he says of Kazan, "Kazan was not in the process of going around giving the names of people whom he thought were hostile to the society he had come to love. But the Committee faced him with a problem. Up to that point he didn't have a problem. All he had was a disagreement politically with some people. Since they were old friends they'd have had these arguments for years. I assume they did, you know. After all, Harold Clurman in *The Fervent Years* tells about the arguments they always had, and they disagreed with each other a hundred times.

"This was something else. This was, Who goes to the concentration camp? Do I go with you or do you go by yourself? That was the real decision he had to face at that time. Now the fact that he no longer sympathized with the political point of view he once shared with these people is irrelevant—no one at this late stage in life attacks his right to change his mind. His opinion about that was not the source of his action. The source of his action was something else. And the ability to make that distinction—between his opinions and his source of action—is the ability to discover where the course of morality lay.

"The fact of the matter is, unless Kazan became a stool pigeon or an informer, whichever one he prefers, under no circumstances whatsoever could he have directed a film in the United States."

Polonsky argues that for most of the people who cooperated with

HUAC, it was not a moral, ethical, or political question at all. It was a practical question—but people don't like to think of it that way because it makes their character less worthy. "In most cases the informers picked a route that seemed to them an easy solution to a difficult problem; in other words, they could handle their own friends, whom they testified against, better than they could handle the U.S. government harassing them." Schulberg, according to Polonsky, "just has to explain one thing: Why did he become an informer when they forced him to? And why didn't he become an informer *before* they forced him to? The reason was that before, he thought it wasn't a good thing to do. What made that change happen was a practical situation. The Nazis pointed a gun up against his head and said, 'Look, give us some names,' and he says, 'Yeah, I hate those guys anyway. You know I hate those guys.' And they say, 'Sure, that's why we're here. So give us their names.' And he gave the names. The question to ask is, Why then and not a week before?

"If you wait till they put a gun up against your head, it's too late to claim that you're doing it for moral-political reasons. Time has passed."

Michael Gordon, Lee Cobb, Isobel Lennart, and Sterling Hayden all concede with remorse that their plan was to name their way back to work. But to this day, other informers deny that they were acting with this sort of self-interest. Schulberg says, "believe it or not," he had long ago turned his back on Hollywood. Elia Kazan says that anyone who says he did it for the money is "simplistic." Richard Collins says that at the time he decided to name names all he knew was that that was what Larry Parks had done and Parks had gotten fired. And so on.

But the evidence is the other way. You *knew* if you took the Fifth Amendment you were blacklisted. "Cooperation" at least kept the door open. Besides, after their HUAC testimony Schulberg and Kazan made *On the Waterfront* and *A Face in the Crowd*. Except for Parks and a very few others, the informers went back to work. Even Leo Townsend, who insists he was on a double blacklist and indeed lost the Warner's job he told the Committee he had been promised he could keep, picked up ten credits in the following five years.

However, reading the informers' testimony and listening to them explain themselves, one suspects that the "reasons why" which they now adduce are not mere after-the-fact rationalizations. The reasons they give seem at a minimum to have functioned as before-the-fact moral tranquilizers; an internal equivalent to the Cohens and Gangs, they served to cancel out the basic presumption against informing, to obfuscate the question of betrayal, to overwhelm compunction.

About informer-motives little can be said with certainty other than that most of them—including those who now profess real regret—insist they were not total sell-outs. Twenty-five years after the fact, each is still careful to delineate where he or she drew the line. As E. E. Cummings put it, " 'There is some s. I will not eat.' "[2] Schulberg didn't name anyone who hadn't been named before. Lennart wouldn't name anyone who hadn't been named at least ten times before. Collins named only the dead, those already called, and those who had quit the Party. Michael Gordon wouldn't name anybody until he was persuaded that the time for symbolic resistance to the Committee had passed and then he insisted on the privacy of his testimony. David Raksin combined his name-naming with a defense of his idealistic reasons for joining the Party in the first place. Clifford Odets lectured the Committee even while he acceded to it. Roy Huggins drew the line at spelling—he would give the names but not the letters. A combination of self-justification and line-drawing apparently freed otherwise honorable people to violate their norms by minimizing damage to their own self-image.

Since motive must remain a mystery, it is all the more important to ask whether the exculpations and justifications—the "reasons why"—can withstand critical scrutiny. The degree to which they cannot—and the evidence of trouble on both the analytic and empirical fronts is considerable—may be the measure by which decent men and women lost touch with their sense of self. Although circumstance varied with individuals, collectively they advanced four different types of explanation for what they did, none of them in the last analysis persuasive, all of them at first blush plausible. Let us examine them one by one.

I Didn't Hurt Anybody. If there is one refrain that keeps asserting itself—almost like a chorus—in the reminiscences and explanations of those who played the informer, it is, "I only named those who were already named." The idea seemed to function as a sort of security blanket not merely for those who now profess shame but also for those who express ambivalence about what they did, as well as those who defend their acting as informer.

Even though spontaneous mention of this argument is often coupled with a disclaimer ("I know that's not the point"), the implication ("I therefore wasn't as cold-blooded as some suspect") is clear. Thus one is astonished to discover that much of the time the claim turns out to be false.*

---

* I have drawn on the lists of Howard Suber (unpublished) and Robert Vaughn (published) as well as on my own reading of the public testimonies before HUAC in determining when individuals were publicly named for the first time.

Roland Kibbee recalled, "Bill Wheeler contacted me. I told him (a) I had no new names, (b) I couldn't say under oath who was or wasn't a member of the CP, (c) I knew nothing." On further prodding he said, "Whether it was considered cooperative or uncooperative I don't know. . . . I named those who named me. I walked a narrow line. There wasn't a human being in the world I could have exposed." Under oath Kibbee had identified sixteen peers as Party members, plus a Party labor organizer named Luke Hinman whose name had never been publicly mentioned and which he spelled out.

Lee J. Cobb took little solace from the idea, yet thought it worth mentioning, that the Committee representatives said to him, "Any names we already have and have been confirmed and reconfirmed—all you have to do at this point . . . is concur." But he was the only one publicly to name Lloyd Bridges (although Bridges had furnished an executive statement a year and a half before Cobb testified). And he was the first one publicly to identify the actors Ludwig Donath and Shimen Ruskin, and the actresses Rose Hobart and Gerry Schlein.

"By plain good luck I gave them nobody new. I didn't deliver anybody over," Sylvia Richards mentions. And since she is quite open about her belief that she made a mistake in cooperating and would do it differently if she had it to do over, she has no "status incentive" to misrepresent the record. But she was the only witness publicly to identify the writer Lee Gold as a Communist and the only one to mention the writer Tamara Hovey.

The writer-producer Roy Huggins says today, "I ended up agreeing that people who had already been mentioned many times were indeed known to me as Communists. . . . There was literally no one in the Communist Party that I had ever known who hadn't already been publicly listed many, many times." But among those Huggins named who had not previously been publicly identified as Communists were the writer Leslie Edgly; Robert Richards, who he said was the dues secretary of his Party unit; and Elliott Grenard (when asked who was the head of his cell, Huggins said that Grenard was the nominal head at one time or another, though he had "no idea" how the name was spelled).

Isobel Lennart ("My criterion was that I would mention no name that had not been mentioned ten times before—not eight but ten") said she mentioned "about ten to twelve names." As it happened, Miss Lennart, although she named no new ones among the twenty-one people she cited, did name more than half a dozen who had been named less than ten times.

Leo Townsend remembered that "I didn't name anyone that hadn't been named." But of the thirty-seven people he named as Communists, he was the first publicly to mention the director Joseph Losey and his wife Louise Losey, the writer Ben Bengal, the screenwriters Ben and Norma Barzman, the actress Phoebe Brand, the songwriter Jay Gorney, the writer Daniel James, the writer Henry Meyers, the writer Mortimer Offner, the writer Maurice Rapf, the writer Bess Taffel, and the agent John Weber.

The Schulberg correction of the *Times* obituary of Herbert Biberman said: "Biberman, as one of the most outspoken of the original Communist leaders, had been mentioned by many previous witnesses before the Committee. Schulberg simply corroborated a list of names that had already been corroborated many times over." In fact, Budd Schulberg was only the third in a round of witnesses (after Meta Rosenberg and Edward Dmytryk) to identify Herbert Biberman as a Party member—although he had been named as early as 1942 by Rena Vale before the California Committee on Un-American Activities. (After Schulberg, Biberman was named by more than a dozen others.) But Schulberg himself named a dozen other persons as having been in the Party, including the writer Tillie Lerner, whom he was the *only* person publicly to identify.

Even Edward Dmytryk, who had done time as a member of the Hollywood Ten before he changed his mind and testified, responded, "How?" when a television interviewer rhetorically asked whether it wasn't true that those he named had suffered. "They suffered through their careers," said Tristram Powell of the BBC. "Not necessarily," replied Dmytryk. "Not a single person I named hadn't already been named at least a half-dozen times and wasn't already on the blacklist. . . . I don't think I put anybody in trouble because of the names I mentioned because they had all been mentioned before."[3] Well, not quite. He was the first publicly to mention the directors Bernard Vorhaus and Michael Gordon and the writer Maurice Clark, and the only one to mention the writer George Corey (*Mr. Winkle Goes to War* [1944]).

Thus memory is frequently belied by testimony. Moreover, even where the Committee's counsel told a potential informer ahead of time that HUAC already "had" the names, the witness had no knowledge of exactly who had or had not been named or called, and no way of knowing whether his own list would be made public. The Committee had three sources of names: those it heard in public, those it heard in private, and those uncovered by its research but never officially publicized. And because testimony taken privately might be released (or leaked) at the Committee's discretion, no witness could ever be certain that his own information would not be publicized in a way which might injure one who had or hadn't already been identified publicly.

That naming as Communists people whom the Committee already knew as Communists was *not* harmless or morally neutral seems to have been implicitly understood by many of those who testified. That, presumably, is why Richard Collins telephoned Cleo Trumbo to tell her that although he was going to name names, he would omit Dalton's. "I like Collins," says Bill Wheeler, "but in naming twenty-three names, he lied. He was one of the whip horses in there. He knew about three hundred people, I guess. I got them—I had their names—he gave them to me later. But he didn't want to name them all." Or, for another, there was Budd Schulberg, who, asked by the Committee who had represented him during the period of his break with the Party, was at first reluctant to say, explaining, "My only hesitation—at times through no fault of your own, sir, people read things in the papers and say, 'I saw your name in the paper. You must be in some kind of trouble.'" All of these people understood on some level that the publication of names, even the second and third time around, could have consequences. The writer Abram Ginnes recalls a multiply named friend from television: "Every time he started to work his way back—it was like one of those Mack Sennett comedies, and he'd get hit in the face with another pie."

Each naming went out like a burglar alarm to the free-lance enforcer network, reminding them that there was a subversive to be fired, harassed, or embarrassed, a career to be derailed; reminding his children and their friends that they had a pariah for a parent; reminding neighbors that they had best keep their distance. The enforcers devoured the Committee's annual indexes and supplements, reference manuals such as *Red Channels,* newsletters like *Counterattack,* and columnists like Winchell and Sokolsky. Their appetite for names was insatiable. They may have preferred new names but were content to recycle old ones, so long as they had something to keep in circulation.

Even where no "objective" damage was done, the target didn't always see it that way. When I asked Polonsky, years later, how he felt toward the people who named him he said, "There were too many to count." Told it was less than a dozen, he was genuinely surprised and said, "It seemed like thirty or forty—at least that's the feeling I had when I was out in the rain. It may be that it was just raining in two or three places, but I thought it was raining everywhere."

By not protesting against HUAC's request for names one collaborated in the fiction that the Committee's quest was part of a legislative rather than a punitive process. Each informer made it that much more difficult for the next witness to resist. And by supplying names one did the Committee's dirty work of advertising its targets. Moreover, virtually every cooperative witness contributed to the corruption of the process by swearing to tell the *whole* truth and then providing only a selective part of it. (The one exception, Martin Berkeley, who named everyone he knew, also corrupted the process by adding to the list some who didn't belong.)

They Deserved What They Got. The obverse of "I didn't hurt anybody" is, "They had it coming to them, they got what they deserved." Essentially the argument is that however evil HUAC was, the Communist Party was worse. To the accusation that he betrayed his former comrades, Kazan makes the point that when he gets around to telling his story he will detail how *they* betrayed *him* eighteen years earlier. Appearing before the Committee, but also writing in the popular magazines of the day and speaking to and through the mass media, many informers by implication justified their cooperation with HUAC by reference to the evil they were exposing. Call it blaming the victim, or the Fallacy of the Greater Evil.

Many Hollywood writers who thought nothing of cranking out formula pictures using recycled plots on pedestrian themes, presented themselves before HUAC as artists shocked by the aesthetic and political demands of Party politics, free spirits mauled by the thought-controllers. Even the talented ones, who had no complaint with Harry Cohn's or Cecil B. De Mille's transformation of art into commerce, complained in the 1950s of the Party's crude attempt to judge their movies or stories by Marxist canons. And then there were serious writers who managed to reconcile themselves to the corruption of the Hollywood system but felt constrained to complain out loud about the corruption of the Party system. To hear them tell it, truth and beauty were the victims and the Party censor, the executioner.

Clifford Odets made it quite clear in his HUAC testimony that he left the Party because he lost his respect for its literary and cultural critics. His evidence: "when my plays came out, they received fantastically bad notices [in the Communist press], although a play like *Waiting for Lefty* was widely used, not only by the Communists but by all liberal organizations and trade-union movements. I not only disagreed with their critical statements of my work, but disagreed with their critical estimates of anybody's work, writers that I didn't know, like Steinbeck and Hemingway."

A close reading of his rowdy testimony (which includes an amusing account of his Party-sponsored trip to Cuba, some militant talk on where he learned his hatred of poverty, and a self-conscious refusal to kowtow to the Committee's demands that he denounce the Communist Party as a revolutionary organization) reveals that he decided it was "not for me" because he wearied of wasting his time on the literary haggling.[4]

After Odets testified—and named names—he was distressed that his message had been missed; he thought he had showed the Committee "the face of a radical," but nobody he cared about heard anything but the names. A month later he wrote his friend the writer Benjamin Appel:

> For the most part the judgments (so judgmental everyone is!) of what I did and said in Washington have been disgustingly mechanical, based on a few lines printed in newspapers, right or left, when actually there were three hundred pages of typed transcript. Personally I find this a disturbingly immoral time and this immorality exists as much on the left as on the right. Personal clarity, in my opinion, is the first law of the day—that plus a true and real search for personal identity. I don't believe in any party or group doing my thinking or directing for me.[5]

Budd Schulberg's testimony, it may be recalled, had mainly to do with how the Party criticized his short stories as decadent and then tried to get him to rewrite *What Makes Sammy Run?*, his Hollywood novel, as a proletarian novel that satisfied the critical canons of socialist realism and the reigning cultural commissars, John Howard Lawson and V. J. Jerome. As he recalled it for the Committee, "The feeling was that [my book] was a destructive idea; that . . . it was much too individualistic; that it didn't begin to show what were called the progressive forces in Hollywood"— all of which was ironic to Schulberg, who believed that his account of Sammy Glick on the make was the first to tell the story of the Screen Writers Guild from the union's perspective. Although he talked briefly about other reasons for defecting, the thrust of his testimony was that it was the literary roughing-up that caused him to quit the group, pay no more dues, flee Hollywood, leave the Party. Why should such crude commissars have a say about his art?

Edward Dmytryk, his second time around in April 1951, gave the Committee one of the rare examples of Communists actually trying to control the content of a picture (there were less than half a dozen of these; eventually the Committee stopped looking for them) when he told of Communist objections to *Cornered,* which he made with Adrian Scott in 1945. "This is the thing," he said, "which actually got me out of the Party."

The cartoonist Zachary Schwartz preceded his naming of names in 1953 with an expression of outrage at a lecture the artist Edward Biberman had given on "Marxism and Art":

> I was completely disgusted . . . because it brought me face to face with the demands that I accept ideas that were utterly ridiculous, and that I paint that way or draw that way or think that way. . . . I got into a discussion with the lecturer around the whole idea of what he called the utilitarian aspects of art, and my argument with him was that art in any form—whether it be painting, writing, mosaic—anything creative . . . is a thing of the spirit and you can't control it or handle it the way you would a frying pan and the manufacture of a piece of utilitarian material of that kind.[6]

The journalist Louis Fischer observed that for every Communist who became an ex-Communist there was a single last straw, an event that transformed doubt into decision, that caused him to leave and then oppose the Party.[7] He called these moments "Kronstadts," after the defection from the Bolshevik cause of Alexander Berkman, the anarchist-supporter of the revolution who jumped off the train of history when he was repelled by the bloody Soviet repression of the sailor-rebels at the Kronstadt naval base in 1921. For some it was Kronstadt, for others the purge trials of the late 1930s, the Nazi-Soviet Pact, Khrushchev's speech to the Twentieth Party Congress denouncing Stalin, the suppression of the Hungarian uprising in 1956, the invasion of Czechoslovakia in 1968. For many of the Hollywood ex-Communists—if one trusts their testimony before HUAC—their Kronstadt was, more than anything else, what Kazan called "the disgusting spectacle" of the recantation of Albert Maltz. Indeed, the event took on a symbolic significance that extended well beyond Hollywood. An index of its effect on the liberal left is found in a letter written in 1952 by I. F. Stone, a consistent champion of the rights of cold war victims, to Dashiell Hammett, setting forth his reasons for declining the honor of sponsoring a rally-tribute on behalf of V. J. Jerome, by then one of the sixteen New York Smith Act defendants:

> VJ is a hell of a nice guy personally but politically he has tried to ride herd on the intellectuals in a way most offensive to anyone who believes in intellectual and cultural freedom, as has *New Masses,* often in

most humiliating ways—as in the belly-crawl forced some years ago on Albert Maltz. I'd feel like a stultified ass to speak at a meeting for Jerome without making clear my own sharp differences with the dogmatic, Talmudic, and dictatorial mentality he represents. I intend to go on defending him as a Smith Act victim but I can't pretend he's a libertarian, so I'd better stay away.[8]

What was this Hollywood Kronstadt, which not only shocked the conscience of civil libertarians such as Stone but also cost the Party some of its best talents? It is worth exploring in detail if for no other reason than because it provided so many ex-Communists with their most vivid grievance, their best argument for revenge against the commissars: It was cited by many witnesses as partial grounds for their cooperation with the House Un-American Activities Committee.

Briefly, the cause of the uproar was four thousand nonrevolutionary words on the subject "What Shall We Ask of Writers?" published in the *New Masses* in February 1946. Maltz carefully mentioned at the outset that he was going to take the assets of the literary left for granted, apologized for what might be too "sweeping" language, and said that he would focus on where things have gone wrong and why.

"The source of the problem," he wrote, "is the vulgarization of the theory of art which lies behind left-wing thinking, namely 'art is a weapon.'" Broadly speaking art *is* a weapon, he observed, but as narrowly applied the emphasis has been too much on the weapon and not enough on the nature of art.

It is wrong, Maltz believed, to judge creative works "*primarily* by their formal ideology," for when you do that you end up with absurdities such as the *New Masses* critic attacking Lillian Hellman's *Watch on the Rhine* when it was produced as a play in 1940, because its anti-Nazi politics were anathema during the period of the Stalin-Hitler Pact, and then hailing it as a film in 1942 after Hitler's invasion of Russia. You can't, he said, write a novel and an editorial at the same time. John Steinbeck, James T. Farrell, John Galsworthy, and Richard Wright were examples of writers who were ideologically out of step and still functioned as great artists. Engels understood that about Balzac. "Having a tactical ax to grind," he wrote, "usually requires the artificial manipulation of character."[9]

In other words, Maltz spoke uncommon sense. Isidor Schneider, the editor of *New Masses*, who had asked writers to think out loud about the relationship of art to politics, seemed to embrace Maltz's unrevolutionary views in a companion piece called "Background to Error," where he wrote: "In our day-to-day reviewing we should avoid the mistakes so clearly shown by Maltz. . . . The first confusion has been in elevating political tactics into political principles. . . . The second confusion has been to stretch the artistic evaluation to cover the political evaluation."[10]

And then the rains came. Howard Fast, still a decade away from his own defection from the Party, charged in *New Masses* that Maltz was calling for "the ideology of liquidation." His summary of Maltz's position:

> Art and politics do not mix. Therefore, salvation—and, of course, achievement—for the artist lies only in a separation from the Communist movement, the most highly political of all movements today. No matter how he slices it, embroiders it, or disguises it, that is what Maltz advocates. He advocates, for the artist, retreat. He pleads with him to get out of the arena of life. The fact that life shows, and has shown for a generation now, that such retreat is tantamount to artistic death and personal degradation, cuts no ice with Maltz.[11]

Joseph North wrote that Maltz would chop down "the fruitful tree of Marxism" to cure some weak branches.[12] Alvah Bessie viewed Maltz's basic contentions as "not only un-Marxist, but actually anti-Marxist":

> Perhaps I do Maltz a disservice in thus associating him with Marxism, for he nowhere identifies himself in his article as anything more than "a working writer," whatever that may be. He nowhere states his frame of reference or identifies the point of departure from which he launches what is, objectively, not only an attack on Marxism but a defense of practically every renegade writer of recent years who ever flirted with the working-class movement. . . . No. We need more than "free" artists. We need *Party* artists. We need artists deeply . . . rooted in the working class who realize the truth of Lenin's assertion that the absolute freedom they seek "is nothing but a bourgeois or anarchist phrase. . . ."[13]

Michael Gold, Samuel Sillen (literary editor of the *Daily Worker*), even the new head of the Party, William Z. Foster, all took their turn,[14] and on March 19 John Howard Lawson too found Maltz out of context:

> We cannot divorce the views expressed by Maltz from the historical moment he selects for the presentation of these views. He writes at a

time of decisive struggle. The democratic victories achieved in the Second World War are threatened by the still powerful forces of imperialism and reaction, which are especially strong in the United States. . . .
Can we regard it as merely an oversight that Maltz does not say one
word about the class struggle? . . .[15]

Indeed, for parochial Party reasons if no others, Maltz had picked a
dubious "historical moment" for his reflections. "Had he written it during the United Front days of 1935–39 or in the war years of Soviet-
American cooperation, when everybody from Monsignor Fulton Sheen
to Captain Eddie Rickenbacker had kind words for the Stalin regime,"
observed the literary historian Daniel Aaron, "it might have slipped by
without official censure. It appeared, however, well after the famous
Jacques Duclos letter of May 1945 presaged the end of peaceful collaboration between the United States and the Soviet Union and the bank-
ruptcy of 'Browderism.' " A week before Maltz's article appeared,
Browder, once hailed as "the beloved leader of our movement," had been
expelled from the Party as a "social imperialist."[16]

Maltz was briefly a pariah. Richard Collins, who was midway on his
journey from enforcer of social realism to HUAC informer, recalls the
Party meeting called to denounce Maltz. "I noticed, which I probably
wouldn't have five years before, that no one was sitting near Albert. So I
made a point of sitting down next to him. I felt about the men who were
attacking him that some of them were talentless; some of the loudest
voices were the least talented. I felt what people must have felt about me
before—that it was outrageous and impudent."

The writer Leopold Atlas prefaced his own naming of names before
the Un-American Activities Committee with an unforgettable description
of the occasion:

> This was truly a ghastly business. Here one saw the wolf pack in full
> operation, working on one of their own long-term members. The mere
> recalling of the incident is abhorrent to me. . . .
> When I heard of Maltz's article and read it, I was enormously
> pleased. This was not only a further indication to me that the Commu-
> nist Political Association had honestly broken with the tenets of the
> Communist Party, but also that Albert Maltz, after long contempla-
> tion, had fought his way clear through to the liberal humanitarian way
> of thinking and writing.
> Albert and I worked at Warner's at the time and I recall going over

to his office to congratulate him on the independent position he had taken. . . .

A week later the roof fell in, and that is a very mild way of putting it. By his article, Maltz evidently had been guilty of some great heresy, and the execution squad, shipped in from the East, came marching in . . . the intellectual goon squad.

Knowing that Maltz was in trouble, I was prepared to defend his position, despite the fact that I was sorely aware of my deficiencies as a public speaker.

From this point on I can only give you my impressions of that meeting. It was a nightmarish and shameful experience.

I remember that Albert tried to explain his thoughts on the article. I remember that almost instantly all sorts of howls went up in protest against it. I remember that I and one or two others made small attempts to speak in favor of Maltz, and we were literally shouted down. I think I remember seeing Leonardo Bercovici trying to defend the article. But the wolves were loose and you should have seen them. It was a spectacle for all time. [The writer Arnold] Manoff, from whom I had expected some statements in defense, said nothing.

From one corner Alvah Bessie, with bitter vituperation and venom, rose up and denounced Maltz. From another corner Herbert Biberman rose and spouted elaborate mouthfuls of nothing, his every accent dripping with hatred. Others from every part of the room jumped in on the kill.

Aside from the merits of the article in question, this spectacle was appalling to me, for one simple reason: Maltz, I knew, was an associate of theirs of long standing. He was at that time a person of some literary stature and, as I then believed, a man of considerable personal integrity. The least one might have accorded him, even in disagreement, was some measure of understanding, some measure of consideration. But not they. They worked over him with every verbal fang and claw at their command; every ax and bludgeon, and they had plenty. They evidently were past masters at this sort of intellectual cannibalism.

The meeting was finally adjourned, to be reconvened the next week at the same place. I firmly resolved in heart and mind that if at the next meeting Maltz decided to renounce them all and stick by his guns, I would be the first to follow him out. However, at the next meeting they completely broke him.

The hyena attack—that is the only way I can describe them—continued with a rising snarl of triumph, and made him crawl and recant. This entire episode is an extremely distasteful thing for me to recall.

I remember feeling a deep anguish for him as a human being, that his closest friends for years, or at least associates, would treat him so shamefully, so uncharitably, so wolfishly. Whatever the cause, his friends had no right, in all decency, to humiliate and break him in this fashion. Or if they did they were not his friends. And whatever they stood for should have been proof eternal to him that they were wrong and evil.

Maltz's martyrdom, if that is what it was, was false, sterile and destructive.

Further, in that hour he betrayed not only himself and his justly derived thoughts but also all those who had entered and remained in the organization, in a large measure, due to him. So long as he was there, one felt some good was there. A sense of justice to which one could always appeal . . .

After this I knew positively that I had to get out. But how, I frankly didn't know. I believe I have already mentioned that they were placed in strategic positions throughout the industry. That withdrawal from them would have meant professional and economic suicide. I had already seen the utterly ruthless, unprincipled, cutthroat act of character assassination they had performed on Albert Maltz and others. . . .

I had two little babies, one newly born and the other a two-year-old child. I had to protect them at whatever cost to myself, though . . . despite all this, I did leave them voluntarily and of my own free will, accepting with certain knowledge retaliatory measures. I could no longer compromise with my principles.[17]

On April 9, 1946, two months after his initial effort, Albert Maltz published a second article in the *New Masses,* this one called "Moving Forward." It retracted the first. After summarizing the criticism of his original piece he said, "I consider now that my article—by what I have come to agree was a one-sided, non-dialectical treatment of complex issues—could not . . . contribute to the development of left-wing criticism and creative writing." He took responsibility for opening the way for the social democratic *New Leader* magazine to seize on his comments to "support its unprincipled slanders against the left." He also pleaded guilty to separating "the organic connection" of art and ideology. And he told those who had read his earlier article with approval that it was revisionist in approach and in it he had ignored "the basic problem of an honest writer in capitalist society."

Then, looking at the bright side of things, he found that "the intense, ardent, and sharp discussion" seemed to have been "a healthy and necessary one," and he sidestepped the harsh tone of some of his critics, saying, "The question is not how fair they were or Howard Fast was, but what was the substance of what he had to say?"[18]

⸻

It is this sequence of challenge and Party intervention and submission that has been seized on by embittered ex-Communists to explain their alienation from the Party and, in a number of cases, partially to justify their decision to play the informer.

Since John Howard Lawson lives on as the cruel face of the Party in the testimony of so many Hollywood informers, it seemed worth hearing his side of it. Before he died in 1977, Lawson was an arthritic and heartsick old man who could function only for about fifteen minutes at a time. But in those stretches he seemed to have his total wits about him and made an impressive case for the role he tried to play in his years as cultural honcho of the Hollywood Party.

What about Schulberg's charge that he tried to get *Sammy* to conform to the Party line? What about Lee Cobb's recollection that he tried to reconcile Stanislavski and Marx? Didn't he try to smuggle the Party line into *Blockade* (1938) and give tips to others on how to do it? And, finally, what about his role in the recantation of Albert Maltz?

Lawson's self-image, it quickly became apparent, had little to do with that of cultural functionary-dictator. He saw himself as a 1930s playwright, a 1940s union organizer and screenwriter, and a 1950s cultural scholar and cultural leader of the Party—as ever struggling to work out a satisfactory understanding of the relationship between art and the social forces that helped to shape and were in turn shaped by it.

The first president of the Screen Writers Guild, author of the experimental plays *Marching Song* and *Processional*, the most militant of the Hollywood Ten, Lawson helped organize the First Writers Congress in 1935 and out of that came *Hollywood Quarterly*, which became *Film Quarterly*. A serious scholar of film and theater and sometime hack-contributor to Party journals, he regarded the blacklist as only one part of the McCarthyite program, which he saw as aiming to control America's mass communications through a new and total censorship. He believed that the cultural blacklist involved a basic struggle concerning control of mass media—a struggle that began with the first sound picture and is still going on. "The role of art is too essential to be dismissed (or at least defined) as part of a general struggle of a political or social kind centering around an 'odd' phenomenon called 'McCarthyism.' The technological revolution has made control of media a burning issue, and we shall all be badly burned if we do not understand its implications."

He believed that the question was not whether Hollywood witnesses before HUAC were great artists but what service did they perform in fighting against thought-control. How one values the social function of the artist helps to determine how one assesses the utility of his action.

"The question of freedom of speech in the motion-picture industry is one with which I had long been concerned. I have always felt there was a struggle against monopolies, and within that framework the whole creative community had to conduct a struggle. The framework is the decline of the arts and the struggle to deal freely with one's material.

"The questions around the blacklist involve the nature of monopoly power. The main issue developed in the Hollywood hearings was the defense of the writers to express their opinions freely—and refuse to cooperate if they wanted to. We were doing a great service, and the film industry is still suffering from the fear of the McCarthy era."

But wasn't it true that he himself was simply one contestant in the fight to control the Communist Party? And didn't he try to smuggle Communist content into his films? Wasn't the reason he criticized Maltz related to Maltz's deviation from the Party line on socialist realism?

"The Maltz discussion," said Lawson, "has been totally misunderstood, in my opinion, because it has been regarded as a dispute about freedom of expression solely, whereas what was involved was a deeper understanding of the nature of the artistic experience. The whole problem of the artist is to deepen and extend and strengthen the character of his work. And this is a very hard undertaking. I have always made my own judgments on my work and not been affected by judgments coming from any political source." When *Processional,* originally produced by the guild in 1935, was revived in 1939, it was violently attacked by the Communist papers as an example of Dada and surrealism. "I can't recall that that had any devastating effect on me." He got a frantic telegram from V. J. Jerome saying the play went against all the principles of socialist realism. Lawson replied, " 'Sorry, I disagree.' Besides, forty people's jobs depended on it, so I let it run." Lawson also remembered the time Michael Gold criticized one of his plays as the work of a "bourgeois Hamlet. . . . I didn't like it, but it wasn't the end of the world."

What about Cobb's charge that he tried to convert the Stanislavski method to Marxism? "I felt that Stanislavski's method was very limited, and I still think that. We have a tendency to idealize Stanislavski in ways that are confusing. We have on the one hand the code of Brecht—his theory of estrangement, sometimes it's called alienation, his theory of jest. At the same time it's true that the best actors have been trained in the Stanislavski method and their training doesn't make a bit of sense for nine out of ten plays they do in the United States. Nobody has tried to examine this contradiction. I've tried and failed."

Originally Lawson believed that film was a "people's art" and as such there could be no permanent interference with it—the technology guaranteed its own ultimate independence. Now he felt this was confused and optimistic. "You can't have people's art under capitalism, you have to take account of the class struggle when analyzing the possibilities of Hollywood."

Maltz never had Lawson's pretensions as a student of Marxist aesthetics, but to understand his role in the *New Masses* dispute one must understand how he got into the Party and why he and so many other decent, intelligent, and socially concerned individuals stayed in. Maltz's extended answer to these questions merits space here not only because of his historic importance but also because, despite his latter-day disillusionment with the Soviet Union, he seems to recapture perfectly the perspective of his cohorts. His involvement started as far back as high school, he told me, when "The stories of the imperialist nature of World War I began to come out—that the munitions makers never bombed each other's plants, that there were secret meetings of capitalists from both sides in Switzerland . . . in which they reached agreements on things. The fact that this was a struggle of capitalism amongst themselves and had nothing to do with making-the-world-safe-for-democracy kind of thing. This began to come out, and I know that also the bloodbath that WWI had been affected me enormously so that my political stand was that of being a pacifist. I didn't want to participate in anything like that, to kill or be killed.

"By the time I was in college, I became very alert to the question of racial discrimination, and I remember one of my first writing attempts . . . had to do with a lynching. I graduated in 1930, that was in New York, Columbia, and I went up to the Yale Drama School for two years. But this was a period in which the most extraordinary people moved left. They may not have stayed too long but it was a period when Edmund Wilson was writing in the *New Republic* that he was a Marxist, and when he and Malcolm Cowley and a whole slew of others signed as supporters for William Z. Foster.

"By the time I came down from Yale, I was already more radicalized and had begun to read *New Masses* and presently came to hear about

German fascism. And one already knew something about Italian fascism. I remember attending a meeting . . . called by, I think, the old John Reed Club in New York and sending telegrams about the Reichstag fire trial and the burning of books in Germany.

"Well, in those years people concerned about the future of the world had a great deal of interest in or excitement about the Soviet Union. What was going on behind the scenes in the Soviet Union in terms of, let's say, deportation of farmers who wouldn't accept collectivization, the imprisonment, starvation, and death—this was hidden. The Soviet Union did a magnificent propaganda job. On the other hand, one heard things that were very exciting to intellectuals—that abortions were free, that divorce and marriage were up to the people to decide, as well as the fact that they had no unemployment and we had tremendous unemployment.

"And then if you began to observe the domestic scene, you found that the Communist movement at that time stood for many good things. It was the Communist movement that was organizing the unemployed. It was the Communist movement that raised the slogan of 'Black and white, unite and fight!' and that spoke out against world racial discrimination. It was the Communist movement that first proposed social security, which became the law of the land. It was the Communist movement that was very important in the organizing of the CIO and the industrial unions.

"And if you furthermore had read in the Marxist classics, you found what I still think to be the noblest set of ideals ever penned by man. The fact that many of them have been so ill-realized in the Soviet Union today didn't matter. But where else in political literature do you find thinkers saying that we were going to end all forms of human exploitation? Wage exploitation, exploitation of women by men (which the lib movement is now playing up but that the Communist movement was fighting then), the exploitation of people of color by white peoples, the exploitation of colonial countries by imperialist countries. And Marx spoke of the fact that socialism will be the kingdom of freedom, where man realizes himself in a way that humankind has never seen before. This was an inspiring body of literature to read.

"And there was another reason why, say, when the [Moscow show] trials came along, there were many like myself who believed that these people must be guilty, because we couldn't conceive that Bolsheviks who had fought together against the tsars and through civil wars would turn on each other and frame each other. This was inconceivable. I wouldn't have framed anybody else I knew. I didn't know anybody who would have framed me. We were starry-eyed and innocent.

"As soon as fascism came up, the other countries like England and France began to play with it; the Soviet Union opposed it. And the Soviet Union was the only friend that Republican Spain had in any consistent way. The nonintervention farce came up and Franklin Roosevelt went along with it. It was the Soviet Union that sent planes to Spain and the Soviet Union that had ships that were sunk in the Mediterranean.

"So the kind of loyalty that I had for the Communist movement when I joined in 1935 was based upon the belief that mankind's future was to be found there. Certainly, millions who joined it the world over, like myself, didn't join it for profit. There was nothing to be gained out of joining it: It could be time-consuming. It could prevent you from reading x number of books that you wanted to read or go to x number of films because you were doing other things. But there was the belief that you were working with others toward making the world a better place to live in.

"And for that reason one also had, or many had, a disgust of those who were considered to be renegades. We considered that the Isaac Don Levines [anti-Communist journalists] were liars, and of course as you know a great many lies were told about the Soviet Union in the beginning. Walter Lippmann inaugurated his career by exposing them. But that didn't mean that in, say, the 1950s Harrison Salisbury's reporting on the Soviet Union wasn't very accurate. But it permitted—because of the history and because of the hostility of the press in general to the Soviet Union—one to say, well, he's just an enemy.

"Now all of this is background to what happened when I wrote the article I did and got the reaction I did. I had had dissatisfactions in literary matters within the Communist movement all along—not on everything, but things came up. For instance, in 1935 a play I wrote was produced by the Action Theater; *Black Pit* has as its central figure a trade unionist who under pressure becomes an informer for the mine company. Well, the rumor on the left (by the left I mean Communist Party people but also . . . fellow travelers) got started, before the play opened, that I had written a play glorifying the stool pigeon. The psychological basis for the rumor is that Communist intellectuals, I think, at that time tended to be . . . let's say they [saw] a new world was on the horizon and they only wanted to hear things like Odets's "Stormbirds of the working class, awaken!" or however he ended *Waiting for Lefty*. That excited the hell out of them. But this sober picture of a trade unionist under pressure becoming a stool pigeon—which God knows was an omnipresent thing in the trade-union movement at that time and which I had learned about in the minefields of Pennsylvania, where I spent some time—ran against the grain of a certain type of person, so that . . . there was a small controversy over my play. At the trade union, there was a Sunday-night debate in which a number of people took one side of it, and a man called Clarence Hathaway—who had been editor of the *Daily Worker* and was a member then, I guess of the Central Committee, whatever the hell it was—took the stand that the play was absolutely sound and that the trade-union movement had this grave problem of stool pigeons. So I had accumulated dissatisfactions and early signs of discontent. I forget when the theory of socialist realism became full-blown, but I certainly know that by the time 1941 came along I was in a fury about it and was trying to work out an extended answer to it, which I never succeeded in doing because I'm not really a sound theoretical person. I don't have that kind of mind. But there was this earlier intimation of socialist realism coming along, however it was formulated, and I just knew from my own work that it wasn't right, that it was a straitjacket and I didn't like it.

"In this issue of *New Masses* several editors invited open discussion. One of the guys who wrote was a man called Isidor Schneider; he seemed to me an awfully nice man who had run some other sort of invited discussions and that was what prompted my article. My article appeared coincidentally at a time when the Communist movement was in a furor over criticisms of it that had been made by one French Communist, Duclos. And at some Party meeting in New York, I think a man who had been a World War II veteran hero . . . just arbitrarily (or maybe it was not arbitrarily) used my piece as an example from the literary world of discredited Browderism. That caused an immediate onslaught against my article by a series of people—one primarily: a series of articles that appeared in the *Daily Worker,* by Samuel Sillen. Now it was my feeling at that time that Sillen had made certain criticisms of my article that were sound. And I have not, in general . . . been someone who for emotional reasons had always to defend every position they ever took to the death. I'm willing to concede that I am wrong if it's pointed out to me. It doesn't hurt my ego.

"However, beside the intellectual perception that maybe he had made certain sound points, what was much more at issue in the emotional sense was my desire not to be made to become a renegade—my desire not to be expelled from the Party. I considered it to be an honor to be a member of the Party, and by the way I haven't changed my mind about that now. I would not be a member of any Communist Party, because of what life has taught me, and especially the American Communist Party, which in certain things I think is absolutely disgusting. (Its silence, for instance, on Polish anti-Semitism around 1968 which drove Jews out of Poland is, I think, just disgusting. There's no other word for it.)

"But when I look back upon how things were in those years and what the Party stood for in the 1930s and 1940s, without knowing about the Gulag Archipelago (because if I had known that I would never have kept silent myself) . . . it was a matter of my personal integrity to remain a Communist. And when I received the amount of criticism I did and was given the opportunity to reply to it with another article, I know that emotionally I wanted to reply in a way that would keep me in the Communist movement. And I'm sure . . . I could have said many things [in the first article] that I said in the second article, if I had chosen, and I could have reaffirmed certain of the criticisms I made in the first article and said they still held—and I didn't do that. I was in a kind of shell-shocked state. The criticism had been so enormous—I had gotten a tremendous number of letters as well—that I started to think, Well, now, who am I? Nobody stood up for me, with the exception of certain letters I got. But I started to say, Well, Jesus Christ, I must be wrong, I must be mistaken; and I didn't think of myself as a theoretician, you know, who knew the answers to this and that and therefore was willing to say, Well, all right, I'll set up my own party. I wanted to remain a Communist, I didn't want to become a renegade.

"I believe I got a letter from one of the editors, like Isidor Schneider, congratulating me on my article before they printed it. And [the criticism] came like lightning out of the blue sky—I had no knowledge that there was going to be that kind of criticism. If I had known then I would have taken a position on—how shall I say—fundamental principles, such as when I signed a statement in protest of Poland's actions against the Jews in 1968. That was a matter of fundamental principles. . . . But this was an article I had written; it had not been thought out as a matter of fundamental principle where I was saying, No matter what happens, this is where I stand. There's a real difference.

"There were people who spoke out very sharply against my article. Some of them, I think, spoke unjustly and went overboard, but except in one case where I *know* there was some underlying personal malice, in no case was there any personal malice. But remember there was a strong tradition—begun by Lenin, I think, if not earlier by Marx and Engels—of extremely sharp wordings when you were dealing with political matters. And polemics were not gentle. I think these people were reacting sincerely, but that doesn't mean their sincerity had not been given a push by the fact that the top leadership [of the Party] had spoken.

"But you see, nobody was holding any gun to my head to cause me to write that second article. I could have said, 'Screw you,' to all of them and I would have gotten applause from certain magazines and newspapers for what they would have called my brave act, or something. And that would have been just as inaccurate as saying I crawled, which is the way in which my second article has been characterized. Perhaps I won't blame certain people who don't understand the period for using a word like that. That's how they see it. But it was much more profound than that. The easiest thing in the world, you know, was to leave the Communist movement. I remember reading figures that go back to—oh, about the time before I left the movement, that in about twenty years about a million Americans had joined the Communist movement and left it. And at its highest I think the Party was about seventy-five thousand. So it was a very simple thing to leave the Communist movement. All you did was quit. And I stayed at that time because I believed in it as a whole, in what it stood for."

What, then, can be said about the recantation of Albert Maltz? First, it was not merely a case of Communist authoritarians crushing yet another free spirit. There were mixed motives on all sides. Albert Maltz was trying to preserve a dream as well as a status. The American Communist Party was caught between the heritage of World War II US-USSR cooperation and the imperatives of cold war antagonisms. Some of the Marxist aestheticians, undoubtedly sensitive to Party-line directives from New York or farther East, were nevertheless genuinely grappling with the peculiar task of analyzing truth and beauty in a class context. Some writers undoubtedly were doing their best to enhance their self-esteem by establishing their credentials as tough-minded leftists. That libertarian values were not a dominant concern of even the most sensitive artists on the left may be gathered from a *New Masses* symposium published less than a year earlier on the subject, "Should Ezra Pound Be Shot?" (for broadcasting fascist propaganda during wartime). None of the five symposiasts (including a young playwright named Arthur Miller) had said no. Albert Maltz, another symposiast, argued, "It is because he is a poet that he should be hanged, not once, but twice—for treason as a citizen, and for his poet's betrayal of all that is decent in civilization."[19]

Second, it should be noted that HUAC had a bureaucratic stake in publicizing the Maltz episode. At the outset of its inquiries, there had been much hoopla about Communist propaganda in the movies, but all that the Committee had come up with was *Mission to Moscow,* which was written by a non-Communist (Howard Koch) at the request of President Roosevelt, and one-liners like Lela Rogers' story of how her daughter Ginger had refused a role in *Sister Carrie* because it was "open propaganda," or that Lionel Stander had been caught whistling the "Internationale" while waiting for an elevator. Even after Lawson died, and a *New York Times* writer reported that he "used to give his colleagues tips on how to get the Party viewpoint across in his dialogue," Ring Lardner sent a letter to the editor setting the record straight: "Actually he regarded anything of that sort as a puerile approach to the politicization of screenwriting."[20] Undoubtedly some Soviet sympathizers considered it a blow for the cause when Harold Medford (whatever his politics) wrote the line in *Berlin Express* (1948) on the occasion of a Nazi who had escaped the death sentence, "Well, he's been sent to the Russian front, it's the same thing," but even the Committee must have understood that Soviet sympathizers inserted such "messages" in the movies much in the way that the cartoonist Al Hirschfeld puts his Ninas in his drawings for the Sunday *New York Times* Arts and Leisure section—a kick for the cognoscenti, invisible to anybody who is not in on the joke. The few examples of genuine interference had mostly to do with books, not movies.

Comes now the Maltz episode, at last, possible pay dirt. Here was at least an inkling of Communist concern for content, so the Committee kept coming back to it.

Any serious student of Party-line aesthetics knows that for more than a decade before the Maltz episode, leftist literary hacks indulged in crudely violent polemics against their artistic superiors. But to portray Lawson or even the cultural bureaucrat V. J. Jerome as nothing but censors may be to miss their most complicated aspect. Lawson told me, "I thought it was idiotic to talk about realism, for instance in the Soviet Union, where they make a whole issue of socialist realism yet the art they admire is the Russian ballet, which is not realistic at all and which is of an aristocratic origin, obviously." As Lardner pointed out in his letter to the *Times,* Lawson believed in making revolutionary movies, but he didn't think they would come from monkeying with scripts. Rather, he thought that more revolutionary movies would come from the interdependence of form and content and the deeper penetration of human character, especially in neglected sections of the population. To Jerome's younger, less philosophic disciples, Lardner wrote, "his counseling sometimes seemed remote from the immediate struggle." A sort of test case of his *modus operandi* was recorded by Dorothy Jones, who did a study of Lawson's work on the original screenplay for an antiwar and anti-Nazi picture entitled *Four Sons* (1940). Lawson's writing on the film covered the period from January 1939 to March 1940, which was neatly punctuated by the signing of the Nazi-Soviet Pact. She found that "a careful comparison of various stages of script over this period of time shows that the material prepared prior to the Nazi-Soviet Pact did not differ in any significant respect from versions of the same material prepared three months after the signing of the pact,"[21] suggesting that Lawson-the-scriptwriter was not automatically following the zigzags in the Party line. Even good old reliable V. J. Jerome, who took these matters as seriously as anybody, eventually came to see that his authoritarian style interfered with his efforts at developing a Marxist aesthetic. The only "overt act" mentioned at his trial (he had been indicted under the Smith Act) was a pamphlet he had written called Grasp the Weapon of Culture. Although today it seems less calculated to inspire action than somnolence, its message was that cultural activity was an essential phase of the Party's ideological work. But after he was released from prison in 1957, Jerome wrote to Maltz, "In looking back upon the field of my own activity, the cultural field, I can see that where the method was by fiat, the purpose—clarification through discussion—was less than served. 'Long is the way/And hard, that out of hell leads up to light.' "[22]

The recantation of Albert Maltz caused much disillusion, but to draw on it as a justification for informing, one finally concludes, is to misuse a complex episode in the Party's history. It should not be overlooked that the one man who might conceivably have been justified in invoking the logic of they-deserved-it, Albert Maltz himself, went to prison rather than become a cooperator. The Party's humbling of Maltz in 1946 provides no rationale for the naming (and possible betrayal) of former comrades in the 1950s. And resentment against the Party's brutally imposed proletarian aesthetic seems a poor excuse for dignifying the Committee's comic-book aesthetic, and no excuse at all for acceding to its ritualistic requirement of names.

I Wasn't Responsible for My Actions. The third justification is really the defense of helplessness, picturing the informer as the victim of forces beyond his control: not that it was a harmless thing to do or the right thing to do, but the only thing left to do. Such a defense has been offered on behalf of the late writer-director Robert Rossen, who was one of the most talented men in Hollywood (his films included Body and Soul [1947], All the King's Men [1949], and The Hustler [1961]) and one of the more articulate witnesses to appear before the House Un-American Activities Committee—both times. (It will be recalled that on the occasion of his second appearance, on May 7, 1953, when he named fifty names, he told the Committee, "I don't think, after two years of thinking, that any one individual can even indulge himself in the luxury of individual morality."[23]*)

Rossen died in 1966; his widow, Sue Rossen, pointed out to me that, "Right from the beginning my husband, who was one of the Hollywood Nineteen first called, wanted to say, 'I'm a member of the Communist Party and fuck you.' Bob told me that in the privacy of the living room, although he was willing to go along with the Ten [in saying nothing]. At that time I was bringing up my kids; I felt he understood it and I didn't. During that time a meeting took place in our house—it was in 1947, after the Nineteen had been subpoenaed but before they appeared—and he came out to the kitchen and said, 'We apparently just can't tell the truth.' The lawyers were trying to protect the Communist Party.

"Bob was informed through Leon Kaplan, an attorney here who looked after his business, that Edward Bennett Williams would be interested in handling his case. Leon led Bob to believe—that Williams could get Bob up there and not have to name names. We went to see two attorneys in Washington. One had plush offices and he was charging seventy-five dollars a minute and he was very formal and proper and distant. Then we went to see Ed Williams, who was in a cubbyhole, informal, sitting there in his shirt-sleeves. He was impressive. I said, 'To use one of Bob's favorite expressions, It's the difference between chicken shit and chicken salad.' Ed thought he could get Bob up there without giving names—at least not in public, but that's not what happened. It ended up with [being a choice between] Bob doing what he did or dying by attrition—because Bob couldn't get a job writing, and in my book if he couldn't write he couldn't live.

"He was totally rejected by everybody. He couldn't even get an offer in New York. He didn't know New York theatrical people that well. He was just boxed in on every side. The idea was to go to New York and pick up a pad and pencil and write, but he couldn't. His handwriting on a page would start out large and end up small and be about the Committee. He was scared about money, terribly frightened.

"I remember his telling me a story about his rabbi. When he was a kid

---

* In 1953 Rossen had been living in Mexico with a colony of political refugees, and when he was subpoenaed he told his friend the screenwriter John Bright that he was going to challenge the Committee, "just like Dimitroff" challenged the Nazis' attempt to frame him for the Reichstag fire. When Rossen finally named the names, Bright sent him a wire: "How do you spell Dimitroff?" (From Bright interview with author.)

he asked the rabbi, 'When you are starving and you know that all there is to eat is pork and either you eat pork or you will die, what should you do?' And the rabbi said, 'You eat it.' That's the way I felt. It was his life. I made it quite clear I felt he ought to go up there and get it over with.

"In retrospect, he needed me to say, 'Don't do it,' or, 'Do it.' My feelings were the whole thing was ridiculous. You're not hurting anybody by testifying since they already have all the names and you'll be able to work."

The actor Marc Lawrence said, "I came right out of an asylum to testify." Lee Cobb said he was flat on his back and his friends had abandoned him.

Consider the situation of the talented choreographer Jerome Robbins, who had the following demeaning colloquy with Congressman Clyde Doyle of the Committee on May 5, 1953:

MR. DOYLE: What is it in your conscience, or what was it in your experience, that makes you certainly, one of the top men in your profession, one who has reached the pinnacle in your art, willing to come here, in spite of the fact that you knew some other people, who claim to be artists or authors or musicians, would put you down as a stool pigeon, and voluntarily testify as you have today?

MR. ROBBINS: I've examined myself. I think I made a great mistake before in entering the Communist Party, and I feel that I am doing the right thing as an American.

MR. DOYLE: Well, so do I. Again, I want to compliment you. You are in a wonderful place, through your art, your music, your talent, which God blessed you with, to perhaps be very vigorous and positive in promoting Americanism in contrast to Communism. Let me suggest to you that you use that great talent which God has blessed you with to put into ballet in some way, to put into music in some way, that interpretation.

MR. ROBBINS: Sir, all my works have been acclaimed for its [sic] American quality particularly.

MR. DOYLE: I realize that, but let me urge you to even put more of that in it, where you can appropriately.[24]

Years later, when I asked one of the Hollywood Ten about the rumor, which Robbins now denies, that he testified under threat by the Committee's staff of disclosing intimate details about his sex life, Ring Lardner said, "I don't know whether it's true or not, but if you were Jerry Robbins, wouldn't you like to have people believe that's the reason you did it?"

When Roy Huggins says, "The terror was undoubtedly upon me," referring to his fleeting belief that his only "choice" was to name names or desert his wife, children, and family for a concentration camp; when Lee Cobb says, "I had to be employable again"; when Sylvia Richards says, "My decisions were passive—those of a woman" and describes her intellectual world as bounded by her attorney, her therapist, her boss, and an anti-Communist boyfriend—what all of these people are really saying is that they weren't in charge of themselves. They were billiard balls subject to the forces of history. They had temporarily lost control of their own destiny. They were more acted upon than acting.

It is not only the informers who make this case for themselves. Beatrice Buchman Rosenfeld, whose late husband the writer Sidney Buchman (*Mr. Smith Goes to Washington* [1939], *Here Comes Mr. Jordan* [1941]) had refused to name names for the Committee, enjoins, "Don't lump all the informers together. Some had 'good' reasons to inform. Those include one who had lied to the FBI, homosexuals, people who were afraid of deportation, a woman afraid of going to jail because she would be leaving a two-year-old son. . . ." The case for distinguishing among motives seems both compelling and appropriately compassionate. And yet it cannot be forgotten that for each informer there were two resisters, some in virtually identical circumstances, who refused to go along.*

Sidney Buchman himself, for example, having decided not to name names, could have avoided all personal risk by invoking the Fifth Amendment.† Instead, he took the First Amendment and used the occasion to refute testimony by Martin Berkeley that could have gotten his wife subpoenaed and testimony by Edward Dmytryk that could have gotten his friends the Coreys deported. (Dmytryk had placed the Coreys at a Communist Party meeting held at the Buchmans, but Buchman told HUAC: "I haven't the faintest knowledge that Mr. and Mrs. George Corey were ever Communists or, by the way, intended to join. . . . Mr. Corey was a man who worked with me and I knew him at the studio. He became a very good friend. . . . He was often at my house for dinner. . . . There can be any one of several explanations for Mr. Corey's presence.")[25]

---

* See above, p. ixn.

† Although many of those interviewed believe that Buchman's Columbia employer, Harry Cohn, bribed the Committee to get him off, no evidence has been produced to substantiate this claim.

Undoubtedly the state leaned on some people more than others, and thresholds of pain—moral, physical, and psychological—vary from person to person. But the example of the Hollywood Ten, of Buchman, Arthur Miller, Lillian Hellman, Pete Seeger, and others are there to be reckoned with. There is no evidence that the informers as a class were subjected to greater pressures—by the state, vigilantes, or personal problems—than the resisters. Some were under greater strain than others, and perhaps in isolated cases the force of circumstance disqualified traditional norms as a test of personal probity. But as a general proposition the notion that one was more acted upon than acting is either a tautology or a cop-out—akin to the claim by a number of witnesses who told HUAC they had joined the CP in the first place because they had been "duped" and didn't know what they were doing. If people don't take responsibility for their actions, no one else will.

I Was Acting in Obedience to a Higher Loyalty. Two arguments are advanced by those who feel they were obliged for reasons of some sort of higher loyalty to cooperate with the Committee: First, there are those like Huggins who simply felt that he owed it to his family not to go to jail, or as he put it, why "be a hero" for something in which he no longer believed, when he did believe in giving aid and comfort to his wife, two children, and his mother? Why "be a martyr" to the Communist cause when he had abandoned the Communist Party? It's one thing to refuse to cooperate "if you have religion," as Collins said, "but I didn't have it anymore."

But without minimizing the real conflict between duty to loved ones and duty to principle, to cite one's defection from the CP as a reason to testify before the Committee is to miss the point. The principle at stake was not the well-being of the Communist Party but rather the rights of all Americans and the well-being of the First Amendment. If resistance was required, it was not to protect the Communist Party (except insofar as *its* rights were violated) so much as to prevent the abuse of power by the state.

More interesting are those like Elia Kazan, Budd Schulberg, Leo Townsend, and others who have suggested that they had a moral obligation to reveal the dimensions of the Communist evil. None of them professed any enthusiasm for cooperating with the Committee, and in fact Schulberg says that he criticized it. But all of them suggest they acted in response to a higher loyalty. Kazan spelled out some of his thinking on the matter of competing obligations in his 1952 ad. Townsend pins his action to his research on Soviet treatment of Jews, and emphasized to me that while he thoroughly disliked McCarthyism his higher obligation was to expose Soviet anti-Semitism.

Budd Schulberg, who still gets visibly agitated when he talks about it, has worked out a sort of moral syllogism which suggests that cooperating with HUAC was not merely an option for ex-Communists but a moral duty. To summarize: Anyone complicit in the Soviet death camps had an obligation to expose and denounce them; Schulberg, Ring Lardner, and others who paid dues to the American Communist Party and defended the Soviet Union's internal and external policies were early deniers of and/or apologists for and thereby complicit in the Soviet death camps. Therefore no matter how distasteful the means (including the naming of names before HUAC), there was an obligation to denounce and expose Communism and Communists.

A year after he testified, Schulberg wrote an article for *Saturday Review* called "Collision with the Party Line" in which he elaborated the connection in his mind between the American Party's attempt to interfere with his conception of *Sammy* and the Soviet Union's brutal treatment of writers. He recalled his visit to Russia, how he thrilled at the Meyerhold Theater's revolutionary interpretation of Ostrovsky's *The Forest*, how he talked with Vakhtangov's widow about her husband's theatrical innovations (which explored a middle course between the realism of Stanislavski and the mechanistic approach of Meyerhold), how he visited the young Afinogenov, whose play *Fear* was one of the hits of the season. He recalled hearing Gorky extol socialist realism (not a straitjacket, but a step beyond the traditional bourgeois realism of the great nineteenth-century writers Balzac, Tolstoy, and Stendhal). He heard the novelist Yuri Olesha honestly discuss how the First Five Year Plan failed to inspire him as a literary theme. He heard Bukharin himself praise Boris Pasternak, "Russia's finest living poet," whose avoidance of topical subjects and experimentalism made him anathema to the Party-minded versifiers. Returning from this inspirational experience Schulberg shortly found himself a member of the Young Communists and stayed in the Party until he had his disillusioning experience with *Sammy*.

> I do not think I am indulging in melodramatics if I invoke a comparison between this easy victory over would-be cultural commissars in America and the systematic violence used by actual Soviet commissars on Russian writers who dare assert their independence and individuality. . . .

For a Soviet writer to buck official criticism or to withdraw from the Party is to invite a one-way ticket to the uranium mines. For the American who wishes to regain and reassert his independence the penalties are merely a certain amount of emotional wear-and-tear involved in breaking the quasi-religious grip in which the movement has held him, and the rupture of friendships with a number of people he has been fond of as individuals, who, while kind and well-meaning, do not realize that the collective will of their organization has twisted their original warm-hearted ideals and crippled their sensibilities. . . .

How these intelligent and personally fair-minded gentlemen could show genuine concern for the political harassment of creative writers in the United States and yet blind themselves to the ever-tightening restrictions strangling the creative arts in the Soviet Union is one of those fascinating doublethinks that riddle our time.

Schulberg's view of V. J. Jerome was that if he were in power he would

righteously murder truth, freedom, and art with exactly that rigidity, fanaticism and "witch-hunting hysteria" he now cries out so righteously against. . . . As a taxpayer I can't help wondering if the expenses of [Jerome's Smith Act] trial could not be better used in the service of free institutions if he were sent on a tour of American writers. Half-an-hour's exposure to this unfortunate man's views of art and politics is guaranteed to convince anyone with literary integrity that in this Pooh-Bah he has met the enemy, the prototype of the authoritarian, that frightening twentieth-century phenomenon—the politician who turns to art as to a hand grenade.

Schulberg saw the *Daily Worker*'s second and antagonistic review of *Sammy* as the same Party line referred to by Mayakovsky in the years before his own plays were banned for their biting criticism of Soviet bureaucracy: "I believe that the best poetic work will be written in accordance with the social command laid down by the Communist International."

Oblivious to the irony of his own recantation before HUAC, Schulberg wrote with insight that the American Communist movement is a reflection of a familiar Soviet literary phenomenon—"the organized attack on books and writers and the stylized recantation that almost invariably follows."

In 1946, for instance, the Central Committee attacked two of Russia's outstanding writers, the brilliant Zoshchenko and the lyrical poet

Akhmatova. . . . Zoshchenko is described in the *Portable Russian Reader* as "Soviet Russia's foremost humorist and probably the best-loved one since Chekhov." But the Central Committee called him a "scum of literature" who "specializes in writing empty, fatuous, vulgar stuff and in preaching a rotten lack of ideas, apoliticalness, designed to lead our youth astray and to poison its consciousness." Anna Akhmatova was branded by [Andrei] Zhdanov, then High Executioner of Soviet Literature, "an out-and-out individualist, a representative of the bourgeois-aristocratic estheticism and decadence whose work could only breed depression and pessimism and a desire to escape into the narrow world of personal emotions, and thus poison the minds of young people."

Thus two of Soviet Russia's most original voices were silenced. There was little subtlety to their choice—either to write the Zoshchenko and Akhmatova way and follow Pilniak, Babel, Terassov-Rodionov, the poet Mandelstam, the leading critic Voronsky, and the others to some dark and dread oblivion, or to write the Central Committee's way, like Simonov, Alexei Tolstoy, Ehrenberg, and other members of the charmed circle of literary millionaires.

He told how his instructor in Russian literature in 1934 was denounced and arrested in 1935 (according to the bulletin of the Russian Literary Fund), and died in Siberian exile for the crime of "failing to fawn over a novel by Fadeiev that enjoyed Kremlin approval." He told how Meyerhold fell into disgrace in 1937 and his theater was "liquidated" for failure to practice socialist realism, and how subsequent to a courageous public speech in 1939, he was arrested and vanished and his name and speech removed from the book of the First Convention of Theatrical Directors where he had given it. He told how Gorky died under mysterious circumstances in 1936. "Indeed, to call a roll of the principal speakers of the First Writers Congress who fired my enthusiasm for Soviet literature in 1934 is to summon up the dead. Gorky, Bukharin, Radek, Babel, Pilniak, I. Kataev, Tretyakov." As Pasternak summed it up in a bitter understatement, Schulberg reported, "Mayakovsky committed suicide and I translate."

He then made clear that while the United States had no Central Committee Directives on art to punish us for the sin of originality,

In the name of patriotism, powerful pressure groups . . . continue to harass Hollywood with their police-state mentalities and their indiscriminate loyalty probes. As the Hollywood correspondent for *The New York Times* said recently, "Now, perhaps as never before in its recent turbulent history, the creative element in Hollywood is experiencing a form of censorship unparalleled in the experience of the average individual in this country."

He said of course these things shouldn't be compared with what was happening in Russia, but "a healthy body should be able to throw off the disease after a mild attack. . . . We have seen how the same Revolution that promised to make a free man of Isaac Babel in 1917 crushed him under its monolithic weight twenty years later." Schulberg added, "I decline to accept any suppression of creative individuality as a necessary step in the defense of our culture. . . . Art must always wither and die when it comes under the control of any censorship that judges a writer by his willingness to conform." Schulberg identified two ways to respond to the Soviet trauma: either retreat in fear or reassert our commitment to democratic dignity.[26]

These last are extremely high-sounding sentiments and one would have assumed that they constituted a caution against cooperating with the Committee and presumed that naming names was an ultimate indignity. But revisiting the scene of the crime, so to speak, fails to confirm such suppositions.

Inspection of the testimony shows that Leo Townsend devoted only a couple of sentences of his thirty-four-page testimony to the Jews, and Schulberg dwelt mainly upon his literary roughing-up, with only a few paragraphs on how that related to what went on in the Soviet Union— and not even a wrist slap for HUAC. The anti-HUAC coda in Schulberg's *Saturday Review* piece is really not present in his testimony before HUAC. Indeed, he conspicuously bypassed the invitation to denounce HUAC's methods, not to mention its goals. When asked by the Committee why he signed a petition for the abolition of HUAC only two years before, he replied that that didn't mean he was fundamentally against the Committee; the truth was his feelings were not "a hundred to nothing" but "fifty-five or sixty percent in favor or forty or forty-five percent against," and "that day" he had a "definite concern . . . that people should be called in and their political views should be inquired into," although, he added, there was certainly "information about the CP and the CP operation that could be of no value to the American people."

Schulberg also added that he had some personal pique at Dies because when the Dies Committee had come to town in 1940, it refused to return his call. "Wasn't most of this agitation to eliminate this Committee started by Communist groups that realized that sooner or later this Committee would expose some of their machination?" asked Chairman Walter. "Undoubtedly Communists would join for that reason," said Schulberg.

When Congressman Jackson asked whether he advised others to come forward and "make a clean breast of it" before HUAC, Schulberg replied, "Sir, it would be my own personal advice." He added that HUAC should help cooperative witnesses get work. Jackson then asked about resisters to HUAC: "Should the same amnesty be extended to them by industry or by the American people at the box office?" Schulberg's answer: "Frankly, I haven't quite decided that problem myself. I don't feel it is the same as the other. I do feel there is some difference, but I haven't quite made up my own mind. I can understand certain hesitance on the part of the industry and the American people. It is something I would like to think more about."

What we must ask, then, is not whether the deathlist is worse than the blacklist. Of course it was. Of course Stalin's terror, torture, deceptions, paranoia, murders, and gulags were worse than McCarthy's red hunt. The question, though, is whether to fight the deathlist it was necessary to support the blacklist, whether collaboration with the American informer system was the price of fighting the Soviet gulag system.

Whatever the motives of those who say they were fighting "thought control" and Stalinist terror with names, the means chosen were known to be inappropriate. The congressional investigators were seen by center liberals and conservatives, as well as by the hard-core radical left, as careerists who evidenced no serious concern for the victims of Stalinist purges and death camps; they seemed bent more on punishing the Hollywood naïfs than on exposing the practitioners of terror. Men like Dies, Thomas, Velde, Nixon, and McCarthy had in common political opportunism and a demagogic capacity to exploit nativism and know-nothing passions.

Moreover, to say as Huggins, Schulberg, and others did, that they saw no "honest" alternative to "taking the Fifth" seems peculiar. The decision not to defy HUAC and risk prison may be defensible, but honesty had nothing to do with it. Virtually all of the cooperative witnesses (except Berkeley) were by their own admission less than honest when it came to naming those they knew in the Party. As a matter of fact, by systematically naming "only those already named," or at any rate naming some but not others, they told less than the whole truth and thereby contributed to the wholesale corruption of the system. The sort of selective "honesty" that justifies stigmatizing some (but not all) others while clearing oneself seems difficult to defend on grounds of a higher political imperative.

Schulberg's question today of the resisters—what have they done lately?—also seems irrelevant to the issue. His own continued involvement in politics is ample evidence that his social conscience persists; but whether that makes him morally superior to Lillian Hellman, say, whose Committee for Public Justice carries on its battles on the civil-liberties front, or Arthur Miller, who is in the forefront of protests against the mistreatment of writers throughout the world, or Ring Lardner, who joined the fight to abolish HUAC immediately after he was out of prison and trying to go back to work, is questionable. Such exercises in comparative latter-day moral commitment seem futile. Many honest men and women were burned out during the cold war years.

———

As a theoretical matter, then, the principal justifications won't wash. The "I didn't hurt anybody" argument (a) turns out to be not true, and (b) in any event seems to go more to what lawyers call mitigation of damages than to be a real defense of naming names. Those who insist that their testimony caused no harm are really saying that they did not wish to harm those they named. But if they indeed perceived their cause as just, then they ought to believe that those they named deserved to be harmed. Yet the "just desserts" justification doesn't hold, either. If those they named behaved wickedly in the past, they deserved punishment in the past. A 1950s investigating committee would seem the wrong forum to administer the wrong punishment at the wrong time.

Undoubtedly the pressure of events incited many to act against their better instincts, but to seek exculpation in such pressures begs the question. Again, the "nonresponsibility" argument sounds more like an attempt to earn compassion (in some cases undoubtedly deserved) than to defend a course of action, especially when it is made by people who are patently ashamed—or at least not proud—of their behavior.

Which leaves the "appeal to higher loyalties." Where the "higher loyalty" is asserted to be family support or other personal commitments, one must concede that conflict and pain may have accompanied the choice (although to do so is not, of course, to endorse the ethics of the decision). But where the higher loyalty is asserted to be an ideological imperative and/or a commitment to "truth," the defense seems inadequate not only because so many of the name-namers told less than the whole truth, and because they waited so many years to tell it, but because as many of these people will now freely concede, the congressional committees were obviously an inappropriate forum for the realization of such high ideals.

There was moral myopia on all sides, but one's victim's inability to distinguish right from wrong is not justification for one's own misdeeds.

Moreover, such justifications ignore the political effect of naming names—of confirming who was and who was not active in left-wing politics, of creating a climate of concern and fear. The effect was to create an exact parallel of McCarthyism: namely, the purging of the cultural apparatus of alien forces, just as McCarthyism was the purging of the state apparatus, an exercise in political purification.

Both resisters and informers claim they were acting according to their lights. The difference may be that the former were true to their mistaken convictions, whereas the latter were untrue to their correct ones—they knew better than to condone Stalinism but they also knew better than to cooperate with McCarthyism.

10.
Degradation Ceremonies

ON ONLY ONE ISSUE did the House Un-American Activities Committee and its most visible victims, Kazan and Polonsky, the blacklisters and the Hollywood Ten, Sokolsky and the *Daily Worker*, all agree: the test for friend or foe was the willingness to inform. Why did such a consensus develop on the meaning of the names test? Why did the Committee insist on it?

Suspend the search for individual motives and consider the underreported testimony of one William Ward Kimple. On June 30, 1955, Kimple appeared as a witness before the Committee and told a story whose significance may have been lost at the time. He was not a star witness. The hearings had stopped making news. The dozen or so names he read into the record were those of mostly anonymous Party functionaries. In other words, who cared . . .

—that he had been a member of the intelligence unit of the Los Angeles Police Department from 1924 to 1944;

—that from 1928 until September 1939 he was a member of the Communist Party under the name William Wallace;

—that he served the Party as unit literary agent, unit educational director, unit organizer, alternate on the county-level disciplinary committee, and, last but not least, assistant to the L.A. County membership director;

—that in this latter capacity he had all the membership records;

—that during the years 1936, 1937, 1938, and 1939—years of the Popular Front, when Party membership skyrocketed—he had charge of the membership lists and kept them in his own possession;

—that there had been 100 members of the Communist Party in Los Angeles when he joined, and 2880 when he left in September 1939;

—that it was his extracurricular duty "to keep the police department informed ... of the 'who and what and when' and the 'where and the why' of the Communist movement and activities."

As he put it in his testimony before the Committee:

My duties ... were to keep the membership records of the Communist Party in order to assist in the annual registration of Communist Party members, to assist in the mid-year control of the Communist Party membership books. That was an activity taken about the first of July—to check on all Communist Party members, to see to it that they were paid up in dues and when. ... When their books were inspected and [they were] found to be paid-up members, then a control card was detached from the membership book and sent back to the membership commission.

Then I, as assistant membership director, would check against the records and show that they were Communist Party members in good standing. I would also assist in the transfer of Communist Party members from one unit to another, one section to another; see to it that their Communist Party cards were kept in place so that at all times we knew where each CP member was and where he was functioning and what his duty was supposed to be.

The following dialogue then took place with Frank Tavenner, counsel to the Committee:

MR. TAVENNER: Then it would be correct to say that you had in your custody or under your control at one time or another the record of memberships in the Communist Party in the Los Angeles area?

MR. KIMPLE: Yes, sir. ... I furnished [my police superior] copies of the CP membership records and, where possible, I furnished him copies of the Communist Party membership registration and, where possible, I turned in to him the Communist Party membership books which were picked up at the end of the year when the new books were issued, and the old books I turned over to him. ...

My instructions were to destroy the old books and the method I used was to turn them over to the police department.

MR. TAVENNER: Did you follow that practice with regard to the entire membership of the Communist Party during this period that you were membership director? I mean, did you furnish the department with the records of membership of all the members?

MR. KIMPLE: Yes, sir. ...

MR. TAVENNER: ... You said you had some assistance in this work from another person employed by the police department. In what way did she assist you in that work?

MR. KIMPLE: Well, sir, we worked as a team all the time and she was the Los Angeles County dues secretary for the Hollywood subsection, dues secretary at the time she was in the new unit.

She was also secretary of the Los Angeles County disciplinary committee of the Communist Party. And working together we kept the police department pretty well informed.

MR. TAVENNER: Have you recently been in a position to review the reports and records which you and the person whom you later married turned over to the police department?

MR. KIMPLE: I have, yes, sir; many of them, not all of them.

At the close of Kimple's testimony, Congressman Donald Jackson thanked him, and observed:

It is by virtue of informed testimony such as this that it has been possible to piece together across the years the nature and the extent and the objectives of the Communist Party in the United States. Of course, anyone who serves on this Committee is automatically a heel in the eyes of the comrades. Your future will be that of a stool pigeon.

MR. KIMPLE: I have been so labeled many times.

MR. JACKSON: However I feel that that will reflect a very small vocal minority viewpoint and that by and large the people of the city of Los Angeles, California in general, and of the Nation owe to you and other people who have been willing to take on assignments of this kind in the line of official duty, separating yourself in large part, as I know you must have, from family associations, social things you would very much have preferred to do, a debt of gratitude.

Jackson then asked whether the witness was in a position to give the Committee additional names. "I am in the position, sir," said Kimple, "to positively identify the Communist Party membership of close to a thousand people."

MR. JACKSON: A thousand people?

MR. KIMPLE: In Los Angeles, yes, sir.

MR. JACKSON: Is the Committee in possession of that information?

MR. KIMPLE: They are.

MR. JACKSON: Thank you very much.[1]

Three years before Kimple testified, in 1952, the Committee had heard from one Max Silver, who had been the paid full-time organizational secretary for the Southern California Communist Party from 1938 to 1945. In other words, Silver's West Coast duties commenced the year before Kimple had retired. Silver guessed that there were four thousand members in the Los Angeles County Party.[2] So between Silver and Kimple alone, the Committee had access to all of the Party's local names from 1936 through 1945. And then, to bring the Committee up-to-date on the postwar period, it had witnesses such as Roy Erwin, a Hollywood radio worker who had joined the Party in 1945 and who doubled as an FBI informant and Party member from 1947 to 1949.[3]

The testimony of Kimple, Silver, and Erwin, combined with intelligence from the FBI* and countless other government sources in the business of trading information (with such as the good-natured investigator Bill Wheeler and his colleagues on HUAC†), meant that the last thing the Committee needed to do its job was to accumulate more names.

Moreover, almost all the witnesses who named names publicly preceded their public testimony with a private, executive-session rehearsal, which means that the public hearings were indeed largely ceremonial. Why did they agree to participate in the ceremony?

Lest there remain any doubt about the informational irrelevance of the public naming, let us remember Wheeler's own injunction to the penitent Martin Berkeley: "When Berkeley came down with his list of 154†† peo-

---

* Throughout the cold war the left charged and the internal-security bureaucracy denied that there was behind-the-scenes cooperation between the FBI and the various congressional committees. Irrefutable evidence of such cooperation is provided by the FBI file of Larry Parks, which I obtained in 1979 under the Freedom of Information Act. It includes a memorandum from Mr. D. M. Ladd to the director, dated September 12, 1947, that begins: "Pursuant to your request, there is attached hereto a blind memorandum concerning the above-captioned individual [Larry Parks] for transmittal to Representative Parnell Thomas." The memorandum then quotes "highly confidential sources" and goes on to list questions Parks ought to be asked by the Committee.

† As Wheeler told me, "Every time I got a witness, I sent him down to the FBI first, 'cause they knew fifty times more about it than I did and would naturally have a guy recollect a little bit more, you know, of what he'd forgotten. . . . I didn't even go in with them. . . . Then I gave the FBI a list of people I was going to subpoena. They wanted to know that."

†† My own count is that Berkeley named 161 names, but I include such public Communists as Earl Browder, V. J. Jerome, et al., which may account for the discrepancy.

ple, I told him, I said, 'Don't name that many. You're just going to get yourself in big, deep trouble.' I said, 'We don't need all this. Put the rest of it in executive testimony.' " Names were turned on and off like water by the Committee's counsel and investigator, depending on the symbolic goal of the day. Thus, on January 21, 1952, Wheeler reined in Max Silver: "I advised him not to identify too many people because I told him I wanted from him the theory of Communism, the story of the way the Hollywood section of the Party was divorced from the Los Angeles section and how they got their directives from New York, and the fight about how New York picked up all the money. I wanted the hearings to focus on the big argument about whether under the Hollywood tithing system they got ten percent of the gross or ten percent of the net. Well, I think he still named about thirty people or something like that, and there were the usual big headlines in all the Los Angeles papers—you know, Ex-Communist Identifies Thirty, and they left out all the theory, they just skipped it."

And the Committee's critics are further confirmed in one of their several indictments of its activities: The purpose of the public hearing was *not*, as HUAC and its defenders insisted it was, to gather information for legislation. The information it demanded in public it already had, and other information that might have been useful to it was rejected. (When Lillian Hellman, Arthur Miller, Robert Rossen, Larry Parks, Sidney Buchman, and others offered to tell all about themselves as long as they weren't required to name others, the Committee said no.) Its "official" reason for demanding the naming of names was perhaps most forcefully stated by Congressman Jackson, who believed that only the naming of names was the final proof that a witness had broken with his past. He said: "I personally will place no credence in the testimony of any witness who is not prepared to come before this Committee and fully cooperate with respect to activities within the Communist Party."[4] And naming names was "the ultimate test" of a witness's cooperation. In theory the failure to name names left open the possibility that one was still in the business of protecting one's old comrades.

Jackson's test may help to explain why the practice was inaugurated but not why it persisted. Nor are we given much guidance in the histories, political analyses, or legal briefs of the period, which concern themselves primarily with matters of the separation and abuse of powers, and the reputation of various constitutional amendments.

One turns instead to the sociologists and anthropologists, students of ritual, ceremony, and symbolism, of the meaning of deviance, the visiting of stigma, and the persistence of social evil. For the lesson of Kimple, Silver, et al. is surely that whatever the practical consequences of the naming of names, the ritual's real significance was symbolic. That this was sensed by many participants in the process may be gathered from the quality of the calculus which the informer Richard Collins reports he undertook with the informer Meta Rosenberg. When they limited the names they would turn over to the Committee into three categories—the dead, the already called, and the long-time ex-Communists—they persuaded themselves they would do minimal damage. Yet if Collins was under no illusion that he was supplying the Committee with important information, did it occur to him that he was supplying it with something more central to its purposes—a body, an instrument without which it could not have carried out its ritual, its degradation ceremony?

The HUAC hearings were degradation ceremonies. Their job was not to legislate or even to discover subversives (that had already been done by the intelligence agencies and their informants) so much as it was to stigmatize.

For a degradation ceremony to work it needs a denouncer. And the most credible denouncer, with the most impeccable credentials, is the one who has been there himself. The ex-Communists constituted a steady supply of denouncers.

A successful status-degradation ceremony must be fueled by moral indignation. The anti-Communist hysteria of the cold war provided an ideal environment.

What makes the degradation ceremony so serious an occasion is the nature of the public denunciation. As Harold Garfinkel, a UCLA sociologist who has written an important article on degradation rites, describes the process, the public, through its agent, delivers a curse which says in effect, "I call upon all men to bear witness that he [the denounced person] is not as he appears but is otherwise and in essence of a lower species." The target becomes in the eyes of his condemners literally "different," "a new person." It is not that new attributes are added to the old identity. He is not changed; he is, rather, reconstituted, transformed. "The man at whose hands a neighbor suffered death becomes a 'murderer.'" The former identity, at best, is seen as something of a sham appearance. The new identity is the "basic reality."[5]

Scholars who undertook to challenge the work of the congressional committees during the cold war years focused for the most part on rights rather than rites. But of course most scholarship of the period divorced itself from concern with the content of actions. In literature the New

Critics focused on form over content, in philosophy the positivists were preoccupied with the verifiable rather than the meaningful, in psychology the behaviorists rejected Gestalt analysis in favor of stimulus-response studies. Even in the relatively new discipline of sociology, whose subject was largely contemporary society, confrontation with McCarthy, the man or the ism, took the form of esoteric studies in conformity. But perhaps there is some sort of unwritten law on the inevitability of relevance, which says that contemporary moral, political, and social issues are inescapable. At any rate, one of the more obscure developments in the sociology of the 1950s turns out to offer perhaps the most useful framework for understanding the politics of that time—namely, the study of "the deviant," by which was usually meant a juvenile delinquent, a mental patient, or a religious fanatic. Thus the sociologist Kai Erikson's description of a community's decision to bring what he calls "deviant sanctions" against one of its members turns out to be a description of the elements of the sort of status-degradation ceremony I have been talking about:

> To begin with, the community's decision to bring deviant sanctions against one of its members is not a simple act of censure. It is an intricate rite of transition, at once moving the individual out of his ordinary place in society and transferring him into a special deviant position. The ceremonies which mark this change of status generally have a number of related phases. They supply a formal stage on which the deviant and his community can confront one another [as in a HUAC hearing]; they make an announcement about the nature of his deviancy [the witness is named as a Communist or former Communist]; and they place him in a particular role which is thought to neutralize the harmful effects of his misconduct [he is put on a blacklist which renders him unemployable]. These commitment ceremonies tend to be occasions of wide public interest and ordinarily take place in a highly dramatic setting [the HUAC hearings, frequently televised, often made page one]. . . .
>
> Now an important feature of these ceremonies in our own culture is that they are almost irreversible. Most provisional roles conferred by society—those of the student or conscripted soldier, for example—include some kind of terminal ceremony to mark the individual's movement back out of the role once its temporary advantages have been exhausted. But the roles allotted the deviant seldom make allowance for this type of passage. He is ushered into the deviant position by a decisive and often dramatic ceremony, yet is retired from it with scarcely a word of public notice. And as a result, the deviant often returns home

with no proper license to resume a normal life in the community. Nothing has happened to cancel out the stigmas imposed upon him by earlier commitment ceremonies; nothing has happened to revoke the verdict or diagnosis pronounced upon him at that time. It should not be surprising, then, that the people of the community are apt to greet the returning deviant with a considerable degree of apprehension and distrust, for in a very real sense they are not at all sure who he is.[6]

The congressional degradation ceremony served the purposes of too many constituencies to be easily discarded. From the perspective of the state, it functioned to reinforce group solidarity. The apparent willingness of former Communists to engage in wholesale denunciations of their former comrades confirmed the state in its conviction that the ceremonies were warranted. The process of stigmatizing individuals as subversives, as agents of a foreign power, as conspirators, as having rejected the American heritage, reassured middle Americans of their own patriotism. Americans have always defined themselves largely by what they are against: America is for Americans; go back to where you came from; the foreign, the different, the strange, the subversive should get out of town.

From the perspective of the Committee, the ceremonies not only brought publicity but alerted the free-lance blacklisters, who functioned as the enforcement arm. Those who were denounced at HUAC had broken no law, and under the American system where there is no crime the state visits no punishment. But the ceremonies enabled the Committee to perpetrate the fiction that the mere publicizing and publication of names—in the form of testimony, indexes, supplements, and cumulative indexes, in effect blacklist deskbooks—was no punishment. No one asked, "Why are you turning out these interminable lists with the taxpayers' money?" The ritual masked the fact that these lists were never intended to help Congress pass any laws.

From the perspective of the free-lance enforcers, the degradation ceremonies promised a continuous generation and supply of the raw material of their trade. The hearings were free advertising, a preview of coming attractions, and an identification of the next round of targets.

From the perspective of the informers, the hearings insulated them from direct contact with the moral dilemmas of betrayal. The anthropologist Ernest Becker has described the age-old dynamic of sacrificial scapegoating as "the sadistic formula *par excellence*: break the bones and spill the blood of the victim in service of some 'higher truth' that the sacrificers alone possess."[7] But the ceremonies shielded the informers from the consequences of their action. By pronouncing a particular set of former friends as Communists (or unrepentant ex-Communists), as deviants, unclean, foreign, they were by definition absolving themselves of moral responsibility: The "subversives" had the same opportunity as the informers did to "come clean," to "purge" themselves; if they chose not to do so, that was not the informer's responsibility. And of course on a more mundane level the hearings generally provided the informers with a ticket back to employment, simultaneously exonerating the witness who wished to go back to work and the employer who wished to employ him. It was a form of stigma transfer—from namer to namee. For some, the very act of denouncing was a form of assimilation, of status elevation. Some critics called Lillian Hellman a snob for speculating in her memoir, *Scoundrel Time,* that "The children of timid immigrants are often remarkable people: energetic, intelligent, hardworking; and often they make it so good that they are determined to keep it at any cost."[8] But the truth was that by denouncing fellow immigrants (or children of immigrants) before HUAC, one consolidated one's identification with the dominant society. The practice came with the prestige of the state conferred upon it; it legitimated betrayal.

The degradation ceremonies satisfied the needs of the mass media, which were either incapable of, or uninterested in, exposing the ways in which the ritual distorted truth when it lent itself so elegantly to reproduction on radio and television. And the degradation ceremonies exploited the peculiar vulnerability of mass media to the pseudo-event. The phrase "pseudo-event" was, appropriately enough, introduced into the language by Daniel J. Boorstin, now Librarian of Congress, distinguished historian, and participant in the degradation ceremonies of 1953, when he named five of his former Harvard colleagues before the Committee. In his elegantly written book called *The Image, or What Happened to the American Dream* (1961), Boorstin offered a four-part definition of the term "pseudo-event":

1. It is not spontaneous, but comes about because someone has planned, planted, or incited it. Typically, it is not a train wreck or an earthquake, but an interview.
2. It is planted primarily (not always exclusively) for the immediate purpose of being reported or reproduced. Therefore, its occurrence is arranged for the convenience of the reporting or reproducing media. Its success is measured by how widely it is reported.... The question "Is it real?" is less important than, "Is it newsworthy?"

3. Its relation to the underlying reality of the situation is ambiguous. Its interest arises largely from this very ambiguity. . . . While the news interest in a train wreck is in *what* happened and in the real consequences, the interest in an interview is always, in a sense, in *whether* it really happened and in what might have been the motives. Did the statement really mean what it said?
4. Usually it is intended to be a self-fulfilling prophecy.

Pseudo-events are staged to give people something to talk about. They become a test for being informed. "Once we have tasted the charm of pseudo-events," Boorstin observed, "we are tempted to believe they are the only important events. Our progress poisons the sources of our experience. And the poison tastes so sweet that it spoils our appetite for plain fact."[9]

The degradation ceremony used the press to promote the ritual, the message, the Committee, the myth, the image of the Communist as conspirator. It repackaged for home entertainment the trivial and sometimes dull, boring, and meaningless experiences of misspent youth into melodramatic morality plays for a national audience. Yet one cannot but believe that, consciously or otherwise, Boorstin's formulation was informed by his own experience as a public denouncer.

The degradation ceremony complemented the status needs of certain former Communists, socialists, and others of the liberal left who were, as we have already seen, caught in the net of the red hunters of the day. To the extent that the ritual public denunciations succeeded in stigmatizing Communists and unrepentant former Communists, by implication they exonerated from intimations of guilt other members of the anti-Communist left. The degree of *trahison* of these particular *clercs* may be measured in terms of their willingness to participate in the degradation ceremonies of the day. It is true that there was a small minority of non-Communist liberals who saw McCarthyism and domestic repression as the enemy and thought it counterproductive to participate in any way.* For their troubles they were dismissed by cold war liberals as fellow trav-

---

* These included men like Carey McWilliams of *The Nation*; H. H. Wilson, politics professor at Princeton; Thomas I. Emerson of the Yale Law School; Bernard De Voto of *Harper's*; Vern Countryman and Fowler Harper of the Yale Law School; Mark deWolfe Howe of the Harvard Law School; Robert Hutchins of the Fund for the Republic; Albert Einstein; the historian Henry Steele Commager; Alan Barth of *The Washington Post*; and Harold Taylor of Sarah Lawrence.

elers. There was also a tiny minority of anti-Stalinist socialists who fought the persecution of Communists at every step.* Their journal was *Dissent,* and their message was that while Stalinism was an unqualified social evil, domestic Communists were entitled to the same rights and presumptions as the rest of our citizens. They denounced the congressional hearings and their adjuncts as intrusions on individual liberty.

But the majority of center liberals lived in the penumbra of the degradation ceremony and reinforced it by playing its game. McCarthy and McCarthyism were to be feared not because they represented a threat to individual rights so much as because they represented an interference in the fight against Communism. The degradation ceremony was deficient only to the extent that it confused an occasional "innocent" (anti-Stalinist) with the "guilty" (those unwilling to denounce Communism). But as long as it succeeded in delivering up bona fide reds the ceremony was to be supported.

The extent to which the center liberal had internalized the assumptions underlying and the myths advanced by the degradation ceremonies may be gathered from an article written in 1954 in *Commentary* by Alan Westin, later editor of the *Civil Liberties Review.* In assessing the effect of the Army-McCarthy hearings on American opinion, Westin considered the message of a 25¢ pamphlet called *McCarthy on Trial,* which itself used the degradation ceremony as a device by "trying" McCarthy in "the court of public opinion."

> By this time most readers will have recognized *McCarthy on Trial* for what it is—a full-strength dose of Communist propaganda peddled under the label of anti-McCarthyism. It is probably unnecessary to name the booklet's editor as Albert E. Kahn (*The Great Conspiracy against Russia*); to note that the "jury" had such trade-union affiliations as the Fur and Leather Workers, the Mine, Mill and Smelter Workers, and the United Electrical, Radio, and Machine Workers; to learn that the chief prosecution counsel was president of the New York City chapter of the National Lawyers Guild; or to go deeply into the political character of witnesses like Howard Fast, Mrs. Paul Robeson, and James Aronson (the executive editor of the *National Guardian*). Actually, the reader can get his bearings simply by looking at the books advertised by the same publisher (Cameron & Kahn) on the back cover of the

---

* These included scholars and journalists like Michael Harrington, Irving Howe, Paul Goodman, C. Wright Mills, and Erich Fromm.

pamphlet: *Eyewitness in Indochina* by Joseph Starobin, "the only American newspaperman yet to travel behind the Viet Minh lines, to interview Ho Chi Minh . . ." (and who just happens to be foreign correspondent for the *Daily Worker*); or *The Truth about Julius and Ethel Rosenberg* by John Wexley (also author of *They Shall Not Die* and *The Last Mile*). Nor is it difficult to see the book's conclusion for what it really is—an attempt by the Communists and Communist collaborators to slip back into respectability through the door of a new "popular front" against McCarthyism, and to exploit the fight against that unsavory and sinister politician solely in their own equally unsavory and sinister interest.[10]

What is at issue here is not the accuracy of Westin's analysis, but the genesis of his standards and assumptions. His assumptions about the National Lawyers Guild were informed by the attorney general's list, which although arbitrarily assembled had been legitimized partly through incessant invocation at countless investigative sessions as evidence that the deviant witnesses belonged to deviant organizations, Communist fronts. (Eventually the Lawyers Guild fought its way off the lists.) His assumptions about Angus Cameron (of Cameron & Kahn), one of America's most distinguished book editors, were informed by the fact that he was forced out of his job as editor-in-chief of Little, Brown less because of the undeniable political coloration of his list, than because of his well-known leftist politics and his refusal to ratify the rituals of the various committees which subpoenaed him. Where Westin is not assuming, he is playing the Committee's own game of intimation, as in his references to James Aronson and John Wexley. Thus did a committed libertarian, accepting the labels and definitions and symbols of the cold war, use them to degrade those men whose rights one would have thought he would defend.

Even when taking action against the cold war ceremonies, liberals could not always resist imitating them, so deeply had the rituals been internalized. We have already seen how James Wechsler chose to try to beat McCarthy at his own game, attempting to use his ritual against him and to play the unfriendly informer. The extraordinarily perceptive and talented journalist Richard Rovere, himself a former Young Communist Leaguer, provides a more poignant example of the same tactic.

Rovere was sitting in the press gallery one day when he heard Senator McCarthy begin to describe his latest case. A good listener with a better memory, Rovere quickly recognized that the suspect was someone who he had reason to believe was actually an unconfessed former Communist.

"I had the feeling, sitting there and listening to McCarthy harangue a practically nonexistent audience, that he might be on the point of enjoying his first real success."

Rovere saw a way of depriving the senator of his victory. As he wrote about it:

> Reluctantly—for it involved an intervention in politics which is something that, as a correspondent, I had always sought to avoid—I took it upon myself to go to an official of X's agency and tell him my story.... I made my point. And it turned out that X, in the course of the various security and loyalty checks he had been through, had chosen to conceal his Communist past—a choice that might allow any one of several moral judgments, but one that, to his misfortune, exposed him to charges of perjury. He was advised that it would be necessary to reopen the case. Within a few days, he quit the government.[11]

As John Caughey of UCLA later asked: "How does one explain a man, much opposed to McCarthy, acting to deny the senator a possible triumph but taking in stride that the means employed were pure McCarthyism? The king was dead, but his kingdom was well institutionalized on the conscious and unconscious levels. McCarthyism marched on."[12]

=====

With the years the blacklist passed. Its death was symbolized in publications, credits, prizes, honors, speeches, ceremonies. In 1952 the ACLU sponsored Merle Miller's *The Judges and the Judged,* an exposé of blacklisting in television, although his unhappy findings caused, as we have seen, a split in the ACLU's board of directors and a criticism by one ACLU board member for failing to give equal time to blacklisting by the left. In 1954 *Frontier* magazine published its blacklist exposé, "The Hollywood Story" by Elizabeth Poe Kerby, and in 1956 the Fund for the Republic's two-volume *Report on Blacklisting* appeared (which confirmed the earlier findings of Miller and *Frontier*); this prompted Congress to investigate not blacklisting but the fund and the authors of the report on what Chairman Walter called "so-called blacklisting."

In 1955 at the Cannes Film Festival, the blacklisted director Jules Dassin won an award for *Rififi* as a French entry. When an interviewer commented, *"Quelle belle revanche,"* Dassin said, "The truth is, it made me sad."[13] In 1956 the Academy Award for the best motion-picture story went to one "Robert Rich" for *The Brave One,* and when he failed to show up to accept it (those in attendance were told he was at the bedside of his wife who was about to give birth to their first baby), rumors spread that Rich also traveled under the name of Dalton Trumbo.

In 1957 the Oscar for best screenplay went to Pierre Boulle for *The Bridge On the River Kwai,* even though it was an open secret that the true screenwriters were the blacklisted Carl Foreman and Michael Wilson.

In 1958 an Academy Award was won by "Nathan E. Douglas" and Harold Jacob Smith for their joint screenplay of *The Defiant Ones.* Douglas turned out to be the blacklisted Ned Young (who, in an inside joke, appeared on the screen while the Douglas credit appeared).

In 1959 the Motion Picture Academy rescinded its bylaw prohibiting awards to those who refused to cooperate with HUAC. In 1960 Otto Preminger announced (and *The New York Times* reported on its front page) that Dalton Trumbo had written his upcoming United Artists release *Exodus.* Later in the same year Frank Sinatra declared in an ad in *Variety* that he had hired the blacklisted Albert Maltz to write the screenplay for *The Execution of Private Slovik,* although public pressure from the American Legion, the Catholic War Veterans, and the Hearst press (plus, it was rumored, a private request from presidential candidate John F. Kennedy's father) caused Sinatra to renege. And shortly after his election, the president-elect and his brother Robert crossed American Legion picket lines to see *Spartacus,* whose screenplay was openly credited to Trumbo.

In 1962 John Henry Faulk was awarded $3.5 million (later reduced to $550,000) in his six-year libel suit against his blacklisters—the fanatical Lawrence A. Johnson, owner of a chain of supermarkets in Syracuse, New York, who had mounted a campaign based largely on material from *Counterattack* and aimed directly at sponsors, agencies, and networks to prevent them from employing Faulk and other of "Stalin's little agents." Since about 60 percent of television advertising revenue came from goods sold in supermarkets, Johnson's campaign was effective. Other defendants in Faulk's suit were the professional anti-Communist Vincent Hartnett and his Aware, Inc., the organization which cleared for a fee the performers it exposed.

In 1963 CBS-Television presented a special drama entitled "Blacklist" on its long-running series *The Defenders,* by Ernest Kinoy, about a blacklisted actor in the 1950s. In 1965, *Inquisition in Eden,* Alvah Bessie's combative memoir on life under the blacklist and in prison was published by Macmillan. That same year Millard Lampell, accepting an Emmy for his Hallmark television drama "Eagle in a Cage," said simply, "I think I ought to mention I was blacklisted for ten years," and received a roaring ovation. In 1968 the blacklisted writer Waldo Salt won an Oscar for the screenplay of *Midnight Cowboy,* and the next year Ring Lardner, Jr., won for *M.A.S.H.* In 1969 the winner of Hollywood's coveted Laurel Award (given by the Screen Writers Guild) was the blacklisted director Carl Foreman, of whom his introducer said, "Those of us who lived through the era of fear in Hollywood have some slight conception of the guts it took for one man to stand up and risk his livelihood and his future in defense of a principle; to face exile from the country of his birth rather than compromise what he felt was his honor. It was six long and troubled years after he won the guild's award for his screenplay of *High Noon* before his name again appeared officially among the screen credits of a motion picture . . . and unlike the rest of us, he couldn't blame his agent."[14] The next year the Laurel Award went to Dalton Trumbo.

By 1975 CBS-TV and Xerox had won nationwide press coverage for David Rintels' special dramatization of "Fear on Trial," the story of how CBS-Radio and Aware, Inc., ganged up on John Henry Faulk. And then there was that evening in 1976 when the Screen Writers Guild chose Foreman to present the Laurel Award to Michael Wilson, and he proposed that they jointly send a letter to Pierre Boulle, the French author of *Bridge over the River Kwai,* credited with the screenplay they had written: "Dear Pierre. Hello there, how are you? We are fine, and hope you are the same. Say, by the way, do you think you might send us our Oscar, COD, and we will work out the custody for same between us. Thanking you in advance, yours truly, Mike and Carl."[15]

That same year saw the release of *The Front,* starring Woody Allen. The film was written by the blacklisted Walter Bernstein, produced and directed by the blacklisted Martin Ritt, and in the credits after each actor's name—Zero Mostel, John Randolph, Lloyd Gough, Joshua Shelley, Herschel Bernardi—appeared the date on which he was blacklisted. And the Motion Picture Academy amidst cheers and tears honored Lillian Hellman, whose just-published memoir, *Scoundrel Time*—entitled partly for the informers who the author felt should have known better—was a best-seller.

The sociologists of deviance, then, proved only partially correct prophets. These particular deviants, the blacklistees, reversed the "irreversible." They returned home and eventually resumed a "normal" life in their abnormal Hollywood. They invented their own rituals of return. They turned the tables. Events conspired to make having been a blacklistee something of a status symbol. They shed their stigma, transformed it into a badge of honor.

But the degradation ceremony had done its work too well. Even as the blacklistees reentered polite society, the myth of the informer as hero, the informer as patriot, passed from our culture. And when that happened, the denouncers themselves became victims of the ceremonies they had made possible. Now society at large began to see them the way their victims saw them—not as heroes but as villains, not as patriots but as betrayers. The stigmatizers became the stigmatized. If it was no longer possible to regard a Trumbo or a Lardner as an agent of a foreign power, it was all too easy to regard Parks or Kazan or Collins as informers "in essence." The denouncers rather than the denounced were stuck with their new identity. It was the informer who was now seen as "what he was all along." The sociologist Harold Garfinkel has explained that the paradigm of moral indignation is public denunciation. Remember the curse: "I call upon all men to bear witness that he is not as he appears but is otherwise and in essence of a lower species." As he elaborates in a footnote, "The person who passes on information to enemies is really, i.e. 'in essence,' 'in the first place,' 'all along,' 'in the final analysis,' 'originally,' an informer."[16]

They named the names because they thought nobody would remember, but it turned out to be the one thing that nobody can forget.

PART III
VICTIMS

THE SOCIAL COSTS of what came to be called McCarthyism have yet to be computed. By conferring its prestige on the red hunt, the state did more than bring misery to the lives of hundreds of thousands of Communists, former Communists, fellow travelers, and unlucky liberals. It weakened American culture and it weakened itself.

Unlike the Palmer Raids of the early 1920s, which were violent hit-and-run affairs that had no long-term effect, the vigilante spirit McCarthy represented still lives on in legislation accepted as a part of the American political way. The morale of the United States' newly reliable and devoted civil service was savagely undermined in the 1950s, and the purge of the Foreign Service contributed to our disastrous miscalculations in Southeast Asia in the 1960s and the consequent human wreckage. The congressional investigations of the 1940s and 1950s fueled the anti-Communist hysteria which eventually led to the investment of thousands of billions of dollars in a nuclear arsenal, with risks that boggle the minds of even those who specialize in "thinking about the unthinkable." Unable to tolerate a little subversion (however one defines it)—if that is the price of freedom, dignity, and experimentation—we lost our edge, our distinctiveness. McCarthyism decimated its alleged target—the American Communist Party, whose membership fell from about seventy-five thousand just after World War II to less than ten thousand in 1957 (probably a high percentage of these lost were FBI informants)—but the real casualties of that assault were the walking wounded of the liberal left and the already impaired momentum of the New Deal. No wonder a new generation of radical idealists came up through the peace and civil-rights movements rather than the Democratic Party.[1]

The damage was compounded by the state's chosen instruments of destruction, the professional informers—those ex-Communists whom the sociologist Edward Shils described in 1956 as a host of frustrated, previously anonymous failures, whose "fantasies of destroying American society and harming their fellow citizens, having fallen out with their equally villainous comrades, now provide a steady stream of information and misinformation about the extent to which Communists, as coherent and stable in character as themselves, penetrated and plotted to subvert American institutions."[2] Specific error can harm individuals, but the institutionalization of misinformation by way of the informer system may have contributed to the falsification of history. "As a rule, our memories romanticize the past," wrote Arthur Koestler. "But when one has renounced a creed or been betrayed by a friend, the opposite mechanism sets to work. In the light of that later knowledge, the original experience loses its innocence, becomes tainted and rancid in recollection.... Those who were caught in the great illusion of our time, and have lived through its moral and intellectual debauch, either give themselves up to a new addiction of the opposite type, or are condemned to pay with a lifelong hangover."[3]

Our lawmakers relied on, our media magnified, and our internal-security bureaucracy exploited and reinforced the images of Communism unleashed by the most sensational and therefore often least reliable of the ex-Communists. (Thoughtful if embittered men like Koestler were heeded in the academy but passed over in the popular press in favor of the Crouches, Cvetics, and Matusows.) Americans' political perspective was therefore distorted, their ability to distinguish myth from fact fatally compromised.

It is no easier to measure the impact of McCarthyism on culture than on politics, although emblems of the terror were ever on display. In the literary community, for example, generally thought to be more permissive than the mass media (a book can be produced for less than a fraction of what it costs to make a movie or a television show, and is harder to picket), the distinguished editor-in-chief of the distinguished publisher Little, Brown & Co. was forced to resign because he refused to repudiate his progressive politics and he became unemployable. Such liberal publications as the *New York Post* and the *New Republic* refused to accept ads for the *transcript* of the trial of Julius and Ethel Rosenberg. Albert Maltz's short story "The Happiest Man on Earth," which had won the O'Henry Memorial Short Story Award in 1938 and been republished seventy-six times in magazines, newspapers, and anthologies, didn't get reprinted again from the time he entered prison in 1950 until 1963. Ring Lardner, Jr., had to go to England to find a publisher for his critically acclaimed novel *The Ecstasy of Owen Muir.* (It didn't find a major publisher here until the 1960s, when it was reissued as part of a series of "classics" by New American Library.) The FBI had a permanent motion-picture crew stationed across the street from the Four Continents Bookstore in New York, which specialized in literature sympathetic to the Soviet Union's brand of Marxism. How to measure a thousand such pollutions of the cultural environment?

Sylvia Jarrico, former wife of the blacklisted Paul Jarrico, who was fired from her job as an editor with *Hollywood Quarterly* because she refused to sign the University of California loyalty oath, says simply, "We lived with the constant sense of being hunted." There is no knowing what intellectual losses were suffered by the widespread insistence on loyalty oaths at state universities, but George Stewart, reporting on the impact of the loyalty oath at the University of California in *The Year of the Oath* (1950), wrote that his colleagues exhibited "worry, depression, fatigue, fear, insomnia, drinking, headache, indigestion, failure to function well, worsening of relations to colleagues, suspicion, distrust, loss of self-respect." In May 1952 *The New York Times* reported intimidation of librarians across the nation by Legionnaires, by Sons and Daughters of the American Revolution, by Minutemen in Texas and California. School texts showing city slums, UNESCO material, all books by such threats to the free world as Howard Fast were purged from school libraries. Even the world of sports was not immune to the terror and the absurd assumptions it bred. The sportscaster Bill Stern observed over the Mutual Broadcasting System as late as October 6, 1958, that the lack of interest in "big time" football at New York University, Chicago, Harvard, and City College "is due to the widespread acceptance of Communism at the universities."[4]

Paul Tillett, the Rutgers University political scientist, in a study of McCarthyism, concluded:

> While it would be difficult to prove and probably inaccurate to say that loyalty purges as they affected Hollywood and television and the other performing arts created the vast wasteland that is American popular entertainment, the anti-Communist hysteria in cultural matters does put the quietus effectively on one branch of the argument for commercialism in culture. The repression of Communists—near, crypto and won't tell varieties—destroyed the notion that commercialism was a more effective guarantee of diversity than state-owned and -directed cultural enterprise.

When the question was raised, the moguls of Hollywood and Madison Avenue came to heel at the behest of a congressional committee without formal authority over them as meekly as the most obedient member of the Soviet cultural committees under Stalin and Khrushchev.[5]

It is simplistic to single out the blacklist, as its victims did at the time, as sole cause of the decline of American movies in the 1950s. Too many other factors complicated the picture and the pictures: the European market, which until then had subsisted on a diet of American films, had begun to discover its own filmmakers, so American films lost some of their overseas market; after World War II, general economic conditions in the film business had deteriorated; and the Supreme Court's ruling in 1948 that many distribution and exhibition practices were illegal meant that studios no longer had guaranteed distribution for their product. "The situation in which it was impossible to make a flop turned completely around," recalls Michael Gordon, who remembers a cost-cutting meeting at Universal where it was explained that all but two of the studio's twenty-four films were in the red. Then there was the installation of the coaxial cable for television in the late 1940s, which brought with it the first network television on a nationwide basis. Dalton Trumbo told me, "Even though we attributed the great box-office decline, which began in 1948 and reached its nadir in 1952, to lack of us, that wasn't true. It was the rise of television." And, to make matters more difficult, the currency freeze in Great Britain, France, Italy, and West Germany under which a studio could spend credits in these countries but not take all of its earnings out of them eliminated the margin of profit on most films; this contributed to a sense of alarm.

We do not, of course, know what we have lost in the way of movies unmade, ideas unhatched, scripts not written, talent undeveloped, careers abandoned, consciousnesses unrevised. And we cannot verify the belief of people like the screenwriter Paul Jarrico, who saw "a direct relation between the blacklist and the increasing emphasis of the Hollywood film on prowar and antihuman themes. We have seen more and more pictures of violence-for-the-sake-of-violence, more and more unmotivated brutality on the screen as the blacklist grew."[6] (One difficulty with his argument is that after the blacklist died the violence continued to escalate.)

Was the blacklist, as John Howard Lawson and others contended, a form of thought-control? Did it succeed, as Mark Jacobson, writing in the mid-1970s, claimed, in smashing "the hopes of the New York crowd for a cinema of ideas in this country"?[7] The screenwriter Ian McClellan

Hunter said yes: "We really felt that sooner or later the Louis B. Mayers and the other studio people would die off and we would be able to make more provocative films. . . . The blacklist stopped us right in our tracks."

Perhaps in the absence of the blacklist the political culture of the 1930s and 1940s would have given birth to a newly experimental cinema in the 1950s. Perhaps *Salt of the Earth* (1954), product of the blacklist underground, which, whatever its limitations, anticipated both the feminist and independent film-producing movements by more than a decade (not to mention its premature concern for the Chicano), is but a crude specimen of what might have been. Or perhaps not. The point is that we will never know. We will also never know how many of the taboos that have beset commercial television in the United States since the late 1940s—when its habits, values, assumptions, and basic perspective on the world were being shaped—were determined by the blacklist atmosphere.

For a while it was fashionable to downgrade the talent of the blacklistees. Murray Kempton wrote an entertaining chapter in *Part of Our Time* (1955) listing the trash films that some of these people had committed. Arthur Schlesinger, Jr., argued that they tithed by night to make up for their hackery by day.[8] But as we have already seen the blacklistees won too many delayed awards to be collectively discounted as hacks. Michael Wilson was right when he observed that a majority of them were younger writers who were just beginning to come into their own, as the subsequent careers of men like Lardner and Salt would seem to prove. "As to other of the so-called no-talent writers, well, it's true their talents do get rusty after fifteen years without employment, and if they've turned to other ways of life and other kinds of jobs, it doesn't mean they never had talent, it means that they never had a chance to develop or prove it."

It is one of the minor ironies of the period that while HUAC found little evidence of Communist influence in films, Dorothy Jones, in her study for the Fund for the Republic, found considerable evidence of the impact of HUAC. From 1950 to 1952 there were fewer social-theme movies like the earlier *The Best Years of Our Lives* (1946), *Crossfire* (1947), and *Naked City* (1948), and more "pure entertainment," war movies, and anti-Communist films, the latter including such duds as *The Conspirator* (1950), *Peking Express* (1951), and *Red Planet Mars* (1952). (In 1952 alone, thirteen anti-Communist films were released.) "Probably never before in the history of Hollywood," wrote Jones, "had such a large number of films been produced which the industry itself doubted would prove really profitable at the box office. During the years 1947–52 only one major studio, Universal-International, did not make any so-called anti-Communist films.[9]

A short-lived publication sponsored by blacklistees and their friends,

Hollywood Review (1955), took the trouble to try to trace the blacklist's effect on film content. An interesting article by Adrian Scott, one of the Hollywood Ten, reveals the methodological problems of such an enterprise. First, he listed distinguished films made by writers and directors who then were blacklisted: *Watch on the Rhine, Our Vines Have Tender Grapes, Mr. Smith Goes to Washington, Here Comes Mr. Jordan, The Naked City, Action in the North Atlantic, The Talk of the Town,* and *Thirty Seconds over Tokyo.*

Scott then compared the contemporary work of nonblacklisted writers and directors with their earlier films. He contrasted John Ford's early films such as *The Informer* (1935), *The Grapes of Wrath* (1940), and *How Green Was My Valley* (1941) with his more recent *The Quiet Man* (1952)—"stereotyped Irish quaintness"—and *The Long Gray Line* (1954)—"sentimentalized West Point." William Dieterle's early "tributes to the capacity of the human intellect"—films on Pasteur, Zola, and *Dr. Ehrlich's Magic Bullet* (1940)—found no counterpart in *Elephant Walk* (1954), a romantic drama about white plantation owners. Scott juxtaposed William Wyler's *The Little Foxes* (1941) with his "watered down" *Carrie* (1951). He contrasted *Dead End* (1937) with *Detective Story* (1951)—the earlier film presenting "juvenile delinquency as a social problem requiring a social solution," while the later "dealt with police brutality wholly in terms of the personality of an individual ... without relation to social responsibility in how he wields his authority." Nunnally Johnson's screenplay for *The Grapes of Wrath* (1940) far overshadowed his later *How to Marry a Millionaire* (1953) or *How to Be Very, Very Popular* (1955). Scott also argued that the industry had ended a cycle of films about American race relations (*Home of the Brave, Intruder in the Dust*) which might have led to a new consciousness. Instead it inaugurated a campaign to glorify the businessman (*Executive Suite, Sabrina, Patterns*).

The change in the political climate could be seen, Scott wrote, in a content-analysis of the films of Elia Kazan. *Boomerang, A Tree Grows in Brooklyn*, and *Gentleman's Agreement* were "excellent liberal films" contrasted with *Viva Zapata* ("theme: power corrupts revolutionaries"), *On the Waterfront* ("theme: courageous stool pigeon frees sheeplike longshoremen from tyranny of corrupt union") and *East of Eden* ("theme: good is really evil and evil really good in this hopeless, meaningless world").

Scott did not pretend to analyze the anti-Communist films—which were for the most part low-budget items made by second-rate talent. Looking at the best Hollywood had to offer, he concluded: "Few if any of

the films made by these men and their colleagues since 1947 have drama-
tized the humanist, democratic, and antifascist values that illuminated
their work in the Roosevelt era. Their talents remain, but the ideas to
which they applied their talents have been eroded and forbidden." Thus
"the blacklisting of other men was in reality the blacklisting of the liberals' own ideas."[10]

Although Scott's somewhat mechanistic, ideologically culture-bound
political aesthetic consigned clearly superior films like *Waterfront* and
arguably superior ones like *Eden* to critical purgatory because he did not
like their values, his catalogue if not his analysis usefully suggests the
magnitude of our loss.

———

Even if it were possible to disentangle the effects of the various elements in the McCarthy period—the informer system, Hollywood division, the blacklist system, the congressional investigations, the larger
repression, the international cold war—the prospect of quantifying the
social cost of any one of them is overwhelming. Nevertheless, since institutions were transformed, content influenced, individuals injured, and
vast public and private resources expended, it seems important to try separately to trace the effect of the informer alone, without whom the blacklist and many other aspects of the purge would not have been possible.
To single out the informer is not to minimize the significance of the investigating committees themselves and the entire internal-security bureaucracy as causal agents of repression; it is merely to affirm that without the
informer—who was seen as the proximate cause of evil by many of the
most visible victims—Hollywood's overnight disintegration could not
have happened in quite the way it did.

The Greek word "stigma" originally referred to a bodily sign to indicate the bearer was "a blemished person, ritually polluted, to be avoided,
especially in public places."[11] In this definition lies a clue to the nature of
the treble damages inflicted by the informer—on his intended victims, on
the collectivity, on himself.

11.

The Intended Victim

DEATH IMAGERY and the odor of contagious disease pervade the literature about the informer. Stefan Kanfer aptly called his study of the blacklist *A Journal of the Plague Years,* after the Defoe novel that followed the progress of a disease sweeping across an entire society.

The blacklist involved hundreds at the center and thousands at the periphery, but in the tales about the blacklist the names that keep recurring, like entries in a Domesday Book, are Mady Christians, Canada Lee, John Garfield, Philip Loeb, and J. Edward Bromberg, all of whom seemed to die of blacklist.

Mady Christians, the Mama of *I Remember Mama* (1948), was a veteran of more than sixty pictures when she was listed in *Red Channels.* Her sin had been compassion for Spanish civil war veterans and exiled German writers, and membership in organizations like the American Committee for the Protection of the Foreign-Born, which acted on her interests but also were on the attorney general's list of Communist-front organizations. She was visited by the usual retinue of investigators, and soon her phone stopped ringing, the jobs stopped coming. She grew ill, tired, her blood pressure went up. Her health took a turn for the better when the Maugham TV Theater offered her a role in *The Mother,* sponsored by Tintair. A week before rehearsals were to begin the producer called to say it was all a mistake: She could have the salary but not the role. Shortly afterward she was hospitalized and wrote a friend, "I cannot bear yet to think of the thing which led to my breakdown. One day I shall put them down as a record of something unbelievable." On October 28, 1951, she collapsed at the home of a Connecticut friend and died of a cerebral hemorrhage.

Canada Lee, it will be recalled, had been banned from forty television shows and died penniless and alone.

Philip Loeb was Papa on *The Goldbergs*, for many years a top-rated weekly television series. His wife was dead, his son an institutionalized schizoid. His *Red Channels* listing was long, including such items as his having signed a petition defending the Moscow purge trials, his membership in the Council for Pan-American Democracy, an organization to End Jim Crow in Baseball, and other relics on the attorney general's list. He had also been active in AFTRA politics. General Foods wanted him fired from *The Goldbergs*, which it sponsored, but Gertrude Berg, the owner-writer-star of the show (she played Molly), said no, and CBS dropped the show. NBC picked it up but nobody would sponsor it. Gertrude Berg came to Loeb with an offer of settlement: If he would take $85,000 the show could go on. He would be out of work, but the forty other people on the show could continue. "I'm sorry," he said, "I have no price." But as the months passed he couldn't meet the expenses he had in keeping his son in a private mental institution, and by 1951 he had accepted the settlement, which had dwindled to $40,000. In 1953 he got his last job—in a revival, at $87.50 a week—his son was in a state home in Massachusetts, and the *American Mercury* ran a story by Vincent Hartnett on "New York's Great Red Way" which featured Loeb as "one of the loudest noises on the popular front." At the age of sixty-one, in 1955, he checked into a room at the Hotel Taft and took the pills that took his life. His sister wept and said, "He's been hurt so terribly. Now see what they did to him. They took his living away. They took his life away. A person can only stand so much."[1]*

J. Edward Bromberg, Group Theatre alumnus, guru, chess master, and character actor, presented the Committee in 1951 with a doctor's certificate that described his rheumatic heart condition, said he had recently experienced an attack of congestive failure, and asked that he be excused. Congressman Walter said he knew from experience "that you can get doctors to make statements as to almost anything" and refused the request (although previous postponements had been granted). Under obvious physical stress on the stand, Bromberg was asked by Congressman Wood if he'd like "a little recess" but he pridefully declined.[2]

In 1946, his son Conrad remembers, he was jumping all over the stage in *Volpone* with no ill effects. Named that year before California's Fact-Finding Committee on Un-American Activities, known as the Tenney

---

*In *The Front*, starring Woody Allen and the once blacklisted Zero Mostel, Mostel, playing the role of a blacklisted borscht-belt comedian, enters a hotel room and, like Philip Loeb, on whom the character was partly based, goes out the window.

Committee, there followed five years of FBI visits, harassment, uncertainty, and chronic unemployment. In 1951, having worked only two weeks in all that time, he had to be carried up a hill at Crystal Lake after his performance in Dalton Trumbo's comedy *The Biggest Thief in Town*—his first job in months. He died in 1952 in London, where he had gone to do a play. "He took the risk of going to London," according to his son, "because he considered the job almost a statement, showing that the English would take him when the Americans wouldn't."

On one level, these case studies in martyrdom are misleading: They collectively appear to suggest that the victims of the blacklist were primarily cases of mistaken identity, since of the lot, only J. Edward Bromberg had been a Communist Party member; but the overwhelming majority of HUAC's immediate targets *were* Communists and former Communists. Although it served the Party's interest to present the "witch-hunters" as indiscriminate smearers, in fact HUAC came to specialize in red-baiting reds and former reds. The real vice of HUAC was not that it bagged the wrong quarry but that it had no moral, political, or constitutionally legitimate hunting license in the first place. On a deeper level, though, the death imagery is appropriate—as a metaphor for jobs lost, careers smashed, marriages broken, promises unfulfilled throughout the plague years. The informer's disease was contagious. Once the germ of suspicion, mistrust, and betrayal was in the air, there was no telling who would be HUAC's next victim, and no knowing for sure exactly who were its present ones.

Few people actually died as a result of being informed against, and after the discovery that the timely invocation of the Fifth Amendment would provide the legal protection that the Hollywood Ten had lacked, few went to prison, but the pain was no less for those on the periphery. Witness the case of R. Lawrence ("Larry") Siegel, preeminent attorney, special counsel to the ACLU, who represented, among others, Sarah Lawrence College, the writer-producer Sidney Buchman, the choreographer Jerome Robbins, the superstar Gloria Swanson, and, as a *pro bono* client, *The Nation* magazine. When Harvey Matusow came to *The Nation* in 1954 with his tale of false-witnessing against HUAC targets, the magazine's editor, Carey McWilliams, sent him to see Siegel. Told that Siegel was at his client Gloria Swanson's apartment, young Harvey, always entranced by show-biz, barged in on Siegel, Swanson, and a man involved in a matrimonial action in which Swanson was a potential corespondent and commenced to regale them with tales of his misspent youth as an informer which he blamed for his failure to launch a career as an entertainer. Siegel returned to his office and, as was his habit, dictated a memorandum summarizing the conversation.

Later, after Matusow claimed that he had fabricated testimony in a Smith Act case at Roy Cohn's request, the government suspected a conspiracy to get Matusow to recant involving *The Nation*, its counsel, and its associate publisher, Martin Solow (who alerted the Mine, Mill and Smelter Workers Union to Matusow's recantation since his testimony had helped convict one of their staff). Siegel was called before a grand jury and asked to produce his memoranda. To spare Swanson (whose contract included a "morals clause") some embarrassment, his law associate had already exorcised the names from the retyped notes that Siegel now turned over. Siegel says that before entering the grand jury room he told the prosecutor, Thomas Bolan, that the notes had been retyped to spare a client embarrassment, but Bolan insisted that the omissions were intended to cover up the *Nation* conspiracy. Solow took the Fifth Amendment. Siegel and his associate were subjected to criminal investigation and prosecution, which, given the climate of the times, was disastrous. Thirty-five lawyers declined to handle Siegel's case.

It may seem superfluous to add yet more pages to the seemingly endless catalogue of misfortunes, but the screenwriter Ben Barzman's recollection of a brief moment in his life in France suggests the grand circumference of damage done:

> In 1956 when Jules Dassin and I had done *He Who Must Die,* which was selected to represent France in the Cannes Film Festival, the American delegation consistently avoided us. Marcel Pagnol, the president of the Cannes jury, whom I met on the train returning to Paris after the festival, told me openly that pressure had been brought on him and the other French members of the jury, by elements of the American delegation, to avoid giving our film a major prize—[the situation was complicated by the fact that the previous two awards had gone to offbeat French entries, but this alone would not have justified the Americans' threat to withdraw permanently from the festival]. . . . He also indicated that even Jean Cocteau, who had also been on the jury, had submitted to the pressure.[3]

The career contamination survived in time as well as space. (That agents, very late in the game, spared their clients' egos by telling them that works which were turned down on the merits were victims of political discrimination, merely escalated the paranoia and the pain.) Lester Cole of the Hollywood Ten, who believes that there is still a special presumption going against him when he deals with politically controversial material, recalls that as late as 1965, when he wrote a screenplay of *Born Free* for Columbia, Michael Frankovich, its president, "was so fearful that he wanted to throw my screenplay out and start over, but this the producer [Carl Foreman] refused to do, so we ended up with a pseudonym."

As the infection frequently spread beyond the Hollywood community, the idea that being named served to inoculate one against further disability turned out to be untrue. The agent George Willner, for instance, lost his partnership at the Goldstone Agency after he was first named before HUAC. Since he had been a furniture salesman and a car salesman before he became a talent salesman, he got himself a job selling textiles and became best friends with the two brothers who were the main buyers of the textiles he was selling. "Well, when Mel Levy named George [in January 1952] it appeared on the front pages of the L.A. papers," recalls George Sklar, a blacklisted writer, "and these two guys were dumbfounded. They called up George's boss and they said, 'Look, if this guy is a Commie, you've got to fire him. We're not going to buy anything from him, we're not going to do business with you if you've got a Communist selling stuff.' And he was fired."

Multiple naming, leading to multiple punishment, sometimes seemed accidental, as in Willner's case, and other times it seemed inevitable. Thus being named before a state Un-American Activities Committee was, like a rash on the skin, often a symptom of more serious trouble to come. One actor, for example, was named before the Canwell Committee in Seattle in 1948, was fired, and, thirty years later observed:

> I was compelled to leave Seattle, where I had lived for twenty-five years, because the theater I had helped found and in which I had invested twenty years of my life and a great deal of personal sacrifice, had been destroyed and I was no longer able to earn a living, either in or out of the theater, there. There were a lot of other painful personal results: item, the night before the Canwell hearings commenced, my mother fell and broke her hip in the most Freudian of accidents; she never walked again and this hastened her death within three years, preceded by the dissipation of all her assets (and any inheritance my brother and I might have shared) to pay for nursing care. Item, a love affair was seriously undermined by differences over the hearings; it lingered on and received the coup de grace as a result of the House Committee hearings. Item, as a result of the House Committee-spawned *Counterattack,* Aware, Inc., and Lawrence Johnson's attention, I was a

second time deprived of a chance to make a living at my chosen profession and had to turn typist because legitimate theater (especially off-Broadway) income alone was insufficient to (as the phrase has it) sustain life. (This last was more of a wrench than I daresay it should have been; it was an honorable way to earn part of a living, but it was a bitter pill; I thought the holder of a Phi Beta Kappa key ought to be able to do better than that, but I learned otherwise.) I lost a few friends as a result of the hearings, but surprisingly few, and some of those have returned; I do not count this as a matter of large importance.[4]

It is true that some Hollywood writers could work on the black market (it was more difficult for directors and virtually impossible for actors). But even work on the black market took its toll. The conditions under which one labored—pay at a fraction of one's worth, no credit, an inability to decline work on uncongenial projects, no contact with producer and/or director—were calculated to spread cynicism, corruption, contempt. Michael Wilson noted: "The degree of hysteria or fear or degradation depended on how close or how far away one was from Hollywood. In France I had no problems. But before I left Hollywood I had one job where I never went to the producer. He was so frightened of being associated with me he would bring cash to the corner druggist, a pharmacist. The degradation came when the man didn't like what I had done and I couldn't even get a hearing to prove to the man I was working for—whom I never met—that the way I wanted to do it was right."

Millard Lampell recalled that he spent nine months finishing the assignments of a well-known writer who had writer's block, until one night the man appeared at his door and said Lampell had to stop, on advice of his analyst: "He says I'm losing my identity."[5]

In the course of litigation challenging the blacklist, John Howard Lawson was asked by an attorney if he really thought his black-market script for a B picture called *Terror in a Texas Town* was worth more than the $5000 he was paid; Lawson pointed out that in ordinary times he might have gotten $100,000 or $150,000 for such a script. But was it worth that? asked the attorney. "No, I would not have done a picture of that type if I had not been in the black market. And furthermore, if it had not been for that situation, I would have been able to work with the producer and director, and the picture would have been, in my opinion, a success. I was placed in an impossible situation in relation to the preparation and production of that film, which was recognized by the producer as well as by myself."[6]

Walter Bernstein, the screenwriter who wrote *The Front* and himself had about a dozen fronts over a period of eight years, recalled how he got his own name back on screen. The director Sidney Lumet arranged for him to do a screenplay for the Italian producer Carlo Ponti. After the screenplay, *That Kind of Woman* (1959), was finished, it was rumored that Bernstein might be served with a subpoena to testify before HUAC. A meeting was called and Ponti flew in from Italy, and the situation was explained to him. "He rattled off a stream of Italian," Bernstein recalls, "and then his interpreter turned to us and said, 'Mr. Ponti would like to know who has to be fixed and how much it will cost.'"

"Most of us," says a character in Studs Terkel's book *Working,* "are looking for a calling, not a job. Most people have jobs too small for their spirit." Many of the intended victims of the informer system in Hollywood were people who thought they had found a calling—or at least were in the process of discovering one, in a rich and rapidly developing medium. To see their right to practice their art and craft suddenly taken away for what appeared to be reasons of political malice, or sometimes, more pettily, someone else's convenience,* seemed cruel and unusual punishment.

---

* In 1954, with approximately 25,000 members in the Hollywood guilds, only 438 were under term contract, and only 1,543 received unemployment insurance (of whom two-thirds were in production and distribution). Thus only 514 out of 24,518 unemployed guild workers had enough part-time work to accrue some unemployment insurance benefits. The blacklist, which rendered at least 300 unemployable, lessened the competition for guild jobs. (Figures: cited in a letter to Frank Donner from Alice Orans, 10 June 1955, private files of Frank Donner.)

12.
The Community as Victim

THE BLACKLIST SAVAGED PRIVATE LIVES, but the informer's particular contribution was to pollute the public well, to poison social life in general, to destroy the very possibility of a community; for the informer operates on the principle of betrayal and a community survives on the principle of trust.

In Hollywood during the HUAC days, friend became afraid of friend, client suspected agent, actors feared that other actors who wanted their parts were turning them in. "You didn't know who was for you or against you," recalls Conrad Bromberg. "One of the confusions of the period was between the prosecution and the defense. Victor Riesel or George Sokolsky would contact Dad and say, 'How do you feel? We understand that there is a picture being made at Fox,' and the implication was that they had the ear of the major studios. So there was always the chance of changing your mind and becoming an informer. It was like option time. Over a five-year period they'd call maybe twenty times . . . . You'd have to make the same decision over and over. So you'd ask yourself what is this man doing for me or against me? You were never quite sure."

Two men in a parked car across the street from one's house meant that the FBI was watching you. If you didn't get a part, it had nothing to do with talent, looks, age, or style—it meant you were black- or graylisted. If old friends weren't heard from, it was not because they were away or preoccupied or even insulted, but because they were afraid to see you, either because you were tarnished or because they were about to inform. "Our best friends called the night we testified and told us not to come to a party that Friday night at their house," says Helen Levitt, wife of the blacklisted writer Al Levitt. The surround no longer seemed neutral.

If the blacklisted people occasionally overestimated the dangers and perils of their situation, that would be only natural, for they had to compensate for having underestimated them before. Many lived in a state of constant apprehension, because generalized fear had destroyed their capacity to screen signs of danger out of their line of vision. Moreover, while one could grieve for lost friends, one couldn't grieve for an "informer," and this merely added to the pain. "The day one of my closest friends reeled off his list, all mutual close friends, I felt the first sharp twinge in my guts," says the actor Philip Brown (who had fled to England). "What a terrifying dilemma to be faced with! How could I be angry with him? Do you get angry with someone you love because they have fallen victim to an illness? Can you hate a man who you knew was finding the simplest act of facing himself in the mirror to shave an almost unbearable experience? Can you castigate a man who must keep away from his familiar haunts for fear of running into friends whose lives he has wrecked? Can you forgive him?" Often the loss of friendship was bemoaned but not the friends, which led to disconnectedness, alienation, depression, and further loss of a sense of community.

So profound were the alienation and ambiguity that thirty years later it is still impossible to be certain where shrewd and prudent suspicion stopped and paranoia began. The blacklisted writer Millard Lampell wrote in 1966, "There was no way of getting proof that I was actually on a list, no easy way to learn the damning details. My income simply dropped from a comfortable five figures to $2000 a year. Finally I ran into an old friend, a producer who had downed a few too many martinis, and he leveled with me. 'Pal, you're dead. I submitted your name for a show and they told me I couldn't touch you with a barge pole.' He shrugged unhappily. 'It's a rotten thing, I hate it, but what can I do?' And with a pat on my cheek: 'Don't quote me, pal, because I'll deny I said it.' "[1]

Robert Rossen's son Stephen recalls that when his father was named, his parents explained to him that years before his father had joined the Communist Party, "which was then a good party dedicated to social causes of the sort that we as poor Jews from New York were interested in. Then we stopped being Communists, and now they were trying to use it against us.

"So I told my best friend that I thought I should explain it to him, and I went through the whole song and dance, and my friend didn't seem to know what I was talking about. But I went back to California twenty-five years later and I looked him up—an old friend from the neighborhood. And all the time when the Communist Party was having scotch and soda in our house (which is all they did, really), the FBI evidently was en-sconced at my friend's father's house, across the street. He was a doctor, and he said, 'I don't care what you do, just don't make a mess.' My best friend's mother had told my best friend, 'You better not go over to that house anymore, because Robert Rossen is in trouble and [his wife] is in it too.' So I said, 'Why didn't you tell me? What kind of a friend are you?' "

Disaster studies indicate that the trauma experienced by survivors of earthquakes, floods, airplane crashes, or such generally occurs in two phases. According to Kai Erikson, first there is numbness of spirit, rage, anxiety, depression, apathy, insomnia, loneliness, anomie, inability to concentrate, helplessness, preoccupation with death, a retreat into depen-dency, a heightened apprehension about the environment, a general loss of ego functions—in other words, the very symptoms exhibited by the blacklistees. Phase two, however, is supposed to be euphoria, when the survivors discover they outnumber the victims after all, that all is not lost, that things are not as bad as they at first appeared.[2] But the destruc-tion of the Hollywood community yielded no such euphoria. For Holly-wood, despite all the jokes ("Strip away the phony tinsel and you'll find the real tinsel underneath"), was not merely a place where people lived. It was a unique company town whose inhabitants invested their energies in and defined themselves by the community life. And when the sense of community died so did a part of themselves.

Even the members of the red subculture defined themselves by more than their political commitments. They had their work (often an elabo-rate collaboration among agent, actor, director, producer, et al., a truly collective effort); their contracts (often for seven years, with an option clause that the studio, but not the talent, could cancel on six months' no-tice); their love-hate relationship with the founding moguls (whom they mocked as vulgarians and fought as exploiters but on whose favor and sentimental support they counted in time of trouble); their shared status system (credits, salaries, sexual conquests, swimming pools). Over the years the Hollywood red subculture had earned a weird coherence by the way it held these contrary tendencies in balance. Their secret CP mem-bership combined with their open "antifascist" work, their aesthetic sen-sibilities combined with their writing to formula, their identification with the proletariat combined with incomes that varied from unemployment compensation to "the high six figures"—all of these were interwoven in a network of personal relationships and business and social bonds that gave a fragile but nevertheless real integration to the life of the community; these happy (and unhappy) few would take care of one another. The secrecy provided a context for intimacy, the community of three hundred "friends"—who were always meeting or discussing or going to a cause party together—provided a cushion for pain, an overnight sense of tradition, and, within the strange values of Hollywood, a moral anchor.

No matter where they fled, members of the community seemed to carry the blacklist in their hearts. Their sense of isolation was not eased by the discovery that few people outside their community knew about it. "We lived the blacklist every day from 1946 to 1951," recalls Conrad Bromberg. "After my father died in January 1952 I went to work in an auto factory of seven thousand workers in L.A., and not one man there had heard of the blacklist. It was a very dim image on the part of anybody who had not been close to it, though they were fascinated once you started to talk about it. This was the blacklist—it's the story of the middle class in America, a raging battle fought in a very small room. For most people it was, not prison or bread. It was the frustration of the American dream—that you won't be a star. Instead of making fifty thousand dollars a year acting or writing, you'll have to do it another way." Thus was Ring Lardner able to parody the conspicuous-consumption ethic of the American middle class when he placed a classified ad in the "Houses for Sale/Owner Going Abroad" section of *Variety* reading, "House for Sale/Owner Going to Prison!"

Even before the blacklist, many members of the movie colony felt they were inhabitants of a political-cultural schizophrenia. "Now we hated what we were doing, and we were living in a kind of—what I would call a fascist society," says the Brooklyn-born screenwriter Leonard Spigelgass. "If you worked for Fox, if you worked for Louis B. Mayer, you did what you were told to do. At the end of the Depression most of the men and some of the women out here were doing very well, making between two hundred fifty dollars and a thousand dollars a week and everybody else was starving to death. Now we recognized when a film was cheesy and awful and appalling, but my God, what do you do? Leave five hundred dollars and one thousand dollars a week and go back to New York and not make anything a week? Not that we were conscious of it at the time, but we began to become lefter and lefter to help those who were not so fortunate. It was a form of compensation."

Some argue that because the blacklisted Hollywood people were "swimming-pool Communists" who had been fighting neither for their lives nor for bread, they weren't really victims in any serious sense and one needn't feel too sorry for them after all. But the fact is that one's membership in the middle class may define the nature of, but cannot isolate one from, the pain that comes with joblessness. Virtually every member of the old left community in Hollywood was wounded, hurt, devastated, traumatized. If it had only been a matter of losing jobs or changing professions or cutting back on salary, it might have been manageable—many writers survived in body and spirit by working the black market, no matter how this might have corrupted the soul. But people were forced to sell their homes, to leave the community, to move on to something else. And one's house and friends and work and place were a part of one's self. Funny and elitist as it sounds, one's swimming pool was often part of one's identity—the evidence not so much of *where* one belonged but *that* one belonged to a special status hierarchy. To sell one's status was to give up a part of one's identity. And one couldn't go into the commissary and talk it over with and seek solace from one's colleagues, because one was banned from the studio lot. One couldn't even commiserate with friends and neighbors, because often one's neighbors and occasionally one's friends feared that the FBI might be watching the house or tapping the phone—at a time when it was believed that the FBI thought that friendship meant comradeship meant red complicity. Albert Maltz, according to one FBI informant, was "a colonel in the Red Army."

It is difficult to recapture the sense of isolation felt by these spiritual refugees. Betrayed by close friends, lacking the insulation provided by community solidarity, they felt especially vulnerable and exposed to the hostility of the state, whose agents often followed up public denunciation with private harassment. "The U.S. government can really harass you, I want to tell you," says Abe Polonsky, the writer-director. "They went around to where people were on jobs and got them fired. Even the jobs that had nothing to do with writing. Not only that, but if people moved into an apartment house, the FBI would show up and talk to the janitor or whoever. The landlord would say, for instance, 'Well, maybe if this guy is a criminal we ought to get him out of here.' And they would say, 'Oh, no, he's not a criminal, but we just want to be sure he's still living here.' Well, now you know there's something wrong with this guy, and everybody hears about it. Obviously it was possible for the FBI to find out if someone was living in an apartment house without going around and asking questions about it. And this was only one of hundreds of routine kinds of checks on people."

When the state didn't attempt direct punishment, individuals frequently imposed sanctions on themselves. Guilt was in the air, and, in the absence of community support, many people internalized the larger society's verdict. They behaved like criminals even though they had committed no crime. Goldie Bromberg, Conrad's mother, would come home every night, cook supper, go into her room, close the door, and cry. She didn't want to hear the outside world. "She has survived," says her son, "by blocking it out." George Sklar recalls walking with his wife in Beverly Hills and seeing "one of them" coming down the street. This is enemy territory, he remembers thinking to himself, and he vowed to stay away from the area. Many actually fled to Mexico—some to avoid subpoenas, others for fear they would be framed "like the Rosenbergs," others in hope of finding tranquillity.

Suspicion, it can be argued, was a healthy response to the situation, since there was more than enough to be suspicious about. Lester Cole's contretemps with the writer Melvin Levy provides a sad case study in the anatomy of such suspicion. Cole, waiting to go to prison as one of the Hollywood Ten, was offered a black-market job writing a film script in 1950, provided he come up with a front—a collaborator who could go on the studio payroll and complete the script when and if Cole went to prison. He came up with Levy; they came up with a script outline; it found favor; and they had started on the screenplay when Cole went to prison. Levy continued to go to the studio every day, but, according to Cole, a few weeks later the checks to Mrs. Cole stopped coming. "When my wife called Levy to ask what had happened," says Cole, "Levy said, 'Do you mind if I skip a week? I'll make it up.' Well, he skipped one week, then two, and after that he wasn't returning her calls. We later found out that he remained on the payroll eight weeks and then he was fired."

A few months later, in the Danbury, Connecticut, federal prison, Cole and his fellow inmates were listening one day to the four o'clock news when who should come on the air as a HUAC witness but Levy, who proceeded to mention Cole's name not once but a number of times.[3] "By repeating my name many times he was seeking psychologically to destroy me," theorizes Cole. "Or maybe he was simply trying to blot me out of his memory because of what he had done to me."

Levy offers a different if more obscure version. "I went to Washington [to testify] for one reason—because somebody, at my request, had stuck her neck out to do a great favor for Lester Cole, and in order that she not be denounced I went to Washington. Lester got the money up until the moment when I didn't have any more, and then he didn't get any more. His wife said, 'We've got a lot and you haven't any, so don't worry about it.'

"Lester thinks I made a deal with the Committee. If I had, I wouldn't have been blacklisted for ten years. I lived selling my blood and getting two hundred and fifty dollars while someone else got fifteen hundred and two thousand dollars for the same work. I came home one day literally ready to blow my brains out when the phone rang. It was a producer who wanted to help. I ran to the studio, and as I entered all these people whom I hadn't seen for ten years said, 'Mel, where have you been?' "

The issue here isn't who is telling the truth, who has the better memory. The point is that suspicion knows no neat boundaries, especially when it is born of friend betraying friend. Other things being equal in the Hollywood of the 1950s, an appropriate amount of paranoia might have functioned as a social preservative. Petty deception became the rule, and, as a result, for many people routine social life became intolerable, a counterfeit, an upside-down moral universe in which honesty and openness came to seem like cruelty or insensitivity. To drop one's guard was to offend. When the writer Vera Caspary returned to America after writing *Wedding in Paris,* a London musical, she and "I.G.," her producer-husband, reopened their Hollywood house, and one night they had a blacklisted writer named Josef Mischel and his wife, Florence, to dinner. Caspary remembers: "An actress who had worked in a picture and had become very fond of my husband called up and said she would like to come up after the movies with her new husband. And with them were two people, including a guy who had named names, Roland Kibbee, whom we all liked very much. But I suddenly realized that here was a guy who was blacklisted over for dinner and here was one who sang. And I lied. I said, 'We're very tired, it's getting late, I.G. has a reading or something in the morning, and we'd like to get to bed early; come some other time.' And after it was over and the Mischels had gone, I said, 'I've never done a thing like that in my life. I've never lied to my friends. I've never told people to stay away from my house.' But the spirit was like that all over Hollywood. You couldn't go to a restaurant and talk to one group of people without another group looking down on you. I was so afraid to have a party because somebody might crash, and I couldn't bear the idea of people not talking to each other in my house. And this was not me alone. I was sensitive to it but it was all over Hollywood. This became a most ghastly town. It was as if a gray cloud had descended over it."

And because one was never sure whom one could trust, there was a reluctance to talk which further exacerbated the murky mix of rumor and paranoia. Even at cocktail parties with good friends, recalls the writer Milt Gelman, "you didn't talk politics or religion. All you talked was sex and you played *the* game—that's what it was called, *the* game—charades."

As suspicion invaded friendships, it turned natural allies against each other. Accidental victories were seen to be fixes, nonbelligerent style was mistaken as collaboration, legal stratagems were misperceived as signs of malice. Hence, for example, the confusion and rumors surrounding Sidney Buchman's decision to invoke the First rather than the Fifth Amendment when he went before HUAC in 1951 and refused to name names. Buchman, whose style was accommodating and self-deprecatory, offered (as Lillian Hellman and Arthur Miller did later) to tell the Committee about himself but not to talk about others. He was cited for contempt of Congress but eventually evaded prison on what appeared to be a legal technicality. To this day, many on the left are certain that the fix was in—that Harry Cohn, who regarded Buchman as his protégé, paid off the Committee. Here is an excerpt from a letter sent in 1951 by one member of the Hollywood Ten to another with reference to Buchman's testimony:

> I was astonished to receive a letter from another friend in Los Angeles who himself was named and who is remaining very firm, in which he said "Sidney's categoric defiance made them look rather sick—in fact it had a most salutary effect on the community." This is a comment of incredible naïveté. Not only was a fix apparent to me from the very first brief account of his testimony which I read in the *Times,* even before your letters and more detailed coverage had arrived, but one thing else should surely be apparent—that no possible constitutional or moral principle can be involved in Sidney's type of declination to answer.[4]

As it happens, if one believes the late Sidney Buchman's former wife, Beatrice, and there is no reason not to, there was no fix at all. The main reason Buchman didn't take the Fifth Amendment, it will be recalled, had to do with protecting friends in danger of deportation as a result of Dmytryk's accusation. "Sidney was outraged that Dmytryk named his friend as a Communist, a man who was at the meeting but who had never joined the Party because he was not a citizen and had been terrified of reprisals. Sidney wanted the opportunity to call Dmytryk a liar."

Had the national Communist Party been an open organization or had more faith in the protective freedoms, perhaps it might have transcended the ecology of suspicion. Instead, it became what it was accused of being—an underground conspiracy, albeit a defensive one. A small contingent went to Mexico to set up an underground organization in case the Party's national committee had to go into exile. Party cards were destroyed, membership lists eliminated, even dues went unreceipted. The Party adopted a "system of threes"—three to a cell, only one of whom knew who was next up in the hierarchy. The Hollywood branch was not directly involved in any of this, but neither were its members immune to the new distrust, which had moved from company town on down to the underground in swift silence.[5]

Survivor guilt, another disaster aftermath, also contributed to the collective malaise. "Guilt was like a bed companion," says the blacklisted writer Clancy Sigal. The free-floating guilt that was in the air visited the innocent—Communist and non-Communist alike. An affecting example may be found in an article written by Warren Hoge in *The New York Times* in 1976, when in the course of an extended interview with the nonpolitical actress Mildred Dunnock, he reported:

> Even the stable life of a banker's wife and a large lack of interest in public affairs didn't insulate her from the political harassment of theater people in the 1950s. *Red Channels*, the right-wing pamphlet that periodically identified people as "Communist sympathizers," listed her in one issue because of her friendships with Arthur Miller, Lillian Hellman and Elia Kazan. Suddenly, job offers—particularly from television—stopped coming. Her husband promptly succeeded in obtaining a retraction and in disabusing the networks by making some threatening noises through banking and business associates. But the experience has left its mark.
>
> "It gave me an emotional understanding of being accused," she said. "I felt contaminated, I felt I had leprosy, I felt I had incriminated my husband, a conventional man."[6]

In his studies of Vietnam veterans, Robert Lifton has described how the survivor's guilt mechanism works:

> His reactions suggest the soldier-survivor's sense of having betrayed his buddies by letting them die while he stayed alive—at the same time feeling relieved and even joyous that it was *he* who survived, his pleasure in surviving becoming a further source of guilt ... he becomes bound to an unconscious perception of an organic social balance which makes him feel that his survival was made possible by others' deaths: if they had not died, he would have had to; if he had not survived, someone else would have. His transgression, then, lies in having purchased his own life at the cost of another's.[7]

Without at all suggesting that the death of the film community *was* a life-and-death matter, if we substitute "career" for "life" we can see that Lifton has captured an important aspect of guilt as it expressed itself in the Hollywood of the early 1950s. Some "fronts" felt guilty that they were getting credit for work not their own; some black-market writers felt guilty that they were working while others were not, and that they were grade-A writers turning out grade-B scripts. Some ex-Party members felt ambivalent about the suffering inflicted on their families as a result of their activity in a party whose program turned out to be so flawed. Others, frustrated at their inability to do anything about the repression of the state, turned against their own families, punishing their loved ones and themselves for their not being able to protect their own. Some liberals who had flirted with leftist causes in the 1930s and 1940s understood, at one or another level, that the Fifth Amendment–takers were making a sacrifice that benefited them, so lurking in the subconscious of many working survivors was the suspicion that their careers were a debt on some huge principal owed the blacklistees.

A decade later, when the blacklisted agent George Willner persuaded the Marvin Josephson Agency to let him back into the business, he found, "There was so much guilt around that there was no script I couldn't sell, no matter how high the price."

There was even a little guilt left over for the other side. In 1972 Robert Rossen's widow was in the south of France and she called Sidney Buchman to say hello. Three years before, Buchman had encountered Mrs. Rossen's daughter Carol, who had applied for a part in a movie he was producing. Now "he had the *need* to tell me that he wanted me to be sure to understand why, when Carol went for an interview for that picture, she didn't get the part. Here it was three years later and Sidney Buchman said, 'I want you to know it had nothing to do with any animosity. It was [Sidney] Lumet's [the director's] decision.' "

Kai Erikson, in his study of the Buffalo Creek flood disaster in West Virginia, found that among the symptoms of extreme trauma is a sense of vulnerability, "a feeling that one has lost a certain natural immunity to misfortune, a growing conviction, even, that the world is no longer a safe place to be." Erikson showed how the Buffalo Creek community had helped to absorb the pressures of mountain life. But when the flood deprived it of house, home, neighbors, emotional shelter, when people think they have no one to warn them, to rescue them, to care for them, to mourn them, "their own bodies become the tissue, as it were, on which disturbances in the surrounding world are recorded in painful detail."

The pressures of life draw in "so tightly that they can scarcely breathe, and that they [are] drained of vigor and spirit."[8] Not until people have experienced such a disaster do they understand to what extent they have defined themselves in terms of their community.

In the case of refugees from Hollywood, they found in some instances that such intimate ties as the bond of marriage had depended on the community for validation and without the community there was no more marriage. As Estelle Foreman describes her own situation: "Carl went to England, and when I joined him he was a different man. He suffered terribly and I think he felt at that time that nothing was any use anymore, including loyalty to one's spouse. So he began leading a completely different life. We had a very happy marriage until then. It was quite the reverse afterward."

For many, the Hollywood red subculture had served as an emotions bank, and when it went under they realized for the first time the extent to which they had invested their lives in it. Since this was a nontransferable investment that could not, as far as anyone could see, be recovered, the loss of communality meant that life was irreparably diminished.

Suspicion, guilt, and shame in turn bred obsession. Perhaps that helps to account for the fact that to this day, many who lived through the blacklist judge themselves and each other less by what they have become than by how they behaved then, what they did when the pressure was on. Scores are still being evened. This is particularly true of those who lost their careers and never made it back, but it goes beyond the career failures. Thus in 1965 Lillian Hellman mentioned, "Recently I was asked to sign a protest about Polish writers. I signed it, it was a good protest, I thought, and went out to mail it. But I tore it up when I realized not one of the people protesting had ever protested about any of us."

In *Pentimento* Hellman tells about how she evened the ideological score with Tallulah Bankhead, who publicly announced that *The Little Foxes,* in which she was starring, would give a benefit for Finnish refugees, following the Russian invasion of 1939. But Tallulah and the rest of the cast had refused Hellman's earlier request to do a benefit for refugees of the Spanish civil war in the aftermath of Franco's victory, so Hellman canceled the benefit, and the two didn't speak to each other for almost thirty years.[9]

The director Joseph Losey moved to England to escape the blacklist's long reach and stayed there because the Hollywood he had known was no more; his last memory was of hiding in a darkened home to avoid service of a subpoena. But after twenty-five years, neither time nor distance has cured his distaste for the name-namer who cost him his community. What for some is obsession, for others might more appropriately be termed moral memory. Either way, few can forget. Losey's story is worth hearing because its theme—the informer trying to resume relations with the informee—is a recurrent one in the experience of many who were blacklisted:

"There was a man I used to know quite well in Hollywood. Very well, in fact. I sometimes lent him my house when I was away. He used to be around quite a lot. In those days he was a bachelor. He was in advertising and then went into an agency and I remember just before I went to Europe I met him in New York one day and discussed the situation, and I told him that I thought he was in danger of being involved. I asked him what he would do. He said it wouldn't happen. But he was involved. And what he did was inform on a lot of people, including me and my wife.

"About five years later I got a call from somebody asking me if I'd be interested in a certain project which this man was producing. I said no, I wouldn't be. And that was the end of that.

"Then, roughly twelve years ago he called me and said he had a project. In the meantime he had produced a number of films and become more or less successful as an independent producer, and I gather he was living in Switzerland most of the time—made some money in Switzerland. Got married also, to a nice woman from a fairly wealthy background—I don't know, but I don't believe she was aware that he was involved. Anyway, he called me two or three times. I was able to avoid speaking to him. And then he got through, and he talked as though nothing had happened, as though no time had elapsed. He said, 'I've got a very interesting screenplay written by my wife, and we think you're the best person to direct it.' I said, 'I'm busy.' But he persisted in writing and phoning and so forth, and finally I said, 'Oh for Christ's sake, send it around.' And he sent it around and it was an extremely interesting project.

"So he said, 'We'll have breakfast at Brown's Hotel.' I went with some considerable fear as to how I was going to behave. I had no intention of accepting the project, but I had a kind of curiosity about the whole business. He had been a particularly nasty witness and had involved my wife (she was by that time my ex-wife). He asked about my son and all this kind of stuff, and then finally said, 'Well, will you do the project?' And I said, 'No.' And he said, 'Why not?' And I said, 'Well, you should know why I won't.' And he said, 'What do you mean?' And I said, 'Do you want me to tell you?' And he said, 'Yes.' And I said, 'Well, you informed on me and my wife, and we had a particularly close relationship. [In fact, Losey learned later that his friend had also betrayed him in other ways.] So what the hell is all this about? You know it's ridiculous.' And he said, 'Oh, well.'

"It had been in private testimony. He gave private testimony. But it so happens that some of the private testimony got into print, particularly in *Variety,* although I hadn't seen it. He said, 'If you think I did that, I can see how you would find it impossible to work with me.' I said, 'Well, didn't you?' And he said, 'Certainly not.' I said, 'Friends saw it in the press. I don't see how I could be mistaken on something of this sort. Friends saw it, I'm sure!'

"Then his wife arrived, and I talked with her. I went away and thought, I suppose after a great many years one could make a mistake, or the information could be mistaken. So I wrote him a letter and said, 'If you're prepared to write a letter saying that you never testified giving names, denying this, denying that, I will consider myself mistaken on the whole proposition.' At the same time I wrote to a man who had been my lawyer at the time and said, 'Can I have been mistaken about this, because it would be awful if it were a mistake.' And I got a letter back from the lawyer saying that when he had gotten my letter he had been absolutely astonished that this man had approached me, because he was as sure as I that my recollection was correct. And he said, 'I went alone to the basement where all my files are stored, and I found the testimony, and I'm sending you a photostatic copy of it.' And I read this thing, and it was much worse than what was reported. It was absolutely shocking, because not only did he inform on me and my wife, and a lot of other people, but he *lied* about himself, and to my personal knowledge he misrepresented his own position totally. Needless to say, I have never heard from him again. He didn't answer my letter.

"But the end of the story is that I told it some years later to someone who was seeing this man and his wife and I said, 'How can they sustain a marriage—what is the basis for this marriage?' And she told his wife, and his wife didn't know anything about it and tried to kill herself. Very upsetting."

The persistent efforts by informers to reestablish contact with those they named suggests something beyond an application for forgiveness—especially since, as in the case of Losey's namer, they often chose to preserve the anonymity of their earlier act. Perhaps they suspected somewhat sentimentally that although the community they helped to destroy could never be reconstructed, a nongeographical community lives on among exiles and others, which carries with it, for better or worse, many of the values that gave their lives meaning and fellowship in an earlier time.

The collective memory of a community is often preserved in tales passed on from one generation to the next. But during the blacklist years many—though not all—preferred not to talk about it. As a result, a generation was almost robbed of its history. The ways in which the story of the blacklist was and wasn't passed on may be one of the more depressing indicators of the community's passage from cohesion to confusion.

What do you tell the children? Larry Parks, in his plea not to be forced to name names, asked the Committee: "I have two boys, one thirteen months, one two weeks. Is this the kind of heritage that I must hand down to them? Is this the kind of heritage that you would like to hand down to your children?"

Different families handled it in different ways. Dalton Trumbo said of his children, "It is impossible for a child to live thirteen or fourteen years in the house of a blacklisted, disgraced, jailbird writer and not be affected by it. We did everything we could to ameliorate the wounds that did occur. . . . And of course the first thing we did was to tell them the absolute truth about everything so that they were in no doubt. There was no Fifth Amendment with our children."

"Our son was four when we testified," says Helen Levitt. "He turned on the radio and heard me spelling our family name. How do you explain to a four-year-old what the blacklist was? Blacklisted kids were ostracized. I explained when he was five or six and told him that he wouldn't understand now but one day he would be proud, and he said, 'Oh, Mommy, I'm so proud of you now.' But here we are in the 1970s and he's found it hard to relate to."

Others, however, followed an alternative strategy. At the time the Hollywood Ten went to jail, the George Sklars had three children who were nine, seven, and one. As Sklar remembers it, "People who were in our boat were saying, 'We've got to be straightforward, tell the kids and try to explain it to them.' And Miriam sort of went along with that thinking, and I was very violently opposed to it. I said, 'Look, Albert [Maltz] is my best friend. They've seen Albert almost every day, two or three times a week at least. If they find out that Albert is going to jail, the next thing that's going to come into their minds is, 'Is Poppa going to have to go to jail?' So I said, 'Let's take the chance that they will not be told by some stranger and let's try and wait until they're old enough (a couple of years older) so at least the two oldest kids can get some sense out of this thing, because they're not going to understand it. Their emotions will be swayed by this.' And we didn't tell them.

"What happened was, a couple of years later there was someone who had been our friend whom we stopped seeing because he had cooperated with the Committee, and I just didn't want any part of seeing him after that. Then Dan, our second child, suddenly asked one day, 'Why don't we see this guy anymore?' At this point I looked at Miriam and sort of felt that this was the time. So we tried to explain in the simplest way possible, and Judy, who is the oldest, listened to all this and was sort of bewildered, and then ended up by saying, 'But I can still get my new bathing suit, can't I?' And Dan burst into tears and said, 'I'm too young to understand this.' He was really terribly upset. That was the immediate reaction. Later Judy went to junior high school and met the kids of other blacklisted people, and they began to feel each other out and to communicate and they called themselves the FC's (the Friendly Conspirators) and they would talk about these things among themselves."

Stephen Rossen was about fourteen when his father returned to Washington for his second testimony. "That was a big crisis, and he said he wanted some help. He wanted to know what I would do if I had this situation. It killed him not to work. He was torn between his desire to work and his desire not to talk, and he didn't know what to do. What I think he wanted to know was, what would I think of him if he talked? He didn't say it in that way, though. Then he explained to me the politics of it—how the studios were in on it, and there was never any chance of his working. He had also had a personal failure, I think, with a play he did here, *Cool World.* He was under pressure, he was sick, his diabetes was bad, and he was drinking. By this time I understood that he had refused to talk before and had done his time, from my point of view. What could any kid say at that point? You say, 'I love you and I'm behind you.' I don't think I could have decided. I had no idea what the issues were.

"Later my mother and father talked about the times when they would walk into the Brown Derby and see friends who would no longer talk to them. When I got older, eighteen or nineteen, if I wanted to find out about the stuff, I had to press, I had to ask the questions, even in the 1960s. It ate away at him. I think it had a physical effect on him. It made him sick. He was one of those guys who took things internally."

Jacoba Atlas was brought up by her father, the Hollywood screenwriter Leopold Atlas, and her mother to believe that only ratfinks inform, that the honorable thing to do, if summoned, was to keep one's silence. But at the age of twenty-two, sixteen years after her father died, she was taking a graduate seminar in film studies at UCLA, and one afternoon the subject was the blacklist. After class, Ms. Atlas mentioned to her professor, one Howard Suber, who, as it happened, had written his dissertation on the Hollywood Ten, that her father had been blacklisted.

"Was he Leopold Atlas?" asked Professor Suber.

"Yes," she said. "I'm his daughter."

"Well, he was one of the cooperative witnesses."

"No, you're mistaken. He never testified."

The professor said he thought he had read Atlas's testimony. Ms. Atlas said that was impossible, so the professor said, "'Well, there's one way to find out," and they went to the library to look up the hearings. There was Leopold Atlas's bitter testimony of March 12, 1953, which in addition to giving the most graphic depiction of Maltz's recantation before the Party, named thirty-seven names.[10]

The Committee had been after Atlas to testify since about 1949, it turned out, and he had held out, and gotten sicker and sicker with three massive heart attacks ("the heart attacks had started when the blacklisting started," says Jacoba). Right before he died he testified—in a hotel room in executive session—but Jacoba had never been told about it. "Apparently he had told my mother that he did not name any names, that he did not testify, that he stood the same ground that he had always stood, which was, 'I won't testify.' That was the way it had been explained to my sister and me. We were brought up with rather the same feeling—that the people who testified were somehow the villains of the piece, and the people who didn't were the heroes. Most of the children of leftist parents would have had that kind of feeling.

"When I confronted my mother with the information, first of all she said, 'That's not true.' I had to bring her the testimony. And then . . . she let out with a kind of barrage, trying to explain the real hysteria of the era. She felt my father had been destroyed, and she blamed the left far more than she blamed the right for what happened to him. She thought he had been ostracized by the left—it was after he did the story of *GI Joe,* which was nominated for an Academy Award around the end of the war. . . . I accept a certain amount of that version, knowing Hollywood and knowing the kinds of things that go into making who gets jobs and who doesn't."

But Jacoba isn't sure exactly what to think. "I was brought up with one kind of thinking—heroes and villains. Then naturally when confronted with the other evidence, you know you love your father and you want to try to understand what he did, so I go back and try to find out some other kind of basis for what might have gone on. I don't think politics had as much to do with what was going on then as a kind of personal paranoia that went on between people—who said the correct things, who went to the correct parties. From what I learned at Berkeley during the free speech movement in the 1960s, I know that it can all be just as dogmatic as the right ever dreamed of being.

"In 1970 my mother said to me, 'I would have been glad to testify to get back at those bastards for what they did. . . .' But I suspected, from my own experiences working within the Hollywood system, that people used the blacklist as a way of getting back at other people for things that had nothing to do with politics. And that's not unique, because it happens in academe too. A lot of people who testified did so to get back at people who had gotten jobs away from them, who had won assignments. It was an opportune moment; in a very cynical way it was a golden opportunity. This was the government who wanted your testimony. It was sanctioned."

Jacoba thinks her father was ashamed of what he had done. "I don't think anybody holds out for as long as he did, and then testifies, and thinks he is making the right moral choice. It sent me kind of spiraling to find out what went on."

At the time I saw Jacoba Atlas in 1976 she was working in a Hollywood public-relations agency and finishing her dissertation on the history of Hollywood labor unions. At the end of our talk I asked her if there was anything we had not covered, and she said no, but then she remembered: "When I was at Berkeley and all involved in the free speech movement, I called home and said, 'We're on strike.' My mother's first comment was, 'Don't sign anything. Do whatever you want, but don't sign anything.' "

Although a resister, J. Edward Bromberg, like Atlas, kept his own counsel. He kept his silence at home as he did before the Committee. It was part of the atmosphere. "All I remember is his sitting, waiting for a phone call, with the FBI guys mysteriously appearing or waiting across the street," says Conrad.

"To this day I have a great reluctance to talk to policemen. To this day I file my income tax early. I did get to see where the power is. There were daily visits with the FBI people. You'd have to make the same decision over and over. I never knew who this guy was who would show up at our door, and Father was very reluctant to talk about it. He would say, 'I'd just as soon you didn't know because it will make it easier for you if you don't know.' I think that was a mistake. If it ever happens again, I'll tell my daughter because I want her to know where the bastards are and how they get there. If you don't know, the paranoia spreads over everybody. The progressive-school thinking of the era said, Don't burden the kids with things they can't handle. But the one thing a kid can't handle is not knowing.

"For the first three years of it, all I got were snatches of conversations in Beverly Hills at the dinner table. He'd report conversations with his agent. 'He thinks I'm in trouble with Metro.' This was the period of the graylist. There was no great discussion at home that the children were privy to. There were meetings, but I think the decision was made to protect the children. We didn't even know the testimony was happening until it broke on the front page. They may have wanted to protect my nine-year-old brother or they may have wanted to get it over and done with and not bother anybody. We were very middle-class children. We were all very sun-tanned, going to the beach every day, kind of living out the American dream, and I don't think they wanted to explode it. By 1949 my father hadn't worked in a year, and it had become palpably clear that he wasn't wanted. After that we came back to New York and then it was out on the table. There was an FBI car parked outside every morning, and he was ducking subpoenas.

"It became like the reign of terror with everybody naming everybody. That's what began to worry Eisenhower about McCarthy—the mad dog thing. He thought he had him on a leash but the leash was loose.

"The enemy is not the guy who names you. He's as much a victim as you are. He just gets a bigger paycheck. You don't get to face your real enemy. Because you don't get to face the real enemy, you take it out on your family and friends—the inversion of reality. My mother blocked out the whole period, and that accounts for her survival."

Even the children of the blacklisters lived in the shadows. Constance Walter, daughter of HUAC's chairman, spent the blacklist years at Sarah Lawrence College, where Harold Taylor, its unorthodox president, told her, "We can't choose our parents, and you lost the toss." In the mid-1970s, Constance Walter Weaver, now a liberal suburbanite in Montgomery County, Maryland, found herself involved in a community dispute over school busing. My interview with her coincided with a meeting of her faction, and she explained her absence on the grounds that she was being interviewed for "a book which involves my father." Asked who her father was, she told me, she still, after all this time, couldn't say. "It's interesting. I feel guilt. I said I would really rather not say because I am associated in Montgomery County with the liberal faction and my father was not a liberal. . . ."

The informer preferred to see himself as a tiny cog in the intricate machinery of the purge, occupying but a small space on the landscape of the cold war. But for those who were banished from the collectivity this perspective is not possible. For many of them, the informer was a magnet that attracted their generalized hostility. Albert Maltz, in writing to Herbert Biberman on the occasion of Edward Dmytryk's decision to name names, revealed how this deeply ingrained hatred of the informer was related to the bitter polarization that had divided Hollywood. His comments on Dmytryk may be read as the birth of an obsession, the death of a sense of community.

April 12, 1951

I was not prepared, really, for the news you give us of Dmytryk. When he made the prison statement . . . I asked him squarely how far he was willing to go to get work in Hollywood. Only this far and no further, he said. This is only a maneuver—maybe it won't work—my beliefs have not changed—of course they will try to make a stool pigeon out of me, but that they will never do. And so on. This was the man who, about only a month before, had read of the grovelling of Lee Pressman with contempt. This man left me in friendliness, differing with me on certain things, perhaps, but brothers under the skin, etc., etc. It is sick and sorrowful and contemptible, and I wait in horror for what he will do. I even hope you are wrong, but I know you are not or you would not have written as you have.

May 3, 1951

. . . Now that Dmytryk has testified I think it becomes clear that he had advanced further toward being a stool pigeon, much further and more consciously . . . than he let me know or I guessed. It is my conjecture that he held off long enough to establish: (1) that there was no work for him in Hollywood despite his statement; (2) that he could not get a passport to work in England. At that point he was all too prepared to see a quick, ideological light and become, not a cowardly stool pigeon, of course, but a big man (as you say) who follows the logic of his principles. And see what a big man he is—why, he even went to prison for his principles. What other member of the MPA ever did that? Why, in a few years, he will hold office in that organization.

. . . He always evaded being pinned down. I don't know if, in my last letter, I told you that in an unguarded moment, very casually, Eddie said to me that he never would go to prison again. I paused and looked at him and took it up, saying that I also *hoped* I would never go to prison again, but to say that I *never* would was quite a different thing. How far was he prepared to go in order *not* to go to prison? He never answered squarely, he evaded. He is a good evader, that scientist.

Now I am not surprised that he accepted your invitations, was host and guest and warm friend—all the while whetting the knife. Don't you see—it was for reasons of pure idealism? Oh, shit. I don't care what happens to some of the other little sheep, like Parks, but I hope, I hope, Dmytryk still doesn't get film work. Let's have a little retribution as we go along.

Yet this I will say, about him and all the others: that if the last fifteen years he survived politically and historically, it will be seen that it was possible for a man to think he had taken a brave political stand with great sincerity—without its being difficult for him for most of that time, and a key thing, without his holding in his heart anything but a reformist position, without his allegiance to being against the mainstream. Collins tried to express this in his testimony. It may or may not be true of him but it is true of many. No more on this now, but I think it is a historic aspect to this flight from conviction that we must realize. And as you say, at the same time how inspiring the solidarity of the others. More difficult what they do than we had to do, it seems to me. For we were fighting a public principle in a flaming way they cannot, and we had the hope of winning. But . . . the other good, good people have a smaller torch to carry, yet the same consequences; have less support, and more certainty that they are walking the plank. In a way we reached bed-rock only when the court turned us down; they begin walking bed-rock from the first moment.

May 31, 1951

. . . Your letter of May 14, which I have been so slow in answering, was sad. Commencing with Eddie Dmytryk and his television program. No matter how deeply one may understand the historical phenomenon of betrayal, it is nauseatingly ugly when someone you have known, someone who fought by your side, went with you into prison—becomes such an eager wretch, such a fawning informer, such a zealous axe-man of others. I must confess that I would have real pity, I think, if a man or woman were to break after really severe trials—torture, endless years of imprisonment, etc. But Dmytryk's actions have no excuse at all, not even poverty. He just couldn't bear to think that he would no longer be at the top, no longer have real money. It is the cheapest sellout of the day.

. . . A lesson for the future: You will recall that I did a black-market film during the period of our fight. This film was not released until we were in prison. It was quite well received and successful and I, who had told no one, not even you, which film it was—since the way to keep a secret of any importance is to keep it—was tempted in prison to tell my colleague, my comrade, the man who had been manacled hand and foot with me, the man who plucked chickens with me and sifted sand and gravel in a stream with me, the man who expressed such fine sentiments to me . . . what the name of the film was I had written. In prison, lonely, wanting to share, I almost did so. But I did not. If it had involved only me, I surely would have. But it did involve the welfare of others still in the industry. Can you imagine, if I had told him, what he would have done with it? It could have been a special tid-bit for the Committee. Oh my stars, what a lesson.[11]

=====

"The Hollywood writer," wrote Arthur Schlesinger, Jr., in 1949, "feels he has sold himself out; he has abandoned his serious work in exchange for large weekly paychecks; and he resents a society which corrupts him. . . . He has qualms of conscience, however, for making so much while others make so little. So he believes that he can buy indulgences by participating in the Communist movement, just as men in the Middle Ages bought remission of sins from wandering monks."[12]

A nice formulation, but too neat. Men like Maltz, Lawson, Odets, Kazan, early activists in the theater of social protest, had come to the Party before they came to Hollywood, they had come in response to Depression at home and fascism abroad. Others, like Trumbo, who didn't actually join the Party until 1943, never had any guilt feelings about making money. Born into the working class, and having served as a baker for eight years before he came to Hollywood, he cheerfully told me, "I never considered the working class anything other than something to get out of."

What the pre-purged Hollywood community did was to provide a supportive context of unspoken assumptions, accommodations, a hard-won heritage within which different members reconciled the continuing tensions between a high sense of craft and the competing demands of ideological and commercial imperatives, between a desire to strike it rich and a genuine impulse to work for a better world, between the political commitment to the *ideal* of socialism which they believed to be exemplified in the Soviet experiment, and their simultaneous belief in American democracy.

And even as they joked, complained about, fought, organized against, and libeled the moguls, they also counted on studio support in times of trouble. Isobel Lennart's reminiscence is singular in its particulars, but not untypical: "I had a very peculiar relationship with Metro. I came there at nineteen in the fan-mail department, thirteen dollars a week, and I organized the union and I got fired right away. . . . But I came back there as a writer. I never worked anyplace else, and I had the most intense child-parent relationship with them, especially [producer] Eddie Mannix, [studio executive L. K.] Sidney, even L. B. [Louis B. Mayer, production head of M-G-M]. It was like I was one of their kids. . . . You know, most screenwriters come from having been writers; they come in as more mature people. I sold my first story and I wrote my first screenplay at Metro before I was twenty-one, and then I spent my life there, and so it wasn't so much [a matter of] how good a writer I was. These were tough but very sentimental men, and they wanted me to work and I was good at my job. I had a couple of years where I was in bad shape, and it was a whole thing just to work. . . . These awful people, Eddie Mannix and Sidney, really were people with some heart. They tried to protect all of us who were involved there—they really did, and when they let us go, it was only after a struggle. It was a family thing. They called me in and said, 'We can't protect you any longer, and this time you're going to have to testify.' "[13]

The ancient custom of killing the messenger who bears the bad news explains *some* of the attitude toward that hapless liberal Dore Schary, whose job it was to inform the Writers Guild in 1947 that the producers (over his objection) were going to fire the Hollywood Ten and blacklist Communists and other "subversives" after all. But a better explanation of why Adrian Scott, in the throes of a postoperative dream he had shortly before he died of cancer in 1973, hallucinated the death of Schary along with that of Dmytryk,[14] was that Schary represented family. The feeling about the failure of the producers in general and Schary in particular to support the blacklisted writers was that they had committed something akin to filicide—the studios had not lived up to the obligations of their own paternalism.

———

Early on in Congress's entanglement with Hollywood (November 14, 1947), Congressman John Rankin indulged in one of his periodic racist harangues:

> They sent this petition to Congress [on behalf of the Hollywood Ten] and I want to read you the names.

One of the names is June Havoc.

We found out from the *Motion Picture Almanac* that her real name is June Hovick.

Another name was Danny Kaye, and we found out that his real name was David Daniel Kaminsky. . . .

Another one is Eddie Cantor, whose real name is Edward Isskowitz.

There is one who calls himself Edward Robinson. His real name is Emanuel Goldenberg.

There is another one who calls himself Melvyn Douglas, whose real name is Melvyn Hesselberg.

There are others too numerous to mention. They are attacking the Committee for doing its duty in trying to protect this country and save the American people from the horrible fate the Communists have meted out to the unfortunate Christian people of Europe.

THE SPEAKER: The time of the gentleman from Mississippi has expired.[15]

Because of their anti-Semitic intent, Rankin's remarks were denounced or ignored by the cognoscenti. In fact, however, he had come close to a truth about the community he was smearing—many of its inhabitants were known by their pseudo-identities rather than their real ones. Hollywood was engaged in the manufacture of myths and dreams, and its inhabitants, stars and writers alike, had come to confuse their self-created images with their selves. One function of a community is to preserve the myths people create about themselves and to give comfort when outsiders attack them. Familiar setting alone—of friends, neighborhood, job—can have a healing effect.

The philosopher Sissela Bok's dictum in her treatise *Lying* that there is a need to protect social trust from lies applies to informing as well: the veneer of social trust is often thin, and as betrayal—lying or informing—spreads, trust is damaged. "Yet trust is a social good to be protected just as much as the air we breathe or the water we drink. When it is damaged, the community as a whole suffers; and when it is destroyed, societies falter and collapse."[16]

Ultimately it was the informer's contribution to spoil the possibility of trust and thereby the sense of community. People in Hollywood lost not only their myths (of the happy ending, among others), their careers, possessions, place, status, and space, but also their sense of self. The disintegration of social bonds abruptly threw people back on their own resources. Marriages broke, personalities dissolved in alcohol, some went to court, some into exile, and some into mental institutions. Others found themselves and their true identities, but life was never the same again.

The impact of the informer on the collectivity was devastating. And for many the trauma came as much in reaction to being disconnected from a familiar network of unspoken understandings as from any job or other loss suffered directly as a result of being called a Communist or being put on a list.

13.
The Informer as Victim

WHEN DALTON TRUMBO told an audience of writers in 1970 apropos the blacklist, "It will do no good to search for villains or heroes or saints or devils because there were none; there were only victims,"[1] his speech—intended to be healing—caused a controversy that still simmers. The truth is, of course, that informers suffered too (even if, as Abe Polonsky puts it, "they suffered more victoriously in the beginning"). To acknowledge this indisputable fact is not to engage the diversionary issue—whether they suffered "more" or "equally" or "less" than those they informed on. That they suffered does not make their informing right. But that they informed does not negate the pain of their suffering.

Informers endured three types of penalty. First, some—but not most—of them suffered the same sort of employment discrimination visited upon those who refused to cooperate with the House Un-American Activities Committee. Second, most—but not all—of them suffered a loss of self-esteem. And finally, virtually all of them were subjected to a variety of social penalties, some of which persist to this day.

Larry Parks was the first man in Hollywood to inform before HUAC, but the combination of his reluctance to do so, the publicity that attended his "performance," his failure to employ an attorney like Martin Gang to work out a behind-the-scenes advance scenario with the Committee staff, and his consequent controversiality resulted in the end of a career that had been on the brink of superstardom. His memorable line, "Do not make me crawl through the mud like an informer," was remembered, and the names he named were forgotten by those in the blacklisting business. At the time John Wayne told an MPAPAI audience at the American Legion auditorium that Parks had waited too long. Victor Riesel shouted, "To hell with Larry Parks!" Hedda Hopper added, "The life of one American soldier is worth all the careers in Hollywood. We must be careful lest we give sympathy to those who do not deserve it—and Parks certainly does not." *The Los Angeles Times* editorialized, "Before Parks is praised too much . . . his attitude may be contrasted with that of Whittaker Chambers, who under somewhat parallel circumstances did sacrifice his career on the altar of patriotism and who did give valuable information, which resulted in the conviction of Alger Hiss and the unmasking of others."[2]

In his testimony Parks had proved prophetic: "It is doubtful whether, after appearing before this Committee, my career will continue." Having abased himself, Parks seemed to have no fight left. Because the studio had only one unreleased picture of his, it had no immediate dollars riding on his rehabilitation, and although Parks's contract called for two more pictures, he told Harry Cohn of Columbia, through an intermediary, that if the studio didn't want him to make the two films, he was willing to cancel the contract. Cohn accepted the offer,[3] and Parks went into real estate.

Two years later Parks tried again, and on July 15, 1953, sent the Committee a "clarifying" letter which read:

> After careful consideration I wish to file a clarifying statement of my point of view on the Communist problem with your Committee. . . . I am now convinced that [my previous testimony] improperly reflects my true attitude toward the malignancy of the Communist Party.
>
> If there is any way in which I can further aid in exposing the methods of entrapment and deceit through which Communist conspirators have gained the adherence of American idealists and liberals, I hope the Committee will so advise me. Perhaps some of the confusion now apparent to me in my testimony before your Committee can best be explained by the fact that I was the first cooperative witness from Hollywood to appear before your Committee and at the time I was under really great strain and tension. Upon reflection I see that I did not adequately express my true beliefs—beliefs which have even deepened and strengthened since my appearance.
>
> Above all, I wish to make it clear that I support completely the objectives of the House Committee on Un-American Activities. I believe fully that Communists and Communist intrigues should be thoroughly exposed and isolated and thus rendered impotent.
>
> In the light of events which have transpired since I appeared as a witness before your Committee, it is crystal clear that no one who really believes in a progressive program for humanity can support any part of the Communist program. No true liberal can doubt that Soviet

Communism constitutes as grave a threat to the rights of man today as once did Hitler's fascism. . . .

Liberals must now embrace the cause of anti-Communism with the same dedication and zeal as we once did that of anti-Nazism. The enemy is the same though the labels have changed.

It is my conviction that to assist your Committee in obtaining full information about the Communist Party and its activities is the duty of all who possess such evidence. Certainly, if I were to testify today I would not testify as I did in 1951—that to give such testimony is to "wallow in the mud"—but on the contrary I would recognize that such cooperation would help further the cause in which many of us were sincerely interested when we were duped into joining and taking part in the Communist Party.

. . . I want my sons to participate fully in the search for democratic answers to the continuing threat of totalitarianism—Communist or fascist. To that end, I will do all within my power as one who once was duped but has since learned the hard way about the guileful traps which Communism can set for an unwary idealist or liberal.

I sincerely hope the Committee will publish the statement of my militant anti-Communist beliefs at the earliest possible date.[4]

Between then and 1976, when he died, Parks played in only three more movies, none of them in more than supporting roles. It was not always possible for out-of-work informers to know whether their problem was marginal talent or marginal politics. Melvin Levy was certain it was the latter, but his agent says it was the former. Leo Townsend, who had complimented Warner Brothers in his testimony on their promise not to fire him for going public about his ex-Communist past, says, "Two weeks after I testified I was fired from my writing job at Warner Brothers I could not get work—at least this is my own feeling—for two reasons. I was a victim of the double-blacklist. The conservative element—the hiring people, the studios—would not hire me because I had been a Communist; and what I call the bleeding-heart liberals—you know, the closet Communists who didn't join the Party but contributed—they wouldn't hire me because I was now considered an outcast because I'd testified for the government. It must have been a couple of years I couldn't get work at all, and I finally got a writing assignment on *The Perry Como Show* on CBS, but I had to file an affidavit saying that I was no longer a member of the Communist Party; otherwise they wouldn't hire me."

A number of people who named names did so only after years of holding out, of refusing to bend to public and private pressure. These unhappy few thus experienced both the emotional torture, harassment, and inconvenience of life on and under the blacklist, *and* the subsequent obloquy of having played the role of informer. The director Michael Gordon, it will be remembered, took the Fifth Amendment in 1951 because he thought the whole concept of being an informer "repugnant and repellent." George Sklar once asked him why he didn't get a job at a small college teaching and running a theater where he would have a choice of which plays he wanted to direct, and he said he couldn't work with amateurs. But after eight years on the blacklist, which yielded among other things an ulcer, a coronary, and a couple of theatrical flops that diminished the possibility of working on Broadway, Gordon agreed to go through the name-naming motions in the privacy of a hotel room. There followed the successful *Pillow Talk*, starring Doris Day and Rock Hudson, and some other credits, but he soon took a job teaching at UCLA. Lee J. Cobb endured what he called "unspeakable tortures"—he was penniless, friendless, and his wife was in an institution—before he "broke." The writer Ben Maddow, too, held out for years, but barely before the list expired he is said to have capitulated privately in order to work publicly. For men such as these, informing was the capstone to their suffering rather than evidence that they had been spared it.

If informing was a way of generating job vacancies and settling scores, both those who were named and those who identified with them were not above malicious retaliation. Revenge and vindictiveness were found on both sides of the street. Even the good-natured, hail-fellow-well-met agent George Willner couldn't resist the opportunity to get in his dig: thus when he met Roy Huggins in a parking lot shortly after the latter testified, "I got so mad I said, 'The smell of horseshit is so bad I can't stand it.' He heard that."

Richard Collins, who had made in-Party enemies as a doctrinaire functionary and post-Party enemies as a HUAC collaborator, found himself on the receiving end of a variety of unpleasantnesses. "My son, who was about six, was mirror-writing, and I took him to a doctor who had been recommended by somebody, and he wouldn't take him on. He said, 'You are a stool pigeon and I won't have your son as a patient.' So I said, 'That's scarcely got to do with him.' He said, 'I don't care, I don't want him.' That was the way it worked."

One day, at the writers' table at Warner's, Collins sat down and an old friend came by. "He said he felt sorry for me because I had gone crazy and had to be put away, and he understood I was out now. He hoped I was feeling well. I may have gone crazy, but nobody knew about it, including me."

And when he got a two-week job rewriting something called *Women of Venus*, the producer got a call from another producer who said that Collins had put one over on him, that since his testimony he had had writer's block, and they would never see any pages and if they did the pages would be terrible. "Little things like that. On the other hand, it was war from their point of view. But I survived it."

Edward Dmytryk, regarded as a renegade by his nine co-convicts, also felt the sting of social retribution. "We bumped into Dmytryk one night in a restaurant sometime in 1956 or 1957," says Mrs. Adrian Scott. "We were seated in a booth adjoining Dmytryk, his wife, and a guest. Dmytryk pretended not to see Adrian. Adrian said in an aside to me, 'Dmytryk is sitting there with his wife.' So I said, 'Do you want to move?' Adrian said, 'Hell, no. I want to look.' And he sat and stared and Dmytryk refused to look back. He just drank. Dmytryk was miserable." The snubs themselves were less traumatic than the constant sense that at any time—in social or business contexts—one might be embarrassed, compromised, humiliated as a result of the past.

Another category of informer suffering was, to a degree, self-inflicted. The composer David Raksin, it will be recalled, had a vision of the nightingale and the rose, where the nightingale presses herself against the rose and then dies from the thorn—after which she decides to "sing." Raksin, who named names but would not say all of the other things his attorney Martin Gang told him the ritual demanded, believed then and still does that "the only decent thing a person could do was not talk." He has yet to forgive himself.

We have already seen how the informer was transformed from stigmatizer to stigmatized. But here we refer to the way in which the act of informing lowered a person's own self-esteem. "No one who went through that experience," says Michael Gordon, "was without ambivalence." The very fact that an informer knows he has betrayed his former friends— even if only symbolically—depresses him. In some cases, he regards his act as betrayal, as "despicable," a mark against his own integrity. Lee J. Cobb covered his face when he saw the son of a man he had named. Mike Gordon ran into some old friends on his return from Hollywood soon after he testified in executive session at a hotel room. They invited him to a party and his response was, "You wouldn't want me."

In some cases informers requested "permission" to name names, or visited those they had named after the fact to beg forgiveness. There was about such actions the odor of humiliation. The informer tended to regard those he named as well as those named by others as his enemy and his judge. "Bob would cross the street when he saw someone coming he thought was going to cut us, and I was not proud of him for it," says Robert Rossen's widow, Sue.

The informer knows that his credibility and respect were damaged in the community of his peers, the community in which he had invested his most cherished creative energies. Leslie Weiner, who took a playwriting seminar with Clifford Odets, recalls visiting Odets in California after his belligerent appearance before the Un-American Activities Committee, when he simultaneously named names but gave the Committee a hard and boisterous time. "He had all the testimony in a bound book and he told me he tried to get Charlie Chaplin to read the whole thing but Chaplin wouldn't do it. That hurt him a lot. People were reacting to the headlines and not listening to what he said and he resented that and was frustrated by it." He wanted to be thought of as a resister, not a namer.

The informer knew or quickly learned that having informed once, he was subject to recall before other forums. The FBI came around flashing pictures, asking for new identifications. The Immigration and Naturalization Office needed witnesses for deportation hearings. Columnists converted the informer's renewed affirmations of patriotism into copy. Once the patriotic barriers were down, the informer often found himself at sea, unable to maintain a moral anchor. Sissela Bok's aperçu about a first lie applies to a first act of betrayal as well: The first "must be thatched with another, or it will rain through."[5] Once you named one, you were regarded as having crossed the line, and were called on to name others. If you refused you could be blacklisted anew, and since there was no grand principle at stake, why not go along?

Like everybody else, the informer travels through life with a social convoy, people whose opinion he values, whose judgment he trusts, whose norms he has internalized. Since in most cases the decision to inform was a wrenching one, self-esteem was often vulnerable to the disesteem of loved ones.

Ultimately the only sanction that was experienced by virtually all informers and that persists to this day is the social penalty—the snub, the cut, the missing handshake, the silent treatment. "For one person to look directly at another and not acknowledge the other's bow is such a breach of civility that only an unforgivable misdemeanor can warrant the rebuke," Emily Post says.[6] Such "punishments" may seem trivial in comparison with the horrors that other victims of the era had to endure, yet they cannot be ignored, for cumulatively they took their toll, and as Herbert Spencer observed, "The government of manners was the original force of social control."[7]

Budd Schulberg is more famous than most, more feisty than most, and, with his goatee, prominent nose, sweet smile, and a life-style that once involved considerable bar-hopping, fight-going, and partying, more visible than most. So perhaps he has endured more than his share of such encounters, but his experiences (reported by others) are typical:

Schulberg meets the Lardners in a restaurant and Ring shakes his hand ("I shake hands with anybody. I don't believe in blacklisting") and Frances Chaney Lardner turns the other way because she does not believe in talking with informers.

Schulberg comes out of Sardi's with the writer Harvey Breit as John Wexley (a Bucks County, Pennsylvania, neighbor and blacklisted playwright) is walking in. Wexley shakes Breit's hand but freezes when he sees Budd. "John, it's Budd," says Breit. "I know it's Budd," says Wexley (who later reported, "It was very painful but I couldn't do it").

Beyond embarrassment, a more serious social penalty was loss of friendship. Michael Blankfort's friendship with Albert Maltz, for example, was a painful casualty of the informer syndrome. Blankfort, Maltz, and George Sklar had been best friends through the 1930s and 1940s. They were novelists, playwrights, and critics together before they were screenwriters. Maltz dedicated his first novel, in part, to Blankfort. They were contemporaries, politically sympathetic, inseparable. Blankfort, it will be recalled, had an ambiguous experience before the Committee. When Congressman Jackson asked at the close of his testimony, "Do you, either through blood or marital relationships, have any relatives who are or have been members [of the Communist Party]?" he is reported to have answered, "You are referring to my ex-wife Laurie and my cousin Henry—I have no knowledge of either." As Blankfort tells it, the names were just blurted out. The trade papers picked it up, and although Gang got it expunged from the record, Blankfort has never lived it down. He has gone on to write a total of ten novels, and a few years ago was president of the Screen Writers Guild, but he has never made it back to his friendship with Albert Maltz and George Sklar. "Why did he say 'you are referring to' and give two specific names?" asks Sklar.

When one talks with Blankfort one detects a mix of nostalgia and hurt. "You would get—what is the phrase they use at West Point?—you would be put in Coventry. You'd be sitting at a writers' table at one of the studio commissaries, and this guy that two days ago you were pals with would give you the cold shoulder, or he would say, 'For Christ's sake, what the hell are you doing, you selling out?' and all kinds of shit that you didn't like, since all of us are born with a great element in us that wants to be loved." When he talks of Maltz's refusal to renew their friendship, one can see that the wound still festers: "As I say, there were a few people who were very angry with me for cooperating with the Committee, to whom I would say, 'But I didn't name names,' who would say, 'Yes, but you betrayed us because you were willing to answer their questions,' and the one man who has never forgiven me is Albert Maltz. Over the years I've made several efforts—through third parties—to talk with him because there are a lot of things he doesn't know about, but he won't do it. I guess he's the only one. I have talked to Trumbo, Lardner, Sidney Buchman—all of them. I don't mean to say they're now my friends, but they weren't my friends before, either. The only friend among the Ten was Albert. It is a matter of real grief to me that he has acted this way. . . . He wouldn't acknowledge the death of my father, whom he knew quite well. He wouldn't drop me a note at all. He wouldn't do anything, though I have called him and written him a few times saying, Now that we're getting on how about a moment of just talking?

"Albert's a very rigid man, and yet he has the most extraordinary compassion. But as [Edmund] Bergler, the psychiatrist, used the phrase, he's an 'injustice collector.' And he really collects. I myself have never felt that way about any person. By the way, that was one of the things that turned me off about the Party—when they saw old friends they'd cross the street in order to avoid saying hello to each other, because one had become a Trotskyite. . . . So when I'm seventy, I'll write Albert another letter."

In 1978 Maltz explained to two interviewers why he refuses to speak to Blankfort: "I have contempt for him. And you know, apropos of this—because it involves the whole question of the behavior of these people—I have a phrase that is very important to me, and that is: To understand all is not to forgive all."[8]

Obviously, a wide variety of motives determine the behavior of those who choose not to have truck with informers. The sometimes comical result is to keep both sides on constant social guard lest they or a spouse commit a moral *faux pas.*

Susan d'Usseau told me, "One time Meta Rosenberg walked into a dressing room, and a girl I know who is near-sighted said 'Hi,' and then put on her glasses. She was furious."

There are those like Adrian Scott's widow, Joan, who made sure to avoid informers as a matter of policy. She recalls the night Frank Tarloff brought an informer to a London party given by the actor Martin Balsam. Everybody, including many blacklisted expatriates, was civilized, but the Scotts decided to leave. Tarloff asked, "How long can this go on?" Joan said she would propose a statute of limitations—when the last victim is no longer a victim. "Frank put his arm around Adrian and said, 'Well, we needn't worry anyway because the cream always rises.'" The Scotts left and it wasn't until the next morning that Joan thought of the comeback: "The scum also rises."

"Maybe if I hadn't lived with a man whose guts were torn out by it, I'd feel differently," adds Mrs. Scott. "But I feel personally responsible not to let anyone think he is forgiven."

There are those like George Sklar whose avoidance of those who named names is visceral. He just doesn't want to have anything to do with them. "They make me sick." Says Sklar, "I remember (and this is kind of silly, I suppose), Miriam, my wife, used to say to me, 'Why should *you* want to avoid or be ashamed or be embarrassed? *They*'re the ones who should be embarrassed.' We were at a play. During intermission we started to go out and I saw this face and said, 'Let's sit.' And that's when Miriam said that. But nonetheless I had this feeling."

"My attitude toward informers has remained from the start unforgiving," Michael Wilson told me. "I'm not one who says, Let bygones be bygones. I don't defend my attitude in terms of principle. It's just a visceral reaction, that's all. I just don't like the fuckers. Socially I don't acknowledge their existence. I wouldn't say hello. I have good friends who don't do that—and that's their right. It is simply not my attitude."

Then there is what might be called the Raskolnikov phenomenon—those who insist, like Joseph Losey's former friend, on returning to the scene of the crime. Carl Foreman remembers that when he finally returned to the United States after twenty years in exile, his phone rang and it was the cartoonist and writer David Lang, a man who had been very close to Foreman and his wife but had subsequently named them in secret testimony. "He had the gall to call me, and my heart began to pound. I said, 'Who is this?' He said, 'David Lang.' I said, 'I don't know any David Lang.'"

But Foreman himself telephoned Richard Collins after he testified. Collins, greatly surprised, recalls: "He said he was very unhappy with Dmytryk and six or seven other guys. I said, 'What makes me different?' He said, 'Well, I trust you.' I said, 'Why?' He said, 'Well, because you were nice to me years ago when I was on my ass. You were the only one that listened to me.' So that's just a phenomenon. It's so strange, because I was no different from men that he was inveighing against, except for some personal reason he wasn't so angry with me as he was with some of the others."

Martin Gang suffered some of the same social penalties as those he represented did. "One lady turned her back on me just because I represented the people who did what she didn't like. She was the sister of a very good friend of mine. I later found out that she was a member of the Communist Party."

Each informer has evolved his own strategies for dealing with such unpleasantness. Richard Collins, for one, seems to roll with the punches: "A month or two after I testified I went to a Writers Guild meeting at the Hotel Roosevelt. I knew almost every writer in the guild, and there were only three who said hello to me: Bob Pirosh, whom I didn't know well; Curtis Kenyon, who was a writer with me when I started with Fox a long time before; and Boris Ingster, who was a Russian who had been around the Party for a while. But everybody else—and not just Party people—gave me the cold shoulder.

"I recognized that you have to pay your dues no matter what you do. I had been in the Party, and there was a certain penalty that had to be paid for that; and I had gotten out, and so obviously there was a penalty to be paid for that, too. The question was to survive and not to indulge in one of those great swings that some guys get involved with—as, for instance, when they become Catholics."

Ben Maddow, who did not inform for a period of six or seven years then apparently decided that working was more important, has a counterstrategy. "When he runs into people," says one of those who has run into him, "he doesn't give them a chance to disregard or snub him, he just is there with his hand out or with an embrace. He just rushes. Others are embarrassed, most of them."

"It's a hard thing to go through, but it's minor-league to suffer from the attitude of disapproval," says the informer David Raksin, "yet I had the feeling that this is the kind of thing you die over."

Excerpt from the journal of Millard Lampell:

Walking down Broadway, someone catches my elbow from behind. It is R, whom I have known for fifteen years, and who recently appeared as a "cooperative witness" before the Committee. He asks plaintively why I passed him without saying hello, and I explain that I didn't see him. He shakes his head, "No, no, you stared right at me." He grimaces, "I don't blame you. I'm disgusting. Do you think I'm disgusting?" I am not particularly proud of the fact that I nodded yes and

walked away. Who appointed me his judge? He's as much a victim as
the rest of us.[9]

Evidence that these social awkwardnesses weigh heavily on the informers may be found in the delight with which they give examples of those
who have chosen to violate the taboo. The screenwriter Lester Cole had
said that "he would not demean himself to speak or contact any so-called
informers" and, as it happened, I put the statement in an article I wrote
for *The New York Times Magazine* in 1973. When I subsequently interviewed the informer Leo Townsend, he was quite anxious to let me know
of a recent communication from Cole. "I got a letter from Lester from
San Francisco. We had done a treatment together, and he wanted to
know if I had a copy of it because he thought that maybe he could turn it
into a screenplay. He wrote me and I wrote him back, and he wrote
again, a very friendly letter. . . . And this is the man who said he wouldn't
speak to one of us."

That Townsend is sensitive to these matters is evident from his other
reports: "I saw Albert Maltz in Mexico City one time. I was getting out
of an elevator and he was coming in. It's possible he didn't recognize me.
But I recognized him, and I started to say hello, and I thought, Well, forget it, he's not going to talk to me; I'm one of the traitors. And Hugo
Butler, you know him? He's dead. I went to a restaurant in Mexico City
with a lady lawyer whom I met, and at the next table were Hugo and his
wife, and they obviously ignored me."

Townsend's favorite story is of what happened the day he testified.
That evening he and his wife went to a black-tie film premiere. "Behind
me was a guy named Stanley Roberts, a writer who had been in the Party. He wouldn't speak to me. And as we were going in a director named
Lazlo Benedek, who had been a close friend—he and his wife— saw me
and immediately turned. He called about three weeks later, and he said,
'Leo, I want to apologize. I saw you.' And I said, 'I know you did.' And
he said, 'I turned my back on you and that was a terrible thing I did.
May I come out and apologize in person?' So he came out and he was
crying. . . . So then we became friends again, which I thought was nice.
He wasn't in the Party. He was one of those sympathizers. Most of his
friends were Party people. It was a crazy time."

Isobel Lennart reminisced about how deeply she regretted the lost
friendships. "I was cut off from all the people who went in, some of them
my closest friends, for a very long time. I cut myself off because I was so
overcome with shame and guilt. The few nasty letters I got I felt were

justified. I felt tremendous misery about it as the years went on, and a number of people approached me and said, 'It's time to stop this nonsense,' and I'd say, 'It's not nonsense, but I hope you can accept it now."

When Lennart was working on *Funny Girl* (1968) in New York the phone rang and it was George Willner, whom she hadn't heard from in fifteen years. "I couldn't believe it. I got on the phone and said, 'George, if you are calling me to tell me to drop dead, don't bother, I am.' You know he said, 'No, I was just thinking. I'm in New York and I read you wrote *Funny Girl* and this is so stupid, you know, so many years have gone by and we love you and want to see you.' I started bawling.

"I tell you that for three years I couldn't go to the commissary at M-G-M. I would get as far as the door and I'd get nauseated. I just couldn't do it. It was shame and guilt and nothing else.

"I must admit, I never really got the terrible kicking around that other people like Collins got—probably because I was a woman. My tough time was all within myself.

"It used to be interesting—to go to a restaurant and see one of my liberal friends, who had never been involved but would call himself a liberal, steeling himself to come over to say hello, to show me that I was not ostracized. Sometimes I felt like saying, 'Don't strain, it's all right.' "[10]

The point, really, is that the situation was inescapable. Twenty years after the fact, the daughter of a blacklisted entertainer went up to a classmate on their first day at Sarah Lawrence and asked, "Are you Ellen Rossen? Our fathers were both blacklisted—isn't that terrific?" Miss Rossen, who now works as a writer with ABC-TV News, says, "I said I didn't see what was so terrific about it. She had the morality of suffering. . . . After my father died, my sister Carol was in California and she had a three-year-old in nursery school. The widow who ran the school was planning to stop by my sister's house one evening and Carol happened to mention that our mother was visiting, and the other woman looked upset and said, 'Well, in that case I had better not come over.' It all had to do with her husband having gone one way and my father having gone the other. Imagine that, the two principals—my father and her husband—were both dead and here it was twenty years later and she still wouldn't come!"

Martin Berkeley long ago moved to Marbella, Spain. He's in touch only with Richard Collins and more rarely William Wheeler. Today many of the survivor-informers are more or less integrated into the life of the community. The new generation is often only dimly aware that such people were "involved" or "controversial" or "blacklisted." If they know more, they are too polite to say. Contemporaries include some who never knew, some who have forgotten, others who have forgiven, but also some who will never forget. To spare the hostess embarrassment, the prudent informer still checks the guest list before he accepts an invitation to dinner.

Manners, it has been observed, are the lowest common denominator of ethical experience. Etiquette is ritual and rituals are the means by which mores are inculcated and preserved. Cicero has written that "the moral function of manners is to give the appearance of being just, the political function is to persuade men to act justly."[11] The social penalties are not the most painful, but for one who would understand the unfinished moral business of the blacklist years, they may be the most significant.

PART IV
LESSONS

IN 1970, WHEN DALTON TRUMBO WAS NOTIFIED that he had been chosen to receive the Screen Writers Guild's highest honor, the Laurel Award, he mulled it over for four days and then decided to make the most of another one of those symbolic occasions where the guild was in effect saying, "We made a mistake." Always the astonisher, Trumbo seized the moment of the award-giving to make his "Only victims" speech. It began with a short history of the guild's beginnings and ended with a tribute to the man after whom the award was originally named, Robert Meltzer, who was killed in World War II. In between, he made remarks that still seem stunning to many who were in the audience:

> I presume that over half of our members have no memory of that blacklist because they were children when it began, or not yet born. To them I would say only this: that the blacklist was a time of evil, and that no one on either side who survived it came through untouched by evil. Caught in a situation that had passed beyond the control of mere individuals, each person reacted as his nature, his needs, his convictions, and his particular circumstances compelled him to. There was bad faith and good, honesty and dishonesty, courage and cowardice, selflessness and opportunism, wisdom and stupidity, good and bad on both sides; and almost every individual involved, no matter where he stood, combined some or all of these antithetical qualities in his own person, in his own acts.
>
> When you who are in your forties or younger look back with curiosity on that dark time, as I think occasionally you should, it will do no good to search for villains or heroes or saints or devils because there were none; there were only victims. Some suffered less than others, some grew and some diminished, but in the final tally we were *all* victims because almost without exception each of us felt compelled to say

things he did not want to say, to do things he did not want to do, to deliver and receive wounds he truly did not want to exchange. That is why none of us—right, left, or center—emerged from that long nightmare without sin.[1]

He paused and repeated the final phrase, "none without sin."

Two and a half years later I walked into Albert Maltz's Hollywood home to interview him for the article I was writing for *The New York Times Magazine* on the Hollywood Ten. The peg for the story was the avalanche of retrospectives then appearing on the blacklist—a subject which the establishment press, including *The New York Times,* had blatantly ignored when it was in operation.

Now, a generation later, Eric Bentley had collected, annotated, and arranged selected testimony in his book *Thirty Years of Treason,* and transformed the material into a play, *Are You Now or Have You Ever Been?* which had bookings in New Haven, New York, and Los Angeles. Robert Vaughn had written and published his doctoral dissertation on the blacklist under the title he borrowed from Trumbo's speech—*Only Victims.* The first history of the blacklist, Stefan Kanfer's biting *Journal of the Plague Years,* was about to appear, Lillian Hellman was at work on *Scoundrel Time,* a UCLA professor (Howard Suber) had contracted with a university press to have a revised version of his doctoral dissertation on HUAC in Hollywood published. Various television and radio specials were in the works. Trumbo's own 1949 polemical pamphlet against the blacklist, *The Time of the Toad,* was reissued along with two other Trumbo essays on the period. Doubtless, interest in the phenomenon was being sparked by the presence in the White House of HUAC-alumnus Richard M. Nixon, who after all had sat through the Hollywood hearings and had used the HUAC investigation of Alger Hiss to catapult his own career from a local to the national arena.

When possible I avoid tape recorders, because I feel ill at ease in their presence (always afraid a battery will give out, a wired connection malfunction) and because I believe note-taking is intrinsic to the rhythm of an interview. But given the historic role of the Hollywood Ten, I thought there might be some value in taping my interviews with them.

"If you don't mind," I said to Maltz, "I'd like to tape our talk."

"Mind? This subject is too important not to be taped," he said soberly. "I am taping it myself." He showed me his more elaborate equipment.

And so we sat down to talk, Maltz taping me taping him. After about an hour, during which Maltz would occasionally go off-the-record and we would press our "off" buttons, he noted that my tape was still running whereas his had played out. "How can that be?" he asked.

"Perhaps one of them is broken?" I offered helpfully. We agreed that if *mine* had broken (he assured me that his was in perfect working order), I should call him before I left town and he would make me a tape of his tape. And that is what happened.

I mention this technological minuet only to underline the point that Albert Maltz is an extremely careful, methodical, and precise man when it comes to matters he cares about. And so I assumed he had a message he was intent on getting out when he handed me two documents, and said of the second: "For reasons you will understand after you read it, I will give you this only on condition that you agree to print it in its entirety. If you cannot give me that assurance, I may take out a full-page ad in *Variety* and run it there. This is a subject of extreme importance."

The first document was a carbon copy of a letter he had just sent off to *The New York Times,* publicly offering his bountiful ruble royalties (earned on the many Russian-language versions of his various books, plays, and stories and held in a nontransferable account in his name in Russia) to the increasingly voluble dissident novelist Alexander Solzhenitsyn, then still living in Russia, where he was, as Maltz put it, "suffering blacklist."

The second document consisted of about five hundred words neatly typed on foolscap. Before reading it I suggested that because *The New York Times Magazine* had given me a word-limit of about five thousand words for my whole article, it might turn out that I would be unable to use his whole statement (and/or I might contrive to fit it in, but my editors might feel it interfered with the flow), in which case I would clear any cuts with him, leaving him the withdrawal option. He was amenable to this arrangement.

The paper he gave me became the opening salvo in an extraordinary three-month correspondence between Maltz and Trumbo. It reads in its entirety:

There is currently in vogue a thesis pronounced first by Dalton Trumbo which declares that everyone during the years of blacklist was equally a "victim." This is factual nonsense and represents a bewildering moral position.

To put the point sharply: If an informer in the French underground who sent a friend to the torture chambers of the Gestapo was equally a victim, then there can be no right or wrong in life that I understand.

Adrian Scott was the producer of the notable film *Crossfire* in 1947 and Edward Dmytryk was its director. *Crossfire* won wide critical acclaim, many awards, and commercial success. Both of these men were members of the Hollywood Ten and opposed the practices of the House Committee on Un-American Activities and refused to cooperate with its attempted invasion of their civil rights. Both were held in contempt of the Committee and subsequently went to jail. When Dmytryk emerged from his prison term he did so with a new set of principles. He suddenly saw the heavenly light, testified as a friend of the Committee, praised its purposes and practices and denounced all who opposed it. Dmytryk immediately found work as a director, and has worked all down the years since. Adrian Scott, who came out of prison with his principles intact, could not produce a film for a studio again until 1970. He was blacklisted for twenty-one years. To assert that he and Dmytryk were equally victims is beyond my comprehension.

He did not advance this doctrine in private or public during the years in which *he* was blacklisted, or at the time he wrote his magnificent pamphlet *The Time of the Toad*. How he can in the same period republish *The Time of the Toad* and present the doctrine that there were "only victims" I cannot say—but he does not speak for me or many others. Let it be noted, however, that his ethic of "equal victims" has been ecstatically embraced by all who cooperated with the Committee on Un-American Activities when there were penalties for not doing so.

Maltz had a lot more to say. When I suggested that perhaps what Trumbo had in mind was the sort of thing John Howard Lawson had meant when he told me (earlier that day) that he found life on the black market corrupting because you worked on scripts you didn't believe in, had no communication with director or producer, and in general labored under conditions that guaranteed an inferior product, Maltz said that the use of the word "corrupted" in that context was meaningless. He explained why:

"Do you remember that at one point Eugene Debs was put into prison and ran for president from the penitentiary in Atlanta? Now being in prison he couldn't travel whistle-stops the way Truman did in 1948, so in that sense his campaign for the presidency was corrupted. But that use of the word corrupted is utterly meaningless. It has no moral value. If you put a man in prison and you chain him to a wall, he can't take exercise. In that sense his life is corrupted, but that's a meaningless use of the word corruption. What Trumbo was saying was that there was no one in that period without sin. He used that—we were all equally compelled to do things we didn't want to do, inflict wounds we didn't want to deliver, to suffer injuries we didn't want to suffer. This is what he said, and I can read you from it again if you want to refresh your memory."

Maltz had recently seen a revival of Arthur Miller's *The Crucible,* which he found to be a magnificent play, but he said he couldn't believe it was written by the same man who wrote *After the Fall.* "In *After the Fall* he gives to the informer as complete a justification as he gives to the man upon whom he informs and whose career he ruined. And I was told that Kazan paused in rehearsals and said proudly, 'That man is me.' Miller had embraced him and absolved him."

This was clearly a position that Maltz deeply opposed. He went on: " 'In the final tally,' Trumbo says, 'we are all victims because almost without exception each of us felt compelled to say things he didn't want to say.' But that isn't true of the Hollywood Ten. To me this makes a mockery of the struggle, which was essentially [about] the right of the Un-American Activities Committee to compel people to follow its political position or pay the price of their careers."

Maltz reeled off example after example of people who never made it back, and he ranged far beyond the movie colony.

"To say, 'None of us emerged from that long nightmare without sin,' is to me ridiculous. To say we're equally without sin—what does that mean? What did we fight for? What did people suffer for?"

What does Trumbo say, I asked, when you put this to him?

"I don't know. He does double-talk to me. I don't understand it, and I want to tell you, others don't understand it. Of course, because Trumbo has been a well-loved and properly admired man, nobody has spoken out before this. But my cup has run over now and I'm speaking out. I'm not going to let this go unchallenged. I should have been warned about it when I told Robert Vaughn what I thought of the 'Only Victims' thesis and he said, 'Well, it makes a nice title.' But the thesis goes on and it gets repeated. It's become a clarion call."

The following afternoon I arrived at the Trumbo household—just a block and a half away on the other side of St. Ives Drive. Where Maltz was methodical Trumbo was casual, where Maltz was solemn Trumbo was jocular. Maltz drank tea, Trumbo drank scotch. He was amenable to my taping the interview and even lent me a tape when my own ran out (that damn machine again). He didn't have his famed parrot on his shoulder, but he did sport the cigarette holder I had seen in pictures, and he kept popping up during our talk for whiskey and books and phone calls.

I made what I later decided was a tactical error in showing him

Maltz's statement shortly after we sat down. I say an error only because it preoccupied Trumbo for the rest of our two hours together. He couldn't get over it. "Do you mean Albert has been stewing over that for two and a half years?" he asked incredulously. "Let me see that thing again," he would say, picking up the paper, scrutinizing it, and shaking his head. Eventually he asked if he could Xerox it. I was reluctant to say yes, because while I was convinced that showing him the statement was the right thing to do for purposes of comment, I thought I ought to have Maltz's okay before I passed it on. (I also confess, somewhat guiltily, that I was probably concerned to keep what I regarded as a minor scoop for myself, and feared that once I let it out of my hands, Xeroxing being what it is, the message would probably find its way into the public domain.*) Anyway, when I asked what he thought about it, he took a few puffs on his cigarette holder, downed what remained of his highball, paused, and said, not unkindly, "Fuck Albert Maltz!"

"What are you to do, for example," Trumbo went on, "about a homosexual caught by the FBI and given the choice of informing or being exposed—in a time when homosexuality was regarded differently than it is now? What were you going to say to that man? It's a choice I wouldn't have wanted to make, and I'm not prepared to damn him. Lillian Hellman once said, 'Forgiveness is God's job, not mine.' Well, so is vengeance, you know. I really am not concerned about it, having lived with it for twenty-five years. Hate is just a goddamned unhealthy thing."

Trumbo volunteered that on the very few occasions when he was the guest of a host who did not know that another guest and he had been on opposite sides, twenty or twenty-five years earlier, "I was unable not to acknowledge that person's presence, and I am physically unable to insult him. . . . I can't do it. There are many of them whom I do not want to see—most of them, in fact—whom I find embarrassing to see. But, you know, to concentrate on them is to forget the enemy. The enemy was the goddamned Committee."

It wasn't that Trumbo advocated automatic amnesty for all informers—he was more selective than that. When Kazan's name came up, for instance, he said: "Kazan is one of those for whom I feel contempt, be-

---

* As I remember it, I never did get around to asking Maltz if I might give Trumbo a copy of his statement. Partly, I guess, because I didn't like the role of go-between, a preference that proved irrelevant, as Maltz later wrote to Trumbo that he had authorized me to show him the statement. This may have been true, but if it was, I didn't remember it, and it wasn't on my tape!

cause he carried down men much less capable of defending themselves than he. And he could have at a minimum continued in the theater, perhaps with somewhat diminished activity, but his reputation would have withstood this blow. If not, he could have gone into smaller theater and he would inevitably have come back, as we all now know. But he brought down people in the theatrical and film world who had much more to lose than he and much less ability to function than he. And that is not nice. I just say that that's not a nice thing. That's the way I feel about him. Why did he bother to kill Tony Kraber?"

It was time, Trumbo seemed to be saying, for forgiveness, but not without discrimination; a time for demythification, a time to stop living off past glories, a time for moral humility.

"Another thing," he said. "The Ten were virgins. We went into an unprecedented situation, which had results we could not predict. (As a matter of fact, we felt we were going to win on the constitutional issue.) No one had ever been blacklisted, nor were they until two or three weeks after [our] hearings. So we could not be certain we would lose our jobs; neither could we have been certain we would go to jail; neither could we be certain that we would become so notorious that there would be no way we could clean ourselves up for a decade. Now, cut to two years later: Everybody else who comes before the Committee knows exactly what the penalty is. All the people who took the First and the Fifth amendments after us knew something we had not known, namely, that they would not work for years. Now I say that those people are in a better position to make a moral judgment of informers than we are, who went in without knowing. We didn't know how hot the water was."

How about those who were able to go back to work by denouncing themselves and managing not to mention others? For example, how about Carl Foreman? "Well, I think that opportunity was only offered by one studio and was only accomplished in two instances. Obviously there was corruption somewhere, but so long as a man didn't inform, if he had been fucked by a corrupt system and could take advantage of that corruption without harming anyone else, possibly without harming himself (except to the degree he did something that he preferred not to do), I see no harm in it. It seems a mild sin, a venial one, and with a few exceptions forgiveness can be granted. I don't admire it, but then, I'm not called upon to admire it."

A few days later I was back in New York when my phone rang. It was Trumbo, and he had a favor to ask. While he understood that I would want to run Maltz's statement, he would appreciate it if I would omit any personal references he might have made regarding Albert, because he thought it unseemly that he get into a public squabble with another member of the Hollywood Ten. "It's the goddamn Committee we should be talking about," he repeated. I told him that what I had done was to quote from his observations on the *issues* Maltz had raised, but that I had omitted any personal references since they seemed irrelevant. This seemed satisfactory, Trumbo said, and we said good-bye.

As is sometimes their wont, the editors of *The New York Times Magazine* saw ways of improving the article, first by calling for additions and later for subtractions; and so it was three months (March 25) before "To Name or Not to Name" found its way into print, by which time Maltz had sent on a slightly amended version of his statement, which I was able to include in its entirety.

It was not until some years later that I discovered that my visits had either triggered or accidentally coincided with—to this day I am not certain which—the postal combat that came in its wake.

On December 23, 1972, Maltz wrote to Trumbo that the time had come for directness. He was outraged, he wrote, by Trumbo's current behavior. Had he not admired him, he would not bother to write, but how could Trumbo, the author of that magnificent polemic *The Time of the Toad,* with its principled vitriol, its scorn for those who "ate toad-meat," sit on a platform at a film retrospective that included one of his own works, and listen without protest to Michael Blankfort, who had toadied to the Committee twenty years before and was now toadying to Trumbo? Elia Kazan, interviewed on the writing of his most recent book, had stated, "I didn't find any heroes or villains in life, so I didn't write any. We're all victims." Where, Maltz asked rhetorically, did that phrasing originate and why did Kazan find it so congenial? How come this philosophic bond between *Toad*'s author and these toadies?

Maltz ended his letter by contrasting the dramatically different fates of Adrian Scott, who did not have his name on a film from 1947 until 1970, with his former collaborator, Edward Dmytryk, who after naming names worked. He, Maltz, was both sad and outraged at Trumbo's "Only Victims" speech, and his conscience required him to make clear that Trumbo did not speak for him.

December 29, 1972

Dear Albert:

My current behavior which you "cannot stomach" appears to center on a speech I delivered two years and nine months ago. It started with a short history of the Guild's clandestine beginnings, in the course of which three members of the Ten were mentioned by name, and ended with the story of a screenwriter who was killed in World War II and blacklisted twelve years after his death by the Guild itself:

If Vaughn, Kazan, Blankfort, and Maltz choose to advance their various ideological precepts by ripping a paragraph or two of that speech out of context, there is nothing I can do to stop one of the oldest tricks in the history of rhetoric.

In a country which, after a reasonable period of punishment, returns murderers and rapists to society on the humane theory that it is still possible for them to become decent and even valuable citizens, I have no intention of fanning the embers of justifiable hatred which burned so brightly twenty-five years ago.

I confess that among those who turned informer there are two or three whose deaths I once actually fantasized, and whom I still view with nothing short of horror. As for the others, I do not associate with them and cannot bring myself to trust them. When, however, chance throws me in the same room with one of them—as, three times in twenty-five years, it has—my sense of personal virtue is not large enough to prevent me from recognizing their existence and accepting their recognition of mine if it is offered.

The retrospective which troubles you so greatly was arranged by the Los Angeles County Museum, the American Film Institute, and the Writers Guild. I had nothing to do with the selection of its principal film, and did not know who the chairman would be until I read the museum's printed circular.

His introductory remarks were so fulsome that I felt obliged to call them a eulogy and remind the audience that I was not yet dead. I'm sorry I offended you by smiling. I rather hope you would have smiled in the same circumstances.

I'm also sorry it didn't occur to me to preface my rather brief remarks with a declaration that I was speaking for myself, and not for Albert Maltz. The truth is that during the past two years I have expressed my political and other opinions on a dozen national TV shows as well as in scores of newspaper and magazine interviews, and not once has it entered my mind that even one of those millions of viewers and readers would leap to the conclusion that I had been chosen to express your opinions rather than my own.

Did you, on the other hand, believe that you spoke for me when you donated a bad debt to poor Solzhenitsyn, who already has more uncollectable accounts than a man in his position actually needs? Or when, on an earlier occasion, you responded to a tribute much more fulsome than mine at the museum by hailing the German Democratic Republic, whose citizens had been so kind to Jews and heretics, as the harbinger of a new era in the history of human freedom and cultural excellence—did you, or your audience, truly believe that you were speaking for Dalton Trumbo? I didn't. Neither did anyone who knows me.

I emphasize the point because your letter of December 23, received on December 26, concludes with a warning: "When opportunities come, it will be a matter of conscience for me to make clear that you are speaking for yourself, and not for me."

Being thus put on notice, how could I have suspected that at least one opportunity had already come and been seized upon?—that a full three weeks earlier you had delivered an excoriation of my acts and wrong thinking to *The New York Times* with the admonition that it be published in full or returned so that you could publish it yourself in a paid advertisement? Don't you think that a letter so boldly characterized as "blunt" might have contained just the slightest hint that, without my knowledge, you had already accomplished what your letter only threatened to accomplish at some point in future time?

Although a man can be charged with murder in one sentence, it often requires a hundred pages to prove his innocence. In the peculiar and somewhat tricky circumstances with which you now confront me, I'm sure you understand how foolish I would be to respond privately to charges which you intend to develop in public. I shall therefore withhold a detailed answer until the issue is joined. . . .

Sincerely,
Dalton

P.S. I reject your remarks about Adrian altogether. Had you loved him more, you could not have found it possible to score a mere debater's point by invoking his illness and death.

The issue *was* joined, and the far-ranging correspondence that followed was alternately serious, hilarious, generous, bitter, trivial, brilliant, obtuse, illuminating, petty, profound, glib, talmudic, vitriolic, inspirational, gossipy, and philosophical—a mix of dialectical glee, bile, and insight. But the themes that emerged from this eccentric exchange eventually transcended its flavor, not least because they were the obsessions of men whose past conduct—they resisted unjust authority at personal risk when it counted—eloquently informed and qualified their respective calls for compassion and justice.

Trumbo's statement must have been written when he was in his cups,

Maltz answered, because there *were* villains, there *were* heroes, there *were* constitutional rights at stake, there *was* a crisis of conscience to be addressed. If everybody was equally a victim, what had the Ten been fighting about? Maltz challenged Trumbo to explain to him about the wounds they inflicted on each other which made everyone "equally a victim." He closed with an offer: if Trumbo could explain this in a way that made sense, Maltz would refrain from criticizing his speech.

Trumbo's answer (January 12) began by allowing as how he would rather "have stayed in bed," but, "The challenge of explaining *anything* in a way that can make sense to you, combined with the prospect of persuading you not to publish a critical word about a speech delivered thirty-four months ago, is much too exciting for a man of my diseased temperament to resist." The remainder of the letter consisted of pieces of Maltz's letter cut, clipped, and pasted, interspersed with Trumbo's gloss on each passage. He explained he had adopted this expedient because he was leaving soon for location work in the Caribbean (where he made *Papillon,* a film about escaped convicts, which has long passages on the informer) and planned to answer by fits and starts. "With any luck at all we should be able to wrap the whole thing up in a hundred pages, give or take ten or fifteen, which should give us plenty of time and energy for the next hot issue—Base and Superstructure, for example, or Therapeutic Vengeance in the Age of Total Despair." He denied he was in his cups, confessed that he *tried* to wound particular informers, and said that at least two of the Ten *felt* wounded by their brethren. He noted that Adrian Scott got off the blacklist in London in 1961 and that his subsequent misfortunes were caused by Committee resisters, among others; denied that he consorted with informers; and surmised that Maltz was really angry at Blankfort, and that's what this whole thing was about. Then:

> The fact that in your first letter you make no mention of informers at all indicates to me that you drew a line which included in your category of the damned all who ate "toad meat" before the Committee—an immensely larger number of people to be avoided including, of course, Mike Blankfort. While I don't give a damn what Blankfort and scores of others said so long as they weren't informers, you do.
>
> Fair enough. You drew your line here; I drew mine there. My line stopped at informers (my first letter rather precisely defined my attitude toward them, so it need not be repeated here). Your line stopped at everyone, whether informer or not, whose testimony before the

Committee did not, in some way, resemble ours. Your line makes Blankfort verboten; mine does not. I'm perfectly willing for you to observe your line, but you are *not* willing for me to observe mine. On the contrary, you insist that I abandon mine and govern my actions by yours. That is the worm at the heart of our current disagreement—that I crossed your line and appeared with Blankfort.

Trumbo explicated his *Time of the Toad* and other of his writings to show that over the years his target had always been the Committee rather than informers, and he suggested that Maltz, who was in Mexico ("no, no—wait a minute there. I'm not blaming you for where you lived during those years"), was out of touch. He went into the dictionary definitions of heroes and villains to prove that the Ten were not heroic, and argued that their primary aim "was to avoid being informers," that they were men "who in that particular moment and situation chose to behave with honor." The informers, Trumbo suggested, had not been villains when they joined the Communist Party, and their preference in the 1950s was not to be informers.

Why did they do what they did?

There were all kinds of motives: a man, to support a business venture, had hypothecated everything he possessed in anticipation of future income, without which he would be bankrupted; a man caught in a homosexual act and given the choice of informing or facing exposure and prosecution in a time when it was more disgraceful to be a homosexual than a Communist; a woman who had worked her way from secretary to writer, now three months' pregnant, the sole support of herself and . . . husband, whose brother had a long record of crime and imprisonment; a man who had left the CP to avoid constant attempts to meddle with the ideological content of his writing; a foreign-born citizen threatened with revocation of his naturalization papers; a man who left the Party because he could not stomach its insistence that the early phases of World War II offered no choice between Hitler and the West; a person whose spouse suffered from recurrent spells of melancholia which, in such a crisis as political exposure, could have resulted in suicide; a person whose disagreement with the CP had turned to forthright hostility and who, when the crunch came, saw no reason to sacrifice his career in defense of the rights of people he now hated; a resident alien threatened with deportation; a person who had been unjustly treated and testified to get even—and then, of course (since fear rarely brings out the best in any of us), the weak, the cunning, the ambitious and the greedy.

Whatever their faults, those sixty-odd unwilling witnesses were ordinarily decent people put to a test which you and I have declared to be immoral, illegal and impermissible. They failed the test and became informers. Had they not been put to the test, they would not have informed. They were, like us, victims of an ordeal that should not be imposed on anybody, and of the Committee which imposed it. As for calling them villains, that cannot be done until the history and definition of *villain* is rewritten to conform with what you believe it should mean even though it doesn't.

So, Trumbo asked Maltz, "what the hell are you bleeding about? This victim business? Forget it. Unless you adulterate it by faking an 'equally' in there, the facts aren't with you."

There was a lot more to Trumbo's forty-one-page letter, but that's the gist. Four days later (January 16) Maltz (in two pages, since he had a novel to finish) reminded Trumbo that the Ten took the First Amendment not to avoid being informers but, rather, to challenge and hope to destroy the Committee's authority, at the risk of spending time in jail.

Trumbo riposted (February 7) with seven cut-and-paste pages reminding Maltz that the Ten barely mentioned the First Amendment, that instead of declining to answer questions, they pretended to be answering them in their own way (which was to attack the Committee's right to ask), the purpose of which was to protect their legal position. "The truth of the debt you say we owe to history," he wrote, "will be this: that confronted with the stark choice between perjury and informing, we decided not to inform and went to jail for it," but that out of self-interest (i.e., their desire to avoid jail) they had fudged the issue.

And so the correspondence continued—until late March, when Maltz, learning of the cancer that had attacked Trumbo and was eventually to kill him, refrained from burdening Trumbo with a final, already written, four pages.*

On the surface the debate is a stand-off. Why did the Hollywood Ten not invoke the Fifth Amendment? Well, since the Supreme Court didn't say until 1950 (in the Blau case) that a witness could avoid being in con-

---

* Cleo Trumbo had returned Maltz's last letter unopened. When Trumbo appeared temporarily on the road to recovery, Maltz, having learned of the serious nature of the illness, kept his final letter to himself.

tempt of court or Congress by invoking the Fifth Amendment on the question of Communist Party membership, and this was three years after the Ten were called, neither the Ten nor their counsel could have been certain that "taking the Fifth" would get them off the hook. Score one for Trumbo. Did the Hollywood Ten behave as they did so as to avoid being informers? Well, none of them *wanted* to be informers, but that issue had not come into sharp focus when they testified, since HUAC's first round of friendly witnesses were people who hadn't been Party members and therefore had no names to name. Score one for Maltz. Were the Hollywood Ten and the informers "*equally* victims"? Obviously not. Score another one for Maltz. But Trumbo had never used the word "equally," which originated with Maltz. Score one for Trumbo. And so on. Trumbo wins on polemics—he's funnier. And Maltz wins on biology—viscerally one responds to his sense of outrage.

But precisely what does all of this writing and typing and cutting and pasting signify, aside from Trumbo's epistolary flair and Maltz's passion to set the record straight? It could be argued that this was merely a personal feud, but it is far from that. Trumbo has died, and the argument still goes on. Lester Cole, who says that "Trumbo's 'Only Victims' speech was like Ford pardoning Nixon, if you ask me,"[2] wrote a letter to the editor of *The New York Times* in 1978 attacking Ring Lardner,[3] who carried on his own correspondence with Maltz after Trumbo died.

Or, one could chalk the moral indignation up to resentment. Consider the circumstance of Albert Maltz. Pre-blacklist, he had been a leading theoretician of the Communist Party, an influential playwright in the revolutionary theater, a top Hollywood screenwriter whose work on such films as *This Gun for Hire* (1942) and *Pride of the Marines* (1945) met both entertainment and "cause" criteria. Maltz emerged from prison in 1951 disillusioned with socialist realism, out-of-touch, blacklisted. He never made it back as theorist, novelist, or screenwriter. Trumbo, on the other hand, who never had Maltz's literary aspirations or pretensions, was back hacking away with the best of them (*Spartacus, Exodus, Lonely Are the Brave, The Sandpiper, Hawaii, Papillon, The Fixer*, and his own more experimental *Johnny Got His Gun*). And the gracefully noisy Trumbo was celebrated in the mass media as the blacklist-breaker. He had become for a new generation the symbol of blacklistee redivivus. To grant informers the status of victim, to downgrade the Hollywood Ten from heroes to mere honorable men, might be said to dilute Maltz's most enduring claim to the benefit of history's doubt, to jeopardize his position as noble victim.

But this sociological approach to moral indignation misses the merits. And if we are to learn from the experience of the blacklist, it is important to address directly the moral issues that pervade the Maltz-Trumbo exchange and haunt the blacklist generation. For interwoven in this dispute are concerns and insights that help to illuminate the conditions under which some people resist and others succumb to unjust authority; the symbolic relationship of etiquette to morality; the tension between public and private virtue; and the role of forgiveness and vengeance in the pursuit of justice.

Robert Rossen's son Stephen laughed when he heard of the Maltz-Trumbo argument. "That's it," he said. "It all comes down to which way do you pass the butter? Do you give it to the guy on your left or do you insult him by sending it all the way around the table?" Yet to say that it all comes down to the path of the butter plate is to ignore the fact that when matters of social etiquette are transformed into symbolic politics, the consequences are real. Life in the penumbra of perpetual social embarrassment can be unpleasant, as we have seen in the case of the informers, to the point of being unbearable (which the people on the blacklist learned when they were themselves among the stigmatized). Had the informers been accused of legal crimes rather than moral ones, had they been punished by courts of law, perhaps their victims would let the matter rest. But these victims never had the satisfaction of expiation. Their living-room morality may be regarded as an attempt to complete the unfinished business of the war between the liberals. Where the Committee demanded of its cooperative witnesses fake renunciation and penitence, its victims will not be satisfied with anything less than the real thing. Sterling Hayden, who renounced and denounced his own informing from coast to coast, speaking on demand at meetings organized by the Committee to Abolish HUAC/HISC, has won a measure of forgiveness even from Albert Maltz, but he is the exception who proves the rule.

Far from trivial, the underlying issue has to do with classic and complex dilemmas. Is there a statute of limitations on moral crimes? How does one reconcile the tension between the impulse to forgive and the impulse to punish, between generosity and accountability, between mercy and justice, compassion and vengeance?

14.
The Question of Forgiveness

MORAL PHILOSOPHERS ask at least three questions about the issues in dispute.[1] First, there are the utilitarians who ask, How can we achieve the greatest good for the greatest number?

Dalton Trumbo's answer was simple: *not* by focusing on the informer, which is to ignore the real enemy—the House Un-American Activities Committee—and beyond the investigators, the deeper social and economic forces of counterrevolution that gave rise to the Committee itself. To focus on the informer, in this perspective, is to divert valuable moral energy from root causes.

Sylvia Jarrico objects to the sort of amnesty Trumbo proposed, also for utilitarian reasons. She sees the social insult, the symbolic gesture, the silent treatment, not as ways of preserving personal purity but, rather, as a means of protecting the polity. "There is an ease among my friends in the industry that I don't feel," says Sylvia Jarrico, who left Hollywood for Paris in 1957 and came back in 1964. "When I left Los Angeles in 1957 I had a tender feeling toward people who had been able to resist the blandishments of the industry. I respected all the people who were willing to take a beating for a point of view—a point of view that was not in their best interests but in everybody's best interest.

"About informers—I know there are differences among them—I accepted that they were dangerous and irresponsible people as a class. I felt there was value in holding them responsible for what they had done, expressing that view to others and regarding them as dangerous people to associate with. On my return, what had changed was that most people had accommodated to the point where they could work with or for informers. Certain kinds of ideas that were unspeakable in the early sixties could be widely and publicly discussed. The Levitts will tell you that you can't function seriously as a working writer in the industry and not work with informers in a civilized way."

For Sylvia Jarrico, the argument over who suffered more—informer or informed-against—trivializes the evil wrought by betrayal. Her suggestion is that yesterday's informer should today be held in obloquy, not by way of punishment, but because "you have to be in advance of the stereotyping and prevailing thinking of your own times, and that's what requires eternal vigilance. That's what the phrase 'eternal vigilance is the price of liberty' has come to mean for me. It's terribly important for people to act on their own convictions, and to do so in such a way that there's no doubt about what the convictions are. In times like ours, the only security one has is to make oneself known."

A second sort of moral philosopher asks questions of duty, promise, obligation. Trumbo's view was that the informers had for the most part paid their debt to society and therefore, "in a country which, after a reasonable period of punishment, returns murderers and rapists to society on the humane theory that it is still possible for them to become decent and even valuable citizens, I have no intention of fanning the embers of justifiable hatred which burned so brightly twenty-five years ago." After all, they had suffered enough; in loss of self-esteem alone their debt has been paid.

Maltz contends that it is our duty to the "real" victims of the blacklist—men like Adrian Scott and Canada Lee and J. Edward Bromberg—to honor their martyrdom by carrying on the fight. People who commit crimes, even moral ones, must be punished, and if the punishment is merely social ostracism, then all the more reason to maintain it; otherwise there is moral crime without punishment. Informing was not merely a political and ideological mistake but a moral one. Not to recognize it as such at this late date is to demonstrate the depth of man's commitment to rationalizing his own errors. It may be true, as Spinoza said, that if men do evil, it is only because they "fall hostage to imperfect reasoning, to external causes and confusing passions."[2] But that does not make people less responsible for their actions. Responsibility is there to be taken and assigned. As the psychiatrist Walter Reich wrote, when asking himself what was the responsibility of Soviet psychiatrists for sending Russian political dissidents to "mental institutions," "Maybe the universe can be absolved from evil, but not man. So long as he has the capacity to see evil in himself, he cannot be allowed to deny it forever. He has to be told it's there. And if he fails to listen, he has to be condemned."[3]

Finally, there are those who ask, How would a good man act? What would a virtuous man, a person of character and conscience, do? Trumbo teaches the virtue of forgiveness and generosity of spirit. Maltz reminds us that a virtuous man keeps a decent distance from the carriers of social evil.

And as might be expected, the spectrum contains more subtle hues.

The blacklisted writer Arnaud d'Usseau says, "It's not a question of forgiving your enemies. It's a question of forgetting them." Whenever Abe Polonsky goes to Paris, sooner or later the French, who have a special interest in both Polonsky and Kazan, whom they regard as great film directors, ask what he thinks about Kazan having informed.* "Well, he did a bad thing," says Polonsky. "But he doesn't want to admit it. That's his problem, that isn't my problem. I consider that he did a bad thing. That's all I say—from the point of view of being a street boy and no other point of view. You see, he *only did a bad thing*. He did not destroy the universe. He treats it as if he were face-to-face with the ultimate judgment, as do many of the other stool pigeons and many of the non-stool pigeons. But, actually, we passed through a tremendous hysterical event. Some people acted one way, some people acted the other. I think a lot of them acted pretty lousy. These are new times and new circumstances, let them act well now. I have nothing against them. The damage is done. I don't want to crucify them; it's a waste of time to crucify someone who isn't the son of the Lord.

"I just don't have anything to do with them on the grounds that it's undignified. No, that's a wrong word. It's just I don't feel pleasant toward them because they did a bad thing to me. I don't like people who named me. I wish they would leave me alone and get out of here. That's the way I feel about them now.

"I wish they had acted better, but they're not all Adolf Hitlers. That's all. I myself don't want to have anything to do with them. After all, I was on the ship and they got off and let us go down. In fact, the only way they could get off was by putting us down. That's the peculiar feeling: It wasn't only that they took the lifeboats from the *Titanic,* you know; they pulled the plugs. That leaves a disagreeable feeling about them—but no more than I have about other people who have done horrible things. There were fellas in the war who tried to kill me; they shot guns at me. I don't forgive them either. But I don't go to their country, now, and shoot them down, do I?"

To identify social evil is one thing; to know what to do about it twenty-five years later is another. Simon Wiesenthal, famous for tracking down

* The critic Robert Benayoun argued that the informer-Kazan and the resister-Polonsky reflected their politics in their films. Using Kazan's *East of Eden* (1955) and Polonsky's *Force of Evil* (1949), he found that each director manipulated the Cain and Abel story to justify his own attitude toward HUAC. Kazan in *East of Eden* said good and evil are ambiguous, and Polonsky in *Force of Evil* said capitalism corrupts. ("Cain, Abel et le Dollar," *Positif,* May 1967, 19–24.)

escaped Nazis, a professional in the business of delayed justice, has, appropriately enough, posed a relevant ethical riddle. He tells the story of how he, as a young Jew, was called to the bedside of a dying SS man who confessed to having participated in an action where the inhabitants of a Jewish village were burned alive. The soldier asked forgiveness. Wiesenthal, torn between horror and compassion, said nothing and left, and the SS man died. Years later, he was still asking himself and others, Was his action right?

Of the various answers he considers, there is one in particular which seems apropos. "I cannot forgive you for what you have done to everybody else," Wiesenthal says. "Only the victim—or God—can forgive that. I can forgive you only for what you have done to me." Forgetting is something that time may take care of, but forgiveness is "an act of volition" and "only the sufferer is qualified to make that decision."[4] Individuals who belong to "victim collectivities" are entitled to complete freedom of judgment. The right to revenge thus has the same status as the right to forgiveness. Maltz and Trumbo as victims are each entitled to their own moral style. Indeed, it is useful to remind ourselves of the extent to which their difference is less over value than moral style.

Both men saw the House Un-American Activities Committee as the enemy. Both men agreed that the honorable course of action was to resist the Committee. Both agreed that the informers failed the test. Both had a sense of solidarity with a community of values that motivated them to join the Party in the first place. As Trumbo wrote to Maltz:

> Whatever else may be said of Communists and the goals they pursued, I think you and I can agree that those who joined the Party were animated by a sincere desire to change the world and make it better, even at the cost of affiliating with an organization that had, from its beginnings, been subject to constant federal harassment, popular hatred, and sometimes physical violence. . . . The impulses which caused them to affiliate with the CP were *good* impulses, and the men and women who acted on them were good people.[5]

Despite their disenchantment with the Communist Party, each remained involved with the community of those who share socialist-humanist values: Trumbo would strengthen it by inviting the informers back in from the cold; Maltz would protect it from contamination by those he regards as still unclean. And, not least important, both shared the assumption that moral argument can make a difference and—in contrast to those informers who would prefer not to talk about it—that moral activity must be susceptible of public defense. Trumbo preferred not to argue with another member of the Hollywood Ten in public, but he took the trouble to make his "Only Victims" speech in public on an occasion of maximum political symbolism. And Maltz took the trouble to question it, in the press and in private.

Let history decide whether the resisters as a class were heroes and the informers as a class were villains or whether, as Ring Lardner later put it, "The choice we faced was between being 'heroes' and being complete shits."[6] Since we cannot know the deepest motives of any individual on either side, perhaps it is the beginning of wisdom to acknowledge that, whatever their motives, the resisters did the right thing, and, whatever *their* motives, the informers did not. "You feel here," Murray Kempton observed of Lillian Hellman, but he could have been talking about the resisters as a community, "the operations of a general nobility, and no small part of a shrewd instinct about the future, an awareness—and such senses have much to do with honor—of how the thing would look in due course."

Kempton thinks of Hellman as "inclined to be a hanging judge of the motives of persons whose opinions differ from their own." Nevertheless, he honors her for her moment. "It is her summit. We can ask from her nothing more; I do not suppose that in the only crucial sense we really need to. The most important thing is never to forget that here is someone who knew how to act when there was nothing harder on earth than knowing how to act."

The lesson Kempton draws, and it is one that has general application, is that "there comes a time when you have to go into capital, and be ready to face up to the loss of a lot, because you are wise enough to sense that the alternative is to lose everything."[7]

Hellman, Trumbo, Maltz, and their comrades resisted and prevailed. Perhaps they behaved as they did out of status-anxiety. Perhaps they were salivating in response to the bell of Party discipline. Perhaps they did it for the rest of us. Perhaps they did it because it was the right thing to do. By risking in some cases their careers and in other cases their freedom as well, by doing their time (in prison and in career-purgatory), they have emerged in the culture as moral exemplars; they taught us how to act, and as a result appear to have made it more difficult to happen again; and as a group they have earned the right to be taken seriously, to be heard. Individuals among them may even have something to teach individuals among us.

15.

The Question of Obedience

IT IS APPROPRIATE that a Nazi-tracker like Simon Wiesenthal should have something to teach the blacklist alumni, for a recurring image in the discourse of many of them is the concentration camp. "If an informer in the French underground who sent a friend to the torture chambers of the Gestapo was equally a victim, then there can be no right and wrong in life that I understand,"[1] wrote Albert Maltz. "If all he had was a disagreement politically with some people he named," says Abe Polonsky of Elia Kazan, "they wouldn't have fought him; they would have disagreed with him. . . . This was something else. This was, Who goes to the concentration camp? Do I go with you or do you go by yourself?"

"This is the beginning," Dalton Trumbo shouted at the gavel-pounding J. Parnell Thomas, "of an American concentration camp!"

Yet despite the undeniable parallels, it seems a mistake and, worse, it risks the trivialization of man's most monstrous crimes against his fellow man to suggest—as the Communist Party was all too anxious to do in its contemporary tracts—that the loss of swimming pools and huge salaries suffered by the Hollywood Communists was in any way comparable to the mass murder and torture characteristic of the concentration camp. No such connection is intended here. The literature on the behavior of human beings in extreme situations does provide, however, a rich repository of clues to the unwritten laws governing man's behavior under stress. Looking at the history of the blacklist in that perspective, one asks oneself, What does this literature tell us about the conditions under which men accept and resist the moral authority of their oppressors? How does the experience of the Hollywood informers fit these findings, and what does it add to our understanding of the issues at stake?

Two dominant tendencies emerge from the literature on life in the

Nazi concentration camps of the 1930s and 1940s. First, the SS deliberately tried to break up all social ties among the inmates and to reduce them to an undifferentiated, degraded mass. At the same time, presumably because they needed some minimal cooperation to carry out the day's routine, they appointed some inmates "Kapos" to carry out their orders. As the sociologist Barrington Moore has noted, these two tendencies enabled the SS "to pervert social cooperation into exploitation."[2] The destruction of prior social ties was also the technique of the NKVD during the Soviet purges. All "suspects" were asked two questions: Who recruited you? Whom did you recruit? The insistence that men betray their fellows and inform was not of course peculiar to the Nazi or Soviet camps but may be found in varying degree in virtually any repressive arrangement.

The insistence of HUAC's Congressman Donald Jackson that the willing naming of names was "the ultimate test of the credibility of a witness before the Committee" served, as we have seen, as a double degradation ritual—of the stigmatizer and the stigmatized. It enhanced the power of HUAC and its members. But it also functioned to cut the ties that bound the old left together. Betrayal ended camaraderie, poisoned the community well.

When Martin Gang and Philip Cohen and indeed some of the mainstream Jewish organizations and their representatives worked with HUAC to help separate the "innocent" from the "guilty," it would be excessive to accuse them of "playing the Kapo role," but it would be obtuse to ignore that they were doing the authorities' dirty work. "During the time of the Spanish Inquisition," Gang said, "I suppose if a poor son of a bitch was supposed to be a Jew but wasn't, he had to go to a lawyer and try to convince the Inquisition he ain't a Jew. . . . What would a lawyer do in a case like that? What would you do if you were in my position?"

On entering the Nazi camps, the prisoners faced "welcoming ceremonies," traumatic rites of passage of a brutalizing nature. Uniforms and numbers take away individuality. HUAC's own degradation ceremonies were not nearly so brutal, but the Committee's insistence that all witnesses recite its incantations was calculated to subvert the ethic of individualism in favor of an ethic of going-alongism.

Bruno Bettelheim, himself a survivor of the Nazi camps, noted in his study of camp life, *The Informed Heart,* that many inmates lost the capacity to resist, even in the privacy of their thoughts and even though it would have brought them self-respect to do so. They blamed their condition on the bureaucracy and administrative oversight and error, rather than seeing the SS as the enemy.[3] Those who were most likely to survive were those with strong religious or political convictions, like the Jehovah's Witnesses and the Communists. In Hollywood, as we have seen, the "reasons why" disillusioned ex-Party members collaborated were as plentiful as second features. Doctrinaire Communists, however, were among the fiercest opponents of and organizers against the Committee. No admittedly then-current member of the Communist Party was subpoenaed who failed to take the Fifth Amendment. If this be "Party discipline," here is a case where they made the most of it.

One unexpected finding of scholars like Bettelheim and Moore has been that prisoners feared not only the SS but other prisoners. In Hollywood, "You didn't know who was for you or against you," said Conrad Bromberg of his father's perpetual dilemma. The domestic cold war led first to moral confusion and eventually to a moral numbing. The sins of the parents were attributed to the children. Anything short of informing was sanctified among some, and nothing but was good enough for others.

For many inmates, hostility in the camps was directed less toward the captors than toward the resisters, because official retaliation for individual acts of resistance was taken against all. The delicate system of compromise and corruption that is the basis of prison life is upset by the heroic resister. The war between the liberals was fought, as we have noted, mostly in print, and the stakes had more to do with political, social, and economic status than with life and death; but it was, one suspects, fear of being identified with less respectable resisters that caused otherwise humanist and libertarian organizations like the Anti-Defamation League and the American Jewish Committee to respond to the Jewish Communist Louis Harap's noisy charges of anti-Semitism against HUAC not by denouncing the Committee, which was harassing citizens for their beliefs and affiliations, but by denouncing the denouncer. Thus the conference where executives of the Jewish organizations told HUAC chairman Velde that if he "had consulted the files of the AJC and the ADL the Committee would have been prepared to deflate and deflect Harap's testimony." It was, perhaps, the same impulse which led various officers and board members of the ACLU to work behind the scenes with the FBI to ferret out Communists and sympathizers in their own organization.

Scholars of the Holocaust have offered a variety of explanations for the camp inmates' acceptance of their captors' dubious moral authority, but three in particular seem relevant even to such relatively banal circumstances as those confronting the HUAC informers in the 1950s.

The first was values shared with the enemy. Many "patriotic" Germans shared beliefs adhered to by the SS (in the superiority of the Aryan race, Germany's right to expansion via annexation, and so on), and many of those who named names agreed with HUAC that Communism was the enemy. Elia Kazan spoke for many when he said in his ad, "Secrecy serves the Communists. At the other pole, it serves those who are interested in silencing liberal voices. The employment of a lot of good liberals is threatened because they have allowed themselves to become associated with or silenced by the Communists. Liberals must speak out."

A second cause of camp docility can be described as peer pressures against solo heroics—those single acts of defiance which risked mass retaliation and as such were condemned by the group as threatening its survival. Hollywood producers and agents pressured their talent not to make trouble lest the entire industry suffer. And the ill-advised efforts of the organized Jewish community to help the Committee and other agents of the repression weed out the "innocent" from the "guilty" undoubtedly sprang from a genuine fear that the Jewish community as a whole was bound to suffer from the visible resistance of the few, especially where the few were tainted as "subversive" of established authority for following the Party line.

Third, the inmates in the camps were encouraged to imitate and beat the guards at their own sadistic games. Thus inmates occasionally went beyond SS brutality—prisoners in charge of others sometimes behaved more cruelly than the SS officers themselves; prisoners eliminated traitors in their midst with SS tactics of torture and slow death. Our modest repression has no equivalent. But it should not be forgotten that the willingness of organizations to beat HUAC, McCarthy, or the FBI to it by purging their own ranks of Communists was expressed in the loyalty oaths not merely adopted by talent guilds and read into the morals clauses by the studios but also codified by the ACLU, the ABA, the NAACP, and many other organizations that espoused a humanist and libertarian rhetoric. In the argot of the day, they were being "tough-minded realists," as opposed to "mush-headed idealists."

A final factor, which partakes of the nature of a self-fulfilling prophecy, was detected by Barrington Moore not only in the camps but in a number of other extreme contexts. "It is possible," he writes, "to discern a general pattern of cultural explanation that stifles the impulse to do anything about suffering. The explanation produces the effect by making suffering appear as part of the cosmic order, hence inevitable and in a sense justified. Even more significantly, the form of explanation helps to turn aggressive impulses that suffering and frustration produce against the self."[4]

In Germany in the 1930s it was said that the system was not at fault, merely its application. In America in the 1950s it was said that by the sloppiness of his methods McCarthy was giving anti-Communism a bad name. It was suggested that procedures could be perfected so that the wrong guys would not get caught. And the contribution of many cold war intellectuals was to explain why the McCarthy phenomenon was the inevitable reaction to liberal "softness on Communism."

The penalties paid by blacklist victims obviously cannot be compared to the price of the camps. McCarthy was not Hitler. But the mechanisms of repression underlying McCarthyism had something in common with the mechanisms of repression of both fascist and Communist bureaucrats—namely, the joining of cultural, corporate, and political forces of domination, a phenomenon identified and analyzed in the literature on totalitarianism, and elaborated in the anti-utopian fiction of such writers as Orwell, Huxley, and Koestler.

It should quickly be added, however, that in recognizing the evils intrinsic to totalitarian societies, it would be a mistake to repeat one of the great political confusions of the 1950s—the merging of Nazi Germany and Soviet Russia in the American image of totalitarianism. Norman Thomas, who should have known better, talked of red fascism. Shortly after Germany invaded Russia in June 1941, *The Wall Street Journal* observed, "The American people know that the principal difference between Mr. Hitler and Mr. Stalin is the size of their respective mustaches."[5] Hannah Arendt's strictures on the evils of the totalitarian state[6] make a profound contribution to our understanding of contemporary politics, but they should not be manipulated to obscure the profound difference between Marxists, who identified with the weak and spoke the language of social justice, and fascists, who identified with an elite and spoke the language of racism and violence. While Stalinist cynicism undoubtedly accounts for the continued loyalty of some of the Party members, it was precisely this important difference between fascism and Marxism that helps to explain why it took others of the Hollywood Communists so long to let go of their illusions about the Soviet Union, and why they were so reluctant to name former comrades, even after they themselves had lost the faith. The simplistic "Look, Ma, he's a totalitarian" tone of much of the rhetoric concerning so-called totalitarian societies and individuals should be replaced with a vocabulary that frankly acknowledges that the identification of a totalitarian, like the identification of a pluralist, is but the beginning of a set of presumptions from which one must always struggle toward the truth.

Another literature, much closer to home, which by its nature is free of such ideological pitfalls but which bears directly on the conditions under which men do and don't go along, may be found in two famous undertakings in social psychology: the Asch and Milgram experiments described below. Each presents a vivid demonstration of how easy it is to manipulate the individual in a group context, even where his senses provide evidence that is blatantly contrary to his instructions.*

The object of the experiment of Solomon E. Asch was to discover the effect of group pressure on individuals. The subject was asked to compare the length of a line with three unequal lines, while others in the room performed the same task. Unbeknownst to the subject, all the others were confederates. In the midst of his monotonous matching task, the subject suddenly found his judgment unanimously contradicted by the others. On the average, 32 percent—or just short of one-third of the subjects— conformed their estimates to the opinions of their fellows. The statistic is a fascinating one, for approximately one-third of the witnesses called before HUAC at the height of its investigations into the entertainment business turned out to be informers.

(In a variation on the main experiment, one confederate gave the correct answer before the real subject could speak, while all the remaining confidants gave the wrong answers; yet the proportion of subjects who went along with the incorrect majority dropped to 5.5 percent. So if the experiment reveals the frightening power of group pressure, it also reveals that a single ally can provide sufficient support to enable a person to make a "correct" judgment—at least in this simplified situation.[7])

Sylvia Richards seems a good example of someone who "knew" that the naming of names constituted a betrayal, that it was wrong. But on hearing her doctor, her boss, her lawyer, indeed the vast majority of her culture deny the evidence of her moral senses, she went along with the crowd. Perhaps Asch's experiment has special meaning for the 1950s, which was, after all, the decade of the organization man, the other-directed man, the man in the gray flannel suit, the age of conformity, the silent

---

* Both experiments, especially the Milgram, have been attacked on methodological and moral grounds. Here we needn't pretend to concern ourselves with the morality of the experiments, a fascinating subject in itself, but only with their results. I don't have the technical expertise to pass judgment on the methodology, hence I cite them only for their analogical rather than their evidential value.

generation, and so forth. Arthur Schlesinger, Jr., called it "the bland leading the bland."

The Milgram experiment, reported in Stanley Milgram's book *Obedience to Authority*, had as its purpose to discover the conditions under which human beings cease to obey legitimate authority when its commands become obviously cruel. The volunteers were told that they would be asked to give or receive electric shocks in order to advance scientific information about the connection between punishment and learning. Each subject entered the laboratory in the company of another "volunteer" (actually a trained actor) who was ostensibly the "student," to whom the real subject in the role of "teacher" would administer increasingly severe electric shocks.

The subject-"teacher" was presented with a panel of switches marked from 15 to 450 in eight steps, culminating in a legend that read, "Danger—Severe Shock" at 375, and "XXX" up to 450. He was instructed (by the "experimenter" in a white laboratory coat) to administer increasingly severe shocks to the "student" as the latter made mistakes. The "student" made intentional mistakes, and with each "shock" gave increasing signs of pain, twisting and writhing and pounding on the wall and finally calling for the experiment to be ended. The "experimenter" told the "teacher" that the experiment "required" that he continue to administer shocks, adding that "although the shocks may be painful, there is no permanent tissue damage, so please go on."

Milgram's purpose was to see at what point the subjects, who believed they were inflicting real pain, would refuse to obey orders, and was shocked to find that most subjects went all the way or nearly all the way to the "XXX" shocks.

(In one variation, confederate "teachers" refused to go along, and given this example most of the subject-"teachers" rebelled. As in the Asch experiment a single ally was enough to liberate subjects to follow their best instincts.)

The interpreted finding: "Pure moral autonomy in the form of lone resistance to an apparently benign authority is very rare. With support from peers, on the other hand, the same kind of resistance increases enormously."[8]

Was the outbreak of name-naming, the pervasive betrayal, the celebration of collaboration that characterized the Hollywood informers in the 1950s an aberration, a departure from our history, our culture, and, more generally, the conventional conduct of man? The literature of the concentration camp says no. People betray their comrades in situations they perceive as extreme. The experiments of the social psychologists say no. People betray themselves, or at least their values and senses, when significant pressures toward conformity are part of the environment. The cultural history of the domestic cold war says no. It was not merely that the informers were wrong in their analyses of obligations and outcomes. As Robert Lifton observed, apropos a group of Vietnam veterans, "The only thing worse than absurd evil is to have that evil rationalized and justified by the guardians of the spirit." The guardians of the spirit to whom Lifton had reference were the chaplains and psychologists, who formed an unholy alliance not only with the military command but with corrupt elements in the soldiers' individual psyches. He speaks of the existence of a "counterfeit universe," in which an all-pervasive, spiritually reinforced inner corruption becomes the price of survival. "In such an inverted moral universe whatever residual ethical sensitivity impels the individual against adjusting to evil is under constant internal and external assault."[9] In much the same way did many liberals form an unholy alliance not only with the congressional investigators but with the whole entourage of informers, collaborators, guilty bystanders, and go-alongers. It was as if Larry Parks and all the rest of the cooperative witnesses had volunteered to be subjects in an experiment whose confederates included their lawyers, guilds, doctors, lobbies, producers, agents, and the rest. It was, in other words, as if the culture had converted into a colossal laboratory for the duration of the cold war.

Consider the investigations into subversion in the entertainment community in the 1950s as a Milgram experiment: the subjects are those subpoenaed to appear before HUAC as witnesses. They receive instructions that they are to name names in order to advance the scientific information about the connection between the Communist conspiracy and the mass-communications industry.

A witness enters the laboratory of HUAC willing to collaborate in the enterprise of revealing information. The names he is asked to name are like the switches in the Milgram experiment. Those who have already been named publicly are at the lower end of the spectrum. But when he is asked to name new names, he is in effect asked to hit the "Danger—Severe Shock" switch, i.e., loss of job, career, or whatever.

When he pleads to be exonerated from inflicting such pain, the Committee, the "experimenter," tells him that the experiment "requires" that he continue to administer shocks, i.e., to name names. And even as Milgram's experimenter mentioned that "although the shocks may be painful there is no permanent tissue damage, so please go on," so did

Congressman Walter try to soothe Larry Parks's conscience as he observed, "I think you could get some comfort out of the fact that the people whose names have been mentioned have been subpoenaed so that if they ever do appear here it won't be as a result of anything that you have testified to."

Even as Milgram's subjects turned out not to be inflicting "real" pain, so did many witnesses in the HUAC experiment turn out to name the names the Committee already had.

And even as Milgram's "teachers" turned out to be victims—morally stigmatized with having agreed to torture the innocent—so did Larry Parks and his confreres turn out to leave the experiment with permanent stigmata and scars.

The HUAC experiment "worked" because almost everybody played by the rules. Even many witnesses who took the Fifth Amendment preferred not to talk about it after they left the Committee room. A few noisy souls like Trumbo and Lardner and Howard Da Silva and John Randolph railed against the blacklist at every opportunity. But by and large, the culture, including especially the establishment press, whose job it should have been to expose it, seemed to accept the weird ground rules of the experimenter. (Elizabeth Poe [Kerby] managed a scoop-exposé of the blacklist in tiny *Frontier* magazine, not through innovative investigative journalism but because *The New York Times,* for example, chose not to write about what everybody knew. It wasn't exactly a conspiracy of silence, since the trade papers themselves had no compunctions about printing revisions in the day-to-day rules of the experiment: for instance, their reports on the American Legion's letter-writing project read as matter-of-factly as schedules for catching a railroad back to respectability.) And while the gossip columnists of the tabloid press zeroed in on the central transaction of the informer system—the naming of names—the way an arbitrageur might pounce on a newly valued currency, their purpose was not to question or expose or reveal or even report but to join the transaction, to trade in and profit by the currency of the day. They were connection points in a network they serviced rather than challenged.

The assumed and thus invisible feature of the Milgram experiment, as in most laboratory tests, is a controlled environment. The experimenter determines the total situation. The environment is truly totalitarian.

In the McCarthy era, the cooperators, collaborators, name-namers, and, no less critical, the silent spectators had in common that they all lent themselves to the assumptions of the experimental situation. The failure to write about it, to denounce it, to open it up for inspection, to identify and analyze the elements of the informer system, and, yes, to name the names of the betrayal network and tell how it worked, was a failure not merely of courage but in many cases of perspective. The *Times* reported that Arthur Miller and Elia Kazan had stopped working together because they had had a falling-out, but neglected to say over what. The mass media did not realize they were part of the pathology.

It was a period when virtually everybody played the game. There were no confederates in white coats, but it was the time of the big charade. Only where the "players" abide by the received rules of communication can charades or experiments survive. As a country and a culture Americans were, during the cold war, governed by the questions they didn't ask.

16.

The Question of Candor

IN THE FIRST HALF OF THE THIRD CENTURY A.D., in the city of Lydda, there was an incident involving the prophet Elijah, Joshua Ben Levi, the leading rabbi in Israel, and Ulla bar Quosheb, a refugee wanted by the government, who was hiding in Joshua's attic.

The refugee had committed a political crime against the government. The authorities sent troops and threatened to destroy Lydda unless he was handed over.

Joshua went up to his attic and persuaded Ulla, who was not one of his own flock, to give himself up, even though it would mean his life. The rabbi argued, "It is better that one man should be slain than that the community should be punished on his account."

For the next thirty days Elijah stayed away from the home of Joshua Ben Levi, and the rabbi fasted. On the thirtieth day Elijah returned, and the rabbi asked why he had not been around. "Am I an associate of betrayers?" asked the prophet. The rabbi protested. The teaching of the Talmud, he said, lays down that, "If a company of Jews walking down the road is threatened by heathens who say, 'Give us one of you that we may kill him, otherwise we shall kill you all,' they must rather all be killed. However, if the demand is for a named individual like Sheeba, son of Bichri, then in order to avoid wholesale slaughter, he should be surrendered." It was on the strength of this last clause, said Joshua Ben Levi, that he delivered Ulla.[1]

But there is conflicting authority. In Genesis it says, "Though they all be killed, they shall not surrender a single soul from Israel" (the Hebrew word for surrender is *masar*—to give up, to betray, to denounce).

The distinctions get finer and finer. Where the request is for someone specific, it may be a slightly different matter but not much. Another authority says that to surrender someone, he must "be deserving of death."

What if two, three, five are claimed? Two out of a group of six? A group of two thousand? Suppose a village is requested, by way of reprisal, to hand over three inhabitants—any odd three—not for execution but to be put in captivity or to have their eyes put out, or for they know not what? Suppose the demand is semispecific—as for a member of a specific family? The rabbis were divided then, and the scholars are divided now. The talmudic scholar clearly says, "This is an area where much must be left to conscience, the weighing up of moral and practical necessities and opportunities in the actual emergency."[2]

Like Joshua Ben Levi, some liberals surrendered the Communists and fellow travelers to the authorities. At best, they did so not merely to save their own skins but to save the city—to preserve the future of liberalism. The informers in this paradigm were the executioners, the front-line soldiers in the war between the liberals, the ones whose hands got dirtiest. But by their lack of candor, their failure to admit and defend what they were, they make it difficult to clarify and learn about the issues of conscience.

Indeed, the Hollywood Ten fudged the issue when, on legal advice, each witness coupled his First Amendment refusal to respond to constitutionally objectionable are-you-or-have-you-ever-been questions with the pretense that by denouncing the Committee he was "answering" it "in my own way." (The mistaken theory was that a jury might acquit him on the grounds that Committee harassment prevented him from answering.) In their public-relations campaign which followed upon their convictions, the Ten sloughed off this legalistic trick; instead, they emphasized that their refusals had been motivated by their determination to defend the First Amendment and the Constitution as a whole. In the overheated political atmosphere of the time such a contention was much closer to the truth than the contentions of their enemies—that these Hollywood Marxists constituted a conspiratorial threat to the Republic, that HUAC was engaged in an honest fact-finding mission, that Hollywood had been subverted.

As we have seen in the Trumbo-Maltz debate, the Ten differed over the issue of *why* they did it. Maltz says they did it to destroy the Committee. Trumbo says they did it to avoid being informers.

But that is not what their critics refer to when they talk of "lack of candor." To them, the Hollywood Ten and all the witnesses who "hid behind the Fifth" were "Stalinists" masquerading as Jeffersonians. To the art critic Hilton Kramer, for example, the silence of these people about their real political commitments tainted the entire liberal community and led to the confusion of liberals with Communists, without which McCarthyism as a national phenomenon would not have been possible. The Ten, Lillian Hellman, and the rest were in this view apologists for Stalinism and for a system of government that arrested and tortured millions.[3]

"What one was asked to defend," writes the editor of *Partisan Review* William Phillips, "was their right to lie about it." Eric Bentley joined the issue most directly in his *Thirty Years of Treason*, when he wrote: ". . . to radicalism, candor is no adornment, it is of the essence. . . . So, in the HUAC hearings, the rhetoric of John Howard Lawson merely counterbalances that of the Committee. Bullshit equals bullshit."[4]

Serious charges in a 1970s rerun of the 1950s war between the liberals. But they confuse rather than illuminate. On the literal question of candor before the Committee a critical distinction should quickly be made. It was the Hollywood Ten's public expression of their political opinion which explains why they were caught. It wasn't lack of candor or concealment of their political views that got them in their pickle. It was the fact that all of them in one way or another had been very forthright in announcing what they thought about every controversial issue that came up. There was no lack of candor there. The Ten tried to draw the line at the difference between expression of opinion and confession of affiliation. As many of them have pointed out, the Committees of Correspondence, the Sons of Liberty, the abolitionists who ran the underground railroad during the Civil War, and even CIO organizers in the 1930s all denied affiliation for tactical reasons. John Howard Lawson, who told me he had "always taken pride in having given a good part of my life to the struggle against thought control," took understandable offense at Bentley's equation of his and HUAC's rhetoric. "Where Bentley got the idea that candor is the hallmark of the true revolutionary is beyond me. The idea that real radicals are obligated to adhere to the rules of disclosure imposed by their oppressors seems too fantastic to merit serious discussion."

Still, one may ask why the Hollywood Ten didn't publicly declare, "Yes, we are members of the CP, it is perfectly legal, and to hell with you. But we're still not going to answer the Committee." "To do that," Dalton Trumbo argued, "is to imperil the whole principle of the right of political privacy because by throwing it away in public you do not really preserve it."

Albert Maltz adds, "I know that the Communist Party leadership in America was eager for everyone who possibly could to be an open Communist. They wanted people to say, 'Yes I am a Communist, this is what I stand for, let's discuss it.' But the actualities of life in America . . . were that if you were an open Communist, you couldn't hold a job. Suppose you were a teacher? What open Communist could hold a job in the American public-school system or an American university? What man working in a Ford assembly-line plant in the year 1930 could announce that he was a member of the Communist Party? It was the repressive nature of democratic American society that caused many members of the Communist Party to remain secret members. It is quite true that if the Party had been open, that might have made it less easy for the congressional committees to do the job they did, but under the circumstances of historic growth, there was no other way to function."

Notwithstanding such disclaimers, it seems quite clear that the CP—with its wooden, inflammatory rhetoric, its so-called democratic centralism, its clandestine style, its overresponsiveness to Soviet policy and the consequent abrupt flip-flops in its Party line, its fortress mentality (an understandable reaction to the red hunt), and its lack of faith in the protective freedoms—was a contributor to its own problems. A dismal failure at making a politics out of its repression, its sole success was in reinforcing those who had the backbone to resist. But to blame the CP or its ex-members for McCarthyism is an absurd and classic case of blaming the victim—like blaming the deer for hunting season.

The Hollywood Ten drew their line at telling the Committee about themselves. Later resisters—Lillian Hellman and Arthur Miller among them—were willing to tell the Committee about themselves but not about others. Some of these witnesses, too, have been accused of lack of candor in improperly invoking the Fifth Amendment since it was designed to protect a witness and not his friends. But Telford Taylor, the lawyer-general who served as the American presiding judge at the Nuremberg trials, has disposed of this legalistic objection with his distinction between "motive" and "basis."[5] Miss Hellman's *motive* for not cooperating may have been her disinclination to bring trouble to others, but the legal *basis* for invoking the Fifth Amendment was the possibility that her testimony—she had, after all, attended Party functions with Dashiell Hammett—could have been used to implicate her in an alleged conspiracy. In the context of those times, such considerations were not merely legally permissible but conventionally prudent.

In an open society there is a presumption in favor of candor, even as there is a presumption against informing. But presumptions are meant to be tested and can be rebutted. If the Communists were simply "lying" because they regarded capitalists as class enemies against whom all forms of deceit are permitted, then little beyond Marxist platitude can be said on their behalf. But in certain contexts openness can be destructive—to oneself and one's values—and the question is whether this was one of those contexts. Sissela Bok has argued that those who lie to enemies out of a conviction that justice allows it fail to take into account the effect of the lies on themselves, on others, and on the general level of trust. But even Professor Bok concedes that in times of persecution honest answers to inquiries into political beliefs "may rob people of their freedom, their employment, respect in their communities. Refusal to give information that could blacklist a friend is then justified. . . . One has a right to protect oneself from illegitimate inquiries."[6]

My own view is that the resisters, since they would suffer the stigma anyway, no matter how they testified, had nothing to lose and society something to gain by a spirited, nonrhetorical, discriminating defense of their political pasts (or presents), in or out of the Committee room (their preference). The dialogue they avoided because "it would have been political suicide" could only have eased the atmosphere. But mine is a political rather than a moral judgment made now rather than then, a footnote to the more important fact of their resistance at a time when resistance became identical with morality. If nothing else, the Maltz-Trumbo difference over why the Hollywood Ten did what they did gives the lie to the portrait of Communist and ex-Communist witnesses as automaton-Stalinists misleading the rest of us as to their motives and purposes. "Is it not possible to be a Marxist, a Communist, and be for the First Amendment? Why are they mutually exclusive?" asks Martin Popper, a Marxist and militant and articulate New York lawyer who was part of the Ten's defense team and who himself testified before HUAC and took the First Amendment, which he came to believe and today argues persuasively everyone should have taken as the best means of mobilizing the country against the Committee mentality. The folksinger Pete Seeger took the First Amendment before HUAC even after it was established that the Fifth would keep him out of prison and the First might not.[7] "Look," he said, "the Fifth means they can't ask *me*, the First means they can't ask anybody." Abe Polonsky, on the other hand, is an example of a Communist who proudly took the Fifth Amendment. "The most amazing reason put forward for taking the First was that it would be easier to get employment—people would respect you more. The trouble with that reasoning is that if you take the First you are going to have a court case and a court case is going to cost a hundred thousand dollars if you take it all the way up. But if you take the Fifth you save some money. And everyone who took the First had to have a Committee of Friends to help raise the money, right? It became a cause. You can't afford to have a hundred causes."

Beyond the reputation of the amendments, critics claim that "Stalinist apologists" like Trumbo, Maltz, and Hellman were complicit in a greater evil than those who may have resisted McCarthyism with insufficient vigor. Stalin's defenders then are said to have no business giving moral lectures now to those who were Stalin's early enemies. The celebration of books like *Scoundrel Time,* and the "new wave of revisionism" that neglects to mention "other blacklists," it is said, honors the people who were blacklisted at the expense of anti-Stalinist informers; such enterprises are particularly offensive because, they believe, a new generation is being misled.

The trouble with these truths is that they are partial—in both senses. Domestic Stalinists helped their friends and Party colleagues and occasionally bullied their ideological enemies, but to equate these faults with the institutionalized HUAC–*Red Channels*–MPAPAI–industry blacklist against the left smacks of what George Orwell called forged history. The immediate context of McCarthyism was not Stalinism in the Soviet Union but wildly exaggerated images of a red menace in the United States.

It is, in any event, a waste to refight the civil war among the liberals of the 1950s, especially when what is also going on is a competition for the redistribution of moral prestige. As survivors approach the end of their days, we should be alert to arguments framed in political or ideological or historical terms that turn out to be autobiographical protectionism in the guise of history, case studies in the same old struggle over "immortality."

> Let him try to explain in any other way the life-and-death viciousness of all ideological disputes. Each person nourishes his immortality in the ideology of self-perpetuation to which he gives his allegiance; this gives his life the only abiding significance it can have. No wonder men go into a rage over fine points of belief: if your adversary wins the argument about truth, *you die.* Your immortality system has been shown to be fallible, your life becomes fallible. History, then, can be understood as the succession of ideologies that console for death. Or, more momentously, *all* cultural forms are *in essence sacred* because they seek the perpetuation and redemption of the individual life.[8]

One needn't adopt the anthropologist Ernest Becker's metaphysics to observe that to ask that we put McCarthyism in a Stalinist context is a request that we mitigate our disappointment in those who went along with the blacklist. "How can anybody get upset about blacklisting," Aryeh

Neier, a former director of the ACLU, has pointed out, "if it must be viewed in the context of the carnage perpetrated by the Stalinist regime? Would the same critics insist that any attack on the sins of the Soviet regime must also point out how bad things were under the tsar? Are Solzhenitsyn's works defective if he is silent about the torture practiced by the Okhrana?"[9]

When the informers and those who premised their politics on the government's right to investigate what it judged to be "threats" to its security are confronted with the fact that they are defending collaboration with unjust authority (and today few of them would defend either the motives or methods of the congressional red hunters), betrayal of friendship and the sacrifices of others to save the self, rather than concede that abandoning men and women like Bromberg, Kraber, Bessie, Levitt, and the rest to the enemy was by any standard unacceptable, they prefer to change the subject to Stalin. Who, then, lacks candor?

The Hollywood progressives were wrong about many things, and some of them had bullying political styles. Trumbo points out that the Hollywood Ten were reluctant heroes at best, expecting to win and fudging the First Amendment as a self-serving strategy. Maltz reminds us that Lillian Hellman, who despite her eloquence did not risk prison, portrays herself in her memoir as alone against the McCarthyite crowd, when in fact she was a private in a virtual army of resisters, many of whom risked and suffered more than she. Hellman's wisecrack that Arthur Miller, who told HUAC he had "been to hell and back and seen the devil," must have gone as a tourist—meant that he was too cozy with the Committee for her taste, too willing to grant their right to ask the questions in the first place. More fundamentally, the center liberals point out that these people were collectively wrong about Stalin, failed to see the great moral crime of their day.

Yet all of the resisters took personal risk for the common good. Some put it in terms of conscience, others, like Lawson, put it in terms of the struggle for control of the media, or as a constitutional issue, or as a chance to break HUAC, to cut off the witch-hunt at its inception. Whatever the motive, they did not permit the state to take over *their* values; they defined their own situation, and by risking self and career they emerged as moral exemplars. Tarnished exemplars, but exemplars nonetheless. Their presentation of themselves today—however self-serving or patronizing to those who named them—cannot and should not obscure what they did yesterday.

The blacklist experience suggests that the old assumption that the public interest is composed of the sum of private interests just doesn't work.

We learn from our study of Hollywood's guilds, trade associations, agents, lawyers, religious and civic organizations, and the industry itself that the utilitarian ethic, and the liberal individualism it presupposes, wasn't good enough. When each organization operated in its own interest, the sum of private interests turned out not to equal the public interest. A flaw in the calculus of pluralism. Adam Smith doesn't work in the marketplace of moral issues.

And so it is with the less consequential but no less difficult discriminations that must be made in the case of the film community's informers. The collective experience of those who were tested under pressure should help us to clarify our ethical norms. Some failed the test, others survived damage to the spirit and found moral energy in resistance. We should try not to shirk the task of articulating the lessons to be learned from that experience, however tentative, fragmentary, and unpleasant some of them may be.

We learn from the literature of men under stress that human beings tend to go along, to move with the mob, to bend the knee to their oppressor, to obey dubious authority. But we also learn that given models of courage, men are inspired to resist. How many were assisted in their own determination to resist because of the examples of the Hollywood Ten, Arthur Miller, Lillian Hellman, Pete Seeger, et al., and what will the example mean for the future? We learn from the celebration of imperfect souls like Miss Hellman that the moral exemplar has the power to reach persons in ways and to a degree that no law can touch. We learn from the performance of the resisters not that loyalty is more important than truth or even, with E. M. Forster, that it is better to betray one's country than one's friends, but rather that one must abide by one's code.

I suspect that those who in the 1950s considered the informer as patriot intuitively understood that it was necessary to rationalize this violation of the primitive instinct to protect one's own. Hence the twin myths of the day: the presentation of Party members as cunning participants in an international espionage conspiracy and of the informer as folk hero. If the purpose of the latter was mythification, the purpose of the former was to persuade the public and the informer himself that here was an extreme situation where human choice is intolerably restricted, where, as the philosophers tell us, survival alone may count and moral considerations be obliterated; where the moral personality is crushed, the ability to choose is destroyed.

But America in the early 1950s was not an extreme situation. In every compact—whether of friendship or membership—there are unwritten escape clauses, but when one would invoke such a clause to turn in a former comrade to the state one must be prepared to defend the action publicly, and to suffer the guilt and other consequences of playing the informer. Those who truly saw the situation as the sort of national emergency that justified suspension of traditional comradely expectations misread the environment and remind us of the need for true perspective.

The informer's highest claim to virtue is that he told the truth, but we learn that as a class they were involved in a fiction. The informers' particular lie was that they were telling all when they only told some. *Un*friendly less-than-truth-tellers were prosecuted for contempt of Congress and perjury (witness Harvey Matusow, Frank Wilkinson, and the Hollywood Ten), but the friendlies were celebrated. Such selective prosecution signified a corrupt system, and set a pattern and precedents that linger in unspoken ways. It also provided the informers with a strategy for dealing with shame, made it more comfortable to collaborate, made self-deception possible, if not the deception of others. To the extent that name-naming was a charade, to that extent they could persuade themselves they had done no damage to their former friends and comrades.

We learn from the images of the epoch, and the explanations citizens give for their actions, how easy it is to persuade oneself that a predicament is a crisis, a mere difficulty a life-and-death emergency, a discomfort an extreme situation. People prefer to be freed from traditional moral constraints. We learn from the cooperation between humanistic organizations and repressive intelligence agencies, between enlightened lawyers and the House Committee on Un-American Activities, how important it is to recognize the enemy.

We judge from the nature of the congressional hearings themselves that their purpose was the obverse of what is was advertised to be. These were not information-gathering investigations so much as they were degradation ceremonies. Ironically it was the informer who was degraded, because the informer represented a threat not merely to the person he named but to the community. He was regarded as a polluter— and became a perpetual outsider.

We deduce that silence—although in many circumstances necessary to the protection of privacy and a right to be preserved—was nevertheless an unwise strategy and kept important issues out of the discussion. Moral positions must be capable of public defense. Mystification, whether by informer or resister, is the enemy of enlightenment.

We deduce from the survey of damage done that, as Dalton Trumbo said, the informer, too, was a victim. But if the community benefits from the example of the moral exemplar, those who believe there are lessons to be learned from moral obloquy must be granted the right to treat the informer as moral leper—to keep him at bay and in the limelight. In either event, we infer from Barrington Moore that it is a tactical error for victims to engage in internecine dispute. Fragmentation plays into the hands of the enemy. And Simon Wiesenthal teaches us that only the victim has the right to forgive and then only on behalf of himself.

Remembering Santayana's familiar injunction that those who do not learn from the mistakes of the past are doomed to repeat them, it seems that much more important for the general community to recognize its complicity in the larger social evil. It is impossible to know the extent to which those pariahs who do the dirty work of society are really acting as agents for the rest of us.

Ernest Becker has argued that what man really fears is not so much extinction but extinction with insignificance. Man wants to know that his life has somehow counted, if not for himself then at least in a larger scheme of things, that it has left a trace, a trace that has meaning. Man's "natural" and "inevitable" urge to deny mortality and achieve a heroic self-image are the root causes of much human evil, and when we see the dynamic of victimization and scapegoating across history, what we are looking at is the offering of the other man's body in order to buy off one's own death. "It is true that a weak man will . . . buy off his own death by taking another. . . . Most men will not usually kill unless it is under the banner of some kind of fight against evil."[10]

Some of the informers have resorted to mesmerization and mystification to avoid facing the wrongs they have done—to the community, to their fellows, to themselves. If they could achieve self-knowledge, the hardest kind, we might move from there to recognition that they were doing the dirty work not merely of the nonresisters, but also of those resisters who instead of turning over their conscience to the state had turned it over to the Communist Party.

Some socialists and liberals were critical both of Stalinists and of informers who cooperated with the committees, but, as we have seen, all too many decent people accept the fallacy of the greater evil in their revisits to the thirties, forties, and fifties. There is no moral abacus that enables one to ignore the consequences of petty transactions in favor of some theoretical grand total. Discussions of comparative evils become not merely frivolous but invidious, diversionary, and occasionally dishonest. Even where the disagreement is an honest and profound one, the invocation of the greater evil muddles the issue, confuses the possibility of clarity, postpones facing-up.

We have seen that our culture presented the informer as a moral hero in order to justify the unjustifiable. We have seen how our guilds, trade associations, artists, and lawyers all accepted the illusion of inevitability and in so doing collaborated in the perpetuation of social evil. We have seen how trust, our most cherished of possessions, was dissipated and the possibility of true community polluted by the advent of symbolic betrayal and literal collaboration. Morality, we are told, is a voice of conscience from within in harmony with a voice of authority from without. We have seen what happens when the citizen delegates his conscience to the state.

Afterword

When I turned in the manuscript for *Naming Names*, I felt I had stopped, rather than finished. I had been reading and interviewing for eight years, but there were more people to see, questions to ask, mysteries to solve. Now, a decade later, it is possible to supply some of the missing pieces. The director Elia Kazan, contrary to my suggestion that his reticence was strategic, has given us a sprawling, in some respects spell-binding, 848-page account of why he did what he did and how he feels about it (ambivalent then, but unapologetic now). Although he doesn't say where he got the notion, he writes, "I concluded that what these fellows were conducting was a degradation ceremony, in which the acts of informing were more important than the information conveyed" (thank you very much). But he named the names anyway on the theory that exposing communist hypocrisy was worth it. Courtesy of the widow of the writer Carl Foreman and of the daughter of his lawyer Sidney Cohn, I have now read Foreman's secret testimony before Congressman Walter's committee of one. If you believed him at the time, Foreman was alone in his managing to go back to work without having to name any names, and contradictory rumors flourished about what he had, or hadn't, done. I can now warrant that he did not name names after all. Although he did comply with the committee's other conditions (ritualistic denunciation of the Communist party and affirmation of HUAC's role in wounding it), he created a counter-ritual of his own, deploring the uses to which its findings were put, without denouncing the hearings themselves.

The Freedom of Information Act was in its infancy when I started my research, and although I had obtained the FBI file of the late actor Larry Parks, whose testimony established the naming names litmus, his file was the sole piece of evidence to bolster the suspicion, harbored by many on the left, that, despite their denials, the FBI and HUAC had been in cahoots. Further FOIA filings were, I believed, destined to yield further documentation. In his book *Hoover and the UnAmericans: The FBI, HUAC and the Red Menace* (Temple, 1983) an enterprising young scholar, Kenneth O'Reilly, definitively documents the extensive behind-the-scenes exchange of information between the FBI and HUAC.

And then there is the matter of a minor character in the blacklist years, who seemed not particularly relevant one way or the other to the question of the informer: the president of the Screen Actors Guild, Ronald Reagan. A month after *Naming Names* was originally published, Ronald Reagan was elected president of the United States. Formerly uninterested talk show hosts now asked me, "How did you know when you began your research in 1972 that the subject would be so timely?" Neither they, nor I, understood the real resonance of the question. I knew that, as president of the Screen Actors Guild, Reagan was the one who had turned down Gale Sondergaard's request for assistance when she received her HUAC subpoena (see p. 128). I knew that, just prior to the Republican nominating convention of 1980, candidate Reagan had told Robert Scheer of the *Los Angeles Times* that "there was no such thing as a blacklist," thus repeating the official industry line of thirty years earlier. And I knew that, such protestations notwithstanding, the blacklist had played Cupid to Reagan and an attractive young MGM contract player, Nancy Davis. Apparently Miss Davis was upset that her name had landed on some left-wing mailing lists, and she consulted her friend the director Mervyn LeRoy, who suggested that they bring the matter to the attention of the Guild president Reagan. Reagan consulted union membership files, found that Miss Davis's name had been confused with that of another actress, and invited her to dinner to give her the good news. "It was in this manner," concluded E. L. Doctorow, writing in *The Nation*, "after giving her a loyalty check, that Ronald Reagan met his wife to be." What I had not known, until it came out via the Freedom of Information Act late in 1985, was that as early as April 10, 1947, Reagan was secretly passing on the names of suspected communists in the Guild to the FBI. So regularly did he deal with the Bureau that he was given an informer's code number, T-10, and was included on a list of eighteen such informers. This early consolidation of his links with Hoover's FBI makes one wonder to what extent his naming of names facilitated his transformation from Hollywood character actor to political contender.

* * *

Reagan's election only reinforced my sense that *Naming Names* involved unfinished business. It was not merely Reagan's anticommunist rhetoric but the omnipresence of the so-called New Right in his corner that led many to talk of Cold War II, a New McCarthyism. The House Committee on Un-American Activities and the old Senate Internal Security Committee were gone by the end of the 70s, but a new Senate Subcommittee on Security and Terrorism was in place. The American Legion, with its cartoon patriotism, was not much in evidence, but on the eve of Reagan's inauguration, the Heritage Foundation, a right-wing think tank, issued a 3,000-page, 9-volume report with the blessing and participation of the president-elect's chief counsel and soon to be attorney general, Edwin Meese. It called for the revival of HUAC (and hundreds of House signatures were quickly gathered on a petition that could make that happen). Its intelligence chapter read like an agenda for repression. It asked for the legalization of breaking and entering, bugging and tapping, and overtly advocated the placing of informers in antinuclear and other dissident organizations. Its message: Whenever civil liberty is thought to be in tension with national safety, the former must give way to the latter. Congress quickly passed the Names of Agents bill, which for the first time made it a crime to publish certain information, even when that information—the names of intelligence agents of the revelation of their techniques—was previously a matter of public record. The vocabulary was new, but not the concept—communist propaganda was now disinformation; where once we had been warned against espionage agents, now we were told to beware of agents of influence. *Terrorist* joined *communist* as a scare word, although the two were not mutually exclusive by a long shot. By June of 1981, hundreds of civil liberties groups across the country could join in a day-long protest under the rubric "No More Witch-Hunts!"

Reagan gave civil libertarians much to protest about. The evil empire became his all-purpose excuse for expanding the role of the intelligence agencies, reclassifying desclassified documents, across-the-board cutbacks on information and liberty. As the journalist–historian Walter Karp noted, the Reagan administration, which came to power promising to "get government off the backs of the people," ended up subjecting and habituating the people to polygraph tests, drug tests, blood tests, urine tests, roadside police checks, surveillance, snooping, official harassment, and various forms of censorship. And George Bush, when his turn came, reached back to the language of McCarthyism as he accused his opponent of being "a card-carrying member of the ACLU," and to the techniques of McCarthyism when he aired a guilt-by-association television commercial about the black rapist Willie Horton. Nevertheless, for a variety of reasons the much-feared New McCarthyism never took hold. Senator Jeremiah Denton, the chairman of the Security and Terrorism subcommittee, turned out to lack Senator McCarthy's flair and staying power; J. Edgar Hoover was not around to mobilize the internal security establishment and intimidate the other establishment; Mikhail Gorbachev, with his glasnost and perestroika, undermined the image of a Kremlin-based international, monolithic, communist conspiracy; and, once elected, George Bush seemed to stop pushing the fear-buttons.

But if a new domestic cold war never materialized, a new spirit of intolerance, energized by, but independent of, Washington, did. PEN, the organization of poets, essayists, and novelists, faithfully chronicled its manifestations, among them: In Onida, South Carolina, birth control information was removed from the high school guidance office, and the word "evolution" was banned from advanced biology. In Piano, Texas, teachers stopped asking students their opinions because to do so, they were told, is to deny absolute right and wrong. In Des Moines, Iowa, a high school production of *Grease*, the hit broadway musical, was banned. In Mount Diabolo, California, *Ms.*, the feminist magazine, was taken off the shelves. In 7-11s across the land, *Playboy* and *Penthouse* disappeared. Vonnegut, Salinger, Judy Blume, Jonathan Swift, and countless other modern and classic writers fell victim to scared school library committees. Even the Mark Twain High School in West Virginia removed a copy of *Huckleberry Finn* from its library shelves! And the president of the Pro-Family Forum in Fort Worth, Texas, explained why all of this was happening in a leaflet titled "Is Humanism Molesting Your Child?" The answer? "Humanism is everywhere. It is destructive in our nation, destructive in the family, destructive to the individual."

At the tail end of the Reagan administration, Attorney General Meese took his antipornography commission on the road, where it played to fundamentalists and others already threatened by the urban, cosmopolitan, sophisticated sensibility that seemed to pervade so much of the electronic media. And after Bush became president, North Carolina's Senator Jesse Helms got into the act with a carefully calculated campaign against the National Endowment for the Arts, which was accused of spending taxpayer dollars on homoerotic art and other degeneracies. We were off to the culture wars.

In human terms, the casualties of the culture wars were trivial compared to those of the cold war, but the metaphor was too obvious to resist. Once again the target group was the creative community, only this time instead of filmmakers trafficking in enemy propaganda, it was artists trafficking in images of religion, unmentionable bodily fluids, sex, and violence. The old loyalty oath now took the form of the anti-obscenity pledge that all NEA grant recipients were required to sign. The NEA chairman's attempt to preempt more drastic congressional action by personally vetoing four previously recommended grants reminds one of nothing so much as Ronald Reagan's efforts while on the Motion Picture Industry Council, whose purpose was to show Congress that the motion picture industry could "clean its own house," by beating Congress to it. And even as Red Channels and Aware, Inc. and scores of free enterprise blacklisters fueled the anticommunist crusade of the 50s, the Reverend Donald Wildman and his American Family Association had the company of the Traditional Values Coalition in California, Phyllis Schafly's Eagle Forum, Pat Robertson and his Christian Coalition, and so forth. Just as John Henry Faulk and others tried to break the blacklist with lawsuits, so the New School for Social Research sued the Endowment, claiming a violation of First Amendment rights. Joe Papp, himself an alumnus of the blacklist, was among the first to turn down an NEA grant on principle. And when the Coalition for Freedom of Expression, representing 250 arts organizations, set up a fund to redistribute grant money to the four vetoed performance artists via contributions from their own NEA grants or regular operating budgets, they called their fund the Anti-blacklist Fund.

But hold that metaphor. As commentators incessantly pointed out, this particular culture war involved merely grant deprivation, not career cut-off. And there is a deeper, more significant difference. As the cold war wound down and the culture war heated up, America seemed to be discovering a new enemy—not an unimportant matter in a country which has historically defined itself by what it is against. Philip Green, the Smith College political scientist, observed as long ago as 1982 that "for all McCarthy's occasional references to 'Commie rats' and his denunciations of 'twenty years of treason,' for him and his followers the enemy of the American way of life was ultimately external." Those who were to be read out of the body politic were spies, traitors, or dupes. Un-Americans were literally un-American: They had alien ideas, they were instruments of the international conspiracy. But as the definition of the enemy yielded diminishing returns, the definition of the enemy changed. Now the enemy was becoming internal. As Green wrote, "It is us, us and our degenerate, cosmopolitan, relativistic secular ideas. . . ."

Remember, this gradual replacement of Karl Marx by John Stuart Mill all took place *before* the East European revolutions of 1989 deprived us of our familiar red enemy. As I write, historians, op editorialists, and others debate who "won" the cold war. The mainstream U.S. consensus is that Americans are "victors" in the cold war because the peoples of Eastern Europe chose capitalism (Milton Friedmanism, yet) over communism. For myself, the question of who won the cold war is itself a cold war appendage. Personally, I agree with the social historian E. P. Thompson, who argues that the "victors" are those who brought the cold war to an end: the forces of democracy and renewal in East and Central Europe, who liberated themselves from the cold war dynamic, and who, with luck, will no longer be pawns in the superpower game.

. Nor do I see in the new revelations of communist brutality in Europe grounds for reopening the question of appropriate witness behavior before HUAC, whose operation assumed a nonexistent internal red menace in the U.S. A non sequitur is a non sequitur.

But there is a message in the revolutions of 1989 that speaks directly to citizens enmeshed in the culture wars, even as it speaks to citizens who tried to reconcile questions of personal morality with matters of community obligation in the context of the cold war. Its courier is none other than that Czech jailbird-playwright-president, Vaclav Havel. And, appropriately enough, he carried this message to the same U.S. Congress whose committees and demagogues have made so much mischief. "Consciousness," he said, "precedes being, and not the other way around. . . ." Congress broke into hearty applause and the press, when they got around to writing about it, into hearty laughter. "Whaaat?! A real live philosophical notion? Discussed in front of congresspeople? What gives? Hey folks, The Man is an intellectual," wrote a reporter for *The Boston Globe*. Only Jay Rosen, in *Deadline*, an obscure newsletter published by the Center for War, Peace, and the News Media, picked it up. "When Havel said that consciousness precedes being he was saying that the human mind was not a mere product of the social structure. He was calling for a revolution, a global revolution in the sphere of human consciousness, without which a more humane society will not emerge." He was calling on people in the public realm to put morality ahead of science, politics, economics. It was a call to conscience, a rejection of all thought police.

Victor Navasky

August 6, 1990

Notes on Sources

BECAUSE A NUMBER of excellent bibliographies exist on the period (see especially *The Great Fear* by David Caute, pp. 621–50) and on political Hollywood (see especially *The Inquisition in Hollywood* by Larry Ceplair and Steven Englund, pp. 478–504), I have resisted as redundant the temptation to provide yet another list of sources. This system has the defect of omitting direct reference to such a valuable source as Cedric Belfrage's *The American Inquisition*. I have, however, included in the text or in the following notes all direct citations to published and unpublished sources. All other material is taken from personal interviews which I conducted from the spring of 1972 through the winter of 1979–80. Wherever relevant, the source of these questions is identified in the text, except for a small number of anonymous comments that were offered on a not-for-attribution basis. In the case of Chapter 8, "The Reasons Why," I have indicated in the notes which of these extended quotations are based on taped interviews, which are based on notes, and which are reconstructed from interviews given to others or from published works.

Among those I interviewed and/or spoke to are the following:

Larry Adler
Benjamin Appel
James Aronson
Jacoba Atlas
Harry Belafonte
Cedric Belfrage
Eric Bentley
Walter Bernstein
Alvah Bessie
Michael Blankfort
Kermit Bloomgarden
Thomas A. Bolan
Patricia Bosworth
Leonard Boudin

Millen Brand
Roy M. Brewer
John Bright
Conrad Bromberg
Phil Brown
Angus Cameron
Vera Caspary
Stanley Chase
Stephen Chodorov
Harold Clurman
Lee J. Cobb
(Ernest) Philip Cohen
Sidney Cohn
Lester Cole

Richard Collins
Howard Da Silva
Curt Demster
Edward Dmytryk
Frank Donner
Arnaud d'Usseau
Susan d'Usseau
Edward Eliscu
Henry Ephron
Pierre Epstein
John Henry Faulk
M. I. Finley
Pauline Lauber Finn
H. William Fitelson
Carl Foreman
Estelle Foreman
Arnold Forster
Ray Franklin
Judy Freed
Martin Gang
Milton Gelman
Phil Gersh
Lou Gilbert
Abraham Ginness
Abraham Goldstein
Ira Gollobin
Michael Gordon
William Goyen
Gilbert Green
Ulu Grosbard
John Harding
Harold Hecht
Lillian Hellman
Edward Huebsch
Roy Huggins
Paul Jacobs
Sam Jaffe
Paul Jarrico
Sylvia Jarrico
Leon Kaplan
Charles Katz
Elia Kazan

Alfred Kazin
Robert Kenny
Elizabeth Poe Kerby
Roland Kibbee
Carolyn Kizer
Howard Koch
Joel Kovell
Tony Kraber
Stanley Kramer
Ilse Lahn
Ring Lardner, Jr.
Marc Lawrence
John Howard Lawson
Alfred Levitt
Helen Levitt
Melvin Levy
Joseph Losey
Kate Foreman Lovenheim
Richard Low
Jerome Lurie
Albert Maltz
Esther Maltz
Ben Margolis
Judd Marmor
William Marshall
Carl Marzani
Harvey Matusow
Carey McWilliams
Michael Meeropol
Arthur Miller
Florence Mischel
Herbert Mitgang
Sam Moore
Charles Morgan
Seymour Peck
Abraham Polonsky
Martin Popper
James Proctor
David Raksin
John Randolph
Joseph Rauh
Walter Reich

William Reuben
Sylvia Richards
David Rintels
Martin Ritt
Allen Rivkin
Earl Robinson
Jill Robinson
Joseph Roos
Beatrice Buchman Rosenfeld
Ellen Rossen
Stephen Rossen
Susan Rossen
Norman Rosten
Dore Schary
Dorothy Schiff
Bernard Schoenfeld
Sidney Schreiber
Budd Schulberg
Henry Schwartzschild
Joan Scott
Earl Shorris
Lawrence Siegel
Clancy Sigal
Susanna Buchman Silver
Helen Silvermaster
George Sklar
Miriam Sklar
Zachary Sklar
George Slaff

Gale Sondergaard
Leonard Spigelgass
Donald Ogden Stewart
Edith Tiger
Leon Townsend
Dalton Trumbo
William Ullman
Willard Van Dyke
Constance Walter Weaver
F. Palmer Weber
James Wechsler
Abe Weiler
Leslie Weiner
Hannah Weinstein
John Wexley
William Wheeler
Mrs. William ("Billie") Wheeler
Alden Whitman
Frank Wilkinson
Mel Williamson
George Willner
Tiba Willner
H. H. Wilson
Michael Wilson
Rosanna Wilson
Ella Winter
Sidney Zion
Isidore Ziferstein

Foreword

1. See *The New York Times,* 22 March 1951, 1.
2. U.S. Congress, House Committee on Un-American Activities, *Communist Infiltration of Hollywood Motion Picture Industry,* Hearings, Eighty-second Congress, 1951, Part 1, 21 March. Hereinafter cited as *Motion Picture Hearings,* 1951. The testimony taken from Parks in executive session on 21 March 1951 was released in 1953: U.S. Congress, House Committee on Un-American Activities, *Investigation of Communist Ac-*

tivities in the Los Angeles Area, Hearings, Eighty-third Congress, Part 6, 2299–2308. Hereinafter cited as *Hearings, Los Angeles.*

3. *Motion Picture Hearings,* 1951, Part 5, 24 September.

4. E. M. Forster, "What I Believe," in *Two Cheers for Democracy* (London: Edward Arnold, 1972), 66.

5. Liam O'Flaherty, *The Informer* (New York: Alfred A. Knopf, 1925), 101, 47–48, 77. See also George Bluestone, *Novels into Film* (Berkeley: University of California Press, 1971), 66–78.

6. Quoted in Bertil Gartner, *Iscariot,* trans. Victor Gruhn (Philadelphia: Fortress Press, 1971), ix.

7. Rabbi Abraham A. Rapaport, "The Informer in Jewish Literature" (unpublished Ph.D. thesis, Yeshiva University, 1952), 5, 96, 3. See also Diane Heller, "Informing in Jewish Law" (paper prepared for Rabbi Rackman, New York Law School, February 1977).

8. Arnaud d'Usseau, interview with author.

9. See Dan E. Moldea, *The Hoffa Wars* (New York: Paddington Press, 1978), 124.

A Note on Vocabulary

1. U.S. Congress, House Committee on Un-American Activities, *Investigation of Communist Activities in the New York City Area,* Hearings, Eighty-third Congress, Part 4, 7 May 1953. Hereinafter cited as *Hearings, New York City.*

2. Quoted in Frank Donner, "Political Informers," in *Investigating the FBI,* ed. Pat Watters and Stephen Gillers (New York: Doubleday, 1973), 339–40.

3. Edwin Newman, interview with Elia Kazan on *Speaking Freely,* WNBC-TV, 1972.

4. Whittaker Chambers, *Witness* (New York: Random House, 1952), 65, 453–56.

5. Richard H. Rovere, "The Kept Witnesses," *Harper's* magazine, May 1955, 23–34.

INTRODUCTION: THE INFORMER AS PATRIOT

1. The Espionage Informer

1. Congressman Charles A. Eaton, quoted in Les K. Adler and Thomas G. Paterson, "Red Fascism: The Merger of Nazi Germany and Soviet Russia in the American Image of Totalitarianism, 1930s–1950s," *American Historical Review,* April 1970, 1055.

2. Quoted in William A. Reuben, *The Honorable Mr. Nixon* (New York: Action Books, 1958), 88.

3. Chambers, *Witness*, 742.

4. Arthur M. Schlesinger, Jr., "Whittaker Chambers & His Witness," *Saturday Review*, 24 May 1952.

5. John Dos Passos, "Mr. Chambers's Descent into Hell," ibid., 11.

6. Elizabeth Bentley, *Out of Bondage* (London: Hart-Davis, 1952), 309.

7. Dissent by Learned Hand, *United States* v. *William Walter Remington* (U.S. Court of Appeals for the Second Circuit, October term, 1953), 169–73.

8. Petition for a writ of certiorari to the U.S. Court of Appeals for the Second Circuit, *United States* v.*William Walter Remington* (Supreme Court of the United States, October term, 1953), 26–27.

9. Quoted in program note cards of the 14 March 1954 episode of the radio series *Last Man Out*, produced by Richard English, written by Richard George Pedicini, NBC-Radio, Archives of the National Broadcasting Company, Inc.

10. Edward A. Shils, *The Torment of Secrecy* (New York: The Free Press, 1956), 144.

11. *The New York Times*, 22 March 1954, 19.

12. Material on Budenz, Crouch, and Johnson is drawn primarily from Frank Donner, "The Informer," *The Nation*, 10 April 1954, 302–306; Richard H. Rovere, "The Kept Witnesses"; Joseph Alsop, "The Strange Case of Louis Budenz," *Atlantic Monthly*, April 1952, 29–33; Herbert L. Packer, *Ex-Communist Witnesses* (Stanford: Stanford University Press, 1962), 121–77; and Cedric Belfrage, *The American Inquisition, 1945–1960* (Indianapolis: Bobbs-Merrill, 1973).

13. Richard C. Donnelly, "Judicial Control of Informants, Spies, Stool Pigeons, and Agents Provocateurs," *Yale Law Journal*, November 1951, 1126.

14. Dorothy B. Jones, "Communism and the Movies: A Study of Film Content," in John Cogley, *Report on Blacklisting*, Vol. 1, *The Movies* (New York: Arno Press, 1972; originally published by The Fund for the Republic, Inc., 1956).

15. Nora Sayre, "Cold War Cinema II," *The Nation*, 3 March 1979, 245.

16. John Strachey, *The Strangled Cry* (New York: William Sloan Associates, 1962).

17. Herbert Philbrick, *I Led Three Lives* (New York: McGraw-Hill, 1953), 62, 64.

18. Angela Calomiris, *Red Masquerade* (Philadelphia: Lippincott, 1950), 32–33, 265.

19. Quoted in Adler and Paterson, "Red Fascism," 1064.

2. The Conspiracy Informer

1. Quoted in the papers of Paul Tillett, "Social Costs—Hollywood" (from the private collection of the late H. H. Wilson, Department of Politics, Princeton University).

2. Quoted in Eric F. Goldman, *The Crucial Decade* (New York: Alfred A. Knopf, 1956), 125.

3. McCarthy and Graham quoted in Lawrence S. Wittner, *Rebels Against War* (New York: Columbia University Press, 1969), 213, 215.

4. See David Caute, *The Great Fear* (New York: Simon & Schuster, 1978), 114.

5. On the CPUSA see Caute, *The Great Fear;* Irving Howe and Lewis Coser, *The American Communist Party: A Critical History* (New York: Praeger, 1962); Theodore Draper, *American Communism and Soviet Russia* (New York: Viking, 1960); David A. Shannon, *The Decline of American Communism: A History of the Communist Party of the United States since 1945* (London: Atlantic Books, 1959); Peter Steinberg, "The Great Red Menace: U.S. Prosecution of American Communists 1947–1951" (unpublished Ph.D. dissertation, New York University, 1979).

6. Steinberg, "The Great Red Menace," 139, 157.

7. Carey McWilliams, "Demagogues and Democracy," *Chicago Jewish Forum,* Winter 1951–52, 136–40.

8. Steinberg, "The Great Red Menace," 278.

9. Peter Viereck, "The Revolt Against the Elite," in *The Radical Right,* ed. Daniel Bell (New York: Doubleday, 1971), 136.

10. Richard H. Rovere, "The Conscience of Arthur Miller," *The New Republic,* 17 June 1957, 13–15.

11. Alsop, "The Strange Case of Louis Budenz," 29.

12. Material on the Smith Act prosecutions is drawn primarily from Brief for Appellants and Brief for the Appellee, *United States* v. *Dennis,* 183 F. 2d 201 (2d Cir. 1950); Michal R. Belknap, "The Smith Act and the Communist Party: A Study in Political Justice" (Ph.D. thesis, University of Wisconsin, 1973, published as *Cold War Political Justice* [Westport: Conn., Greenwood Press, 1978]); George Marion, *The Communist Trial: An American Crossroad* (New York: Fairplay, 1949); Paul S. Sarbanes, "The Smith Act: A Denial of American Freedom" (unpublished senior thesis, Princeton University, 1954); A. L. Wirin and Sam Rosenwein, "The Smith Act Prosecutions," *The Nation,* 12 December 1953, 487.

13. Packer, *Ex-Communist Witnesses,* 12.

14. Quoted in Belknap, "The Smith Act and the Communist Party," 197.

15. Quoted in ibid., 204.

16. Philbrick, *I Led Three Lives,* 290.

17. *United States* v. *Dennis,* 183 F. 2d 201 (1950), 212.

18. *Rogers* v. *United States,* 340 U.S. 367 (1951).

19. *The New York Times,* 20 November 1952, 16.

20. See Steve Nelson, *The 13th Juror: The Inside Story of My Trial* (New York: Masses & Mainstream, 1955).

21 *The New York Times,* 28 August 1953, 1.

22. Quoted in Donner, "Political Informers," 340–41.

23. Quoted in Rovere, "The Kept Witnesses," 27n.

24. See Melvin Rader, *False Witness* (Seattle: University of Washington Press, 1969); Carey McWilliams, *Witch Hunt* (Boston: Little, Brown, 1950), 144–55.

25. Rovere, "The Kept Witnesses," 27.

26. See program note cards from *Last Man Out* (NBC-Radio). The Crouch program was broadcast 4 October 1953; Sunoo, 7 and 14 February 1954; Butler, 28 March 1954.

27. Sidney Hook, "Heresy, Yes—But Conspiracy, No," *The New York Times Magazine,* 9 July 1950, 12, 38–39; *Heresy, Yes—Conspiracy, No* (New York: John Day, 1953). The essay was also published and distributed as a pamphlet by the American Committee for Cultural Freedom.

28. Michael Harrington, *Fragments of the Century* (New York: Saturday Review Press, 1973), 78.

29. Michael Harrington, "The Post-McCarthy Atmosphere," *Dissent,* Autumn 1955, 291.

30. Zechariah Chafee, Jr., "Spies Into Heroes," *The Nation,* 28 June 1952, 618.

3. The Liberal Informer

1. Lillian Hellman, *Scoundrel Time* (Boston: Little, Brown, 1976), 93, 61.

2. Lillian Hellman, interview with author.

3. U.S. Congress, Senate Permanent Subcommittee on Investigations of the Committee on Government Operations, *State Department Information Program,* Hearings, Eighty-third Congress, 1953, Part 4, 24 April, 268. Hereinafter cited as *State Department Hearings.*

4. For an overview of the conflicts within each of these three organizations see Mary McAuliffe, *Crisis on the Left* (Amherst: University of Massachusetts Press, 1978).

5. Quoted in Richard J. Walton, *Henry Wallace, Harry Truman, and the Cold War* (New York: Viking, 1976), 288.

6. Corliss Lamont, ed., *The Trial of Elizabeth Gurley Flynn by the Ameri-*

can Civil Liberties Union (New York: Modern Reader Paperbacks, 1968), 45.

7. Jerold S. Auerbach, "The Depression Decade," in *The Pulse of Freedom: American Liberties: 1920–1970s,* ed. Alan Reitman (New York: New American Library, 1976), 73.

8. Ibid., 71.

9. Lamont, ed., *The Trial of Elizabeth Gurley Flynn,* 23.

10. See *The New York Times,* 4 August 1977, B5; see also Aryeh Neier, "Adhering to Principle: Lessons from the 1950s," *The Civil Liberties Review,* November/December 1977, 26–32.

11. Quoted in McAuliffe, *Crisis on the Left,* 77.

12. Ibid., 49.

13. Arthur M. Schlesinger, Jr., "The Life of the Party," *Saturday Review,* 16 July 1949, 34.

14. Arthur M. Schlesinger, Jr., *New York Post,* column of 4 May 1952.

15. See Christopher Lasch, "The Cultural Cold War: A Short History of the Congress for Cultural Freedom," in *Towards a New Past: Dissenting Essays in American History,* ed. Barton J. Bernstein (New York: Pantheon, 1968); see also the ACCF files at the State Historical Society of Wisconsin.

16. Quoted material from McAuliffe, *Crisis on the Left,* 116, 117.

17. James Rorty and Moshe Decter, *McCarthy and the Communists* (Boston: Beacon Press, 1954), 140–41.

18. See Sigmund Diamond, "Veritas at Harvard," and "An Exchange on 'Veritas at Harvard,' " *New York Review of Books,* 28 April, 26 May, 14 July, 1977.

19. *State Department Hearings,* Part 4, 24 April 1953.

20. *State Department Hearings,* Part 4, 5 May 1953.

21. *State Department Hearings,* Part 4, 24 April 1953.

22. Richard H. Rovere, *Senator Joe McCarthy* (New York: Harper & Row, 1973), 166–67.

23. Cited in James Aronson, *The Press and the Cold War* (Indianapolis: Bobbs-Merrill, 1953), 100.

PART I: NAMING NAMES

1. Beck: *Motion Picture Hearings,* 1951, Part 5, 25 September.

2. *Hearings, Los Angeles,* Part 1, 25 March and Part 2, 26 March 1953.

3. *Hearings, New York City,* Part 4, 7 May 1953.

4. *Hearings, New York City,* Part 1, 4 May 1953.
5. Schulberg: *Motion Picture Hearings,* 1951, Part 3, 23 May. Dare: *Hearings, Los Angeles,* Part 1, 23 March 1953.
6. Odets: *Motion Picture Hearings,* 1952, Part 8, 19 and 20 May. Bela: U.S. Congress, House Committee on Un-American Activities, *Communist Methods of Infiltration (Entertainment),* Hearings, Eighty-third Congress, Part 2, 14 December 1954.
7. Hecht: *Hearings, Los Angeles,* Part 1, 23 March 1953. Atlas: ibid., Part 5, 12 March 1953. Wexley: *Motion Picture Hearings,* 1951, Part 4, 18 September.
8. See *The New York Times,* 12 April 1952, 7. Gordon's testimony was taken in executive session and never released.
9. *Motion Picture Hearings,* 1952, Part 10, 12 November.
10. Max Benoff: *Hearings, Los Angeles,* Part 1, 24 March; Mildred Benoff: ibid., Part 5, 17 February 1953.
11. Ibid., Part 2, 28 March 1953; Maddow's second testimony was never released but it is believed to have been in the late 1950s.
12. *Hearings, Los Angeles,* Part II, 6 June 1956.
13. *Hearings, New York City,* Part 2, 5 May 1953.
14. *Hearings, Los Angeles,* Part 5, 12 March 1953.
15. *Motion Picture Hearings,* 1951, Part 2, 23 April; Richard English, "What Makes a Hollywood Communist?" *Saturday Evening Post,* 19 May 1951.
16. Hayden: *Motion Picture Hearings,* 1951, Part 1, 10 April. Levy: ibid., 1952, Part 7, 28 January. Collins: ibid., 1951, Part 1, 12 April. Berkeley: ibid., Part 4, 19 September.

4. HUAC in Hollywood

1. Alvah Bessie, interview with author.
2. Quoted in Cogley, *Report on Blacklisting,* Vol. 1, *The Movies,* 3.
3. U.S. Congress, House Committee on Un-American Activities, *Hearings Regarding the Communist Infiltration of the Motion Picture Industry,* Eightieth Congress. Hereinafter cited as *Motion Picture Hearings,* 1947. Warner: 20 October; Taylor: 22 October; Rogers: 24 October; Disney: 24 October; Rand: 20 October.
4. See Walter Goodman, *The Committee* (New York: Farrar, Straus & Giroux, 1964), 215.
5. *Motion Picture Hearings,* 1947, 30 October.
6. Stander: *Hearings, New York City,* Part 1, 4 May 1953.
7. Seeger: U.S. Congress, House Committee on Un-American Activities,

Investigation of Communist Activities, New York Area (Entertainment), Hearings, Eighty-fourth Congress, 1955, Part 8, 18 August 1955. Hereinafter cited as *Entertainment Hearings*.

8. Ibid., Part 8, 14 October 1955.

9. Material on the American Legion is drawn from documents relating to *Young* v. *MPAA*; documents relating to *IPC* v. *Loew's*; Howard Suber, "The Anti-Communist Blacklist in the Hollywood Motion-Picture Industry"; Elizabeth Poe, "The Hollywood Story," *Frontier*, May 1954; Stefan Kanfer, *A Journal of the Plague Years* (New York: Atheneum, 1978); and back issues of the *American Legion Magazine*.

10. Thomas A. Bolan made this remark at a class I taught at New York University in 1973. Bolan, who served as attorney for the blacklisters in the landmark John Henry Faulk case, was also the assistant U.S. attorney who brought the case against Harvey Matusow.

11. *Los Angeles Times*, Letters, 27 July 1979.

12. Cogley, *Report on Blacklisting*, 84.

13. See Paul Jacobs, *Is Curly Jewish?* (New York: Random House, 1973), 199.

14. Freeman Exhibit 1 for identification, *Independent Production Corp.* v. *Loew's, Inc. et al.* (U.S. District Court, Southern District of New York, Civil Action 110–304, 4 May 1964). Hereinafter cited as *IPC* v. *Loew's*.

15. Arthur Exhibits 9 and 12 for identification, *IPC* v. *Loew's*.

16. Arthur Exhibits 13 and 16 for identification, *IPC* v. *Loew's*.

17. Brewer Exhibit 46 for identification and deposition of Martin Gang taken on 23 March 1964 in Los Angeles, 112, *IPC* v. *Loew's*.

18. O'Neil Exhibit 8B, *IPC* v. *Loew's*.

19. *People's World*, 31 December 1952.

20. Bell Exhibits 2 and 4, *IPC* v. *Loew's*. See also Lee Israel, "Judy Holliday," *MS*, December 1976, 72–74, 90–96.

21. Brewer Exhibit 68 for identification, *IPC* v. *Loew's*.

22. Harburg's letters are Plaintiff's Exhibits 182, 183, and 187, *IPC* v. *Loew's*.

23. Quoted in Kanfer, *A Journal of the Plague Years*, 234–35.

5. The Collaborators

1. Letter dated 26 November 1947, in the Robert Kenny/Robert Morris Collection, Wisconsin Center for Theatre Research.

2. *Motion Picture Hearings*, 1952, Part 7, 24 January.

3. Brewer Exhibit 43 for identification, *IPC* v. *Loew's*.

4. Papers of Martin Gang, Archives of the American Jewish Committee.

5. Koch to Brown, Howard Koch Collection, Wisconsin Center for Theatre Research.

6. See deposition of Martin Gang, *IPC* v. *Loew's,* 30, 35.

7. Brewer Exhibit 39 for identification, *IPC* v. *Loew's.*

8. Brewer Exhibit 40 for identification, *IPC* v. *Loew's.*

9. Deposition of Martin Gang, *IPC* v. *Loew's,* 39, 17–48.

10. Ibid., 65–67, 97–98; Brewer Exhibits 34 and 33, *IPC* v. *Loew's.*

11. Deposition of Martin Gang, *IPC* v. *Loew's,* 26, 88.

12. Goodman, *The Committee,* 173–74.

13. For a detailed description of the corruption under Browne and Bioff see Jesse George Murray, *The Legacy of Al Capone* (New York: Putnam, 1975). See also Poe, "The Hollywood Story," 19–23; Cogley, *Report on Blacklisting,* 17–18.

14. Irving Howe, *World of Our Fathers* (New York: Harcourt Brace Jovanovich, 1976), 342.

15. Unless otherwise cited, material on the Jewish community's response to the cold war is based on research in the library and records of the American Jewish Committee, Institute of Human Relations, New York City.

16. Jacobs, *Is Curly Jewish?,* 193.

17. See Merle Miller, "The Judges and the Judged," in John Cogley, *Report on Blacklisting,* Vol. II, *Radio-Television* (New York: Arno Press, 1972), 155–56; Miller's report was originally published by The American Civil Liberties Union in 1952.

18. Material on Martin Gang's activities here and below from Martin Gang, "The Citizens Committee for Cooperation with Congress," with covering letter, 10 March 1952, Gang Exhibit 2 for identification, *IPC* v. *Loew's*; deposition of Martin Gang, *IPC* v. *Loew's,* statement appended to page 73; Gang to Dales, Breen, and Heller, 13 January 1953, Gang Exhibit 3, *IPC* v. *Loew's.*

19. Ernest Jones, "The Psychology of Quislingism," *International Journal of Psycho-Analysis,* January 1941, 2.

20. Quoted in Poe, "The Hollywood Story," 15.

21. Arthur Laurents, *The Way We Were* (New York: Harper & Row, 1972), 173.

22. Alvah Bessie, *Inquisition in Eden* (New York: Macmillan, 1965), 234–35.

23. Sterling Hayden, *Wanderer* (London: Longmans, Green, 1964), 370–86 passim.

24. Joseph Wortis, "The Psychoanalytic Tradition," *New Masses,* 2 October 1945, 10.

25. Henry Winston, "Psychoanalysis: Ideological Instrument of Imperialism," *Political Affairs,* December 1950, 61–73.

26. Joseph C. Clayton, "Some Problems in the Struggle Against Psychoanalysis," *Political Affairs,* April 1954, 40.
27. Hayden, *Wanderer,* 363.
28. *Motion Picture Hearings,* 1951, Part 5, 21 September.
29. Poe, "The Hollywood Story," 15.

6. Guilty Bystanders

1. See Tino Balio, ed., *The American Film Industry* (Madison: University of Wisconsin Press, 1976), Part III; Charles Higham and Joel Greenberg, *Hollywood in the Forties* (New York: Paperback Library, 1970), 7–19; *The New York Times,* 6 February 1955, 5.
2. Figures are from Alice Orans, correspondence with Frank Donner, 10 June 1955, private files of Frank Donner.
3. Ezra Goodman, *The Fifty-Year Decline and Fall of Hollywood* (New York: Simon & Schuster, 1961), 17.
4. Robert Alan Aurthur, "Hanging Out," *Esquire,* October 1972, 14.
5. Kanfer, *A Journal of the Plague Years,* 128.
6. O'Neil Exhibits 11 and 12, *IPC* v. *Loew's.*
7. Deposition of Samuel Goldwyn, *Nedrick Young et al.,* v. *Motion Picture Association of America, Inc., et al.* (U.S. District Court, District of Columbia, Civil Action 4189–60, 30 December 1960). 9. Hereinafter cited as *Young* v. *MPAA.*
8. Hayden, *Wanderer,* 392.
9. Quoted in *The Washington Post,* 30 June 1975, C3.
10. *Daily Mirror,* New York, 6 October 1947.
11. Ibid., 6 December 1947.
12. Ibid., 28 July 1947.
13. *Daily News,* New York, 30 March 1955.
14. Quoted in Bob Thomas, *King Cohn* (New York: Putnam, 1967), 319.
15. *Motion Picture Hearings,* 1951, Part 5, 24 September.
16. *Motion Picture Hearings,* 1952, Part 7, 21 January.
17. *Writers Guild of America News,* May 1976, 22.
18. Hy Kraft, *On My Way to the Theater* (New York: Macmillan, 1971), 196.
19. *Motion Picture Hearings,* 1951, Part 2, 25 April.
20. Affidavit of Nedrick Young, *Young* v. *MPAA,* 61.
21. Howard Koch Collection, Wisconsin Center for Theatre Research.
22. Ibid.

23. Affidavit of Robert Loring Richards, *Young* v. *MPAA,* 87–88.
24. Helen Manfull, ed., *Additional Dialogue: Letters of Dalton Trumbo, 1942–1962* (New York: M. Evans, 1970), 112–19 passim.
25. Figures are from Larry Ceplair and Steven Englund, *The Inquisition in Hollywood* (New York: Anchor Press, 1980), 45.
26. Caute, *The Great Fear,* 488.
27. From Tristram Powell, "Hollywood on Trial," BBC-Television documentary, broadcast 4 November 1973.
28. *Motion Picture Hearings,* 1947, 29 October.
29. Quoted in Millard Lampell, "I Think I Ought to Mention I Was Blacklisted," *The New York Times,* 21 August 1966, D13.
30. Herbert Biberman/Gale Sondergaard Collection, Wisconsin Center for Theatre Research.
31. See "The Iniquitous Blacklist," *Equity,* October 1950, 3, 15; "Subpoenas, Blacklisting and Communism," *Equity,* June 1952, 13; *Variety,* 3 and 10 June 1953; *Equity,* November 1953, 10.
32. *The New York Times,* 11 August 1955.
33. Material on the Screen Directors Guild is drawn from clipping file, Screen Directors Guild, New York Library of the Performing Arts at Lincoln Center; Robert Parrish, *Growing Up in Hollywood* (New York: Harcourt Brace Jovanovich, 1976), 201–10; Kenneth L. Geist, *Pictures Will Talk* (New York: Scribners, 1978), 173–206.
34. "Minutes of meeting of current board and Plaintiffs in the Black-List Suit with Thurman Arnold on January 12, 1953," Stulberg Exhibit 4, *IPC* v. *Loew's.*
35. Affidavit of John Howard Lawson, *Young* v. *MPAA,* 95.
36. *The New York Times,* 24 April 1953.
37. Michael Wilson, speech on accepting the 1976 Laurel Award for Screen Writing, reprinted in *Writers Guild of America West News,* May 1976, 22.
38. This and following quotations from U.S. Congress, House Committee on Un-American Activities, *Hearings Regarding Communist Infiltration of Minority Groups,* Eighty-first Congress, Part 1, 18 July 1949. Hereinafter cited as *Minority Group Hearings.*
39. *The New York Times,* 18 July 1948.
40. For example, in April 1976 ABC-Television broadcast "The Tallest Tree in the Forest," a documentary on Robeson's life produced by Gil Noble.
41. U.S. Congress, House Committee on Un-American Activities, *Investigation of the Unauthorized Use of U.S. Passports,* Eighty-fourth Congress, Part 3, 12 June 1956. Hereinafter cited as *Passport Hearings.*
42. Abner Berry, "The Heavy Burden of Canada Lee," *Daily Worker,* 13 May 1952, 3.

43. See Kanfer, *A Journal of the Plague Years,* 180–81.

44. *Minority Group Hearings,* Part 3, 1 September 1950.

45. Material relating to Hughes's testimony before the Senate Permanent Sub-Committee on Investigations as well as the letter from Hughes to Reeves, 8 April 1853, are from the James Weldon Johnson Memorial Collection, Beinecke Rare Book and Manuscript Library, Yale University. See also *State Department Hearings,* Part 4, 24–26 March 1953.

46. *The Daily Compass,* New York, 9 October 1951, 3.

47. Martin Gang, interview with author.

PART II: STARS, STRIPES, AND STIGMAS

7. Elia Kazan and the Case for Silence

1. *The New York Times,* c. 1953 (undated clipping filed under "Arthur Miller" in *Times* morgue).

2. Richard H. Rovere, "The Conscience of Arthur Miller," *The New Republic,* 17 June 1957, 13.

3. From Michel Ciment, *Kazan on Kazan* (New York: Viking, 1974), 12.

4. Art Smith and Elia Kazan, "Dimitroff," *New Theatre,* July/August 1934, 20.

5. *Motion Picture Hearings,* 1952, Part 7, 10 April; Kazan's first executive session appearance, 14 January 1952, was never released.

6. *Daily Worker,* 4 May 1952, 7.

7. *Entertainment Hearings,* Part 6, 18 August 1955.

8. Ciment, *Kazan on Kazan,* 83–84.

9. Peter Biskind, "The Politics of Power in 'On the Waterfront,' " *Film Quarterly,* Fall 1975, 33.

10. Arthur Miller, "The Crucible," in *Arthur Miller's Collected Plays* (New York: Viking, 1957), 326, 327. Hereinafter cited as *Collected Plays.*

11. Miller said this during a question-and-answer session at the 92nd Street YM-YWHA's Poetry Center's Playwright Series in New York City in May 1972, which I attended.

12. Arthur Miller, "It Could Happen Here—And Did," *The New York Times,* 30 April 1967, D17.

13. From the program of *The Crucible* produced at the Vivian Beaumont Theater, Lincoln Center, New York City, 1972, 8.

14. Stuart Byron and Martin Rubin, "Elia Kazan Interview," *Movie 19,* Winter 1971–72, 7.

15. Arthur Miller, "The Year It Came Apart," *New York* magazine, 30 December 1974, 43–44.

16. Arthur Miller, "A View from the Bridge," in *Collected Plays*, 388–89, 424.
17. *Passport Hearings*, Part 4, 21 June 1956.
18. Brief for the Appellant, *Arthur Miller* v. *United States of America* (U.S. Court of Appeals, District of Columbia Circuit, No. 14, 057, February 1958), 65.
19. Rovere, "The Conscience of Arthur Miller," 13–15.
20. "A View from the Bridge," in *Collected Plays*, 439.
21. *The New York Times*, 24 January 1964.
22. Tom Prideaux, "A Desperate Search by a Troubled Hero," *Life*, 7 February 1964, 64d.
23. Arthur Miller, "With Respect for Her Agony—But with Love," *Life*, 7 February 1964, 66.
24. Edwin Newman, interview with Elia Kazan on *Speaking Freely*, WNBC-Television, 1972.
25. Elia Kazan, "View from a Turkish Prison," *The New York Times Magazine*, 4 February 1979, 33–35.

8. The Reasons Why

1. Erving Goffman, *Stigma* (Englewood Cliffs, N.J.: Prentice-Hall, 1963), 24.
2. Studs Terkel, *Working* (New York: Pantheon, 1972), xviii.
3. See *Los Angeles Times*, 1952: 22 October, 2; 23 October, 32; 24 October, 3; 31 October, 25.
4. My taped interview with Richard Collins was conducted in the spring of 1975 in the presence of Jessica Perrin Silvers. Collins testimony: *Motion Picture Hearings*, 1951, Part 1, 12 April.
5. Manfull, ed., *Additional Dialogue: Letters of Dalton Trumbo, 1942–1962*, 149.
6. Letters: Maltz to Dmytryk, 23 November 1948; Jean Dmytryk to Kenny, 15 May 1949; Dmytryk to Kenny, 12 February 1949, from the Robert Kenny/Robert Morris Collection, Wisconsin Center for Theatre Research.
7. I spoke briefly with Edward Dmytryk on the telephone in the winter of 1973 but he was "unenthusiastic" about talking and on his way to Europe. The material quoted here is taken from his memoir, *It's a Hell of a Life But Not a Bad Living* (New York: Times Books, 1979), and from Tristram Powell, "Hollywood on Trial." Dmytryk: *Motion Picture Hearings*, 1947, October 29; *Motion Picture Hearings*, 1951, Part 2, 25 April.
8. Doug Ireland, interview with author.

9. Filed under "Schulberg" in the morgue of *The New York Times.*

10. My interviews with Budd Schulberg were conducted at his home in Long Island in the summers of 1973 and 1976 and over the telephone; we also exchanged some correspondence. He preferred that no tape recorder be used. Schulberg testimony: *Motion Picture Hearings,* 1951, Part 3, 23 May.

11. Jessica Perrin Silvers taped a preliminary interview with Leo Townsend in the summer of 1973 and I taped a subsequent interview in the winter of 1974. Townsend testimony: *Motion Picture Hearings,* 1951, Part 4, 18 September.

12. I taped an interview with David Raksin in the spring of 1975 but the tape recorder malfunctioned so I have reconstructed his comments from notes. Raksin testimony: *Motion Picture Hearings,* 1951, Part 4, 20 September.

13. Robert Vaughn conducted the interview with Isobel Lennart in 1970 in connection with his doctoral dissertation, later published as *Only Victims* (New York: Putnam, 1972). I interviewed Lennart's husband, John Harding, in Hollywood in the winter of 1974, and took notes. Lennart testimony: *Motion Picture Hearings,* 1952, Part 8, 20 May.

14. I taped an interview with Roy Huggins in the winter of 1973. Huggins testimony: *Motion Picture Hearings,* 1952, Part 9, 29 September.

15. I interviewed Sylvia Richards at a playground in Hollywood in the winter of 1974, and took notes. Richards testimony: *Hearings, Los Angeles,* Part 1, 25 March 1953.

16. Bessie, *Inquisition in Eden,* 243–45.

17. I interviewed Lee J. Cobb in the winter of 1974 and took notes. Cobb testimony: *Hearings, Los Angeles,* Part 6, 2 June 1953.

18. I interviewed Roland Kibbee in the spring of 1975; the interview is reconstructed from notes. Kibbee testimony: *Hearings, Los Angeles,* Part 6, 2 June 1953.

19. I interviewed Michael Gordon in the spring of 1975 at his office in the film department of UCLA. He preferred that I not use a tape recorder. Gordon testimony: *Motion Picture Hearings,* 1951, 17 September; Gordon's second testimony in 1958 was never made public.

9. The Reasons Considered

1. See C. Wright Mills, "Situated Actions and Vocabularies of Motive," *American Sociological Review,* October 1940, 904–13.

2. E. E. Cummings, "i sing of Olaf glad and big," in *Collected Poems* (New York: Harcourt Brace, 1926), 204.

3. Powell, "Hollywood on Trial."

4. *Motion Picture Hearings,* 1952, Part 8, 19 and 20 May.

5. See Benjamin Appel, "Odets University," *The Literary Review,* Summer 1976, 470–75.

6. *Hearings, New York City,* Part 4, 7 May 1953.

7. Louis Fischer chapter in *The God That Failed,* Richard Crossman, ed. (New York: Harper & Bros., 1949), 204.

8. Typed note from I. F. Stone to Dashiell Hammett, added to a letter from Hammett to Stone, 18 March 1952. V. J. Jerome Collection, Sterling Library, Yale University.

9. Albert Maltz, "What Shall We Ask of Writers?" *New Masses,* 12 February 1946, 19–20.

10. Isidore Schneider, "Background to Error," ibid., 23–25.

11. Howard Fast, "Art and Politics," *New Masses,* 26 February 1946, 6.

12. Joseph North, ibid., 8.

13. Alvah Bessie, *New Masses,* 12 March 1946, 8.

14. Michael Gold, *Daily Worker,* 12 and 23 February, 2 and 16 March 1946; Samuel Sillen, *Daily Worker,* 11–16 February 1946; William Z. Foster, *New Masses,* 23 April 1946.

15. John Howard Lawson, *New Masses,* 19 March 1946, 18.

16. Daniel Aaron, *Writers on the Left* (New York: Avon Books, 1961), 399.

17. *Hearings, Los Angeles,* Part 5, 12 March 1953.

18. Albert Maltz, "Moving Forward," *New Masses,* 9 April 1946, 8–10, 21–22.

19. *New Masses,* 25 December 1945.

20. *The New York Times,* letter from Ring Lardner, Jr., 26 August 1977, 20.

21. Dorothy Jones, "Communism and the Movies: A Study of Film Content," 222.

22. Letter from Jerome to Maltz, 29 October 1957, V. J. Jerome Collection, Sterling Library, Yale University.

23. *Hearings, New York City,* Part 1, 7 May 1953.

24. *Hearings, New York City,* Part 1, 5 May 1953.

25. *Motion Picture Hearings,* 1951, Part 5, 25 September.

26. Budd Schulberg, "Collision with the Party Line," *Saturday Review,* 30 August 1952, 6–8, 31–37.

10. Degradation Ceremonies

1. *Hearings, Los Angeles,* Part 2, 30 June 1955.

2. U.S. Congress, House Committee on Un-American Activities, *Commu-*

    nist Activities among Professional Groups in the Los Angeles Area, Hearings, Eighty-second Congress, 1952, Part 1, 21 January.

3. *Hearings, Los Angeles,* Part 3, 31 March 1953.

4. Jackson's statement was made at the end of Carl Foreman's testimony: *Motion Picture Hearings,* 1951, Part 5, 24 September.

5. Harold Garfinkel, "Conditions of Successful Degradation Ceremonies," *American Journal of Sociology,* January 1956, 420–24.

6. Kai T. Erikson, *Wayward Puritans* (New York: John Wiley, 1966), 15–16.

7. Ernest Becker, *Escape from Evil* (New York: Free Press, 1975), 159.

8. Lillian Hellman, *Scoundrel Time,* 40–41.

9. Daniel J. Boorstin, *The Image* (New York: Atheneum, 1972), 11–12, 44 (originally published in 1961 as *The Image, or What Happened to the American Dream*).

10. Alan F. Westin, "Winning the Fight against McCarthy," *Commentary,* July 1954, 12–13.

11. Rovere, *Senator Joe McCarthy,* 158–59.

12. John W. Caughey, "McCarthyism Rampant," in Reitman, ed., *The Pulse of Freedom: American Liberties, 1920–1970,* 153.

13. *The New York Times,* 16 October 1960, Section II, 9.

14. Comments by Melville Shavelson reprinted in *Writers Guild of America West News,* April 1969, 12.

15. Reprinted in *Writers Guild of America West News,* May 1976, 22.

16. Garfinkel, "Conditions of Successful Degradation Ceremonies," 421.

PART III: VICTIMS

1. See, for instance, Howe and Coser, *The American Communist Party: A Critical History,* 480; Hannah Arendt, "Home to Roost: A Bicentennial Address," *The New York Review of Books,* 26 June 1975, 3–6; David Halberstam, *The Best and the Brightest* (New York: Random House, 1969): Fred J. Cook, *The Nightmare Decade* (New York: Random House, 1971).

2. Shils, *The Torment of Secrecy,* 195.

3. Arthur Koestler in *The God That Failed,* 55–56.

4. See Paul Tillett papers in the collection of H. H. Wilson, "The Social Costs of the Loyalty Programs, A Preliminary Draft (1965)," 10.

5. Ibid., 69–70.

6. Paul Jarrico, response to unidentified questionnaire of 28 January 1955 (private files of Frank Donner).

7. Mark Jacobson, "New York, You Oughta Be in Pictures," *New York* magazine, Year-end issue, 1975, 40.
8. Murray Kempton, "The Day of the Locust," in *Part of Our Time* (New York: Simon & Schuster, 1955), 181–83; Arthur M. Schlesinger, Jr., *The Vital Center* (Boston: Houghton Mifflin, 1949), 125.
9. Jones, "Communism and the Movies: A Study of Film Content," 231.
10. Adrian Scott, "Blacklist—the Liberal's Straitjacket and Its Effect on Content," *Hollywood Review,* September/October 1955, 1, 3–6.
11. Goffman, *Stigma,* 1.

11. The Intended Victim

1. Material on Christians and Loeb is from Stefan Kanfer, *A Journal of the Plague Years,* 154–55.
2. *Motion Picture Hearings,* 1951, Part 3, 25 June.
3. Ben Barzman, response to Robert Vaughn questionnaire of 1970, and letter to author, 22 January 1980.
4. Anonymous response to Robert Vaughn questionnaire.
5. Lampell, "I Think I Ought to Mention I Was Blacklisted," D13.
6. Deposition of John Howard Lawson, *Young* v. *MPAA.*

12. The Community as Victim

1. Lampell, "I Think I Ought to Mention I Was Blacklisted," D13.
2. Kai T. Erikson, *Everything in Its Path* (New York: Simon & Schuster, 1976), Part III.
3. *Motion Picture Hearings,* 1952, Part 7, 28 January.
4. Letter to Herbert Biberman, 3 October 1951, Herbert Biberman/Gale Sondergaard Collection, Wisconsin Center for Theatre Research.
5. Steinberg, "The Great Red Menace," 311.
6. *The New York Times,* 24 September 1976, C4.
7. Robert Jay Lifton, *Home from the War* (New York: Simon & Schuster, 1973), 105–106.
8. Erikson, *Everything in Its Path,* 234.
9. John Phillips and Anne Hollander, "Lillian Hellman—An Interview," *Paris Review,* Spring 1965, 86; Lillian Hellman, *Pentimento* (Boston: Little, Brown, 1973) 183–84.
10. *Hearings, Los Angeles,* Part 5, 12 March 1953.
11. Letters in the Herbert Biberman/Gale Sondergaard Collection, Wisconsin Center for Theatre Research.

12. Schlesinger, *The Vital Center*, 125.
13. Isobel Lennart, interview with Robert Vaughn.
14. Joan LaCour Scott, interview with author.
15. Quoted in Gordon Kahn, *Hollywood on Trial* (New York: Boni & Gaer, 1948), 176–77.
16. Sissela Bok, *Lying* (New York: Pantheon, 1978), 26–27.

13. The Informer as Victim

1. Trumbo's speech is reprinted in Manfull, ed., *Additional Dialogue: Letters of Dalton Trumbo, 1942–1962*, 569–70.
2. These responses to Parks's testimony are cited in Eric Bentley, *Thirty Years of Treason* (New York: Viking, 1971), 300–301.
3. Bob Thomas, *King Cohn*, 300.
4. *Hearings, Los Angeles*, Part 6, included in the released testimony of 21 March 1951.
5. Bok, *Lying*, 25.
6. Quoted in Donald Clark Hodges, "Ethics and Manners" (unpublished Ph.D. dissertation, Columbia University, 1954), 27.
7. Ibid., 13.
8. David Talbot and Barbara Zheutlin, *Creative Differences* (Boston: South End Press, 1978), 48.
9. Lampell, "I Think I Ought to Mention I Was Blacklisted," D16.
10. Isobel Lennart, interview with Robert Vaughn.
11. Quoted in Hodges, "Ethics and Manners," 62.

PART IV: LESSONS

1. Trumbo's speech is reprinted in Manfull, ed., *Additional Dialogue: Letters of Dalton Trumbo, 1942–1962*, 569–70.
2. Quoted in Bruce Cook, *Dalton Trumbo* (New York: Scribner's, 1977), 310.
3. *The New York Times*, 7 April 1978.

14. The Question of Forgiveness

1. See Lee C. McDonald, "Private Ethics and Civic Virtue," paper delivered at the 1978 Annual Meeting of the American Political Science Association, New York City, September 1978.

2. Quoted in Walter Reich, "Diagnosing Soviet Dissidents," *Harper's*, August 1978, 37.
3. Ibid.
4. Simon Wiesenthal, *The Sunflower* (New York: Schocken Books, 1976), passim.
5. Letter, Trumbo to Maltz, 12 January 1972.
6. Letter, Lardner to Maltz, 29 October 1977.
7. Murray Kempton, review of *Scoundrel Time* in *The New York Review of Books*, 10 June 1976, 25.

15. The Question of Obedience

1. From Maltz's statement given to the author for publication in *The New York Times Magazine*.
2. Barrington Moore, Jr., *Injustice: The Social Bases of Obedience and Revolt* (White Plains: M. E. Sharpe, 1978), 65. This book, especially chapters 2, 3, 12, 13, 14, has informed much of the discussion that follows.
3. Bruno Bettelheim, *The Informed Heart* (New York: The Free Press, 1960).
4. Moore, *Injustice*, 78.
5. *The Wall Street Journal*, 25 June 1941.
6. See Hannah Arendt, *Origins of Totalitarianism* (New York: Harcourt Brace, 1951).
7. Moore, *Injustice*. 93–94; Solomon E. Asch, "Effects of Group Pressure upon the Modification and Distortion of Judgments," in Harold S. Guetzkow, ed., *Groups, Leadership, and Men: Research in Human Relations* (New Brunswick, N.J.: Rutgers University Press, 1951), 177–90.
8. Moore, Injustice, 94–100; Stanley Milgram, *Obedience to Authority* (New York: Harper & Row, 1974).
9. Lifton, *Home from the War*, 166–67.

16. The Question of Candor

1. David Daube, *Collaboration with Tyranny in Rabbinic Law* (London: Oxford University Press, 1965), 5–7.
2. See Rapaport, "The Informer in Jewish Literature," 153–55; Heller, "Informing in Jewish Law."
3. See Hilton Kramer, "The Blacklist and the Cold War," *The New York Times*, 3 October 1976, Section II, and letters regarding Kramer's article, *The New York Times*, 17 October and 7 November 1976.

4. William Phillips, "What Happened in the Fifties?" *Partisan Review,* 1976, IV, 338; Bentley, *Thirty Years of Treason,* 245–46.

5. Telford Taylor, *Grand Inquest: The Story of Congressional Investigations* (New York: Simon & Schuster, 1955), passim.

6. Bok, *Lying,* 139, 150.

7. Popper testimony: U.S. Congress, House Committee on Un-American Activities, *Passport Security Hearings,* Eighty-sixth Congress, 1959, Part 2, 5 June; Seeger testimony: *Entertainment Hearings,* Part 8, 18 August 1955.

8. Becker, *Escape from Evil,* 64.

9. Aryeh Neier, "The Critics and 'The Front,'" *Civil Liberties Review,* December 1976/January 1977, 8.

10. Becker, *Escape from Evil,* 141.

Acknowledgments

SO MANY PEOPLE AND INSTITUTIONS have helped in so many different ways since I started work on this book in the spring of 1972 that I cannot give adequate thanks to them all here. This is especially true of all those who agreed to sit for interviews and otherwise cooperate in helping me to reconstruct an experience filled in many cases with grief and pain.

At *The New York Times,* where this book began, I owe special thanks to Harvey Shapiro, Roger Jellinek, Seymour Peck, William Honan, Walter Goodman, Harriet Wilson, and James Schwartz, whose assignments, editing, and/or extracurricular assistance helped to get me going.

The John Simon Guggenheim Foundation saw me through 1974–75 and the Russell Sage Foundation through 1975–76; I am grateful to both. At Russell Sage I had the intelligent assistance of Madeline Spitaleri, who typed the transcripts for many of my taped interviews, and I also received help from Anne Balding and Ellen Liebowitz. Talks with Stanton Wheeler, Arnold Shore, Walter Wallace, and Herbert McClosky deepened my understanding of the subject and Hugh Cline was unfailingly supportive in every aspect of my life at the foundation.

To Professors Clement Vose and my students at Wesleyan University, Neil Postman and my students in New York University's Department of Media Ecology, and Edward Sullivan and my students in the Politics and the Press seminar at Princeton University (where Natalie Cruickshank kept all in order), I owe the chance to have tested half-formed hypotheses on rare critical intelligences. At Princeton my talks with Robert C. Tucker, Robert Scott, Reiko Hasuike, and Randall Rothenberg were especially helpful.

Scholars of the period who have been unfailingly generous with their time, ideas, and documents include Eric Bentley, Stefan Kanfer, Robert Vaughn (who made available to me his invaluable taped interview with the late Isobel Lennart), Howard Suber, Frank Donner (who let me invade his voluminous files), Ronald Radosh, Edith Tiger, the late Paul Jacobs, and the late H. H. Wilson, whose memory and analyses were as rare as his archives. I had useful conversations with Bruce Cook, and reading galleys of Vivian Gornick's *The Romance of American Communism* helped me to think about "The Reasons Considered." William Reuben was always available to supply a fact, challenge an interpretation, offer an informed dissent. Tristram Powell of the BBC arranged for a special showing of his documentary "Hollywood on Trial."

In Hollywood, I had the diligent assistance of Jessica Perrin Silvers and the helpful counsel of Mae Churchill and David Rintels.

Others who put their diverse wisdom and expertise at my disposal include Erving Goffman, Jonathan Rubinstein, Edward Jay Epstein, Steven Scheuer, Walter Reich, Ira Gollobin, Sissela Bok, Joel Kovel, Philip Pochoda, Paula Newberg, John Murray Cuddihy, Cynthia Buchanan, Peter Davis, Michael Harrington, Marcus Raskin, Nancy Schwartz, and Earl Shorris. I also received assists from Marilyn Berger, Mary Kay Schilling, Harriet Heyman, Paula Glatzer, Roberta Gratz, Tony Kraber, Martin Solow, Sidney Schreiber, Stephen Schwartz, Barbara Scott, Ken Lerer, Lucia Suarez, Willard Van Dyke, and Richard Low.

John Rosenberg read portions of my manuscript, and Carey McWilliams, E. L. Doctorow, Irving Louis Horowitz, and Sanford Levinson read the complete manuscript. My gratitude for their respective critiques and enthusiasms resists adequate reproduction here; but in the case of Sandy Levinson—while he no more than any of the others is responsible for what I have written—it would be a grievous omission to fail to mention the scores of hours of lonely conversation with him before, during and after the manuscript, without which it is difficult to imagine its having taken its present form.

I am indebted to the following archives, collections, and organizations for the use of their materials: the Motion Picture Association of America, Inc., the State Historical Society of Wisconsin, the Wisconsin Center for Theatre Research, the New York Library of the Performing Arts at Lincoln Center, the American Jewish Committee, the James Weldon Johnson Memorial Collection of Negro Arts and Letters at the Beinecke Rare Book and Manuscript Library at Yale (where I saw the papers of Langston Hughes with the kind permission of the executors of his estate), the Museum of Modern Art, which arranged a special screening of "The Hollywood Ten," the Oral History Projects at UCLA, Columbia University, and the University of Wyoming, the Harry S. Truman Library in Independence, Missouri, The Sterling Memorial Library at Yale, the Humanities Research Center at the University of Texas, the Meiklejohn Civil Liberties Institute at the University of California at Berkeley, and the Southern California Library for Social Studies and Research.

My agent, Lynn Nesbit, was there before the beginning and a wise adviser throughout. At The Viking Press, Thomas Guinzburg and Irving Goodman were generous in their support of the project; my editor, Elisabeth Sifton, counselor, guide, and conscience, served as a perpetual lobbyist for excellence. She was ably assisted by Jennifer Snodgrass, and by Altie Karper, who typed and retyped.

I thank my partner, Hamilton Fish, and my other colleagues at *The Nation* for their unfailing enthusiastic encouragement, even at the cost of extra burdens on themselves. Shirley Sulat and Ola Lyon both helped in emergencies. And to Karen Wilcox, researcher, de facto editor, fact checker, and chapter-notes preparer, my gratitude.

Finally I thank my wife, Annie, and my children Bruno, Miri, and Jenny for getting along without me, but now that this is over, put them on notice that I intend to break that habit.

Index

Malcolm X, 193

Malden, Karl, 209

Malin, Patrick Murphy, 51

Maltz, Albert, 224, 275, 276, 351, 360, 422

   during blacklist, 185, 327, 334

   Blankfort and, 377–78

   on candor, 419–20

   debate between Trumbo and, 388–401, 403, 405–406, 407, 418, 421

   dispute over *New Masses* article of, 226, 237, 266, 287–302, 362

   Dmytryk and, 232–34, 365–67

   on Hellman, 423

   Kazan on, 208

   as one of Hollywood Ten, 81, 82, 113

   Townsend, L., and, 381

Mandell, William, 118–19

Mandelstam, Osip, 309

Manfull, Helen, 232

Mankiewicz, Joseph L., 104, 179–81, 195

Mann, Thomas, 93 n

Mannix, Eddie, 108, 251, 368

Manoff, Arnold, 291

Marcantonio, Vito, 26

Margolis, Ben, 161

Marshall, William, 192, 193, 195

Martin, Dean, 149

Marvin Josephson Agency, 356

Marx, Groucho, 80

Marx, Karl, 131, 132, 142, 259, 296, 299

   Staniskavski and, 293–95

Marxists, 411

Massing, Hede, 17, 41

Matthews, J. B., 86, 152

Mature, Victor, 184

Matusow, Harvey, xxii, 40–41, 334, 342–43, 425

Max, Alan, 35

Mayakovsky, Vladimir, 308, 309

Mayer, Louis B., 109, 176, 337, 350, 368

MCA. *See* Music Corporation of America.

Medford, Howard, 301

Medina, Harold, 33–35, 124

Meltzer, Robert, 387

Menjou, Adolphe, 89, 170

Metro-Goldwyn-Mayer (M-G-M), 107, 144, 145, 156, 252, 255, 257, 368, 382

Meyerhold, Vsevolod, 307, 309

Meyers, Henry, 283

M-G-M. *See* Metro-Goldwyn-Mayer.

Milestone, Lewis, 98, 113

Milgram, Stanley, 412–15

Miller, Allen, 228

Miller, Arthur, 300, 312, 391, 424

   Cobb and, 269, 273

   guilt by association with, 355

   Hellman on, 423

   HUAC testimony of, 34, 61 n, 224, 306, 318, 354, 420

   Kazan and, 199, 200, 202, 203, 206, 207, 210–19, 221, 416

Miller, Merle, 326

Mills, C. Wright, 279, 324 n

Milosz, Czeslaw, 90

Minton, Sherman, 84

Mischel, Florence, 353

Mischel, Josef, 353

Mission to Moscow (film, Michael Curtiz), 104, 167, 300

Monroe, Marilyn, 207, 216–18

Moore, Barrington, Jr., 408–11, 426

Morgan, Charles, 48

Morley, Karen, 100 n

Morros, Boris, 17

Mortimer, Lee, 58

FOR THE BEST IN PAPERBACKS, LOOK FOR THE

In every corner of the world, on every subject under the sun, Penguin represents quality and variety—the very best in publishing today.

For complete information about books available from Penguin—including Pelicans, Puffins, Peregrines, and Penguin Classics—and how to order them, write to us at the appropriate address below. Please note that for copyright reasons the selection of books varies from country to country.

In the United Kingdom: For a complete list of books available from Penguin in the U.K., please write to *Dept E.P., Penguin Books Ltd, Harmondsworth, Middlesex, UB7 0DA.*

In the United States: For a complete list of books available from Penguin in the U.S., please write to *Consumer Sales, Penguin USA, P.O. Box 999— Dept. 17109, Bergenfield, New Jersey 07621-0120.* VISA and MasterCard holders call 1-800-253-6476 to order all Penguin titles.

In Canada: For a complete list of books available from Penguin in Canada, please write to *Penguin Books Canada Ltd, 10 Alcorn Avenue, Suite 300, Toronto, Ontario, Canada M4V 3B2.*

In Australia: For a complete list of books available from Penguin in Australia, please write to the *Marketing Department, Penguin Books Ltd, P.O. Box 257, Ringwood, Victoria 3134.*

In New Zealand: For a complete list of books available from Penguin in New Zealand, please write to the *Marketing Department, Penguin Books (NZ) Ltd, Private Bag, Takapuna, Auckland 9.*

In India: For a complete list of books available from Penguin, please write to *Penguin Overseas Ltd, 706 Eros Apartments, 56 Nehru Place, New Delhi, 110019.*

In Holland: For a complete list of books available from Penguin in Holland, please write to *Penguin Books Nederland B.V., Postbus 195, NL-1380AD Weesp, Netherlands.*

In Germany: For a complete list of books available from Penguin, please write to *Penguin Books Ltd, Friedrichstrasse 10-12, D-6000 Frankfurt Main I, Federal Republic of Germany.*

In Spain: For a complete list of books available from Penguin in Spain, please write to *Longman, Penguin España, Calle San Nicolas 15, E-28013 Madrid, Spain.*

In Japan: For a complete list of books available from Penguin in Japan, please write to *Longman Penguin Japan Co Ltd, Yamaguchi Building, 2-12-9 Kanda Jimbocho, Chiyoda-Ku, Tokyo 101, Japan.*

FOR THE BEST IN HISTORY, LOOK FOR THE

FOR THE BEST IN HISTORY, LOOK FOR THE

☐ **THE FACE OF BATTLE**
John Keegan

In this study of three battles from three different centuries, John Keegan examines war from the fronts—conveying its reality for the participants at the "point of maximum danger."

366 pages   *ISBN: 0-14-004897-9*

☐ **VIETNAM: A HISTORY**
Stanley Karnow

Stanley Karnow's monumental narrative—the first complete account of the Vietnam War—puts events and decisions of the day into sharp, clear focus. "This is history writing at its best."—*Chicago Sun-Times*

752 pages   *ISBN: 0-14-007324-8*

☐ **MIRACLE AT MIDWAY**
Gordon W. Prange
with Donald M. Goldstein and Katherine V. Dillon

The best-selling sequel to *At Dawn We Slept* recounts the battles at Midway Island—events which marked the beginning of the end of the war in the Pacific.

470 pages   *ISBN: 0-14-006814-7*

☐ **THE MASK OF COMMAND**
John Keegan

This provocative view of leadership examines the meaning of military heroism through four prototypes from history—Alexander the Great, Wellington, Grant, and Hitler—and proposes a fifth type of "post-heroic" leader for the nuclear age.   *368 pages*   *ISBN: 0-14-011406-8*

☐ **THE SECOND OLDEST PROFESSION**
Spies and Spying in the Twentieth Century
Phillip Knightley

In this fascinating history and critique of espionage, Phillip Knightley explores the actions and missions of such noted spies as Mata Hari and Kim Philby, and organizations such as the CIA and the KGB.

436 pages   *ISBN: 0-14-010655-3*

☐ **THE STORY OF ENGLISH**
Robert McCrum, William Cran, and Robert MacNeil

"Rarely has the English language been scanned so brightly and broadly in a single volume," writes the *San Francisco Chronicle* about this journey across time and space that explores the evolution of English from Anglo-Saxon Britain to Reagan's America.   *384 pages*   *ISBN: 0-14-009435-0*

FOR THE BEST IN HISTORY, LOOK FOR THE

☐ THE WORLD SINCE 1945
T. E. Vadney

This magnificent survey of recent global history charts all the major developments since the end of World War II, including the Cold War, Vietnam, the Middle East wars, NATO, the emergence of sovereign African states, and the Warsaw Pact. *570 pages   ISBN: 0-14-022723-7*

☐ THE ECONOMIC CONSEQUENCES OF THE PEACE
John Maynard Keynes
Introduction by Robert Lekachman

First published in 1920, Keynes's brilliant book about the cost of the "Carthaginian" peace imposed on Germany after World War I stands today as one of the great economic and political works of our time. *336 pages   ISBN: 0-14-011380-0*

☐ A SHORT HISTORY OF AFRICA
Sixth Edition
Roland Oliver and J. D. Fage

While the centers of European culture alternately flourished and decayed, empires in Africa rose, ruled, resisted, and succumbed. In this classic work, the authors have drawn on the whole range of literature about Africa, taking its study a step forward. *304 pages   ISBN: 0-14-022759-8*

☐ RUSSIA
Broken Idols, Solemn Dreams
David K. Shipler

A national best-seller, this involving personal narrative by the former Moscow bureau chief of *The New York Times* crystallizes what is truly Russian behind the facade of stereotypes and official government rhetoric. *404 pages   ISBN: 0-14-007408-2*

FOR THE BEST IN HISTORY, LOOK FOR THE

☐ **MOVE YOUR SHADOW**
South Africa, Black & White
Joseph Lelyveld

Drawing on his two tours as a correspondent for *The New York Times*, Lelyveld offers a vivid portrait of a troubled country and its people, illuminating the history, society, and feelings that created and maintain apartheid.

402 pages   ISBN: 0-14-009326-5

☐ **THE PELICAN HISTORY OF THE WORLD**
Revised Edition
J. M. Roberts

This comprehensive and informative survey of the growth of the modern world analyzes the major forces of our history and emphasizes both their physical and psychological effects.

1056 pages   ISBN: 0-14-022785-7